# INTRODUCTION TO
# LINEAR ALGEBRA

## CUSTOM EDITION FOR RENSSELAER POLYTECHNIC INSTITUTE

Taken From:

*Introduction to Linear Algebra*, Fifth Edition
by Lee W. Johnson, R. Dean Riess, and Jimmy T. Arnold

### Learning Solutions

New York   Boston   San Francisco
London   Toronto   Sydney   Tokyo   Singapore   Madrid
Mexico City   Munich   Paris   Cape Town   Hong Kong   Montreal

Taken from:

*Introduction to Linear Algebra*, Fifth Edition
by Lee W. Johnson, R. Dean Riess, and Jimmy T. Arnold
Copyright © 2002 by Pearson Education, Inc.
Published by Addison-Wesley
Upper Saddle River, New Jersey 07458

This special edition published in cooperation with Pearson Learning Solutions.

Pearson Learning Solutions, 501 Boylston Street, Suite 900, Boston, MA 02116
A Pearson Education Company
www.pearsoned.com

Printed in the United States of America

1 2 3 4 5 6 VOZU 14 13 12 11 10

000200010270085063

RR

ISBN 10: 0-558-75722-7
ISBN 13: 978-0-558-75722-9

# PREFACE

Linear algebra is an important component of undergraduate mathematics, particularly for students majoring in the scientific, engineering, and social science disciplines. At the practical level, matrix theory and the related vector-space concepts provide a language and a powerful computational framework for posing and solving important problems. Beyond this, elementary linear algebra is a valuable introduction to mathematical abstraction and logical reasoning because the theoretical development is self-contained, consistent, and accessible to most students.

Therefore, this book stresses both practical computation and theoretical principles and centers on the principal topics of the first four chapters:

matrix theory and systems of linear equations,

elementary vector-space concepts, and

the eigenvalue problem.

This core material can be used for a brief (10-week) course at the late-freshman/sophomore level. There is enough additional material in Chapters 5–7 either for a more advanced or a more leisurely paced course.

## FEATURES

Our experience teaching freshman and sophomore linear algebra has led us to carefully choose the features of this text. Our approach is based on the way students learn *and* on the tools they need to be successful in linear algebra as well as in related courses.

We have found that students learn more effectively when the material has a consistent level of difficulty. Therefore, in Chapter 1, we provide early and meaningful coverage of topics such as linear combinations and linear independence. This approach helps the student negotiate what is usually a dramatic jump in level from solving systems of linear equations to working with concepts such as basis and spanning set.

### TOOLS STUDENTS NEED (WHEN THEY NEED THEM)

The following examples illustrate how we provide students with the tools they need for success.

*An early introduction to eigenvalues.* In Chapter 3, elementary vector-space ideas (subspace, basis, dimension, and so on) are introduced in the familiar setting of $R^n$. Therefore, it is possible to cover the eigenvalue problem very early and in much greater depth than is usually possible. A brief introduction to determinants is given in Section 4.2 to facilitate the early treatment of eigenvalues.

*An early introduction to linear combinations.* In Section 1.5, we observe that the matrix-vector product $A\mathbf{x}$ can be expressed as a linear combination of the columns of

$A$, $A\mathbf{x} = x_1\mathbf{A}_1 + x_2\mathbf{A}_2 + \cdots + x_n\mathbf{A}_n$. This viewpoint leads to a simple and natural development for the theory associated with systems of linear equations. For instance, the equation $A\mathbf{x} = \mathbf{b}$ is consistent if and only if $\mathbf{b}$ is expressible as a linear combination of the columns of $A$. Similarly, a consistent equation $A\mathbf{x} = \mathbf{b}$ has a unique solution if and only if the columns of $A$ are linearly independent. This approach gives some early motivation for the vector-space concepts (introduced in Chapter 3) such as subspace, basis, and dimension. The approach also simplifies ideas such as rank and nullity (which are then naturally given in terms of dimension of appropriate subspaces).

*Applications to different fields of study.*     Some applications are drawn from difference equations and differential equations. Other applications involve interpolation of data and least-squares approximations. In particular, students from a wide variety of disciplines have encountered problems of drawing curves that fit experimental or empirical data. Hence, they can appreciate techniques from linear algebra that can be applied to such problems.

*Computer awareness.*     The increased accessibility of computers (especially personal computers) is beginning to affect linear algebra courses in much the same way as it has calculus courses. Accordingly, this text has somewhat of a numerical flavor, and (when it is appropriate) we comment on various aspects of solving linear algebra problems in a computer environment.

### A Comfort in the Storm

We have attempted to provide the type of student support that will encourage success in linear algebra—one of the most important undergraduate mathematics courses that students take.

*A gradual increase in the level of difficulty.*     In a typical linear algebra course, the students find the techniques of Gaussian elimination and matrix operations fairly easy. Then, the ensuing material relating to vector spaces is suddenly much harder. We do three things to lessen this abrupt midterm jump in difficulty:

1.  We introduce linear independence early in Section 1.7.
2.  We include a new Chapter 2, "Vectors in 2-Space and 3-Space."
3.  We first study vector space concepts such as subspace, basis, and dimension in Chapter 3, in the familiar geometrical setting of $R^n$.

*Clarity of exposition.*     For many students, linear algebra is the most rigorous and abstract mathematical course they have taken since high-school geometry. We have tried to write the text so that it is accessible, but also so that it reveals something of the power of mathematical abstraction. To this end, the topics have been organized so that they flow logically and naturally from the concrete and computational to the more abstract. Numerous examples, many presented in extreme detail, have been included in order to illustrate the concepts. The sections are divided into subsections with boldface headings. This device allows the reader to develop a mental outline of the material and to see how the pieces fit together.

*Extensive exercise sets.*     We have provided a large number of exercises, ranging from routine drill exercises to interesting applications and exercises of a theoretical nature. The more difficult theoretical exercises have fairly substantial hints. The computational exercises are written using workable numbers that do not obscure the point with a mass of cumbersome arithmetic details.

*Trustworthy answer key.*    Except for the theoretical exercises, solutions to the odd-numbered exercises are given at the back of the text. We have expended considerable effort to ensure that these solutions are correct.

*Spiraling exercises.*    Many sections contain a few exercises that hint at ideas that will be developed later. Such exercises help to get the student involved in thinking about extensions of the material that has just been covered. Thus the student can anticipate a bit of the shape of things to come. This feature helps to lend unity and cohesion to the material.

*Historical notes.*    We have a number of historical notes. These assist the student in gaining a historical and mathematical perspective of the ideas and concepts of linear algebra.

*Supplementary exercises.*    We include, at the end of each chapter, a set of supplementary exercises. These exercises, some of which are true–false questions, are designed to test the student's understanding of important concepts. They often require the student to use ideas from several different sections.

*Integration of MATLAB.*    We have included a collection of MATLAB projects at the end of each chapter. For the student who is interested in computation, these projects provide hands-on experience with MATLAB.

*A short MATLAB appendix.*    Many students are not familiar with MATLAB. Therefore, we include a *very* brief appendix that is sufficient to get the student comfortable with using MATLAB for problems that typically arise in linear algebra.

*The vector form for the general solution.*    To provide an additional early introduction to linear combinations and spanning sets, in Section 1.5 we introduce the idea of the vector form for the general solution of $A\mathbf{x} = \mathbf{b}$.

## SUPPLEMENTS

### SOLUTIONS MANUALS

*An Instructor's Solutions Manual and a Student's Solutions Manual are available.* The odd-numbered computational exercises have answers at the back of the book. The student's solutions manual (ISBN 0-201-65860-7) includes detailed solutions for these exercises. The instructor's solutions manual (ISBN 0-201-75814-8) contains solutions to all the exercises.

*New Technology Resource Manual.*    This manual was designed to assist in the teaching of the MATLAB, Maple, and Mathematica programs in the context of linear algebra. This manual is available from Addison-Wesley (ISBN 0-201-75812-1) or via [our website,] http://www.aw.com/jra.

### ORGANIZATION

To provide greater flexibility, Chapters 4, 5, and 6 are essentially independent. These chapters can be taken in any order once Chapters 1 and 3 are covered. Chapter 7 is a mélange of topics related to the eigenvalue problem: quadratic forms, differential equations, $QR$ factorizations, Householder transformations, generalized eigenvectors, and so on. The sections in Chapter 7 can be covered in various orders. A schematic diagram illustrating the chapter dependencies is given below. Note that Chapter 2, "Vectors in 2-Space and 3-Space," can be omitted with no loss of continuity.

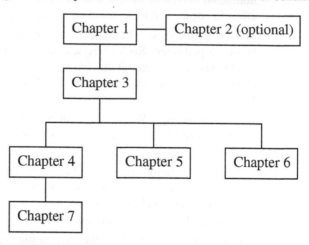

We especially note that Chapter 6 (Determinants) can be covered before Chapter 4 (Eigenvalues). However, Chapter 4 contains a brief introduction to determinants that should prove sufficient to users who do not wish to cover Chapter 6.

A very short but useful course at the beginning level can be built around the following sections:

Section 1.1–1.3, 1.5–1.7, 1.9

Sections 3.1–3.6

Sections 4.1–4.2, 4.4–4.5

**A syllabus that integrates abstract vector spaces.**     Chapter 3 introduces elementary vector-space ideas in the familiar setting of $R^n$. We designed Chapter 3 in this way so that it is possible to cover the eigenvalue problem much earlier and in greater depth than is generally possible. Many instructors, however, prefer an integrated approach to vector spaces, one that combines $R^n$ and abstract vector spaces. The following syllabus, similar to ones used successfully at several universities, allows for a course that integrates abstract vector spaces into Chapter 3. This syllabus also allows for a detailed treatment of determinants:

Sections 1.1–1.3, 1.5–1.7, 1.9

Sections 3.1–3.3, 5.1–5.3, 3.4–3.5, 5.4–5.5

Sections 4.1–4.3, 6.4–6.5, 4.4–4.7

**Augmenting the core sections.**     As time and interest permit, the core of Sections 1.1–1.3, 1.5–1.7, 1.9, 3.1–3.6, 4.1–4.2, and 4.4–4.5 can be augmented by including various combinations of the following sections:

(a) *Data fitting and approximation:* 1.8, 3.8–3.9, 7.5–7.6.

(b) *Eigenvalue applications:* 4.8, 7.1–7.2.

**(c)** *More depth in vector space theory:* 3.7, Chapter 5.

**(d)** *More depth in eigenvalue theory:* 4.6–4.7, 7.3–7.4, 7.7–7.8.

**(e)** *Determinant theory:* Chapter 6.

To allow the possibility of getting quickly to eigenvalues, Chapter 4 contains a brief introduction to determinants. If the time is available and if it is desirable, Chapter 6 (Determinants) can be taken after Chapter 3. In such a course, Section 4.1 can be covered quickly and Sections 4.2–4.3 can be skipped.

Finally, in the interest of developing the student's mathematical sophistication, we have provided proofs for almost every theorem. However, some of the more technical proofs (such as the demonstration that $\det(AB) = \det(A)\det(B)$) are deferred to the end of the sections. As always, constraints of time and class maturity will dictate which proofs should be omitted.

## ACKNOWLEDGMENTS

A great many valuable contributions to the Fifth Edition were made by those who reviewed the manuscript as it developed through various stages:

Idris Assani, University of North Carolina, Chapel Hill

Satish Bhatnagar, University of Nevada, Las Vegas

Richard Daquila, Muskingum College

Robert Dobrow, Clarkson University

Branko Grunbaum, University of Washington

Isom Herron, Rennsselaer Polytechnic Institute

Diane Hoffoss, Rice University

Richard Kubelka, San Jose State University

Tong Li, University of Iowa

David K. Neal, Western Kentucky University

Eileen Shugart, Virginia Institute of Technology

Nader Vakil, Western Illinios University

Tarynn Witten, Trinity University

Christos Xenophontos, Clarkson University

In addition, we wish to thank Michael A. Jones, Montclair State University and Isom Herron, Rennsselaer Polytech Institute for their careful work in accuracy checking this edition.

*Blacksburg, Virginia*                                                                L.W.J.
                                                                                                   R.D.R.
                                                                                                   J.T.A.

# CONTENTS

# Matrices and Systems of Linear Equations

**1**

---

OVERVIEW

In this chapter we discuss systems of linear equations and methods (such as Gauss-Jordan elimination) for solving these systems. We introduce matrices as a convenient language for describing systems and the Gauss-Jordan solution method.

We next introduce the operations of addition and multiplication for matrices and show how these operations enable us to express a linear system in matrix-vector terms as

$$Ax = b.$$

Representing the matrix $A$ in column form as $A = [\mathbf{A}_1, \mathbf{A}_2, \ldots, \mathbf{A}_n]$, we then show that the equation $A\mathbf{x} = \mathbf{b}$ is equivalent to

$$x_1\mathbf{A}_1 + x_2\mathbf{A}_2 + \cdots + x_n\mathbf{A}_n = \mathbf{b}.$$

The equation above leads naturally to the concepts of linear combination and linear independence. In turn, those ideas allow us to address questions of existence and uniqueness for solutions of $A\mathbf{x} = \mathbf{b}$ and to introduce the idea of an inverse matrix.

---

CORE SECTIONS

## 1.1 INTRODUCTION TO MATRICES AND SYSTEMS OF LINEAR EQUATIONS

In the real world, problems are seldom so simple that they depend on a single input variable. For example, a manufacturer's profit clearly depends on the cost of materials, but it also depends on other input variables such as labor costs, transportation costs, and plant overhead. A realistic expression for profit would involve all these variables. Using mathematical language, we say that profit is a *function of several variables.*

In linear algebra we study the simplest functions of several variables, the ones that are *linear*. We begin our study by considering linear equations. By way of illustration, the equation

$$x_1 + 2x_2 + x_3 = 1$$

is an example of a linear equation, and $x_1 = 2$, $x_2 = 1$, $x_3 = -3$ is one solution for the equation. In general a **linear equation** in $n$ unknowns is an equation that can be put in the form

$$a_1 x_1 + a_2 x_2 + \cdots + a_n x_n = b. \tag{1}$$

In (1), the coefficients $a_1, a_2, \ldots, a_n$ and the constant $b$ are known, and $x_1, x_2, \ldots, x_n$ denote the unknowns. A **solution** to Eq. (1) is any sequence $s_1, s_2, \ldots, s_n$ of numbers such that the substitution $x_1 = s_1, x_2 = s_2, \ldots, x_n = s_n$ satisfies the equation.

Equation (1) is called linear because each term has degree one in the variables $x_1, x_2, \ldots, x_n$. (Also, see Exercise 37.)

EXAMPLE 1    Determine which of the following equations are linear.

(i)  $x_1 + 2x_1 x_2 + 3x_2 = 4$

(ii)  $x_1^{1/2} + 3x_2 = 4$

(iii)  $2x_1^{-1} + \sin x_2 = 0$

(iv)  $3x_1 - x_2 = x_3 + 1$

*Solution*    Only Eq. (iv) is linear. The terms $x_1 x_2$, $x_1^{1/2}$, $x_1^{-1}$, and $\sin x_2$ are all nonlinear.    ■

### Linear Systems

Our objective is to obtain simultaneous solutions to a system (that is, a set) of one or more linear equations. Here are three examples of systems of linear equations.

(a)  $x_1 + x_2 = 3$
     $x_1 - x_2 = 1$

(b)  $x_1 - 2x_2 - 3x_3 = -11$
     $-x_1 + 3x_2 + 5x_3 = 15$

(c)  $3x_1 - 2x_2 = 1$
     $6x_1 - 4x_2 = 6$

In terms of solutions, it is easy to check that $x_1 = 2$, $x_2 = 1$ is one solution to system (a). Indeed, it can be shown that this is the *only* solution to the system.

On the other hand, $x_1 = -4$, $x_2 = 2$, $x_3 = 1$ and $x_1 = -2$, $x_2 = 6$, $x_3 = -1$ are both solutions to system (b). In fact, it can be verified by substitution that $x_1 = -3 - x_3$ and $x_2 = 4 - 2x_3$ yields a solution to system (b) for any choice of $x_3$. Thus, this system has infinitely many solutions.

Finally, note that the equations given in (c) can be viewed as representing two parallel lines in the plane. Therefore, system (c) has no solution. (Another way to see that (c) has no solution is to observe that the second equation in (c), when divided by 2, reduces to $3x_1 - 2x_2 = 3$. Because the first equation requires $3x_1 - 2x_2 = 1$, there is no way that both equations can be satisfied.)

In general, an *(m $\times$ n) system of linear equations* is a set of equations of the form:

$$
\begin{aligned}
a_{11}x_1 + a_{12}x_2 + \cdots + a_{1n}x_n &= b_1 \\
a_{21}x_1 + a_{22}x_2 + \cdots + a_{2n}x_n &= b_2 \\
\vdots \qquad\qquad \vdots \quad \vdots \\
a_{m1}x_1 + a_{m2}x_2 + \cdots + a_{mn}x_n &= b_m.
\end{aligned}
\qquad (2)^*
$$

For example, the general form of a $(3 \times 3)$ system of linear equations is

$$
\begin{aligned}
a_{11}x_1 + a_{12}x_2 + a_{13}x_3 &= b_1 \\
a_{21}x_1 + a_{22}x_2 + a_{23}x_3 &= b_2 \\
a_{31}x_1 + a_{32}x_2 + a_{33}x_3 &= b_3.
\end{aligned}
$$

A *solution* to system (2) is a sequence $s_1, \ldots, s_n$ of numbers that is simultaneously a solution for each equation in the system. The double subscript notation used for the coefficients is necessary to provide an "address" for each coefficient. For example, $a_{32}$ appears in the third equation as the coefficient of $x_2$.

### EXAMPLE 2

(a) Display the system of equations with coefficients $a_{11} = 2$, $a_{12} = -1$, $a_{13} = -3$, $a_{21} = -2$, $a_{22} = 2$, and $a_{23} = 5$, and with constants $b_1 = -1$ and $b_2 = 3$.

(b) Verify that $x_1 = 1$, $x_2 = 0$, $x_3 = 1$ is a solution for the system.

*Solution*

(a) The system is

$$
\begin{aligned}
2x_1 - \phantom{2}x_2 - 3x_3 &= -1 \\
-2x_1 + 2x_2 + 5x_3 &= \phantom{-}3.
\end{aligned}
$$

(b) Substituting $x_1 = 1$, $x_2 = 0$, and $x_3 = 1$ yields

$$
\begin{aligned}
2(1) - \phantom{2}(0) - 3(1) &= -1 \\
-2(1) + 2(0) + 5(1) &= \phantom{-}3.
\end{aligned}
$$

---

*For clarity of presentation, we assume throughout the chapter that the constants $a_{ij}$ and $b_i$ are real numbers, although all statements are equally valid for complex constants. When we consider eigenvalue problems, we will occasionally encounter linear systems having complex coefficients, but the solution technique is no different. In Chapter 4 we will discuss the technical details of solving systems that have complex coefficients.

### Geometric Interpretations of Solution Sets

We can use geometric examples to get an initial impression about the nature of solution sets for linear systems. For example, consider a general $(2 \times 2)$ system of linear equations

$$a_{11}x_1 + a_{12}x_2 = b_1 \quad (a_{11}, a_{12} \text{ not both zero})$$
$$a_{21}x_1 + a_{22}x_2 = b_2 \quad (a_{21}, a_{22} \text{ not both zero}).$$

Geometrically, the solution set for each of these equations can be represented as a line in the plane. A solution for the system, therefore, corresponds to a point $(x_1, x_2)$ where the lines intersect. From this geometric interpretation, it follows that there are exactly three possibilities:

1. The two lines are coincident (the same line), so there are infinitely many solutions.
2. The two lines are parallel (never meet), so there are no solutions.
3. The two lines intersect at a single point, so there is a unique solution.

The three possibilities are illustrated in Fig. 1.1 and in Example 3.

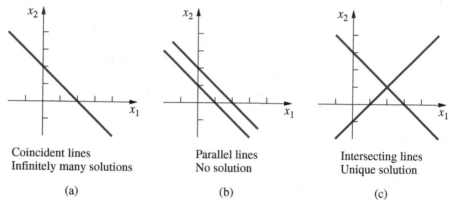

Coincident lines
Infinitely many solutions

(a)

Parallel lines
No solution

(b)

Intersecting lines
Unique solution

(c)

*Figure 1.1*     The three possibilities for the solution set of a $(2 \times 2)$ system.

EXAMPLE 3     Give a geometric representation for each of the following systems of equations.

**(a)**  $x_1 + x_2 = 2$
$2x_1 + 2x_2 = 4$

**(b)**  $x_1 + x_2 = 2$
$x_1 + x_2 = 1$

**(c)**  $x_1 + x_2 = 3$
$x_1 - x_2 = 1$

*Solution*     The representations are displayed in Fig. 1.1.

The graph of a linear equation in three variables, $ax_1 + bx_2 + cx_3 = d$, is a plane in three-dimensional space (as long as one of $a$, $b$, or $c$ is nonzero). So, as another example, let us consider the general $(2 \times 3)$ system:

$$a_{11}x_1 + a_{12}x_2 + a_{13}x_3 = b_1$$
$$a_{21}x_1 + a_{22}x_2 + a_{23}x_3 = b_2.$$

Because the solution set for each equation can be represented by a plane, there are two possibilities:

1. The two planes might be coincident, or they might intersect in a line. In either case, the system has infinitely many solutions.

2. The two planes might be parallel. In this case, the system has no solution.

Note, for the case of the general $(2 \times 3)$ system, that the possibility of a unique solution has been ruled out.

As a final example, consider a general $(3 \times 3)$ system:

$$a_{11}x_1 + a_{12}x_2 + a_{13}x_3 = b_1$$
$$a_{21}x_1 + a_{22}x_2 + a_{23}x_3 = b_2$$
$$a_{31}x_1 + a_{32}x_2 + a_{33}x_3 = b_3.$$

If we view this $(3 \times 3)$ system as representing three planes, it is easy to see from the geometric perspective that there are three possible outcomes: infinitely many solutions, no solution, or a unique solution (see Fig. 1.2). Note that Fig. 1.2(b) does not illustrate every possible case of a $(3 \times 3)$ system that has no solution. For example, if just two of three planes are parallel, then the system has no solution even though the third plane might intersect each of the two parallel planes.

We conclude this subsection with the following remark, which we will state formally in Section 1.3 (see Corollary to Theorem 3). This remark says that the possible outcomes suggested by the geometric interpretations shown in Figs. 1.1 and 1.2 are typical for any system of linear equations.

**Remark** An $(m \times n)$ system of linear equations has either infinitely many solutions, no solution, or a unique solution.

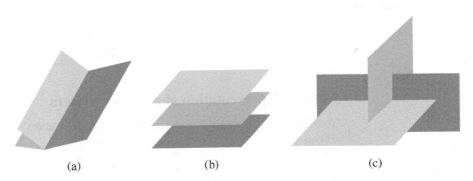

(a)   (b)   (c)

*Figure 1.2* The general $(3 \times 3)$ system may have (a) infinitely many solutions, (b) no solution, or (c) a unique solution.

In general, a system of equations is called *consistent* if it has at least one solution, and the system is called *inconsistent* if it has no solution. By the preceding remark, a consistent system has either one solution or an infinite number of solutions; it is not possible for a linear system to have, for example, exactly five solutions.

## Matrices

We begin our introduction to matrix theory by relating matrices to the problem of solving systems of linear equations. Initially we show that matrix theory provides a convenient and natural symbolic language to describe linear systems. Later we show that matrix theory is also an appropriate and powerful framework within which to analyze and solve more general linear problems, such as least-squares approximations, representations of linear operations, and eigenvalue problems.

The rectangular array

$$\begin{bmatrix} 1 & 3 & -1 & 2 \\ 4 & 2 & 1 & -3 \\ 0 & 2 & 0 & 3 \end{bmatrix}$$

is an example of a matrix. More generally, an $(m \times n)$ *matrix* is a rectangular array of numbers of the form

$$A = \begin{bmatrix} a_{11} & a_{12} & \cdots & a_{1n} \\ a_{21} & a_{22} & \cdots & a_{2n} \\ \vdots & & & \vdots \\ a_{m1} & a_{m2} & \cdots & a_{mn} \end{bmatrix}.$$

Thus an $(m \times n)$ matrix has $m$ rows and $n$ columns. The subscripts for the entry $a_{ij}$ indicate that the number appears in the $i$th row and $j$th column of $A$. For example, $a_{32}$ is the entry in the third row and second column of $A$. We will frequently use the notation $A = (a_{ij})$ to denote a matrix $A$ with entries $a_{ij}$.

EXAMPLE 4    Display the $(2 \times 3)$ matrix $A = (a_{ij})$, where $a_{11} = 6$, $a_{12} = 3$, $a_{13} = 7$, $a_{21} = 2$, $a_{22} = 1$, and $a_{23} = 4$.

*Solution*

$$A = \begin{bmatrix} 6 & 3 & 7 \\ 2 & 1 & 4 \end{bmatrix}$$

## Matrix Representation of a Linear System

To illustrate the use of matrices to represent linear systems, consider the $(3 \times 3)$ system of equations

$$\begin{aligned} x_1 + 2x_2 + x_3 &= 4 \\ 2x_1 - x_2 - x_3 &= 1 \\ x_1 + x_2 + 3x_3 &= 0. \end{aligned}$$

If we display the coefficients and constants for this system in matrix form,

$$B = \begin{bmatrix} 1 & 2 & 1 & 4 \\ 2 & -1 & -1 & 1 \\ 1 & 1 & 3 & 0 \end{bmatrix},$$

then we have expressed compactly and naturally all the essential information. The matrix $B$ is called the *augmented matrix* for the system.

In general, with the $(m \times n)$ system of linear equations

$$\begin{aligned}
a_{11}x_1 + a_{12}x_2 + \cdots + a_{1n}x_n &= b_1 \\
a_{21}x_1 + a_{22}x_2 + \cdots + a_{2n}x_n &= b_2 \\
\vdots \qquad\qquad\qquad \vdots \quad &\ \ \vdots \\
a_{m1}x_1 + a_{m2}x_2 + \cdots + a_{mn}x_n &= b_m,
\end{aligned} \tag{3}$$

we associate two matrices. The **coefficient matrix** for system (3) is the $(m \times n)$ matrix $A$ where

$$A = \begin{bmatrix} a_{11} & a_{12} & \cdots & a_{1n} \\ a_{21} & a_{22} & \cdots & a_{2n} \\ \vdots & & & \vdots \\ a_{m1} & a_{m2} & \cdots & a_{mn} \end{bmatrix}.$$

The **augmented matrix** for system (3) is the $[m \times (n+1)]$ matrix $B$ where

$$B = \begin{bmatrix} a_{11} & a_{12} & \cdots & a_{1n} & b_1 \\ a_{21} & a_{22} & \cdots & a_{2n} & b_2 \\ \vdots & & & \vdots & \vdots \\ a_{m1} & a_{m2} & \cdots & a_{mn} & b_m \end{bmatrix}.$$

Note that $B$ is nothing more than the coefficient matrix $A$ augmented with an extra column; the extra column is the right-hand side of system (3).

The augmented matrix $B$ is usually denoted as $[A \mid \mathbf{b}]$, where $A$ is the coefficient matrix and

$$\mathbf{b} = \begin{bmatrix} b_1 \\ b_2 \\ \vdots \\ b_m \end{bmatrix}.$$

EXAMPLE 5 Display the coefficient matrix $A$ and the augmented matrix $B$ for the system

$$\begin{aligned}
x_1 - 2x_2 + x_3 &= 2 \\
2x_1 + x_2 - x_3 &= 1 \\
-3x_1 + x_2 - 2x_3 &= -5.
\end{aligned}$$

*Solution*    The coefficient matrix $A$ and the augmented matrix $[A \mid \mathbf{b}]$ are given by

$$A = \begin{bmatrix} 1 & -2 & 1 \\ 2 & 1 & -1 \\ -3 & 1 & -2 \end{bmatrix} \quad \text{and} \quad [A \mid \mathbf{b}] = \begin{bmatrix} 1 & -2 & 1 & 2 \\ 2 & 1 & -1 & 1 \\ -3 & 1 & -2 & -5 \end{bmatrix}. \quad ∎$$

## Elementary Operations

As we shall see, there are two steps involved in solving an $(m \times n)$ system of equations. The steps are:

1. Reduction of the system (that is, the elimination of variables).
2. Description of the set of solutions.

The details of both steps will be left to the next section. For the remainder of this section, we will concentrate on giving an overview of the reduction step.

   The goal of the reduction process is to simplify the given system by eliminating unknowns. It is, of course, essential that the reduced system of equations have the same set of solutions as the original system.

DEFINITION 1

Two systems of linear equations in $n$ unknowns are *equivalent* provided that they have the same set of solutions.

Thus the reduction procedure must yield an equivalent system of equations. The following theorem provides three operations, called *elementary operations*, that can be used in reduction.

THEOREM 1

If one of the following elementary operations is applied to a system of linear equations, then the resulting system is equivalent to the original system.

1. Interchange two equations.
2. Multiply an equation by a nonzero scalar.
3. Add a constant multiple of one equation to another.    ∎

(In part 2 of Theorem 1, the term *scalar* means a constant; that is, a number.) The proof of Theorem 1 is included in Exercise 41 of Section 1.1.

   To facilitate the use of the elementary operations listed above, we adopt the following notation:

| *Notation* | *Elementary Operation Performed* |
| --- | --- |
| $E_i \leftrightarrow E_j$ | The $i$th and $j$th equations are interchanged. |
| $kE_i$ | The $i$th equation is multiplied by the nonzero scalar $k$. |
| $E_i + kE_j$ | $k$ times the $j$th equation is added to the $i$th equation. |

The following simple example illustrates the use of elementary operations to solve a $(2 \times 2)$ system. (The complete solution process for a general $(m \times n)$ system is described in detail in the next section.)

**EXAMPLE 6** Use elementary operations to solve the system

$$x_1 + x_2 = 5$$
$$-x_1 + 2x_2 = 4.$$

*Solution* The elementary operation $E_2 + E_1$ produces the following equivalent system:

$$x_1 + x_2 = 5$$
$$3x_2 = 9.$$

The operation $\frac{1}{3}E_2$ then leads to

$$x_1 + x_2 = 5$$
$$x_2 = 3.$$

Finally, using the operation $E_1 - E_2$, we obtain

$$x_1 \quad = 2$$
$$x_2 = 3.$$

By Theorem 1, the system above is equivalent to the original system. Hence the solution to the original system is also $x_1 = 2, x_2 = 3$. ◼

(*Note:* Example 6 illustrates a *systematic* method for solving a system of linear equations. This method is called ***Gauss-Jordan elimination*** and is described fully in the next section.)

## Row Operations

As noted earlier, we want to use an augmented matrix as a shorthand notation for a system of equations. Because equations become translated to rows in the augmented matrix, we want to perform elementary operations on the rows of a matrix. Toward that end, we introduce the following terminology.

**DEFINITION 2** The following operations, performed on the rows of a matrix, are called ***elementary row operations:***

1. Interchange two rows.
2. Multiply a row by a nonzero scalar.
3. Add a constant multiple of one row to another.

As before, we adopt the following notation:

| Notation | Elementary Row Operation |
|---|---|
| $R_i \leftrightarrow R_j$ | The $i$th and $j$th rows are interchanged. |
| $k R_i$ | The $i$th row is multiplied by the nonzero scalar $k$. |
| $R_i + k R_j$ | $k$ times the $j$th row is added to the $i$th row. |

We say that two $(m \times n)$ matrices, $B$ and $C$, are **row equivalent** if one can be obtained from the other by a sequence of elementary row operations. Now if $B$ is the augmented matrix for a system of linear equations and if $C$ is row equivalent to $B$, then $C$ is the augmented matrix for an equivalent system. This observation follows because the elementary row operations for matrices exactly duplicate the elementary operations for equations.

Thus, we can solve a linear system with the following steps:

1. Form the augmented matrix $B$ for the system.
2. Use elementary row operations to transform $B$ to a row equivalent matrix $C$ which represents a "simpler" system.
3. Solve the simpler system that is represented by $C$.

We will specify what we mean by a simpler system in the next section. For now, we illustrate in Example 7 how using elementary row operations to reduce an augmented matrix is exactly parallel to using elementary operations to reduce the corresponding system of equations.

EXAMPLE 7    Consider the $(3 \times 3)$ system of equations

$$\begin{aligned}
2x_2 + x_3 &= -2 \\
3x_1 + 5x_2 - 5x_3 &= 1 \\
2x_1 + 4x_2 - 2x_3 &= 2.
\end{aligned}$$

Use elementary operations on equations to reduce the following system. Simultaneously use elementary row operations to reduce the augmented matrix for the system.

Solution    In the left-hand column of the following table, we will reduce the given system of equations using elementary operations. In the right-hand column we will perform the analogous elementary row operations on the augmented matrix. (**Note:** At each step of the process, the system of equations obtained in the left-hand column is equivalent to the original system. The corresponding matrix in the right-hand column is the augmented matrix for the system in the left-hand column.)

Our initial goal is to have $x_1$ appear in the first equation with coefficient 1, and then to eliminate $x_1$ from the remaining equations. This can be accomplished by the following steps:

| *System:* | *Augmented Matrix:* |
|---|---|

$$
\begin{aligned}
2x_2 + x_3 &= -2 \\
3x_1 + 5x_2 - 5x_3 &= 1 \\
2x_1 + 4x_2 - 2x_3 &= 2
\end{aligned}
\qquad
\begin{bmatrix}
0 & 2 & 1 & -2 \\
3 & 5 & -5 & 1 \\
2 & 4 & -2 & 2
\end{bmatrix}
$$

$E_1 \leftrightarrow E_3$:  $\qquad\qquad\qquad\qquad$  $R_1 \leftrightarrow R_3$:

$$
\begin{aligned}
2x_1 + 4x_2 - 2x_3 &= 2 \\
3x_1 + 5x_2 - 5x_3 &= 1 \\
2x_2 + x_3 &= -2
\end{aligned}
\qquad
\begin{bmatrix}
2 & 4 & -2 & 2 \\
3 & 5 & -5 & 1 \\
0 & 2 & 1 & -2
\end{bmatrix}
$$

$(1/2)E_1$:  $\qquad\qquad\qquad\qquad$  $(1/2)R_1$:

$$
\begin{aligned}
x_1 + 2x_2 - x_3 &= 1 \\
3x_1 + 5x_2 - 5x_3 &= 1 \\
2x_2 + x_3 &= -2
\end{aligned}
\qquad
\begin{bmatrix}
1 & 2 & -1 & 1 \\
3 & 5 & -5 & 1 \\
0 & 2 & 1 & -2
\end{bmatrix}
$$

$E_2 - 3E_1$:  $\qquad\qquad\qquad\qquad$  $R_2 - 3R_1$:

$$
\begin{aligned}
x_1 + 2x_2 - x_3 &= 1 \\
- x_2 - 2x_3 &= -2 \\
2x_2 + x_3 &= -2
\end{aligned}
\qquad
\begin{bmatrix}
1 & 2 & -1 & 1 \\
0 & -1 & -2 & -2 \\
0 & 2 & 1 & -2
\end{bmatrix}
$$

The variable $x_1$ has now been eliminated from the second and third equations. Next, we eliminate $x_2$ from the first and third equations and leave $x_2$, with coefficient 1, in the second equation. We continue the reduction process with the following operations:

$(-1)E_2$:  $\qquad\qquad\qquad\qquad$  $(-1)R_2$:

$$
\begin{aligned}
x_1 + 2x_2 - x_3 &= 1 \\
x_2 + 2x_3 &= 2 \\
2x_2 + x_3 &= -2
\end{aligned}
\qquad
\begin{bmatrix}
1 & 2 & -1 & 1 \\
0 & 1 & 2 & 2 \\
0 & 2 & 1 & -2
\end{bmatrix}
$$

$E_1 - 2E_2$:  $\qquad\qquad\qquad\qquad$  $R_1 - 2R_2$:

$$
\begin{aligned}
x_1 \qquad - 5x_3 &= -3 \\
x_2 + 2x_3 &= 2 \\
2x_2 + x_3 &= -2
\end{aligned}
\qquad
\begin{bmatrix}
1 & 0 & -5 & -3 \\
0 & 1 & 2 & 2 \\
0 & 2 & 1 & -2
\end{bmatrix}
$$

$E_3 - 2E_2$:  $\qquad\qquad\qquad\qquad$  $R_3 - 2R_2$:

$$
\begin{aligned}
x_1 \qquad - 5x_3 &= -3 \\
x_2 + 2x_3 &= 2 \\
-3x_3 &= -6
\end{aligned}
\qquad
\begin{bmatrix}
1 & 0 & -5 & -3 \\
0 & 1 & 2 & 2 \\
0 & 0 & -3 & -6
\end{bmatrix}
$$

The variable $x_2$ has now been eliminated from the first and third equations. Next, we eliminate $x_3$ from the first and second equations and leave $x_3$, with coefficient 1, in the third equation:

**System:**

**$(-1/3)E_3$:**

$$
\begin{aligned}
x_1 &&- 5x_3 &= -3 \\
&& x_2 + 2x_3 &= 2 \\
&& x_3 &= 2
\end{aligned}
$$

**Augmented Matrix:**

**$(-1/3)R_3$:**

$$
\begin{bmatrix}
1 & 0 & -5 & -3 \\
0 & 1 & 2 & 2 \\
0 & 0 & 1 & 2
\end{bmatrix}
$$

**$E_1 + 5E_3$:**

$$
\begin{aligned}
x_1 && &= 7 \\
&& x_2 + 2x_3 &= 2 \\
&& x_3 &= 2
\end{aligned}
$$

**$R_1 + 5R_3$:**

$$
\begin{bmatrix}
1 & 0 & 0 & 7 \\
0 & 1 & 2 & 2 \\
0 & 0 & 1 & 2
\end{bmatrix}
$$

**$E_2 - 2E_3$:**

$$
\begin{aligned}
x_1 && &= 7 \\
&& x_2 &= -2 \\
&& x_3 &= 2
\end{aligned}
$$

**$R_2 - 2R_3$:**

$$
\begin{bmatrix}
1 & 0 & 0 & 7 \\
0 & 1 & 0 & -2 \\
0 & 0 & 1 & 2
\end{bmatrix}
$$

The last system above clearly has a unique solution given by $x_1 = 7$, $x_2 = -2$, and $x_3 = 2$. Because the final system is equivalent to the original given system, both systems have the same solution. ∎

The reduction process used in the preceding example is known as **Gauss-Jordan elimination** and will be explained in Section 1.2. Note the advantage of the shorthand notation provided by matrices. Because we do not need to list the variables, the sequence of steps in the right-hand column is easier to perform and record.

Example 7 illustrates that row equivalent augmented matrices represent equivalent systems of equations. The following corollary to Theorem 1 states this in mathematical terms.

**COROLLARY**　Suppose $[A \mid \mathbf{b}]$ and $[C \mid \mathbf{d}]$ are augmented matrices, each representing a different $(m \times n)$ system of linear equations. If $[A \mid \mathbf{b}]$ and $[C \mid \mathbf{d}]$ are row equivalent matrices, then the two systems are also equivalent. ∎

## 1.1　EXERCISES

Which of the equations in Exercises 1–6 are linear?

**1.** $x_1 + 2x_3 = 3$　　　　**2.** $x_1 x_2 + x_2 = 1$

**3.** $x_1 - x_2 = \sin^2 x_1 + \cos^2 x_1$

**4.** $x_1 - x_2 = \sin^2 x_1 + \cos^2 x_2$

**5.** $|x_1| - |x_2| = 0$　　　**6.** $\pi x_1 + \sqrt{7} x_2 = \sqrt{3}$

In Exercises 7–10, coefficients are given for a system of the form (2). Display the system and verify that the given values constitute a solution.

**7.** $a_{11} = 1$, 　$a_{12} = 3$, 　$a_{21} = 4$, 　$a_{22} = -1$,
　　$b_1 = 7$, 　$b_2 = 2$; 　$x_1 = 1$, 　$x_2 = 2$

**8.** $a_{11} = 6$, $\quad a_{12} = -1$, $\quad a_{13} = 1$, $\quad a_{21} = 1$,
$a_{22} = 2$, $\quad a_{23} = 4$, $\quad b_1 = 14$, $\quad b_2 = 4$;
$x_1 = 2$, $\quad x_2 = -1$, $\quad x_3 = 1$

**9.** $a_{11} = 1$, $\quad a_{12} = 1$, $\quad a_{21} = 3$, $\quad a_{22} = 4$,
$a_{31} = -1$, $\quad a_{32} = 2$, $\quad b_1 = 0$, $\quad b_2 = -1$,
$b_3 = -3$; $\quad x_1 = 1$, $\quad x_2 = -1$

**10.** $a_{11} = 0$, $\quad a_{12} = 3$, $\quad a_{21} = 4$, $\quad a_{22} = 0$,
$b_1 = 9$, $\quad b_2 = 8$; $\quad x_1 = 2$, $\quad x_2 = 3$

In Exercises 11–14, sketch a graph for each equation to determine whether the system has a unique solution, no solution, or infinitely many solutions.

**11.** $2x + y = 5$
$x - y = 1$

**12.** $2x - y = -1$
$2x - y = \phantom{-}2$

**13.** $3x + 2y = \phantom{-}6$
$-6x - 4y = -12$

**14.** $2x + \phantom{-}y = 5$
$x - \phantom{-}y = 1$
$x + 3y = 9$

**15.** The $(2 \times 3)$ system of linear equations

$$a_1 x + b_1 y + c_1 z = d_1$$
$$a_2 x + b_2 y + c_2 z = d_2$$

is represented geometrically by two planes. How are the planes related when:

**a)** The system has no solution?

**b)** The system has infinitely many solutions?

Is it possible for the system to have a unique solution? Explain.

In Exercises 16–18, determine whether the given $(2 \times 3)$ system of linear equations represents coincident planes (that is, the same plane), two parallel planes, or two planes whose intersection is a line. In the latter case, give the parametric equations for the line; that is, give equations of the form $x = at + b$, $y = ct + d$, $z = et + f$.

**16.** $2x_1 + x_2 + x_3 = 3$
$-2x_1 + x_2 - x_3 = 1$

**17.** $x_1 + 2x_2 - x_3 = 2$
$x_1 + \phantom{2}x_2 + x_3 = 3$

**18.** $x_1 + 3x_2 - 2x_3 = -1$
$2x_1 + 6x_2 - 4x_3 = -2$

**19.** Display the $(2 \times 3)$ matrix $A = (a_{ij})$, where $a_{11} = 2$, $a_{12} = 1$, $a_{13} = 6$, $a_{21} = 4$, $a_{22} = 3$, and $a_{23} = 8$.

**20.** Display the $(2 \times 4)$ matrix $C = (c_{ij})$, where $c_{23} = 4$, $c_{12} = 2$, $c_{21} = 2$, $c_{14} = 1$, $c_{22} = 2$, $c_{24} = 3$, $c_{11} = 1$, and $c_{13} = 7$.

**21.** Display the $(3 \times 3)$ matrix $Q = (q_{ij})$, where $q_{23} = 1$, $q_{32} = 2$, $q_{11} = 1$, $q_{13} = -3$, $q_{22} = 1$, $q_{33} = 1$, $q_{21} = 2$, $q_{12} = 4$, and $q_{31} = 3$.

**22.** Suppose the matrix $C$ in Exercise 20 is the augmented matrix for a system of linear equations. Display the system.

**23.** Repeat Exercise 22 for the matrices in Exercises 19 and 21.

In Exercises 24–29, display the coefficient matrix $A$ and the augmented matrix $B$ for the given system.

**24.** $x_1 - x_2 = -1$
$x_1 + x_2 = \phantom{-}3$

**25.** $x_1 + x_2 - x_3 = 2$
$2x_1 \phantom{+ x_2} - x_3 = 1$

**26.** $x_1 + 3x_2 - x_3 = 1$
$2x_1 + 5x_2 + x_3 = 5$
$x_1 + \phantom{5}x_2 + x_3 = 3$

**27.** $x_1 + \phantom{3}x_2 + 2x_3 = 6$
$3x_1 + 4x_2 - \phantom{2}x_3 = 5$
$-x_1 + \phantom{4}x_2 + \phantom{2}x_3 = 2$

**28.** $x_1 + \phantom{2}x_2 - 3x_3 = -1$
$x_1 + 2x_2 - 5x_3 = -2$
$-x_1 - 3x_2 + 7x_3 = \phantom{-}3$

**29.** $x_1 + \phantom{3}x_2 + \phantom{3}x_3 = 1$
$2x_1 + 3x_2 + \phantom{3}x_3 = 2$
$x_1 - \phantom{3}x_2 + 3x_3 = 2$

In Exercises 30–36, display the augmented matrix for the given system. Use elementary operations on equations to obtain an equivalent system of equations in which $x_1$ appears in the first equation with coefficient one and has been eliminated from the remaining equations. Simultaneously, perform the corresponding elementary row operations on the augmented matrix.

**30.** $2x_1 + 3x_2 = 6$
$4x_1 - \phantom{3}x_2 = 7$

**31.** $x_1 + 2x_2 - \phantom{2}x_3 = 1$
$x_1 + \phantom{2}x_2 + 2x_3 = 2$
$-2x_1 + \phantom{2}x_2 \phantom{+ 2x_3} = 4$

**32.** $x_2 + \phantom{2}x_3 = 4$
$x_1 - x_2 + 2x_3 = 1$
$2x_1 + x_2 - \phantom{2}x_3 = 6$

**33.** $x_1 + x_2 = 9$
$x_1 - x_2 = 7$
$3x_1 + x_2 = 6$

**34.** $x_1 + x_2 + x_3 - x_4 = 1$
$-x_1 + x_2 - x_3 + x_4 = 3$
$-2x_1 + x_2 + x_3 - x_4 = 2$

**35.** $x_2 + \phantom{2}x_3 - \phantom{7}x_4 = 3$
$x_1 + 2x_2 - \phantom{2}x_3 + \phantom{7}x_4 = 1$
$-x_1 + \phantom{2}x_2 + 7x_3 - \phantom{7}x_4 = 0$

**36.** $x_1 + x_2 = 0$
$x_1 - x_2 = 0$
$3x_1 + x_2 = 0$

**37.** Consider the equation $2x_1 - 3x_2 + x_3 - x_4 = 3$.

**a)** In the six different possible combinations, set any two of the variables equal to 1 and graph the equation in terms of the other two.

**b)** What type of graph do you always get when you set two of the variables equal to two fixed constants?

**c)** What is one possible reason the equation in formula (1) is called *linear*?

**38.** Consider the $(2 \times 2)$ system

$$a_{11}x_1 + a_{12}x_2 = b_1$$
$$a_{21}x_1 + a_{22}x_2 = b_2.$$

Show that if $a_{11}a_{22} - a_{12}a_{21} \neq 0$, then this system is equivalent to a system of the form

$$c_{11}x_1 + c_{12}x_2 = d_1$$
$$c_{22}x_2 = d_2,$$

where $c_{11} \neq 0$ and $c_{22} \neq 0$. Note that the second system always has a solution. [*Hint:* First suppose that $a_{11} \neq 0$, and then consider the special case in which $a_{11} = 0$.]

**39.** In the following $(2 \times 2)$ linear systems (A) and (B), $c$ is a nonzero scalar. Prove that any solution, $x_1 = s_1$, $x_2 = s_2$, for (A) is also a solution for (B). Conversely, show that any solution, $x_1 = t_1$, $x_2 = t_2$, for (B) is also a solution for (A). Where is the assumption that $c$ is nonzero required?

**(A)**
$$a_{11}x_1 + a_{12}x_2 = b_1$$
$$a_{21}x_1 + a_{22}x_2 = b_2$$

**(B)**
$$a_{11}x_1 + a_{12}x_2 = b_1$$
$$ca_{21}x_1 + ca_{22}x_2 = cb_2$$

**40.** In the $(2 \times 2)$ linear systems that follow, the system (B) is obtained from (A) by performing the elementary operation $E_2 + cE_1$. Prove that any solution, $x_1 = s_1$, $x_2 = s_2$, for (A) is a solution for (B). Similarly, prove that any solution, $x_1 = t_1$, $x_2 = t_2$, for (B) is a solution for (A).

**(A)**
$$a_{11}x_1 + a_{12}x_2 = b_1$$
$$a_{21}x_1 + a_{22}x_2 = b_2$$

**(B)**
$$a_{11}x_1 + a_{12}x_2 = b_1$$
$$(a_{21} + ca_{11})x_1 + (a_{22} + ca_{12})x_2 = b_2 + cb_1$$

**41.** Prove that any of the elementary operations in Theorem 1 applied to system (2) produces an equivalent system. [*Hint:* To simplify this proof, represent the $i$th equation in system (2) as $f_i(x_1, x_2, \ldots, x_n) = b_i$; so

$$f_i(x_1, x_2, \ldots, x_n) = a_{i1}x_1 + a_{i2}x_2 + \cdots + a_{in}x_n$$

for $i = 1, 2, \ldots, m$. With this notation, system (2) has the form of (A), which follows. Next, for example, if a multiple of $c$ times the $j$th equation is added to the $k$th equation, a new system of the form (B) is produced:

| **(A)** | **(B)** |
|---|---|
| $f_1(x_1, x_2, \ldots, x_n) = b_1$ | $f_1(x_1, x_2, \ldots, x_n) = b_1$ |
| $\vdots$ | $\vdots$ |
| $f_j(x_1, x_2, \ldots, x_n) = b_j$ | $f_j(x_1, x_2, \ldots, x_n) = b_j$ |
| $\vdots$ | $\vdots$ |
| $f_k(x_1, x_2, \ldots, x_n) = b_k$ | $g(x_1, x_2, \ldots, x_n) = r$ |
| $\vdots$ | $\vdots$ |
| $f_m(x_1, x_2, \ldots, x_n) = b_m$ | $f_m(x_1, x_2, \ldots, x_n) = b_m$ |

where $g(x_1, x_2, \ldots, x_n) = f_k(x_1, x_2, \ldots, x_n) + cf_j(x_1, x_2, \ldots, x_n)$, and $r = b_k + cb_j$. To show that the operation gives an equivalent system, show that any solution for (A) is a solution for (B), and vice versa.]

**42.** Solve the system of two nonlinear equations in two unknowns

$$x_1^2 - 2x_1 + x_2^2 = 3$$
$$x_1^2 \qquad - x_2^2 = 1.$$

# 1.2    ECHELON FORM AND GAUSS-JORDAN ELIMINATION

As we noted in the previous section, our method for solving a system of linear equations will be to pass to the augmented matrix, use elementary row operations to reduce the augmented matrix, and then solve the simpler but equivalent system represented by the reduced matrix. This procedure is illustrated in Fig. 1.3.

The objective of the Gauss-Jordan reduction process (represented by the middle block in Fig. 1.3) is to obtain a system of equations simplified to the point where we

***Figure 1.3*** Procedure for solving a system of linear equations

can immediately describe the solution. See, for example, Examples 6 and 7 in Section 1.1. We turn now to the question of how to describe this objective in mathematical terms—that is, how do we know when the system has been simplified as much as it can be? The answer is: The system has been simplified as much as possible when it is in reduced echelon form.

## Echelon Form

When an augmented matrix is reduced to the form known as *echelon form*, it is easy to solve the linear system represented by the reduced matrix. The formal description of echelon form is given in Definition 3. Then, in Definition 4, we describe an even simpler form known as *reduced echelon form*.

DEFINITION 3

An $(m \times n)$ matrix $B$ is in ***echelon form*** if:

1. All rows that consist entirely of zeros are grouped together at the bottom of the matrix.
2. In every nonzero row, the first nonzero entry (counting from left to right) is a 1.
3. If the $(i + 1)$-st row contains nonzero entries, then the first nonzero entry is in a column to the right of the first nonzero entry in the $i$th row.

Put informally, a matrix $A$ is in echelon form if the nonzero entries in $A$ form a staircase-like pattern, such as the four examples shown in Fig. 1.4. (***Note:*** Exercise 46 shows that there are exactly seven different types of echelon form for a $(3 \times 3)$ matrix. Figure 1.4 illustrates four of the possible patterns. In Fig. 1.4, the entries marked $*$ can be zero or nonzero.)

$$A = \begin{bmatrix} 1 & * & * \\ 0 & 1 & * \\ 0 & 0 & 1 \end{bmatrix} \quad A = \begin{bmatrix} 1 & * & * \\ 0 & 1 & * \\ 0 & 0 & 0 \end{bmatrix} \quad A = \begin{bmatrix} 1 & * & * \\ 0 & 0 & 1 \\ 0 & 0 & 0 \end{bmatrix} \quad A = \begin{bmatrix} 0 & 1 & * \\ 0 & 0 & 1 \\ 0 & 0 & 0 \end{bmatrix}$$

***Figure 1.4*** Patterns for four of the seven possible types of $(3 \times 3)$ matrices in echelon form. Entries marked $*$ can be either zero or nonzero.

Two examples of matrices in echelon form are

$$A = \begin{bmatrix} 1 & -1 & 4 & 3 & 0 & 2 & 0 \\ 0 & 0 & 1 & 8 & -4 & 3 & 2 \\ 0 & 0 & 0 & 1 & 2 & 1 & 2 \\ 0 & 0 & 0 & 0 & 0 & 1 & 3 \\ 0 & 0 & 0 & 0 & 0 & 0 & 0 \end{bmatrix} \quad B = \begin{bmatrix} 0 & 1 & -1 & 4 & 3 \\ 0 & 0 & 1 & 6 & -5 \\ 0 & 0 & 0 & 0 & 1 \end{bmatrix}.$$

We show later that every matrix can be transformed to echelon form with elementary row operations. It turns out, however, that echelon form is not unique. In order to guarantee uniqueness, we therefore add one more constraint and define a form known as *reduced echelon form*. As noted in Theorem 2, reduced echelon form is unique.

---

**DEFINITION 4**

A matrix that is in echelon form is in ***reduced echelon form*** provided that the first nonzero entry in any row is the only nonzero entry in its column.

---

Figure 1.5 gives four examples (corresponding to the examples in Fig. 1.4) of matrices in reduced echelon form.

$$A = \begin{bmatrix} 1 & 0 & 0 \\ 0 & 1 & 0 \\ 0 & 0 & 1 \end{bmatrix} \quad A = \begin{bmatrix} 1 & 0 & * \\ 0 & 1 & * \\ 0 & 0 & 0 \end{bmatrix} \quad A = \begin{bmatrix} 1 & * & 0 \\ 0 & 0 & 1 \\ 0 & 0 & 0 \end{bmatrix} \quad A = \begin{bmatrix} 0 & 1 & 0 \\ 0 & 0 & 1 \\ 0 & 0 & 0 \end{bmatrix}$$

*Figure 1.5*    Patterns for four of the seven possible types of $(3 \times 3)$ matrices in reduced echelon form. Entries marked $*$ can be either zero or nonzero.

Two examples of matrices in reduced echelon form are

$$A = \begin{bmatrix} 1 & 0 & 0 & 2 \\ 0 & 1 & 0 & -1 \\ 0 & 0 & 1 & 3 \end{bmatrix} \quad B = \begin{bmatrix} 1 & 2 & 0 & 1 & -1 \\ 0 & 0 & 1 & 3 & 4 \\ 0 & 0 & 0 & 0 & 0 \end{bmatrix}.$$

As can be seen from these examples and from Figs. 1.4 and 1.5, the feature that distinguishes reduced echelon form from echelon form is that the leading 1 in each nonzero row has only 0's above and below it.

**EXAMPLE 1**    For each matrix shown, choose one of the following phrases to describe the matrix.

(a)  The matrix is not in echelon form.

(b)  The matrix is in echelon form, but not in reduced echelon form.

(c)  The matrix is in reduced echelon form.

$$A = \begin{bmatrix} 1 & 0 & 0 \\ 2 & 1 & 0 \\ 3 & -4 & 1 \end{bmatrix}, \qquad B = \begin{bmatrix} 1 & 3 & 2 \\ 0 & -1 & 1 \\ 0 & 0 & 1 \end{bmatrix},$$

$$C = \begin{bmatrix} 0 & 1 & -1 & 0 \\ 0 & 0 & 0 & 1 \\ 0 & 0 & 0 & 0 \end{bmatrix}, \qquad D = \begin{bmatrix} 1 & 2 & 3 & 4 & 5 \\ 0 & 0 & 1 & 2 & 3 \\ 0 & 0 & 0 & 1 & 0 \end{bmatrix}, \qquad E = \begin{bmatrix} 1 \\ 0 \\ 0 \end{bmatrix},$$

$$F = \begin{bmatrix} 0 \\ 0 \\ 1 \end{bmatrix}, \qquad G = [1 \quad 0 \quad 0], \qquad H = [0 \quad 0 \quad 1].$$

*Solution*    $A$, $B$, and $F$ are not in echelon form; $D$ is in echelon form but not in reduced echelon form; $C$, $E$, $G$, and $H$ are in reduced echelon form. ◼

## Solving a Linear System Whose Augmented Matrix Is in Reduced Echelon Form

Software packages that can solve systems of equations typically include a command that produces the reduced echelon form of a matrix. Thus, to solve a linear system on a machine, we first enter the augmented matrix for the system and then apply the machine's reduce command. Once we get the machine output (that is, the reduced echelon form for the original augmented matrix), we have to interpret the output in order to find the solution. The next example illustrates this interpretation process.

Example 2    Each of the following matrices is in reduced echelon form and is the augmented matrix for a system of linear equations. In each case, give the system of equations and describe the solution.

$$B = \begin{bmatrix} 1 & 0 & 0 & 3 \\ 0 & 1 & 0 & -2 \\ 0 & 0 & 1 & 7 \\ 0 & 0 & 0 & 0 \end{bmatrix}, \qquad C = \begin{bmatrix} 1 & 0 & -1 & 0 \\ 0 & 1 & 3 & 0 \\ 0 & 0 & 0 & 1 \end{bmatrix},$$

$$D = \begin{bmatrix} 1 & -3 & 0 & 4 & 2 \\ 0 & 0 & 1 & -5 & 1 \\ 0 & 0 & 0 & 0 & 0 \end{bmatrix}, \qquad E = \begin{bmatrix} 1 & 2 & 0 & 5 \\ 0 & 0 & 1 & 0 \\ 0 & 0 & 0 & 0 \end{bmatrix}.$$

*Solution*

***Matrix B:***    Matrix $B$ is the augmented matrix for the following system:

$$\begin{aligned} x_1 \qquad\qquad &= \quad 3 \\ x_2 \qquad &= -2 \\ x_3 &= \quad 7. \end{aligned}$$

Therefore, the system has the unique solution $x_1 = 3$, $x_2 = -2$, and $x_3 = 7$.

***Matrix C:***    Matrix $C$ is the augmented matrix for the following system

$$x_1 \qquad\quad -x_3 = 0$$
$$x_2 + 3x_3 = 0$$
$$0x_1 + 0x_2 + 0x_3 = 1.$$

Because no values for $x_1$, $x_2$, or $x_3$ can satisfy the third equation, the system is inconsistent.

***Matrix D:***    Matrix $D$ is the augmented matrix for the following system

$$x_1 - 3x_2 \qquad + 4x_4 = 2$$
$$x_3 - 5x_4 = 1.$$

We solve each equation for the leading variable in its row, finding

$$x_1 = 2 + 3x_2 - 4x_4$$
$$x_3 = 1 + 5x_4.$$

In this case, $x_1$ and $x_3$ are the dependent (or constrained) variables whereas $x_2$ and $x_4$ are the independent (or unconstrained) variables. The system has infinitely many solutions, and particular solutions can be obtained by assigning values to $x_2$ and $x_4$. For example, setting $x_2 = 1$ and $x_4 = 2$ yields the solution $x_1 = -3$, $x_2 = 1$, $x_3 = 11$, and $x_4 = 2$.

***Matrix E:***    The second row of matrix $E$ sometimes leads students to conclude erroneously that the system of equations is inconsistent. Note the critical difference between the third row of matrix $C$ (which did represent an inconsistent system) and the second row of matrix $E$. In particular, if we write the system corresponding to $E$, we find

$$x_1 + 2x_2 \qquad = 5$$
$$x_3 = 0.$$

Thus, the system has infinitely many solutions described by

$$x_1 = 5 - 2x_2$$
$$x_3 = 0$$

where $x_2$ is an independent variable.    ◼

As we noted in Example 2, if an augmented matrix has a row of zeros, we sometimes jump to the conclusion (an *erroneous* conclusion) that the corresponding system of equations is inconsistent (see the discussion of matrix $E$ in Example 2). Similar confusion can arise when the augmented matrix has a column of zeros. For example, consider the matrix

$$\begin{bmatrix} 1 & 0 & 0 & -2 & 0 & 3 \\ 0 & 0 & 1 & -4 & 0 & 1 \\ 0 & 0 & 0 & 0 & 1 & 2 \end{bmatrix},$$

where $F$ is the augmented matrix for a system of 3 equations in 5 unknowns. Thus, $F$ represents the system

$$x_1 \qquad\quad - 2x_4 \qquad = 3$$
$$x_3 - 4x_4 \qquad = 2$$
$$x_5 = 2.$$

The solution of this system is $x_1 = 3 + 2x_4$, $x_3 = 1 + 4x_4$, $x_5 = 2$, and $x_4$ is arbitrary. Note that the equations place no constraint whatsoever on the variable $x_2$. That does not mean that $x_2$ must be zero; instead, it means that $x_2$ is also arbitrary.

## Recognizing an Inconsistent System

Suppose $[A \mid \mathbf{b}]$ is the augmented matrix for an $(m \times n)$ linear system of equations. If $[A \mid \mathbf{b}]$ is in reduced echelon form, you should be able to tell at a glance whether the linear system has any solutions. The idea was illustrated by matrix $C$ in Example 2.

In particular, we can show that if the last nonzero row of $[A \mid \mathbf{b}]$ has its leading 1 in the last column, then the linear system has no solution. To see why this is true, suppose the last nonzero row of $[A \mid \mathbf{b}]$ has the form

$$[0, 0, 0, \dots, 0, 1].$$

This row, then, represents the equation

$$0x_1 + 0x_2 + 0x_3 + \cdots + 0x_n = 1.$$

Because this equation cannot be satisfied, it follows that the linear system represented by $[A \mid \mathbf{b}]$ is inconsistent. We list this observation formally in the following remark.

***Remark***    Let $[A \mid \mathbf{b}]$ be the augmented matrix for an $(m \times n)$ linear system of equations, and let $[A \mid \mathbf{b}]$ be in reduced echelon form. If the last nonzero row of $[A \mid \mathbf{b}]$ has its leading 1 in the last column, then the system of equations has no solution.

When you are carrying out the reduction of $[A \mid \mathbf{b}]$ to echelon form by hand, you might encounter a row that consists entirely of zeros except for a nonzero entry in the last column. In such a case, there is no reason to continue the reduction process since you have found an equation in an equivalent system that has no solution; that is, the system represented by $[A \mid \mathbf{b}]$ is inconsistent.

## Reduction to Echelon Form

The following theorem guarantees that every matrix can be transformed to one and only one matrix that is in reduced echelon form.

**THEOREM 2**    Let $B$ be an $(m \times n)$ matrix. There is a unique $(m \times n)$ matrix $C$ such that:

    **(a)**   $C$ is in reduced echelon form

and

    **(b)**   $C$ is row equivalent to $B$.      ◼

Suppose $B$ is the augmented matrix for an $(m \times n)$ system of linear equations. One important consequence of this theorem is that it shows we can always transform $B$ by a series of elementary row operations into a matrix $C$ which is in reduced echelon form. Then, because $C$ is in reduced echelon form, it is easy to solve the equivalent linear system represented by $C$ (recall Example 2).

The following steps show how to transform a given matrix $B$ to reduced echelon form. As such, this list of steps constitutes an informal proof of the existence portion of Theorem 2. We do not prove the uniqueness portion of Theorem 2. The steps listed assume that $B$ has at least one nonzero entry (because if $B$ has only zero entries, then $B$ is already in reduced row echelon form).

---

### Reduction to Reduced Echelon Form for an $(m \times n)$ Matrix

*Step 1.* Locate the first (left-most) column that contains a nonzero entry.

*Step 2.* If necessary, interchange the first row with another row so that the first nonzero column has a nonzero entry in the first row.

*Step 3.* If $a$ denotes the leading nonzero entry in row one, multiply each entry in row one by $1/a$. (Thus, the leading nonzero entry in row one is a 1.)

*Step 4.* Add appropriate multiples of row one to each of the remaining rows so that every entry below the leading 1 in row one is a 0.

*Step 5.* Temporarily ignore the first row of this matrix and repeat Steps 1–4 on the submatrix that remains. Stop the process when the resulting matrix is in echelon form.

*Step 6.* Having reached echelon form in Step 5, continue on to reduced echelon form as follows: Proceeding upward, add multiples of each nonzero row to the rows above in order to zero all entries above the leading 1.

---

The next example illustrates an application of the six-step process just described. When doing a small problem by hand, however, it is customary to alter the steps slightly— instead of going all the way to echelon form (sweeping from left to right) and then going from echelon to reduced echelon form (sweeping from bottom to top), it is customary to make a single pass (moving from left to right) introducing 0's above and below the leading 1. Example 3 demonstrates this single-pass variation.

**EXAMPLE 3**    Use elementary row operations to transform the following matrix to reduced echelon form

$$
A = \begin{bmatrix}
0 & 0 & 0 & 0 & 2 & 8 & 4 \\
0 & 0 & 0 & 1 & 3 & 11 & 9 \\
0 & 3 & -12 & -3 & -9 & -24 & -33 \\
0 & -2 & 8 & 1 & 6 & 17 & 21
\end{bmatrix}.
$$

*Solution*    The following row operations will transform $A$ to reduced echelon form.

$R_1 \leftrightarrow R_3, (1/3)R_1$:     Introduce a leading 1 into the first row of the first nonzero column.

$$\begin{bmatrix} 0 & 1 & -4 & -1 & -3 & -8 & -11 \\ 0 & 0 & 0 & 1 & 3 & 11 & 9 \\ 0 & 0 & 0 & 0 & 2 & 8 & 4 \\ 0 & -2 & 8 & 1 & 6 & 17 & 21 \end{bmatrix}$$

$R_4 + 2R_1$:     Introduce 0's below the leading 1 in row 1.

$$\begin{bmatrix} 0 & 1 & -4 & -1 & -3 & -8 & -11 \\ 0 & 0 & 0 & 1 & 3 & 11 & 9 \\ 0 & 0 & 0 & 0 & 2 & 8 & 4 \\ 0 & 0 & 0 & -1 & 0 & 1 & -1 \end{bmatrix}$$

$R_1 + R_2, R_4 + R_2$:     Introduce 0's above and below the leading 1 in row 2.

$$\begin{bmatrix} 0 & 1 & -4 & 0 & 0 & 3 & -2 \\ 0 & 0 & 0 & 1 & 3 & 11 & 9 \\ 0 & 0 & 0 & 0 & 2 & 8 & 4 \\ 0 & 0 & 0 & 0 & 3 & 12 & 8 \end{bmatrix}$$

$(1/2)R_3$:     Introduce a leading 1 into row 3.

$$\begin{bmatrix} 0 & 1 & -4 & 0 & 0 & 3 & -2 \\ 0 & 0 & 0 & 1 & 3 & 11 & 9 \\ 0 & 0 & 0 & 0 & 1 & 4 & 2 \\ 0 & 0 & 0 & 0 & 3 & 12 & 8 \end{bmatrix}$$

$R_2 - 3R_3, R_4 - 3R_3$:     Introduce 0's above and below the leading 1 in row 3.

$$\begin{bmatrix} 0 & 1 & -4 & 0 & 0 & 3 & -2 \\ 0 & 0 & 0 & 1 & 0 & -1 & 3 \\ 0 & 0 & 0 & 0 & 1 & 4 & 2 \\ 0 & 0 & 0 & 0 & 0 & 0 & 2 \end{bmatrix}$$

$(1/2)R_4$:     Introduce a leading 1 into row 4.

$$\begin{bmatrix} 0 & 1 & -4 & 0 & 0 & 3 & -2 \\ 0 & 0 & 0 & 1 & 0 & -1 & 3 \\ 0 & 0 & 0 & 0 & 1 & 4 & 2 \\ 0 & 0 & 0 & 0 & 0 & 0 & 1 \end{bmatrix}$$

$R_1 + 2R_4, R_2 - 3R_4, R_3 - 2R_4$:     Introduce 0's above the leading 1 in row 4.

$$\begin{bmatrix} 0 & 1 & -4 & 0 & 0 & 3 & 0 \\ 0 & 0 & 0 & 1 & 0 & -1 & 0 \\ 0 & 0 & 0 & 0 & 1 & 4 & 0 \\ 0 & 0 & 0 & 0 & 0 & 0 & 1 \end{bmatrix}$$

Having provided this example of how to transform a matrix to reduced echelon form, we can be more specific about the procedure for solving a system of equations that is diagrammed in Fig. 1.3.

---

### Solving a System of Equations

Given a system of equations:

***Step 1.***   Create the augmented matrix for the system.

***Step 2.***   Transform the matrix in Step 1 to reduced echelon form.

***Step 3.***   Decode the reduced matrix found in Step 2 to obtain its associated system of equations. (This system is equivalent to the original system.)

***Step 4.***   By examining the reduced system in Step 3, describe the solution set for the original system.

---

The next example illustrates the complete process.

**EXAMPLE 4**   Solve the following system of equations:

$$
\begin{aligned}
2x_1 - 4x_2 + \phantom{1}3x_3 - \phantom{1}4x_4 - 11x_5 &= \phantom{-1}28 \\
-x_1 + 2x_2 - \phantom{1}x_3 + 2x_4 + \phantom{1}5x_5 &= -13 \\
- \phantom{1}3x_3 + \phantom{1}x_4 + \phantom{1}6x_5 &= -10 \\
3x_1 - 6x_2 + 10x_3 - 8x_4 - 28x_5 &= \phantom{-1}61.
\end{aligned}
$$

*Solution*   We first create the augmented matrix and then transform it to reduced echelon form. The augmented matrix is

$$
\begin{bmatrix}
2 & -4 & 3 & -4 & -11 & 28 \\
-1 & 2 & -1 & 2 & 5 & -13 \\
0 & 0 & -3 & 1 & 6 & -10 \\
3 & -6 & 10 & -8 & -28 & 61
\end{bmatrix}.
$$

The first step is to introduce a leading 1 into row 1. We can introduce the leading 1 if we multiply row 1 by 1/2, but that would create fractions that are undesirable for hand work. As an alternative, we can add row 2 to row 1 and avoid fractions.

$R_1 + R_2:$

$$
\begin{bmatrix}
1 & -2 & 2 & -2 & -6 & 15 \\
-1 & 2 & -1 & 2 & 5 & -13 \\
0 & 0 & -3 & 1 & 6 & -10 \\
3 & -6 & 10 & -8 & -28 & 61
\end{bmatrix}
$$

$R_2 + R_1, R_4 - 3R_1$:     Introduce 0's below the leading 1 in row 1.

$$\begin{bmatrix} 1 & -2 & 2 & -2 & -6 & 15 \\ 0 & 0 & 1 & 0 & -1 & 2 \\ 0 & 0 & -3 & 1 & 6 & -10 \\ 0 & 0 & 4 & -2 & -10 & 16 \end{bmatrix}$$

$R_1 - 2R_2, R_3 + 3R_2, R_4 - 4R_2$:     Introduce 0's above and below the leading 1 in row 2.

$$\begin{bmatrix} 1 & -2 & 0 & -2 & -4 & 11 \\ 0 & 0 & 1 & 0 & -1 & 2 \\ 0 & 0 & 0 & 1 & 3 & -4 \\ 0 & 0 & 0 & -2 & -6 & 8 \end{bmatrix}$$

$R_1 + 2R_3, R_4 + 2R_3$:     Introduce 0's above and below the leading 1 in row 3.

$$\begin{bmatrix} 1 & -2 & 0 & 0 & 2 & 3 \\ 0 & 0 & 1 & 0 & -1 & 2 \\ 0 & 0 & 0 & 1 & 3 & -4 \\ 0 & 0 & 0 & 0 & 0 & 0 \end{bmatrix}$$

The matrix above represents the system of equations

$$\begin{aligned} x_1 - 2x_2 \qquad + 2x_5 &= 3 \\ x_3 \quad - x_5 &= 2 \\ x_4 + 3x_5 &= -4. \end{aligned}$$

Solving the preceding system, we find:

$$\begin{aligned} x_1 &= 3 + 2x_2 - 2x_5 \\ x_3 &= 2 \qquad + x_5 \\ x_4 &= -4 \qquad - 3x_5 \end{aligned} \qquad (1)$$

In Eq. (1) we have a nice description of all of the infinitely many solutions to the original system—it is called the **general solution** for the system. For this example, $x_2$ and $x_5$ are viewed as independent (or unconstrained) variables and can be assigned values arbitrarily. The variables $x_1$, $x_3$, and $x_4$ are dependent (or constrained) variables, and their values are determined by the values assigned to $x_2$ and $x_5$. For example, in Eq. (1), setting $x_2 = 1$ and $x_5 = -1$ yields a **particular solution** given by $x_1 = 7$, $x_2 = 1$, $x_3 = 1$, $x_4 = -1$, and $x_5 = -1$.

## Electronic Aids and Software

One testimony to the practical importance of linear algebra is the wide variety of electronic aids available for linear algebra computations. For instance, many scientific calculators can solve systems of linear equations and perform simple matrix operations. For computers there are general-purpose computer algebra systems such as Derive, Mathematica, and Maple that have extensive computational capabilities. Special-purpose linear algebra software such as MATLAB is very easy to use and can perform virtually any type of matrix calculation.

In the following example, we illustrate the use of MATLAB. From time to time, as appropriate, we will include other examples that illustrate the use of electronic aids.

**EXAMPLE 5**      In certain applications, it is necessary to evaluate sums of powers of integers such as

$$1 + 2 + 3 + \cdots + n,$$
$$1^2 + 2^2 + 3^2 + \cdots + n^2,$$
$$1^3 + 2^3 + 3^3 + \cdots + n^3, \quad \text{and so on.}$$

Interestingly, it is possible to derive simple formulas for such sums. For instance, you might be familiar with the formula

$$1 + 2 + 3 + \cdots + n = \frac{n(n + 1)}{2}.$$

Such formulas can be derived using the following result: If $n$ and $r$ are positive integers, then there are constants $a_1, a_2, \ldots, a_{r+1}$ such that

$$1^r + 2^r + 3^r + \cdots + n^r = a_1 n + a_2 n^2 + a_3 n^3 + \cdots + a_{r+1} n^{r+1}. \tag{2}$$

Use Eq. (2) to find the formula for $1^3 + 2^3 + 3^3 + \cdots + n^3$. (***Note:*** Eq. (2) can be derived from the theory of linear difference equations.)

***Solution***      From Eq. (2) there are constants $a_1, a_2, a_3$, and $a_4$ such that

$$1^3 + 2^3 + 3^3 + \cdots + n^3 = a_1 n + a_2 n^2 + a_3 n^3 + a_4 n^4.$$

If we evaluate the formula just given for $n = 1$, $n = 2$, $n = 3$, and $n = 4$, we obtain four equations for $a_1, a_2, a_3$, and $a_4$:

$$
\begin{array}{rcll}
a_1 + a_2 + a_3 + a_4 & = & 1 & (n = 1) \\
2a_1 + 4a_2 + 8a_3 + 16a_4 & = & 9 & (n = 2) \\
3a_1 + 9a_2 + 27a_3 + 81a_4 & = & 36 & (n = 3) \\
4a_1 + 16a_2 + 64a_3 + 256a_4 & = & 100. & (n = 4)
\end{array}
$$

The augmented matrix for this system is

$$A = \begin{bmatrix} 1 & 1 & 1 & 1 & 1 \\ 2 & 4 & 8 & 16 & 9 \\ 3 & 9 & 27 & 81 & 36 \\ 4 & 16 & 64 & 256 & 100 \end{bmatrix}.$$

We used MATLAB to solve the system by transforming $A$ to reduced echelon form. The steps, as they appear on a computer screen, are shown in Fig. 1.6. The symbol $>>$ is a prompt from MATLAB. At the first prompt, we entered the augmented matrix $A$

```
>>A=[1,1,1,1,1;2,4,8,16,9;3,9,27,81,36;4,16,64,256,100]

A=
      1          1          1          1          1
      2          4          8         16          9
      3          9         27         81         36
      4         16         64        256        100

>>C=rref(A)

C=
 1.0000          0                     0          0          0
      0     1.0000                     0          0     0.2500
      0          0                1.0000          0     0.5000
      0          0                     0     1.0000     0.2500

>>C

C=
      1          0          0          0          0
      0          1          0          0        1/4
      0          0          1          0        1/2
      0          0          0          1        1/4
```

*Figure 1.6*  Using MATLAB in Example 5 to row reduce the matrix $A$
to the matrix $C$.

and then MATLAB displayed $A$. At the second prompt, we entered the MATLAB row-reduction command, $C = \text{rref}(A)$. The new matrix $C$, as displayed by MATLAB, is the result of transforming $A$ to reduced echelon form.

MATLAB normally displays results in decimal form. To obtain a rational form for the reduced matrix $C$, from the submenu *numerical form* we selected *rat* and entered $C$, finding

$$C = \begin{bmatrix} 1 & 0 & 0 & 0 & 0 \\ 0 & 1 & 0 & 0 & 1/4 \\ 0 & 0 & 1 & 0 & 1/2 \\ 0 & 0 & 0 & 1 & 1/4 \end{bmatrix}.$$

From this, we have $a_1 = 0$, $a_2 = 1/4$, $a_3 = 1/2$, and $a_4 = 1/4$. Therefore, the formula for the sum of the first $n$ cubes is

$$1^3 + 2^3 + 3^3 + \cdots + n^3 = \frac{1}{4}n^2 + \frac{1}{2}n^3 + \frac{1}{4}n^4$$

or, after simplification,

$$1^3 + 2^3 + 3^3 + \cdots + n^3 = \frac{n^2(n+1)^2}{4}.$$

ADDING INTEGERS   Mathematical folklore has it that Gauss discovered the formula $1 + 2 + 3 + \cdots + n = n(n + 1)/2$ when he was only ten years old. To occupy time, his teacher asked the students to add the integers from 1 to 100. Gauss immediately wrote an answer and turned his slate over. To his teacher's amazement, Gauss had the only correct answer in the class. Young Gauss had recognized that the numbers could be put in 50 sets of pairs such that the sum of each pair was 101:

$$(50 + 51) + (49 + 52) + (48 + 53) + \cdots + (1 + 100) = 50(101) = 5050.$$

Soon his brilliance was brought to the attention of the Duke of Brunswick, who thereafter sponsored the education of Gauss.

## 1.2   EXERCISES

Consider the matrices in Exercises 1–10.

**a)** Either state that the matrix is in echelon form or use elementary row operations to transform it to echelon form.

**b)** If the matrix is in echelon form, transform it to reduced echelon form.

**1.** $\begin{bmatrix} 1 & 2 \\ 0 & 1 \end{bmatrix}$

**2.** $\begin{bmatrix} 1 & 2 & -1 \\ 0 & 1 & 3 \end{bmatrix}$

**3.** $\begin{bmatrix} 2 & 3 & 1 \\ 4 & 1 & 0 \end{bmatrix}$

**4.** $\begin{bmatrix} 0 & 1 & 1 \\ 1 & 2 & 3 \end{bmatrix}$

**5.** $\begin{bmatrix} 0 & 0 & 2 & 3 \\ 2 & 0 & 1 & 4 \end{bmatrix}$

**6.** $\begin{bmatrix} 2 & 0 & 3 & 1 \\ 0 & 0 & 1 & 2 \end{bmatrix}$

**7.** $\begin{bmatrix} 1 & 3 & 2 & 1 \\ 0 & 1 & 4 & 2 \\ 0 & 0 & 1 & 1 \end{bmatrix}$

**8.** $\begin{bmatrix} 2 & -1 & 3 \\ 0 & 1 & 1 \\ 0 & 0 & -3 \end{bmatrix}$

**9.** $\begin{bmatrix} 1 & 2 & -1 & -2 \\ 0 & 2 & -2 & -3 \\ 0 & 0 & 0 & 1 \end{bmatrix}$

**10.** $\begin{bmatrix} -1 & 4 & -3 & 4 & 6 \\ 0 & 2 & 1 & -3 & -3 \\ 0 & 0 & 0 & 1 & 2 \end{bmatrix}$

In Exercises 11–21, each of the given matrices represents the augmented matrix for a system of linear equations. In each exercise, display the solution set or state that the system is inconsistent.

**11.** $\begin{bmatrix} 1 & 1 & 0 \\ 0 & 1 & 0 \end{bmatrix}$

**12.** $\begin{bmatrix} 1 & 1 & 0 \\ 0 & 0 & 2 \end{bmatrix}$

**13.** $\begin{bmatrix} 1 & 2 & 1 & 0 \\ 0 & 1 & 3 & 1 \end{bmatrix}$

**14.** $\begin{bmatrix} 1 & 2 & 2 & 1 \\ 0 & 1 & 0 & 0 \end{bmatrix}$

**15.** $\begin{bmatrix} 1 & 1 & 1 & 0 \\ 0 & 1 & 0 & 0 \\ 0 & 0 & 0 & 1 \end{bmatrix}$

**16.** $\begin{bmatrix} 1 & 2 & 0 & 1 \\ 0 & 1 & 1 & 0 \\ 0 & 0 & 2 & 0 \end{bmatrix}$

**17.** $\begin{bmatrix} 1 & 0 & 1 & 0 & 0 \\ 0 & 0 & 1 & 1 & 0 \\ 0 & 0 & 0 & 1 & 0 \end{bmatrix}$

**18.** $\begin{bmatrix} 1 & 2 & 1 & 3 \\ 0 & 0 & 0 & 2 \\ 0 & 0 & 0 & 0 \end{bmatrix}$

**19.** $\begin{bmatrix} 1 & 0 & 0 & 1 \\ 0 & 1 & 0 & 1 \\ 0 & 0 & 0 & 1 \end{bmatrix}$

**20.** $\begin{bmatrix} 1 & 1 & 2 & 0 & 2 & 0 \\ 0 & 1 & 1 & 1 & 0 & 0 \\ 0 & 0 & 1 & 2 & 1 & 2 \end{bmatrix}$

**21.** $\begin{bmatrix} 2 & 1 & 3 & 2 & 0 & 1 \\ 0 & 0 & 1 & 1 & 2 & 1 \\ 0 & 0 & 0 & 0 & 3 & 0 \end{bmatrix}$

In Exercises 22–35, solve the system by transforming the augmented matrix to reduced echelon form.

**22.**  $\begin{aligned} 2x_1 - 3x_2 &= 5 \\ -4x_1 + 6x_2 &= -10 \end{aligned}$

**23.**  $\begin{aligned} x_1 - 2x_2 &= 3 \\ 2x_1 - 4x_2 &= 1 \end{aligned}$

**24.** $x_1 - x_2 + x_3 = 3$
$\quad 2x_1 + x_2 - 4x_3 = -3$

**25.** $x_1 + x_2 = 2$
$\quad 3x_1 + 3x_2 = 6$

**26.** $x_1 - x_2 + x_3 = 4$
$\quad 2x_1 - 2x_2 + 3x_3 = 2$

**27.** $x_1 + x_2 - x_3 = 2$
$\quad -3x_1 - 3x_2 + 3x_3 = -6$

**28.** $2x_1 + 3x_2 - 4x_3 = 3$
$\quad x_1 - 2x_2 - 2x_3 = -2$
$\quad -x_1 + 16x_2 + 2x_3 = 16$

**29.** $x_1 + x_2 - x_3 = 1$
$\quad 2x_1 - x_2 + 7x_3 = 8$
$\quad -x_1 + x_2 - 5x_3 = -5$

**30.** $x_1 + x_2 \quad\quad - x_5 = 1$
$\quad x_2 + 2x_3 + x_4 + 3x_5 = 1$
$\quad x_1 \quad\quad - x_3 + x_4 + x_5 = 0$

**31.** $x_1 \quad\quad + x_3 + x_4 - 2x_5 = 1$
$\quad 2x_1 + x_2 + 3x_3 - x_4 + x_5 = 0$
$\quad 3x_1 - x_2 + 4x_3 + x_4 + x_5 = 1$

**32.** $x_1 + x_2 = 1$
$\quad x_1 - x_2 = 3$
$\quad 2x_1 + x_2 = 3$

**33.** $x_1 + x_2 = 1$
$\quad x_1 - x_2 = 3$
$\quad 2x_1 + x_2 = 2$

**34.** $x_1 + 2x_2 = 1$
$\quad 2x_1 + 4x_2 = 2$
$\quad -x_1 - 2x_2 = -1$

**35.** $x_1 - x_2 - x_3 = 1$
$\quad x_1 \quad\quad + x_3 = 2$
$\quad x_2 + 2x_3 = 3$

In Exercises 36–40, find all values $a$ for which the system has no solution.

**36.** $x_1 + 2x_2 = -3$
$\quad ax_1 - 2x_2 = 5$

**37.** $x_1 + 3x_2 = 4$
$\quad 2x_1 + 6x_2 = a$

**38.** $2x_1 + 4x_2 = a$
$\quad 3x_1 + 6x_2 = 5$

**39.** $3x_1 + ax_2 = 3$
$\quad ax_1 + 3x_2 = 5$

**40.** $x_1 + ax_2 = 6$
$\quad ax_1 + 2ax_2 = 4$

In Exercises 41 and 42, find all values $\alpha$ and $\beta$ where $0 \le \alpha \le 2\pi$ and $0 \le \beta \le 2\pi$.

**41.** $2\cos\alpha + 4\sin\beta = 3$
$\quad 3\cos\alpha - 5\sin\beta = -1$

**42.** $2\cos^2\alpha - \sin^2\beta = 1$
$\quad 12\cos^2\alpha + 8\sin^2\beta = 13$

**43.** Describe the solution set of the following system in terms of $x_3$:
$$x_1 + x_2 + x_3 = 3$$
$$x_1 + 2x_2 \quad\quad = 5.$$
For $x_1, x_2, x_3$ in the solution set:

**a)** Find the maximum value of $x_3$ such that $x_1 \ge 0$ and $x_2 \ge 0$.

**b)** Find the maximum value of $y = 2x_1 - 4x_2 + x_3$ subject to $x_1 \ge 0$ and $x_2 \ge 0$.

**c)** Find the minimum value of $y = (x_1 - 1)^2 + (x_2 + 3)^2 + (x_3 + 1)^2$ with no restriction on $x_1$ or $x_2$. [*Hint:* Regard $y$ as a function of $x_3$ and set the derivative equal to 0; then apply the second-derivative test to verify that you have found a minimum.]

**44.** Let $A$ and $I$ be as follows:
$$A = \begin{bmatrix} 1 & d \\ c & b \end{bmatrix}, \quad I = \begin{bmatrix} 1 & 0 \\ 0 & 1 \end{bmatrix}.$$
Prove that if $b - cd \ne 0$, then $A$ is row equivalent to $I$.

**45.** As in Fig. 1.4, display all the possible configurations for a $(2 \times 3)$ matrix that is in echelon form. [*Hint:* There are seven such configurations. Consider the various positions that can be occupied by one, two, or none of the symbols.]

**46.** Repeat Exercise 45 for a $(3 \times 2)$ matrix, for a $(3 \times 3)$ matrix, and for a $(3 \times 4)$ matrix.

**47.** Consider the matrices $B$ and $C$:
$$B = \begin{bmatrix} 1 & 2 \\ 2 & 3 \end{bmatrix}, \quad C = \begin{bmatrix} 1 & 2 \\ 3 & 4 \end{bmatrix}.$$
By Exercise 44, $B$ and $C$ are both row equivalent to matrix $I$ in Exercise 44. Determine elementary row operations that demonstrate that $B$ is row equivalent to $C$.

**48.** Repeat Exercise 47 for the matrices
$$B = \begin{bmatrix} 1 & 4 \\ 3 & 7 \end{bmatrix}, \quad C = \begin{bmatrix} 1 & 2 \\ 2 & 1 \end{bmatrix}.$$

**49.** A certain three-digit number $N$ equals fifteen times the sum of its digits. If its digits are reversed, the resulting number exceeds $N$ by 396. The one's digit is one larger than the sum of the other two. Give a linear system of three equations whose three unknowns are the digits of $N$. Solve the system and find $N$.

**50.** Find the equation of the parabola, $y = ax^2 + bx + c$, that passes through the points $(-1, 6)$, $(1, 4)$, and $(2, 9)$. [*Hint:* For each point, give a linear equation in $a$, $b$, and $c$.]

**51.** Three people play a game in which there are always two winners and one loser. They have the understanding that the loser gives each winner an amount equal to what the winner already has. After three games, each has lost just once and each has $24. With how much money did each begin?

**52.** Find three numbers whose sum is 34 when the sum of the first and second is 7, and the sum of the second and third is 22.

**53.** A zoo charges $6 for adults, $3 for students, and $.50 for children. One morning 79 people enter and pay a total of $207. Determine the possible numbers of adults, students, and children.

**54.** Find a cubic polynomial, $p(x) = a+bx+cx^2+dx^3$, such that $p(1) = 5$, $p'(1) = 5$, $p(2) = 17$, and $p'(2) = 21$.

In Exercises 55–58, use Eq. (2) to find the formula for the sum. If available, use linear algebra software for Exercises 57 and 58.

**55.** $1 + 2 + 3 + \cdots + n$

**56.** $1^2 + 2^2 + 3^2 + \cdots + n^2$

**57.** $1^4 + 2^4 + 3^4 + \cdots + n^4$

**58.** $1^5 + 2^5 + 3^5 + \cdots + n^5$

# CONSISTENT SYSTEMS OF LINEAR EQUATIONS

We saw in Section 1.1 that a system of linear equations may have a unique solution, infinitely many solutions, or no solution. In this section and in later sections, it will be shown that with certain added bits of information we can, without solving the system, either eliminate one of the three possible outcomes or determine precisely what the outcome will be. This will be important later when situations will arise in which we are not interested in obtaining a specific solution, but we need to know only how many solutions there are.

To illustrate, consider the general $(2 \times 3)$ linear system

$$a_{11}x_1 + a_{12}x_2 + a_{13}x_3 = b_1$$
$$a_{21}x_1 + a_{22}x_2 + a_{23}x_3 = b_2.$$

Geometrically, the system is represented by two planes, and a solution corresponds to a point in the intersection of the planes. The two planes may be parallel, they may be coincident (the same plane), or they may intersect in a line. Thus the system is either inconsistent or has infinitely many solutions; the existence of a unique solution is impossible.

## Solution Possibilities for a Consistent Linear System

We begin our analysis by considering the $(m \times n)$ system of linear equations

$$\begin{aligned}
a_{11}x_1 + a_{12}x_2 + \cdots + a_{1n}x_n &= b_1 \\
a_{21}x_1 + a_{22}x_2 + \cdots + a_{2n}x_n &= b_2 \\
\vdots \qquad\qquad\qquad \vdots \quad\; \vdots \\
a_{m1}x_1 + a_{m2}x_2 + \cdots + a_{mn}x_n &= b_m.
\end{aligned} \tag{1}$$

Our goal is to deduce as much information as possible about the solution set of system (1) without actually solving the system.

To that end, let $[A \,|\, \mathbf{b}]$ denote the augmented matrix for system (1). We know we can use row operations to transform the $[m \times (n + 1)]$ matrix $[A \,|\, \mathbf{b}]$ to a row equivalent matrix $[C \,|\, \mathbf{d}]$ where $[C \,|\, \mathbf{d}]$ is in reduced echelon form. Hence, instead of trying to deduce the various possibilities for the solution set of (1), we will focus on the simpler problem of analyzing the solution possibilities for the *equivalent* system represented by the matrix $[C \mid \mathbf{d}]$.

We begin by making four remarks about an $[m \times (n + 1)]$ matrix $[C \mid \mathbf{d}]$ that is in reduced echelon form. Our first remark recalls an observation made in Section 1.2.

***Remark 1:***   The system represented by the matrix $[C \mid \mathbf{d}]$ is inconsistent if and only if $[C \mid \mathbf{d}]$ has a row of the form $[0, 0, 0, \ldots, 0, 1]$.

Our second remark also follows because $[C \mid \mathbf{d}]$ is in reduced echelon form. In particular, we know every nonzero row of $[C \mid \mathbf{d}]$ has a leading 1. We also know there are no other nonzero entries in a column of $[C \mid \mathbf{d}]$ that contains a leading 1. Thus, if $x_k$ is the variable corresponding to a leading 1, then $x_k$ can be expressed in terms of other variables that do not correspond to any leading ones in $[C \mid \mathbf{d}]$. Therefore, we obtain

***Remark 2:***   Every variable corresponding to a leading 1 in $[C \mid \mathbf{d}]$ is a dependent variable. (That is, each "leading-one variable" can be expressed in terms of the independent or "nonleading-one variables.")

We illustrate Remark 2 with the following example.

**EXAMPLE 1**   Consider the matrix $[C \mid \mathbf{d}]$ given by

$$[C \mid \mathbf{d}] = \begin{bmatrix} 1 & 2 & 0 & 3 & 0 & 4 & 1 \\ 0 & 0 & 1 & 2 & 0 & 3 & 2 \\ 0 & 0 & 0 & 0 & 1 & 1 & 2 \\ 0 & 0 & 0 & 0 & 0 & 0 & 0 \\ 0 & 0 & 0 & 0 & 0 & 0 & 0 \end{bmatrix}.$$

The matrix $[C \mid \mathbf{d}]$ is in reduced echelon form and represents the consistent system

$$\begin{aligned} x_1 + 2x_2 + \qquad 3x_4 + \qquad + 4x_6 &= 1 \\ x_3 + 2x_4 + \qquad + 3x_6 &= 2 \\ x_5 + \quad x_6 &= 2. \end{aligned}$$

The dependent variables (corresponding to the leading 1's) are $x_1$, $x_3$, and $x_5$. They can be expressed in terms of the other (independent) variables as follows:

$$\begin{aligned} x_1 &= 1 - 2x_2 - 3x_4 - 4x_6 \\ x_3 &= 2 \qquad\quad - 2x_4 - 3x_6 \\ x_5 &= 2 \qquad\qquad\qquad - x_6. \end{aligned}$$

Our third remark gives a bound on the number of nonzero rows in $[C \mid \mathbf{d}]$. Let $r$ denote the number of nonzero rows in $[C \mid \mathbf{d}]$. (Later we will see that the number $r$ is called the "rank" of $C$.) Since every nonzero row contains a leading 1, the number $r$ is equal to the number of leading 1's. Because the matrix is in echelon form, there cannot be more leading 1's in $[C \mid \mathbf{d}]$ than there are columns. Since the matrix $[C \mid \mathbf{d}]$ has $n + 1$ columns, we conclude:

***Remark 3:***   Let $r$ denote the number of nonzero rows in $[C \mid \mathbf{d}]$. Then, $r \le n + 1$.

Our fourth remark is a consequence of Remark 1 and Remark 3. Let $r$ denote the number of nonzero rows in $[C \mid \mathbf{d}]$. If $r = n+1$, then $[C \mid \mathbf{d}]$ has a row of the form $[0, 0, \ldots, 0, 1]$ and hence the system represented by $[C \mid \mathbf{d}]$ must be inconsistent. Therefore, if the system is consistent, we need to have $r < n + 1$. This observation leads to:

***Remark 4:***     Let $r$ denote the number of nonzero rows in $[C \mid \mathbf{d}]$. If the system represented by $[C \mid \mathbf{d}]$ is consistent, then $r \leq n$.

In general, let $[C \mid \mathbf{d}]$ be an $[m \times (n + 1)]$ matrix in reduced echelon form where $[C \mid \mathbf{d}]$ represents a consistent system. According to Remark 2, if $[C \mid \mathbf{d}]$ has $r$ nonzero rows, then there are $r$ dependent (constrained) variables in the solution of the system corresponding to $[C \mid \mathbf{d}]$. In addition, by Remark 4, we know $r \leq n$. Since there are $n$ variables altogether in this $(m \times n)$ system, the remaining $n-r$ variables are independent (or unconstrained) variables. See Theorem 3.

**THEOREM 3**     Let $[C \mid \mathbf{d}]$ be an $[m \times (n + 1)]$ matrix in reduced echelon form, where $[C \mid \mathbf{d}]$ represents a consistent system. Let $[C \mid \mathbf{d}]$ have $r$ nonzero rows. Then $r \leq n$ and in the solution of the system there are $n - r$ variables that can be assigned arbitrary values.     ◼

Theorem 3 is illustrated below in Example 2.

**EXAMPLE 2**     Illustrate Theorem 3 using the results of Example 1.

***Solution***     The augmented matrix $[C \mid \mathbf{d}]$ in Example 1 is $(5 \times 6)$ and represents a consistent system since it does not have a row of the form $[0, 0, 0, 0, 0, 1]$. The matrix has $r = 3$ nonzero rows and hence must have $n - r = 6 - 3 = 3$ independent variables. The 3 dependent variables and 3 independent variables are displayed in Example 1.     ◼

The remark in Section 1.1 that a system of linear equations has either infinitely many solutions, no solution, or a unique solution is an immediate consequence of Theorem 3. To see why, let $[A \mid \mathbf{b}]$ denote the augmented matrix for a system of $m$ equations in $n$ unknowns. Then $[A \mid \mathbf{b}]$ is row equivalent to a matrix $[C \mid \mathbf{d}]$ that is in reduced echelon form. Since the two augmented matrices represent equivalent systems, both of the systems have the same solution set. By Theorem 3, we know the only possibilities for the system represented by $[C \mid \mathbf{d}]$ (and hence for the system represented by $[A \mid \mathbf{b}]$) are:

1. The system is inconsistent.

2. The system is consistent and, in the notation of Theorem 3, $r < n$. In this case there are $n - r$ unconstrained variables, so the system has infinitely many solutions.

3. The system is consistent and $r = n$. In this case there are no unconstrained variables, so the system has a unique solution.

We can also use Theorem 3 to draw some conclusions about a general $(m \times n)$ system of linear equations in the case where $m < n$. These conclusions are given in the following corollary. Note that the hypotheses do not require the augmented matrix for the system to be in echelon form. Nor do the hypotheses require the system to be consistent.

COROLLARY     Consider an $(m \times n)$ system of linear equations. If $m < n$, then either the system is inconsistent or it has infinitely many solutions.

*Proof*     Consider an $(m \times n)$ system of linear equations where $m < n$. If the system is inconsistent, there is nothing to prove. If the system is consistent, then Theorem 3 applies. For a consistent system, suppose that the augmented matrix $[A \mid \mathbf{b}]$ is row equivalent to a matrix $[C \mid \mathbf{d}]$ that is in echelon form and has $r$ nonzero rows. Because the given system has $m$ equations, the augmented matrix $[A \mid \mathbf{b}]$ has $m$ rows. Therefore the matrix $[C \mid \mathbf{d}]$ also has $m$ rows. Because $r$ is the number of nonzero rows for $[C \mid \mathbf{d}]$, it is clear that $r \leq m$. But $m < n$, so it follows that $r < n$. By Theorem 3, there are $n - r$ independent variables. Because $n - r > 0$, the system has infinitely many solutions. ◼

EXAMPLE 3     What are the possibilities for the solution set of a $(3 \times 4)$ system of linear equations? If the system is consistent, what are the possibilities for the number of independent variables?

*Solution*     By the corollary to Theorem 3, the system either has no solution or has infinitely many solutions. If the system reduces to a system with $r$ equations, then $r \leq 3$. Thus $r$ must be 1, 2, or 3. (The case $r = 0$ can occur only when the original system is the trivial system in which all coefficients and all constants are zero.) If the system is consistent, the number of free parameters is $4 - r$, so the possibilities are 3, 2, and 1. ◼

EXAMPLE 4     What are the possibilities for the solution set of the following $(3 \times 4)$ system?

$$2x_1 - x_2 + x_3 - 3x_4 = 0$$
$$x_1 + 3x_2 - 2x_3 + x_4 = 0$$
$$-x_1 - 2x_2 + 4x_3 - x_4 = 0$$

*Solution*     First note that $x_1 = x_2 = x_3 = x_4 = 0$ is a solution, so the system is consistent. By the corollary to Theorem 3, the system must have infinitely many solutions. That is, $m = 3$ and $n = 4$, so $m < n$. ◼

## Homogeneous Systems

The system in Example 4 is an example of a homogeneous system of equations. More generally, the $(m \times n)$ system of linear equations given in (2) is called a ***homogeneous*** system of linear equations:

$$\begin{aligned}
a_{11}x_1 + a_{12}x_2 + \cdots + a_{1n}x_n &= 0 \\
a_{21}x_1 + a_{22}x_2 + \cdots + a_{2n}x_n &= 0 \\
&\vdots \\
a_{m1}x_1 + a_{m2}x_2 + \cdots + a_{mn}x_n &= 0.
\end{aligned} \qquad (2)$$

Thus system (2) is the special case of the general $(m \times n)$ system (1) given earlier in which $b_1 = b_2 = \cdots = b_m = 0$. Note that a homogeneous system is always consistent, because $x_1 = x_2 = \cdots = x_n = 0$ is a solution to system (2). This solution is called the ***trivial solution*** or ***zero solution***, and any other solution is called a ***nontrivial solution.*** A homogeneous system of equations, therefore, either has the trivial solution as the unique solution or also has nontrivial (and hence infinitely many) solutions. With these observations, the following important theorem is an immediate consequence of the corollary to Theorem 3.

THEOREM 4    A homogeneous $(m \times n)$ system of linear equations always has infinitely many nontrivial solutions when $m < n$. ◼

EXAMPLE 5    What are the possibilities for the solution set of

$$x_1 + 2x_2 + \quad x_3 + 3x_4 = 0$$
$$2x_1 + 4x_2 + 3x_3 + \quad x_4 = 0$$
$$3x_1 + 6x_2 + 6x_3 + 2x_4 = 0?$$

Solve the system.

*Solution*    By Theorem 4, the system has infinitely many nontrivial solutions. We solve by reducing the augmented matrix:

$$\begin{bmatrix} 1 & 2 & 1 & 3 & 0 \\ 2 & 4 & 3 & 1 & 0 \\ 3 & 6 & 6 & 2 & 0 \end{bmatrix}.$$

$R_2 - 2R_1, R_3 - 3R_1$:

$$\begin{bmatrix} 1 & 2 & 1 & 3 & 0 \\ 0 & 0 & 1 & -5 & 0 \\ 0 & 0 & 3 & -7 & 0 \end{bmatrix}$$

$R_3 - 3R_2, R_1 - R_2$:

$$\begin{bmatrix} 1 & 2 & 0 & 8 & 0 \\ 0 & 0 & 1 & -5 & 0 \\ 0 & 0 & 0 & 8 & 0 \end{bmatrix}$$

$(1/8)R_3, R_1 - 8R_3, R_2 + 5R_3$:

$$\begin{bmatrix} 1 & 2 & 0 & 0 & 0 \\ 0 & 0 & 1 & 0 & 0 \\ 0 & 0 & 0 & 1 & 0 \end{bmatrix}.$$

Note that the last column of zeros is maintained under elementary row operations, so the given system is equivalent to the homogeneous system

$$x_1 + 2x_2 \qquad\qquad = 0$$
$$x_3 \qquad = 0$$
$$x_4 = 0.$$

Therefore, we obtain

$$x_1 = -2x_2$$
$$x_3 = \quad 0$$
$$x_4 = \quad 0$$

as the solution. ◼

||| EXAMPLE 6   What are the possibilities for the solution set of

$$2x_1 + 4x_2 + 2x_3 = 0$$
$$-2x_1 - 2x_2 + 2x_3 = 0$$
$$2x_1 + 6x_2 + 9x_3 = 0?$$

Solve the system.

*Solution*   Theorem 4 no longer applies because $m = n = 3$. However, because the system is homogeneous, either the trivial solution is the unique solution or there are infinitely many nontrivial solutions. To solve, we reduce the augmented matrix

$$\begin{bmatrix} 2 & 4 & 2 & 0 \\ -2 & -2 & 2 & 0 \\ 2 & 6 & 9 & 0 \end{bmatrix}.$$

$(1/2)R_1, R_2 + 2R_1, R_3 - 2R_1$:

$$\begin{bmatrix} 1 & 2 & 1 & 0 \\ 0 & 2 & 4 & 0 \\ 0 & 2 & 7 & 0 \end{bmatrix}$$

$(1/2)R_2, R_1 - 2R_2, R_3 - 2R_2$:

$$\begin{bmatrix} 1 & 0 & -3 & 0 \\ 0 & 1 & 2 & 0 \\ 0 & 0 & 3 & 0 \end{bmatrix}$$

$(1/3)R_3, R_1 + 3R_3, R_2 - 2R_3$:

$$\begin{bmatrix} 1 & 0 & 0 & 0 \\ 0 & 1 & 0 & 0 \\ 0 & 0 & 1 & 0 \end{bmatrix}.$$

Therefore, we find $x_1 = 0$, $x_2 = 0$, and $x_3 = 0$ is the only solution to the system. ■

||| EXAMPLE 7   For the system of equations

$$x_1 - 2x_2 + 3x_3 = b_1$$
$$2x_1 - 3x_2 + 2x_3 = b_2$$
$$-x_1 \qquad + 5x_3 = b_3,$$

determine conditions on $b_1$, $b_2$, and $b_3$ that are necessary and sufficient for the system to be consistent.

*Solution*   The augmented matrix is

$$\begin{bmatrix} 1 & -2 & 3 & b_1 \\ 2 & -3 & 2 & b_2 \\ -1 & 0 & 5 & b_3 \end{bmatrix}.$$

The augmented matrix reduces to

$$\begin{bmatrix} 1 & 0 & -5 & -3b_1 + 2b_2 \\ 0 & 1 & -4 & -2b_1 + b_2 \\ 0 & 0 & 0 & -3b_1 + 2b_2 + b_3 \end{bmatrix}.$$

If $-3b_1 + 2b_2 + b_3 \neq 0$ the system is inconsistent. On the other hand, if $-3b_1 + 2b_2 + b_3 = 0$, then the system has general solution

$$x_1 = -3b_1 + 2b_2 + 5x_3$$
$$x_2 = -2b_1 + b_2 + 4x_3.$$

Thus, the given system is consistent if and only if $-3b_1 + 2b_2 + b_3 = 0$.    ◼

## Conic Sections and Quadric Surfaces

An interesting application of homogeneous equations involves the quadratic equation in two variables:

$$ax^2 + bxy + cy^2 + dx + ey + f = 0. \tag{3}$$

If Eq. (3) has real solutions, then the graph is a curve in the $xy$-plane. If at least one of $a$, $b$, or $c$ is nonzero, the resulting graph is known as a **conic section.** Conic sections include such familiar plane figures as parabolas, ellipses, hyperbolas, and (as well) certain degenerate forms such as points and lines. Objects as diverse as planets, comets, man-made satellites, and electrons follow trajectories in space that correspond to conic sections. The earth, for instance, travels in an elliptical path about the sun, with the sun at one focus of the ellipse.

In this subsection we consider an important data-fitting problem associated with Eq. (3), namely:

> *Suppose we are given several points in the xy-plane, $(x_1, y_1)$, $(x_2, y_2)$, ..., $(x_n, y_n)$. Can we find coefficients $a, b, \ldots, f$ so that the graph of Eq. (3) passes through the given points?*

For example, if we know an object is moving along an ellipse, can we make a few observations of the object's position and then determine its complete orbit? As we will see, the answer is yes. In fact, if an object follows a trajectory that corresponds to the graph of Eq. (3), then five or fewer observations are sufficient to determine the complete trajectory.

The following example introduces the data-fitting technique. As you will see, Example 8 describes a method for finding the equation of the line passing through two points in the plane. This is a simple and familiar problem, but its very simplicity is a virtue because it suggests methods we can use for solving more complicated problems.

EXAMPLE 8    The general equation of a line is $dx + ey + f = 0$. Find the equation of the line through the points $(1, 2)$ and $(3, 7)$.

*Solution*    In an analytic geometry course, we would probably find the equation of the line by first calculating the slope of the line. In this example, however, we are interested in developing methods that can be used to find equations for more complicated curves; and we do not want to use special purpose techniques, such as slopes, that apply only to lines.

Since the points (1, 2) and (3, 7) lie on the line defined by $dx + ey + f = 0$, we insert these values into the equation and find the following conditions on the coefficients $d, e,$ and $f$:

$$d + 2e + f = 0$$
$$3d + 7e + f = 0.$$

We are guaranteed from Theorem 4 that the preceding homogeneous linear system has nontrivial solutions; that is, we can find a line passing through the two given points. To find the equation of the line, we need to solve the system. We begin by forming the associated augmented matrix

$$\begin{bmatrix} 1 & 2 & 1 & 0 \\ 3 & 7 & 1 & 0 \end{bmatrix}.$$

The preceding matrix can be transformed to reduced echelon form, yielding

$$\begin{bmatrix} 1 & 0 & 5 & 0 \\ 0 & 1 & -2 & 0 \end{bmatrix}.$$

It follows that the solution is $d = -5f, e = 2f,$ and hence the equation of the line is

$$-5fx + 2fy + f = 0.$$

Canceling the parameter $f$, we obtain an equation for the line:

$$-5x + 2y + 1 = 0.$$    ◼

Example 8 suggests how we might determine the equation of a conic that passes through a given set of points in the $xy$-plane. In particular, see Eq. (3); the general conic has six coefficients, $a, b, \ldots, f$. So, given any five points $(x_i, y_i)$ we can insert these five points into Eq. (3) and the result will be a homogeneous system of five equations for the six unknown coefficients that define the conic section. By Theorem 4, the resulting system is guaranteed to have a nontrivial solution—that is, we can guarantee that any five points in the plane lie on the graph of an equation of the form (3). Example 9 illustrates this point.

EXAMPLE 9    Find the equation of the conic section passing through the five points $(-1, 0)$, $(0, 1)$, $(2, 2)$, $(2, -1)$, $(0, -3)$. Display the graph of the conic.

*Solution*    The augmented matrix for the corresponding homogeneous system of five equations in six unknowns is listed below. In creating the augmented matrix, we formed the rows in the same order the points were listed and formed columns using the same order the unknowns were listed in Eq. (3). For example, the third row of the augmented matrix arises from inserting (2, 2) into Eq. (3):

$$4a + 4b + 4c + 2d + 2e + f = 0.$$

In particular, the augmented matrix is

$$\begin{bmatrix} 1 & 0 & 0 & -1 & 0 & 1 & 0 \\ 0 & 0 & 1 & 0 & 1 & 1 & 0 \\ 4 & 4 & 4 & 2 & 2 & 1 & 0 \\ 4 & -2 & 1 & 2 & -1 & 1 & 0 \\ 0 & 0 & 9 & 0 & -3 & 1 & 0 \end{bmatrix}.$$

We used MATLAB to transform the augmented matrix to reduced echelon form, finding

$$\begin{bmatrix} 1 & 0 & 0 & 0 & 0 & 7/18 & 0 \\ 0 & 1 & 0 & 0 & 0 & -1/2 & 0 \\ 0 & 0 & 1 & 0 & 0 & 1/3 & 0 \\ 0 & 0 & 0 & 1 & 0 & -11/18 & 0 \\ 0 & 0 & 0 & 0 & 1 & 2/3 & 0 \end{bmatrix}.$$

Thus, the coefficients of the conic through these five points are given by

$$a = -7f/18, b = f/2, c = -f/3, d = 11f/18, e = -2f/3.$$

Setting $f = 18$, we obtain a version of Eq. (3) with integer coefficients:

$$-7x^2 + 9xy - 6y^2 + 11x - 12y + 18 = 0.$$

The graph of this equation is an ellipse and is shown in Fig. 1.7. The graph was drawn using the contour command from MATLAB. Contour plots and other features of MATLAB graphics are described in the Appendix.  ◼

Finally, it should be noted that the ideas discussed above are not limited to the $xy$-plane. For example, consider the quadratic equation in three variables:

$$ax^2 + by^2 + cz^2 + dxy + exz + fyz + gx + hy + iz + j = 0. \qquad (4)$$

The graph of Eq. (4) is a surface in three-space; the surface is known as a **quadric surface**. Counting the coefficients in Eq. (4), we find ten. Thus, given any nine points in three-space, we can find a quadric surface passing through the nine points (see Exercises 30–31).

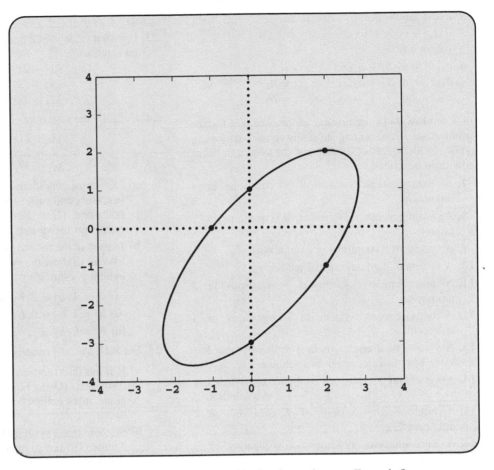

*Figure 1.7* The ellipse determined by five data points, see Example 9.

## 1.3 EXERCISES

In Exercises 1–4, transform the augmented matrix for the given system to reduced echelon form and, in the notation of Theorem 3, determine $n$, $r$, and the number, $n - r$, of independent variables. If $n - r > 0$, then identify $n - r$ independent variables.

1.
$$2x_1 + 2x_2 - \phantom{4}x_3 = \phantom{-}1$$
$$-2x_1 - 2x_2 + 4x_3 = \phantom{-}1$$
$$2x_1 + 2x_2 + 5x_3 = \phantom{-}5$$
$$-2x_1 - 2x_2 - 2x_3 = -3$$

2.
$$2x_1 + 2x_2 = \phantom{-}1$$
$$4x_1 + 5x_2 = \phantom{-}4$$
$$4x_1 + 2x_2 = -2$$

3.
$$\phantom{x_1 +} -x_2 + \phantom{2}x_3 + x_4 = 2$$
$$x_1 + 2x_2 + 2x_3 - x_4 = 3$$
$$x_1 + 3x_2 + \phantom{2}x_3 \phantom{+ x_4} = 2$$

4.
$$x_1 + 2x_2 + 3x_3 + 2x_4 = 1$$
$$x_1 + 2x_2 + 3x_3 + 5x_4 = 2$$
$$2x_1 + 4x_2 + 6x_3 + \phantom{7}x_4 = 1$$
$$-x_1 - 2x_2 - 3x_3 + 7x_4 = 2$$

In Exercises 5 and 6, assume that the given system is consistent. For each system determine, in the notation of Theorem 3, all possibilities for the number, $r$ of nonzero rows and the number, $n - r$, of unconstrained variables. Can the system have a unique solution?

**5.** $ax_1 + bx_2 = c$
$dx_1 + ex_2 = f$
$gx_1 + hx_2 = i$

**6.** $a_{11}x_1 + a_{12}x_2 + a_{13}x_3 + a_{14}x_4 = b_1$
$a_{21}x_1 + a_{22}x_2 + a_{23}x_3 + a_{24}x_4 = b_2$
$a_{31}x_1 + a_{32}x_2 + a_{33}x_3 + a_{34}x_4 = b_3$

In Exercises 7–18, determine all possibilities for the solution set (from among infinitely many solutions, a unique solution, or no solution) of the system of linear equations described.

**7.** A homogeneous system of 3 equations in 4 unknowns.

**8.** A homogeneous system of 4 equations in 5 unknowns.

**9.** A system of 3 equations in 2 unknowns.

**10.** A system of 4 equations in 3 unknowns.

**11.** A homogeneous system of 3 equations in 2 unknowns.

**12.** A homogeneous system of 4 equations in 3 unknowns.

**13.** A system of 2 equations in 3 unknowns that has $x_1 = 1, x_2 = 2, x_3 = -1$ as a solution.

**14.** A system of 3 equations in 4 unknowns that has $x_1 = -1, x_2 = 0, x_3 = 2, x_4 = -3$ as a solution.

**15.** A homogeneous system of 2 equations in 2 unknowns.

**16.** A homogeneous system of 3 equations in 3 unknowns.

**17.** A homogeneous system of 2 equations in 2 unknowns that has solution $x_1 = 1, x_2 = -1$.

**18.** A homogeneous system of 3 equations in 3 unknowns that has solution $x_1 = 1, x_2 = 3, x_3 = -1$.

In Exercises 19–22, determine by inspection whether the given system has nontrivial solutions or only the trivial solution.

**19.** $2x_1 + 3x_2 - x_3 = 0$
$x_1 - x_2 + 2x_3 = 0$

**20.** $x_1 + 2x_2 - x_3 + 2x_4 = 0$
$2x_1 + x_2 + x_3 - x_4 = 0$
$3x_1 - x_2 - 2x_3 + 3x_4 = 0$

**21.** $x_1 + 2x_2 - x_3 = 0$
$x_2 + 2x_3 = 0$
$4x_3 = 0$

**22.** $x_1 - x_2 = 0$
$3x_1 = 0$

$2x_1 + x_2 = 0$

**23.** For what value(s) of $a$ does the system have nontrivial solutions?

$x_1 + 2x_2 + x_3 = 0$
$-x_1 - x_2 + x_3 = 0$
$3x_1 + 4x_2 + ax_3 = 0.$

**24.** Consider the system of equations

$x_1 + 3x_2 - x_3 = b_1$
$x_1 + 2x_2 = b_2$
$3x_1 + 7x_2 - x_3 = b_3.$

a) Determine conditions on $b_1$, $b_2$, and $b_3$ that are necessary and sufficient for the system to be consistent. [*Hint:* Reduce the augmented matrix for the system.]

b) In each of the following, either use your answer from a) to show the system is inconsistent or exhibit a solution.

   i) $b_1 = 1, b_2 = 1, b_3 = 3$

   ii) $b_1 = 1, b_2 = 0, b_3 = -1$

   iii) $b_1 = 0, b_2 = 1, b_3 = 2$

**25.** Let $B$ be a $(4 \times 3)$ matrix in reduced echelon form.

a) If $B$ has three nonzero rows, then determine the form of $B$. (Using Fig. 1.5 of Section 1.2 as a guide, mark entries that may or may not be zero by $*$.)

b) Suppose that a system of 4 linear equations in 2 unknowns has augmented matrix $A$, where $A$ is a $(4 \times 3)$ matrix row equivalent to $B$. Demonstrate that the system of equations is inconsistent.

In Exercises 26–31, follow the ideas illustrated in Examples 8 and 9 to find the equation of the curve or surface through the given points. For Exercises 28–29, display the graph of the equation as in Fig. 1.7.

**26.** The line through $(3, 1)$ and $(7, 2)$.

**27.** The line through $(2, 8)$ and $(4, 1)$.

**28.** The conic through $(-4, 0)$, $(-2, -2)$, $(0, 3)$, $(1, 1)$, and $(4, 0)$.

**29.** The conic through $(-4, 1)$, $(-1, 2)$, $(3, 2)$, $(5, 1)$, and $(7, -1)$.

**30.** The quadric surface through $(0, 0, 1)$, $(1, 0, 1)$, $(0, 1, 0)$, $(3, 1, 0)$, $(2, 0, 4)$, $(1, 1, 2)$, $(1, 2, 1)$, $(2, 2, 3)$, $(2, 2, 1)$.

**31.** The quadric surface through $(1, 2, 3)$, $(2, 1, 0)$, $(6, 0, 6)$, $(3, 1, 3)$, $(4, 0, 2)$, $(5, 5, 1)$, $(1, 1, 2)$, $(3, 1, 4)$, $(0, 0, 2)$.

In Exercises 32–33, note that the equation of a circle has the form

$$ax^2 + ay^2 + bx + cy + d = 0.$$

Hence a circle is determined by three points. Find the equation of the circle through the given points.

**32.** (1, 1), (2, 1), and (3, 2)

**33.** (4, 3), (1, 2), and (2, 0)

# APPLICATIONS (OPTIONAL)

In this brief section we discuss networks and methods for determining flows in networks. An example of a network is the system of one-way streets shown in Fig. 1.8. A typical problem associated with networks is estimating the flow of traffic through this network of streets. Another example is the electrical network shown in Fig. 1.9. A typical problem consists of determining the currents flowing through the loops of the circuit.

(*Note:* The network problems we discuss in this section are kept very simple so that the computational details do not obscure the ideas.)

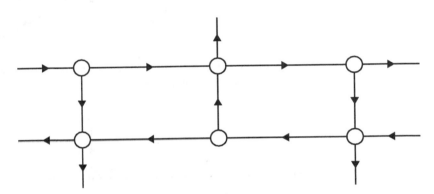

*Figure 1.8*    A network of one-way streets

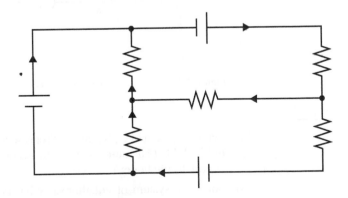

*Figure 1.9*    An electrical network

## Flows in Networks

Networks consist of branches and nodes. For the street network shown in Fig. 1.8, the branches are the streets and the nodes are the intersections. We assume for a network that the total flow into a node is equal to the total flow out of the node. For example, Fig. 1.10 shows a flow of 40 into a node and a total flow of $x_1 + x_2 + 5$ out of the node. Since we assume that the flow into a node is equal to the flow out, it follows that the flows $x_1$ and $x_2$ must satisfy the linear equation $40 = x_1 + x_2 + 5$, or equivalently,

$$x_1 + x_2 = 35.$$

As an example of network flow calculations, consider the system of one-way streets in Fig. 1.11, where the flow is given in vehicles per hour. For instance, $x_1 + x_4$ vehicles per hour enter node $B$, while $x_2 + 400$ vehicles per hour leave.

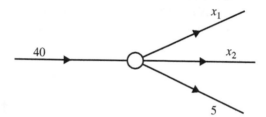

**Figure 1.10**    Since we assume that the flow into a node is equal to the flow out, in this case, $x_1 + x_2 = 35$.

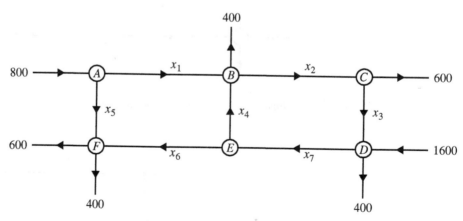

**Figure 1.11**    The traffic network analyzed in Example 1

### EXAMPLE 1

**(a)** Set up a system of equations that represents traffic flow for the network shown in Fig. 1.11. (The numbers give the average flows into and out of the network at peak traffic hours.)

**(b)** Solve the system of equations. What is the traffic flow if $x_6 = 300$ and $x_7 = 1300$ vehicles per hour?

*Solution*

(a) Since the flow into a node is equal to the flow out, we obtain the following system of equations:

$$800 = x_1 + x_5 \qquad \text{(Node } A\text{)}$$
$$x_1 + x_4 = 400 + x_2 \qquad \text{(Node } B\text{)}$$
$$x_2 = 600 + x_3 \qquad \text{(Node } C\text{)}$$
$$1600 + x_3 = 400 + x_7 \qquad \text{(Node } D\text{)}$$
$$x_7 = x_4 + x_6 \qquad \text{(Node } E\text{)}$$
$$x_5 + x_6 = 1000. \qquad \text{(Node } F\text{)}$$

(b) The augmented matrix for the system above is

$$\begin{bmatrix} 1 & 0 & 0 & 0 & 1 & 0 & 0 & 800 \\ 1 & -1 & 0 & 1 & 0 & 0 & 0 & 400 \\ 0 & 1 & -1 & 0 & 0 & 0 & 0 & 600 \\ 0 & 0 & 1 & 0 & 0 & 0 & -1 & -1200 \\ 0 & 0 & 0 & 1 & 0 & 1 & -1 & 0 \\ 0 & 0 & 0 & 0 & 1 & 1 & 0 & 1000 \end{bmatrix}.$$

Some calculations show that this matrix is row equivalent to

$$\begin{bmatrix} 1 & 0 & 0 & 0 & 0 & -1 & 0 & -200 \\ 0 & 1 & 0 & 0 & 0 & 0 & -1 & -600 \\ 0 & 0 & 1 & 0 & 0 & 0 & -1 & -1200 \\ 0 & 0 & 0 & 1 & 0 & 1 & -1 & 0 \\ 0 & 0 & 0 & 0 & 1 & 1 & 0 & 1000 \\ 0 & 0 & 0 & 0 & 0 & 0 & 0 & 0 \end{bmatrix}.$$

Therefore, the solution is

$$x_1 = x_6 - 200$$
$$x_2 = x_7 - 600$$
$$x_3 = x_7 - 1200$$
$$x_4 = x_7 - x_6$$
$$x_5 = 1000 - x_6.$$

If $x_6 = 300$ and $x_7 = 1300$, then (in vehicles per hour)

$$x_1 = 100, \qquad x_2 = 700, \qquad x_3 = 100, \qquad x_4 = 1000, \qquad x_5 = 700. \qquad ■$$

We normally want the flows in a network to be nonnegative. For instance, consider the traffic network in Fig. 1.11. If $x_6$ were negative, it would indicate that traffic was flowing from $F$ to $E$ rather than in the prescribed direction from $E$ to $F$.

EXAMPLE 2    Consider the street network in Example 1 (see Fig. 1.11). Suppose that the streets from $A$ to $B$ and from $B$ to $C$ must be closed (that is, $x_1 = 0$ and $x_2 = 0$). How might the traffic be rerouted?

Solution    By Example 1, the flows are

$$x_1 = x_6 - 200$$
$$x_2 = x_7 - 600$$
$$x_3 = x_7 - 1200$$
$$x_4 = x_7 - x_6$$
$$x_5 = 1000 - x_6.$$

Therefore, if $x_1 = 0$ and $x_2 = 0$, it follows that $x_6 = 200$ and $x_7 = 600$. Using these values, we then obtain $x_3 = -600$, $x_4 = 400$, and $x_5 = 800$. In order to have nonnegative flows, we must reverse directions on the street connecting $C$ and $D$; this change makes $x_3 = 600$ instead of $-600$. The network flows are shown in Fig. 1.12.

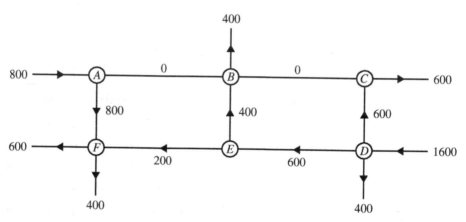

Figure 1.12    The traffic network analyzed in Example 2

## Electrical Networks

We now consider current flow in simple electrical networks such as the one illustrated in Fig. 1.13. For such networks, current flow is governed by Ohm's law and Kirchhoff's laws, as follows.

**Ohm's Law:** The voltage drop across a resistor is the product of the current and the resistance.

**Kirchhoff's First Law:** The sum of the currents flowing into a node is equal to the sum of the currents flowing out.

**Kirchhoff's Second Law:** The algebraic sum of the voltage drops around a closed loop is equal to the total voltage in the loop.

(**Note:** With respect to Kirchhoff's second law, two basic closed loops in Fig. 1.13 are the counterclockwise paths $BDCB$ and $BCAB$. Also, in each branch, we make a tentative

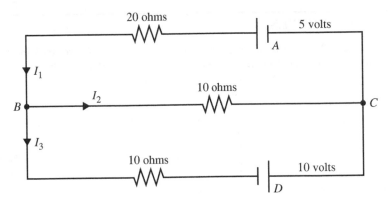

*Figure 1.13*    The electrical network analyzed in Example 3

assignment for the direction of current flow. If a current turns out to be negative, we then reverse our assignment for that branch.)

EXAMPLE 3    Determine the currents $I_1$, $I_2$, and $I_3$ for the electrical network shown in Fig. 1.13.

*Solution*    Applying Kirchhoff's second law to the loops *BDCB* and *BCAB*, we obtain equations

$$-10I_2 + 10I_3 = 10 \quad (BDCB)$$
$$20I_1 + 10I_2 = 5 \quad (BCAB).$$

Applying Kirchhoff's first law to either of the nodes *B* or *C*, we find $I_1 = I_2 + I_3$. Therefore,

$$I_1 - I_2 - I_3 = 0.$$

The augmented matrix for this system of three equations is

$$\begin{bmatrix} 1 & -1 & -1 & 0 \\ 0 & -10 & 10 & 10 \\ 20 & 10 & 0 & 5 \end{bmatrix}.$$

This matrix can be row reduced to

$$\begin{bmatrix} 1 & 0 & 0 & 0.4 \\ 0 & 1 & 0 & -0.3 \\ 0 & 0 & 1 & 0.7 \end{bmatrix}.$$

Therefore, the currents are

$$I_1 = 0.4, \quad I_2 = -0.3, \quad I_3 = 0.7.$$

Since $I_2$ is negative, the current flow is from *C* to *B* rather than from *B* to *C*, as tentatively assigned in Fig. 1.13.

## 1.4    EXERCISES

In Exercises 1 and 2, (a) set up the system of equations that describes traffic flow; (b) determine the flows $x_1$, $x_2$, and $x_3$ if $x_4 = 100$; and (c) determine the maximum and minimum values for $x_4$ if all the flows are constrained to be nonnegative.

In Exercises 3 and 4, find the flow of traffic in the rotary if $x_1 = 600$.

**1.**

**2.**

**3.**

**4.**

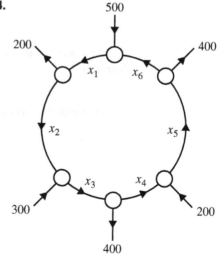

In Exercises 5–8, determine the currents in the various branches.

**5.**

**8.**

**9. a)** Set up the system of equations that describes the traffic flow in the accompanying figure.

   **b)** Show that the system is consistent if and only if $a_1 + b_1 + c_1 + d_1 = a_2 + b_2 + c_2 + d_2$.

**6.**

**7.**

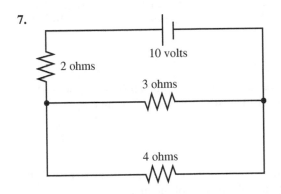

**10.** The electrical network shown in the accompanying figure is called a **Wheatstone bridge**. In this bridge, $R_2$ and $R_4$ are known resistances and $R_3$ is a known resistance that can be varied. The resistance $R_1$ is unknown and is to be determined by using the bridge. The resistance $R_5$ represents the internal resistance of a voltmeter attached between nodes $B$ and $D$. The bridge is said to be balanced when $R_3$ is adjusted so that there is no current flowing in the branch between $B$ and $D$. Show that, when the bridge is balanced, $R_1 R_4 = R_2 R_3$. (In particular, the unknown resistance $R_1$ can be found from $R_1 = R_2 R_3 / R_4$ when the bridge is balanced.)

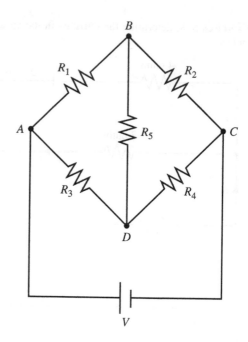

## 1.5    MATRIX OPERATIONS

In the previous sections, matrices were used as a convenient way of representing systems of equations. But matrices are of considerable interest and importance in their own right, and this section introduces the arithmetic operations that make them a useful computational and theoretical tool.

In this discussion of matrices and matrix operations (and later in the discussion of vectors), it is customary to refer to numerical quantities as *scalars*. For convenience we assume throughout this chapter that all matrix (and vector) entries are real numbers; hence the term *scalar* will mean a real number. In later chapters the term *scalar* will also be applied to complex numbers. We begin with a definition of the equality of two matrices.

---

**DEFINITION 5**

Let $A = (a_{ij})$ be an $(m \times n)$ matrix, and let $B = (b_{ij})$ be an $(r \times s)$ matrix. We say that $A$ and $B$ are *equal* (and write $A = B$) if $m = r$, $n = s$, and $a_{ij} = b_{ij}$ for all $i$ and $j$, $1 \le i \le m$, $1 \le j \le n$.

---

Thus two matrices are equal if they have the same size and, moreover, if all their corresponding entries are equal. For example, no two of the matrices

$$A = \begin{bmatrix} 1 & 2 \\ 3 & 4 \end{bmatrix}, \quad B = \begin{bmatrix} 2 & 1 \\ 4 & 3 \end{bmatrix}, \quad \text{and} \quad C = \begin{bmatrix} 1 & 2 & 0 \\ 3 & 4 & 0 \end{bmatrix}$$

are equal.

## Matrix Addition and Scalar Multiplication

The first two arithmetic operations, matrix addition and the multiplication of a matrix by a scalar, are defined quite naturally. In these definitions we use the notation $(Q)_{ij}$ to denote the $ij$th entry of a matrix $Q$.

DEFINITION 6

Let $A = (a_{ij})$ and $B = (b_{ij})$ both be $(m \times n)$ matrices. The **sum**, $A + B$, is the $(m \times n)$ matrix defined by

$$(A + B)_{ij} = a_{ij} + b_{ij}.$$

Note that this definition requires that $A$ and $B$ have the same size before their sum is defined. Thus if

$$A = \begin{bmatrix} 1 & 2 & -1 \\ 2 & 3 & 0 \end{bmatrix}, \quad B = \begin{bmatrix} -3 & 1 & 2 \\ 0 & -4 & 1 \end{bmatrix}, \quad \text{and} \quad C = \begin{bmatrix} 1 & 2 \\ 3 & 1 \end{bmatrix},$$

then

$$A + B = \begin{bmatrix} -2 & 3 & 1 \\ 2 & -1 & 1 \end{bmatrix},$$

while $A + C$ is undefined.

DEFINITION 7

Let $A = (a_{ij})$ be an $(m \times n)$ matrix, and let $r$ be a scalar. The **product**, $rA$, is the $(m \times n)$ matrix defined by

$$(rA)_{ij} = ra_{ij}.$$

For example,

$$2 \begin{bmatrix} 1 & 3 \\ 2 & -1 \\ 0 & 3 \end{bmatrix} = \begin{bmatrix} 2 & 6 \\ 4 & -2 \\ 0 & 6 \end{bmatrix}.$$

EXAMPLE 1

Let the matrices $A$, $B$, and $C$ be given by

$$A = \begin{bmatrix} 1 & 3 \\ -2 & 7 \end{bmatrix}, \quad B = \begin{bmatrix} 6 & 1 \\ 2 & 4 \end{bmatrix}, \quad \text{and} \quad C = \begin{bmatrix} 1 & 2 & -1 \\ 3 & 0 & 5 \end{bmatrix}.$$

Find each of $A + B$, $A + C$, $B + C$, $3C$, and $A + 2B$, or state that the indicated operation is undefined.

*Solution*    The defined operations yield

$$A + B = \begin{bmatrix} 7 & 4 \\ 0 & 11 \end{bmatrix}, \quad 3C = \begin{bmatrix} 3 & 6 & -3 \\ 9 & 0 & 15 \end{bmatrix}, \quad \text{and} \quad A + 2B = \begin{bmatrix} 13 & 5 \\ 2 & 15 \end{bmatrix},$$

while $A + C$ and $B + C$ are undefined. ◼

## Vectors in $R^n$

Before proceeding with the definition of matrix multiplication, recall that a point in $n$-dimensional space is represented by an ordered $n$-tuple of real numbers $\mathbf{x} = (x_1, x_2, \ldots, x_n)$. Such an $n$-tuple will be called an ***n-dimensional vector*** and will be written in the form of a matrix,

$$\mathbf{x} = \begin{bmatrix} x_1 \\ x_2 \\ \vdots \\ x_n \end{bmatrix}.$$

For example, an arbitrary three-dimensional vector has the form

$$\mathbf{x} = \begin{bmatrix} x_1 \\ x_2 \\ x_3 \end{bmatrix},$$

and the vectors

$$\mathbf{x} = \begin{bmatrix} 1 \\ 2 \\ 3 \end{bmatrix}, \quad \mathbf{y} = \begin{bmatrix} 3 \\ 2 \\ 1 \end{bmatrix}, \quad \text{and} \quad \mathbf{z} = \begin{bmatrix} 2 \\ 3 \\ 1 \end{bmatrix}$$

are distinct three-dimensional vectors. The set of all $n$-dimensional vectors with real components is called ***Euclidean n-space*** and will be denoted by $R^n$. Vectors in $R^n$ will be denoted by boldface type. Thus $R^n$ is the set defined by

$$R^n = \left\{ \mathbf{x} \colon \mathbf{x} = \begin{bmatrix} x_1 \\ x_2 \\ \vdots \\ x_n \end{bmatrix} \quad \text{where} \quad x_1, x_2, \ldots, x_n \text{ are real numbers} \right\}.$$

As the notation suggests, an element of $R^n$ can be viewed as an $(n \times 1)$ real matrix, and conversely an $(n \times 1)$ real matrix can be considered an element of $R^n$. Thus addition and scalar multiplication of vectors is just a special case of these operations for matrices.

## Vector Form of the General Solution

Having defined addition and scalar multiplication for vectors and matrices, we can use these operations to derive a compact expression for the general solution of a consistent system of linear equations. We call this expression the ***vector form for the general solution***.

The idea of the vector form for the general solution is straightforward and is best explained by a few examples.

**EXAMPLE 2** The matrix $B$ is the augmented matrix for a homogeneous system of linear equations. Find the general solution for the linear system and express the general solution in terms of vectors

$$B = \begin{bmatrix} 1 & 0 & -1 & -3 & 0 \\ 0 & 1 & 2 & 1 & 0 \end{bmatrix}.$$

**Solution** Since $B$ is in reduced echelon form, it is easy to write the general solution:

$$x_1 = x_3 + 3x_4, \qquad x_2 = -2x_3 - x_4.$$

In vector form, therefore, the general solution can be expressed as

$$\mathbf{x} = \begin{bmatrix} x_1 \\ x_2 \\ x_3 \\ x_4 \end{bmatrix} = \begin{bmatrix} x_3 + 3x_4 \\ -2x_3 - x_4 \\ x_3 \\ x_4 \end{bmatrix} = \begin{bmatrix} x_3 \\ -2x_3 \\ x_3 \\ 0 \end{bmatrix} + \begin{bmatrix} 3x_4 \\ -x_4 \\ 0 \\ x_4 \end{bmatrix}$$

$$= x_3 \begin{bmatrix} 1 \\ -2 \\ 1 \\ 0 \end{bmatrix} + x_4 \begin{bmatrix} 3 \\ -1 \\ 0 \\ 1 \end{bmatrix}.$$

This last expression is called the *vector form for the general solution.* ◼

In general, the vector form for the general solution of a homogeneous system consists of a sum of well-determined vectors multiplied by the free variables. Such expressions are called "linear combinations" and we will use this concept of a linear combination extensively, beginning in Section 1.7. The next example illustrates the vector form for the general solution of a nonhomogeneous system.

**EXAMPLE 3** Let $B$ denote the augmented matrix for a system of linear equations

$$B = \begin{bmatrix} 1 & -2 & 0 & 0 & 2 & 3 \\ 0 & 0 & 1 & 0 & -1 & 2 \\ 0 & 0 & 0 & 1 & 3 & -4 \end{bmatrix}.$$

Find the vector form for the general solution of the linear system.

**Solution** Since $B$ is in reduced echelon form, we readily find the general solution:

$$x_1 = 3 + 2x_2 - 2x_5, x_3 = 2 + x_5, x_4 = -4 - 3x_5.$$

Expressing the general solution in vector form, we obtain

$$
\mathbf{x} = \begin{bmatrix} x_1 \\ x_2 \\ x_3 \\ x_4 \\ x_5 \end{bmatrix} = \begin{bmatrix} 3 + 2x_2 - 2x_5 \\ x_2 \\ 2 + x_5 \\ -4 - 3x_5 \\ x_5 \end{bmatrix} = \begin{bmatrix} 3 \\ 0 \\ 2 \\ -4 \\ 0 \end{bmatrix} + \begin{bmatrix} 2x_2 \\ x_2 \\ 0 \\ 0 \\ 0 \end{bmatrix} + \begin{bmatrix} -2x_5 \\ 0 \\ x_5 \\ -3x_5 \\ x_5 \end{bmatrix}
$$

$$
= \begin{bmatrix} 3 \\ 0 \\ 2 \\ -4 \\ 0 \end{bmatrix} + x_2 \begin{bmatrix} 2 \\ 1 \\ 0 \\ 0 \\ 0 \end{bmatrix} + x_5 \begin{bmatrix} -2 \\ 0 \\ 1 \\ -3 \\ 1 \end{bmatrix}.
$$

Thus, the general solution has the form $\mathbf{x} = \mathbf{b} + a\mathbf{u} + b\mathbf{v}$, where $\mathbf{b}$, $\mathbf{u}$, and $\mathbf{v}$ are fixed vectors in $R^5$. ◼

## Scalar Product

In vector calculus, the *scalar product* (or *dot product*) of two vectors

$$
\mathbf{u} = \begin{bmatrix} u_1 \\ u_2 \\ \vdots \\ u_n \end{bmatrix} \quad \text{and} \quad \mathbf{v} = \begin{bmatrix} v_1 \\ v_2 \\ \vdots \\ v_n \end{bmatrix}
$$

in $R^n$ is defined to be the number $u_1 v_1 + u_2 v_2 + \cdots + u_n v_n = \sum_{i=1}^{n} u_i v_i$. For example, if

$$
\mathbf{u} = \begin{bmatrix} 2 \\ 3 \\ -1 \end{bmatrix} \quad \text{and} \quad \mathbf{v} = \begin{bmatrix} -4 \\ 2 \\ 3 \end{bmatrix},
$$

then the scalar product of $\mathbf{u}$ and $\mathbf{v}$ is $2(-4) + 3(2) + (-1)3 = -5$. The scalar product of two vectors will be considered further in the following section, and in Chapter 3 the properties of $R^n$ will be more fully developed.

## Matrix Multiplication

Matrix multiplication is defined in such a way as to provide a convenient mechanism for describing a linear correspondence between vectors. To illustrate, let the variables $x_1, x_2, \ldots, x_n$ and the variables $y_1, y_2, \ldots, y_m$ be related by the linear equations

$$
\begin{array}{rcl}
a_{11}x_1 + a_{12}x_2 + \cdots + a_{1n}x_n &=& y_1 \\
a_{21}x_1 + a_{22}x_2 + \cdots + a_{2n}x_n &=& y_2 \\
\vdots & & \vdots \quad \vdots \\
a_{m1}x_1 + a_{m2}x_2 + \cdots + a_{mn}x_n &=& y_m.
\end{array} \tag{1}
$$

If we set

$$\mathbf{x} = \begin{bmatrix} x_1 \\ x_2 \\ \vdots \\ x_n \end{bmatrix} \quad \text{and} \quad \mathbf{y} = \begin{bmatrix} y_1 \\ y_2 \\ \vdots \\ y_m \end{bmatrix},$$

then (1) defines a correspondence $\mathbf{x} \rightarrow \mathbf{y}$ from vectors in $R^n$ to vectors in $R^m$. The $i$th equation of (1) is

$$a_{i1}x_1 + a_{i2}x_2 + \cdots + a_{in}x_n = y_i,$$

and this can be written in a briefer form as

$$\sum_{j=1}^{n} a_{ij}x_j = y_i. \tag{2}$$

If $A$ is the coefficient matrix of system (1),

$$A = \begin{bmatrix} a_{11} & a_{12} & \cdots & a_{1n} \\ a_{21} & a_{22} & \cdots & a_{2n} \\ \vdots & & & \vdots \\ a_{m1} & a_{m2} & \cdots & a_{mn} \end{bmatrix},$$

then the left-hand side of Eq. (2) is precisely the scalar product of the $i$th row of $A$ with the vector $\mathbf{x}$. Thus if we define the product of $A$ and $\mathbf{x}$ to be the $(m \times 1)$ vector $A\mathbf{x}$ whose $i$th component is the scalar product of the $i$th row of $A$ with $\mathbf{x}$, then $A\mathbf{x}$ is given by

$$A\mathbf{x} = \begin{bmatrix} \sum_{j=1}^{n} a_{1j}x_j \\ \sum_{j=1}^{n} a_{2j}x_j \\ \vdots \\ \sum_{j=1}^{n} a_{mj}x_j \end{bmatrix}.$$

Using the definition of equality (Definition 5), we see that the simple matrix equation

$$A\mathbf{x} = \mathbf{y} \tag{3}$$

is equivalent to system (1).

In a natural fashion, we can extend the idea of the product of a matrix and a vector to the product, $AB$, of an $(m \times n)$ matrix $A$ and an $(n \times s)$ matrix $B$ by defining the $ij$th entry of $AB$ to be the scalar product of the $i$th row of $A$ with the $j$th column of $B$. Formally, we have the following definition.

**DEFINITION 8**

Let $A = (a_{ij})$ be an $(m \times n)$ matrix, and let $B = (b_{ij})$ be an $(r \times s)$ matrix. If $n = r$, then the *product* $AB$ is the $(m \times s)$ matrix defined by

$$(AB)_{ij} = \sum_{k=1}^{n} a_{ik}b_{kj}.$$

If $n \neq r$, then the product $AB$ is not defined.

The definition can be visualized by referring to Fig. 1.14.

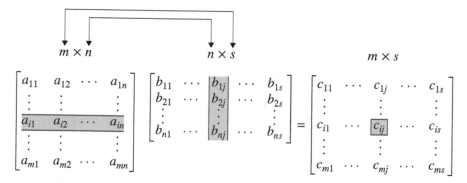

*Figure 1.14*    The $ij$th entry of $AB$ is the scalar product of the $i$th row of $A$ and the $j$th column of $B$.

Thus the product $AB$ is defined only when the inside dimensions of $A$ and $B$ are equal. In this case the outside dimensions, $m$ and $s$, give the size of $AB$. Furthermore, the $ij$th entry of $AB$ is the scalar product of the $i$th row of $A$ with the $j$th column of $B$. For example,

$$\begin{bmatrix} 2 & 1 & -3 \\ -2 & 2 & 4 \end{bmatrix} \begin{bmatrix} -1 & 2 \\ 0 & -3 \\ 2 & 1 \end{bmatrix}$$

$$= \begin{bmatrix} 2(-1) + 1(0) + (-3)2 & 2(2) + 1(-3) + (-3)1 \\ (-2)(-1) + 2(0) + 4(2) & (-2)2 + 2(-3) + 4(1) \end{bmatrix} = \begin{bmatrix} -8 & -2 \\ 10 & -6 \end{bmatrix},$$

whereas the product

$$\begin{bmatrix} 2 & 1 & -3 \\ -2 & 2 & 4 \end{bmatrix} \begin{bmatrix} -1 & 0 & 2 \\ 2 & -3 & 1 \end{bmatrix}$$

is undefined.

| | | EXAMPLE 4    Let the matrices $A$, $B$, $C$, and $D$ be given by

$$A = \begin{bmatrix} 1 & 2 \\ 2 & 3 \end{bmatrix}, \qquad B = \begin{bmatrix} -3 & 2 \\ 1 & -2 \end{bmatrix},$$

$$C = \begin{bmatrix} 1 & 0 & -2 \\ 0 & 1 & 1 \end{bmatrix}, \quad \text{and} \quad D = \begin{bmatrix} 3 & 1 \\ -1 & -2 \\ 1 & 1 \end{bmatrix}.$$

Find each of $AB$, $BA$, $AC$, $CA$, $CD$, and $DC$, or state that the indicated product is undefined.

*Solution*    The definition of matrix multiplication yields

$$AB = \begin{bmatrix} -1 & -2 \\ -3 & -2 \end{bmatrix}, \quad BA = \begin{bmatrix} 1 & 0 \\ -3 & -4 \end{bmatrix}, \quad \text{and} \quad AC = \begin{bmatrix} 1 & 2 & 0 \\ 2 & 3 & -1 \end{bmatrix}.$$

The product $CA$ is undefined, and

$$CD = \begin{bmatrix} 1 & -1 \\ 0 & -1 \end{bmatrix} \quad \text{and} \quad DC = \begin{bmatrix} 3 & 1 & -5 \\ -1 & -2 & 0 \\ 1 & 1 & -1 \end{bmatrix}. \qquad ◼$$

Example 4 illustrates that matrix multiplication is not commutative; that is, normally $AB$ and $BA$ are different matrices. Indeed, the product $AB$ may be defined while the product $BA$ is undefined, or both may be defined but have different dimensions. Even when $AB$ and $BA$ have the same size, they usually are not equal.

| | | EXAMPLE 5    Express each of the linear systems

$$\begin{aligned} x_1 &= 2y_1 - y_2 \\ x_2 &= -3y_1 + 2y_2 \\ x_3 &= y_1 + 3y_2 \end{aligned} \quad \text{and} \quad \begin{aligned} y_1 &= -4z_1 + 2z_2 \\ y_2 &= 3z_1 + z_2 \end{aligned}$$

as a matrix equation and use matrix multiplication to express $x_1$, $x_2$, and $x_3$ in terms of $z_1$ and $z_2$.

*Solution*    We have

$$\begin{bmatrix} x_1 \\ x_2 \\ x_3 \end{bmatrix} = \begin{bmatrix} 2 & -1 \\ -3 & 2 \\ 1 & 3 \end{bmatrix} \begin{bmatrix} y_1 \\ y_2 \end{bmatrix} \quad \text{and} \quad \begin{bmatrix} y_1 \\ y_2 \end{bmatrix} = \begin{bmatrix} -4 & 2 \\ 3 & 1 \end{bmatrix} \begin{bmatrix} z_1 \\ z_2 \end{bmatrix}.$$

Substituting for $\begin{bmatrix} y_1 \\ y_2 \end{bmatrix}$ in the left-hand equation gives

$$\begin{bmatrix} x_1 \\ x_2 \\ x_3 \end{bmatrix} = \begin{bmatrix} 2 & -1 \\ -3 & 2 \\ 1 & 3 \end{bmatrix} \begin{bmatrix} -4 & 2 \\ 3 & 1 \end{bmatrix} \begin{bmatrix} z_1 \\ z_2 \end{bmatrix} = \begin{bmatrix} -11 & 3 \\ 18 & -4 \\ 5 & 5 \end{bmatrix} \begin{bmatrix} z_1 \\ z_2 \end{bmatrix}.$$

Therefore,

$$x_1 = -11z_1 + 3z_2$$
$$x_2 = \phantom{-}18z_1 - 4z_2$$
$$x_3 = \phantom{-1}5z_1 + 5z_2.$$

The use of the matrix equation (3) to represent the linear system (1) provides a convenient notational device for representing the $(m \times n)$ system

$$
\begin{aligned}
a_{11}x_1 + a_{12}x_2 + \cdots + a_{1n}x_n &= b_1 \\
a_{21}x_1 + a_{22}x_2 + \cdots + a_{2n}x_n &= b_2 \\
\vdots \qquad \vdots \qquad\qquad \vdots \qquad \vdots \\
a_{m1}x_1 + a_{m2}x_2 + \cdots + a_{mn}x_n &= b_m
\end{aligned}
\tag{4}
$$

of linear equations with unknowns $x_1, \ldots, x_n$. Specifically, if $A = (a_{ij})$ is the coefficient matrix of (4), and if the unknown $(n \times 1)$ matrix $\mathbf{x}$ and the constant $(m \times 1)$ matrix $\mathbf{b}$ are defined by

$$
\mathbf{x} = \begin{bmatrix} x_1 \\ x_2 \\ \vdots \\ x_n \end{bmatrix}
\quad \text{and} \quad
\mathbf{b} = \begin{bmatrix} b_1 \\ b_2 \\ \vdots \\ b_m \end{bmatrix},
$$

then the system (4) is equivalent to the matrix equation

$$\mathbf{Ax} = \mathbf{b}. \tag{5}$$

**EXAMPLE 6** Solve the matrix equation $A\mathbf{x} = \mathbf{b}$, where

$$
A = \begin{bmatrix} 1 & 3 & -1 \\ 2 & 5 & -1 \\ 2 & 8 & -2 \end{bmatrix},
\quad
\mathbf{x} = \begin{bmatrix} x_1 \\ x_2 \\ x_3 \end{bmatrix},
\quad \text{and} \quad
\mathbf{b} = \begin{bmatrix} 2 \\ 6 \\ 6 \end{bmatrix}.
$$

*Solution* The matrix equation $A\mathbf{x} = \mathbf{b}$ is equivalent to the $(3 \times 3)$ linear system

$$
\begin{aligned}
x_1 + 3x_2 - \phantom{2}x_3 &= 2 \\
2x_1 + 5x_2 - \phantom{2}x_3 &= 6 \\
2x_1 + 8x_2 - 2x_3 &= 6.
\end{aligned}
$$

This system can be solved in the usual way—that is, by reducing the augmented matrix—to obtain $x_1 = 2$, $x_2 = 1$, $x_3 = 3$. Therefore,

$$
\mathbf{s} = \begin{bmatrix} 2 \\ 1 \\ 3 \end{bmatrix}
$$

is the unique solution to $A\mathbf{x} = \mathbf{b}$.

## Other Formulations of Matrix Multiplication

It is frequently convenient and useful to express an $(m \times n)$ matrix $A = (a_{ij})$ in the form

$$A = [\mathbf{A}_1, \mathbf{A}_2, \ldots, \mathbf{A}_n], \tag{6}$$

where for each $j$, $1 \leq j \leq n$, $\mathbf{A}_j$ denotes the $j$th column of $A$. That is, $\mathbf{A}_j$ is the $(m \times 1)$ column vector

$$\mathbf{A}_j = \begin{bmatrix} a_{1j} \\ a_{2j} \\ \vdots \\ a_{mj} \end{bmatrix}.$$

For example, if $A$ is the $(2 \times 3)$ matrix

$$A = \begin{bmatrix} 1 & 3 & 6 \\ 2 & 4 & 0 \end{bmatrix}, \tag{7}$$

then $A = [\mathbf{A}_1, \mathbf{A}_2, \mathbf{A}_3]$, where

$$\mathbf{A}_1 = \begin{bmatrix} 1 \\ 2 \end{bmatrix}, \quad \mathbf{A}_2 = \begin{bmatrix} 3 \\ 4 \end{bmatrix}, \quad \text{and} \quad \mathbf{A}_3 = \begin{bmatrix} 6 \\ 0 \end{bmatrix}.$$

The next two theorems use Eq. (6) to provide alternative ways of expressing the matrix products $A\mathbf{x}$ and $AB$; these methods will be extremely useful in our later development of matrix theory.

**THEOREM 5** Let $A = [\mathbf{A}_1, \mathbf{A}_2, \ldots, \mathbf{A}_n]$ be an $(m \times n)$ matrix whose $j$th column is $\mathbf{A}_j$, and let $\mathbf{x}$ be the $(n \times 1)$ column vector

$$\mathbf{x} = \begin{bmatrix} x_1 \\ x_2 \\ \vdots \\ x_n \end{bmatrix}.$$

Then the product $A\mathbf{x}$ can be expressed as

$$A\mathbf{x} = x_1\mathbf{A}_1 + x_2\mathbf{A}_2 + \cdots + x_n\mathbf{A}_n.$$

The proof of this theorem is not difficult and uses only Definitions 5, 6, 7, and 8; the proof is left as an exercise for the reader. To illustrate Theorem 5, let $A$ be the matrix

$$A = \begin{bmatrix} 1 & 3 & 6 \\ 2 & 4 & 0 \end{bmatrix},$$

and let $\mathbf{x}$ be the vector in $R^3$,

$$\mathbf{x} = \begin{bmatrix} x_1 \\ x_2 \\ x_3 \end{bmatrix}.$$

Then

$$Ax = \begin{bmatrix} 1 & 3 & 6 \\ 2 & 4 & 0 \end{bmatrix} \begin{bmatrix} x_1 \\ x_2 \\ x_3 \end{bmatrix}$$

$$= \begin{bmatrix} x_1 + 3x_2 + 6x_3 \\ 2x_1 + 4x_2 + 0x_3 \end{bmatrix}$$

$$= x_1 \begin{bmatrix} 1 \\ 2 \end{bmatrix} + x_2 \begin{bmatrix} 3 \\ 4 \end{bmatrix} + x_3 \begin{bmatrix} 6 \\ 0 \end{bmatrix};$$

so that $Ax = x_1\mathbf{A}_1 + x_2\mathbf{A}_2 + x_3\mathbf{A}_3$. In particular, if we set

$$\mathbf{x} = \begin{bmatrix} 2 \\ 2 \\ -3 \end{bmatrix},$$

then $Ax = 2\mathbf{A}_1 + 2\mathbf{A}_2 - 3\mathbf{A}_3$.

From Theorem 5, we see that the matrix equation $Ax = \mathbf{b}$ corresponding to the $(m \times n)$ system (4) can be expressed as

$$x_1\mathbf{A}_1 + x_2\mathbf{A}_2 + \cdots + x_n\mathbf{A}_n = \mathbf{b}. \tag{8}$$

Thus, Eq. (8) says that solving $Ax = \mathbf{b}$ amounts to showing that $\mathbf{b}$ can be written in terms of the columns of $A$.

**EXAMPLE 7**  Solve

$$x_1 \begin{bmatrix} 1 \\ 2 \\ 2 \end{bmatrix} + x_2 \begin{bmatrix} 3 \\ 5 \\ 8 \end{bmatrix} + x_3 \begin{bmatrix} -1 \\ -1 \\ -2 \end{bmatrix} = \begin{bmatrix} 2 \\ 6 \\ 6 \end{bmatrix}.$$

*Solution*  By Theorem 5, the given equation is equivalent to the matrix equation $Ax = \mathbf{b}$, where

$$A = \begin{bmatrix} 1 & 3 & -1 \\ 2 & 5 & -1 \\ 2 & 8 & -2 \end{bmatrix}, \quad \mathbf{x} = \begin{bmatrix} x_1 \\ x_2 \\ x_3 \end{bmatrix}, \quad \text{and} \quad \mathbf{b} = \begin{bmatrix} 2 \\ 6 \\ 6 \end{bmatrix}.$$

This equation was solved in Example 6 giving $x_1 = 2, x_2 = 1, x_3 = 3$, so we have

$$2 \begin{bmatrix} 1 \\ 2 \\ 2 \end{bmatrix} + \begin{bmatrix} 3 \\ 5 \\ 8 \end{bmatrix} + 3 \begin{bmatrix} -1 \\ -1 \\ -2 \end{bmatrix} = \begin{bmatrix} 2 \\ 6 \\ 6 \end{bmatrix}. \qquad \blacksquare$$

Although Eq. (8) is not particularly efficient as a computational tool, it is useful for understanding how the internal structure of the coefficient matrix affects the possible solutions of the linear system $Ax = \mathbf{b}$.

Another important observation, which we will use later, is an alternative way of expressing the product of two matrices, as given in Theorem 6.

THEOREM 6    Let $A$ be an $(m \times n)$ matrix, and let $B = [\mathbf{B}_1, \mathbf{B}_2, \ldots, \mathbf{B}_s]$ be an $(n \times s)$ matrix whose $k$th column is $\mathbf{B}_k$. Then the $j$th column of $AB$ is $A\mathbf{B}_j$, so that

$$AB = [A\mathbf{B}_1, A\mathbf{B}_2, \ldots, A\mathbf{B}_s].$$

*Proof*    If $A = (a_{ij})$ and $B = (b_{ij})$, then the $j$th column of $AB$ contains the entries

$$\sum_{k=1}^{n} a_{1k}b_{kj}$$

$$\sum_{k=1}^{n} a_{2k}b_{kj}$$

$$\vdots$$

$$\sum_{k=1}^{n} a_{mk}b_{kj};$$

and these are precisely the components of the column vector $A\mathbf{B}_j$, where

$$\mathbf{B}_j = \begin{bmatrix} b_{1j} \\ b_{2j} \\ \vdots \\ b_{nj} \end{bmatrix}.$$

It follows that we can write $AB$ in the form $AB = [A\mathbf{B}_1, A\mathbf{B}_2, \ldots, A\mathbf{B}_s].$    ■

To illustrate Theorem 6, let $A$ and $B$ be given by

$$A = \begin{bmatrix} 2 & 6 \\ 0 & 4 \\ 1 & 2 \end{bmatrix} \quad \text{and} \quad B = \begin{bmatrix} 1 & 3 & 0 & 1 \\ 4 & 5 & 2 & 3 \end{bmatrix}.$$

Thus the column vectors for $B$ are

$$\mathbf{B}_1 = \begin{bmatrix} 1 \\ 4 \end{bmatrix}, \quad \mathbf{B}_2 = \begin{bmatrix} 3 \\ 5 \end{bmatrix}, \quad \mathbf{B}_3 = \begin{bmatrix} 0 \\ 2 \end{bmatrix}, \quad \text{and} \quad \mathbf{B}_4 = \begin{bmatrix} 1 \\ 3 \end{bmatrix}$$

and

$$A\mathbf{B}_1 = \begin{bmatrix} 26 \\ 16 \\ 9 \end{bmatrix}, \quad A\mathbf{B}_2 = \begin{bmatrix} 36 \\ 20 \\ 13 \end{bmatrix}, \quad A\mathbf{B}_3 = \begin{bmatrix} 12 \\ 8 \\ 4 \end{bmatrix}, \quad \text{and} \quad A\mathbf{B}_4 = \begin{bmatrix} 20 \\ 12 \\ 7 \end{bmatrix}.$$

Calculating $AB$, we see immediately that $AB$ is a $(3 \times 4)$ matrix with columns $A\mathbf{B}_1$, $A\mathbf{B}_2$, $A\mathbf{B}_3$, and $A\mathbf{B}_4$; that is,

$$AB = \begin{bmatrix} 26 & 36 & 12 & 20 \\ 16 & 20 & 8 & 12 \\ 9 & 13 & 4 & 7 \end{bmatrix}.$$

## 1.5   EXERCISES

The $(2 \times 2)$ matrices listed in Eq. (9) are used in several of the exercises that follow.

$$A = \begin{bmatrix} 2 & 1 \\ 1 & 3 \end{bmatrix}, \qquad B = \begin{bmatrix} 0 & -1 \\ 1 & 3 \end{bmatrix},$$

$$C = \begin{bmatrix} -2 & 3 \\ 1 & 1 \end{bmatrix}, \qquad Z = \begin{bmatrix} 0 & 0 \\ 0 & 0 \end{bmatrix} \tag{9}$$

Exercises 1–6 refer to the matrices in Eq. (9).

**1.** Find (a) $A + B$; (b) $A + C$; (c) $6B$; and (d) $B + 3C$.

**2.** Find (a) $B + C$; (b) $3A$; (c) $A + 2C$; and (d) $C + 8Z$.

**3.** Find a matrix $D$ such that $A + D = B$.

**4.** Find a matrix $D$ such that $A + 2D = C$.

**5.** Find a matrix $D$ such that $A + 2B + 2D = 3B$.

**6.** Find a matrix $D$ such that $2A + 5B + D = 2B + 3A$.

The vectors listed in Eq. (10) are used in several of the exercises that follow.

$$\mathbf{r} = \begin{bmatrix} 1 \\ 0 \end{bmatrix}, \qquad \mathbf{s} = \begin{bmatrix} 2 \\ -3 \end{bmatrix},$$

$$\mathbf{t} = \begin{bmatrix} 1 \\ 4 \end{bmatrix}, \qquad \mathbf{u} = \begin{bmatrix} -4 \\ 6 \end{bmatrix} \tag{10}$$

In Exercises 7–12, perform the indicated computation, using the vectors in Eq. (10) and the matrices in Eq. (9).

**7. a)** $\mathbf{r} + \mathbf{s}$      **8. a)** $\mathbf{t} + \mathbf{s}$
  **b)** $2\mathbf{r} + \mathbf{t}$         **b)** $\mathbf{r} + 3\mathbf{u}$
  **c)** $2\mathbf{s} + \mathbf{u}$         **c)** $2\mathbf{u} + 3\mathbf{t}$

**9. a)** $A\mathbf{r}$         **10. a)** $B\mathbf{t}$
  **b)** $B\mathbf{r}$           **b)** $C(\mathbf{r} + \mathbf{s})$
  **c)** $C(\mathbf{s} + 3\mathbf{t})$     **c)** $B(\mathbf{r} + \mathbf{s})$

**11. a)** $(A + 2B)\mathbf{r}$   **12. a)** $(A + C)\mathbf{r}$
  **b)** $(B + C)\mathbf{u}$       **b)** $(2B + 3C)\mathbf{s}$

Exercises 13–20 refer to the vectors in Eq. (10). In each exercise, find scalars $a_1$ and $a_2$ that satisfy the given equation, or state that the equation has no solution.

**13.** $a_1\mathbf{r} + a_2\mathbf{s} = \mathbf{t}$     **14.** $a_1\mathbf{r} + a_2\mathbf{s} = \mathbf{u}$

**15.** $a_1\mathbf{s} + a_2\mathbf{t} = \mathbf{u}$     **16.** $a_1\mathbf{s} + a_2\mathbf{t} = \mathbf{r} + \mathbf{t}$

**17.** $a_1\mathbf{s} + a_2\mathbf{u} = 2\mathbf{r} + \mathbf{t}$     **18.** $a_1\mathbf{s} + a_2\mathbf{u} = \mathbf{t}$

**19.** $a_1\mathbf{t} + a_2\mathbf{u} = 3\mathbf{s} + 4\mathbf{t}$     **20.** $a_1\mathbf{t} + a_2\mathbf{u} = 3\mathbf{r} + 2\mathbf{s}$

Exercises 21–24 refer to the matrices in Eq. (9) and the vectors in Eq. (10).

**21.** Find $\mathbf{w}_2$, where $\mathbf{w}_1 = B\mathbf{r}$ and $\mathbf{w}_2 = A\mathbf{w}_1$. Calculate $Q = AB$. Calculate $Q\mathbf{r}$ and verify that $\mathbf{w}_2$ is equal to $Q\mathbf{r}$.

**22.** Find $\mathbf{w}_2$, where $\mathbf{w}_1 = C\mathbf{s}$ and $\mathbf{w}_2 = A\mathbf{w}_1$. Calculate $Q = AC$. Calculate $Q\mathbf{s}$ and verify that $\mathbf{w}_2$ is equal to $Q\mathbf{s}$.

**23.** Find $\mathbf{w}_3$, where $\mathbf{w}_1 = C\mathbf{r}$, $\mathbf{w}_2 = B\mathbf{w}_1$, and $\mathbf{w}_3 = A\mathbf{w}_2$. Calculate $Q = A(BC)$ and verify that $\mathbf{w}_3$ is equal to $Q\mathbf{r}$.

**24.** Find $\mathbf{w}_3$, where $\mathbf{w}_1 = A\mathbf{r}$, $\mathbf{w}_2 = C\mathbf{w}_1$, and $\mathbf{w}_3 = B\mathbf{w}_2$. Calculate $Q = B(CA)$ and verify that $\mathbf{w}_3$ is equal to $Q\mathbf{r}$.

Exercises 25–30 refer to the matrices in Eq. (9). Find each of the following.

**25.** $(A + B)C$        **26.** $(A + 2B)A$

**27.** $(A + C)B$        **28.** $(B + C)Z$

**29.** $A(BZ)$           **30.** $Z(AB)$

The matrices and vectors listed in Eq. (11) are used in several of the exercises that follow.

$$A = \begin{bmatrix} 2 & 3 \\ 1 & 4 \end{bmatrix}, \quad B = \begin{bmatrix} 1 & 2 \\ 1 & 4 \end{bmatrix}, \quad \mathbf{u} = \begin{bmatrix} 1 \\ 3 \end{bmatrix},$$

$$\mathbf{v} = [\, 2, 4 \,], \quad C = \begin{bmatrix} 2 & 1 \\ 4 & 0 \\ 8 & -1 \\ 3 & 2 \end{bmatrix}, \tag{11}$$

$$D = \begin{bmatrix} 2 & 1 & 3 & 6 \\ 2 & 0 & 0 & 4 \\ 1 & -1 & 1 & -1 \\ 1 & 3 & 1 & 2 \end{bmatrix}, \quad \mathbf{w} = \begin{bmatrix} 2 \\ 3 \\ 1 \\ 1 \end{bmatrix}.$$

Exercises 31–41 refer to the matrices and vectors in Eq. (11). Find each of the following.

**31.** $AB$ and $BA$        **32.** $DC$

**33.** $A\mathbf{u}$ and $\mathbf{v}A$        **34.** $\mathbf{u}\mathbf{v}$ and $\mathbf{v}\mathbf{u}$

**35.** $\mathbf{v}(B\mathbf{u})$           **36.** $B\mathbf{u}$

**37.** $CA$               **38.** $CB$

**39.** $C(B\mathbf{u})$           **40.** $(AB)\mathbf{u}$ and $A(B\mathbf{u})$

**41.** $(BA)\mathbf{u}$ and $B(A\mathbf{u})$

In Exercises 42–49, the given matrix is the augmented matrix for a system of linear equations. Give the vector form for the general solution.

**42.** $\begin{bmatrix} 1 & 0 & -1 & -2 & 0 \\ 0 & 1 & 2 & 3 & 0 \end{bmatrix}$

**43.** $\begin{bmatrix} 1 & 0 & -1 & -2 \\ 0 & 1 & 2 & 3 \end{bmatrix}$

**44.** $\begin{bmatrix} 1 & 0 & -1 & 0 & -1 \\ 0 & 1 & 2 & 0 & 1 \\ 0 & 0 & 0 & 1 & 1 \end{bmatrix}$

**45.** $\begin{bmatrix} 1 & 0 & -1 & 0 & -1 & 0 \\ 0 & 1 & 2 & 0 & 1 & 0 \\ 0 & 0 & 0 & 1 & 1 & 0 \end{bmatrix}$

**46.** $\begin{bmatrix} 1 & 0 & -1 & -2 & -3 & 1 \\ 0 & 1 & 2 & 3 & 4 & 0 \end{bmatrix}$

**47.** $\begin{bmatrix} 1 & 0 & -1 & -2 & -3 & 0 \\ 0 & 1 & 2 & 3 & 4 & 0 \end{bmatrix}$

**48.** $\begin{bmatrix} 1 & 0 & -1 & 0 & -1 & -2 & 0 \\ 0 & 1 & 2 & 0 & 1 & 2 & 0 \\ 0 & 0 & 0 & 1 & 1 & 1 & 0 \end{bmatrix}$

**49.** $\begin{bmatrix} 1 & -1 & 0 & -2 & 0 & 0 \\ 0 & 0 & 1 & 2 & 0 & 0 \\ 0 & 0 & 0 & 0 & 1 & 0 \end{bmatrix}$

**50.** In Exercise 40, the calculations $(AB)\mathbf{u}$ and $A(B\mathbf{u})$ produce the same result. Which calculation requires fewer multiplications of individual matrix entries? (For example, it takes two multiplications to get the $(1, 1)$ entry of $AB$.)

**51.** The next section will show that all the following calculations produce the same result:

$C[A(B\mathbf{u})] = (CA)(B\mathbf{u}) = [C(AB)]\mathbf{u} = C[(AB)\mathbf{u}].$

Convince yourself that the first expression requires the fewest individual multiplications. [*Hint:* Forming $B\mathbf{u}$ takes four multiplications, and thus $A(B\mathbf{u})$ takes eight multiplications, and so on.] Count the number of multiplications required for each of the four preceding calculations.

**52.** Refer to the matrices and vectors in Eq. (11).

    **a)** Identify the column vectors in $A = [\mathbf{A}_1, \mathbf{A}_2]$ and $D = [\mathbf{D}_1, \mathbf{D}_2, \mathbf{D}_3, \mathbf{D}_4]$.

    **b)** In part (a), is $\mathbf{A}_1$ in $R^2$, $R^3$, or $R^4$? Is $\mathbf{D}_1$ in $R^2$, $R^3$, or $R^4$?

    **c)** Form the $(2 \times 2)$ matrix with columns $[AB_1, AB_2]$, and verify that this matrix is the product $AB$.

    **d)** Verify that the vector $D\mathbf{w}$ is the same as $2\mathbf{D}_1 + 3\mathbf{D}_2 + \mathbf{D}_3 + \mathbf{D}_4$.

**53.** Determine whether the following matrix products are defined. When the product is defined, give the size of the product.

    **a)** $AB$ and $BA$, where $A$ is $(2 \times 3)$ and $B$ is $(3 \times 4)$

    **b)** $AB$ and $BA$, where $A$ is $(2 \times 3)$ and $B$ is $(2 \times 4)$

    **c)** $AB$ and $BA$, where $A$ is $(3 \times 7)$ and $B$ is $(6 \times 3)$

    **d)** $AB$ and $BA$, where $A$ is $(2 \times 3)$ and $B$ is $(3 \times 2)$

    **e)** $AB$ and $BA$, where $A$ is $(3 \times 3)$ and $B$ is $(3 \times 1)$

    **f)** $A(BC)$ and $(AB)C$, where $A$ is $(2 \times 3)$, $B$ is $(3 \times 5)$, and $C$ is $(5 \times 4)$

    **g)** $AB$ and $BA$, where $A$ is $(4 \times 1)$ and $B$ is $(1 \times 4)$

**54.** What is the size of the product $(AB)(CD)$, where $A$ is $(2 \times 3)$, $B$ is $(3 \times 4)$, $C$ is $(4 \times 4)$, and $D$ is $(4 \times 2)$? Also calculate the size of $A[B(CD)]$ and $[(AB)C]D$.

**55.** If $A$ is a matrix, what should the symbol $A^2$ mean? What restrictions on $A$ are required in order that $A^2$ be defined?

**56.** Set

$$O = \begin{bmatrix} 0 & 0 \\ 0 & 0 \end{bmatrix},$$

$$A = \begin{bmatrix} 2 & 0 \\ 0 & 2 \end{bmatrix}, \quad \text{and}$$

$$B = \begin{bmatrix} 1 & b \\ b^{-1} & 1 \end{bmatrix},$$

where $b \neq 0$. Show that $O$, $A$, and $B$ are solutions to the matrix equation $X^2 - 2X = O$. Conclude that this quadratic equation has infinitely many solutions.

**57.** Two newspapers compete for subscriptions in a region with 300,000 households. Assume that no household subscribes to both newspapers and that the following table gives the probabilities that a household will change its subscription status during the year.

|        | *From A* | *From B* | *From None* |
|--------|----------|----------|-------------|
| **To A**    | .70 | .15 | .30 |
| **To B**    | .20 | .80 | .20 |
| **To None** | .10 | .05 | .50 |

For example, an interpretation of the first column of the table is that during a given year, newspaper A can expect to keep 70% of its current subscribers while losing 20% to newspaper B and 10% to no subscription.

At the beginning of a particular year, suppose that 150,000 households subscribe to newspaper A, 100,000 subscribe to newspaper B, and 50,000 have no subscription. Let $P$ and $\mathbf{x}$ be defined by

$$P = \begin{bmatrix} .70 & .15 & .30 \\ .20 & .80 & .20 \\ .10 & .05 & .50 \end{bmatrix} \quad \text{and} \quad \mathbf{x} = \begin{bmatrix} 150{,}000 \\ 100{,}000 \\ 50{,}000 \end{bmatrix}.$$

The vector $\mathbf{x}$ is called the **state vector** for the beginning of the year. Calculate $P\mathbf{x}$ and $P^2\mathbf{x}$ and interpret the resulting vectors.

**58.** Let $A = \begin{bmatrix} 1 & 2 \\ 3 & 4 \end{bmatrix}$.

a) Find all matrices $B = \begin{bmatrix} a & b \\ c & d \end{bmatrix}$ such that
   $AB = BA$.

b) Use the results of part (a) to exhibit $(2 \times 2)$ matrices $B$ and $C$ such that $AB = BA$ and $AC \neq CA$.

**59.** Let $A$ and $B$ be matrices such that the product $AB$ is defined and is a square matrix. Argue that the product $BA$ is also defined and is a square matrix.

**60.** Let $A$ and $B$ be matrices such that the product $AB$ is defined. Use Theorem 6 to prove each of the following.

a) If $B$ has a column of zeros, then so does $AB$.

b) If $B$ has two identical columns, then so does $AB$.

**61. a)** Express each of the linear systems i) and ii) in the form $A\mathbf{x} = \mathbf{b}$.

   i) $2x_1 - x_2 = 3$       ii) $x_1 - 3x_2 + x_3 = 1$
      $x_1 + x_2 = 3$            $x_1 - 2x_2 + x_3 = 2$
                                 $x_2 - x_3 = -1$

b) Express systems i) and ii) in the form of Eq. (8).

c) Solve systems i) and ii) by Gaussian elimination. For each system $A\mathbf{x} = \mathbf{b}$,

represent $\mathbf{b}$ as a linear combination of the columns of the coefficient matrix.

**62.** Solve $A\mathbf{x} = \mathbf{b}$, where $A$ and $\mathbf{b}$ are given by

$$A = \begin{bmatrix} 1 & 1 \\ 1 & 2 \end{bmatrix}, \quad \mathbf{b} = \begin{bmatrix} 2 \\ 3 \end{bmatrix}.$$

**63.** Let $A$ and $I$ be the matrices

$$A = \begin{bmatrix} 1 & 1 \\ 1 & 2 \end{bmatrix}, \quad I = \begin{bmatrix} 1 & 0 \\ 0 & 1 \end{bmatrix}.$$

a) Find a $(2 \times 2)$ matrix $B$ such that $AB = I$.
   [*Hint:* Use Theorem 6 to determine the column vectors of $B$.]

b) Show that $AB = BA$ for the matrix $B$ found in part (a).

**64.** Prove Theorem 5 by showing that the $i$th component of $A\mathbf{x}$ is equal to the $i$th component of $x_1\mathbf{A}_1 + x_2\mathbf{A}_2 + \cdots + x_n\mathbf{A}_n$, where $1 \leq i \leq m$.

**65.** For $A$ and $C$, which follow, find a matrix $B$ (if possible) such that $AB = C$.

a) $A = \begin{bmatrix} 1 & 3 \\ 1 & 4 \end{bmatrix}$, $C = \begin{bmatrix} 2 & 6 \\ 3 & 6 \end{bmatrix}$

b) $A = \begin{bmatrix} 1 & 1 & 1 \\ 0 & 2 & 1 \\ 2 & 4 & 3 \end{bmatrix}$, $C = \begin{bmatrix} 1 & 0 & 0 \\ 1 & 2 & 0 \\ 1 & 3 & 5 \end{bmatrix}$

c) $A = \begin{bmatrix} 1 & 2 \\ 2 & 4 \end{bmatrix}$, $C = \begin{bmatrix} 0 & 0 \\ 0 & 0 \end{bmatrix}$,

   where $B \neq C$.

**66.** A $(3 \times 3)$ matrix $T = (t_{ij})$ is called an **upper-triangular** matrix if $T$ has the form

$$T = \begin{bmatrix} t_{11} & t_{12} & t_{13} \\ 0 & t_{22} & t_{23} \\ 0 & 0 & t_{33} \end{bmatrix}.$$

Formally, $T$ is upper triangular if $t_{ij} = 0$ whenever $i > j$. If $A$ and $B$ are upper-triangular $(3 \times 3)$ matrices, verify that the product $AB$ is also upper triangular.

**67.** An $(n \times n)$ matrix $T = (t_{ij})$ is called upper triangular if $t_{ij} = 0$ whenever $i > j$. Suppose that $A$ and $B$ are $(m \times n)$ upper-triangular matrices. Use Definition 8 to prove that the product $AB$ is upper triangular. That is, show that the $ij$th entry of $AB$ is zero when $i > j$.

In Exercises 68–70, find the vector form for the general solution.

**68.** $x_1 + 3x_2 - 3x_3 + 2x_4 - 3x_5 = -4$
$\quad 3x_1 + 9x_2 - 10x_3 + 10x_4 - 14x_5 = 2$
$\quad 2x_1 + 6x_2 - 10x_3 + 21x_4 - 25x_5 = 53$

**69.** $14x_1 - 8x_2 + 3x_3 - 49x_4 + 29x_5 = 44$
$\quad -8x_1 + 5x_2 - 2x_3 + 29x_4 - 16x_5 = -24$
$\quad 3x_1 - 2x_2 + x_3 - 11x_4 + 6x_5 = 9$

**70.** $18x_1 + 18x_2 - 10x_3 + 7x_4 + 2x_5 + 50x_6 = 26$
$\quad -10x_1 - 10x_2 + 6x_3 - 4x_4 - x_5 - 27x_6 = -13$
$\quad 7x_1 + 7x_2 - 4x_3 + 5x_4 + 2x_5 + 30x_6 = 18$
$\quad 2x_1 + 2x_2 - x_3 + 2x_4 + x_5 + 12x_6 = 8$

**71.** In Exercise 57 we saw that the state vector giving the number of newspaper subscribers in year $n$ could be found by forming $P^n \mathbf{x}$ where $\mathbf{x}$ is the initial state. Later, in Section 3.8, we will see that as $n$ grows larger and larger, the vector $P^n \mathbf{x}$ tends toward a limit. Use MATLAB to calculate $P^n \mathbf{x}$ for $n = 1, 2, \ldots, 30$. For ease of reading, display the results using bank format in the MATLAB numeric options menu. What do you think the steady state distribution of newspapers will be?

## 1.6 ALGEBRAIC PROPERTIES OF MATRIX OPERATIONS

In the previous section we defined the matrix operations of addition, multiplication, and the multiplication of a matrix by a scalar. For these operations to be useful, the basic rules they obey must be determined. As we will presently see, many of the familiar algebraic properties of real numbers also hold for matrices. There are, however, important exceptions. We have already noted, for example, that matrix multiplication is not commutative. Another property of real numbers that does not carry over to matrices is the cancellation law for multiplication. That is, if $a$, $b$, and $c$ are real numbers such that $ab = ac$ and $a \neq 0$, then $b = c$. By contrast, consider the three matrices

$$A = \begin{bmatrix} 1 & 1 \\ 1 & 1 \end{bmatrix}, \quad B = \begin{bmatrix} 1 & 4 \\ 2 & 1 \end{bmatrix}, \quad \text{and} \quad C = \begin{bmatrix} 2 & 2 \\ 1 & 3 \end{bmatrix}.$$

Note that $AB = AC$ but $B \neq C$. This example shows that the familiar cancellation law for real numbers does not apply to matrix multiplication.

### Properties of Matrix Operations

The next three theorems list algebraic properties that do hold for matrix operations. In some cases, although the rule seems obvious and the proof simple, certain subtleties should be noted. For example, Theorem 9 asserts that $(r + s)A = rA + sA$, where $r$ and $s$ are scalars and $A$ is an $(m \times n)$ matrix. Although the same addition symbol, $+$, appears on both sides of the equation, two different addition operations are involved; $r + s$ is the sum of two scalars, and $rA + sA$ is the sum of two matrices.

Our first theorem lists some of the properties satisfied by matrix addition.

**THEOREM 7** If $A$, $B$, and $C$ are $(m \times n)$ matrices, then the following are true:

1. $A + B = B + A$.
2. $(A + B) + C = A + (B + C)$.
3. There exists a unique $(m \times n)$ matrix $\mathcal{O}$ (called the **zero matrix**) such that $A + \mathcal{O} = A$ for every $(m \times n)$ matrix $A$.
4. Given an $(m \times n)$ matrix $A$, there exists a unique $(m \times n)$ matrix $P$ such that $A + P = \mathcal{O}$.

These properties are easily established, and the proofs of 2–4 are left as exercises. Regarding properties 3 and 4, we note that the zero matrix, $\mathcal{O}$, is the $(m \times n)$ matrix, all of whose entries are zero. Also the matrix $P$ of property 4 is usually called the additive inverse for $A$, and the reader can show that $P = (-1)A$. The matrix $(-1)A$ is also denoted as $-A$, and the notation $A - B$ means $A + (-B)$. Thus property 4 states that $A - A = \mathcal{O}$.

***Proof of Property 1***   If $A = (a_{ij})$ and $B = (b_{ij})$ are $(m \times n)$ matrices, then, by Definition 6,

$$(A + B)_{ij} = a_{ij} + b_{ij}.$$

Similarly, by Definition 6,

$$(B + A)_{ij} = b_{ij} + a_{ij}.$$

Since addition of real numbers is commutative, $a_{ij}+b_{ij}$ and $b_{ij}+a_{ij}$ are equal. Therefore, $A + B = B + A$. ◼

Three associative properties involving scalar and matrix multiplication are given in Theorem 8.

### THEOREM 8

1. If $A$, $B$, and $C$ are $(m \times n)$, $(n \times p)$, and $(p \times q)$ matrices, respectively, then $(AB)C = A(BC)$.
2. If $r$ and $s$ are scalars, then $r(sA) = (rs)A$.
3. $r(AB) = (rA)B = A(rB)$. ◼

The proof is again left to the reader, but we will give one example to illustrate the theorem.

### EXAMPLE 1   Demonstrate that $(AB)C = A(BC)$, where

$$A = \begin{bmatrix} 1 & 2 \\ -1 & 3 \end{bmatrix}, \quad B = \begin{bmatrix} 2 & -1 & 3 \\ 1 & -1 & 1 \end{bmatrix}, \quad \text{and} \quad C = \begin{bmatrix} 3 & 1 & 2 \\ -2 & 1 & -1 \\ 4 & -2 & -1 \end{bmatrix}.$$

***Solution***   Forming the products $AB$ and $BC$ yields

$$AB = \begin{bmatrix} 4 & -3 & 5 \\ 1 & -2 & 0 \end{bmatrix} \quad \text{and} \quad BC = \begin{bmatrix} 20 & -5 & 2 \\ 9 & -2 & 2 \end{bmatrix}.$$

Therefore, $(AB)C$ is the product of a $(2 \times 3)$ matrix with a $(3 \times 3)$ matrix, whereas $A(BC)$ is the product of a $(2 \times 2)$ matrix with a $(2 \times 3)$ matrix. Forming these products, we find

$$(AB)C = \begin{bmatrix} 38 & -9 & 6 \\ 7 & -1 & 4 \end{bmatrix} \quad \text{and} \quad A(BC) = \begin{bmatrix} 38 & -9 & 6 \\ 7 & -1 & 4 \end{bmatrix}. \quad ◼$$

Finally, the distributive properties connecting addition and multiplication are given in Theorem 9.

**THEOREM 9**

1. If $A$ and $B$ are $(m \times n)$ matrices and $C$ is an $(n \times p)$ matrix, then $(A + B)C = AC + BC$.
2. If $A$ is an $(m \times n)$ matrix and $B$ and $C$ are $(n \times p)$ matrices, then $A(B + C) = AB + AC$.
3. If $r$ and $s$ are scalars and $A$ is an $(m \times n)$ matrix, then $(r + s)A = rA + sA$.
4. If $r$ is a scalar and $A$ and $B$ are $(m \times n)$ matrices, then $r(A + B) = rA + rB$.

**Proof** We will prove property 1 and leave the others to the reader. First observe that $(A + B)C$ and $AC + BC$ are both $(m \times p)$ matrices. To show that the components of these two matrices are equal, let $Q = A + B$, where $Q = (q_{ij})$. Then $(A + B)C = QC$, and the $rs$th component of $QC$ is given by

$$\sum_{k=1}^{n} q_{rk}c_{ks} = \sum_{k=1}^{n}(a_{rk} + b_{rk})c_{ks} = \sum_{k=1}^{n} a_{rk}c_{ks} + \sum_{k=1}^{n} b_{rk}c_{ks}.$$

Because

$$\sum_{k=1}^{n} a_{rk}c_{ks} + \sum_{k=1}^{n} b_{rk}c_{ks}$$

is precisely the $rs$th entry of $AC + BC$, it follows that $(A + B)C = AC + BC$. ◼

## The Transpose of a Matrix

The concept of the transpose of a matrix is important in applications. Stated informally, the transpose operation, applied to a matrix $A$, interchanges the rows and columns of $A$. The formal definition of transpose is as follows.

**DEFINITION 9**

If $A = (a_{ij})$ is an $(m \times n)$ matrix, then the **transpose** of $A$, denoted $A^T$, is the $(n \times m)$ matrix $A^T = (b_{ij})$, where $b_{ij} = a_{ji}$ for all $i$ and $j$, $1 \leq j \leq m$, and $1 \leq i \leq n$.

The following example illustrates the definition of the transpose of a matrix:

**EXAMPLE 2** Find the transpose of $A = \begin{bmatrix} 1 & 3 & 7 \\ 2 & 1 & 4 \end{bmatrix}$.

**Solution** By Definition 9, $A^T$ is the $(3 \times 2)$ matrix

$$A^T = \begin{bmatrix} 1 & 2 \\ 3 & 1 \\ 7 & 4 \end{bmatrix}.$$ ◼

In the preceding example, note that the first row of $A$ becomes the first column of $A^T$, and the second row of $A$ becomes the second column of $A^T$. Similarly, the columns of $A$ become the rows of $A^T$. Thus $A^T$ is obtained by interchanging the rows and columns of $A$.

Three important properties of the transpose are given in Theorem 10.

**THEOREM 10**    If $A$ and $B$ are $(m \times n)$ matrices and $C$ is an $(n \times p)$ matrix, then:

    **1.** $(A + B)^T = A^T + B^T$.
    **2.** $(AC)^T = C^T A^T$.
    **3.** $(A^T)^T = A$.

*Proof*    We will leave properties 1 and 3 to the reader and prove property 2. Note first that $(AC)^T$ and $C^T A^T$ are both $(p \times m)$ matrices, so we have only to show that their corresponding entries are equal. From Definition 9, the $ij$th entry of $(AC)^T$ is the $ji$th entry of $AC$. Thus the $ij$th entry of $(AC)^T$ is given by

$$\sum_{k=1}^{n} a_{jk} c_{ki}.$$

Next the $ij$th entry of $C^T A^T$ is the scalar product of the $i$th row of $C^T$ with the $j$th column of $A^T$. In particular, the $i$th row of $C^T$ is $[c_{1i}, c_{2i}, \ldots, c_{ni}]$ (the $i$th column of $C$), whereas the $j$th column of $A^T$ is

$$\begin{bmatrix} a_{j1} \\ a_{j2} \\ \vdots \\ a_{jn} \end{bmatrix}$$

(the $j$th row of $A$). Therefore, the $ij$th entry of $C^T A^T$ is given by

$$c_{1i} a_{j1} + c_{2i} a_{j2} + \cdots + c_{ni} a_{jn} = \sum_{k=1}^{n} c_{ki} a_{jk}.$$

Finally, since

$$\sum_{k=1}^{n} c_{ki} a_{jk} = \sum_{k=1}^{n} a_{jk} c_{ki},$$

the $ij$th entries of $(AC)^T$ and $C^T A^T$ agree, and the matrices are equal. ◼

The transpose operation is used to define certain important types of matrices, such as positive-definite matrices, normal matrices, and symmetric matrices. We will consider these in detail later and give only the definition of a symmetric matrix in this section.

**DEFINITION 10**    A matrix $A$ is *symmetric* if $A = A^T$.

If $A$ is an $(m \times n)$ matrix, then $A^T$ is an $(n \times m)$ matrix, so we can have $A = A^T$ only if $m = n$. An $(n \times n)$ matrix is called a ***square matrix***; thus if a matrix is symmetric, it must be a square matrix. Furthermore, Definition 9 implies that if $A = (a_{ij})$ is an $(n \times n)$ symmetric matrix, then $a_{ij} = a_{ji}$ for all $i$ and $j$, $1 \leq i, j \leq n$. Conversely, if $A$ is square and $a_{ij} = a_{ji}$ for all $i$ and $j$, then $A$ is symmetric.

EXAMPLE 3  Determine which of the matrices

$$ A = \begin{bmatrix} 1 & 2 \\ 2 & 3 \end{bmatrix}, \quad B = \begin{bmatrix} 1 & 2 \\ 1 & 2 \end{bmatrix}, \quad \text{and} \quad C = \begin{bmatrix} 1 & 6 \\ 3 & 1 \\ 2 & 0 \end{bmatrix} $$

is symmetric. Also show that $B^T B$ and $C^T C$ are symmetric.

*Solution*  By Definition 9,

$$ A^T = \begin{bmatrix} 1 & 2 \\ 2 & 3 \end{bmatrix}, \quad B^T = \begin{bmatrix} 1 & 1 \\ 2 & 2 \end{bmatrix}, \quad \text{and} \quad C^T = \begin{bmatrix} 1 & 3 & 2 \\ 6 & 1 & 0 \end{bmatrix}. $$

Thus $A$ is symmetric since $A^T = A$. However, $B^T \neq B$ and $C^T \neq C$. Therefore, $B$ and $C$ are not symmetric. As can be seen, the matrices $B^T B$ and $C^T C$ are symmetric:

$$ B^T B = \begin{bmatrix} 2 & 4 \\ 4 & 8 \end{bmatrix} \quad \text{and} \quad C^T C = \begin{bmatrix} 14 & 9 \\ 9 & 37 \end{bmatrix}. $$

In Exercise 49, the reader is asked to show that $Q^T Q$ is *always* a symmetric matrix whether or not $Q$ is symmetric.

In the $(n \times n)$ matrix $A = (a_{ij})$, the entries $a_{11}, a_{22}, \ldots, a_{nn}$ are called the ***main diagonal*** of $A$. For example, the main diagonal of a $(3 \times 3)$ matrix is illustrated in Fig. 1.15. Since the entries $a_{ij}$ and $a_{ji}$ are symmetric partners relative to the main diagonal, symmetric matrices are easily recognizable as those in which the entries form a symmetric array relative to the main diagonal. For example, if

**Figure 1.15**
Main diagonal

$$ A = \begin{bmatrix} 2 & 3 & -1 \\ 3 & 4 & 2 \\ -1 & 2 & 0 \end{bmatrix} \quad \text{and} \quad B = \begin{bmatrix} 1 & 2 & 2 \\ -1 & 3 & 0 \\ 5 & 2 & 6 \end{bmatrix}, $$

then, by inspection, $A$ is symmetric, whereas $B$ is not.

## The Identity Matrix

As we will see later, the $(n \times n)$ identity matrix plays an important role in matrix theory. In particular, for each positive integer $n$, the ***identity matrix*** $I_n$ is defined to be the

$(n \times n)$ matrix with ones on the main diagonal and zeros elsewhere:

$$I_n = \begin{bmatrix} 1 & 0 & 0 & \cdots & 0 \\ 0 & 1 & 0 & \cdots & 0 \\ 0 & 0 & 1 & \cdots & 0 \\ \vdots & & & & \vdots \\ 0 & 0 & 0 & \cdots & 1 \end{bmatrix}.$$

That is, the $ij$th entry of $I_n$ is 0 when $i \neq j$, and is 1 when $i = j$. For example, $I_2$ and $I_3$ are given by

$$I_2 = \begin{bmatrix} 1 & 0 \\ 0 & 1 \end{bmatrix} \quad \text{and} \quad I_3 = \begin{bmatrix} 1 & 0 & 0 \\ 0 & 1 & 0 \\ 0 & 0 & 1 \end{bmatrix}.$$

The identity matrix is the multiplicative identity for matrix multiplication. Specifically, let $A$ denote an $(n \times n)$ matrix. Then, as in Exercise 62, it is not hard to show that

$$AI_n = A \quad \text{and} \quad I_n A = A.$$

Identity matrices can also be used with rectangular matrices. For example, let $B$ denote a $(p \times q)$ matrix. Then, as in Exercise 62,

$$BI_q = B \quad \text{and} \quad I_p B = B.$$

By way of illustration, consider

$$A = \begin{bmatrix} 1 & 2 & 0 \\ -1 & 3 & 4 \\ 6 & 1 & 8 \end{bmatrix}, \quad B = \begin{bmatrix} 2 & 3 & 1 \\ 1 & 5 & 7 \end{bmatrix}, \quad C = \begin{bmatrix} -2 & 0 \\ 8 & 3 \\ 6 & 1 \end{bmatrix},$$

and

$$\mathbf{x} = \begin{bmatrix} 1 \\ 0 \\ 3 \end{bmatrix}.$$

Note that

$$I_3 A = A I_3 = A$$
$$B I_3 = B$$
$$I_3 C = C$$
$$I_3 \mathbf{x} = \mathbf{x},$$

whereas the products $I_3 B$ and $C I_3$ are not defined.

Usually the dimension of the identity matrix is clear from the context of the problem under consideration, and it is customary to drop the subscript, $n$, and denote the $(n \times n)$ identity matrix simply as $I$. So, for example, if $A$ is an $(n \times n)$ matrix, we will write

$IA = AI = A$ instead of $I_n A = AI_n = A$. Note that the identity matrix is a symmetric matrix.

## Scalar Products and Vector Norms

The transpose operation can be used to represent scalar products and vector norms. As we will see, a vector norm provides a method for measuring the size of a vector.

To illustrate the connection between transposes and the scalar product, let $\mathbf{x}$ and $\mathbf{y}$ be vectors in $R^3$ given by

$$\mathbf{x} = \begin{bmatrix} 1 \\ -3 \\ 2 \end{bmatrix} \quad \text{and} \quad \mathbf{y} = \begin{bmatrix} 1 \\ 2 \\ 1 \end{bmatrix}.$$

Then $\mathbf{x}^T$ is the $(1 \times 3)$ vector

$$\mathbf{x}^T = [1, -3, 2],$$

and $\mathbf{x}^T\mathbf{y}$ is the scalar (or $(1 \times 1)$ matrix) given by

$$\mathbf{x}^T\mathbf{y} = [1, -3, 2] \begin{bmatrix} 1 \\ 2 \\ 1 \end{bmatrix} = 1 - 6 + 2 = -3.$$

More generally, if $\mathbf{x}$ and $\mathbf{y}$ are vectors in $R^n$,

$$\mathbf{x} = \begin{bmatrix} x_1 \\ x_2 \\ \vdots \\ x_n \end{bmatrix}, \quad \mathbf{y} = \begin{bmatrix} y_1 \\ y_2 \\ \vdots \\ y_n \end{bmatrix},$$

then

$$\mathbf{x}^T\mathbf{y} = \sum_{i=1}^{n} x_i y_i;$$

that is, $\mathbf{x}^T\mathbf{y}$ is the scalar product or dot product of $\mathbf{x}$ and $\mathbf{y}$. Also note that $\mathbf{y}^T\mathbf{x} = \sum_{i=1}^{n} y_i x_i = \sum_{i=1}^{n} x_i y_i = \mathbf{x}^T\mathbf{y}$.

One of the basic concepts in computational work is that of the length or norm of a vector. If

$$\mathbf{x} = \begin{bmatrix} a \\ b \end{bmatrix}$$

**Figure 1.16**
Geometric vector in
two-space

is in $R^2$, then $\mathbf{x}$ can be represented geometrically in the plane as the directed line segment $\overrightarrow{OP}$ from the origin $O$ to the point $P$, which has coordinates $(a, b)$, as illustrated in Fig. 1.16. By the Pythagorean theorem, the length of the line segment $\overrightarrow{OP}$ is $\sqrt{a^2 + b^2}$.

A similar idea is used in $R^n$. For a vector $\mathbf{x}$ in $R^n$,

$$\mathbf{x} = \begin{bmatrix} x_1 \\ x_2 \\ \vdots \\ x_n \end{bmatrix},$$

it is natural to define the *Euclidean length*, or *Euclidean norm* of $\mathbf{x}$, denoted by $\|\mathbf{x}\|$, to be

$$\|\mathbf{x}\| = \sqrt{x_1^2 + x_2^2 + \cdots + x_n^2}.$$

(The quantity $\|\mathbf{x}\|$ gives us a way to measure the size of the vector $\mathbf{x}$.)

Noting that the scalar product of $\mathbf{x}$ with itself is

$$\mathbf{x}^T \mathbf{x} = x_1^2 + x_2^2 + \cdots + x_n^2,$$

we have

$$\|\mathbf{x}\| = \sqrt{\mathbf{x}^T \mathbf{x}}. \tag{1}$$

For vectors $\mathbf{x}$ and $\mathbf{y}$ in $R^n$, we define the Euclidean distance between $\mathbf{x}$ and $\mathbf{y}$ to be $\|\mathbf{x} - \mathbf{y}\|$. Thus the distance between $\mathbf{x}$ and $\mathbf{y}$ is given by

$$\|\mathbf{x} - \mathbf{y}\| = \sqrt{(\mathbf{x} - \mathbf{y})^T (\mathbf{x} - \mathbf{y})}$$
$$= \sqrt{(x_1 - y_1)^2 + (x_2 - y_2)^2 + \cdots + (x_n - y_n)^2}. \tag{2}$$

**EXAMPLE 4**   If $\mathbf{x}$ and $\mathbf{y}$ in $R^3$ are given by

$$\mathbf{x} = \begin{bmatrix} -2 \\ 3 \\ 2 \end{bmatrix} \quad \text{and} \quad \mathbf{y} = \begin{bmatrix} 1 \\ 2 \\ -1 \end{bmatrix},$$

then find $\mathbf{x}^T \mathbf{y}$, $\|\mathbf{x}\|$, $\|\mathbf{y}\|$, and $\|\mathbf{x} - \mathbf{y}\|$.

*Solution*   We have

$$\mathbf{x}^T \mathbf{y} = \begin{bmatrix} -2 & 3 & 2 \end{bmatrix} \begin{bmatrix} 1 \\ 2 \\ -1 \end{bmatrix} = -2 + 6 - 2 = 2.$$

Also, $\|\mathbf{x}\| = \sqrt{\mathbf{x}^T \mathbf{x}} = \sqrt{4 + 9 + 4} = \sqrt{17}$, and $\|\mathbf{y}\| = \sqrt{\mathbf{y}^T \mathbf{y}} = \sqrt{1 + 4 + 1} = \sqrt{6}$. Subtracting $\mathbf{y}$ from $\mathbf{x}$ gives

$$\mathbf{x} - \mathbf{y} = \begin{bmatrix} -3 \\ 1 \\ 3 \end{bmatrix},$$

so $\|\mathbf{x} - \mathbf{y}\| = \sqrt{(\mathbf{x} - \mathbf{y})^T (\mathbf{x} - \mathbf{y})} = \sqrt{9 + 1 + 9} = \sqrt{19}$.    ◼

## 1.6 EXERCISES

The matrices and vectors listed in Eq. (3) are used in several of the exercises that follow.

$$A = \begin{bmatrix} 3 & 1 \\ 4 & 7 \\ 2 & 6 \end{bmatrix}, \quad B = \begin{bmatrix} 1 & 2 & 1 \\ 7 & 4 & 3 \\ 6 & 0 & 1 \end{bmatrix},$$

$$C = \begin{bmatrix} 2 & 1 & 4 & 0 \\ 6 & 1 & 3 & 5 \\ 2 & 4 & 2 & 0 \end{bmatrix}, \quad D = \begin{bmatrix} 2 & 1 \\ 1 & 4 \end{bmatrix},$$

$$E = \begin{bmatrix} 3 & 6 \\ 2 & 3 \end{bmatrix}, \quad F = \begin{bmatrix} 1 & 1 \\ 1 & 1 \end{bmatrix},$$

$$\mathbf{u} = \begin{bmatrix} 1 \\ -1 \end{bmatrix}, \quad \mathbf{v} = \begin{bmatrix} -3 \\ 3 \end{bmatrix} \tag{3}$$

Exercises 1–25 refer to the matrices and vectors in Eq. (3). In Exercises 1–6, perform the multiplications to verify the given equality or nonequality.

**1.** $(DE)F = D(EF)$  **2.** $(FE)D = F(ED)$

**3.** $DE \neq ED$  **4.** $EF \neq FE$

**5.** $F\mathbf{u} = F\mathbf{v}$  **6.** $3F\mathbf{u} = 7F\mathbf{v}$

In Exercises 7–12, find the matrices.

**7.** $A^T$  **8.** $D^T$  **9.** $E^T F$

**10.** $A^T C$  **11.** $(F\mathbf{v})^T$  **12.** $(EF)\mathbf{v}$

In Exercises 13–25, calculate the scalars.

**13.** $\mathbf{u}^T \mathbf{v}$  **14.** $\mathbf{v}^T F \mathbf{u}$  **15.** $\mathbf{v}^T D \mathbf{v}$

**16.** $\mathbf{v}^T F \mathbf{v}$  **17.** $\mathbf{u}^T \mathbf{u}$  **18.** $\mathbf{v}^T \mathbf{v}$

**19.** $\|\mathbf{u}\|$  **20.** $\|D\mathbf{v}\|$  **21.** $\|A\mathbf{u}\|$

**22.** $\|\mathbf{u} - \mathbf{v}\|$  **23.** $\|F\mathbf{u}\|$  **24.** $\|F\mathbf{v}\|$

**25.** $\|(D - E)\mathbf{u}\|$

**26.** Let $A$ and $B$ be $(2 \times 2)$ matrices. Prove or find a counterexample for this statement: $(A - B)(A + B) = A^2 - B^2$.

**27.** Let $A$ and $B$ be $(2 \times 2)$ matrices such that $A^2 = AB$ and $A \neq \mathcal{O}$. Can we assert that, by cancellation, $A = B$? Explain.

**28.** Let $A$ and $B$ be as in Exercise 27. Find the flaw in the following proof that $A = B$.

Since $A^2 = AB$, $A^2 - AB = \mathcal{O}$. Factoring yields $A(A - B) = \mathcal{O}$. Since $A \neq \mathcal{O}$, it follows that $A - B = \mathcal{O}$. Therefore, $A = B$.

**29.** Two of the six matrices listed in Eq. (3) are symmetric. Identify these matrices.

**30.** Find $(2 \times 2)$ matrices $A$ and $B$ such that $A$ and $B$ are symmetric, but $AB$ is not symmetric. [*Hint:* $(AB)^T = B^T A^T = BA$.]

**31.** Let $A$ and $B$ be $(n \times n)$ symmetric matrices. Give a necessary and sufficient condition for $AB$ to be symmetric. [*Hint:* Recall Exercise 30.]

**32.** Let $G$ be the $(2 \times 2)$ matrix that follows, and consider any vector $\mathbf{x}$ in $R^2$ where both entries are not simultaneously zero:

$$G = \begin{bmatrix} 2 & 1 \\ 1 & 1 \end{bmatrix}, \quad \mathbf{x} = \begin{bmatrix} x_1 \\ x_2 \end{bmatrix}; \quad |x_1| + |x_2| > 0.$$

Show that $\mathbf{x}^T G \mathbf{x} > 0$. [*Hint:* Write $\mathbf{x}^T G \mathbf{x}$ as a sum of squares.]

**33.** Repeat Exercise 32 using the matrix $D$ in Eq. (3) in place of $G$.

**34.** For $F$ in Eq. (3), show that $\mathbf{x}^T F \mathbf{x} \geq 0$ for all $\mathbf{x}$ in $R^2$. Classify those vectors $\mathbf{x}$ such that $\mathbf{x}^T F \mathbf{x} = 0$.

If $\mathbf{x}$ and $\mathbf{y}$ are vectors in $R^n$, then the product $\mathbf{x}^T \mathbf{y}$ is often called an *inner product*. Similarly, the product $\mathbf{x}\mathbf{y}^T$ is often called an *outer product*. Exercises 35–40 concern outer products; the matrices and vectors are given in Eq. (3). In Exercises 35–40, form the outer products.

**35.** $\mathbf{u}\mathbf{v}^T$  **36.** $\mathbf{u}(F\mathbf{u})^T$  **37.** $\mathbf{v}(E\mathbf{v})^T$

**38.** $\mathbf{u}(E\mathbf{v})^T$  **39.** $(A\mathbf{u})(A\mathbf{v})^T$  **40.** $(A\mathbf{v})(A\mathbf{u})^T$

**41.** Let $\mathbf{a}$ and $\mathbf{b}$ be given by

$$\mathbf{a} = \begin{bmatrix} 1 \\ 2 \end{bmatrix} \quad \text{and} \quad \mathbf{b} = \begin{bmatrix} 3 \\ 4 \end{bmatrix}.$$

a) Find $\mathbf{x}$ in $R^2$ that satisfies both $\mathbf{x}^T \mathbf{a} = 6$ and $\mathbf{x}^T \mathbf{b} = 2$.

b) Find $\mathbf{x}$ in $R^2$ that satisfies both $\mathbf{x}^T (\mathbf{a} + \mathbf{b}) = 12$ and $\mathbf{x}^T \mathbf{a} = 2$.

**42.** Let $A$ be a $(2 \times 2)$ matrix, and let $B$ and $C$ be given by

$$B = \begin{bmatrix} 1 & 3 \\ 1 & 4 \end{bmatrix} \quad \text{and} \quad C = \begin{bmatrix} 2 & 3 \\ 4 & 5 \end{bmatrix}.$$

a) If $A^T + B = C$, what is $A$?

b) If $A^T B = C$, what is $A$? and

c) Calculate $BC_1$, $B_1^T C$, $(BC_1)^T C_2$, and $\|CB_2\|$.

**43.** Let

$$A = \begin{bmatrix} 4 & -2 & 2 \\ 2 & 4 & -4 \\ 1 & 1 & 0 \end{bmatrix} \quad \text{and} \quad u = \begin{bmatrix} 1 \\ 3 \\ 2 \end{bmatrix}.$$

a) Verify that $Au = 2u$.

b) Without forming $A^5$, calculate the vector $A^5 u$.

c) Give a formula for $A^n u$, where $n$ is a positive integer. What property from Theorem 8 is required to derive the formula?

**44.** Let $A$, $B$, and $C$ be $(m \times n)$ matrices such that $A + C = B + C$. The following statements are the steps in a proof that $A = B$. Using Theorem 7, provide justification for each of the assertions.

a) There exists an $(m \times n)$ matrix $\mathcal{O}$ such that $A = A + \mathcal{O}$.

b) There exists an $(m \times n)$ matrix $D$ such that $A = A + (C + D)$.

c) $A = (A + C) + D = (B + C) + D$.

d) $A = B + (C + D)$.

e) $A = B + \mathcal{O}$.

f) $A = B$.

**45.** Let $A$, $B$, $C$, and $D$ be matrices such that $AB = D$ and $AC = D$. The following statements are steps in a proof that if $r$ and $s$ are scalars, then $A(rB+sC) = (r+s)D$. Use Theorems 8 and 9 to provide reasons for each of the steps.

a) $A(rB + sC) = A(rB) + A(sC)$.

b) $A(rB + sC) = r(AB) + s(AC) = rD + sD$.

c) $A(rB + sC) = (r + s)D$.

**46.** Let $x$ and $y$ be vectors in $R^n$ such that $\|x\| = \|y\| = 1$ and $x^T y = 0$. Use Eq. (1) to show that $\|x - y\| = \sqrt{2}$.

**47.** Use Theorem 10 to show that $A + A^T$ is symmetric for any square matrix $A$.

**48.** Let $A$ be the $(2 \times 2)$ matrix

$$A = \begin{bmatrix} 1 & 2 \\ 3 & 6 \end{bmatrix}.$$

Choose some vector $b$ in $R^2$ such that the equation $Ax = b$ is inconsistent. Verify that the associated

equation $A^T Ax = A^T b$ is consistent for your choice of $b$. Let $x^*$ be a solution to $A^T Ax = A^T b$, and select some vectors $x$ at random from $R^2$. Verify that $\|Ax^* - b\| \le \|Ax - b\|$ for any of these random choices for $x$. (In Chapter 3, we will show that $A^T Ax = A^T b$ is always consistent for any $(m \times n)$ matrix $A$ regardless of whether $Ax = b$ is consistent or not. We also show that any solution $x^*$ of $A^T Ax = A^T b$ satisfies $\|Ax^* - b\| \le \|Ax - b\|$ for all $x$ in $R^n$; that is, such a vector $x^*$ minimizes the length of the residual vector $r = Ax - b$.)

**49.** Use Theorem 10 to prove each of the following:

a) If $Q$ is any $(m \times n)$ matrix, then $Q^T Q$ and $QQ^T$ are symmetric.

b) If $A$, $B$, and $C$ are matrices such that the product $ABC$ is defined, then $(ABC)^T = C^T B^T A^T$. [*Hint:* Set $BC = D$.] *Note:* These proofs can be done quickly without considering the entries in the matrices.

**50.** Let $Q$ be an $(m \times n)$ matrix and $x$ any vector in $R^n$. Prove that $x^T Q^T Qx \ge 0$. [*Hint:* Observe that $Qx$ is a vector in $R^m$.]

**51.** Prove properties 2, 3, and 4 of Theorem 7.

**52.** Prove property 1 of Theorem 8. [*Note:* This is a long exercise, but the proof is similar to the proof of part 2 of Theorem 10.]

**53.** Prove properties 2 and 3 of Theorem 8.

**54.** Prove properties 2, 3, and 4 of Theorem 9.

**55.** Prove properties 1 and 3 of Theorem 10.

In Exercises 56–61, determine $n$ and $m$ so that $I_n A = A$ and $A I_m = A$, where:

**56.** $A$ is $(2 \times 3)$          **57.** $A$ is $(5 \times 7)$

**58.** $A$ is $(4 \times 4)$          **59.** $A$ is $(4 \times 6)$

**60.** $A$ is $(4 \times 2)$          **61.** $A$ is $(5 \times 5)$

**62.** a) Let $A$ be an $(n \times n)$ matrix. Use the definition of matrix multiplication to show that $A I_n = A$ and $I_n A = A$.

b) Let $B$ be a $(p \times q)$ matrix. Use the definition of matrix multiplication to show that $B I_q = B$ and $I_p B = B$.

# LINEAR INDEPENDENCE AND NONSINGULAR MATRICES

Section 1.5 demonstrated how the general linear system

$$a_{11}x_1 + a_{12}x_2 + \cdots + a_{1n}x_n = b_1$$
$$a_{21}x_1 + a_{22}x_2 + \cdots + a_{2n}x_n = b_2$$
$$\vdots \qquad \vdots \qquad \qquad \vdots \qquad \vdots$$
$$a_{m1}x_1 + a_{m2}x_2 + \cdots + a_{mn}x_n = b_m$$

(1)

can be expressed as a matrix equation $A\mathbf{x} = \mathbf{b}$. We observed in Section 1.1 that system (1) may have a unique solution, infinitely many solutions, or no solution. The material in Section 1.3 illustrates that, with appropriate additional information, we can know which of the three possibilities will occur. The case in which $m = n$ is of particular interest, and in this and later sections, we determine conditions on the matrix $A$ in order that an $(n \times n)$ system has a unique solution.

## Linear Independence

If $A = [\mathbf{A}_1, \mathbf{A}_2, \ldots, \mathbf{A}_n]$, then, by Theorem 5 of Section 1.5, the equation $A\mathbf{x} = \mathbf{b}$ can be written in terms of the columns of $A$ as

$$x_1\mathbf{A}_1 + x_2\mathbf{A}_2 + \cdots + x_n\mathbf{A}_n = \mathbf{b}.$$

(2)

From Eq. (2), it follows that system (1) is consistent if, and only if, $\mathbf{b}$ can be written as a sum of scalar multiples of the column vectors of $A$. We call a sum such as $x_1\mathbf{A}_1 + x_2\mathbf{A}_2 + \cdots + x_n\mathbf{A}_n$ a ***linear combination*** of the vectors $\mathbf{A}_1, \mathbf{A}_2, \ldots, \mathbf{A}_n$. Thus $A\mathbf{x} = \mathbf{b}$ is consistent if, and only if, $\mathbf{b}$ is a linear combination of the columns of $A$.

EXAMPLE 1    If the vectors $\mathbf{A}_1, \mathbf{A}_2, \mathbf{A}_3, \mathbf{b}_1$, and $\mathbf{b}_2$ are given by

$$\mathbf{A}_1 = \begin{bmatrix} 1 \\ 2 \\ -1 \end{bmatrix}, \quad \mathbf{A}_2 = \begin{bmatrix} 1 \\ 3 \\ 1 \end{bmatrix}, \quad \mathbf{A}_3 = \begin{bmatrix} 1 \\ 4 \\ 3 \end{bmatrix},$$

$$\mathbf{b}_1 = \begin{bmatrix} 3 \\ 8 \\ 1 \end{bmatrix}, \quad \text{and} \quad \mathbf{b}_2 = \begin{bmatrix} 2 \\ 5 \\ -1 \end{bmatrix},$$

then express each of $\mathbf{b}_1$ and $\mathbf{b}_2$ as a linear combination of the vectors $\mathbf{A}_1, \mathbf{A}_2, \mathbf{A}_3$.

***Solution***    If $A = [\mathbf{A}_1, \mathbf{A}_2, \mathbf{A}_3]$, that is,

$$A = \begin{bmatrix} 1 & 1 & 1 \\ 2 & 3 & 4 \\ -1 & 1 & 3 \end{bmatrix},$$

then expressing $\mathbf{b}_1$ as a linear combination of $\mathbf{A}_1, \mathbf{A}_2, \mathbf{A}_3$ is equivalent to solving the $(3 \times 3)$ linear system with matrix equation $A\mathbf{x} = \mathbf{b}_1$. The augmented matrix for the system is

$$\begin{bmatrix} 1 & 1 & 1 & 3 \\ 2 & 3 & 4 & 8 \\ -1 & 1 & 3 & 1 \end{bmatrix},$$

and solving in the usual manner yields

$$x_1 = 1 + x_3$$
$$x_2 = 2 - 2x_3,$$

where $x_3$ is an unconstrained variable. Thus $\mathbf{b}_1$ can be expressed as a linear combination of $\mathbf{A}_1, \mathbf{A}_2, \mathbf{A}_3$ in infinitely many ways. Taking $x_3 = 2$, for example, yields $x_1 = 3$, $x_2 = -2$, so

$$3\mathbf{A}_1 - 2\mathbf{A}_2 + 2\mathbf{A}_3 = \mathbf{b}_1;$$

that is,

$$3\begin{bmatrix} 1 \\ 2 \\ -1 \end{bmatrix} - 2\begin{bmatrix} 1 \\ 3 \\ 1 \end{bmatrix} + 2\begin{bmatrix} 1 \\ 4 \\ 3 \end{bmatrix} = \begin{bmatrix} 3 \\ 8 \\ 1 \end{bmatrix}.$$

If we attempt to follow the same procedure to express $\mathbf{b}_2$ as a linear combination of $\mathbf{A}_1, \mathbf{A}_2, \mathbf{A}_3$, we discover that the system of equations $A\mathbf{x} = \mathbf{b}_2$ is inconsistent. Therefore, $\mathbf{b}_2$ cannot be expressed as a linear combination of $\mathbf{A}_1, \mathbf{A}_2, \mathbf{A}_3$. ◼

It is convenient at this point to introduce a special symbol, $\boldsymbol{\theta}$, to denote the $m$-dimensional **zero vector**. Thus $\boldsymbol{\theta}$ is the vector in $R^m$, all of whose components are zero:

$$\boldsymbol{\theta} = \begin{bmatrix} 0 \\ 0 \\ \vdots \\ 0 \end{bmatrix}.$$

We will use $\boldsymbol{\theta}$ throughout to designate zero vectors in order to avoid any possible confusion between a zero vector and the scalar zero. With this notation, the $(m \times n)$ homogeneous system

$$\begin{array}{c} a_{11}x_1 + a_{12}x_2 + \cdots + a_{1n}x_n = 0 \\ a_{21}x_1 + a_{22}x_2 + \cdots + a_{2n}x_n = 0 \\ \vdots \qquad \vdots \qquad \qquad \vdots \qquad \vdots \\ a_{m1}x_1 + a_{m2}x_2 + \cdots + a_{mn}x_n = 0 \end{array} \qquad (3)$$

has the matrix equation $A\mathbf{x} = \boldsymbol{\theta}$, which can be written as

$$x_1\mathbf{A}_1 + x_2\mathbf{A}_2 + \cdots + x_n\mathbf{A}_n = \boldsymbol{\theta}. \qquad (4)$$

In Section 1.3, we observed that the homogeneous system (3) always has the trivial solution $x_1 = x_2 = \cdots = x_n = 0$. Thus in Eq. (4), $\boldsymbol{\theta}$ can always be expressed as a linear combination of the columns $A_1, A_2, \ldots, A_n$ of $A$ by taking $x_1 = x_2 = \cdots = x_n = 0$. There could, however, be nontrivial solutions, and this leads to the following definition.

---

**DEFINITION 11**

A set of $m$-dimensional vectors $\{\mathbf{v}_1, \mathbf{v}_2, \ldots, \mathbf{v}_p\}$ is said to be *linearly independent* if the only solution to the vector equation

$$a_1\mathbf{v}_1 + a_2\mathbf{v}_2 + \cdots + a_p\mathbf{v}_p = \boldsymbol{\theta}$$

is $a_1 = 0, a_2 = 0, \ldots, a_p = 0$. The set of vectors is said to be *linearly dependent* if it is not linearly independent. That is, the set is linearly dependent if we can find a solution to $a_1\mathbf{v}_1 + a_2\mathbf{v}_2 + \cdots + a_p\mathbf{v}_p = \boldsymbol{\theta}$ where not all the $a_i$ are zero.

---

Any time you need to know whether a set of vectors is linearly independent or linearly dependent, you should start with the dependence equation:

$$a_1\mathbf{v}_1 + a_2\mathbf{v}_2 + \cdots + a_p\mathbf{v}_p = \boldsymbol{\theta} \tag{5}$$

You would then solve Eq. (5). If there are nontrivial solutions, then the set of vectors is linearly dependent. If Eq. (5) has only the trivial solution, then the set of vectors is linearly independent.

We can phrase Eq. (5) in matrix terms. In particular, let $V$ denote the $(m \times p)$ matrix made up from the vectors $\mathbf{v}_1, \mathbf{v}_2, \ldots, \mathbf{v}_p$:

$$V = [\mathbf{v}_1, \mathbf{v}_2, \ldots, \mathbf{v}_p].$$

Then Eq. (5) is equivalent to the matrix equation

$$V\mathbf{x} = \boldsymbol{\theta}. \tag{6}$$

Thus to determine whether the set $\{\mathbf{v}_1, \mathbf{v}_2, \ldots, \mathbf{v}_p\}$ is linearly independent or dependent, we solve the homogeneous system of equations (6) by forming the augmented matrix $[V \mid \boldsymbol{\theta}]$ and reducing $[V \mid \boldsymbol{\theta}]$ to echelon form. If the system has nontrivial solutions, then $\{\mathbf{v}_1, \mathbf{v}_2, \ldots, \mathbf{v}_p\}$ is a linearly dependent set. If the trivial solution is the only solution, then $\{\mathbf{v}_1, \mathbf{v}_2, \ldots, \mathbf{v}_p\}$ is a linearly independent set.

**EXAMPLE 2**   Determine whether the set $\{\mathbf{v}_1, \mathbf{v}_2, \mathbf{v}_3\}$ is linearly independent or linearly dependent, where

$$\mathbf{v}_1 = \begin{bmatrix} 1 \\ 2 \\ 3 \end{bmatrix}, \quad \mathbf{v}_2 = \begin{bmatrix} 2 \\ -1 \\ 4 \end{bmatrix}, \quad \text{and} \quad \mathbf{v}_3 = \begin{bmatrix} 0 \\ 5 \\ 2 \end{bmatrix}.$$

*Solution*   To determine whether the set is linearly dependent, we must determine whether the vector equation

$$x_1\mathbf{v}_1 + x_2\mathbf{v}_2 + x_3\mathbf{v}_3 = \boldsymbol{\theta} \tag{7}$$

has a nontrivial solution. But Eq. (7) is equivalent to the $(3 \times 3)$ homogeneous system of equations $V\mathbf{x} = \boldsymbol{\theta}$, where $V = [\mathbf{v}_1, \mathbf{v}_2, \mathbf{v}_3]$. The augmented matrix, $[V \mid \boldsymbol{\theta}]$, for this system is

$$\begin{bmatrix} 1 & 2 & 0 & 0 \\ 2 & -1 & 5 & 0 \\ 3 & 4 & 2 & 0 \end{bmatrix}.$$

This matrix reduces to

$$\begin{bmatrix} 1 & 0 & 2 & 0 \\ 0 & 1 & -1 & 0 \\ 0 & 0 & 0 & 0 \end{bmatrix}.$$

Therefore, we find the solution $x_1 = -2x_3$, $x_2 = x_3$, where $x_3$ is arbitrary. In particular, Eq. (7) has nontrivial solutions, so $\{\mathbf{v}_1, \mathbf{v}_2, \mathbf{v}_3\}$ is a linearly dependent set. Setting $x_3 = 1$, for example, gives $x_1 = -2$, $x_2 = 1$. Therefore,

$$-2\mathbf{v}_1 + \mathbf{v}_2 + \mathbf{v}_3 = \boldsymbol{\theta}.$$

Note that from this equation we can express $\mathbf{v}_3$ as a linear combination of $\mathbf{v}_1$ and $\mathbf{v}_2$:

$$\mathbf{v}_3 = 2\mathbf{v}_1 - \mathbf{v}_2.$$

Similarly, of course, $\mathbf{v}_1$ can be expressed as a linear combination of $\mathbf{v}_2$ and $\mathbf{v}_3$, and $\mathbf{v}_2$ can be expressed as a linear combination of $\mathbf{v}_1$ and $\mathbf{v}_3$.  ◼

**EXAMPLE 3**   Determine whether or not the set $\{\mathbf{v}_1, \mathbf{v}_2, \mathbf{v}_3\}$ is linearly dependent, where

$$\mathbf{v}_1 = \begin{bmatrix} 1 \\ 2 \\ -3 \end{bmatrix}, \quad \mathbf{v}_2 = \begin{bmatrix} -2 \\ 1 \\ 1 \end{bmatrix}, \quad \text{and} \quad \mathbf{v}_3 = \begin{bmatrix} 1 \\ -1 \\ -2 \end{bmatrix}.$$

*Solution*   If $V = [\mathbf{v}_1, \mathbf{v}_2, \mathbf{v}_3]$, then the augmented matrix $[V \mid \boldsymbol{\theta}]$ is row equivalent to

$$\begin{bmatrix} 1 & 0 & 0 & 0 \\ 0 & 1 & 0 & 0 \\ 0 & 0 & 1 & 0 \end{bmatrix}.$$

Thus the only solution of $x_1\mathbf{v}_1 + x_2\mathbf{v}_2 + x_3\mathbf{v}_3 = \boldsymbol{\theta}$ is the trivial solution $x_1 = x_2 = x_3 = 0$; so the set $\{\mathbf{v}_1, \mathbf{v}_2, \mathbf{v}_3\}$ is linearly independent.

In contrast to the preceding example, note that $\mathbf{v}_3$ cannot be expressed as a linear combination of $\mathbf{v}_1$ and $\mathbf{v}_2$. If there were scalars $a_1$ and $a_2$ such that

$$\mathbf{v}_3 = a_1\mathbf{v}_1 + a_2\mathbf{v}_2,$$

then there would be a nontrivial solution to $x_1\mathbf{v}_1 + x_2\mathbf{v}_2 + x_3\mathbf{v}_3 = \boldsymbol{\theta}$; namely, $x_1 = -a_1$, $x_2 = -a_2$, $x_3 = 1$.  ◼

We note that a set of vectors is linearly dependent if and only if one of the vectors is a linear combination of the remaining ones (see the exercises). It is also worth noting

THE VECTOR $\mathcal{S}$PACE $R^n$, $n > 3$   The extension of vectors and their corresponding algebra into more than three dimensions was an extremely important step in the development of mathematics. This advancement is attributed largely to Hermann Grassmann (1809–1877) in his *Ausdehnungslehre*. In this work Grassmann discussed linear independence and dependence and many concepts dealing with the algebraic structure of $R^n$ (such as dimension and subspaces), which we will study in Chapter 3. Unfortunately, Grassmann's work was so difficult to read that it went almost unnoticed for a long period of time, and he did not receive as much credit as he deserved.

that any set of vectors that contains the zero vector is linearly dependent (again, see the exercises).

The **unit vectors** $\mathbf{e}_1, \mathbf{e}_2, \ldots, \mathbf{e}_n$ in $R^n$ are defined by

$$\mathbf{e}_1 = \begin{bmatrix} 1 \\ 0 \\ 0 \\ \vdots \\ 0 \end{bmatrix}, \quad \mathbf{e}_2 = \begin{bmatrix} 0 \\ 1 \\ 0 \\ \vdots \\ 0 \end{bmatrix}, \quad \mathbf{e}_3 = \begin{bmatrix} 0 \\ 0 \\ 1 \\ \vdots \\ 0 \end{bmatrix}, \quad \ldots, \quad \mathbf{e}_n = \begin{bmatrix} 0 \\ 0 \\ 0 \\ \vdots \\ 1 \end{bmatrix}. \quad (8)$$

It is easy to see that $\{\mathbf{e}_1, \mathbf{e}_2, \ldots, \mathbf{e}_n\}$ is linearly independent. To illustrate, consider the unit vectors

$$\mathbf{e}_1 = \begin{bmatrix} 1 \\ 0 \\ 0 \end{bmatrix}, \quad \mathbf{e}_2 = \begin{bmatrix} 0 \\ 1 \\ 0 \end{bmatrix}, \quad \text{and} \quad \mathbf{e}_3 = \begin{bmatrix} 0 \\ 0 \\ 1 \end{bmatrix}$$

in $R^3$. If $V = [\mathbf{e}_1, \mathbf{e}_2, \mathbf{e}_3]$, then

$$[V \mid \boldsymbol{\theta}] = \begin{bmatrix} 1 & 0 & 0 & 0 \\ 0 & 1 & 0 & 0 \\ 0 & 0 & 1 & 0 \end{bmatrix},$$

so clearly the only solution of $V\mathbf{x} = \boldsymbol{\theta}$ (or equivalently, of $x_1\mathbf{e}_1 + x_2\mathbf{e}_2 + x_3\mathbf{e}_3 = \boldsymbol{\theta}$) is the trivial solution $x_1 = 0$, $x_2 = 0$, $x_3 = 0$.

The next example illustrates that, in some cases, the linear dependence of a set of vectors can be determined by inspection. The example is a special case of Theorem 11, which follows.

EXAMPLE 4   Let $\{\mathbf{v}_1, \mathbf{v}_2, \mathbf{v}_3\}$ be the set of vectors in $R^2$ given by

$$\mathbf{v}_1 = \begin{bmatrix} 1 \\ 2 \end{bmatrix}, \quad \mathbf{v}_2 = \begin{bmatrix} 3 \\ 1 \end{bmatrix}, \quad \text{and} \quad \mathbf{v}_3 = \begin{bmatrix} 2 \\ 3 \end{bmatrix}.$$

Without solving the corresponding homogeneous system of equations, show that the set is linearly dependent.

*Solution*  The vector equation $x_1\mathbf{v}_1 + x_2\mathbf{v}_2 + x_3\mathbf{v}_3 = \boldsymbol{\theta}$ is equivalent to the homogeneous system of equations $V\mathbf{x} = \boldsymbol{\theta}$, where $V = [\mathbf{v}_1, \mathbf{v}_2, \mathbf{v}_3]$. But this is the homogeneous system

$$x_1 + 3x_2 + 2x_3 = 0$$
$$2x_1 + \ x_2 + 3x_3 = 0,$$

consisting of two equations in three unknowns. By Theorem 4 of Section 1.3, the system has nontrivial solutions; hence the set $\{\mathbf{v}_1, \mathbf{v}_2, \mathbf{v}_3\}$ is linearly dependent. ◼

Example 4 is a particular case of the following general result.

**THEOREM 11**  Let $\{\mathbf{v}_1, \mathbf{v}_2, \ldots, \mathbf{v}_p\}$ be a set of vectors in $R^m$. If $p > m$, then this set is linearly dependent.

*Proof*  The set $\{\mathbf{v}_1, \mathbf{v}_2, \ldots, \mathbf{v}_p\}$ is linearly dependent if the equation $V\mathbf{x} = \boldsymbol{\theta}$ has a nontrivial solution, where $V = [\mathbf{v}_1, \mathbf{v}_2, \ldots, \mathbf{v}_p]$. But $V\mathbf{x} = \boldsymbol{\theta}$ represents a homogeneous $(m \times p)$ system of linear equations with $m < p$. By Theorem 4 of Section 1.3, $V\mathbf{x} = \boldsymbol{\theta}$ has nontrivial solutions. ◼

Note that Theorem 11 does not say that if $p \leq m$, then the set $\{\mathbf{v}_1, \mathbf{v}_2, \ldots, \mathbf{v}_p\}$ is linearly independent. Indeed Examples 2 and 3 illustrate that if $p \leq m$, then the set may be either linearly independent or linearly dependent.

## Nonsingular Matrices

The concept of linear independence allows us to state precisely which $(n \times n)$ systems of linear equations always have a unique solution. We begin with the following definition.

**DEFINITION 12**  An $(n \times n)$ matrix $A$ is ***nonsingular*** if the only solution to $A\mathbf{x} = \boldsymbol{\theta}$ is $\mathbf{x} = \boldsymbol{\theta}$. Furthermore, $A$ is said to be ***singular*** if $A$ is not nonsingular.

If $A = [\mathbf{A}_1, \mathbf{A}_2, \ldots, \mathbf{A}_n]$, then $A\mathbf{x} = \boldsymbol{\theta}$ can be written as

$$x_1\mathbf{A}_1 + x_2\mathbf{A}_2 + \cdots + x_n\mathbf{A}_n = \boldsymbol{\theta},$$

so it is an immediate consequence of Definition 12 that $A$ is nonsingular if and only if the column vectors of $A$ form a linearly independent set. This observation is important enough to be stated as a theorem.

**THEOREM 12**  The $(n \times n)$ matrix $A = [\mathbf{A}_1, \mathbf{A}_2, \ldots, \mathbf{A}_n]$ is nonsingular if and only if $\{\mathbf{A}_1, \mathbf{A}_2, \ldots, \mathbf{A}_n\}$ is a linearly independent set. ◼

**EXAMPLE 5**  Determine whether each of the matrices

$$A = \begin{bmatrix} 1 & 3 \\ 2 & 2 \end{bmatrix} \quad \text{and} \quad B = \begin{bmatrix} 1 & 2 \\ 2 & 4 \end{bmatrix}$$

is singular or nonsingular.

***Solution***    The augmented matrix $[A \mid \theta]$ for the system $A\mathbf{x} = \theta$ is row equivalent to

$$\begin{bmatrix} 1 & 0 & 0 \\ 0 & 1 & 0 \end{bmatrix},$$

so the trivial solution $x_1 = 0, x_2 = 0$ (or $\mathbf{x} = \theta$) is the unique solution. Thus $A$ is nonsingular.

The augmented matrix $[B \mid \theta]$ for the system $B\mathbf{x} = \theta$ is row equivalent to

$$\begin{bmatrix} 1 & 2 & 0 \\ 0 & 0 & 0 \end{bmatrix}.$$

Thus, $B$ is singular because the vector

$$\mathbf{x} = \begin{bmatrix} -2 \\ 1 \end{bmatrix}$$

is a nontrivial solution of $B\mathbf{x} = \theta$. Equivalently, the columns of $B$ are linearly dependent because

$$-2\mathbf{B}_1 + \mathbf{B}_2 = \theta.$$    ◼

The next theorem demonstrates the importance of nonsingular matrices with respect to linear systems.

**THEOREM 13**    Let $A$ be an $(n \times n)$ matrix. The equation $A\mathbf{x} = \mathbf{b}$ has a unique solution for every $(n \times 1)$ column vector $\mathbf{b}$ if and only if $A$ is nonsingular.

***Proof***    Suppose first that $A\mathbf{x} = \mathbf{b}$ has a unique solution no matter what choice we make for $\mathbf{b}$. Choosing $\mathbf{b} = \theta$ implies, by Definition 12, that $A$ is nonsingular.

Conversely, suppose that $A = [\mathbf{A}_1, \mathbf{A}_2, \ldots, \mathbf{A}_n]$ is nonsingular, and let $\mathbf{b}$ be any $(n \times 1)$ column vector. We first show that $A\mathbf{x} = \mathbf{b}$ has a solution. To see this, observe first that

$$\{\mathbf{A}_1, \mathbf{A}_2, \ldots, \mathbf{A}_n, \mathbf{b}\}$$

is a set of $(n \times 1)$ vectors in $R^n$; so by Theorem 11 this set is linearly dependent. Thus there are scalars $a_1, a_2, \ldots, a_n, a_{n+1}$ such that

$$a_1\mathbf{A}_1 + a_2\mathbf{A}_2 + \cdots + a_n\mathbf{A}_n + a_{n+1}\mathbf{b} = \theta; \tag{9}$$

and moreover not all these scalars are zero. In fact, if $a_{n+1} = 0$ in Eq. (9), then

$$a_1\mathbf{A}_1 + a_2\mathbf{A}_2 + \cdots + a_n\mathbf{A}_n = \theta,$$

and it follows that $\{\mathbf{A}_1, \mathbf{A}_2, \ldots, \mathbf{A}_n\}$ is a linearly dependent set. Since this contradicts the assumption that $A$ is nonsingular, we know that $a_{n+1}$ is nonzero. It follows from Eq. (9) that

$$s_1\mathbf{A}_1 + s_2\mathbf{A}_2 + \cdots + s_n\mathbf{A}_n = \mathbf{b},$$

where

$$s_1 = \frac{-a_1}{a_{n+1}}, \quad s_2 = \frac{-a_2}{a_{n+1}}, \ldots, \quad s_n = \frac{-a_n}{a_{n+1}}.$$

Thus $Ax = b$ has a solution $s$ given by

$$s = \begin{bmatrix} s_1 \\ s_2 \\ \vdots \\ s_n \end{bmatrix}.$$

This shows that $Ax = b$ is always consistent when $A$ is nonsingular.

To show that the solution is unique, suppose that the $(n \times 1)$ vector $u$ is any solution whatsoever to $Ax = b$; that is, $Au = b$. Then $As - Au = b - b$, or

$$A(s - u) = \theta;$$

therefore, $y = s - u$ is a solution to $Ax = \theta$. But $A$ is nonsingular, so $y = \theta$; that is $s = u$. Thus $Ax = b$ has one, and only one, solution. ∎

In closing we note that for a specific system $Ax = b$, it is usually easier to demonstrate the existence and/or uniqueness of a solution by using Gaussian elimination and actually solving the system. There are many instances, however, in which theoretical information about existence and uniqueness is extremely valuable to practical computations. A specific instance of this is provided in the next section.

## 1.7    EXERCISES

The vectors listed in Eq. (10) are used in several of the exercises that follow.

$$v_1 = \begin{bmatrix} 1 \\ 2 \end{bmatrix}, \quad v_2 = \begin{bmatrix} 2 \\ 3 \end{bmatrix}, \quad v_3 = \begin{bmatrix} 2 \\ 4 \end{bmatrix},$$

$$v_4 = \begin{bmatrix} 1 \\ 1 \end{bmatrix}, \quad v_5 = \begin{bmatrix} 3 \\ 6 \end{bmatrix},$$

$$u_0 = \begin{bmatrix} 1 \\ 0 \\ 0 \end{bmatrix}, \quad u_1 = \begin{bmatrix} 1 \\ 2 \\ -1 \end{bmatrix}, \quad u_2 = \begin{bmatrix} 2 \\ 1 \\ -3 \end{bmatrix},$$

$$u_3 = \begin{bmatrix} -1 \\ 4 \\ 3 \end{bmatrix}, \quad u_4 = \begin{bmatrix} 4 \\ 4 \\ 0 \end{bmatrix}, \quad u_5 = \begin{bmatrix} 1 \\ 1 \\ 0 \end{bmatrix}$$

(10)

In Exercises 1–14, use Eq. (6) to determine whether the given set of vectors is linearly independent or linearly dependent. If the set is linearly dependent, express one vector in the set as a linear combination of the others.

**1.** $\{v_1, v_2\}$

**2.** $\{v_1, v_3\}$

**3.** $\{v_1, v_5\}$

**4.** $\{v_2, v_3\}$

**5.** $\{v_1, v_2, v_3\}$

**6.** $\{v_2, v_3, v_4\}$

**7.** $\{u_4, u_5\}$

**8.** $\{u_3, u_4\}$

**9.** $\{u_1, u_2, u_5\}$

**10.** $\{u_1, u_4, u_5\}$

**11.** $\{u_2, u_4, u_5\}$

**12.** $\{u_1, u_2, u_4\}$

**13.** $\{u_0, u_1, u_2, u_4\}$

**14.** $\{u_0, u_2, u_3, u_4\}$

**15.** Consider the sets of vectors in Exercises 1–14. Using Theorem 11, determine by inspection which of these sets are known to be linearly dependent.

The matrices listed in Eq. (11) are used in some of the exercises that follow.

$$A = \begin{bmatrix} 1 & 2 \\ 3 & 4 \end{bmatrix}, \quad B = \begin{bmatrix} 1 & 2 \\ 2 & 4 \end{bmatrix}, \quad C = \begin{bmatrix} 1 & 3 \\ 2 & 4 \end{bmatrix},$$

$$D = \begin{bmatrix} 1 & 0 & 0 \\ 0 & 1 & 0 \\ 0 & 1 & 0 \end{bmatrix}, \quad E = \begin{bmatrix} 0 & 1 & 0 \\ 0 & 0 & 2 \\ 0 & 1 & 3 \end{bmatrix},$$

$$F = \begin{bmatrix} 1 & 2 & 1 \\ 0 & 3 & 2 \\ 0 & 0 & 1 \end{bmatrix}$$

(11)

In Exercises 16–27, use Definition 12 to determine whether the given matrix is singular or nonsingular. If a matrix $M$ is singular, give all solutions of $M\mathbf{x} = \boldsymbol{\theta}$.

**16.** $A$          **17.** $B$          **18.** $C$

**19.** $AB$         **20.** $BA$         **21.** $D$

**22.** $F$          **23.** $D + F$      **24.** $E$

**25.** $EF$         **26.** $DE$         **27.** $F^T$

In Exercises 28–33, determine conditions on the scalars so that the set of vectors is linearly dependent.

**28.** $\mathbf{v}_1 = \begin{bmatrix} 1 \\ a \end{bmatrix}$, $\mathbf{v}_2 = \begin{bmatrix} 2 \\ 3 \end{bmatrix}$

**29.** $\mathbf{v}_1 = \begin{bmatrix} 1 \\ 2 \end{bmatrix}$, $\mathbf{v}_2 = \begin{bmatrix} 3 \\ a \end{bmatrix}$

**30.** $\mathbf{v}_1 = \begin{bmatrix} 1 \\ 2 \\ 1 \end{bmatrix}$, $\mathbf{v}_2 = \begin{bmatrix} 1 \\ 3 \\ 2 \end{bmatrix}$, $\mathbf{v}_3 = \begin{bmatrix} 0 \\ 1 \\ a \end{bmatrix}$

**31.** $\mathbf{v}_1 = \begin{bmatrix} 1 \\ 2 \\ 1 \end{bmatrix}$, $\mathbf{v}_2 = \begin{bmatrix} 1 \\ a \\ 3 \end{bmatrix}$, $\mathbf{v}_3 = \begin{bmatrix} 0 \\ 2 \\ b \end{bmatrix}$

**32.** $\mathbf{v}_1 = \begin{bmatrix} a \\ 1 \end{bmatrix}$, $\mathbf{v}_2 = \begin{bmatrix} b \\ 3 \end{bmatrix}$

**33.** $\mathbf{v}_1 = \begin{bmatrix} 1 \\ a \end{bmatrix}$, $\mathbf{v}_2 = \begin{bmatrix} b \\ c \end{bmatrix}$

In Exercises 34–39, the vectors and matrices are from Eq. (10) and Eq. (11). The equations listed in Exercises 34–39 all have the form $M\mathbf{x} = \mathbf{b}$, and all the equations are consistent. In each exercise, solve the equation and express $\mathbf{b}$ as a linear combination of the columns of $M$.

**34.** $A\mathbf{x} = \mathbf{v}_1$          **35.** $A\mathbf{x} = \mathbf{v}_3$

**36.** $C\mathbf{x} = \mathbf{v}_4$          **37.** $C\mathbf{x} = \mathbf{v}_2$

**38.** $F\mathbf{x} = \mathbf{u}_1$          **39.** $F\mathbf{x} = \mathbf{u}_3$

In Exercises 40–45, express the given vector $\mathbf{b}$ as a linear combination of $\mathbf{v}_1$ and $\mathbf{v}_2$, where $\mathbf{v}_1$ and $\mathbf{v}_2$ are in Eq. (10).

**40.** $\mathbf{b} = \begin{bmatrix} 2 \\ 7 \end{bmatrix}$          **41.** $\mathbf{b} = \begin{bmatrix} 3 \\ -1 \end{bmatrix}$

**42.** $\mathbf{b} = \begin{bmatrix} 0 \\ 4 \end{bmatrix}$          **43.** $\mathbf{b} = \begin{bmatrix} 0 \\ 0 \end{bmatrix}$

**44.** $\mathbf{b} = \begin{bmatrix} 1 \\ 2 \end{bmatrix}$          **45.** $\mathbf{b} = \begin{bmatrix} 1 \\ 0 \end{bmatrix}$

In Exercises 46–47, let $S = \{\mathbf{v}_1, \mathbf{v}_2, \mathbf{v}_3\}$.

  **a)** For what value(s) $a$ is the set $S$ linearly dependent?

  **b)** For what value(s) $a$ can $\mathbf{v}_3$ be expressed as a linear combination of $\mathbf{v}_1$ and $\mathbf{v}_2$?

**46.** $\mathbf{v}_1 = \begin{bmatrix} 1 \\ -1 \end{bmatrix}$, $\mathbf{v}_2 = \begin{bmatrix} -2 \\ 2 \end{bmatrix}$, $\mathbf{v}_3 = \begin{bmatrix} 3 \\ a \end{bmatrix}$

**47.** $\mathbf{v}_1 = \begin{bmatrix} 1 \\ 0 \end{bmatrix}$, $\mathbf{v}_2 = \begin{bmatrix} 1 \\ 1 \end{bmatrix}$, $\mathbf{v}_3 = \begin{bmatrix} 3 \\ a \end{bmatrix}$

**48.** Let $S = \{\mathbf{v}_1, \mathbf{v}_2, \mathbf{v}_3\}$ be a set of vectors in $R^3$, where $\mathbf{v}_1 = \boldsymbol{\theta}$. Show that $S$ is a linearly dependent set of vectors. [*Hint:* Exhibit a nontrivial solution for either Eq. (5) or Eq. (6).)]

**49.** Let $\{\mathbf{v}_1, \mathbf{v}_2, \mathbf{v}_3\}$ be a set of nonzero vectors in $R^m$ such that $\mathbf{v}_i^T \mathbf{v}_j = 0$ when $i \neq j$. Show that the set is linearly independent. [*Hint:* Set $a_1\mathbf{v}_1 + a_2\mathbf{v}_2 + a_3\mathbf{v}_3 = \boldsymbol{\theta}$ and consider $\boldsymbol{\theta}^T\boldsymbol{\theta}$.]

**50.** If the set $\{\mathbf{v}_1, \mathbf{v}_2, \mathbf{v}_3\}$ of vectors in $R^m$ is linearly dependent, then argue that the set $\{\mathbf{v}_1, \mathbf{v}_2, \mathbf{v}_3, \mathbf{v}_4\}$ is also linearly dependent for every choice of $\mathbf{v}_4$ in $R^m$.

**51.** Suppose that $\{\mathbf{v}_1, \mathbf{v}_2, \mathbf{v}_3\}$ is a linearly independent subset of $R^m$. Show that the set $\{\mathbf{v}_1, \mathbf{v}_1 + \mathbf{v}_2, \mathbf{v}_1 + \mathbf{v}_2 + \mathbf{v}_3\}$ is also linearly independent.

**52.** If $A$ and $B$ are $(n \times n)$ matrices such that $A$ is nonsingular and $AB = \mathcal{O}$, then prove that $B = \mathcal{O}$. [*Hint:* Write $B = [\mathbf{B}_1, \ldots, \mathbf{B}_n]$ and consider $AB = [A\mathbf{B}_1, \ldots, A\mathbf{B}_n]$.]

**53.** If $A$, $B$, and $C$ are $(n \times n)$ matrices such that $A$ is nonsingular and $AB = AC$, then prove that $B = C$. [*Hint:* Consider $A(B - C)$ and use the preceding exercise.]

**54.** Let $A = [\mathbf{A}_1, \ldots, \mathbf{A}_{n-1}]$ be an $(n \times (n-1))$ matrix. Show that $B = [\mathbf{A}_1, \ldots, \mathbf{A}_{n-1}, A\mathbf{b}]$ is singular for every choice of $\mathbf{b}$ in $R^{n-1}$.

**55.** Suppose that $C$ and $B$ are $(2 \times 2)$ matrices and that $B$ is singular. Show that $CB$ is singular. [*Hint:* By Definition 12, there is a vector $\mathbf{x}_1$ in $R^2$, $\mathbf{x}_1 \neq \boldsymbol{\theta}$, such that $B\mathbf{x}_1 = \boldsymbol{\theta}$.]

**56.** Let $\{\mathbf{w}_1, \mathbf{w}_2\}$ be a linearly independent set of vectors in $R^2$. Show that if $\mathbf{b}$ is any vector in $R^2$, then $\mathbf{b}$ is a linear combination of $\mathbf{w}_1$ and $\mathbf{w}_2$. [*Hint:* Consider the $(2 \times 2)$ matrix $A = [\mathbf{w}_1, \mathbf{w}_2]$.]

**57.** Let $A$ be an $(n \times n)$ nonsingular matrix. Show that $A^T$ is nonsingular as follows:

**a)** Suppose that $\mathbf{v}$ is a vector in $R^n$ such that $A^T\mathbf{v} = \boldsymbol{\theta}$. Cite a theorem from this section that guarantees there is a vector $\mathbf{w}$ in $R^n$ such that $A\mathbf{w} = \mathbf{v}$.

**b)** By part (a), $A^T A\mathbf{w} = \boldsymbol{\theta}$, and therefore $\mathbf{w}^T A^T A\mathbf{w} = \mathbf{w}^T\boldsymbol{\theta} = 0$. Cite results from Section 1.6 that allow you to conclude that $\|A\mathbf{w}\| = 0$. [*Hint:* What is $(A\mathbf{w})^T$?]

**c)** Use parts (a) and (b) to conclude that if $A^T\mathbf{v} = \boldsymbol{\theta}$, then $\mathbf{v} = \boldsymbol{\theta}$; this shows that $A^T$ is nonsingular.

**58.** Let $T$ be an $(n \times n)$ upper-triangular matrix

$$T = \begin{bmatrix} t_{11} & t_{12} & t_{13} & \cdots & t_{1n} \\ 0 & t_{22} & t_{23} & \cdots & t_{2n} \\ 0 & 0 & t_{33} & \cdots & t_{3n} \\ \vdots & & & & \vdots \\ 0 & 0 & 0 & \cdots & t_{nn} \end{bmatrix}.$$

Prove that if $t_{ii} = 0$ for some $i$, $1 \le i \le n$, then $T$ is singular. [*Hint:* If $t_{11} = 0$, find a nonzero vec-

tor $\mathbf{v}$ such that $T\mathbf{v} = \boldsymbol{\theta}$. If $t_{rr} = 0$, but $t_{ii} \neq 0$ for $1, 2, \ldots, r-1$, use Theorem 4 of Section 1.3 to show that columns $\mathbf{T}_1, \mathbf{T}_2, \ldots, \mathbf{T}_r$ of $T$ are linearly dependent. Then select a nonzero vector $\mathbf{v}$ such that $T\mathbf{v} = \boldsymbol{\theta}$.]

**59.** Let $T$ be an $(n \times n)$ upper-triangular matrix as in Exercise 58. Prove that if $t_{ii} \neq 0$ for $i = 1, 2, \ldots, n$, then $T$ is nonsingular. [*Hint:* Let $T = [\mathbf{T}_1, \mathbf{T}_2, \ldots, \mathbf{T}_n]$, and suppose that $a_1\mathbf{T}_1 + a_2\mathbf{T}_2 + \cdots + a_n\mathbf{T}_n = \boldsymbol{\theta}$ for some scalars $a_1, a_2, \ldots, a_n$. First deduce that $a_n = 0$. Next show $a_{n-1} = 0$, and so on.] Note that Exercises 58 and 59 establish that an upper-triangular matrix is singular if and only if one of the entries $t_{11}, t_{22}, \ldots, t_{nn}$ is zero. By Exercise 57 the same result is true for lower-triangular matrices.

**60.** Suppose that the $(n \times n)$ matrices $A$ and $B$ are row equivalent. Prove that $A$ is nonsingular if and only if $B$ is nonsingular. [*Hint:* The homogeneous systems $A\mathbf{x} = \boldsymbol{\theta}$ and $B\mathbf{x} = \boldsymbol{\theta}$ are equivalent by Theorem 1 of Section 1.1.]

# DATA FITTING, NUMERICAL INTEGRATION, AND NUMERICAL DIFFERENTIATION (OPTIONAL)

In this section we present four applications of matrix theory toward the solution of a practical problem. Three of the applications involve numerical approximation techniques, and the fourth relates to solving certain types of differential equations. In each case, solving the general problem depends on being able to solve a system of linear equations, and the theory of nonsingular matrices will guarantee that a solution exists and is unique.

## Polynomial Interpolation

We begin by applying matrix theory to the problem of interpolating data with polynomials. In particular, Theorem 13 of Section 1.7 is used to establish a general existence and uniqueness result for polynomial interpolation. The following example is a simple illustration of polynomial interpolation.

*Figure 1.17*
Points in the $ty$-plane

**EXAMPLE 1**    Find a quadratic polynomial, $q(t)$, such that the graph of $q(t)$ goes through the points $(1, 2)$, $(2, 3)$, and $(3, 6)$ in the $ty$-plane (see Fig. 1.17).

*Solution*    A quadratic polynomial $q(t)$ has the form

$$q(t) = a + bt + ct^2, \tag{1a}$$

so our problem reduces to determining constants $a$, $b$, and $c$ such that

$$q(1) = 2$$
$$q(2) = 3 \tag{1b}$$
$$q(3) = 6.$$

The constraints in (1b) are, by (1a), equivalent to

$$a + b + c = 2$$
$$a + 2b + 4c = 3 \tag{1c}$$
$$a + 3b + 9c = 6.$$

Clearly (1c) is a system of three linear equations in the three unknowns $a$, $b$, and $c$; so solving (1c) will determine the polynomial $q(t)$. Solving (1c), we find the unique solution $a = 3$, $b = -2$, $c = 1$; therefore, $q(t) = 3 - 2t + t^2$ is the unique quadratic polynomial satisfying the conditions (1b). A portion of the graph of $q(t)$ is shown in Fig. 1.18.

**Figure 1.18**
Graph of $q(t)$

Frequently polynomial interpolation is used when values of a function $f(t)$ are given in tabular form. For example, given a table of $n + 1$ values of $f(t)$ (see Table 1.1), an **interpolating polynomial** for $f(t)$ is a polynomial, $p(t)$, of the form

$$p(t) = a_0 + a_1 t + a_2 t^2 + \cdots + a_n t^n$$

such that $p(t_i) = y_i = f(t_i)$ for $0 \le i \le n$. Problems of interpolating data in tables are quite common in scientific and engineering work; for example, $y = f(t)$ might describe a temperature distribution as a function of time with $y_i = f(t_i)$ being observed (measured) temperatures. For a time $\hat{t}$ not listed in the table, $p(\hat{t})$ provides an approximation for $f(\hat{t})$.

**Table 1.1**

| $t$ | $f(t)$ |
|-----|--------|
| $t_0$ | $y_0$ |
| $t_1$ | $y_1$ |
| $t_2$ | $y_2$ |
| $\vdots$ | $\vdots$ |
| $t_n$ | $y_n$ |

EXAMPLE 2    Find an interpolating polynomial for the four observations given in Table 1.2. Give an approximation for $f(1.5)$.

**Solution**    In this case, the interpolating polynomial is a polynomial of degree 3 or less,

$$p(t) = a_0 + a_1 t + a_2 t^2 + a_3 t^3,$$

where $p(t)$ satisfies the four constraints $p(0) = 3$, $p(1) = 0$, $p(2) = -1$, and $p(3) = 6$. As in the previous example, these constraints are equivalent to the $(4 \times 4)$ system of equations

$$a_0 \qquad\qquad\qquad\quad = 3$$
$$a_0 + a_1 + a_2 + a_3 = 0$$
$$a_0 + 2a_1 + 4a_2 + 8a_3 = -1$$
$$a_0 + 3a_1 + 9a_2 + 27a_3 = 6.$$

**Table 1.2**

| $t$ | $f(t)$ |
|-----|--------|
| 0 | 3 |
| 1 | 0 |
| 2 | -1 |
| 3 | 6 |

Solving this system, we find that $a_0 = 3$, $a_1 = -2$, $a_2 = -2$, $a_3 = 1$ is the unique solution. Hence the unique polynomial that interpolates the tabular data for $f(t)$ is

$$p(t) = 3 - 2t - 2t^2 + t^3.$$

The desired approximation for $f(1.5)$ is $p(1.5) = -1.125$.

Note that in each of the two preceding examples, the interpolating polynomial was unique. Theorem 14, on page 83, states that this is always the case. The next example considers the general problem of fitting a quadratic polynomial to three data points and illustrates the proof of Theorem 14.

EXAMPLE 3   Given three distinct numbers $t_0, t_1, t_2$ and any set of three values $y_0, y_1, y_2$, show that there exists a unique polynomial,

$$p(t) = a_0 + a_1 t + a_2 t^2, \tag{2a}$$

of degree 2 or less such that $p(t_0) = y_0$, $p(t_1) = y_1$, and $p(t_2) = y_2$.

**Solution**   The given constraints and (2a) define a $(3 \times 3)$ linear system,

$$
\begin{aligned}
a_0 + a_1 t_0 + a_2 t_0^2 &= y_0 \\
a_0 + a_1 t_1 + a_2 t_1^2 &= y_1 \\
a_0 + a_1 t_2 + a_2 t_2^2 &= y_2,
\end{aligned}
\tag{2b}
$$

where $a_0$, $a_1$, and $a_2$ are the unknowns. The problem is to show that system (2b) has a unique solution. We can write system (2b) in matrix form as $T\mathbf{a} = \mathbf{y}$, where

$$
T = \begin{bmatrix} 1 & t_0 & t_0^2 \\ 1 & t_1 & t_1^2 \\ 1 & t_2 & t_2^2 \end{bmatrix}, \quad
\mathbf{a} = \begin{bmatrix} a_0 \\ a_1 \\ a_2 \end{bmatrix}, \quad \text{and} \quad
\mathbf{y} = \begin{bmatrix} y_0 \\ y_1 \\ y_2 \end{bmatrix}.
\tag{2c}
$$

By Theorem 13, the system is guaranteed to have a unique solution if $T$ is nonsingular. To establish that $T$ is nonsingular, it suffices to show that if

$$
\mathbf{c} = \begin{bmatrix} c_0 \\ c_1 \\ c_2 \end{bmatrix}
$$

is a solution to the homogeneous system $T\mathbf{x} = \boldsymbol{\theta}$, then $\mathbf{c} = \boldsymbol{\theta}$. But $T\mathbf{c} = \boldsymbol{\theta}$ is equivalent to

$$
\begin{aligned}
c_0 + c_1 t_0 + c_2 t_0^2 &= 0 \\
c_0 + c_1 t_1 + c_2 t_1^2 &= 0 \\
c_0 + c_1 t_2 + c_2 t_2^2 &= 0.
\end{aligned}
\tag{2d}
$$

Let $q(t) = c_0 + c_1 t + c_2 t^2$. Then $q(t)$ has degree at most 2 and, by system (2d), $q(t_0) = q(t_1) = q(t_2) = 0$. Thus $q(t)$ has three distinct real zeros. By Exercise 25, if a quadratic polynomial has three distinct real zeros, then it must be identically zero. That is, $c_0 = c_1 = c_2 = 0$, or $\mathbf{c} = \boldsymbol{\theta}$. Hence $T$ is nonsingular, and so system (2b) has a unique solution. ■

The matrix $T$ given in (2c) is the $(3 \times 3)$ Vandermonde matrix. More generally, for real numbers $t_0, t_1, \ldots, t_n$, the $[(n + 1) \times (n + 1)]$ **Vandermonde matrix** $T$

is defined by

$$T = \begin{bmatrix} 1 & t_0 & t_0^2 & \cdots & t_0^n \\ 1 & t_1 & t_1^2 & \cdots & t_1^n \\ \vdots & & & & \vdots \\ 1 & t_n & t_n^2 & \cdots & t_n^n \end{bmatrix}. \tag{3}$$

Following the argument given in Example 3 and making use of Exercise 26, we can show that if $t_0, t_1, \ldots, t_n$ are distinct, then $T$ is nonsingular. Thus, by Theorem 13, the linear system $T\mathbf{x} = \mathbf{y}$ has a unique solution for each choice of $\mathbf{y}$ in $R^{n+1}$. As a consequence, we have the following theorem.

**THEOREM 14** Given $n+1$ distinct numbers $t_0, t_1, \ldots, t_n$ and any set of $n+1$ values $y_0, y_1, \ldots, y_n$, there is one and only one polynomial $p(t)$ of degree $n$ or less, $p(t) = a_0 + a_1 t + \cdots + a_n t^n$, such that $p(t_i) = y_i$, $i = 0, 1, \ldots, n$. ■

## Solutions to Initial Value Problems

The following example provides yet another application of the fact that the Vandermonde matrix $T$ given in (3) is nonsingular when $t_0, t_1, \ldots, t_n$ are distinct. Problems of this sort arise in solving initial value problems in differential equations.

**EXAMPLE 4** Given $n + 1$ distinct numbers $t_0, t_1, \ldots, t_n$ and any set of $n + 1$ values $y_0, y_1, \ldots, y_n$, show that there is one, and only one, function that has the form

$$y = a_0 e^{t_0 x} + a_1 e^{t_1 x} + \cdots + a_n e^{t_n x} \tag{4a}$$

and that satisfies the constraints $y(0) = y_0$, $y'(0) = y_1, \ldots, y^{(n)}(0) = y_n$.

**Solution**  Calculating the first $n$ derivatives of $y$ gives

$$
\begin{aligned}
y &= a_0 e^{t_0 x} + a_1 e^{t_1 x} + \cdots + a_n e^{t_n x} \\
y' &= a_0 t_0 e^{t_0 x} + a_1 t_1 e^{t_1 x} + \cdots + a_n t_n e^{t_n x} \\
y'' &= a_0 t_0^2 e^{t_0 x} + a_1 t_1^2 e^{t_1 x} + \cdots + a_n t_n^2 e^{t_n x} \\
&\ \ \vdots \qquad\quad \vdots \qquad\qquad\qquad \vdots \\
y^{(n)} &= a_0 t_0^n e^{t_0 x} + a_1 t_1^n e^{t_1 x} + \cdots + a_n t_n^n e^{t_n x}.
\end{aligned}
\tag{4b}
$$

Substituting $x = 0$ in each equation of system (4b) and setting $y^{(k)}(0) = y_k$ yields the system

$$
\begin{aligned}
y_0 &= a_0 + a_1 + \cdots + a_n \\
y_1 &= a_0 t_0 + a_1 t_1 + \cdots + a_n t_n \\
y_2 &= a_0 t_0^2 + a_1 t_1^2 + \cdots + a_n t_n^2 \\
&\ \ \vdots \qquad \vdots \qquad\qquad\quad \vdots \\
y_n &= a_0 t_0^n + a_1 t_1^n + \cdots + a_n t_n^n
\end{aligned}
\tag{4c}
$$

with unknowns $a_0, a_1, \ldots, a_n$. Note that the coefficient matrix for the linear system (4c) is

$$T^T = \begin{bmatrix} 1 & 1 & \cdots & 1 \\ t_0 & t_1 & \cdots & t_n \\ t_0^2 & t_1^2 & \cdots & t_n^2 \\ \vdots & & & \vdots \\ t_0^n & t_1^n & \cdots & t_n^n \end{bmatrix}, \tag{4d}$$

where $T$ is the $[(n+1) \times (n+1)]$ Vandermonde matrix given in Eq. (3). It is left as an exercise (see Exercise 57 of Section 1.7) to show that because $T$ is nonsingular, the transpose $T^T$ is also nonsingular. Thus by Theorem 13, the linear system (4c) has a unique solution. ∎

The next example is a specific case of Example 4.

EXAMPLE 5     Find the unique function $y = c_1 e^x + c_2 e^{2x} + c_3 e^{3x}$ that satisfies the constraints $y(0) = 1$, $y'(0) = 2$, and $y''(0) = 0$.

*Solution*     The given function and its first two derivatives are

$$\begin{aligned} y &= c_1 e^x + c_2 e^{2x} + c_3 e^{3x} \\ y' &= c_1 e^x + 2c_2 e^{2x} + 3c_3 e^{3x} \\ y'' &= c_1 e^x + 4c_2 e^{2x} + 9c_3 e^{3x}. \end{aligned} \tag{5a}$$

From (5a) the given constraints are equivalent to

$$\begin{aligned} 1 &= c_1 + c_2 + c_3 \\ 2 &= c_1 + 2c_2 + 3c_3 \\ 0 &= c_1 + 4c_2 + 9c_3. \end{aligned} \tag{5b}$$

The augmented matrix for system (5b) is

$$\begin{bmatrix} 1 & 1 & 1 & 1 \\ 1 & 2 & 3 & 2 \\ 1 & 4 & 9 & 0 \end{bmatrix},$$

and solving in the usual manner yields the unique solution $c_1 = -2$, $c_2 = 5$, $c_3 = -2$. Therefore, the function $y = -2e^x + 5e^{2x} - 2e^{3x}$ is the unique function that satisfies the given constraints. ∎

## Numerical Integration

The Vandermonde matrix also arises in problems where it is necessary to estimate numerically an integral or a derivative. For example, let $I(f)$ denote the definite integral

$$I(f) = \int_a^b f(t)\,dt.$$

If the integrand is fairly complicated or if the integrand is not a standard form that can be found in a table of integrals, then it will be necessary to approximate the value $I(f)$ numerically.

One effective way to approximate $I(f)$ is first to find a polynomial $p$ that approximates $f$ on $[a, b]$,

$$p(t) \approx f(t), \quad a \le t \le b.$$

Next, given that $p$ is a good approximation to $f$, we would expect that the approximation that follows is also a good one:

$$\int_a^b p(t)\,dt \approx \int_a^b f(t)\,dt. \tag{6}$$

Of course, since $p$ is a polynomial, the integral on the left-hand side of Eq. (6) can be easily evaluated and provides a computable estimate to the unknown integral, $I(f)$.

One way to generate a polynomial approximation to $f$ is through interpolation. If we select $n + 1$ points $t_0, t_1, \ldots, t_n$ in $[a, b]$, then the $n$th-degree polynomial $p$ that satisfies $p(t_i) = f(t_i), 0 \le i \le n$, is an approximation to $f$ that can be used in Eq. (6) to estimate $I(f)$.

In summary, the numerical integration process proceeds as follows:

1. Given $f$, construct the interpolating polynomial, $p$.

2. Given $p$, calculate the integral, $\int_a^b p(t)\,dt$.

3. Use $\int_a^b p(t)\,dt$ as the approximation to $\int_a^b f(t)\,dt$.

It turns out that this approximation scheme can be simplified considerably, and step 1 can be skipped entirely. That is, it is not necessary to construct the actual interpolating polynomial $p$ in order to know the integral of $p$, $\int_a^b p(t)\,dt$.

We will illustrate the idea with a quadratic interpolating polynomial. Suppose $p$ is the quadratic polynomial that interpolates $f$ at $t_0, t_1$, and $t_2$. Next, suppose we can find scalars $A_0, A_1, A_2$ such that

$$
\begin{aligned}
A_0 + A_1 + A_2 &= \int_a^b 1\,dt \\
A_0 t_0 + A_1 t_1 + A_2 t_2 &= \int_a^b t\,dt \\
A_0 t_0^2 + A_1 t_1^2 + A_2 t_2^2 &= \int_a^b t^2\,dt.
\end{aligned}
\tag{7}
$$

Now, if the interpolating polynomial $p$ is given by $p(t) = a_0 + a_1 t + a_2 t^2$, then the equations in (7) give

$$\int_a^b p(t)\, dt = \int_a^b [a_0 + a_1 t + a_2 t^2]\, dt$$

$$= a_0 \int_a^b 1\, dt + a_1 \int_a^b t\, dt + a_2 \int_a^b t^2\, dt$$

$$= a_0 \sum_{i=0}^{2} A_i + a_1 \sum_{i=0}^{2} A_i t_i + a_2 \sum_{i=0}^{2} A_i t_i^2$$

$$= \sum_{i=0}^{2} A_i [a_0 + a_1 t_i + a_2 t_i^2]$$

$$= \sum_{i=0}^{2} A_i\, p(t_i).$$

The previous calculations demonstrate the following: If we know the values of a quadratic polynomial $p$ at three points $t_0, t_1, t_2$ and if we can find scalars $A_0, A_1, A_2$ that satisfy system (7), then we can evaluate the integral of $p$ with the formula

$$\int_a^b p(t)\, dt = \sum_{i=0}^{2} A_i\, p(t_i). \tag{8}$$

Next, since $p$ is the quadratic interpolating polynomial for $f$, we see that the values of $p(t_i)$ are known to us; that is, $p(t_0) = f(t_0)$, $p(t_1) = f(t_1)$, and $p(t_2) = f(t_2)$. Thus, combining Eq. (8) and Eq. (6), we obtain

$$\int_a^b p(t)\, dt = \sum_{i=0}^{2} A_i\, p(t_i) = \sum_{i=0}^{2} A_i\, f(t_i) \approx \int_a^b f(t)\, dt,$$

or equivalently,

$$\int_a^b f(t)\, dt \approx \sum_{i=0}^{2} A_i\, f(t_i). \tag{9}$$

The approximation $\sum_{i=0}^{2} A_i\, f(t_i)$ in (9) is known as a numerical integration formula. Observe that once the evaluation points $t_0, t_1, t_2$ are selected, the scalars $A_0, A_1, A_2$ are determined by system (7). The coefficient matrix for system (7) has the form

$$A = \begin{bmatrix} 1 & 1 & 1 \\ t_0 & t_1 & t_2 \\ t_0^2 & t_1^2 & t_2^2 \end{bmatrix},$$

and so we see that $A$ is nonsingular since $A$ is the transpose of a Vandermonde matrix (recall matrix (4d)).

In general, if $t_0, t_1, \ldots, t_n$ are $n + 1$ points in $[a, b]$, we can proceed exactly as in the derivation of formula (9) and produce a numerical integration formula of the form

$$\int_a^b f(t)\, dt \approx \sum_{i=0}^{n} A_i\, f(t_i). \tag{10}$$

The weights $A_i$ in formula (10) would be determined by solving the Vandermonde system:

$$A_0 \ + A_1 \ + \cdots + A_n \ = \int_a^b 1 \, dt$$

$$A_0 t_0 + A_1 t_1 + \cdots + A_n t_n = \int_a^b t \, dt \qquad (11)$$

$$\vdots \qquad \qquad \vdots \qquad \qquad \vdots$$

$$A_0 t_0^n + A_1 t_1^n + \cdots + A_n t_n^n = \int_a^b t^n \, dt.$$

The approximation $\sum_{i=0}^n A_i f(t_i)$ is the same number that would be produced by calculating the polynomial $p$ of degree $n$ that interpolates $f$ at $t_0, t_1, \ldots, t_n$ and then evaluating $\int_a^b p(t) \, dt$.

EXAMPLE 6    For an interval $[a, b]$ let $t_0 = a$, $t_1 = (a+b)/2$, and $t_2 = b$. Construct the corresponding numerical integration formula.

*Solution*    For $t_0 = a$, $t_1 = (a+b)/2$, and $t_2 = b$, the system to be solved is given by (11) with $n = 2$. We write system (11) as $C\mathbf{x} = \mathbf{d}$, where

$$C = \begin{bmatrix} 1 & 1 & 1 \\ a & t_1 & b \\ a^2 & t_1^2 & b^2 \end{bmatrix} \quad \text{and} \quad \mathbf{d} = \begin{bmatrix} b - a \\ (b^2 - a^2)/2 \\ (b^3 - a^3)/3 \end{bmatrix}.$$

It can be shown (see Exercise 23) that the solution of $C\mathbf{x} = \mathbf{d}$ is $A_0 = (b - a)/6$, $A_1 = 4(b-a)/6$, $A_2 = (b-a)/6$. The corresponding numerical integration formula is

$$\int_a^b f(t) \, dt \approx [(b - a)/6]\{f(a) + 4f[(a + b)/2] + f(b)\}. \qquad (12)$$

The reader may be familiar with the preceding approximation, which is known as Simpson's rule.    ■

EXAMPLE 7    Use the integration formula (12) to approximate the integral

$$I(f) = \int_0^{1/2} \cos(\pi t^2/2) \, dt.$$

*Solution*    With $a = 0$ and $b = 1/2$, formula (12) becomes

$$I(f) \approx 1/12[\cos(0) + 4\cos(\pi/32) + \cos(\pi/8)]$$
$$= (1/12)[1.0 + 4(0.995184\ldots) + 0.923879\ldots]$$
$$= 0.492051\ldots. \qquad ■$$

Note that in Example 7, the number $I(f)$ is equal to $C(0.5)$, where $C(x)$ denotes the Fresnel integral

$$C(x) = \int_0^x \cos(\pi t^2/2) \, dt.$$

The function $C(x)$ is important in applied mathematics, and extensive tables of the function $C(x)$ are available. The integrand is not a standard form, and $C(x)$ must be evaluated numerically. From a table, $C(0.5) = 0.49223442\ldots$.

## Numerical Differentiation

Numerical differentiation formulas can also be derived in the same fashion as numerical integration formulas. In particular, suppose that $f$ is a differentiable function and we wish to estimate the value $f'(a)$, where $f$ is differentiable at $t = a$.

Let $p$ be the polynomial of degree $n$ that interpolates $f$ at $t_0, t_1, \ldots, t_n$, where the interpolation nodes $t_i$ are clustered near $t = a$. Then $p$ provides us with an approximation for $f$, and we can estimate the value $f'(a)$ by evaluating the derivative of $p$ at $t = a$:

$$f'(a) \approx p'(a).$$

As with a numerical integration formula, it can be shown that the value $p'(a)$ can be expressed as

$$p'(a) = A_0 p(t_0) + A_1 p(t_1) + \cdots + A_n p(t_n). \tag{13}$$

In formula (13), the weights $A_i$ are determined by the system of equations

$$
\begin{aligned}
q_0'(a) &= A_0 q_0(t_0) + A_1 q_0(t_1) + \cdots + A_n q_0(t_n) \\
q_1'(a) &= A_0 q_1(t_0) + A_1 q_1(t_1) + \cdots + A_n q_1(t_n) \\
&\ \vdots \qquad\qquad \vdots \qquad\qquad\qquad\qquad \vdots \\
q_n'(a) &= A_0 q_n(t_0) + A_1 q_n(t_1) + \cdots + A_n q_n(t_n),
\end{aligned}
$$

where $q_0(t) = 1, q_1(t) = t, \ldots, q_n(t) = t^n$. So if formula (13) holds for the $n + 1$ special polynomials $1, t, \ldots, t^n$, then it holds for every polynomial $p$ of degree $n$ or less.

If $p$ interpolates $f$ at $t_0, t_1, \ldots, t_n$ so that $p(t_i) = f(t_i), 0 \le i \le n$, then (by formula 13) the approximation $f'(a) \approx p'(a)$ leads to

$$f'(a) \approx A_0 f(t_0) + A_1 f(t_1) + \cdots + A_n f(t_n). \tag{14}$$

An approximation of the form (14) is called a numerical differentiation formula.

EXAMPLE 8    Derive a numerical differentiation formula of the form

$$f'(a) \approx A_0 f(a - h) + A_1 f(a) + A_2 f(a + h).$$

*Solution*    The weights $A_0$, $A_1$, and $A_2$ are determined by forcing Eq. (13) to hold for $p(t) = 1$, $p(t) = t$, and $p(t) = t^2$. Thus the weights are found by solving the system

$$
\begin{aligned}
[p(t) = 1] \quad & 0 = A_0 && + A_1 && + A_2 \\
[p(t) = t] \quad & 1 = A_0(a - h) && + A_1(a) && + A_2(a + h) \\
\left[p(t) = t^2\right] \quad & 2a = A_0(a - h)^2 && + A_1(a)^2 && + A_2(a + h)^2.
\end{aligned}
$$

In matrix form, the system above can be expressed as $C\mathbf{x} = \mathbf{d}$, where

$$C = \begin{bmatrix} 1 & 1 & 1 \\ a-h & a & a+h \\ (a-h)^2 & a^2 & (a+h)^2 \end{bmatrix} \quad \text{and} \quad \mathbf{d} = \begin{bmatrix} 0 \\ 1 \\ 2a \end{bmatrix}.$$

By (4d), the matrix $C$ is nonsingular and (see Exercise 24) the solution is $A_0 = -1/2h$, $A_1 = 0$, $A_2 = 1/2h$. The numerical differentiation formula has the form

$$f'(a) \approx [f(a+h) - f(a-h)]/2h. \tag{15}$$

(*Note:* Formula (15) in this example is known as the centered-difference approximation to $f'(a)$.)

The same techniques can be used to derive formulas for estimating higher derivatives.

EXAMPLE 9    Construct a numerical differentiation formula of the form

$$f''(a) \approx A_0 f(a) + A_1 f(a+h) + A_2 f(a+2h) + A_3 f(a+3h).$$

*Solution*    The weights $A_0$, $A_1$, $A_2$, and $A_3$ are determined by forcing the preceding approximation to be an equality for $p(t) = 1$, $p(t) = t$, $p(t) = t^2$, and $p(t) = t^3$. These constraints lead to the equations

$$[p(t) = 1] \quad 0 = A_0 \quad + A_1 \quad + A_2 \quad + A_3$$
$$[p(t) = t] \quad 0 = A_0(a) + A_1(a+h) + A_2(a+2h) + A_3(a+3h)$$
$$[p(t) = t^2] \quad 2 = A_0(a)^2 + A_1(a+h)^2 + A_2(a+2h)^2 + A_3(a+3h)^2$$
$$[p(t) = t^3] \quad 6a = A_0(a)^3 + A_1(a+h)^3 + A_2(a+2h)^3 + A_3(a+3h)^3.$$

Since this system is a bit cumbersome to solve by hand, we decided to use the computer algebra system Derive. (Because the coefficient matrix has symbolic rather than numerical entries, we had to use a computer algebra system rather than numerical software such as MATLAB. In particular, Derive is a popular computer algebra system that is menu-driven and very easy to use.)

Figure 1.19 shows the results from Derive. Line 2 gives the command to row reduce the augmented matrix for the system. Line 3 gives the results. Therefore, the numerical differentiation formula is

$$f''(a) \approx \frac{1}{h^2}[2f(a) - 5f(a+h) + 4f(a+2h) - f(a+3h)].$$

$$\text{2: ROW\_REDUCE} \begin{bmatrix} 1 & 1 & 1 & 1 & 0 \\ a & a+h & a+2h & a+3h & 0 \\ a^2 & (a+h)^2 & (a+2h)^2 & (a+3h)^2 & 2 \\ a^3 & (a+h)^3 & (a+2h)^3 & (a+3h)^3 & 6a \end{bmatrix}$$

$$\text{3:} \begin{bmatrix} 1 & 0 & 0 & 0 & \dfrac{2}{h^2} \\ 0 & 1 & 0 & 0 & -\dfrac{5}{h^2} \\ 0 & 0 & 1 & 0 & \dfrac{4}{h^2} \\ 0 & 0 & 0 & 1 & -\dfrac{1}{h^2} \end{bmatrix}$$

**Figure 1.19**    Using Derive to solve the system of equations in Example 9

## 1.8    EXERCISES

In Exercises 1–6, find the interpolating polynomial for the given table of data. [*Hint:* If the data table has $k$ entries, the interpolating polynomial will be of degree $k-1$ or less.]

1.

| $t$ | 0 | 1 | 2 |
|---|---|---|---|
| $y$ | −1 | 3 | 6 |

2.

| $t$ | −1 | 0 | 2 |
|---|---|---|---|
| $y$ | 6 | 1 | −3 |

3.

| $t$ | −1 | 1 | 2 |
|---|---|---|---|
| $y$ | 1 | 5 | 7 |

4.

| $t$ | 1 | 3 | 4 |
|---|---|---|---|
| $y$ | 5 | 11 | 14 |

5.

| $t$ | −1 | 0 | 1 | 2 |
|---|---|---|---|---|
| $y$ | −6 | 1 | 4 | 15 |

6.

| $t$ | −2 | −1 | 1 | 2 |
|---|---|---|---|---|
| $y$ | −3 | 1 | 3 | 13 |

In Exercises 7–10, find the constants so that the given function satisfies the given conditions.

7. $y = c_1 e^{2x} + c_2 e^{3x}$; $y(0) = 3$, $y'(0) = 7$

8. $y = c_1 e^{(x-1)} + c_2 e^{3(x-1)}$; $y(1) = 1$, $y'(1) = 5$

9. $y = c_1 e^{-x} + c_2 e^x + c_3 e^{2x}$; $y(0) = 8$, $y'(0) = 3$, $y''(0) = 11$

10. $y = c_1 e^x + c_2 e^{2x} + c_3 e^{3x}$; $y(0) = -1$, $y'(0) = -3$, $y''(0) = -5$

As in Example 6, find the weights $A_i$ for the numerical integration formulas listed in Exercises 11–16. [*Note:* It can be shown that the special formulas developed in Exercises 11–16 can be translated to any interval of the general form $[a, b]$. Similarly, the numerical differentiation formulas in Exercises 17–22 can also be translated.]

**11.** $\int_0^{3h} f(t)\, dt \approx A_0 f(h) + A_1 f(2h)$

**12.** $\int_0^h f(t)\, dt \approx A_0 f(0) + A_1 f(h)$

**13.** $\int_0^{3h} f(t)\, dt \approx A_0 f(0) + A_1 f(h) + A_2 f(2h) + A_3 f(3h)$

**14.** $\int_0^{4h} f(t)\, dt \approx A_0 f(h) + A_1 f(2h) + A_2 f(3h)$

**15.** $\int_0^h f(t)\, dt \approx A_0 f(-h) + A_1 f(0)$

**16.** $\int_0^h f(t)\, dt \approx A_0 f(-h) + A_1 f(0) + A_2 f(h)$

As in Example 8, find the weights for the numerical differentiation formulas in Exercises 17–22. For Exercises 21 and 22, replace $p'(a)$ in formula (13) by $p''(a)$.

**17.** $f'(0) \approx A_0 f(0) + A_1 f(h)$

**18.** $f'(0) \approx A_0 f(-h) + A_1 f(0)$

**19.** $f'(0) \approx A_0 f(0) + A_1 f(h) + A_2 f(2h)$

**20.** $f'(0) \approx A_0 f(0) + A_1 f(h) + A_2 f(2h) + A_3 f(3h)$

**21.** $f''(0) \approx A_0 f(-h) + A_1 f(0) + A_2 f(h)$

**22.** $f''(0) \approx A_0 f(0) + A_1 f(h) + A_2 f(2h)$

**23.** Complete the calculations in Example 6 by transforming the augmented matrix $[C \,|\, \mathbf{d}]$ to reduced echelon form.

**24.** Complete the calculations in Example 8 by transforming the augmented matrix $[C \,|\, \mathbf{d}]$ to reduced echelon form.

**25.** Let $p$ denote the quadratic polynomial defined by $p(t) = at^2 + bt + c$, where $a$, $b$, and $c$ are real numbers. Use Rolle's theorem to prove the following: If $t_0$, $t_1$, and $t_2$ are real numbers such that $t_0 < t_1 < t_2$ and if $p(t_0) = 0$, $p(t_1) = 0$, and $p(t_2) = 0$, then $a = b = c = 0$. (Recall that Rolle's theorem states there are values $u_1$ and $u_2$ such that $u_1$ is in $(t_0, t_1)$, $u_2$ is in $(t_1, t_2)$, $p'(u_1) = 0$, and $p'(u_2) = 0$.)

**26.** Use mathematical induction to prove that a polynomial of the form $p(t) = a_n t^n + \cdots + a_1 t + a_0$ can have $n+1$ distinct real zeros only if $a_n = a_{n-1} = \cdots = a_1 = a_0 = 0$. [*Hint:* Use Rolle's theorem, as in Exercise 25.]

Exercises 27–33 concern **Hermite interpolation**, where Hermite interpolation means the process of constructing polynomials that match both function values and derivative values.

In Exercises 27–30, find a polynomial $p$ of the form $p(t) = at^3 + bt^2 + ct + d$ that satisfies the given conditions.

**27.** $p(0) = 2$, $p'(0) = 3$, $p(1) = 8$, $p'(1) = 10$

**28.** $p(0) = 1$, $p'(0) = 2$, $p(1) = 4$, $p'(1) = 4$

**29.** $p(-1) = -1$, $p'(-1) = 5$, $p(1) = 9$, $p'(1) = 9$

**30.** $p(1) = 3$, $p'(1) = 4$, $p(2) = 15$, $p'(2) = 22$

**31.** Suppose that $t_0$ and $t_1$ are distinct real numbers, where $t_0 < t_1$. Prove: If $p$ is any polynomial of the form $p(t) = at^3 + bt^2 + ct + d$, where $p(t_0) = p(t_1) = 0$ and $p'(t_0) = p'(t_1) = 0$, then $a = b = c = d = 0$. [*Hint:* Apply Rolle's theorem.]

**32.** Suppose $t_0$ and $t_1$ are distinct real numbers, where $t_0 < t_1$. Suppose $y_0$, $y_1$, $s_0$, and $s_1$ are given real numbers. Prove that there is one, and only one, polynomial $p$ of the form $p(t) = at^3 + bt^2 + ct + d$ such that $p(t_0) = y_0$, $p'(t_0) = s_0$, $p(t_1) = y_1$, and $p'(t_1) = s_1$. [*Hint:* Set up a system of four equations corresponding to the four interpolation constraints. Use Exercise 31 to show that the coefficient matrix is nonsingular.]

**33.** Let $t_0 < t_1 < \cdots < t_n$ be $n+1$ distinct real numbers. Let $y_0, y_1, \ldots, y_n$ and $s_0, s_1, \ldots, s_n$ be given real numbers. Show that there is one, and only one, polynomial $p$ of degree $2n+1$ or less such that $p(t_i) = y_i$, $0 \le i \le n$, and $p'(t_i) = s_i$, $0 \le i \le n$. [*Hint:* As in Exercise 31, show that all the coefficients of $p$ are zero if $y_i = s_i = 0$, $0 \le i \le n$. Next, as in Exercise 32, write the system of equations corresponding to the interpolation constraints and verify that the coefficient matrix is nonsingular.]

In Exercises 34 and 35, use linear algebra software, such as Derive, to construct the formula.

**34.** $\int_0^{5h} f(x)\, dx \approx \sum_{j=0}^{5} A_j f(jh)$

**35.** $f'(a) \approx A_0 f(a - 2h) + A_1 f(a - h) + A_2 f(a) + A_3 f(a + h) + A_4 f(a + 2h)$

## 1.9 MATRIX INVERSES AND THEIR PROPERTIES

In the preceding sections the matrix equation

$$A\mathbf{x} = \mathbf{b} \tag{1}$$

has been used extensively to represent a system of linear equations. Equation (1) looks, symbolically, like the single linear equation

$$ax = b, \tag{2}$$

where $a$ and $b$ are real numbers. Since Eq. (2) has the unique solution

$$x = a^{-1}b$$

when $a \neq 0$, it is natural to ask whether Eq. (1) can also be solved as

$$\mathbf{x} = A^{-1}\mathbf{b}.$$

In this section we investigate this question. We begin by defining the inverse of a matrix, showing how to calculate it, and then showing how the inverse can be used to solve systems of the form $A\mathbf{x} = \mathbf{b}$.

### The Matrix Inverse

For a nonzero real number $a$, the inverse of $a$ is the unique real number $a^{-1}$ having the property that

$$a^{-1}a = aa^{-1} = 1. \tag{3}$$

In Eq. (3), the number 1 is the multiplicative identity for real number multiplication. In an analogous fashion, let $A$ be an $(n \times n)$ matrix. We now ask if we can find a matrix $A^{-1}$ with the property that

$$A^{-1}A = AA^{-1} = I. \tag{4}$$

(In Eq. (4) $I$ denotes the $(n \times n)$ identity matrix; see Section 1.6.)

We formalize the idea suggested by Eq. (4) in the next definition. Note that the commutativity condition $A^{-1}A = AA^{-1}$ means that $A$ and $A^{-1}$ must be square and of the same size; see Exercise 75.

---

**DEFINITION 13**

Let $A$ be an $(n \times n)$ matrix. We say that $A$ is *invertible* if we can find an $(n \times n)$ matrix $A^{-1}$ such that

$$A^{-1}A = AA^{-1} = I.$$

The matrix $A^{-1}$ is called an *inverse* for $A$.

---

(*Note:* It is shown in Exercise 77 that if $A$ is invertible, then $A^{-1}$ is unique.

As an example of an invertible matrix, consider

$$A = \begin{bmatrix} 1 & 2 \\ 3 & 4 \end{bmatrix}.$$

It is simple to show that $A$ is invertible and that $A^{-1}$ is given by

$$A^{-1} = \begin{bmatrix} -2 & 1 \\ 3/2 & -1/2 \end{bmatrix}.$$

(To show that the preceding matrix is indeed the inverse of $A$, we need only form the products $A^{-1}A$ and $AA^{-1}$ and then verify that both products are equal to $I$.)

Not every square matrix is invertible, as the next example shows.

EXAMPLE 1 Let $A$ be the $(2 \times 2)$ matrix

$$A = \begin{bmatrix} 1 & 2 \\ 3 & 6 \end{bmatrix}.$$

Show that $A$ has no inverse.

*Solution* An inverse for $A$ must be a $(2 \times 2)$ matrix

$$B = \begin{bmatrix} a & b \\ c & d \end{bmatrix}$$

such that $AB = BA = I$. If such a matrix $B$ exists, it must satisfy the following equation:

$$\begin{bmatrix} 1 & 0 \\ 0 & 1 \end{bmatrix} = \begin{bmatrix} 1 & 2 \\ 3 & 6 \end{bmatrix} \begin{bmatrix} a & b \\ c & d \end{bmatrix} = \begin{bmatrix} a+2c & b+2d \\ 3a+6c & 3b+6d \end{bmatrix}.$$

The preceding equation requires that $a + 2c = 1$ and $3a + 6c = 0$. This is clearly impossible, so $A$ has no inverse. ◣

## Using Inverses to Solve Systems of Linear Equations

One major use of inverses is to solve systems of linear equations. In particular, consider the equation

$$A\mathbf{x} = \mathbf{b}, \tag{5}$$

where $A$ is an $(n \times n)$ matrix and where $A^{-1}$ exists. Then, to solve $A\mathbf{x} = \mathbf{b}$, we might think of multiplying both sides of the equation by $A^{-1}$:

$$A^{-1}A\mathbf{x} = A^{-1}\mathbf{b}$$

or

$$\mathbf{x} = A^{-1}\mathbf{b}.$$

The preceding calculations suggest the following: To solve $A\mathbf{x} = \mathbf{b}$ we need only compute the vector $\mathbf{x}$ given by

$$\mathbf{x} = A^{-1}\mathbf{b}. \tag{6}$$

To verify that the vector $\mathbf{x} = A^{-1}\mathbf{b}$ is indeed a solution, we need only insert it into the equation:

$$
\begin{aligned}
A\mathbf{x} &= A(A^{-1}\mathbf{b}) \\
&= (AA^{-1})\mathbf{b} \quad &\text{(by associativity of multiplication)} \\
&= I\mathbf{b} \quad &\text{(by Definition 13)} \\
&= \mathbf{b}. \quad &\text{(because } I \text{ is the identity matrix)}
\end{aligned}
$$

## Existence of Inverses

As we saw earlier in Example 1, some matrices do not have an inverse. We now turn our attention to determining exactly which matrices *are* invertible. In the process, we will also develop a simple algorithm for calculating $A^{-1}$.

Let $A$ be an $(n \times n)$ matrix. If $A$ does have an inverse, then that inverse is an $(n \times n)$ matrix $B$ such that

$$AB = I. \tag{7a}$$

(Of course, to be an inverse, the matrix $B$ must also satisfy the condition $BA = I$. We will put this additional requirement aside for the moment and concentrate solely on the condition $AB = I$.)

Expressing $B$ and $I$ in column form, the equation $AB = I$ can be rewritten as

$$A[\mathbf{b}_1, \mathbf{b}_2, \ldots, \mathbf{b}_n] = [\mathbf{e}_1, \mathbf{e}_2, \ldots, \mathbf{e}_n]$$

or

$$[A\mathbf{b}_1, A\mathbf{b}_2, \ldots, A\mathbf{b}_n] = [\mathbf{e}_1, \mathbf{e}_2, \ldots, \mathbf{e}_n]. \tag{7b}$$

If $A$ has an inverse, therefore, it follows that we must be able to solve each of the following $n$ equations:

$$\begin{aligned} A\mathbf{x} &= \mathbf{e}_1 \\ A\mathbf{x} &= \mathbf{e}_2 \\ &\vdots \\ A\mathbf{x} &= \mathbf{e}_n. \end{aligned} \tag{7c}$$

In particular, if $A$ is invertible, then the $k$th column of $A^{-1}$ can be found by solving $A\mathbf{x} = \mathbf{e}_k, k = 1, 2, \ldots, n$.

We know (recall Theorem 13) that all the equations listed in (7c) can be solved if $A$ is nonsingular. We suspect, therefore, that a nonsingular matrix always has an inverse. In fact, as is shown in Theorem 15, $A$ has an inverse if and only if $A$ is nonsingular.

Before stating Theorem 15, we give a lemma. (Although we do not need it here, the converse of the lemma is also valid; see Exercise 70.)

**LEMMA** Let $P$, $Q$, and $R$ be $(n \times n)$ matrices such that $PQ = R$. If either $P$ or $Q$ is singular, then so is $R$.

*Proof* Suppose first that $Q$ is singular. Then there is a nonzero vector $\mathbf{x}_1$ such that $Q\mathbf{x}_1 = \boldsymbol{\theta}$. Therefore, using associativity of matrix multiplication,

$$\begin{aligned} R\mathbf{x}_1 &= (PQ)\mathbf{x}_1 \\ &= P(Q\mathbf{x}_1) \\ &= P\boldsymbol{\theta} \\ &= \boldsymbol{\theta}. \end{aligned}$$

So, $Q$ singular implies $R$ is singular.

Now, suppose $Q$ is nonsingular but the other factor, $P$, is singular. Then there is a nonzero vector $\mathbf{x}_1$ such that $P\mathbf{x}_1 = \boldsymbol{\theta}$. Also, $Q$ nonsingular means we can find a vector

$\mathbf{x}_2$ such that $Q\mathbf{x}_2 = \mathbf{x}_1$. (In addition, note that $\mathbf{x}_2$ must be nonzero because $\mathbf{x}_1$ is nonzero.) Therefore,

$$
\begin{aligned}
R\mathbf{x}_2 &= (PQ)\mathbf{x}_2 \\
&= P(Q\mathbf{x}_2) \\
&= P\mathbf{x}_1 \\
&= \boldsymbol{\theta}.
\end{aligned}
$$

Thus, if either $P$ or $Q$ is singular, then the product $PQ$ is also singular. ◼

We are now ready to characterize invertible matrices.

**THEOREM 15**   Let $A$ be an $(n \times n)$ matrix. Then $A$ has an inverse if and only if $A$ is nonsingular.

*Proof*   Suppose first that $A$ has an inverse. That is, as in equation (7a), there is a matrix $B$ such that $AB = I$. Now, as Exercise 74 proves, $I$ is nonsingular. Therefore, by the lemma, neither $A$ nor $B$ can be singular. This argument shows that invertibility implies nonsingularity.

For the converse, suppose $A$ is nonsingular. Since $A$ is nonsingular, we see from equations (7a)–(7c) that there is a unique matrix $B$ such that $AB = I$. This matrix $B$ will be the inverse of $A$ if we can show that $A$ and $B$ commute; that is, if we can also show that $BA = I$.

We will use a common algebraic trick to prove $BA = I$. First of all, note that the matrix $B$ must also be nonsingular since $AB = I$. Therefore, just as with equations (7a)–(7c), there is a matrix $C$ such that $BC = I$. Then, combining the expressions $AB = I$ and $BC = I$, we obtain

$$A = AI = A(BC) = (AB)C = IC = C.$$

Since $A = C$, we also have $BA = BC = I$. Therefore, $BA = I$, and this shows that $B$ is the inverse of $A$. Hence, $A$ nonsingular implies that $A$ is invertible. ◼

### Calculating the Inverse

In this subsection we give a simple algorithm for finding the inverse of a matrix $A$, provided that $A$ has an inverse. The algorithm is based on the system of equations (7c):

$$A\mathbf{x} = \mathbf{e}_1, A\mathbf{x} = \mathbf{e}_2, \ldots, A\mathbf{x} = \mathbf{e}_n.$$

We first observe that there is a very efficient way to organize the solution of these $n$ systems; we simply row reduce the associated augmented matrix $[A \mid \mathbf{e}_1, \mathbf{e}_2, \ldots, \mathbf{e}_n]$. The procedure is illustrated in the next example.

**EXAMPLE 2**   Find the inverse of the $(3 \times 3)$ matrix

$$A = \begin{bmatrix} 1 & 2 & 3 \\ 2 & 5 & 4 \\ 1 & -1 & 10 \end{bmatrix}.$$

*Solution*    The augmented matrix $[A \mid \mathbf{e}_1, \mathbf{e}_2, \mathbf{e}_3]$ is given by

$$\begin{bmatrix} 1 & 2 & 3 & 1 & 0 & 0 \\ 2 & 5 & 4 & 0 & 1 & 0 \\ 1 & -1 & 10 & 0 & 0 & 1 \end{bmatrix}.$$

(Note that the augmented matrix has the form $[A \mid I]$.)

We now perform appropriate row operations to transform $[A \mid I]$ to reduced echelon form.

$R_2 - 2R_1, R_3 - R_1$:

$$\begin{bmatrix} 1 & 2 & 3 & 1 & 0 & 0 \\ 0 & 1 & -2 & -2 & 1 & 0 \\ 0 & -3 & 7 & -1 & 0 & 1 \end{bmatrix}$$

$R_1 - 2R_2, R_3 + 3R_2$:

$$\begin{bmatrix} 1 & 0 & 7 & 5 & -2 & 0 \\ 0 & 1 & -2 & -2 & 1 & 0 \\ 0 & 0 & 1 & -7 & 3 & 1 \end{bmatrix}$$

$R_1 - 7R_3, R_2 + 2R_3$:

$$\begin{bmatrix} 1 & 0 & 0 & 54 & -23 & -7 \\ 0 & 1 & 0 & -16 & 7 & 2 \\ 0 & 0 & 1 & -7 & 3 & 1 \end{bmatrix}.$$

Having the reduced echelon form above, we easily find the solutions of the three systems $A\mathbf{x} = \mathbf{e}_1, A\mathbf{x} = \mathbf{e}_2, A\mathbf{x} = \mathbf{e}_3$. In particular,

| $A\mathbf{x} = \mathbf{e}_1$ *has solution:* | $A\mathbf{x} = \mathbf{e}_2$ *has solution:* | $A\mathbf{x} = \mathbf{e}_3$ *has solution:* |
|---|---|---|
| $x_1 = \begin{bmatrix} 54 \\ -16 \\ -7 \end{bmatrix}$ | $x_2 = \begin{bmatrix} -23 \\ 7 \\ 3 \end{bmatrix}$ | $x_3 = \begin{bmatrix} -7 \\ 2 \\ 1 \end{bmatrix}.$ |

Therefore, $A^{-1} = [\mathbf{x}_1, \mathbf{x}_2, \mathbf{x}_3]$ or

$$A^{-1} = \begin{bmatrix} 54 & -23 & -7 \\ -16 & 7 & 2 \\ -7 & 3 & 1 \end{bmatrix}.$$

This procedure illustrated in Example 2 can be summarized by the following algorithm for calculating $A^{-1}$.

---

### Computation of $A^{-1}$

To calculate the inverse of a nonsingular $(n \times n)$ matrix, we can proceed as follows:

*Step 1.* Form the $(n \times 2n)$ matrix $[A \mid I]$.

*Step 2.* Use elementary row operations to transform $[A \mid I]$ to the form $[I \mid B]$.

*Step 3.* Reading from this final form, $A^{-1} = B$.

---

(*Note:* Step 2 of the algorithm above assumes that $[A \mid I]$ can always be row reduced to the form $[I \mid B]$ when $A$ is nonsingular. This is indeed the case, and we ask you to prove it in Exercise 76 by showing that the reduced echelon form for any nonsingular matrix $A$ is $I$. In fact, Exercise 76 actually establishes the stronger result listed next in Theorem 16.)

THEOREM 16 Let $A$ be an $(n \times n)$ matrix. Then $A$ is nonsingular if and only if $A$ is row equivalent to $I$.

The next example illustrates the algorithm for calculating $A^{-1}$ and also illustrates how to compute the solution to $A\mathbf{x} = \mathbf{b}$ by forming $\mathbf{x} = A^{-1}\mathbf{b}$.

EXAMPLE 3 Consider the system of equations

$$x_1 + 2x_2 = -1$$
$$2x_1 + 5x_2 = -10.$$

(a) Use the algorithm to find the inverse of the coefficient matrix $A$.

(b) Use the inverse to calculate the solution of the system.

*Solution*

(a) We begin by forming the $(2 \times 4)$ matrix $[A \mid I]$,

$$[A \mid I] = \begin{bmatrix} 1 & 2 & 1 & 0 \\ 2 & 5 & 0 & 1 \end{bmatrix}.$$

We next row reduce $[A \mid I]$ to $[I \mid B]$ as follows:

$R_2 - 2R_1$:

$$\begin{bmatrix} 1 & 2 & 1 & 0 \\ 0 & 1 & -2 & 1 \end{bmatrix}$$

$R_1 - 2R_2$:

$$\begin{bmatrix} 1 & 0 & 5 & -2 \\ 0 & 1 & -2 & 1 \end{bmatrix}.$$

Thus, $A^{-1}$ is the matrix

$$\begin{bmatrix} 5 & -2 \\ -2 & 1 \end{bmatrix}.$$

**(b)** The solution to the system is $\mathbf{x} = A^{-1}\mathbf{b}$ where

$$\mathbf{b} = \begin{bmatrix} -1 \\ -10 \end{bmatrix}.$$

Now, $A^{-1}\mathbf{b} = [15, -8]^T$, so the solution is $x_1 = 15, x_2 = -8$.　◼

## Inverses for (2 × 2) Matrices

There is a simple formula for the inverse of a $(2 \times 2)$ matrix, which we give in the remark that follows.

***Remark***    Let $A$ be a $(2 \times 2)$ matrix,

$$A = \begin{bmatrix} a & b \\ c & d \end{bmatrix},$$

and set $\Delta = ad - bc$.

**(a)** If $\Delta = 0$, then $A$ does not have an inverse.

**(b)** If $\Delta \neq 0$, then $A$ has an inverse given by

$$A^{-1} = \frac{1}{\Delta} \begin{bmatrix} d & -b \\ -c & a \end{bmatrix}. \tag{8}$$

Part (a) of the remark is Exercise 69. To verify the formula given in (b), suppose that $\Delta \neq 0$, and define $B$ to be the matrix

$$B = \frac{1}{\Delta} \begin{bmatrix} d & -b \\ -c & a \end{bmatrix}.$$

Then

$$BA = \frac{1}{\Delta} \begin{bmatrix} d & -b \\ -c & a \end{bmatrix} \begin{bmatrix} a & b \\ c & d \end{bmatrix} = \frac{1}{\Delta} \begin{bmatrix} ad - bc & 0 \\ 0 & ad - bc \end{bmatrix} = \begin{bmatrix} 1 & 0 \\ 0 & 1 \end{bmatrix}.$$

Similarly, $AB = I$, so $B = A^{-1}$.

The reader familiar with determinants will recognize the number $\Delta$ in the remark as the determinant of the matrix $A$. We make use of the remark in the following example.

EXAMPLE 4    Let $A$ and $B$ be given by

$$A = \begin{bmatrix} 6 & 8 \\ 3 & 4 \end{bmatrix} \quad \text{and} \quad B = \begin{bmatrix} 1 & 7 \\ 3 & 5 \end{bmatrix}.$$

For each matrix, determine whether an inverse exists and calculate the inverse if it does exist.

***Solution*** For the matrix $A$, the number $\Delta$ is

$$\Delta = 6(4) - 8(3) = 0,$$

so, by the remark, $A$ cannot have an inverse. For the matrix $B$, the number $\Delta$ is

$$\Delta = 1(5) - 7(3) = -16.$$

According to formula (8)

$$B^{-1} = -\frac{1}{16} \begin{bmatrix} 5 & -7 \\ -3 & 1 \end{bmatrix}.$$

■

**EXAMPLE 5** Consider the matrix $A$

$$A = \begin{bmatrix} \lambda & 2 \\ 2 & \lambda - 3 \end{bmatrix}.$$

For what values of $\lambda$ is the matrix $A$ nonsingular? Find $A^{-1}$ if $A$ is nonsingular.

***Solution*** The number $\Delta$ is given by

$$\Delta = \lambda(\lambda - 3) - 4 = \lambda^2 - 3\lambda - 4 = (\lambda - 4)(\lambda + 1).$$

Thus, $A$ is singular if and only if $\lambda = 4$ or $\lambda = -1$. For values other than these two, $A^{-1}$ is given by

$$A^{-1} = \frac{1}{\lambda^2 - 3\lambda - 4} \begin{bmatrix} \lambda - 3 & -2 \\ -2 & \lambda \end{bmatrix}.$$

■

## Properties of Matrix Inverses

The following theorem lists some of the properties of matrix inverses.

**THEOREM 17** Let $A$ and $B$ be $(n \times n)$ matrices, each of which has an inverse. Then:

1. $A^{-1}$ has an inverse, and $(A^{-1})^{-1} = A$.
2. $AB$ has an inverse, and $(AB)^{-1} = B^{-1}A^{-1}$.
3. If $k$ is a nonzero scalar, then $kA$ has an inverse, and $(kA)^{-1} = (1/k)A^{-1}$.
4. $A^T$ has an inverse, and $(A^T)^{-1} = (A^{-1})^T$.

***Proof***

1. Since $AA^{-1} = A^{-1}A = I$, the inverse of $A^{-1}$ is $A$; that is, $(A^{-1})^{-1} = A$.
2. Note that $(AB)(B^{-1}A^{-1}) = A(BB^{-1})A^{-1} = A(IA^{-1}) = AA^{-1} = I$. Similarly, $(B^{-1}A^{-1})(AB) = I$, so, by Definition 13, $B^{-1}A^{-1}$ is the inverse for $AB$. Thus $(AB)^{-1} = B^{-1}A^{-1}$.
3. The proof of property 3 is similar to the proofs given for properties 1 and 2 and is left as an exercise.

**4.** It follows from Theorem 10, property 2, of Section 1.6 that $A^T(A^{-1})^T = (A^{-1}A)^T = I^T = I$. Similarly, $(A^{-1})^T A^T = I$. Therefore, $A^T$ has inverse $(A^{-1})^T$. ◼

Note that the familiar formula $(ab)^{-1} = a^{-1}b^{-1}$ for real numbers is valid only because multiplication of real numbers is commutative. We have already noted that matrix multiplication is not commutative, so, as the following example demonstrates, $(AB)^{-1} \neq A^{-1}B^{-1}$.

EXAMPLE 6   Let $A$ and $B$ be the $(2 \times 2)$ matrices

$$A = \begin{bmatrix} 1 & 3 \\ 2 & 4 \end{bmatrix} \quad \text{and} \quad B = \begin{bmatrix} 3 & -2 \\ 1 & -1 \end{bmatrix}.$$

**1.** Use formula (8) to calculate $A^{-1}$, $B^{-1}$, and $(AB)^{-1}$.
**2.** Use Theorem 17, property 2, to calculate $(AB)^{-1}$.
**3.** Show that $(AB)^{-1} \neq A^{-1}B^{-1}$.

*Solution*   For $A$ the number $\Delta$ is $\Delta = 1(4) - 3(2) = -2$, so by formula (8)

$$A^{-1} = \begin{bmatrix} -2 & 3/2 \\ 1 & -1/2 \end{bmatrix}.$$

For $B$ the number $\Delta$ is $3(-1) - 1(-2) = -1$, so

$$B^{-1} = \begin{bmatrix} 1 & -2 \\ 1 & -3 \end{bmatrix}.$$

The product $AB$ is given by

$$AB = \begin{bmatrix} 6 & -5 \\ 10 & -8 \end{bmatrix},$$

so by formula (8)

$$(AB)^{-1} = \begin{bmatrix} -4 & 5/2 \\ -5 & 3 \end{bmatrix}.$$

By Theorem 17, property 2,

$$(AB)^{-1} = B^{-1}A^{-1} = \begin{bmatrix} 1 & -2 \\ 1 & -3 \end{bmatrix} \begin{bmatrix} -2 & 3/2 \\ 1 & -1/2 \end{bmatrix} = \begin{bmatrix} -4 & 5/2 \\ -5 & 3 \end{bmatrix}.$$

Finally,

$$A^{-1}B^{-1} = \begin{bmatrix} -2 & 3/2 \\ 1 & -1/2 \end{bmatrix} \begin{bmatrix} 1 & -2 \\ 1 & -3 \end{bmatrix} = \begin{bmatrix} -1/2 & -1/2 \\ 1/2 & -1/2 \end{bmatrix} \neq (AB)^{-1}. \quad ◼$$

The following theorem summarizes some of the important properties of nonsingular matrices.

THEOREM 18    Let $A$ be an $(n \times n)$ matrix. The following are equivalent:

(a)   $A$ is nonsingular; that is, the only solution of $A\mathbf{x} = \boldsymbol{\theta}$ is $\mathbf{x} = \boldsymbol{\theta}$.

(b)   The column vectors of $A$ are linearly independent.

(c)   $A\mathbf{x} = \mathbf{b}$ always has a unique solution.

(d)   $A$ has an inverse.

(e)   $A$ is row equivalent to $I$.

## Ill-Conditioned Matrices

In applications the equation $A\mathbf{x} = \mathbf{b}$ often serves as a mathematical model for a physical problem. In these cases it is important to know whether solutions to $A\mathbf{x} = \mathbf{b}$ are sensitive to small changes in the right-hand side $\mathbf{b}$. If small changes in $\mathbf{b}$ can lead to relatively large changes in the solution $\mathbf{x}$, then the matrix $A$ is called **ill-conditioned**.

The concept of an ill-conditioned matrix is related to the size of $A^{-1}$. This connection is explained after the next example.

EXAMPLE 7    The $(n \times n)$ Hilbert matrix is the matrix whose $ij$th entry is $1/(i + j - 1)$. For example, the $(3 \times 3)$ Hilbert matrix is

$$
\begin{bmatrix}
1 & 1/2 & 1/3 \\
1/2 & 1/3 & 1/4 \\
1/3 & 1/4 & 1/5
\end{bmatrix}.
$$

Let $A$ denote the $(6 \times 6)$ Hilbert matrix, and consider the vectors $\mathbf{b}$ and $\mathbf{b} + \Delta\mathbf{b}$:

$$
\mathbf{b} = \begin{bmatrix} 1 \\ 2 \\ 1 \\ 1.414 \\ 1 \\ 2 \end{bmatrix}, \qquad
\mathbf{b} + \Delta\mathbf{b} = \begin{bmatrix} 1 \\ 2 \\ 1 \\ 1.4142 \\ 1 \\ 2 \end{bmatrix}.
$$

Note that $\mathbf{b}$ and $\mathbf{b} + \Delta\mathbf{b}$ differ slightly in their fourth components. Compare the solutions of $A\mathbf{x} = \mathbf{b}$ and $A\mathbf{x} = \mathbf{b} + \Delta\mathbf{b}$.

*Solution*    We used MATLAB to solve these two equations. If $\mathbf{x}_1$ denotes the solution of $A\mathbf{x} = \mathbf{b}$, and $\mathbf{x}_2$ denotes the solution of $A\mathbf{x} = \mathbf{b} + \Delta\mathbf{b}$, the results are (rounded to the nearest integer):

$$
x_1 = \begin{bmatrix} -6538 \\ 185706 \\ -1256237 \\ 3271363 \\ -3616326 \\ 1427163 \end{bmatrix} \quad \text{and} \quad
x_2 = \begin{bmatrix} -6539 \\ 185747 \\ -1256519 \\ 3272089 \\ -3617120 \\ 1427447 \end{bmatrix}.
$$

(*Note:* Despite the fact that **b** and **b** + Δ**b** are nearly equal, **x**₁ and **x**₂ differ by almost 800 in their fifth components.)  ◼

Example 7 illustrates that the solutions of $A\mathbf{x} = \mathbf{b}$ and $A\mathbf{x} = \mathbf{b} + \Delta\mathbf{b}$ may be quite different even though Δ**b** is a small vector. In order to explain these differences, let **x**₁ denote the solution of $A\mathbf{x} = \mathbf{b}$ and **x**₂ the solution of $A\mathbf{x} = \mathbf{b} + \Delta\mathbf{b}$. Therefore, $A\mathbf{x}_1 = \mathbf{b}$ and $A\mathbf{x}_2 = \mathbf{b} + \Delta\mathbf{b}$. To assess the difference, $\mathbf{x}_2 - \mathbf{x}_1$, we proceed as follows:

$$A\mathbf{x}_2 - A\mathbf{x}_1 = (\mathbf{b} + \Delta\mathbf{b}) - \mathbf{b} = \Delta\mathbf{b}.$$

Therefore, $A(\mathbf{x}_2 - \mathbf{x}_1) = \Delta\mathbf{b}$, or

$$\mathbf{x}_2 - \mathbf{x}_1 = A^{-1}\Delta\mathbf{b}.$$

If $A^{-1}$ contains large entries, then we see from the equation above that $\mathbf{x}_2 - \mathbf{x}_1$ can be large even though Δ**b** is small.

The Hilbert matrices described in Example 7 are well-known examples of ill-conditioned matrices and have large inverses. For example, the inverse of the $(6 \times 6)$ Hilbert matrix is

$$A^{-1} = \begin{bmatrix} 36 & -630 & 3360 & -7560 & 7560 & -2772 \\ -630 & 14700 & -88200 & 211680 & -220500 & 83160 \\ 3360 & -88200 & 564480 & -1411200 & 1512000 & -582120 \\ -7560 & 211680 & -1411200 & 3628800 & -3969000 & 1552320 \\ 7560 & -220500 & 1512000 & -3969000 & 4410000 & -1746360 \\ -2772 & 83160 & -582120 & 1552320 & -1746360 & 698544 \end{bmatrix}.$$

Because of the large entries in $A^{-1}$, we should not be surprised at the large difference between **x**₁ and **x**₂, the two solutions in Example 7.

## 1.9    EXERCISES

In Exercises 1–4, verify that $B$ is the inverse of $A$ by showing that $AB = BA = I$.

**1.** $A = \begin{bmatrix} 7 & 4 \\ 5 & 3 \end{bmatrix}$, $B = \begin{bmatrix} 3 & -4 \\ -5 & 7 \end{bmatrix}$

**2.** $A = \begin{bmatrix} 3 & 10 \\ 2 & 10 \end{bmatrix}$, $B = \begin{bmatrix} 1 & -1 \\ -.2 & .3 \end{bmatrix}$

**3.** $A = \begin{bmatrix} -1 & -2 & 11 \\ 1 & 3 & -15 \\ 0 & -1 & 5 \end{bmatrix}$, $B = \begin{bmatrix} 0 & 1 & 3 \\ 5 & 5 & 4 \\ 1 & 1 & 1 \end{bmatrix}$

**4.** $A = \begin{bmatrix} 1 & 0 & 0 \\ 2 & 1 & 0 \\ 3 & 4 & 1 \end{bmatrix}$, $B = \begin{bmatrix} 1 & 0 & 0 \\ -2 & 1 & 0 \\ 5 & -4 & 1 \end{bmatrix}$

In Exercises 5–8, use the appropriate inverse matrix from Exercises 1–4 to solve the given system of linear equations.

**5.** $3x_1 + 10x_2 = 6$
$\phantom{3}2x_1 + 10x_2 = 9$

**6.** $7x_1 + 4x_2 = 5$
$\phantom{7}5x_1 + 3x_2 = 2$

**7.** $\phantom{5x_1 + 5}x_2 + 3x_3 = 4$
$5x_1 + 5x_2 + 4x_3 = 2$
$\phantom{5}x_1 + \phantom{5}x_2 + \phantom{4}x_3 = 2$

**8.** $\phantom{-2}x_1 \phantom{+ x_2 + x_3} = 2$
$-2x_1 + \phantom{4}x_2 \phantom{+ x_3} = 3$
$\phantom{-}5x_1 - 4x_2 + x_3 = 2$

In Exercises 9–12, verify that the given matrix $A$ does not have an inverse. [*Hint:* One of $AB = I$ or $BA = I$ leads to an easy contradiction.]

**9.** $A = \begin{bmatrix} 0 & 0 & 0 \\ 1 & 2 & 1 \\ 3 & 2 & 1 \end{bmatrix}$

**10.** $A = \begin{bmatrix} 0 & 4 & 2 \\ 0 & 1 & 7 \\ 0 & 3 & 9 \end{bmatrix}$

**11.** $A = \begin{bmatrix} 2 & 2 & 4 \\ 1 & 1 & 7 \\ 3 & 3 & 9 \end{bmatrix}$ **12.** $A = \begin{bmatrix} 1 & 1 & 1 \\ 1 & 1 & 1 \\ 2 & 3 & 2 \end{bmatrix}$

In Exercises 13–21, reduce $[A \mid I]$ to find $A^{-1}$. In each case, check your calculations by multiplying the given matrix by the derived inverse.

**13.** $\begin{bmatrix} 1 & 1 \\ 2 & 3 \end{bmatrix}$  **14.** $\begin{bmatrix} 2 & 3 \\ 6 & 7 \end{bmatrix}$

**15.** $\begin{bmatrix} 1 & 2 \\ 2 & 1 \end{bmatrix}$  **16.** $\begin{bmatrix} -1 & -2 & 11 \\ 1 & 3 & -15 \\ 0 & -1 & 5 \end{bmatrix}$

**17.** $\begin{bmatrix} 1 & 0 & 0 \\ 2 & 1 & 0 \\ 3 & 4 & 1 \end{bmatrix}$  **18.** $\begin{bmatrix} 1 & 3 & 5 \\ 0 & 1 & 4 \\ 0 & 2 & 7 \end{bmatrix}$

**19.** $\begin{bmatrix} 1 & 4 & 2 \\ 0 & 2 & 1 \\ 3 & 5 & 3 \end{bmatrix}$  **20.** $\begin{bmatrix} 1 & -2 & 2 & 1 \\ 1 & -1 & 5 & 0 \\ 2 & -2 & 11 & 2 \\ 0 & 2 & 8 & 1 \end{bmatrix}$

**21.** $\begin{bmatrix} 1 & 2 & 3 & 1 \\ -1 & 0 & 2 & 1 \\ 2 & 1 & -3 & 0 \\ 1 & 1 & 2 & 1 \end{bmatrix}$

As in Example 5, determine whether the $(2 \times 2)$ matrices in Exercises 22–26 have an inverse. If $A$ has an inverse, find $A^{-1}$ and verify that $A^{-1}A = I$.

**22.** $A = \begin{bmatrix} -3 & 2 \\ 1 & 1 \end{bmatrix}$  **23.** $A = \begin{bmatrix} 2 & -2 \\ 2 & 3 \end{bmatrix}$

**24.** $A = \begin{bmatrix} -1 & 3 \\ 2 & 1 \end{bmatrix}$  **25.** $A = \begin{bmatrix} 2 & 1 \\ 4 & 2 \end{bmatrix}$

**26.** $A = \begin{bmatrix} 6 & -2 \\ 9 & -3 \end{bmatrix}$

In Exercises 27–28 determine the value(s) of $\lambda$ for which $A$ has an inverse.

**27.** $A = \begin{bmatrix} \lambda & 4 \\ 1 & \lambda \end{bmatrix}$  **28.** $A = \begin{bmatrix} 1 & -2 & 3 \\ 4 & -1 & 4 \\ 2 & -3 & \lambda \end{bmatrix}$

In Exercises 29–34, solve the given system by forming $\mathbf{x} = A^{-1}\mathbf{b}$, where $A$ is the coefficient matrix for the system.

**29.** $\begin{aligned} 2x_1 + \ x_2 &= 4 \\ 3x_1 + 2x_2 &= 2 \end{aligned}$  **30.** $\begin{aligned} x_1 + \ x_2 &= 0 \\ 2x_1 + 3x_2 &= 4 \end{aligned}$

**31.** $\begin{aligned} x_1 - \ x_2 &= 5 \\ 3x_1 - 4x_2 &= 2 \end{aligned}$  **32.** $\begin{aligned} 2x_1 + 3x_2 &= 1 \\ 3x_1 + 4x_2 &= 7 \end{aligned}$

**33.** $\begin{aligned} 3x_1 + \ x_2 &= 10 \\ -x_1 + 3x_2 &= \ 5 \end{aligned}$  **34.** $\begin{aligned} x_1 - \ x_2 &= 10 \\ 2x_1 + 3x_2 &= \ 4 \end{aligned}$

The following matrices are used in Exercises 35–45.

$$A^{-1} = \begin{bmatrix} 3 & 1 \\ 0 & 2 \end{bmatrix}, B = \begin{bmatrix} 1 & 2 \\ 2 & 1 \end{bmatrix}, C^{-1} = \begin{bmatrix} -1 & 1 \\ 1 & 2 \end{bmatrix}.$$

(9)

In Exercises 35–45, use Theorem 17 and the matrices in (9) to form $Q^{-1}$, where $Q$ is the given matrix.

**35.** $Q = AC$  **36.** $Q = CA$

**37.** $Q = A^T$  **38.** $Q = A^TC$

**39.** $Q = C^TA^T$  **40.** $Q = B^{-1}A$

**41.** $Q = CB^{-1}$  **42.** $Q = B^{-1}$

**43.** $Q = 2A$  **44.** $Q = 10C$

**45.** $Q = (AC)B^{-1}$

**46.** Let $A$ be the matrix given in Exercise 13. Use the inverse found in Exercise 13 to obtain matrices $B$ and $C$ such that $AB = D$ and $CA = E$, where

$$D = \begin{bmatrix} -1 & 2 & 3 \\ 1 & 0 & 2 \end{bmatrix} \quad \text{and} \quad E = \begin{bmatrix} 2 & -1 \\ 1 & 1 \\ 0 & 3 \end{bmatrix}.$$

**47.** Repeat Exercise 46 with $A$ being the matrix given in Exercise 16 and where

$$D = \begin{bmatrix} 2 & -1 \\ 1 & 1 \\ 0 & 3 \end{bmatrix} \quad \text{and} \quad E = \begin{bmatrix} -1 & 2 & 3 \\ 1 & 0 & 2 \end{bmatrix}.$$

**48.** For what values of $a$ is

$$A = \begin{bmatrix} 1 & 1 & -1 \\ 0 & 1 & 2 \\ 1 & 1 & a \end{bmatrix}$$

nonsingular?

**49.** Find $(AB)^{-1}$, $(3A)^{-1}$, and $(A^T)^{-1}$ given that

$$A^{-1} = \begin{bmatrix} 1 & 2 & 5 \\ 3 & 1 & 6 \\ 2 & 8 & 1 \end{bmatrix} \quad \text{and} \quad B^{-1} = \begin{bmatrix} 3 & -3 & 4 \\ 5 & 1 & 3 \\ 7 & 6 & -1 \end{bmatrix}.$$

**50.** Find the $(3 \times 3)$ nonsingular matrix $A$ if $A^2 = AB + 2A$, where

$$B = \begin{bmatrix} 2 & 1 & -1 \\ 0 & 3 & 2 \\ -1 & 4 & 1 \end{bmatrix}.$$

**51.** Simplify $(A^{-1}B)^{-1}(C^{-1}A)^{-1}(B^{-1}C)^{-1}$ for $(n \times n)$ invertible matrices $A$, $B$, and $C$.

**52.** The equation $x^2 = 1$ can be solved by setting $x^2 - 1 = 0$ and factoring the expression to obtain $(x-1)(x+1) = 0$. This yields solutions $x = 1$ and $x = -1$.

a) Using the factorization technique given above, what $(2 \times 2)$ matrix solutions do you obtain for the matrix equation $X^2 = I$?

b) Show that

$$A = \begin{bmatrix} a & 1 - a^2 \\ 1 & -a \end{bmatrix}$$

is a solution to $X^2 = I$ for every real number $a$.

c) Let $b = \pm 1$. Show that

$$B = \begin{bmatrix} b & 0 \\ c & -b \end{bmatrix}$$

is a solution to $X^2 = I$ for every real number $c$.

d) Explain why the factorization technique used in part (a) did not yield all the solutions to the matrix equation $X^2 = I$.

**53.** Suppose that $A$ is a $(2 \times 2)$ matrix with columns $\mathbf{u}$ and $\mathbf{v}$, so that $A = [\mathbf{u}, \mathbf{v}]$, $\mathbf{u}$ and $\mathbf{v}$ in $R^2$. Suppose also that $\mathbf{u}^T \mathbf{u} = 1$, $\mathbf{u}^T \mathbf{v} = 0$, and $\mathbf{v}^T \mathbf{v} = 1$. Prove that $A^T A = I$. [*Hint:* Express the matrix $A$ as

$$A = \begin{bmatrix} u_1 & v_1 \\ u_2 & v_2 \end{bmatrix}, \quad \mathbf{u} = \begin{bmatrix} u_1 \\ u_2 \end{bmatrix}, \quad \mathbf{v} \begin{bmatrix} v_1 \\ v_2 \end{bmatrix}$$

and form the product $A^T A$.]

**54.** Let $\mathbf{u}$ be a vector in $R^n$ such that $\mathbf{u}^T \mathbf{u} = 1$. Let $A = I - \mathbf{u}\mathbf{u}^T$, where $I$ is the $(n \times n)$ identity. Verify that $AA = A$. [*Hint:* Write the product $\mathbf{u}\mathbf{u}^T \mathbf{u}\mathbf{u}^T$ as $\mathbf{u}\mathbf{u}^T\mathbf{u}\mathbf{u}^T = \mathbf{u}(\mathbf{u}^T \mathbf{u})\mathbf{u}^T$, and note that $\mathbf{u}^T \mathbf{u}$ is a scalar.]

**55.** Suppose that $A$ is an $(n \times n)$ matrix such that $AA = A$, as in Exercise 54. Show that if $A$ has an inverse, then $A = I$.

**56.** Let $A = I - a\mathbf{v}\mathbf{v}^T$, where $\mathbf{v}$ is a nonzero vector in $R^n$, $I$ is the $(n \times n)$ identity, and $a$ is the scalar given by $a = 2/(\mathbf{v}^T \mathbf{v})$. Show that $A$ is symmetric and that $AA = I$; that is, $A^{-1} = A$.

**57.** Consider the $(n \times n)$ matrix $A$ defined in Exercise 56. For $\mathbf{x}$ in $R^n$, show that the product $A\mathbf{x}$ has the form $A\mathbf{x} = \mathbf{x} - \lambda\mathbf{v}$, where $\lambda$ is a scalar. What is the value of $\lambda$ for a given $\mathbf{x}$?

**58.** Suppose that $A$ is an $(n \times n)$ matrix such that $A^T A = I$ (the matrix defined in Exercise 56 is such a matrix). Let $\mathbf{x}$ be any vector in $R^n$. Show that $\|A\mathbf{x}\| = \|\mathbf{x}\|$; that is, multiplication of $\mathbf{x}$ by $A$ produces a vector $A\mathbf{x}$ having the same length as $\mathbf{x}$.

**59.** Let $\mathbf{u}$ and $\mathbf{v}$ be vectors in $R^n$, and let $I$ denote the $(n \times n)$ identity. Let $A = I + \mathbf{u}\mathbf{v}^T$, and suppose $\mathbf{v}^T \mathbf{u} \neq -1$. Establish the **Sherman–Woodberry** formula:

$$A^{-1} = I - a\mathbf{u}\mathbf{v}^T, \quad a = 1/(1 + \mathbf{v}^T\mathbf{u}). \quad (10)$$

[*Hint:* Form $AA^{-1}$, where $A^{-1}$ is given by formula (10).]

**60.** If $A$ is a square matrix, we define the powers $A^2$, $A^3$, and so on, as follows: $A^2 = AA$, $A^3 = A(A^2)$, and so on. Suppose $A$ is an $(n \times n)$ matrix such that

$$A^3 - 2A^2 + 3A - I = \mathcal{O}.$$

Show that $AB = I$, where $B = A^2 - 2A + 3I$.

**61.** Suppose that $A$ is $(n \times n)$ and

$$A^2 + b_1 A + b_0 I = \mathcal{O}, \quad (11)$$

where $b_0 \neq 0$. Show that $AB = I$, where $B = (-1/b_0)[A + b_1 I]$.

It can be shown that when $A$ is a $(2 \times 2)$ matrix such that $A^{-1}$ exists, then there are constants $b_1$ and $b_0$ such that Eq. (11) holds. Moreover, $b_0 \neq 0$ in Eq. (11) unless $A$ is a multiple of $I$. In Exercises 62–65, find the constants $b_1$ and $b_0$ in Eq. (11) for the given $(2 \times 2)$ matrix. Also, verify that $A^{-1} = (-1/b_0)[A + b_1 I]$.

**62.** $A$ in Exercise 13.     **63.** $A$ in Exercise 15.

**64.** $A$ in Exercise 14.     **65.** $A$ in Exercise 22.

**66.** a) If linear algebra software is available, solve the systems $A\mathbf{x} = \mathbf{b}_1$ and $A\mathbf{x} = \mathbf{b}_2$, where

$$A = \begin{bmatrix} 0.932 & 0.443 & 0.417 \\ 0.712 & 0.915 & 0.887 \\ 0.632 & 0.514 & 0.493 \end{bmatrix},$$

$$\mathbf{b}_1 = \begin{bmatrix} 1 \\ 1 \\ -1 \end{bmatrix}, \quad \mathbf{b}_2 = \begin{bmatrix} 1.01 \\ 1.01 \\ -1.01 \end{bmatrix}.$$

Note the large difference between the two solutions.

b) Calculate $A^{-1}$ and use it to explain the results of part (a).

67. a) Give examples of nonsingular $(2 \times 2)$ matrices $A$ and $B$ such that $A + B$ is singular.

   b) Give examples of singular $(2 \times 2)$ matrices $A$ and $B$ such that $A + B$ is nonsingular.

68. Let $A$ be an $(n \times n)$ nonsingular symmetric matrix. Show that $A^{-1}$ is also symmetric.

69. a) Suppose that $AB = \mathcal{O}$, where $A$ is nonsingular. Prove that $B = \mathcal{O}$.

   b) Find a $(2 \times 2)$ matrix $B$ such that $AB = \mathcal{O}$, where $B$ has nonzero entries and where $A$ is the matrix

$$A = \begin{bmatrix} 1 & 1 \\ 1 & 1 \end{bmatrix}.$$

   Why does this example not contradict part (a)?

70. Let $A$, $B$, and $C$ be matrices such that $A$ is nonsingular and $AB = AC$. Prove that $B = C$.

71. Let $A$ be the $(2 \times 2)$ matrix

$$A = \begin{bmatrix} a & b \\ c & d \end{bmatrix},$$

and set $\Delta = ad - bc$. Prove that if $\Delta = 0$, then $A$ is singular. Conclude that $A$ has no inverse. [*Hint:* Consider the vector

$$\mathbf{v} = \begin{bmatrix} d \\ -c \end{bmatrix};$$

also treat the special case when $d = c = 0$.]

72. Let $A$ and $B$ be $(n \times n)$ nonsingular matrices. Show that $AB$ is also nonsingular.

73. What is wrong with the following argument that if $AB$ is nonsingular, then each of $A$ and $B$ is also nonsingular?

   Since $AB$ is nonsingular, $(AB)^{-1}$ exists. But by Theorem 17, property 2, $(AB)^{-1} = B^{-1}A^{-1}$. Therefore, $A^{-1}$ and $B^{-1}$ exist, so $A$ and $B$ are nonsingular.

74. Let $A$ and $B$ be $(n \times n)$ matrices such that $AB$ is nonsingular.

   a) Prove that $B$ is nonsingular. [*Hint:* Suppose $\mathbf{v}$ is any vector such that $B\mathbf{v} = \boldsymbol{\theta}$, and write $(AB)\mathbf{v}$ as $A(B\mathbf{v})$.]

   b) Prove that $A$ is nonsingular. [*Hint:* By part (a), $B^{-1}$ exists. Apply Exercise 72 to the matrices $AB$ and $B^{-1}$.]

75. Let $A$ be a singular $(n \times n)$ matrix. Argue that at least one of the systems $A\mathbf{x} = \mathbf{e}_k$, $k = 1, 2, \ldots, n$, must be inconsistent, where $\mathbf{e}_1, \mathbf{e}_2, \ldots, \mathbf{e}_n$ are the $n$-dimensional unit vectors.

76. Show that the $(n \times n)$ identity matrix, $I$, is nonsingular.

77. Let $A$ and $B$ be matrices such that $AB = BA$. Show that $A$ and $B$ must be square and of the same order. [*Hint:* Let $A$ be $(p \times q)$ and let $B$ be $(r \times s)$. Now show that $p = r$ and $q = s$.]

78. Use Theorem 3 to prove Theorem 16.

79. Let $A$ be $(n \times n)$ and invertible. Show that $A^{-1}$ is unique.

## SUPPLEMENTARY EXERCISES

1. Consider the system of equations

$$\begin{aligned} x_1 \qquad\qquad &= 1 \\ 2x_1 + (a^2 + a - 2)x_2 &= a^2 - a - 4. \end{aligned}$$

For what values of $a$ does the system have infinitely many solutions? No solutions? A unique solution in which $x_2 = 0$?

2. Let

$$A = \begin{bmatrix} 1 & -1 & -1 \\ 2 & -1 & 1 \\ -3 & 1 & -3 \end{bmatrix}, \quad \mathbf{x} = \begin{bmatrix} x_1 \\ x_2 \\ x_3 \end{bmatrix}, \text{ and}$$

$$\mathbf{b} = \begin{bmatrix} b_1 \\ b_2 \\ b_3 \end{bmatrix}.$$

**a)** Determine conditions on $b_1$, $b_2$, and $b_3$ that are necessary and sufficient for the system of equations $A\mathbf{x} = \mathbf{b}$ to be consistent.
[*Hint:* Reduce the augmented matrix $[A \mid \mathbf{b}]$.]

**b)** For each of the following choices of $\mathbf{b}$, either show that the system $A\mathbf{x} = \mathbf{b}$ is inconsistent or exhibit the solution.

i) $\mathbf{b} = \begin{bmatrix} 1 \\ 1 \\ 1 \end{bmatrix}$   ii) $\mathbf{b} = \begin{bmatrix} 5 \\ 2 \\ 1 \end{bmatrix}$

iii) $\mathbf{b} = \begin{bmatrix} 7 \\ 3 \\ 1 \end{bmatrix}$   iv) $\mathbf{b} = \begin{bmatrix} 0 \\ 1 \\ 2 \end{bmatrix}$

**3.** Let

$$A = \begin{bmatrix} 1 & -1 & 3 \\ 2 & -1 & 5 \\ -3 & 5 & -10 \\ 1 & 0 & 4 \end{bmatrix} \quad \text{and} \quad \mathbf{x} = \begin{bmatrix} x_1 \\ x_2 \\ x_3 \end{bmatrix}.$$

**a)** Simultaneously solve each of the systems $A\mathbf{x} = \mathbf{b}_i$, $i = 1, 2, 3$, where

$$\mathbf{b}_1 = \begin{bmatrix} -5 \\ -17 \\ 19 \\ 24 \end{bmatrix}, \quad \mathbf{b}_2 = \begin{bmatrix} 5 \\ 11 \\ -12 \\ 8 \end{bmatrix}, \quad \text{and}$$

$$\mathbf{b}_3 = \begin{bmatrix} 1 \\ 2 \\ -1 \\ 5 \end{bmatrix}.$$

**b)** Let $B = [\mathbf{b}_1, \mathbf{b}_2, \mathbf{b}_3]$. Use the results of part (a) to exhibit a $(3 \times 3)$ matrix $C$ such that $AC = B$.

**4.** Let

$$A = \begin{bmatrix} 1 & -1 & 3 \\ 2 & -1 & 4 \end{bmatrix} \quad \text{and} \quad C = \begin{bmatrix} 1 & 2 \\ 3 & 1 \end{bmatrix}.$$

Find a $(3 \times 2)$ matrix $B$ such that $AB = C$.

**5.** Let $A$ be the nonsingular $(5 \times 5)$ matrix

$$A = [\mathbf{A}_1, \mathbf{A}_2, \mathbf{A}_3, \mathbf{A}_4, \mathbf{A}_5],$$

and let $B = [\mathbf{A}_5, \mathbf{A}_1, \mathbf{A}_4, \mathbf{A}_2, \mathbf{A}_3]$. For a given vector $\mathbf{b}$, suppose that $[1, 3, 5, 7, 9]^T$ is the solution to $B\mathbf{x} = \mathbf{b}$. What is the solution of $A\mathbf{x} = \mathbf{b}$?

**6.** Let

$$\mathbf{v}_1 = \begin{bmatrix} 1 \\ 1 \\ 3 \end{bmatrix}, \quad \mathbf{v}_2 = \begin{bmatrix} 2 \\ 1 \\ 4 \end{bmatrix}, \quad \text{and} \quad \mathbf{v}_3 = \begin{bmatrix} 5 \\ 2 \\ 9 \end{bmatrix}.$$

**a)** Solve the vector equation $x_1\mathbf{v}_1 + x_2\mathbf{v}_2 + x_3\mathbf{v}_3 = \mathbf{b}$, where

$$\mathbf{b} = \begin{bmatrix} 8 \\ 5 \\ 18 \end{bmatrix}.$$

**b)** Show that the set of vectors $\{\mathbf{v}_1, \mathbf{v}_2, \mathbf{v}_3\}$ is linearly dependent by exhibiting a nontrivial solution to the vector equation $x_1\mathbf{v}_1 + x_2\mathbf{v}_2 + x_3\mathbf{v}_3 = \boldsymbol{\theta}$.

**7.** Let

$$A = \begin{bmatrix} 1 & -1 & 3 \\ 2 & -1 & 5 \\ -1 & 4 & -5 \end{bmatrix}$$

and define a function $T: R^3 \to R^3$ by $T(\mathbf{x}) = A\mathbf{x}$ for each

$$\mathbf{x} = \begin{bmatrix} x_1 \\ x_2 \\ x_3 \end{bmatrix}$$

in $R^3$.

**a)** Find a vector $\mathbf{x}$ in $R^3$ such that $T(\mathbf{x}) = \mathbf{b}$, where

$$\mathbf{b} = \begin{bmatrix} 1 \\ 3 \\ 2 \end{bmatrix}.$$

**b)** If $\boldsymbol{\theta}$ is the zero vector of $R^3$, then clearly $T(\boldsymbol{\theta}) = \boldsymbol{\theta}$. Describe all vectors $\mathbf{x}$ in $R^3$ such that $T(\mathbf{x}) = \boldsymbol{\theta}$.

**8.** Let

$$\mathbf{v}_1 = \begin{bmatrix} 1 \\ -1 \\ 3 \end{bmatrix}, \quad \mathbf{v}_2 = \begin{bmatrix} 2 \\ -1 \\ 5 \end{bmatrix}, \quad \text{and} \quad \mathbf{v}_3 = \begin{bmatrix} -1 \\ 4 \\ -5 \end{bmatrix}.$$

Find

$$\mathbf{x} = \begin{bmatrix} x_1 \\ x_2 \\ x_3 \end{bmatrix}$$

so that $\mathbf{x}^T\mathbf{v}_1 = 2$, $\mathbf{x}^T\mathbf{v}_2 = 3$, and $\mathbf{x}^T\mathbf{v}_3 = -4$.

**9.** Find $A^{-1}$ for each of the following matrices $A$

a) $A = \begin{bmatrix} 1 & 2 & 1 \\ 2 & 5 & 4 \\ 1 & 1 & 0 \end{bmatrix}$

b) $A = \begin{bmatrix} \cos\theta & -\sin\theta \\ \sin\theta & \cos\theta \end{bmatrix}$

**10.** For what values of $\lambda$ is the matrix

$$A = \begin{bmatrix} \lambda - 4 & -1 \\ 2 & \lambda - 1 \end{bmatrix}$$

singular? Find $A^{-1}$ if $A$ is nonsingular.

**11.** Find $A$ if $A$ is $(2 \times 2)$ and $(4A)^{-1} = \begin{bmatrix} 3 & 1 \\ 5 & 2 \end{bmatrix}$.

**12.** Find $A$ and $B$ if they are $(2 \times 2)$ and

$$A + B = \begin{bmatrix} 4 & 6 \\ 8 & 10 \end{bmatrix} \quad \text{and} \quad A - B = \begin{bmatrix} 2 & 2 \\ 4 & 6 \end{bmatrix}.$$

**13.** Let

$$A = \begin{bmatrix} 1 & 0 & 0 \\ 0 & -1 & 0 \\ 0 & 0 & -1 \end{bmatrix}.$$

Calculate $A^{99}$ and $A^{100}$.

In Exercises 14–18, $A$ and $B$ are $(3 \times 3)$ matrices such that

$$A^{-1} = \begin{bmatrix} 2 & 3 & 5 \\ 7 & 2 & 1 \\ 4 & -4 & 3 \end{bmatrix} \quad \text{and} \quad B^{-1} = \begin{bmatrix} -6 & 4 & 3 \\ 7 & -1 & 5 \\ 2 & 3 & 1 \end{bmatrix}.$$

**14.** Without calculating $A$, solve the system of equations $Ax = b$, where

$$x = \begin{bmatrix} x_1 \\ x_2 \\ x_3 \end{bmatrix} \quad \text{and} \quad b = \begin{bmatrix} -1 \\ 0 \\ 1 \end{bmatrix}.$$

**15.** Without calculating $A$ or $B$, find $(AB)^{-1}$.

**16.** Without calculating $A$, find $(3A)^{-1}$.

**17.** Without calculating $A$ or $B$, find $(A^T B)^{-1}$.

**18.** Without calculating $A$ or $B$, find $[(A^{-1}B^{-1})^{-1}A^{-1}B]^{-1}$.

## CONCEPTUAL EXERCISES

In Exercises 1–8, answer true or false. Justify your answer by providing a counterexample if the statement is false or an outline of a proof if the statement is true.

**1.** If $A$ and $B$ are symmetric $(n \times n)$ matrices, then $AB$ is also symmetric.

**2.** If $A$ is an $(n \times n)$ matrix, then $A + A^T$ is symmetric.

**3.** If $A$ and $B$ are nonsingular $(n \times n)$ matrices such that $A^2 = I$ and $B^2 = I$, then $(AB)^{-1} = BA$.

**4.** If $A$ and $B$ are nonsingular $(n \times n)$ matrices, then $A + B$ is also nonsingular.

**5.** A consistent $(3 \times 2)$ linear system of equations can never have a unique solution.

**6.** If $A$ is an $(m \times n)$ matrix such that $Ax = \theta$ for every $x$ in $R^n$, then $A$ is the $(m \times n)$ zero matrix.

**7.** If $A$ is a $(2 \times 2)$ nonsingular matrix and $u_1$ and $u_2$ are nonzero vectors in $R^2$, then $\{Au_1, Au_2\}$ is linearly independent.

**8.** Let $A$ be $(m \times n)$ and $B$ be $(p \times q)$. If $AB$ is defined and square, then $BA$ is also defined and square.

In Exercises 9–16, give a brief answer.

**9.** Let $P$, $Q$, and $R$ be nonsingular $(n \times n)$ matrices such that $PQR = I$. Express $Q^{-1}$ in terms of $P$ and $R$.

**10.** Suppose that each of $A$, $B$, and $AB$ are symmetric $(n \times n)$ matrices. Show that $AB = BA$.

**11.** Let $\mathbf{u}_1$, $\mathbf{u}_2$, and $\mathbf{u}_3$ be nonzero vectors in $R^n$ such that $\mathbf{u}_1^T \mathbf{u}_2 = 0$, $\mathbf{u}_1^T \mathbf{u}_3 = 0$, and $\mathbf{u}_2^T \mathbf{u}_3 = 0$. Show that $\{\mathbf{u}_1, \mathbf{u}_2, \mathbf{u}_3\}$ is a linearly independent set.

**12.** Let $\mathbf{u}_1$ and $\mathbf{u}_2$ be linearly dependent vectors in $R^2$, and let $A$ be a $(2 \times 2)$ matrix. Show that the vectors $A\mathbf{u}_1$ and $A\mathbf{u}_2$ are linearly dependent.

**13.** An $(n \times n)$ matrix $A$ is *orthogonal* provided that $A^T = A^{-1}$, that is, if $AA^T = A^TA = I$. If $A$ is an $(n \times n)$ orthogonal matrix, then prove that $\|\mathbf{x}\| = \|A\mathbf{x}\|$ for every vector $\mathbf{x}$ in $R^n$.

**14.** An $(n \times n)$ matrix $A$ is *idempotent* if $A^2 = A$. What can you say about $A$ if it is both idempotent and nonsingular?

**15.** Let $A$ and $B$ be $(n \times n)$ idempotent matrices such that $AB = BA$. Show that $AB$ is also idempotent.

**16.** An $(n \times n)$ matrix $A$ is *nilpotent of index* $k$ if $A^k = \mathcal{O}$ but $A^i \neq \mathcal{O}$ for $1 \leq i \leq k - 1$.

a) Show: If $A$ is nilpotent of index 2 or 3, then $A$ is singular.

b) (Optional) Show: If $A$ is nilpotent of index $k$, $k \geq 2$, then $A$ is singular. [*Hint:* Consider a proof by contradiction.]

## MATLAB EXERCISES

Exercise 1 illustrates some ideas associated with population dynamics. We will look at this topic again in Chapter 4, after we have developed the necessary analytical tools—eigenvalues and eigenvectors.

**1. Population dynamics**   An island is divided into three regions, $A$, $B$, and $C$. The yearly migration of a certain animal among these regions is described by the following table.

|        | *From* A | *From* B | *From* C |
|--------|----------|----------|----------|
| *To* A | 70%      | 15%      | 10%      |
| *To* B | 15%      | 80%      | 30%      |
| *To* C | 15%      | 5%       | 60%      |

For example, the first column in the table tells us, in any given year, that 70% of the population in $A$ remains in region $A$, 15% migrates to $B$, and 15% migrates to $C$.

The total population of animals on the island is expected to remain stable for the foreseeable future and a census finds the current population consists of 300 in region $A$, 350 in region $B$, and 200 in region $C$. Corresponding to the migration table and the census, we define a matrix $A$ and a vector $\mathbf{x}_0$:

$$A = \begin{bmatrix} .70 & .15 & .10 \\ .15 & .80 & .30 \\ .15 & .05 & .60 \end{bmatrix} \qquad \mathbf{x}_0 = \begin{bmatrix} 300 \\ 350 \\ 200 \end{bmatrix}.$$

The matrix $A$ is called the *transition matrix* and the vector $\mathbf{x}_0$ is the initial *state vector*. In general, let $\mathbf{x}_k = [x_1, x_2, x_3]^T$ denote the state vector for year $k$. (The state vector tells us that in year $k$ there are $x_1$ animals in region $A$, $x_2$ in region $B$, and $x_3$ in region $C$.) Then, using the transition matrix, we find in year $k + 1$ that the population distribution is given by

$$\mathbf{x}_{k+1} = A\mathbf{x}_k. \tag{1}$$

**a)** Use Eq. (1) to find the population distribution one year after the census.

**b)** Give a formula for $\mathbf{x}_n$ in terms of powers of $A$ and $\mathbf{x}_0$.

**c)** Calculate the state vectors $\mathbf{x}_1, \mathbf{x}_2, \ldots, \mathbf{x}_{10}$. Observe that the population distribution seems to be reaching a *steady state*. Estimate the steady-state population for each region.

**d)** Calculate $\mathbf{x}_{20}$ and compare it with your estimate from part c).

**e)** Let $\mathbf{x}_{-1}$ denote the state vector one year prior to the census. Calculate $\mathbf{x}_{-1}$.

**f)** Demonstrate that Eq. (1) has not always been an accurate model for population distribution by calculating the state vector four years prior to the census.

**g)** How should we rearrange the population just after the census so that the distribution three years later is $\mathbf{x}_3 = [250, 400, 200]^T$? That is, what should $\mathbf{x}_0$ be in order to hit the target $\mathbf{x}_3$?

We have already seen one example of a *partitioned matrix* (also called a *block matrix*) when we wrote $A$ in column form as $A = [\mathbf{A}_1, \mathbf{A}_2, \ldots, \mathbf{A}_n]$; recall Section 1.6. Exercise 2 expands on this idea and illustrates how partitioned matrices can be multiplied in a natural way.

**2. Partitioned matrices**    A matrix $A$ is a $(2 \times 2)$ *block matrix* if it is represented in the form

$$A = \begin{bmatrix} A_1 & A_2 \\ A_3 & A_4 \end{bmatrix},$$

where each of the $A_i$ are matrices. Note that the matrix $A$ need not be a square matrix; for instance, $A$ might be $(7 \times 12)$ with $A_1$ being $(3 \times 5)$, $A_2$ being $(3 \times 7)$, $A_3$ being $(4 \times 5)$, and $A_4$ being $(4 \times 7)$. We can imagine creating a $(2 \times 2)$ block matrix by dividing the array into four pieces using a horizontal line and a vertical line.

Now suppose $B$ is also a $(2 \times 2)$ block matrix given by

$$B = \begin{bmatrix} B_1 & B_2 \\ B_3 & B_4 \end{bmatrix}.$$

Finally, let us suppose that the product $AB$ can be formed and that $B$ has been partitioned in a way such that the following matrix is defined:

$$\begin{bmatrix} A_1 B_1 + A_2 B_3 & A_1 B_2 + A_2 B_4 \\ A_3 B_1 + A_4 B_3 & A_3 B_2 + A_4 B_4 \end{bmatrix}.$$

It turns out that the product $AB$ is given by this block matrix. That is, if all the submatrix products are defined, then we can treat the blocks in a partitioned matrix as though they were scalars when forming products. It is tedious to prove this result in general, so we ask you to illustrate its validity with some randomly chosen matrices.

**a)** Using the MATLAB command round(10*rand(6, 6)) generate two randomly selected $(6 \times 6)$ matrices $A$ and $B$. Compute the product $AB$. Then write each of $A$ and $B$ as a block matrix of the form

$$A = \begin{bmatrix} A_1 & A_2 \\ A_3 & A_4 \end{bmatrix} \quad B = \begin{bmatrix} B_1 & B_2 \\ B_3 & B_4 \end{bmatrix}.$$

Above, each $A_i$ and $B_i$ should be a $(3 \times 3)$ block. Using matrix surgery (see Section 4 of Appendix A) extract the $A_i$ and $B_i$ matrices and form the new block matrix:

$$\begin{bmatrix} A_1B_1 + A_2B_3 & A_1B_2 + A_2B_4 \\ A_3B_1 + A_4B_3 & A_3B_2 + A_4B_4 \end{bmatrix}.$$

Compare the preceding block matrix with $AB$ and confirm that they are equal.

**b)** Repeat this calculation on three other matrices (not necessarily $(6 \times 6)$ matrices). Break some of these matrices into blocks of unequal sizes. You need to make sure that corresponding blocks are the correct size so that matrix multiplication is defined.

**c)** Repeat the calculation in (a) with the product of a $(2 \times 3)$ block matrix times a $(3 \times 3)$ block matrix.

In Exercise 3, determine how many places were lost to round-off error when $Ax = b$ was solved on the computer?

**3.** This exercise expands on the topic of ill-conditioned matrices, introduced at the end of Section 1.9. In general, a mathematician speaks of a problem as being ***ill conditioned*** if *small* changes in the parameters of the problem lead to *large* changes in the solution to the problem.

Part d) of this exercise also discusses a very practical question:

> *How much reliance can I place in the solution to $Ax = b$ that my computer gives me?*

A reasonably precise assessment of this question can be made using the concept of a **condition number** for $A$.

An easily understood example of an ill-conditioned problem is the equation $Ax = b$ where $A$ is the $(n \times n)$ Hilbert matrix (see Example 7, Section 1.9 for the definition of the Hilbert matrix). When $A$ is the Hilbert matrix, then a small change in any entry of $A$ or a small change in any entry of $b$ will lead to a large change in the solution of $Ax = b$.

Let $A$ denote the $(n \times n)$ Hilbert matrix; in MATLAB, $A$ can be created by the command $A = \text{hilb}(n, n)$.

**a)** Let $B$ denote the inverse of $A$, as calculated by MATLAB. For $n = 8, 9, 10, 11$, and 12, form the product $AB$ and note how the product looks less and less like the identity. In order to have the results clearly displayed, you might want to use the MATLAB Bank format for your output. For each value $n$, list the difference of the $(1, 1)$ entries, $(AB)_{11} - I_{11}$. [Note that it is not MATLAB's fault that the inverse cannot be calculated with any accuracy. MATLAB's calculations are all done with 17-place arithmetic, but the Hilbert matrix is so sensitive that seventeen places are not enough.]

**b)** This exercise illustrates how small changes in $b$ can sometimes dramatically shift the solution of $Ax = b$ when $A$ is an ill-conditioned matrix. Let $A$ denote the $(9 \times 9)$ Hilbert matrix and let $b$ denote the $(9 \times 1)$ column vector consisting entirely of 1's. Use MATLAB to calculate the solution $u = \text{inv}(A)^*b$. Next change the fourth component of $b$ to 1.001 and let $v = \text{inv}(A)^*b$. Compare the difference between the two solution vectors $u$ and $v$; what is the largest component (in absolute value) of the difference vector $u - v$? For ease of comparison, you might form the matrix $[u, v]$ and display it using Bank format.

**c)** This exercise illustrates that different methods of solving $Ax = b$ may lead to wildly different numerical answers in the computer when $A$ is ill-conditioned. For $A$ and $b$

as in part b), compare the solution vector **u** found using the MATLAB command
u = inv(A)*b with the solution **w** found using the MATLAB command
ww = rref([A, b]). For comparison, display the matrix [**u**, **w**] using Bank
format. What is the largest component (in absolute value) of the difference vector
**u** − **w**?

**d)** To give a numerical measure for how ill conditioned a matrix is, mathematicians use
the concept of a ***condition number***. You can find the definition of the condition
number in a numerical analysis text. The condition number has many uses, one of
which is to estimate the error between a machine-calculated solution to $A\mathbf{x} = \mathbf{b}$ and
the true solution. To explain, let $\mathbf{x}_c$ denote the machine-calculated solution and let $\mathbf{x}_t$
denote the true solution. For a machine that uses $d$-place arithmetic, we can bound
the relative error between the true solution and the machine solution as follows:

$$\frac{\|\mathbf{x}_c - \mathbf{x}_t\|}{\|\mathbf{x}_t\|} \leq 10^{-d} \, \text{Cond}(A). \tag{2}$$

In inequality (2), Cond($A$) denotes the condition number. The left-hand side of the
inequality is the ***relative error*** (sometimes also called the ***percentage error***). The relative
error has the following interpretation: If the relative error is about $10^{-k}$, then the two
vectors $\mathbf{x}_c$ and $\mathbf{x}_t$ agree to about $k$ places. Thus, using inequality (2), suppose Cond($A$) is
about $10^c$ and suppose we are using MATLAB so that $d = 17$. Then the right-hand side
of inequality (2) is roughly $(10^{-17})(10^c) = 10^{-(17-c)}$. In other words, we might have as
few as $17 - c$ correct places in the computer-calculated solution (we might have more than
$17 - c$ correct places, but inequality (2) is sharp and so there will be problems for which
the inequality is nearly an equality). If $c = 14$, for instance, then we might have as few as
3 correct places in our answer.

Test inequality (2) using the ($n \times n$) Hilbert matrix for $n = 3, 4, \ldots, 9$. As the
vector **b**, use the $n$-dimensional vector consisting entirely of 1's. For a calculated solution,
use MATLAB to calculate $\mathbf{x}_c = \text{inv}(A)*\mathbf{b}$ where $A$ is the ($n \times n$) Hilbert matrix. For
this illustration we also need to determine the true solution $\mathbf{x}_t$. Now, it is known that the
Hilbert matrix has an inverse with only integer entries, see Example 6 in Section 1.9 for a
listing of the inverse of the ($6 \times 6$) Hilbert matrix. (In fact, there is a known formula giving
the entries of Hilbert matrix inverses.) Therefore, the true solution to our problem is a
vector $\mathbf{x}_t$ that has only integer entries. The calculated solution found by MATLAB can
be rounded in order to generate the true solution. Do so, using the MATLAB rounding
command: $\mathbf{x}_t$ = round($\mathbf{x}_c$). Finally, the MATLAB command cond(A) will calculate the condition number for $A$. Prepare a table listing $n$, the left-hand side of inequality
(2), and the right-hand side of inequality (2) with $d = 17$. Next, using the long format,
display several of the pairs $\mathbf{x}_c$ and $\mathbf{x}_t$ and comment on how well the order of magnitude of
the relative error compares with the number of correct places in $\mathbf{x}_c$.

# VECTORS IN 2-SPACE AND 3-SPACE

Readers already familiar with the material in this chapter
can go directly to Chapter 3 with no loss of continuity.

In this chapter we review the related concepts of physical vectors, geometric vectors, and algebraic vectors. To provide maximum geometric insight, we concentrate on vectors in two-space and three-space.

Later, in Chapter 3, we will generalize many of the ideas developed in this chapter and apply them to a study of vectors in $n$-space, that is, to vectors in $R^n$. A major emphasis in Chapter 3 is on certain fundamental ideas such as subspaces of $R^n$ and the dimension of a subspace. As we will see in Chapter 3, concepts such as subspace and dimension are directly related to the geometrically familiar notions of lines and planes in three-space.

**2.1**

# VECTORS IN THE PLANE

The word *vector* has its origins in physics where it is used to denote a quantity having both magnitude and direction—quantities such as force and velocity. In this chapter we see how matrix algebra can help us solve the problems involving vectors that arise in science and engineering.

## Three Types of Vectors

To minimize confusion, we will be careful to distinguish among three different types of vectors:

(a)   Physical vectors

(b)   Geometric vectors

(c)   Algebraic vectors

We will use the term *physical vector* when we refer to a physical quantity such as a force or a velocity.

If we want to visualize a physical vector, we can draw a directed line segment in the $xy$-plane. We will refer to such a directed line segment as a *geometric vector.*

Finally, as we will see, any geometric vector in the plane can be represented as an ordered pair. We will call such a representation an *algebraic vector.* We will use algebraic vectors when we need to make a calculation.

## Physical Vectors

Some physical quantities, such as air pressure in a tire or the weight of a metal bar, can be described by a single real number. Such quantities are called *scalar quantities.* Frequently, however, a single real number is not sufficient to describe a physical situation. For example, consider a wind blowing from the southwest toward the northeast at 10 miles per hour. This wind has both magnitude and direction and so we need two numbers to describe it.

In general, a physical quantity having both magnitude and direction is called a *vector quantity* or simply, a *vector.* Typical physical vectors are forces, displacements, velocities, and so forth.

## Geometric Vectors

We use geometric vectors to visualize a problem that involves physical vectors. For instance, consider Fig. 2.1, which shows two wires pulling on a pin. If the pin tears loose from the block, which direction will it fly?

We can visualize the problem described in Fig. 2.1 by sketching it in the $xy$-plane; see Fig. 2.2. Note in Fig. 2.2 that the directed line segment $OP$ representing the horizontal force has a length of 50. Similarly, $OQ$, which represents the other force, has a length of 90. The directed line segments (or arrows) in Fig. 2.2 are examples of geometric vectors.

In general, let $A = (a_1, a_2)$ and $B = (b_1, b_2)$ be two points in the $xy$-plane. The directed line segment from $A$ to $B$ is called a *geometric vector* and is denoted by

$$\mathbf{v} = \overrightarrow{AB}.$$

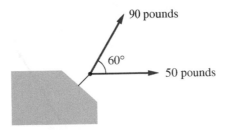

**Figure 2.1** The tension in the horizontal wire is 50 pounds, and the tension in the other wire is 90 pounds. If the pin tears loose from the block, which direction will it fly?

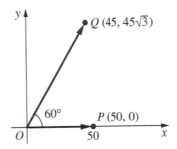

**Figure 2.2** Geometric vectors representing the physical vectors in Fig. 2.1

For a given geometric vector $\overrightarrow{AB}$, the endpoint $A$ is called the ***initial point*** and $B$ is the ***terminal point***. A geometric vector has both magnitude (its length) and direction—therefore, it is natural to represent physical vectors as geometric vectors.

## Equality of Geometric Vectors

Because we are going to use geometric vectors to represent physical vectors, we adopt the following rule:

> *All geometric vectors having the same direction and magnitude will be regarded as **equal**, regardless of whether or not they have the same endpoints.*

For example, in Fig. 2.3, the geometric vectors $\overrightarrow{AB}$, $\overrightarrow{CD}$, and $\overrightarrow{EF}$ are all equal.

We use this definition of equality for geometric vectors because it agrees with the definition of equality for physical vectors. For instance, suppose we place a brick weighing five pounds on a desk. The brick exerts the same five-pound force (directed downward) no matter where we place it on the desk. Similarly, if we move the brick from the desk and place it on the floor, it still exerts a five-pound force directed downward. In other words, the force vector does not change even if its point of application is changed.

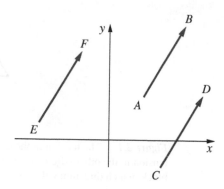

*Figure 2.3*    Even if they have different endpoints, geometric vectors are equal whenever they have the same magnitude and direction. Thus, $\overrightarrow{AB}$, $\overrightarrow{CD}$, and $\overrightarrow{EF}$ are equal geometric vectors.

Since geometric vectors represent physical vectors, we do not want them to change when they are translated in the plane.

There is a simple test for whether two geometric vectors are equal. This test is given later in Theorem 1 and is based on the idea of a *position vector*.

## Position Vectors

Let $\mathbf{v} = \overrightarrow{AB}$ be a geometric vector having initial point $A = (a_1, a_2)$ and having terminal point $B = (b_1, b_2)$; see Fig. 2.4. Among all geometric vectors $\overrightarrow{CD}$ that are equal to $\overrightarrow{AB}$, there is exactly one of the form $\mathbf{v} = \overrightarrow{OP}$ where the initial point $O = (0, 0)$ is at the origin; see Fig. 2.4. This vector $\overrightarrow{OP}$ is called the **position vector** for $\mathbf{v}$. From geometry, it follows that the terminal point $P$ has coordinates equal to $(b_1 - a_1, b_2 - a_2)$.

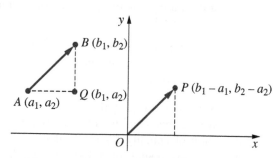

*Figure 2.4*    $\overrightarrow{OP}$ is the position vector for $\overrightarrow{AB}$. From geometry, $P$ has coordinates $(b_1 - a_1, b_2 - a_2)$.

## Components of a Vector

Let $\mathbf{v} = \overrightarrow{OP}$ be the position vector for $\mathbf{v} = \overrightarrow{AB}$. The coordinates of $P$ are called the *components* of $\mathbf{v}$. If $A = (a_1, a_2)$ and $B = (b_1, b_2)$, then we see from Fig. 2.4:

$$\text{The } x\text{-component of } \overrightarrow{AB} \text{ is } b_1 - a_1 \tag{1a}$$

$$\text{The } y\text{-component of } \overrightarrow{AB} \text{ is } b_2 - a_2 \tag{1b}$$

**EXAMPLE 1**   Let $A = (7, 3)$ and $B = (2, 5)$. Find the components of $\mathbf{v} = \overrightarrow{AB}$.

**Solution**   By (1), the $x$-component of $\overrightarrow{AB}$ is $2 - 7 = -5$. Similarly, the $y$-component of $\overrightarrow{AB}$ is $5 - 3 = 2$. (In terms of Fig. 2.4, the position vector $\overrightarrow{OP}$ has its terminal point given by $P = (-5, 2)$.)   ◼

## An Equality Test for Geometric Vectors

As we see from the following theorem, two geometric vectors are equal if and only if they have the same components.

**THEOREM 1**   Let $\overrightarrow{AB}$ and $\overrightarrow{CD}$ be geometric vectors. Then $\overrightarrow{AB} = \overrightarrow{CD}$ if and only if their components are equal.

**Proof**   If two geometric vectors are equal, then they have the same position vector; hence, they have the same components. On the other hand, if two geometric vectors have the same components, then they have the same position vector; hence, they are equal.   ◼

The following example illustrates Theorem 1.

**EXAMPLE 2**   Let $A = (2, 2)$, $B = (4, 5)$, $C = (3, -2)$, and $D = (5, 1)$. Use Theorem 1 to show that $\overrightarrow{AB} = \overrightarrow{CD}$.

**Solution**   Calculating $x$-components, we have

> **For $\overrightarrow{AB}$:**   $b_1 - a_1 = 4 - 2 = 2$
>
> **For $\overrightarrow{CD}$:**   $d_1 - c_1 = 5 - 3 = 2.$

Similarly, calculating $y$-components, we find

> **For $\overrightarrow{AB}$:**   $b_2 - a_2 = 5 - 2 = 3$
>
> **For $\overrightarrow{CD}$:**   $d_2 - c_2 = 1 - (-2) = 3.$

Since both vectors have the same components, Theorem 1 tells us they are equal.   ◼

If we know the components of a geometric vector $\mathbf{v}$, then it is easy to draw $\mathbf{v}$ using any desired initial point or terminal point. For example, suppose we know that $\mathbf{v}$ has an $x$-component $v_1$ and a $y$-component $v_2$. Suppose we want to represent $\mathbf{v}$ as the directed line segment $\overrightarrow{AB}$, where $A = (a_1, a_2)$. The terminal point $B$ is found by moving $v_1$ units in the $x$ direction and then $v_2$ units in the $y$ direction. In other words

$$B = (a_1 + v_1, a_2 + v_2). \qquad (2)$$

If we want to specify the terminal point $B$, a similar calculation is used to find the initial point $A$; see part (**b**) of the next example.

**EXAMPLE 3** A geometric vector **v** has $x$-component 3 and $y$-component $-5$.

    (**a**)   If we want to represent **v** in the form $\mathbf{v} = \overrightarrow{AB}$ where $A = (1, 2)$, what are the coordinates of the terminal point $B$?

    (**b**)   If we want to represent **v** in the form $\mathbf{v} = \overrightarrow{CD}$ where $D = (5, 7)$, what are the coordinates of the initial point $C$?

*Solution*

    (**a**)   By (2), the coordinates of $B$ are $(1 + 3, 2 + (-5)) = (4, -3)$; see Fig. 2.5.

    (**b**)   Given the coordinates of the terminal point $D$, we find the initial point $C$ by moving "backward"; that is, see Fig. 2.5,

$$C = (5 - v_1, 7 - v_2) = (5 - 3, 7 - (-5)) = (2, 12).$$

## Algebraic Vectors

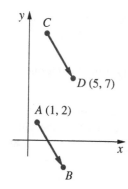

Let **v** be a geometric vector with $x$-component $v_1$ and $y$-component $v_2$. Figure 2.6 shows $\overrightarrow{OP}$, the position vector for **v**, where

$$P = (v_1, v_2).$$

Since **v** is completely characterized by its components, it is natural to associate **v** with the algebraic vector

$$\mathbf{v} = \begin{bmatrix} v_1 \\ v_2 \end{bmatrix}.$$

**Figure 2.5**
A geometric vector **v** has $x$-component 3 and $y$-component $-5$. In Example 3 we saw how to draw **v** with initial point $A$ and how to draw **v** with terminal point $D$.

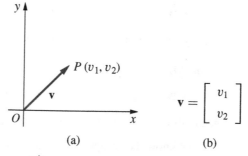

(a)                      (b)

**Figure 2.6**   (a) $\overrightarrow{OP}$ is the position vector for **v**; the *coordinates* of $P$ are equal to the components of **v**. (b) In the algebraic representation for **v**, the *entries* of the column vector are the components of **v**.

The connection between a geometric vector $\mathbf{v} = \overrightarrow{AB}$ and its algebraic representation

$$\mathbf{v} = \begin{bmatrix} v_1 \\ v_2 \end{bmatrix}$$

is so close that we will not distinguish between the two. We simply use the term *vector* to refer to either representation. Each representation for $\mathbf{v}$ has its own advantages. The geometric representation allows us to draw diagrams as an aid for our intuition. On the other hand, the algebraic representation is very efficient when we need to make mathematical calculations.

Table 2.1 summarizes the relationship between geometric vectors and algebraic vectors.

**Table 2.1**

---

(a) Let $\mathbf{v} = \overrightarrow{AB}$ be a geometric vector, with $A = (a_1, a_2)$ and $B = (b_1, b_2)$. Then $\mathbf{v}$ can be represented by the algebraic vector

$$\mathbf{v} = \begin{bmatrix} b_1 - a_1 \\ b_2 - a_2 \end{bmatrix}.$$

(b) Let $\mathbf{v} = \begin{bmatrix} v_1 \\ v_2 \end{bmatrix}$. Given $A = (a_1, a_2)$, $\mathbf{v}$ can be represented as the geometric vector $\overrightarrow{AB}$ where the terminal point $B$ is given by

$$B = (a_1 + v_1, a_2 + v_2).$$

---

## EXAMPLE 4

(a) Let $\mathbf{v} = \overrightarrow{AB}$ where $A = (1, 5)$ and $B = (3, 2)$. Represent $\mathbf{v}$ as an algebraic vector.

(b) Let $\mathbf{u} = \begin{bmatrix} 4 \\ 7 \end{bmatrix}$. Represent $\mathbf{u}$ as a geometric vector with initial point $C = (5, -2)$.

*Solution*

(a) Using part (a) of Table 2.1,

$$\mathbf{v} = \begin{bmatrix} 2 \\ -3 \end{bmatrix}.$$

(b) Using part (b) of Table 2.1, $\mathbf{u} = \overrightarrow{CD}$ where $D = (5 + 4, -2 + 7) = (9, 5)$. ■

## Adding Physical Vectors

As you might recall from your physics or statics courses, physical vectors (forces, displacements, velocities, and so forth) can be summed.

For instance, consider Fig. 2.7 which shows two forces, $\mathbf{F}_1$ and $\mathbf{F}_2$, applied at the same point $A$. We know from physics that the net effect of applying these two forces is exactly the same as applying a single force $\mathbf{F}$. This single force $\mathbf{F}$ is called the ***resultant force*** and can be calculated by adding $\mathbf{F}_1$ and $\mathbf{F}_2$ according to the rules for adding geometric vectors.

*Figure 2.7*
The net effect of the two forces $\mathbf{F}_1$ and $\mathbf{F}_2$ is the same as the effect of the single resultant force $\mathbf{F}$. The resultant force $\mathbf{F}$ can be calculated using the rules for adding geometric vectors.

## Adding Geometric Vectors

You are familiar with the rules for adding geometric vectors from your physics courses. We review those rules now.

As in Fig. 2.8(a), let $\mathbf{u}$ and $\mathbf{v}$ be geometric vectors. The ***sum***, denoted by $\mathbf{u} + \mathbf{v}$, is the geometric vector found as follows [see Fig. 2.8(b)]:

**(a)**    Translate $\mathbf{v}$ so that its initial point coincides with the terminal point of $\mathbf{u}$.

**(b)**    Then, $\mathbf{u} + \mathbf{v}$ is the geometric vector having the same initial point as $\mathbf{u}$ and the same terminal point as the translated vector $\mathbf{v}$.

As will be shown shortly, it does not matter which vector is translated—we can move $\mathbf{v}$ to the tip of $\mathbf{u}$ as in Fig. 2.8(b), or we can move $\mathbf{u}$ to the tip of $\mathbf{v}$. We will always get the same sum, $\mathbf{u} + \mathbf{v}$, in either case.

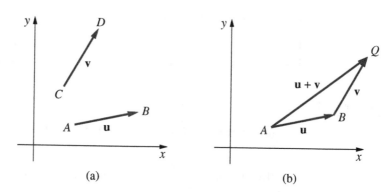

*Figure 2.8*    (a) $\mathbf{u}$ and $\mathbf{v}$ are geometric vectors. (b) The sum $\mathbf{u} + \mathbf{v}$ is formed by translating $\mathbf{v}$ so that its initial point is at the terminal point of $\mathbf{u}$.

The next example illustrates vector addition. The example also suggests that we can use algebraic vectors to calculate the sum of geometric vectors.

EXAMPLE 5    Let $\mathbf{u} = \overrightarrow{AB}$ where $A = (1, 2)$ and $B = (4, 6)$; see Fig. 2.9. Let $\mathbf{v} = \overrightarrow{CD}$ where $C = (-4, 3)$ and $D = (-2, 1)$. Find the sum $\mathbf{u} + \mathbf{v}$.

***Solution*** In Fig. 2.9(b) we translate $\mathbf{v}$ so that its initial point is at $B = (4, 6)$. As can be seen, the terminal point of $\mathbf{v}$ is now at $Q = (6, 4)$. Thus, we see that the sum $\mathbf{u} + \mathbf{v}$ is given by $\mathbf{u} + \mathbf{v} = \overrightarrow{AQ}$.

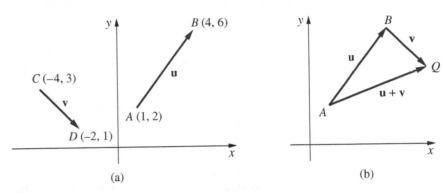

***Figure 2.9*** Forming the sum $\mathbf{u} + \mathbf{v}$, see Example 5

If we examine the geometric construction used in Fig. 2.9, we see that the coordinates of $Q$ are found by adding the *components* of $\mathbf{v}$ to the *coordinates* of $B$. Therefore, Fig. 2.9 suggests that we can use algebraic vectors to calculate vector sums; this idea is stated formally below, in Theorem 2.

## Using Algebraic Vectors to Calculate the Sum of Geometric Vectors

The following theorem shows that we can find the components of $\mathbf{u} + \mathbf{v}$ by adding their corresponding algebraic vector representations. In words: the components of the sum are the sums of the components.

THEOREM 2    Let $\mathbf{u}$ and $\mathbf{v}$ be geometric vectors with algebraic representations given by $\mathbf{u} = \begin{bmatrix} u_1 \\ u_2 \end{bmatrix}$ and $\mathbf{v} = \begin{bmatrix} v_1 \\ v_2 \end{bmatrix}$. Then the sum $\mathbf{u} + \mathbf{v}$ has the following algebraic representation:

$$\mathbf{u} + \mathbf{v} = \begin{bmatrix} u_1 + v_1 \\ u_2 + v_2 \end{bmatrix}.$$

***Proof*** The proof is based on Fig. 2.8 where $\mathbf{u} = \overrightarrow{AB}$. Let $A = (a_1, a_2)$ and let $B = (b_1, b_2)$. Note that, $\mathbf{u} + \mathbf{v} = \overrightarrow{AQ}$ where $Q = (b_1 + v_1, b_2 + v_2)$. Therefore, the components of $\mathbf{u} + \mathbf{v} = \overrightarrow{AQ}$ are:

***The x-component:***    $(b_1 + v_1) - a_1 = (b_1 - a_1) + v_1 = u_1 + v_1$

***The y-component:***    $(b_2 + v_2) - a_2 = (b_2 - a_2) + v_2 = u_2 + v_2.$

EXAMPLE 6    Let $\mathbf{u} = \overrightarrow{AB}$ where $A = (-3, 1)$ and $B = (2, 8)$. Let $\mathbf{v} = \overrightarrow{CD}$ where $C = (1, 3)$ and $D = (4, 7)$.

(a)    Use Theorem 2 to find the components of $\mathbf{u} + \mathbf{v}$.

(b)    Find $S$ so that $\mathbf{u} + \mathbf{v} = \overrightarrow{RS}$ when the initial point is $R = (-1, 1)$.

**Solution**

(a)    As algebraic vectors, $\mathbf{u} = \begin{bmatrix} 2 - (-3) \\ 8 - 1 \end{bmatrix} = \begin{bmatrix} 5 \\ 7 \end{bmatrix}$ and $\mathbf{v} = \begin{bmatrix} 4 - 1 \\ 7 - 3 \end{bmatrix} = \begin{bmatrix} 3 \\ 4 \end{bmatrix}$. Therefore, the components of $\mathbf{u} + \mathbf{v}$ are found from $\mathbf{u} + \mathbf{v} = \begin{bmatrix} 5 \\ 7 \end{bmatrix} + \begin{bmatrix} 3 \\ 4 \end{bmatrix} = \begin{bmatrix} 8 \\ 11 \end{bmatrix}$.

(b)    Having the components of $\mathbf{u} + \mathbf{v}$ we see that the terminal point $S$ is given by $S = (-1 + 8, 1 + 11) = (7, 12)$.    ◼

## Scalar Multiplication

Suppose you initially push on an object with a certain force, but later decide you need to push twice as hard in the same direction. Let $\mathbf{u} = \overrightarrow{OP}$ be the position vector representing the first force, where $P = (u_1, u_2)$. Let $\mathbf{v} = \overrightarrow{OQ}$ represent the second force (see Fig. 2.10). Since $\mathbf{u}$ and $\mathbf{v}$ are in the same direction, $Q$ must be on the line through $O$ and $P$. But, since the second force $\mathbf{v}$ is twice as strong, the line segment $OQ$ is twice as long as the segment $OP$ (again, see Fig. 2.10). Thus, the coordinates of $Q$ are twice that of the coordinates of $P$; that is, $Q = (v_1, v_2) = (2u_1, 2u_2)$.

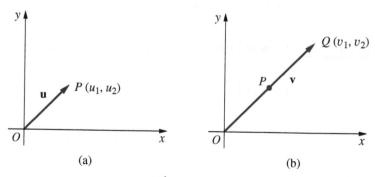

**Figure 2.10**    The vector $\mathbf{v} = \overrightarrow{OQ}$ is twice as long as the vector $u = \overrightarrow{OP}$. We will write $\mathbf{v} = 2\mathbf{u}$.

Interpreting Fig. 2.10 in terms of algebraic vectors, we have

$$\mathbf{v} = \begin{bmatrix} v_1 \\ v_2 \end{bmatrix} = \begin{bmatrix} 2u_1 \\ 2u_2 \end{bmatrix} = 2\mathbf{u}.$$

The rules for forming the scalar multiple of a geometric vector are suggested by Fig. 2.10. In particular, let $\mathbf{u} = \overrightarrow{AB}$ be a geometric vector and let $c$ denote a scalar. The *scalar multiple*, denoted $c\mathbf{u}$, is defined as follows:

**(a)** If $c > 0$, then $c\mathbf{u}$ is the geometric vector having the same direction as $\mathbf{u}$, but with a magnitude that is $c$ times as large.

**(b)** If $c < 0$, then $c\mathbf{u}$ is the geometric vector having the opposite direction as $\mathbf{u}$, but with a magnitude that is $c$ times as large.

The definition of scalar multiplication is illustrated in Fig. 2.11.

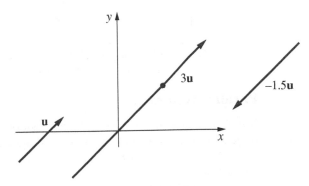

*Figure 2.11*    The vector $3\mathbf{u}$ is three times as long as $\mathbf{u}$, in the same direction. The vector $-1.5\mathbf{u}$ is 1.5 times as long as $\mathbf{u}$, but is in the opposite direction.

Theorem 2 shows how to use algebraic vectors to calculate the components of the sum, $\mathbf{u} + \mathbf{v}$. As might be expected from Fig. 2.11, a similar result holds for scalar multiplication.

THEOREM 3    Let $\mathbf{u}$ be a geometric vector with algebraic representation

$$\mathbf{u} = \begin{bmatrix} u_1 \\ u_2 \end{bmatrix}.$$

Then the scalar multiple $c\mathbf{u}$ has the following algebraic representation:

$$c\mathbf{u} = \begin{bmatrix} cu_1 \\ cu_2 \end{bmatrix}.$$

## Subtracting Geometric Vectors

Having defined the scalar multiple of a geometric vector, we are ready to define the difference, $\mathbf{u} - \mathbf{v}$, of two vectors. We define vector subtraction as follows:

$$\mathbf{u} - \mathbf{v} = \mathbf{u} + (-1)\mathbf{v}.$$

Vector addition and vector subtraction are often visualized in terms of the diagonals of a parallelogram; see Fig. 2.12.

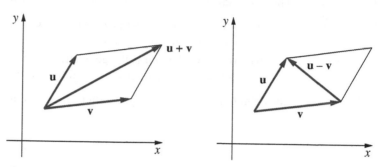

*Figure 2.12*    The parallelogram determined by **u** and **v** has one diagonal equal to **u** + **v** and the other equal to **u** − **v**.

## Parallel Vectors

If $c \neq 0$, then **u** and $c$**u** have collinear position vectors and we say they are "parallel." In general, vectors **u** and **v** are *parallel* if there is a nonzero scalar $c$ such that $\mathbf{v} = c\mathbf{u}$. If $c > 0$, we say **u** and **v** have the *same direction* but if $c < 0$, we say **u** and **v** have the *opposite direction*.

To determine whether vectors are parallel, it is easier to use the algebraic representation than the geometric representation. The next example illustrates this fact.

EXAMPLE 7    Let $\mathbf{u} = \overrightarrow{AB}$ and $\mathbf{v} = \overrightarrow{CD}$ where $A = (1, 2)$, $B = (3, 5)$, $C = (1, 7)$, and $D = (-3, 1)$. Show that **u** and **v** are parallel vectors. Does **v** have the same direction or the opposite direction as **u**?

*Solution*    The algebraic representations for **u** and **v** are (respectively)

$$\mathbf{u} = \begin{bmatrix} 3 - 1 \\ 5 - 2 \end{bmatrix} = \begin{bmatrix} 2 \\ 3 \end{bmatrix} \quad \text{and} \quad \mathbf{v} = \begin{bmatrix} -3 - 1 \\ 1 - 7 \end{bmatrix} = \begin{bmatrix} -4 \\ -6 \end{bmatrix}.$$

We see that $\mathbf{v} = -2\mathbf{u}$. Hence **v** is parallel to **u**, and has the opposite direction.    ■

## Lengths of Vectors and Unit Vectors

The length or magnitude of a geometric vector $\mathbf{u} = \overrightarrow{AB}$ is the length of the line segment joining $A$ and $B$. Therefore, from analytic geometry, the length of $\mathbf{u} = \overrightarrow{AB}$ is equal to

$$\sqrt{(u_1)^2 + (u_2)^2} = \sqrt{(b_1 - a_1)^2 + (b_2 - a_2)^2}.$$

As in Section 1.7, we use the symbol $\|\mathbf{u}\|$, read as the *norm of u*, to denote the length of **u**:

$$\text{If } \mathbf{u} = \begin{bmatrix} u_1 \\ u_2 \end{bmatrix}, \quad \text{then} \quad \|\mathbf{u}\| = \sqrt{(u_1)^2 + (u_2)^2}.$$

If a vector **w** has length equal to 1, we say that **w** is a *unit vector*. That is, **w** is a *unit vector* if and only if

$$\|\mathbf{w}\| = 1.$$

For example, the following vector **w** is a unit vector

$$\mathbf{w} = \begin{bmatrix} 0.6 \\ 0.8 \end{bmatrix}.$$

We often use a unit vector to specify *direction*. In particular, if **u** is any nonzero vector, then Eq. (3) gives a formula for a unit vector **w** in the same direction as **u**,

$$\mathbf{w} = \frac{1}{\|\mathbf{u}\|}\mathbf{u}. \qquad (3)$$

In Exercise 40 we ask you to verify that the vector **w** defined in Eq. (3) is indeed a unit vector. Then, because **w** is a positive scalar multiple of **u**, it will follow that **w** is a unit vector in the direction of **u**. (Similarly, the vector −**w** is a unit vector in the direction opposite to **u**.)

EXAMPLE 8   Find a vector **v** having the opposite direction as $\mathbf{u} = \begin{bmatrix} 1 \\ 7 \end{bmatrix}$ and where $\|\mathbf{v}\| = 10$.

*Solution*   We first choose a unit vector **w** in the direction we want (opposite the direction of **u**) and then multiply **w** by 10 to produce the desired vector **v**. Now, $\|\mathbf{u}\| = \sqrt{50}$. Therefore, using (3), a unit vector **w** having the same direction as **u** is given by

$$\mathbf{w} = \frac{1}{\|\mathbf{u}\|}\mathbf{u} = \frac{1}{\sqrt{50}}\begin{bmatrix} 1 \\ 7 \end{bmatrix}.$$

Since **w** has the same direction as **u**, we know −**w** is a unit vector in the direction opposite **u**. Multiplying −**w** by 10 will produce the vector **v** asked for in this example:

$$\mathbf{v} = -10\mathbf{w} = -\frac{10}{\sqrt{50}}\begin{bmatrix} 1 \\ 7 \end{bmatrix} = -\frac{10}{5\sqrt{2}}\begin{bmatrix} 1 \\ 7 \end{bmatrix} = -\sqrt{2}\begin{bmatrix} 1 \\ 7 \end{bmatrix}. \qquad \blacksquare$$

## The Basic Vectors i and j

Let $\mathbf{u} = \begin{bmatrix} u_1 \\ u_2 \end{bmatrix}$ be a vector. Then:

$$\mathbf{u} = \begin{bmatrix} u_1 \\ u_2 \end{bmatrix} = \begin{bmatrix} u_1 \\ 0 \end{bmatrix} + \begin{bmatrix} 0 \\ u_2 \end{bmatrix} = u_1\begin{bmatrix} 1 \\ 0 \end{bmatrix} + u_2\begin{bmatrix} 0 \\ 1 \end{bmatrix} = u_1\mathbf{i} + u_2\mathbf{j} \qquad (4)$$

where the special vectors **i** and **j** are defined by

$$\mathbf{i} = \begin{bmatrix} 1 \\ 0 \end{bmatrix} \quad \text{and} \quad \mathbf{j} = \begin{bmatrix} 0 \\ 1 \end{bmatrix}.$$

As you can see, the vectors **i** and **j** are unit vectors; they are shown in Fig. 2.13. From Eq. (4) we see that **i** and **j** are *basic* in the sense that any vector **u** can be formed by adding a scalar multiple of **i** to a scalar multiple of **j**.

**Figure 2.13**
The unit vector **i** is parallel to the *x*-axis; **j** is parallel to the *y*-axis.

EXAMPLE 9    Let $\mathbf{u} = 2\mathbf{i} - 4\mathbf{j}$ and $\mathbf{v} = \mathbf{i} + 6\mathbf{j}$. Find the components of $\mathbf{w} = 2\mathbf{u} + \mathbf{v}$.

**Solution**    We find

$$\mathbf{w} = 2(2\mathbf{i} - 4\mathbf{j}) + (\mathbf{i} + 6\mathbf{j}) = 5\mathbf{i} - 2\mathbf{j} = 5\begin{bmatrix} 1 \\ 0 \end{bmatrix} - 2\begin{bmatrix} 0 \\ 1 \end{bmatrix} = \begin{bmatrix} 5 \\ -2 \end{bmatrix}. \quad \blacksquare$$

## 2.1    EXERCISES

In Exercises 1–4, graph the geometric vectors $\mathbf{u} = \overrightarrow{AB}$ and $\mathbf{v} = \overrightarrow{CD}$. Determine by inspection whether the two vectors are equal; then use Theorem 1 to verify your answers.

1. $A = (0, -2)$,    $B = (-4, 3)$,    $C = (1, 2)$,
   $D = (-3, 7)$

2. $A = (-1, 3)$,    $B = (3, -2)$,    $C = (5, -1)$,
   $D = (1, 4)$

3. $A = (-4, -2)$,    $B = (0, 1)$,    $C = (0, -2)$,
   $D = (3, 2)$

4. $A = (3, 1)$,    $B = (-1, 1)$,    $C = (0, 3)$,
   $D = (-6, 0)$

5. Let $\mathbf{u} = \overrightarrow{AB}$ and $\mathbf{v} = \overrightarrow{CD}$ where $A = (-3, 5)$, $B = (2, 2)$, $C = (3, 4)$, $D = (-2, 7)$.

   a) Verify that $\mathbf{u}$ and $\mathbf{v}$ have the same length.
   b) Verify that the line segments $AB$ and $CD$ have the same slope.
   c) Use Theorem 1 to show that $\mathbf{u} \neq \mathbf{v}$.
   d) Graph $\mathbf{u}$ and $\mathbf{v}$ and use the graph to explain why $\mathbf{u} \neq \mathbf{v}$.

In Exercises 6–9, find the unspecified coordinates so that $\overrightarrow{AB} = \overrightarrow{CD}$.

6. $A = (-1, -3)$,    $B = (3, 2)$,    $C = (0, 2)$,
   $D = (d_1, d_2)$

7. $A = (3, -2)$,    $B = (0, 3)$,    $C = (1, 0)$,
   $D = (d_1, d_2)$

8. $A = (-2, 3)$,    $B = (2, -1)$,    $C = (c_1, c_2)$,
   $D = (3, 2)$

9. $A = (3, -2)$,    $B = (3, 4)$,    $C = (c_1, c_2)$,
   $D = (-1, 7)$

10. A force of 10 pounds is directed from left to right along a line at an angle of 30° (measured clockwise) from the horizontal. Represent this force as a geo-

metric vector $\overrightarrow{OP}$ where $O = (0, 0)$. Sketch a graph of $\overrightarrow{OP}$.

In Exercises 11–14, express the geometric vector $\mathbf{v} = \overrightarrow{AB}$ as an algebraic vector $\mathbf{v} = \begin{bmatrix} v_1 \\ v_2 \end{bmatrix}$.

11. $A = (-1, -2)$,    $B = (4, 1)$

12. $A = (1, 3)$,    $B = (6, -1)$

13. $A = (2, -1)$,    $B = (-4, 4)$

14. $A = (3, 2)$,    $B = (0, -2)$

In Exercises 15–16, find $B = (b_1, b_2)$ such that $\mathbf{v} = \overrightarrow{AB}$.

15. $\mathbf{v} = \begin{bmatrix} 2 \\ 5 \end{bmatrix}$    and    $A = (1, -2)$

16. $\mathbf{v} = \begin{bmatrix} -3 \\ 4 \end{bmatrix}$    and    $A = (2, -2)$

In Exercises 17–18, find $A = (a_1, a_2)$ such that $\mathbf{v} = \overrightarrow{AB}$.

17. $\mathbf{v} = \begin{bmatrix} 3 \\ -3 \end{bmatrix}$    and    $B = (5, 1)$

18. $\mathbf{v} = \begin{bmatrix} -4 \\ -1 \end{bmatrix}$    and    $B = (-4, 2)$

19. Let $\mathbf{u} = \begin{bmatrix} 1 \\ 3 \end{bmatrix}$ and $\mathbf{v} = \begin{bmatrix} 2 \\ -2 \end{bmatrix}$, and let $A$ denote the point $(2, -1)$.

   a) Find points $B$ and $C$ such that $\mathbf{u} = \overrightarrow{AB}$, $\mathbf{v} = \overrightarrow{BC}$ and $\mathbf{u} + \mathbf{v} = \overrightarrow{AC}$.
   b) Graph $\mathbf{u} = \overrightarrow{AB}$, $\mathbf{v} = \overrightarrow{BC}$ and $\mathbf{u} + \mathbf{v} = \overrightarrow{AC}$.

**20.** Repeat Exercise 19 for $\mathbf{u} = \begin{bmatrix} -2 \\ 4 \end{bmatrix}$ and $\mathbf{v} = \begin{bmatrix} 3 \\ 1 \end{bmatrix}$ and $A = (0, -1)$.

**21.** Let $\mathbf{u} = \overrightarrow{AB}$ and $\mathbf{v} = \overrightarrow{CD}$, where $A = (-1, 2)$, $B = (3, 5)$, $C = (0, 3)$, $D = (4, -1)$.

  **a)** Find a point $Q$ such that $\mathbf{v} = \overrightarrow{BQ}$ and $\mathbf{u} + \mathbf{v} = \overrightarrow{AQ}$.

  **b)** Graph $\mathbf{u} = \overrightarrow{AB}$, $\mathbf{v} = \overrightarrow{CD}$, $\mathbf{v} = \overrightarrow{BQ}$, and $\mathbf{u} + \mathbf{v} = \overrightarrow{AQ}$.

**22.** Repeat Exercise 21 with $A = (-2, 4)$, $B = (1, -3)$, $C = (0, 1)$, $D = (3, 5)$.

**23.** Let $\mathbf{u} = \begin{bmatrix} 1 \\ 3 \end{bmatrix}$ and $\mathbf{v} = \begin{bmatrix} 2 \\ -2 \end{bmatrix}$, and let $A$ denote the point $(-2, 1)$.

  **a)** Find points $B$ and $C$ such that $\mathbf{u} = \overrightarrow{AB}$, $\mathbf{v} = \overrightarrow{AC}$, and $\mathbf{u} - \mathbf{v} = \overrightarrow{CB}$.

  **b)** Graph $\mathbf{u} = \overrightarrow{AB}$, $\mathbf{v} = \overrightarrow{AC}$, and $\mathbf{u} - \mathbf{v} = \overrightarrow{CB}$.

**24.** Let $\mathbf{u} = \overrightarrow{AB}$ and $\mathbf{v} = \overrightarrow{CD}$ where $A = (-1, 2)$, $B = (3, 5)$, $C = (0, 3)$, $D = (4, -1)$.

  **a)** Find a point $Q$ such that $\mathbf{v} = \overrightarrow{AQ}$ and $\mathbf{u} - \mathbf{v} = \overrightarrow{QB}$.

  **b)** Graph $\mathbf{u} = \overrightarrow{AB}$, $\mathbf{v} = \overrightarrow{CD}$, $\mathbf{v} = \overrightarrow{AQ}$, and $\mathbf{u} - \mathbf{v} = \overrightarrow{QB}$.

**25.** Let $\mathbf{v} = \begin{bmatrix} 3 \\ -2 \end{bmatrix}$ and $A = (0, 5)$.

  **a)** Find points $B$ and $C$ such that $\mathbf{v} = \overrightarrow{AB}$ and $2\mathbf{v} = \overrightarrow{AC}$.

  **b)** Graph $\mathbf{v} = \overrightarrow{AB}$ and $2\mathbf{v} = \overrightarrow{AC}$.

**26.** Let $\mathbf{v} = 2\mathbf{i} + 6\mathbf{j}$ and $A = (-2, 1)$.

  **a)** Find points $B$ and $C$ such that $\mathbf{v} = \overrightarrow{AB}$ and $\left(\dfrac{-1}{2}\right)\mathbf{v} = \overrightarrow{AC}$.

  **b)** Graph $\mathbf{v} = \overrightarrow{AB}$ and $\left(\dfrac{-1}{2}\right)\mathbf{v} = \overrightarrow{AC}$.

**27.** Let $\mathbf{v} = \overrightarrow{AB}$ where $A = (1, 4)$ and $B = (5, -1)$.

  **a)** If $C = (-2, 7)$, find $D$ such that $2\mathbf{v} = \overrightarrow{CD}$.

  **b)** Graph $\mathbf{v} = \overrightarrow{AB}$ and $2\mathbf{v} = \overrightarrow{CD}$.

In Exercises 28–31, find a unit vector $\mathbf{u}$ that has the same direction as the given vector $\mathbf{v}$.

**28.** $\mathbf{v} = \begin{bmatrix} -1 \\ 2 \end{bmatrix}$      **29.** $\mathbf{v} = \begin{bmatrix} 3 \\ 4 \end{bmatrix}$

**30.** $\mathbf{v} = \mathbf{i} + \mathbf{j}$      **31.** $\mathbf{v} = 3\mathbf{i} - 2\mathbf{j}$

In Exercises 32–35, determine the terminal point $B$ such that $\mathbf{v} = \overrightarrow{AB}$.

**32.** $\mathbf{v}$ has the same direction as $\begin{bmatrix} 2 \\ 1 \end{bmatrix}$, $\|\mathbf{v}\| = 4\sqrt{5}$, $A = (-4, -2)$.

**33.** $\mathbf{v}$ has opposite direction to $\begin{bmatrix} 1 \\ 3 \end{bmatrix}$, $\|\mathbf{v}\| = 3\sqrt{10}$, $A = (4, 7)$.

**34.** $\mathbf{v}$ is parallel to $\mathbf{i} + 2\mathbf{j}$, $A = (3, 1)$, $B$ is on the $y$-axis.

**35.** $\mathbf{v}$ is parallel to $\mathbf{i} + 3\mathbf{j}$, $A = (3, 1)$, $B$ is on the line $y = -7$.

In Exercises 36–39, find the components of $\mathbf{u} + \mathbf{v}$ and $\mathbf{u} - 3\mathbf{v}$.

**36.** $\mathbf{u} = \begin{bmatrix} 1 \\ 1 \end{bmatrix}$, $\mathbf{v} = \begin{bmatrix} 1 \\ 2 \end{bmatrix}$

**37.** $\mathbf{u} = \begin{bmatrix} 0 \\ 5 \end{bmatrix}$, $\mathbf{v} = \begin{bmatrix} 2 \\ -1 \end{bmatrix}$

**38.** $\mathbf{u} = \mathbf{i} + 2\mathbf{j}$, $\mathbf{v} = \mathbf{i} - \mathbf{j}$

**39.** $\mathbf{u} = 2\mathbf{i} - \mathbf{j}$, $\mathbf{v} = 2\mathbf{i} + 2\mathbf{j}$

**40.** Let $\mathbf{u} = \begin{bmatrix} a \\ b \end{bmatrix}$ where at least one of $a$ or $b$ is nonzero and set $\mathbf{w} = \dfrac{1}{\|\mathbf{u}\|}\|\mathbf{u}\|$. Verify that $\|\mathbf{w}\| = 1$.

## VECTORS IN SPACE

So far, our study has focused on vectors in the plane, that is, on two-dimensional problems. But, since we live and work in a three-dimensional world, we need to extend vector concepts to three dimensions. As we know, a vector is a quantity that has both direction and magnitude. In order to discuss direction and magnitude in three dimensions, it is convenient to have a coordinate system for three-dimensional space.

### Coordinate Axes in Three Space

**Figure 2.14**
The rectangular axis system consists of three mutually perpendicular axes that meet at the origin, $O$.

There are a number of different coordinate systems we can use in three-dimensional space—for airline navigation we might use a system of geographical coordinates (latitude, longitude, and altitude). The system we introduce here is called the ***rectangular coordinate system*** or the ***Cartesian coordinate system.*** It is a direct generalization of the familiar $xy$-coordinate system for the plane.

We begin with three mutually perpendicular axes, called the $x$-axis, the $y$-axis, and the $z$-axis. We require that these axes intersect at a point designated as the ***origin,*** $O$; see Fig. 2.14.

### The Right-Hand Rule

When the coordinate axes are oriented as in Fig. 2.14, the coordinate system is called a ***right-handed*** system. If the $x$-axis and $y$-axis are interchanged, the system is a ***left-handed*** system. The orientation of the right-handed system can be remembered with the ***right-hand rule***:

> *If the fingers of the right-hand are pointed in the direction of the positive $x$-axis and curled in the direction of the positive $y$-axis, then the thumb points in the direction of the positive $z$-axis.*

We will see the right-hand rule again when we study the cross product of two vectors.

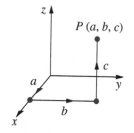

**Figure 2.15**
The point $P$ has rectangular coordinates $(a, b, c)$.

### Rectangular Coordinates for Points in Three Space

Let $P$ denote a point in space. We can locate $P$ by moving a directed distance of $a$ units along the $x$-axis, then $b$ units along the $y$-axis, and then $c$ units along the $z$-axis; see Fig. 2.15. When the point $P$ is located in this fashion, we say that $P$ has coordinates $(a, b, c)$.

The plane containing the $x$ and $y$ axes is called the ***xy-plane.*** Similarly, the ***yz-plane*** contains the $y$ and $z$ axes and the ***xz-plane*** contains the $x$ and $z$ axes. Collectively, these planes are known as the ***coordinate planes.*** The coordinate planes divide three space into eight subregions called ***octants.*** The ***rst octant*** consists of all points $P = (a, b, c)$ where $a > 0$, $b > 0$, and $c > 0$. The other seven octants are usually not given numbers.

**EXAMPLE 1**    Graph the points $P = (2, 3, 2)$ and $Q = (1, -2, 1)$.

**Solution**    The points $P$ and $Q$ are shown in Fig. 2.16.

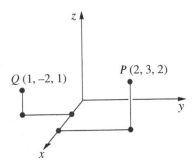

***Figure 2.16***    The points $P = (2, 3, 2)$ and $Q = (1, -2, 1)$; see Example 1.

EXAMPLE 2    Describe the graph of the equation $z = 2$ in three space.

*Solution*    In three space, the graph of $z = 2$ consists of all points that have coordinates of the form $(x, y, 2)$, where $x$ and $y$ are arbitrary. Thus, the graph of $z = 2$ can be viewed as the $xy$-plane translated up 2 units; see Fig. 2.17.

***Figure 2.17***    The graph of the equation $z = 2$; see Example 2

## The Distance Formula

Consider a geometric vector $\mathbf{u} = \overrightarrow{AB}$ in the plane. The magnitude of $\mathbf{u}$ is found by measuring the distance between the endpoints, $A$ and $B$. Similarly, to define the magnitude of a vector in three space, we will need a formula for the distance between two points in space. A formula for the distance between two points in space is given by Theorem 4.

THEOREM 4    Let $P = (p_1, p_2, p_3)$ and $Q = (q_1, q_2, q_3)$ be two points in three space. The distance between $P$ and $Q$, denoted by $d(P, Q)$, is given by

$$d(P, Q) = \sqrt{(q_1 - p_1)^2 + (q_2 - p_2)^2 + (q_3 - p_3)^2}.$$

*Proof*    The proof follows from Fig. 2.18, after two applications of the Pythagorean formula. We ask you to supply the details in Exercise 17.

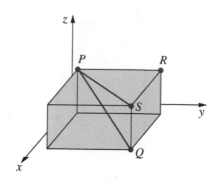

*Figure 2.18*     The triangle *PRS* is in a plane. The Pythagorean theorem gives the length of *PS*. Similarly, the triangle *PSQ* is in a plane and we can use the Pythagorean theorem to find the length of *PQ*.

EXAMPLE 3     Find $d(P, Q)$ where $P = (3, 2, -4)$ and $Q = (1, -1, 2)$.

*Solution*     By Theorem 4,

$$d(P, Q) = \sqrt{(1-3)^2 + ((-1) - 2)^2 + (2 - (-4))^2} = \sqrt{49} = 7.$$

## The Midpoint Formula

Now that we have the distance formula, it is easy to develop a formula for the midpoint of a line segment. The formula is given in Theorem 5.

THEOREM 5     Let $P = (p_1, p_2, p_3)$ and $Q = (q_1, q_2, q_3)$ be two points in three space. Let $M$ denote the midpoint of the line segment joining $P$ and $Q$. Then, $M$ is given by

$$M = \left( \frac{p_1 + q_1}{2}, \frac{p_2 + q_2}{2}, \frac{p_3 + q_3}{2} \right).$$

*Proof*     We leave the proof to the reader—it requires you to establish that $d(P, M) = d(Q, M)$.

EXAMPLE 4     Find the midpoint, $M$, of the line segment joining the points $P = (3, 2, -4)$ and $Q = (1, -6, 2)$.

*Solution*     By the midpoint formula, we find

$$M = \left( \frac{3 + 1}{2}, \frac{2 - 6}{2}, \frac{-4 + 2}{2} \right) = (2, -2, -1).$$

## Geometric Vectors and Their Components

The vector concepts from two dimensions can be extended directly to three dimensions. The next few subsections briefly describe the extension. As we did in the plane, we can represent physical vectors in three dimensions by a directed line segment $\mathbf{v} = \overrightarrow{AB}$. This directed line segment is called a **geometric vector**. The length of the line segment represents the magnitude of the physical vector and the orientation of the line segment represents the direction of the physical vector.

Let $\mathbf{v} = \overrightarrow{AB}$ be a geometric vector with **initial point** $A = (a_1, a_2, a_3)$ and **terminal point** $B = (b_1, b_2, b_3)$. The **components** of $\mathbf{v} = \overrightarrow{AB}$ are defined for three-dimensional vectors just as they are for two-dimensional vectors. In particular:

The $x$-component of $\overrightarrow{AB}$ is $b_1 - a_1$.

The $y$-component of $\overrightarrow{AB}$ is $b_2 - a_2$.

The $z$-component of $\overrightarrow{AB}$ is $b_3 - a_3$.

As before, two geometric vectors are **equal** if they have the same components. Among all geometric vectors $\mathbf{v} = \overrightarrow{CD}$ that are equal to $\mathbf{v} = \overrightarrow{AB}$, there is exactly one of the form $\mathbf{v} = \overrightarrow{OP}$ whose initial point is at the origin. The vector $\mathbf{v} = \overrightarrow{OP}$ is the **position vector** for $\mathbf{v}$. Because $\overrightarrow{OP}$ and $\overrightarrow{AB}$ are equal, we know that $P = (b_1 - a_1, b_2 - a_2, b_3 - a_3)$.

## Algebraic Vectors

Since all geometric vectors equal to $\mathbf{v} = \overrightarrow{AB}$ have the same position vector, we use the following **algebraic vector** to represent $\overrightarrow{AB}$ (as in two dimensions, the **components** of $\mathbf{v}$ are the **coordinates** of $P$):

$$\mathbf{v} = \begin{bmatrix} b_1 - a_1 \\ b_2 - a_2 \\ b_3 - a_3 \end{bmatrix}. \tag{1}$$

EXAMPLE 5    Let $A = (1, -1, 2)$ and $B = (2, 1, 3)$.

    **(a)**   Represent $\mathbf{v} = \overrightarrow{AB}$ as an algebraic vector.

    **(b)**   For $C = (2, 2, 1)$, find the point $D$ such that $\mathbf{v} = \overrightarrow{CD}$.

**Solution**

    **(a)**   Using formula (1), we have

$$\mathbf{v} = \begin{bmatrix} 2 - 1 \\ 1 - (-1) \\ 3 - 2 \end{bmatrix} = \begin{bmatrix} 1 \\ 2 \\ 1 \end{bmatrix}.$$

**(b)** To find the terminal point $D$, we add the components of $\mathbf{v}$ to the coordinates of the initial point $C$. Thus, $D = (2+1, 2+2, 1+1) = (3, 4, 2)$. ◼

## Addition and Scalar Multiplication for Vectors

There is an *addition* and a *scalar multiplication* defined for geometric vectors in three space. These operations are defined exactly as they are for geometric vectors in the plane.

For instance, we find the geometric vector $\mathbf{u} + \mathbf{v}$ by translating $\mathbf{v}$ so that its initial point is at the terminal point of $\mathbf{u}$—the initial point of $\mathbf{u} + \mathbf{v}$ is the initial point of $\mathbf{u}$ while the terminal point of $\mathbf{u} + \mathbf{v}$ is the terminal point of the translated vector $\mathbf{v}$.

As with geometric vectors in the plane, these geometric operations are easily performed using algebraic representations; see Theorem 6.

### THEOREM 6

**(a)** Let $\mathbf{u} = \overrightarrow{AB}$ and $\mathbf{v} = \overrightarrow{CD}$. The algebraic representation for the geometric vector $\mathbf{u} + \mathbf{v}$ is:

$$\mathbf{u} + \mathbf{v} = \begin{bmatrix} u_1 \\ u_2 \\ u_3 \end{bmatrix} + \begin{bmatrix} v_1 \\ v_2 \\ v_3 \end{bmatrix} = \begin{bmatrix} u_1 + v_1 \\ u_2 + v_2 \\ u_3 + v_3 \end{bmatrix}.$$

**(b)** Let $\mathbf{u} = \overrightarrow{AB}$ and let $c$ be a scalar. The algebraic representation for the geometric vector $c\mathbf{u}$ is:

$$c\mathbf{u} = c \begin{bmatrix} u_1 \\ u_2 \\ u_3 \end{bmatrix} = \begin{bmatrix} cu_1 \\ cu_2 \\ cu_3 \end{bmatrix}. \qquad ◼$$

## Parallel Vectors, Lengths of Vectors, and Unit Vectors

As before, if $\mathbf{u} = c\mathbf{v}$ for some nonzero scalar $c$, we say $\mathbf{u}$ is *parallel* to $\mathbf{v}$. If $c$ is positive, then $\mathbf{u}$ has the *same direction* as $\mathbf{v}$. If $c$ is negative, then $\mathbf{u}$ has the *opposite direction* as $\mathbf{v}$.

Let $\mathbf{u}$ be given by

$$\mathbf{u} = \begin{bmatrix} u_1 \\ u_2 \\ u_3 \end{bmatrix}.$$

The *length* of $\mathbf{u}$ (or the *norm* of $\mathbf{u}$) is defined to be:

$$\|\mathbf{u}\| = \sqrt{(u_1)^2 + (u_2)^2 + (u_3)^2}.$$

If a vector $\mathbf{w}$ has length equal to 1, we say $\mathbf{w}$ is a *unit vector.*

In applications we often need to calculate a unit vector in the direction of a given vector. This is an easy task. In particular, given a vector $\mathbf{u}$, the following vector $\mathbf{w}$ is a unit vector in the same direction as **u**:

$$\mathbf{w} = \frac{1}{\|\mathbf{u}\|}\mathbf{u}. \tag{2}$$

If we need a vector **v** having a given length, $m$, and in the same direction as a given vector **u**, we can find **v** with the following formula derived from Eq. (2).

$$\mathbf{v} = m\left(\frac{1}{\|\mathbf{u}\|}\mathbf{u}\right). \tag{3}$$

**EXAMPLE 6**    Find a vector of length 7 in the direction opposite $\mathbf{u} = \begin{bmatrix} 1 \\ 2 \\ 2 \end{bmatrix}$.

*Solution*    A calculation shows $\|\mathbf{u}\| = 3$. Therefore, a unit vector in the direction of **u** is given by

$$\mathbf{w} = \frac{1}{3}\begin{bmatrix} 1 \\ 2 \\ 2 \end{bmatrix} = \begin{bmatrix} 1/3 \\ 2/3 \\ 2/3 \end{bmatrix}.$$

The vector $-\mathbf{w}$ is a unit vector in the direction we are interested in (since $-\mathbf{w}$ is opposite **u**). Thus, the vector **v** we seek is given by $\mathbf{v} = -7\mathbf{w}$:

$$\mathbf{v} = -7\mathbf{w} = \begin{bmatrix} -7/3 \\ -14/3 \\ -14/3 \end{bmatrix}.$$

### The Basic Unit Vectors in Three Space

In three space, the basic unit vectors are denoted **i**, **j**, and **k**. In particular, **i** is along the $x$-axis, **j** is along the $y$-axis, and **k** is along the $z$-axis. These vectors are

$$\mathbf{i} = \begin{bmatrix} 1 \\ 0 \\ 0 \end{bmatrix}, \quad \mathbf{j} = \begin{bmatrix} 0 \\ 1 \\ 0 \end{bmatrix}, \quad \mathbf{k} = \begin{bmatrix} 0 \\ 0 \\ 1 \end{bmatrix}.$$

A given vector $\mathbf{u} = \begin{bmatrix} u_1 \\ u_2 \\ u_3 \end{bmatrix}$ can be expressed in terms of these basic unit vectors:

$$\mathbf{u} = u_1\mathbf{i} + u_2\mathbf{j} + u_3\mathbf{k}.$$

**EXAMPLE 7**    Let $\mathbf{u} = 2\mathbf{i} - \mathbf{j} + 3\mathbf{k}$ and $\mathbf{v} = 6\mathbf{i} + 4\mathbf{j} + \mathbf{k}$. Find a unit vector in the direction of $\mathbf{u} - \mathbf{v}$.

**Solution**  The vector $\mathbf{u} - \mathbf{v}$ is given by $\mathbf{u} - \mathbf{v} = -4\mathbf{i} - 5\mathbf{j} + 2\mathbf{k} = \begin{bmatrix} -4 \\ -5 \\ 2 \end{bmatrix}$. The length of $\mathbf{u} - \mathbf{v}$

is $\sqrt{45} = 3\sqrt{5}$. Thus a unit vector in the direction of $\mathbf{u} - \mathbf{v}$ is

$$\mathbf{w} = \frac{1}{\|\mathbf{u} - \mathbf{v}\|}(\mathbf{u} - \mathbf{v}) = \frac{1}{3\sqrt{5}}\begin{bmatrix} -4 \\ -5 \\ 2 \end{bmatrix}.$$

## 2.2    EXERCISES

In Exercises 1–4, plot the points $P$ and $Q$ and determine $d(P, Q)$.

**1.** $P = (1, 2, 1)$,    $Q = (0, 2, 2)$

**2.** $P = (1, 1, 0)$,    $Q = (0, 0, 1)$

**3.** $P = (1, 0, 0)$,    $Q = (0, 0, 1)$

**4.** $P = (1, 1, 1)$,    $Q = (0, 0, 0)$

In Exercises 5–6, find the coordinates of the segment $PQ$. Calculate the distance from the midpoint to the origin.

**5.** $P = (2, 3, 1)$,    $Q = (0, 5, 7)$

**6.** $P = (1, 0, 3)$,    $Q = (3, 2, 5)$

**7.** Let $A = (-1, 0, -3)$ and $E = (3, 6, 3)$. Find points $B$, $C$, and $D$ on the line segment $AE$ such that $d(A, B) = d(B, C) = d(C, D) = d(D, E) = \frac{1}{4}d(A, E)$.

In Exercises 8–12, identify the given set of points in space as being a plane or a line.

**8.** $\{(x, y, z) : z = 4\}$

**9.** $\{(x, y, z) : x = 4, y = 2\}$

**10.** $\{(x, y, z) : x = y = z\}$

**11.** $\{(x, y, z) : y = 2\}$

**12.** The set of all points equidistant from $(5, 0, 0)$ and $(0, 5, 0)$.

In Exercises 13–16, graph the given region $R$.

**13.** $R = \{(x, y, z) : |x| \le 1, |y| \le 2, |z| \le 3\}$

**14.** $R = \{(x, y, z) : 0 \le x \le 1, 0 \le y \le 2, z = 2\}$

**15.** $R = \{(x, y, z) : 0 \le x \le 1, 0 \le y \le 2x, 0 \le z \le 1\}$

**16.** $R = \{(x, y, z) : 0 \le x, 0 \le y, x + y \le 1,$

$0 \le z \le 1\}$

**17.** Let $P = (p_1, p_2, p_3)$ and $Q = (q_1, q_2, q_3)$ be two points in space. As in Fig. 2.18, let $R = (p_1, q_2, p_3)$ and $S = (q_1, q_2, p_3)$.

**a)** Apply the Pythagorean theorem to the triangle $PRS$ to show that

$$d(P, S) = \sqrt{(q_1 - p_1)^2 + (q_2 - p_2)^2}.$$

**b)** Apply the Pythagorean theorem to the triangle $PSQ$ to establish the distance formula,

$$d(P, Q) = \sqrt{(q_1 - p_1)^2 + (q_2 - p_2)^2 + (q_3 - p_3)^2}.$$

In Exercises 18–21, (a) give the algebraic representation for $\mathbf{v} = \overrightarrow{AB}$; (b) for $C = (-1, 2, 1)$, find $D$ such that $\mathbf{v} = \overrightarrow{CD}$.

**18.** $A = (2, 0, 7)$, $B = (0, 3, 4)$

**19.** $A = (-1, 2, 3)$, $B = (2, 4, 0)$

**20.** $A = (2, 4, 0)$, $B = (-1, 2, 3)$

**21.** $A = (1, -2, 4)$, $B = (1, 3, -3)$

In Exercises 22–25, determine a point $A$ such that $\mathbf{v} = \overrightarrow{AB}$ where $B = (4, 3, 2)$.

**22.** $\mathbf{v} = \begin{bmatrix} 0 \\ 3 \\ 2 \end{bmatrix}$        **23.** $\mathbf{v} = \begin{bmatrix} 1 \\ 1 \\ 1 \end{bmatrix}$

**24.** $\mathbf{v} = 2\mathbf{j}$        **25.** $\mathbf{v} = 6\mathbf{i} + 3\mathbf{k}$

In Exercises 26–29, find: (a) $\mathbf{u} + 2\mathbf{v}$; (b) $\|\mathbf{u} - \mathbf{v}\|$; (c) a vector $\mathbf{w}$ such that $\mathbf{u} + 2\mathbf{w} = \mathbf{v}$.

**26.** $\mathbf{u} = \begin{bmatrix} 1 \\ 3 \\ 2 \end{bmatrix}$,    $\mathbf{v} = \begin{bmatrix} 4 \\ 3 \\ 6 \end{bmatrix}$

**27.** $\mathbf{u} = \begin{bmatrix} 1 \\ 3 \\ 2 \end{bmatrix}$, $\mathbf{v} = \begin{bmatrix} 3 \\ 2 \\ 4 \end{bmatrix}$

**28.** $\mathbf{u} = 9\mathbf{i} - 3\mathbf{j} + 2\mathbf{k}$, $\mathbf{v} = \mathbf{i} + \mathbf{k}$

**29.** $\mathbf{u} = -5\mathbf{i} + 7\mathbf{j}$, $\mathbf{v} = 2\mathbf{i} - 3\mathbf{j} + \mathbf{k}$

In Exercises 30–35, determine a vector $\mathbf{u}$ that satisfies the given conditions.

**30.** $\mathbf{u}$ has the same direction as $\mathbf{v} = \mathbf{i} + \mathbf{j}$ and $\|\mathbf{u}\| = \sqrt{8}$.

**31.** $\mathbf{u}$ has the same direction as $\mathbf{v} = \mathbf{k}$ and $\|\mathbf{u}\| = 2$.

**32.** $\mathbf{u}$ has opposite direction to $\mathbf{v} = \begin{bmatrix} 1 \\ 0 \\ 1 \end{bmatrix}$ and $\|\mathbf{u}\| = \sqrt{32}$.

**33.** $\mathbf{u}$ has opposite direction to $\mathbf{v} = \begin{bmatrix} -1 \\ 2 \\ 2 \end{bmatrix}$ and $\|\mathbf{u}\| = 5$.

**34.** $\mathbf{u}$ is parallel to $\mathbf{v} = \begin{bmatrix} 1 \\ 2 \\ 0 \end{bmatrix}$ and $\mathbf{u} = \overrightarrow{AB}$ where

$A = (1, 1, 1)$ and $B$ is in the $xz$-plane.

**35.** $\mathbf{u}$ is parallel to $\mathbf{v} = \begin{bmatrix} 4 \\ 8 \\ 2 \end{bmatrix}$ and $\mathbf{u} = \overrightarrow{AB}$ where

$A = (1, 1, 1)$ and $B$ is in the $xy$-plane.

# THE DOT PRODUCT AND THE CROSS PRODUCT

Applications such as calculating the work done by a force often require us to determine the angle between two geometric vectors. Figure 2.19 shows the angle $\theta$ between two vectors $\mathbf{u}$ and $\mathbf{v}$. As we will see, $\theta$ can be found using the *dot product,* one of the topics of this section.

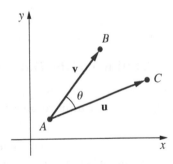

*Figure 2.19*    When geometric vectors $\mathbf{u}$ and $\mathbf{v}$ are translated to have the same initial point, we can measure the angle $\theta$ between them.

### The Dot Product of Two Vectors

To find the angle $\theta$ in Fig. 2.19, we consider the triangle $ABC$ and interpret the vectors $\mathbf{v} = \overrightarrow{AB}$, $\mathbf{u} = \overrightarrow{AC}$, and $\mathbf{u} - \mathbf{v} = \overrightarrow{BC}$ as the sides of $ABC$ (see Fig. 2.20).

Applying the **Law of Cosines** to the triangle in Fig. 2.20, we obtain

$$\|\mathbf{u} - \mathbf{v}\|^2 = \|\mathbf{u}\|^2 + \|\mathbf{v}\|^2 - 2\|\mathbf{u}\|\|\mathbf{v}\| \cos\theta. \tag{1}$$

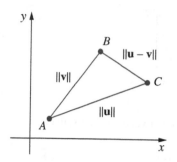

*Figure 2.20*    The sides of the triangle $ABC$ can be interpreted in terms of the lengths of $\mathbf{u}$, $\mathbf{v}$, and $\mathbf{u} - \mathbf{v}$.

To solve (1) for $\cos\theta$, let $\mathbf{u}$ and $\mathbf{v}$ be given by

$$\mathbf{u} = \begin{bmatrix} u_1 \\ u_2 \end{bmatrix}, \quad \mathbf{v} = \begin{bmatrix} v_1 \\ v_2 \end{bmatrix}.$$

If we insert $\mathbf{u}$ and $\mathbf{v}$ into Eq. (1) and simplify, we obtain

$$u_1 v_1 + u_2 v_2 = \|\mathbf{u}\|\|\mathbf{v}\|\cos\theta. \tag{2a}$$

Solving Eq. (2a) for $\cos\theta$, we arrive at

$$\cos\theta = \frac{u_1 v_1 + u_2 v_2}{\|\mathbf{u}\|\|\mathbf{v}\|}.$$

If we now take the inverse cosine of the above expression, we will have the angle $\theta$. The numerator of the above expression is called the ***dot product*** of $\mathbf{u}$ and $\mathbf{v}$. (For $\theta$ to be defined, both $\mathbf{u}$ and $\mathbf{v}$ must be *nonzero* vectors.)

## The Definition of the Dot Product

Although it is a bit more complicated, the calculations leading from Eq. (1) to Eq. (2a) can be carried out in three dimensions as well. In fact, Eq. (2a) becomes (in three dimensions)

$$u_1 v_1 + u_2 v_2 + u_3 v_3 = \|\mathbf{u}\|\|\mathbf{v}\|\cos\theta. \tag{2b}$$

The left-hand side of (2b) defines the dot product in three space. In general,

---

DEFINITION 1

**(a)** If $\mathbf{u}$ and $\mathbf{v}$ are two-dimensional vectors, then the ***dot product*** of $\mathbf{u}$ and $\mathbf{v}$, denoted $\mathbf{u} \cdot \mathbf{v}$, is defined by

$$\mathbf{u} \cdot \mathbf{v} = u_1 v_1 + u_2 v_2.$$

**(b)** If $\mathbf{u}$ and $\mathbf{v}$ are three-dimensional vectors, then

$$\mathbf{u} \cdot \mathbf{v} = u_1 v_1 + u_2 v_2 + u_3 v_3.$$

(*Note:* We actually introduced the dot product (or scalar product) for $n$-dimensional vectors in Section 1.6. In that section we defined the dot product as

$$\mathbf{u}^T\mathbf{v}.$$

Of course, these two definitions are exactly the same in two dimensions or three dimensions. In this chapter, however, we will use the "dot" notation, $\mathbf{u} \cdot \mathbf{v}$, that is customary in the study of geometric vectors rather than $\mathbf{u}^T\mathbf{v}$.)

## The Angle Between Two Vectors

We use the dot product notation to summarize Eq. (2a) and (2b).

**THEOREM 7**   Let $\mathbf{u}$ and $\mathbf{v}$ be two nonzero vectors in the plane or in three space. If $\theta$ denotes the angle between $\mathbf{u}$ and $\mathbf{v}$, then

$$\mathbf{u} \cdot \mathbf{v} = \|\mathbf{u}\|\,\|\mathbf{v}\| \cos\theta.$$

The next example illustrates the use of Theorem 7.

**EXAMPLE 1**   Let $\mathbf{u} = \begin{bmatrix} 1 \\ 3 \\ -2 \end{bmatrix}$ and $\mathbf{v} = \begin{bmatrix} 4 \\ -1 \\ -3 \end{bmatrix}$.

    **(a)**   Calculate $\mathbf{u} \cdot \mathbf{v}$.

    **(b)**   Using Theorem 7, find the angle between $\mathbf{u}$ and $\mathbf{v}$.

*Solution*

    **(a)**   The number $\mathbf{u} \cdot \mathbf{v}$ is given by

$$\mathbf{u} \cdot \mathbf{v} = (1)(4) + (3)(-1) + (-2)(-3) = 4 - 3 + 6 = 7.$$

    **(b)**   Solving for $\cos\theta$ in Theorem 7, we have

$$\cos\theta = \frac{\mathbf{u} \cdot \mathbf{v}}{\|\mathbf{u}\|\,\|\mathbf{v}\|} = \frac{7}{\sqrt{14}\sqrt{26}} = \frac{7}{\sqrt{364}} = 0.366899\ldots.$$

Taking the inverse cosine, we find $\theta = 1.1951\ldots$ radians ($68.4755\ldots$ degrees).

## Algebraic Properties of the Dot Product

The following theorem lists some of the algebraic properties of the dot product.

**THEOREM 8**   Let $\mathbf{u}$, $\mathbf{v}$, and $\mathbf{w}$ denote vectors in space or in the plane, and let $c$ denote a scalar. Then:

    **(a)**  $\mathbf{u} \cdot \mathbf{u} \geq 0$

    **(b)**  $\mathbf{u} \cdot \mathbf{v} = \mathbf{v} \cdot \mathbf{u}$

(c)   $\mathbf{u} \cdot (c\mathbf{v}) = c(\mathbf{u} \cdot \mathbf{v})$

(d)   $\mathbf{u} \cdot (\mathbf{v} + \mathbf{w}) = \mathbf{u} \cdot \mathbf{v} + \mathbf{u} \cdot \mathbf{w}$

We leave the verification of Theorem 8 to the exercises.

## Orthogonal Vectors

Let $\mathbf{u}$ and $\mathbf{v}$ be nonzero vectors and let $\theta$ denote the angle between them. When $\theta = \pi/2$, we say that $\mathbf{u}$ and $\mathbf{v}$ are *perpendicular* or *orthogonal*. By Theorem 7, we see that $\mathbf{u}$ and $\mathbf{v}$ are orthogonal if and only if

$$\mathbf{u} \cdot \mathbf{v} = 0.$$

In the plane, the basic unit vectors $\mathbf{i}$ and $\mathbf{j}$ are orthogonal. In three space, the basic unit vectors $\mathbf{i}$, $\mathbf{j}$, and $\mathbf{k}$ are mutually orthogonal. The next example also illustrates the concept of orthogonality.

EXAMPLE 2    Consider the vectors

$$\mathbf{u} = \begin{bmatrix} 2 \\ -3 \\ 7 \end{bmatrix}, \quad \mathbf{v} = \begin{bmatrix} 1 \\ 3 \\ 1 \end{bmatrix} \quad \text{and} \quad \mathbf{w} = \begin{bmatrix} 3 \\ 2 \\ 0 \end{bmatrix}.$$

Show that $\mathbf{u}$ is orthogonal to both $\mathbf{v}$ and $\mathbf{w}$, but that $\mathbf{v}$ and $\mathbf{w}$ are not orthogonal.

*Solution*    Forming dot products, we find

$$\mathbf{u} \cdot \mathbf{v} = (2)(1) + (-3)(3) + (7)(1) = 2 - 9 + 7 = 0$$
$$\mathbf{u} \cdot \mathbf{w} = (2)(3) + (-3)(2) + (7)(0) = 6 - 6 + 0 = 0$$
$$\mathbf{v} \cdot \mathbf{w} = (1)(3) + (3)(2) + (1)(0) = 3 + 6 + 0 = 9.$$

Thus, $\mathbf{u}$ and $\mathbf{v}$ are orthogonal; $\mathbf{u}$ and $\mathbf{w}$ are orthogonal; but $\mathbf{v}$ and $\mathbf{w}$ are not orthogonal.

## Projections

In applications it is often necessary to express a given vector $\mathbf{u}$ in the form

$$\mathbf{u} = \mathbf{v} + \mathbf{w}$$

where

(a)   The vector $\mathbf{v}$ is parallel to a given nonzero vector $\mathbf{q}$.

(b)   The vector $\mathbf{w}$ is orthogonal to $\mathbf{q}$.

As an example, consider Fig. 2.21, illustrating a block on an inclined plane. In Fig. 2.21, the downward directed force $\mathbf{u}$ is the weight of the block. As you can see, the force $\mathbf{u}$ has been expressed as the sum of two forces:

$$\mathbf{u} = \mathbf{v} + \mathbf{w}.$$

The force $\mathbf{v}$ is normal (perpendicular) to the inclined plane and because of friction it tends to hold the block stationary on the plane. The force $\mathbf{w}$ is tangential to the inclined

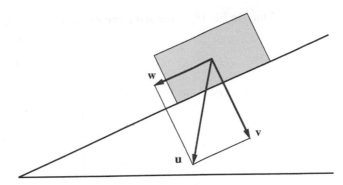

*Figure 2.21*    The vector **u** represents the weight of the block. We want to express **u** in the form **u** = **v** + **w** where **v** is normal to the plane and **w** is parallel to the plane.

plane and because of gravitational forces it tends to make the block slide downward. The relative magnitudes of **v** and **w** (along with the frictional characteristics of the block and the plane) determine whether the block remains stationary or slides.

The situation shown in Fig. 2.21 is a special case of the general problem we discuss next. The general problem is illustrated in Fig. 2.22. As you can see, Fig. 2.22 shows a given vector **u** and a given direction defined by the vector **q**. The vector **v** shown in Fig. 2.22 is parallel to **q** and is called the ***projection of* u *onto* q**. For notation, we write

$$\mathbf{v} = proj_{\mathbf{q}}(\mathbf{u}) \qquad \text{(read as "v is the projection of u onto q").}$$

*Figure 2.22*    The vector **v** is called the projection of **u** onto **q**.

## Calculating the Projection

To calculate the projection **v** shown in Fig. 2.22, we first write **v** as

$$\mathbf{v} = \|\mathbf{v}\| \left( \frac{\mathbf{q}}{\|\mathbf{q}\|} \right).$$

Next, from Fig. 2.22, we see that $\|\mathbf{v}\| = \|\mathbf{u}\| \cos \theta$, and thus we have

$$\mathbf{v} = \|\mathbf{u}\| \cos \theta \left( \frac{\mathbf{q}}{\|\mathbf{q}\|} \right). \tag{3}$$

If we know the angle $\theta$, then Eq. (3) gives us the projection. In certain applications, especially in three dimensions, we might need to use the dot product to find the term $\cos \theta$ that appears in Eq. (3). In such an event, recall from Theorem 7 that $\mathbf{u} \cdot \mathbf{q} = \|\mathbf{u}\| \|\mathbf{q}\| \cos \theta$.

Thus, in Eq. (3), we can replace $\|\mathbf{u}\| \cos\theta$ by $\mathbf{u} \cdot \mathbf{q}/\|\mathbf{q}\|$, finding

$$\mathbf{v} = \frac{\mathbf{u} \cdot \mathbf{q}}{\|\mathbf{q}\|}\left(\frac{\mathbf{q}}{\|\mathbf{q}\|}\right). \tag{4}$$

**EXAMPLE 3**    Find $\mathbf{v} = proj_{\mathbf{q}}(\mathbf{u})$ for the vectors

$$\mathbf{u} = \begin{bmatrix} 2 \\ 1 \\ -3 \end{bmatrix} \quad \text{and} \quad \mathbf{q} = \begin{bmatrix} 1 \\ 0 \\ 2 \end{bmatrix}.$$

*Solution*    According to Eq. (4),

$$\mathbf{v} = \frac{\mathbf{u} \cdot \mathbf{q}}{\|\mathbf{q}\|}\left(\frac{\mathbf{q}}{\|\mathbf{q}\|}\right) = \frac{-4}{\sqrt{5}}\left(\frac{\mathbf{q}}{\sqrt{5}}\right) = \frac{-4}{5}\begin{bmatrix} 1 \\ 0 \\ 2 \end{bmatrix} = \begin{bmatrix} -0.8 \\ 0 \\ -1.6 \end{bmatrix}.$$

(a)

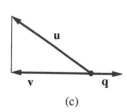

(b)

(c)

Depending on the relative magnitudes of $\mathbf{q}$ and $\mathbf{u}$, the projection of $\mathbf{u}$ onto $\mathbf{q}$ might be longer than $\mathbf{q}$ or shorter than $\mathbf{q}$; see Fig. 2.23. Also, depending on the relative directions of $\mathbf{u}$ and $\mathbf{q}$, the projection of $\mathbf{u}$ onto $\mathbf{q}$ might be in the same direction as $\mathbf{q}$ or it might have the opposite direction; see Fig. 2.23. Although formula (4) was derived from Fig. 2.22, it is valid as well for the configurations shown in Fig. 2.23(b)–(c).

## Expressing u as the Sum of Two Orthogonal Vectors

We began our discussion of projections with the important problem of expressing $\mathbf{u}$ in the form $\mathbf{u} = \mathbf{v} + \mathbf{w}$ where $\mathbf{v}$ is parallel to $\mathbf{q}$ and $\mathbf{w}$ is orthogonal to $\mathbf{q}$. Eq. (4) gives us a formula for $\mathbf{v}$ and we see from Fig. 2.24 that $\mathbf{w} = \mathbf{u} - \mathbf{v}$ is indeed orthogonal to $\mathbf{q}$. That is, the decomposition we sought has the form

$$\mathbf{u} = \mathbf{v} + \mathbf{w} = proj_{\mathbf{q}}(\mathbf{u}) + (\mathbf{u} - proj_{\mathbf{q}}(\mathbf{u})). \tag{5}$$

**Figure 2.23**
The projection of $\mathbf{u}$ onto $\mathbf{q}$ might be shorter or longer than $\mathbf{q}$ and might have the same or opposite direction as $\mathbf{q}$.

**Figure 2.24**    Here, $\mathbf{u} = \mathbf{v} + \mathbf{w}$. The vector $\mathbf{v}$ is the projection of $\mathbf{u}$ along $\mathbf{q}$. The vector $\mathbf{w} = \mathbf{u} - \mathbf{v}$ is orthogonal to $\mathbf{q}$, by construction.

**EXAMPLE 4**    Let $\mathbf{u} = \begin{bmatrix} 4 \\ -2 \\ 3 \end{bmatrix}$ and $\mathbf{q} = \begin{bmatrix} 3 \\ 0 \\ 1 \end{bmatrix}$. Express $\mathbf{u}$ in the form $\mathbf{u} = \mathbf{v} + \mathbf{w}$ where $\mathbf{u}$ is parallel to $\mathbf{q}$ and $\mathbf{w}$ is orthogonal to $\mathbf{q}$; see Eq. (5).

*Solution*  We first calculate the projection **v** as in Example 3:

$$\mathbf{v} = \frac{\mathbf{u} \cdot \mathbf{q}}{\|\mathbf{q}\|}\left(\frac{\mathbf{q}}{\|\mathbf{q}\|}\right) = \frac{15}{\sqrt{10}}\left(\frac{\mathbf{q}}{\sqrt{10}}\right) = \frac{15}{10}\begin{bmatrix} 3 \\ 0 \\ 1 \end{bmatrix} = \begin{bmatrix} 4.5 \\ 0 \\ 1.5 \end{bmatrix}.$$

Then, $\mathbf{w} = \mathbf{u} - \mathbf{v} = \begin{bmatrix} 4 \\ -2 \\ 3 \end{bmatrix} - \begin{bmatrix} 4.5 \\ 0 \\ 1.5 \end{bmatrix} = \begin{bmatrix} -0.5 \\ -2 \\ 1.5 \end{bmatrix}$ . As we see, **v** is parallel

to **q** since $\mathbf{v} = 1.5\mathbf{q}$, **w** is orthogonal to **q**, and $\mathbf{u} = \mathbf{v} + \mathbf{w}$. ◼

## The Cross Product

To introduce the cross product, let us consider the problem stated below and illustrated in Fig. 2.25.

> **Problem:** *Given nonzero vectors* **u** *and* **v** *in three space, find a vector* **w** *that is orthogonal to both* **u** *and* **v**.

A solution to this problem is the *cross product vector*, the topic of the remainder of this section.

**Figure 2.25**
Given vectors **u** and **v** in three space, how do we find a vector **w** that is orthogonal to **u** and to **v**?

## Derivation of the Cross Product

To solve the problem posed in Fig. 2.25, let $\mathbf{u} = \begin{bmatrix} u_1 \\ u_2 \\ u_3 \end{bmatrix}$ and $\mathbf{v} = \begin{bmatrix} v_1 \\ v_2 \\ v_3 \end{bmatrix}$ . We want

a nonzero vector $\mathbf{w} = \begin{bmatrix} x \\ y \\ z \end{bmatrix}$ such that $\mathbf{w} \cdot \mathbf{u} = 0$ and $\mathbf{w} \cdot \mathbf{v} = 0$. In terms of the com-

ponents of **u**, **v**, and **w**, the orthogonality conditions lead to a system of two equations in three unknowns:

$$u_1 x + u_2 y + u_3 z = 0$$
$$v_1 x + v_2 y + v_3 z = 0.$$

The system above is homogeneous and has more unknowns than equations. Thus, we know the system always has nonzero solutions (see Theorem 4 in Section 1.3). In the exercises, we ask you to show that one nonzero solution is

$$x = u_2 v_3 - u_3 v_2, \qquad y = u_3 v_1 - u_1 v_3, \qquad z = u_1 v_2 - u_2 v_1. \tag{6}$$

The vector **w** having components (6) is called the **cross product** of **u** and **v**.

## The Definition of the Cross Product

Drawing on the derivation above, we are led to the following definition.

DEFINITION 2

Let $\mathbf{u} = \begin{bmatrix} u_1 \\ u_2 \\ u_3 \end{bmatrix}$ and $\mathbf{v} = \begin{bmatrix} v_1 \\ v_2 \\ v_3 \end{bmatrix}$ be vectors in three space. The **cross product** of $\mathbf{u}$ and $\mathbf{v}$, denoted by $\mathbf{u} \times \mathbf{v}$, is the vector given by

$$\mathbf{u} \times \mathbf{v} = \begin{bmatrix} u_2 v_3 - u_3 v_2 \\ u_3 v_1 - u_1 v_3 \\ u_1 v_2 - u_2 v_1 \end{bmatrix}.$$

The next example illustrates a typical cross product calculation.

EXAMPLE 5     Find $\mathbf{u} \times \mathbf{v}$ for $\mathbf{u} = \begin{bmatrix} 2 \\ 1 \\ 3 \end{bmatrix}$ and $\mathbf{v} = \begin{bmatrix} 1 \\ -3 \\ 4 \end{bmatrix}$. Verify that the cross product vector is orthogonal to both $\mathbf{u}$ and $\mathbf{v}$.

*Solution*     Using Definition 2, we find the cross product vector

$$\mathbf{u} \times \mathbf{v} = \begin{bmatrix} (1)(4) - (3)(-3) \\ (3)(1) - (2)(4) \\ (2)(-3) - (1)(1) \end{bmatrix} = \begin{bmatrix} 13 \\ -5 \\ -7 \end{bmatrix}.$$

Calculating shows that $(\mathbf{u} \times \mathbf{v}) \cdot \mathbf{u} = 0$ and $(\mathbf{u} \times \mathbf{v}) \cdot \mathbf{v} = 0$.

## Using Determinants to Remember the Form of the Cross Product

We can use a "symbolic determinant" to help us remember the cross product. (A detailed discussion of determinants can be found in Chapters 4 and 6. Many people, however, will recall seeing $(2 \times 2)$ and $(3 \times 3)$ determinants in their high school algebra courses.) The cross product can be remembered as

$$\mathbf{u} \times \mathbf{v} = \begin{vmatrix} \mathbf{i} & \mathbf{j} & \mathbf{k} \\ u_1 & u_2 & u_3 \\ v_1 & v_2 & v_3 \end{vmatrix} = (u_2 v_3 - u_3 v_2)\mathbf{i} - (u_1 v_3 - u_3 v_1)\mathbf{j} + (u_1 v_2 - u_2 v_1)\mathbf{k}. \quad (7)$$

EXAMPLE 6     Use the symbolic determinant (7) to calculate $\mathbf{u} \times \mathbf{v}$ and $\mathbf{v} \times \mathbf{u}$, where

$$\mathbf{u} = \begin{bmatrix} 1 \\ 1 \\ -1 \end{bmatrix} \text{ and } \mathbf{v} = \begin{bmatrix} 2 \\ -1 \\ 3 \end{bmatrix}.$$

***Solution***    Using (7), we obtain

$$\mathbf{u} \times \mathbf{v} = \begin{vmatrix} \mathbf{i} & \mathbf{j} & \mathbf{k} \\ 1 & 1 & -1 \\ 2 & -1 & 3 \end{vmatrix} = (3-1)\mathbf{i} - (3+2)\mathbf{j} + (-1-2)\mathbf{k} = 2\mathbf{i} - 5\mathbf{j} - 3\mathbf{k} = \begin{bmatrix} 2 \\ -5 \\ -3 \end{bmatrix}.$$

To calculate $\mathbf{v} \times \mathbf{u}$, we switch the rows in the symbolic determinant for $\mathbf{u} \times \mathbf{v}$

$$\mathbf{v} \times \mathbf{u} = \begin{vmatrix} \mathbf{i} & \mathbf{j} & \mathbf{k} \\ 2 & -1 & 3 \\ 1 & 1 & -1 \end{vmatrix}.$$

From the properties of determinants, we know that the determinant changes sign when two rows are interchanged. Thus, even without expanding the determinant for $\mathbf{v} \times \mathbf{u}$,

we know that $\mathbf{v} \times \mathbf{u} = -\mathbf{u} \times \mathbf{v} = \begin{bmatrix} -2 \\ 5 \\ 3 \end{bmatrix}.$ ■

## Algebraic Properties of the Cross Product

We have to be careful with cross product calculations since properties that we intuitively expect to hold might not be true. For instance, we saw in Example 6 that the expected equality, $\mathbf{u} \times \mathbf{v} = \mathbf{v} \times \mathbf{u}$, might not be true. A summary of several important algebraic properties of the cross product is given in Theorem 9.

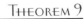 THEOREM 9    Let $\mathbf{u}$, $\mathbf{v}$, and $\mathbf{w}$ be three-dimensional vectors and let $c$ be a scalar. Then

   (a)  $\mathbf{u} \times \mathbf{v} = -\mathbf{v} \times \mathbf{u}$

   (b)  $\mathbf{u} \times \mathbf{u} = \mathbf{0}$

   (c)  $(c\mathbf{u}) \times \mathbf{v} = \mathbf{u} \times (c\mathbf{v}) = c(\mathbf{u} \times \mathbf{v})$

   (d)  $\mathbf{u} \times (\mathbf{v} + \mathbf{w}) = \mathbf{u} \times \mathbf{v} + \mathbf{u} \times \mathbf{w}$

   (e)  $\mathbf{u} \cdot (\mathbf{v} \times \mathbf{w}) = (\mathbf{u} \times \mathbf{v}) \cdot \mathbf{w}$

***Proof***    The proof of Theorem 9 follows from the definition of the cross product. ■

   It is worth noting that the cross product operation is not associative. That is, in general, $(\mathbf{u} \times \mathbf{v}) \times \mathbf{w}$ is not equal to $\mathbf{u} \times (\mathbf{v} \times \mathbf{w})$. See the exercises for an example of this fact.

## The Right-Hand Rule

By Theorem 9, $\mathbf{u} \times \mathbf{v} = -\mathbf{v} \times \mathbf{u}$. Therefore, both of the vectors $\mathbf{u} \times \mathbf{v}$ and $\mathbf{v} \times \mathbf{u}$ are perpendicular to $\mathbf{u}$ and to $\mathbf{v}$. The orientation of $\mathbf{u} \times \mathbf{v}$ can be found by using the ***right-hand rule:***

> *Let $\mathbf{u}$, $\mathbf{v}$, and $\mathbf{u} \times \mathbf{v}$ have a common initial point A. Imagine placing your right hand near A with your fingers pointing along $\mathbf{u}$. Let your fingers curl from $\mathbf{u}$ toward $\mathbf{v}$. Your thumb points in the direction of $\mathbf{u} \times \mathbf{v}$.*

Cross products of the basic unit vectors illustrate the right-hand rule. The first line of cross products can be found using Definition 2 or the determinant (7). The other two lines follow from Theorem 9.

$$\begin{array}{lll}
\mathbf{i} \times \mathbf{j} = \mathbf{k} & \mathbf{j} \times \mathbf{k} = \mathbf{i} & \mathbf{k} \times \mathbf{i} = \mathbf{j} \\
\mathbf{j} \times \mathbf{i} = -\mathbf{k} & \mathbf{k} \times \mathbf{j} = -\mathbf{i} & \mathbf{i} \times \mathbf{k} = -\mathbf{j} \\
\mathbf{i} \times \mathbf{i} = 0 & \mathbf{j} \times \mathbf{j} = 0 & \mathbf{k} \times \mathbf{k} = 0.
\end{array} \tag{8}$$

When **u** and **v** are given in terms of the basic unit vectors, we can use Theorem 9 and Eq. (8) to calculate **u** × **v**. The next example illustrates this idea.

**EXAMPLE 7** Let $\mathbf{u} = 3\mathbf{i} + 2\mathbf{k}$ and let $\mathbf{v} = 4\mathbf{i} + \mathbf{j} + 5\mathbf{k}$. Calculate **u** × **v**.

**Solution** We have

$$\begin{aligned}
\mathbf{u} \times \mathbf{v} &= (3\mathbf{i} + 2\mathbf{k}) \times (4\mathbf{i} + \mathbf{j} + 5\mathbf{k}) \\
&= 12\mathbf{i} \times \mathbf{i} + 3\mathbf{i} \times \mathbf{j} + 15\mathbf{i} \times \mathbf{k} + 8\mathbf{k} \times \mathbf{i} + 2\mathbf{k} \times \mathbf{j} + 10\mathbf{k} \times \mathbf{k} \\
&= (12)\mathbf{0} + (10)\mathbf{0} \\
&= -2\mathbf{i} - 7\mathbf{j} + 3\mathbf{k}.
\end{aligned}$$

## Geometric Properties of the Cross Product

The right-hand rule gives us the direction of **u** × **v**. Theorem 10 tells us the magnitude of **u** × **v**.

**THEOREM 10** Let **u** and **v** be nonzero three-dimensional vectors and let $\theta$ be the angle between **u** and **v**. The length of **u** × **v** is given by

$$\|\mathbf{u} \times \mathbf{v}\| = \|\mathbf{u}\| \|\mathbf{v}\| \sin \theta.$$

We leave the proof of Theorem 10 as an exercise. Note that Theorem 10 can be used as a test of whether or not nonzero vectors **u** and **v** are parallel; see Theorem 12 at the end of this section.

An interesting application of Theorem 10 involves using **u** × **v** to find the area of a parallelogram. Let *ABCD* denote a parallelogram determined by four points *A*, *B*, *C*, and *D*; see Fig. 2.26.

The following result can be established with the help of Fig. 2.26.

**THEOREM 11** Let *ABCD* be the parallelogram where *A* and *D* are opposite vertices. The area of *ABCD* is equal to the length of the cross product vector, $\overrightarrow{AB} \times \overrightarrow{AC}$.

**Proof** We can verify Theorem 11 by appealing to Fig. 2.26:

$$\begin{aligned}
\text{Area} &= \|\overrightarrow{AB}\| h && \text{(area = base × height)} \\
&= \|\overrightarrow{AB}\| \|\overrightarrow{AC}\| \sin \theta && \text{(since } h = \|\overrightarrow{AC}\| \sin \theta) \\
&= \|\overrightarrow{AB} \times \overrightarrow{AC}\| && \text{(by Theorem 2)}
\end{aligned}$$

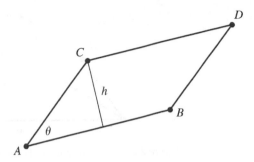

***Figure 2.26*** The parallelogram $ABCD$. The area of $ABCD$ is equal to the magnitude of $\overrightarrow{AB} \times \overrightarrow{AC}$.

EXAMPLE 8     Use Theorem 11 to find the area of the triangle $ABC$ where the vertices are $A = (1, 2, 2)$, $B = (3, 1, 4)$, and $C = (5, 2, 1)$.

***Solution***     From geometry, we know that the triangle $ABC$ has half the area of the parallelogram $ABCD$; see Fig. 2.26. So, as in Fig. 2.26, let $\mathbf{v} = \overrightarrow{AB}$ and let $\mathbf{u} = \overrightarrow{AC}$. Forming $\mathbf{u} \times \mathbf{v}$ we find

$$\mathbf{u} \times \mathbf{v} = \begin{vmatrix} \mathbf{i} & \mathbf{j} & \mathbf{k} \\ 4 & 0 & -1 \\ 2 & -1 & 2 \end{vmatrix} = -\mathbf{i} - 10\mathbf{j} - 4\mathbf{k}.$$

Calculating the magnitude of $\mathbf{u} \times \mathbf{v}$, we obtain $\sqrt{117}$. Thus, the area of the triangle $ABC$ is equal to $\sqrt{117}/2$.

## Triple Products

The products $\mathbf{u} \cdot (\mathbf{v} \times \mathbf{w})$ and $\mathbf{u} \times (\mathbf{v} \times \mathbf{w})$ are called ***triple products***. The triple product $\mathbf{u} \cdot (\mathbf{v} \times \mathbf{w})$ is known as the ***scalar triple product***, and $\mathbf{u} \times (\mathbf{v} \times \mathbf{w})$ is called the ***vector triple product***.

The magnitude of the scalar triple product has an interesting geometric interpretation. Suppose $PQ$, $PR$, and $PS$ are adjacent edges of a parallelepiped, as in Fig. 2.27. Let $\mathbf{u} = \overrightarrow{PQ}$, $\mathbf{v} = \overrightarrow{PR}$, and $\mathbf{w} = \overrightarrow{PS}$. In the exercises we ask you to verify that the volume, $V$, of the parallelepiped is given by

$$V = |\mathbf{u} \cdot (\mathbf{v} \times \mathbf{w})|. \tag{9}$$

## Tests for Collinearity and Coplanarity

Let $AP$ be the area of a parallelogram with adjacent edges $\mathbf{u} = \overrightarrow{AB}$ and $\mathbf{v} = \overrightarrow{AC}$. Then, $AP = 0$ if and only if $\mathbf{u}$ and $\mathbf{v}$ are collinear (see Fig. 2.26). Similarly, let $V$ be the volume of the parallelepiped in Fig. 2.27. We see that $V = 0$ if and only if the vectors $\mathbf{u}$, $\mathbf{v}$, and $\mathbf{w}$ are coplanar.

Combining $AP = 0$ with Theorem 11 and $V = 0$ with Eq. (9), we obtain the following useful test.

*Figure 2.27*     The volume of the parallelepiped is $|\mathbf{u} \cdot (\mathbf{v} \times \mathbf{w})|$.

### THEOREM 12     Let $\mathbf{u}$, $\mathbf{v}$, and $\mathbf{w}$ be nonzero three dimensional vectors.

(a)   $\mathbf{u}$ and $\mathbf{v}$ are collinear if and only if $\mathbf{u} \times \mathbf{v} = \mathbf{0}$.

(b)   $\mathbf{u}$, $\mathbf{v}$, and $\mathbf{w}$ are coplanar if and only if $\mathbf{u} \cdot (\mathbf{v} \times \mathbf{w}) = \mathbf{0}$.

## 2.3     EXERCISES

In Exercises 1–4, calculate the dot product $\mathbf{u} \cdot \mathbf{v}$.

**1.** $\mathbf{u} = \begin{bmatrix} 1 \\ 3 \end{bmatrix}$,     $\mathbf{v} = \begin{bmatrix} 4 \\ -2 \end{bmatrix}$

**2.** $\mathbf{u} = \begin{bmatrix} 2 \\ 3 \end{bmatrix}$,     $\mathbf{v} = \begin{bmatrix} -3 \\ 2 \end{bmatrix}$

**3.** $\mathbf{u} = \begin{bmatrix} 1 \\ -2 \\ 1 \end{bmatrix}$,     $\mathbf{v} = \begin{bmatrix} 3 \\ -1 \\ 2 \end{bmatrix}$

**4.** $\mathbf{u} = 4\mathbf{i} + 2\mathbf{j} - 3\mathbf{k}$,     $\mathbf{v} = -2\mathbf{i} + \mathbf{j} - 2\mathbf{k}$

In Exercises 5–8, determine $\cos \theta$ where $\theta$ is the angle between $\mathbf{u}$ and $\mathbf{v}$.

**5.** $\mathbf{u} = \begin{bmatrix} 3 \\ 1 \end{bmatrix}$,     $\mathbf{v} = \begin{bmatrix} 2 \\ 5 \end{bmatrix}$

**6.** $\mathbf{u} = \begin{bmatrix} 2 \\ 3 \end{bmatrix}$,     $\mathbf{v} = \begin{bmatrix} -3 \\ 1 \end{bmatrix}$

**7.** $\mathbf{u} = \begin{bmatrix} 1 \\ 2 \\ 1 \end{bmatrix}$,     $\mathbf{v} = \begin{bmatrix} 2 \\ -1 \\ 1 \end{bmatrix}$

**8.** $\mathbf{u} = 2\mathbf{i} - 3\mathbf{j} + \mathbf{k}$,     $\mathbf{v} = \mathbf{i} - 2\mathbf{j} + 3\mathbf{k}$

In Exercises 9–12, find $\theta$ (in radians) where $\theta$ is the angle between $\mathbf{u}$ and $\mathbf{v}$.

**9.** $\mathbf{u} = \begin{bmatrix} 3 \\ \sqrt{3} \end{bmatrix}$,     $\mathbf{v} = \begin{bmatrix} 2 \\ 2\sqrt{3} \end{bmatrix}$

**10.** $\mathbf{u} = \begin{bmatrix} \sqrt{3} \\ 1 \end{bmatrix}$,     $\mathbf{v} = \begin{bmatrix} -3 \\ \sqrt{3} \end{bmatrix}$

**11.** $\mathbf{u} = \begin{bmatrix} 1 \\ 3 \\ -1 \end{bmatrix}$,     $\mathbf{v} = \begin{bmatrix} 2 \\ -2 \\ -4 \end{bmatrix}$

**12.** $\mathbf{u} = \mathbf{i} + 2\mathbf{j} + \mathbf{k}$,     $\mathbf{v} = 3\mathbf{i} + 6\mathbf{j} + 3\mathbf{k}$

In Exercises 13–18, there are at most two three-dimensional vectors $\mathbf{u}$ that satisfy the given conditions. Determine these vector(s) $\mathbf{u}$.

**13.** $\mathbf{u} \cdot \mathbf{i} = 1$,     $\mathbf{u} \cdot \mathbf{j} = 3$,     $\mathbf{u} \cdot \mathbf{k} = 4$

**14.** $\mathbf{u} \cdot \mathbf{i} = 0$,     $\mathbf{u} \cdot \mathbf{j} = 0$,     $\mathbf{u} \cdot \mathbf{k} = 4$

**15.** $\mathbf{u} \cdot \mathbf{i} = 3$,     $\mathbf{u} \cdot \mathbf{k} = 4$,     $\|\mathbf{u}\| = 5$

**16.** $\mathbf{u} \cdot \mathbf{i} = 12$,     $\mathbf{u} \cdot \mathbf{k} = 3$,     $\|\mathbf{u}\| = 13$

**17.** $\mathbf{u} \cdot (\mathbf{i} + \mathbf{j}) = 2$,     $\mathbf{u} \cdot (\mathbf{j} + \mathbf{k}) = 4$,     $\mathbf{u} \cdot \mathbf{k} = 1$

**18.** $\mathbf{u} \cdot (\mathbf{i} + \mathbf{j}) = 2$,     $\mathbf{u} \cdot (\mathbf{j} + \mathbf{k}) = 3$,     $\mathbf{u} \cdot \mathbf{k} = 2$

In Exercises 19–22, $\mathbf{u} = \overrightarrow{OP}$, $\mathbf{v} = \overrightarrow{OQ}$ and $\mathbf{w} = proj_q\mathbf{u}$. Find the point $R$ such that $\mathbf{w} = \overrightarrow{OR}$. Graph $\mathbf{u}$, $\mathbf{v}$, and $\mathbf{w}$.

**19.** $P = (2, 5), \quad Q = (6, 2)$

**20.** $P = (7, 6), \quad Q = (4, 1)$

**21.** $P = (-4, 2), \quad Q = (6, 2)$

**22.** $P = (-2, 4), \quad Q = (4, 2)$

In Exercises 23–26, find $\mathbf{u}_1$ and $\mathbf{u}_2$ such that $\mathbf{u}_1 = proj_q\mathbf{u}$, $\mathbf{u}_1$ and $\mathbf{u}_2$ are orthogonal, and $\mathbf{u} = \mathbf{u}_1 + \mathbf{u}_2$.

**23.** $\mathbf{u} = \begin{bmatrix} 7 \\ 3 \end{bmatrix}, \quad \mathbf{q} = \begin{bmatrix} 1 \\ 1 \end{bmatrix}$

**24.** $\mathbf{u} = \begin{bmatrix} 6 \\ 2 \end{bmatrix}, \quad \mathbf{q} = \begin{bmatrix} 1 \\ -1 \end{bmatrix}$

**25.** $\mathbf{u} = \begin{bmatrix} 6 \\ 4 \\ -2 \end{bmatrix}, \quad \mathbf{q} = \begin{bmatrix} 1 \\ 2 \\ 1 \end{bmatrix}$

**26.** $\mathbf{u} = 2\mathbf{i} + \mathbf{j} + 6\mathbf{k}, \quad \mathbf{q} = \mathbf{i} + \mathbf{j} + \mathbf{k}$

In Exercises 27–30,

$$\text{let } \mathbf{u} = \begin{bmatrix} u_1 \\ u_2 \\ u_3 \end{bmatrix}, \mathbf{v} = \begin{bmatrix} v_1 \\ v_2 \\ v_3 \end{bmatrix}, \mathbf{w} = \begin{bmatrix} w_1 \\ w_2 \\ w_3 \end{bmatrix}.$$

**27.** Prove part (**a**) of Theorem 8.

**28.** Prove part (**b**) of Theorem 8.

**29.** Prove part (**c**) of Theorem 8.

**30.** Prove part (**d**) of Theorem 8.

**31.** Let $\mathbf{u} = \begin{bmatrix} u_1 \\ u_2 \end{bmatrix}$ and $\mathbf{v} = \begin{bmatrix} v_1 \\ v_2 \end{bmatrix}$. Show that

Eq. (1) simplifies to Eq. (2a).

In Exercises 32–35, calculate the cross product $\mathbf{u} \times \mathbf{v}$.

**32.** $\mathbf{u} = \begin{bmatrix} 1 \\ 3 \\ 0 \end{bmatrix}, \quad \mathbf{v} = \begin{bmatrix} 4 \\ 1 \\ 0 \end{bmatrix}$

**33.** $\mathbf{u} = \begin{bmatrix} 4 \\ 0 \\ 1 \end{bmatrix}, \quad \mathbf{v} = \begin{bmatrix} 2 \\ 2 \\ 0 \end{bmatrix}$

**34.** $\mathbf{u} = \mathbf{i} + \mathbf{j} + 3\mathbf{k}, \quad \mathbf{v} = 2\mathbf{i} + 2\mathbf{j} + 6\mathbf{k}$

**35.** $\mathbf{u} = \mathbf{1} + 3\mathbf{j}, \quad \mathbf{v} = 2\mathbf{i} + \mathbf{j} + \mathbf{k}$

In Exercises 36–39, find a vector $\mathbf{w}$ such that $\mathbf{u} \cdot \mathbf{w} = 0$ and $\mathbf{v} \cdot \mathbf{w} = 0$.

**36.** $\mathbf{u} = \begin{bmatrix} 3 \\ 1 \\ 2 \end{bmatrix}, \quad \mathbf{v} = \begin{bmatrix} 1 \\ 1 \\ 1 \end{bmatrix}$

**37.** $\mathbf{u} = \begin{bmatrix} 2 \\ 0 \\ 1 \end{bmatrix}, \quad \mathbf{v} = \begin{bmatrix} 1 \\ 2 \\ 3 \end{bmatrix}$

**38.** $\mathbf{u} = \mathbf{i} + \mathbf{j}, \quad \mathbf{v} = \mathbf{i} + \mathbf{k}$

**39.** $\mathbf{u} = \mathbf{i} - 2\mathbf{k}, \quad \mathbf{v} = \mathbf{j} + 3\mathbf{k}$

In Exercises 40–41, find a vector $\mathbf{w}$ that is perpendicular to the plane containing the given points $A$, $B$, and $C$.

**40.** $A = (-1, 1, 2), \quad B = (2, 1, -1),$
$\quad C = (0, -2, 4)$

**41.** $A = (1, 0, 0), \quad B = (0, 1, 0), \quad C = (2, 3, 1)$

In Exercises 42–43, two sides of a parallelogram coincide with the position vectors for $\mathbf{u}$ and $\mathbf{v}$. Find the area of the parallelogram.

**42.** $\mathbf{u} = \begin{bmatrix} 1 \\ 2 \\ 4 \end{bmatrix}, \quad \mathbf{v} = \begin{bmatrix} 0 \\ 2 \\ 1 \end{bmatrix}$

**43.** $\mathbf{u} = \begin{bmatrix} 4 \\ -1 \\ 2 \end{bmatrix}, \quad \mathbf{v} = \begin{bmatrix} 0 \\ 1 \\ 2 \end{bmatrix}$

In Exercises 44–45, find the area of the triangle having the given points as vertices.

**44.** $A = (0, 0, 0), \quad B = (2, 3, 4), \quad C = (1, -1, 2)$

**45.** $A = (5, -1, 1), \quad B = (4, 3, 0), \quad C = (0, 1, 2)$

In Exercises 46–47, three edges of a parallelepiped coincide with the position vectors for $\mathbf{u}$, $\mathbf{v}$, and $\mathbf{w}$. Find the volume of the parallelepiped.

**46.** $\mathbf{u} = \begin{bmatrix} 0 \\ 1 \\ 3 \end{bmatrix}, \quad \mathbf{v} = \begin{bmatrix} -2 \\ 1 \\ 0 \end{bmatrix}, \quad \mathbf{w} = \begin{bmatrix} 0 \\ 4 \\ 1 \end{bmatrix}$

**47.** $\mathbf{u} = \begin{bmatrix} 2 \\ 2 \\ 0 \end{bmatrix}, \quad \mathbf{v} = \begin{bmatrix} 1 \\ 4 \\ 0 \end{bmatrix}, \quad \mathbf{w} = \begin{bmatrix} 1 \\ 2 \\ 4 \end{bmatrix}$

In Exercises 48–49, determine if the three vectors are coplanar.

**48.** $\mathbf{u} = \begin{bmatrix} 1 \\ -1 \\ 0 \end{bmatrix}$, $\quad \mathbf{v} = \begin{bmatrix} 2 \\ 0 \\ 1 \end{bmatrix}$, $\quad \mathbf{w} = \begin{bmatrix} 0 \\ 2 \\ 1 \end{bmatrix}$

**49.** $\mathbf{u} = \begin{bmatrix} 2 \\ -2 \\ 1 \end{bmatrix}$, $\quad \mathbf{v} = \begin{bmatrix} 0 \\ 1 \\ -1 \end{bmatrix}$, $\quad \mathbf{w} = \begin{bmatrix} -1 \\ 0 \\ 3 \end{bmatrix}$

**50.** Verify that $x = u_2 v_3 - u_3 v_2$, $y = u_3 v_1 - u_1 v_3$, $z = u_1 v_2 - u_2 v_1$ is a solution of the system of equations
$$u_1 x + u_2 y + u_3 z = 0$$
$$v_1 x + v_2 y + v_3 z = 0$$

**51.** Show that $(\mathbf{i} \times \mathbf{i}) \times \mathbf{j} \neq \mathbf{i} \times (\mathbf{i} \times \mathbf{j})$.

**52.** Let $\mathbf{u} = \begin{bmatrix} u_1 \\ u_2 \\ u_3 \end{bmatrix}$ and $\mathbf{v} = \begin{bmatrix} v_1 \\ v_2 \\ v_3 \end{bmatrix}$.

  a) Verify that $\|\mathbf{u} \times \mathbf{v}\|^2 = \|\mathbf{u}\|^2 \|\mathbf{v}\|^2 - (\mathbf{u} \cdot \mathbf{v})^2$
  b) Use the equation in part (a) to show $\|\mathbf{u} \times \mathbf{v}\| = \|\mathbf{u}\| \|\mathbf{v}\| \sin \theta$ where $\theta$ is the angle between $\mathbf{u}$ and $\mathbf{v}$.

**53.** Suppose $PQ, PR$, and $PS$ are adjacent edges of a rectangular parallelepiped, as in Fig. 2.27. Let $\mathbf{u} = \overrightarrow{PQ}$, $\mathbf{v} = \overrightarrow{PR}$, $\mathbf{w} = \overrightarrow{PS}$. Show that the volume, $V$, of the parallelepiped is given by $V = |\mathbf{u} \cdot (\mathbf{v} \times \mathbf{w})|$.

## 2.4    LINES AND PLANES IN SPACE

Many physical problems involve motion along a curve in three space. Examples include satellite trajectories, the arc of a slicing golf ball, the flight path of an airliner, and so forth. The simplest curve in three space is a line and we now discuss how lines are defined in three space.

### The Equation of a Line in the $xy$-Plane

As we know, a line in the $xy$-plane is determined by a point on the line and the slope of the line (see Fig. 2.28). If a line $l$ passes through the point $P_0 = (x_0, y_0)$ and if $l$ has slope $m$, then the equation of the line is

$$y = m(x - x_0) + y_0.$$

That is, the line $l$ is completely determined once we specify two pieces of information:

  **(a)**    A direction for the line, given by the slope $m$.
  **(b)**    A point $P_0 = (x_0, y_0)$ on the line.

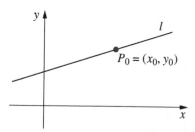

*Figure 2.28*    The line $l$ has slope $m$ and passes through the point $P_0 = (x_0, y_0)$. In general, a line in the $xy$-plane is determined by its direction (the slope of the line) and a point $P_0$ on the line.

## The Vector Form for the Equation of a Line in Three Space

As with lines in the $xy$-plane, a line $L$ in three space is completely determined once we specify the *direction* of the line and a *point* on the line. In three space, vectors are used to specify direction. Therefore, a line $L$ is determined once we specify a direction vector $\mathbf{u}$ for the line and a point $P_0 = (x_0, y_0, z_0)$ on the line (see Fig. 2.29). As you can see from Fig. 2.29, a point $P = (x, y, z)$ is on the line $L$ if and only if the vector $\overrightarrow{P_0P}$ is parallel to $\mathbf{u}$; that is, if and only if $\overrightarrow{P_0P} = t\mathbf{u}$ for some scalar $t$.

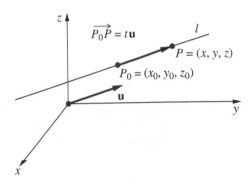

*Figure 2.29* A line $L$ in space is determined by a direction vector, $\mathbf{u}$, and a point $P_0$ on $L$. As we see, a point $P = (x, y, z)$ is on $L$ if and only if $\overrightarrow{P_0P} = t\mathbf{u}$ for some value $t$.

The geometric view given in Fig. 2.29 leads us to the ***vector form for the equation of a line:***

---

**Vector Form for the Equation of a Line**

Let $L$ be the line through $P_0 = (x_0, y_0, z_0)$ having direction vector $\mathbf{u}$. A point $P = (x, y, z)$ is on the line $L$ if and only if

$$\overrightarrow{P_0P} = t\mathbf{u} \text{ for some scalar } t, -\infty < t < \infty.$$

---

## Parametric Equations for a Line in Three Space

We can use the vector form for the equation of a line to derive a formula for the coordinates of every point $P$ on the line. Let $L$ be a line through $P_0 = (x_0, y_0, z_0)$ and let $L$ have direction vector $\mathbf{u}$ where

$$\mathbf{u} = \begin{bmatrix} u_1 \\ u_2 \\ u_3 \end{bmatrix}.$$

Let $P = (x, y, z)$ be any point on the line $L$. The vector $\overrightarrow{P_0P}$ is given by

$$\overrightarrow{P_0P} = \begin{bmatrix} x - x_0 \\ y - y_0 \\ z - z_0 \end{bmatrix}.$$

Since $P$ is on the line $L$, we know there is some scalar $t$ such that $\overrightarrow{P_0P} = t\mathbf{u}$. Therefore,

$$x - x_0 = tu_1$$
$$y - y_0 = tu_2$$
$$z - z_0 = tu_3$$

or

$$x = x_0 + tu_1$$
$$y = y_0 + tu_2$$
$$z = z_0 + tu_3.$$

The equations above are called the **parametric equations of the line**. As such, they constitute a formula that generates the coordinates, $(x, y, z)$, of every point $P$ on the line. The parameter $t$ is allowed to vary from $-\infty$ to $\infty$.

---

**Parametric Equations for a Line**

Let $L$ be a line with direction vector $\mathbf{u} = \begin{bmatrix} u_1 \\ u_2 \\ u_3 \end{bmatrix}$ where $P_0 = (x_0, y_0, z_0)$ is on the line. A point $P = (x, y, z)$ is on the line if and only if
$$x = x_0 + tu_1, \qquad y = y_0 + tu_2, \qquad z = z_0 + tu_3$$
for some real number $t$.

---

EXAMPLE 1   Let $L$ be the line through $P_0 = (2, 1, 6)$, having direction vector $\mathbf{u}$ given by

$$\mathbf{u} = \begin{bmatrix} 4 \\ -1 \\ 3 \end{bmatrix}.$$

**(a)**  Find parametric equations for the line $L$.

**(b)**  Does the line $L$ intersect the $xy$-plane? If so, what are the coordinates of the point of intersection?

*Solution*

**(a)**  One set of parametric equations for $L$ is
$$x = 2 + 4t, \qquad y = 1 - t, \qquad z = 6 + 3t.$$

**(b)** If $L$ intersects the $xy$-plane, it must do so at a point $P_1$ having $z$-coordinate equal to zero—a point of the form $P_1 = (x_1, y_1, 0)$. Since the $z$-coordinate of points on $L$ is given by $z = 6 + 3t$, it follows that $t = -2$. When $t = -2$, we see that $x = -6$ and $y = 3$. Thus, the line $L$ intersects the $xy$-plane at the point $P_1 = (-6, 3, 0)$. ◼

As we know from geometry, two points determine a line. The next example illustrates how we can find the equation of a line $L$ given two points on $L$.

EXAMPLE 2   Find parametric equations for the line $L$ passing through $P_0 = (2, 5, 7)$ and $P_1 = (4, 9, 8)$.

*Solution*   As a direction vector for $L$, we use $\mathbf{u} = \overrightarrow{P_0 P_1}$:

$$\overrightarrow{P_0 P_1} = \begin{bmatrix} 2 \\ 4 \\ 1 \end{bmatrix}.$$

Therefore, one set of parametric equations for $L$ is

$$x = 2 + 2t, \qquad y = 5 + 4t, \qquad z = 7 + t.$$ ◼

(***Note:*** In Examples 1 and 2, we were careful to say that we had found *one* set of parametric equations for the line $L$. In particular, there are many other ways to describe the line $L$. For example, we could replace the parameter $t$ by a new parameter $t^3$ and the parametric equations in Examples 1 and 2 would still trace out the same line $L$.)

## Line Segments

We can use the ideas described above to specify line segments instead of entire lines. To specify the line segment joining $P_0$ and $P_1$, we first find parametric equations for the line passing through $P_0$ and $P_1$, as in Example 2. We then restrict the parameter $t$ to the interval $[0, 1]$; when $t = 0$, we are at $P_0$ and when $t = 1$, we are at $P_1$.

EXAMPLE 3   Find parametric equations for the line segment joining $P_0 = (2, 5, 7)$ and the point $P_1 = (4, 9, 8)$; recall Example 2.

*Solution*   Drawing on the results of Example 2, one set of parametric equations for the line segment is

$$x = 2 + 2t, \qquad y = 5 + 4t, \qquad z = 7 + t, \qquad 0 \le t \le 1.$$

As you can see, $t = 0$ gives $P_0$ and $t = 1$ gives $P_1$. ◼

## Planes in Space and Their Normal Vectors

A line $L$ is determined by a point $P_0$ on the line and a direction vector $\mathbf{u}$ for the line. Similarly, a plane $\Pi$ is determined by a point $P_0$ on the plane and a vector $\mathbf{n}$ that gives us the "orientation"of the plane. In particular, a vector **n** is said to be ***normal*** to the plane Π if **n** is perpendicular (orthogonal) to every vector **u** in the plane (see Fig. 2.30).

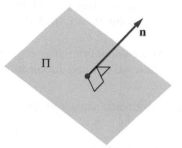

*Figure 2.30*   The vector **n** is normal (that is, perpendicular) to the plane Π. The vector **n** tells us the orientation of the plane.

One way to think of a normal is to imagine that the plane Π is an infinite sheet of plywood. Then a normal is like a nail hammered perpendicularly into the plywood. When we turn the plywood, we can deduce the orientation of the sheet simply by looking at the direction the nail is pointing.

From our work in Section 2.3, we know that two nonzero vectors **r** and **s** are perpendicular if and only if $\mathbf{r} \cdot \mathbf{s} = 0$. Therefore, a vector **n** is normal to a plane Π if and only if

$$\mathbf{n} \cdot \mathbf{u} = 0 \quad \text{for every vector } \mathbf{u} \text{ in } \Pi.$$

The following example illustrates the concept of a normal to a plane.

EXAMPLE 4   Let Π denote the *xy*-plane. Which of the following vectors are normal to Π?

(a)   $\mathbf{n}_1 = \begin{bmatrix} 2 \\ 1 \\ 3 \end{bmatrix}$

(b)   $\mathbf{n}_2 = \begin{bmatrix} 3 \\ 2 \\ 0 \end{bmatrix}$

(c)   $\mathbf{n}_3 = \begin{bmatrix} 0 \\ 0 \\ 5 \end{bmatrix}$

*Solution*   A vector **u** is in the *xy*-plane if and only if **u** has the form

$$\mathbf{u} = \begin{bmatrix} u_1 \\ u_2 \\ 0 \end{bmatrix}.$$

Forming the dot products $\mathbf{n}_1 \cdot \mathbf{u}$, $\mathbf{n}_2 \cdot \mathbf{u}$, and $\mathbf{n}_3 \cdot \mathbf{u}$, we find

$$\mathbf{n}_1 \cdot \mathbf{u} = 2u_1 + u_2$$

$$\mathbf{n}_2 \cdot \mathbf{u} = 3u_1 + 2u_2$$

$$\mathbf{n}_3 \cdot \mathbf{u} = 0.$$

Thus, $\mathbf{n}_3$ is normal to the plane $\Pi$. Observe that $\mathbf{n}_1$ and $\mathbf{n}_2$ are not normal to $\Pi$ because they are not perpendicular to *every* vector $\mathbf{u}$ in $\Pi$. ▬◖

(**Note:** Parallel planes have the same orientation and hence have the same normals. For example, the plane $z = 3$ is parallel to the $xy$-plane. In particular, the plane $z = 3$ consists of all vectors $\mathbf{u}$ having the form

$$\mathbf{u} = \begin{bmatrix} u_1 \\ u_2 \\ 3 \end{bmatrix}.$$

Recalling Example 4, the vector $\mathbf{n}_3$ is normal to the $xy$-plane. Clearly, this vector $\mathbf{n}_3$ is also normal to the plane $z = 3$. Thus, we have an illustration of the fact that parallel planes have the same normals.)

### The Vector Form for the Equation of a Plane in Three Space

Let $\Pi$ be a plane in three space and let $\mathbf{n}$ be a normal for $\Pi$. As noted above, the normal vector $\mathbf{n}$ tells us the orientation of $\Pi$. But, since parallel planes all have the same orientation (that is, the same normals) we also need to give a point $P_0$ on $\Pi$ in order to specify completely.

So, let $\Pi$ be a plane with normal $\mathbf{n}$ where $P_0$ is a point on $\Pi$. If $P$ is any other point on $\Pi$, then the vector $\mathbf{u} = \overrightarrow{PP_0}$ lies in $\Pi$ (see Fig. 2.31). Since $\mathbf{n}$ is normal to $\Pi$, it follows that

$$\mathbf{n} \cdot \overrightarrow{PP_0} = 0.$$

**Figure 2.31** The vector $\mathbf{n}$ is normal to the plane $\Pi$. The point $P = (x, y, z)$ is in $\Pi$ if and only if the vector $\overrightarrow{PP_0}$ lies in $\Pi$ and hence, if and only if $\mathbf{n} \cdot \overrightarrow{PP_0} = 0$.

The geometric view given in Fig. 2.31 leads us to the *vector form for the equation of a plane*:

**Vector Form for the Equation of a Plane**

Let $\Pi$ be the plane containing the point $P_0 = (x_0, y_0, z_0)$ and having normal $\mathbf{n}$. A point $P = (x, y, z)$ is in the plane $\Pi$ if and only if

$$\mathbf{n} \cdot \overrightarrow{PP_0} = 0.$$

## The Scalar Form for the Equation of a Plane

Let $\Pi$ be a plane and let $P_0 = (x_0, y_0, z_0)$ be a point in $\Pi$. Let $\mathbf{n}$ be a normal vector for $\Pi$ where

$$\mathbf{n} = \begin{bmatrix} A \\ B \\ C \end{bmatrix}.$$

As we saw above, a point $P = (x, y, z)$ is in $\Pi$ if and only if $\mathbf{n} \cdot \overrightarrow{PP_0} = 0$. Expanding this dot product condition, we obtain:

$$\begin{bmatrix} A \\ B \\ C \end{bmatrix} \cdot \begin{bmatrix} x - x_0 \\ y - y_0 \\ z - z_0 \end{bmatrix} = 0$$

or,

$$A(x - x_0) + B(y - y_0) + C(z - z_0) = 0.$$

The equation above is the scalar form for the equation of a plane.

**Scalar Form for the Equation of a Plane**

Let $\Pi$ be the plane containing the point $P_0 = (x_0, y_0, z_0)$ and having a normal

$\mathbf{n} = \begin{bmatrix} A \\ B \\ C \end{bmatrix}$. A point $P = (x, y, z)$ is on the plane $\Pi$ if and only if

$$A(x - x_0) + B(y - y_0) + C(z - z_0) = 0. \tag{1}$$

EXAMPLE 5    Find the equation of the plane containing the point $P_0 = (1, 3, -2)$ and having normal

$$\mathbf{n} = \begin{bmatrix} 5 \\ -2 \\ 2 \end{bmatrix}.$$

***Solution*** The equation of the plane is $\mathbf{n} \cdot \overrightarrow{PP_0} = 0$,

$$5(x - 1) - 2(y - 3) + 2(z + 2) = 0$$

or

$$5x - 2y + 2z = -5. \qquad \blacksquare$$

When simplified, the scalar form (1) for the equation of a plane $\Pi$ has the form

$$Ax + By + Cz = D.$$

We can read the components of a normal vector for $\Pi$ from this equation; the components are $A$, $B$, and $C$.

EXAMPLE 6 The equation of a plane $\Pi$ is given by

$$2x + y - 2z = 8.$$

Find a unit normal for $\Pi$ (by a unit normal, we mean a normal vector that has length 1).

***Solution*** From the equation for $\Pi$, we see that a normal vector $\mathbf{n}$ is given by

$$\mathbf{n} = \begin{bmatrix} 2 \\ 1 \\ -2 \end{bmatrix}.$$

We get a *unit* normal, $\mathbf{v}$, by dividing $\mathbf{n}$ by its length:

$$\mathbf{v} = \frac{\mathbf{n}}{\|\mathbf{n}\|} = \frac{1}{3}\mathbf{n} = \begin{bmatrix} 2/3 \\ 1/3 \\ -2/3 \end{bmatrix}. \qquad \blacksquare$$

## Using the Cross Product to Find a Normal

We have often heard that "two points determine a line." Similarly, three points determine a plane. To explain how, suppose $P_0$, $P_1$, and $P_2$ are three points on a plane $\Pi$ (see Fig. 2.32). Clearly, the vectors $\mathbf{u} = \overrightarrow{P_0P_1}$ and $\mathbf{v} = \overrightarrow{P_0P_2}$ lie in the plane $\Pi$. To find a normal for $\Pi$ (a vector $\mathbf{n}$ that is perpendicular to both $\mathbf{u}$ and $\mathbf{v}$), we need only form the cross product of $\mathbf{u}$ and $\mathbf{v}$. Thus, a normal for $\Pi$ is given by:

$$\mathbf{n} = \mathbf{u} \times \mathbf{v}.$$

EXAMPLE 7 Find the equation of the plane passing through the points $P_0 = (1, 3, 2)$, $P_1 = (2, 0, -1)$, and $P_2 = (4, 5, 1)$.

***Solution*** The vectors $\mathbf{u} = \overrightarrow{P_0P_1}$ and $\mathbf{v} = \overrightarrow{P_0P_2}$ are given by

$$\mathbf{u} = \begin{bmatrix} 1 \\ -3 \\ -3 \end{bmatrix} \quad \text{and} \quad \mathbf{v} = \begin{bmatrix} 3 \\ 2 \\ -1 \end{bmatrix}.$$

**Figure 2.32**    Since $P_0$, $P_1$, and $P_2$ are in the plane $\Pi$, the vectors $\mathbf{u} = \overrightarrow{P_0P_1}$ and $\mathbf{v} = \overrightarrow{P_0P_2}$ also lie in $\Pi$. Therefore, $\mathbf{n} = \mathbf{u} \times \mathbf{v}$ is a normal for $\Pi$.

We use a symbolic determinant to find the cross product of $\mathbf{u}$ and $\mathbf{v}$:

$$\mathbf{n} = \mathbf{u} \times \mathbf{v} = \begin{vmatrix} \mathbf{i} & \mathbf{j} & \mathbf{k} \\ 1 & -3 & -3 \\ 3 & 2 & -1 \end{vmatrix} = 9\mathbf{i} - 8\mathbf{j} + 11\mathbf{k} = \begin{bmatrix} 9 \\ -8 \\ 11 \end{bmatrix}.$$

Having $\mathbf{n}$, we use Eq. (1) to calculate the equation of the plane:

$$9(x - 1) - 8(y - 3) + 11(z - 2) = 0$$

or,

$$9x - 8y + 11z = 7. \qquad \blacksquare$$

(*Note:* The method for finding a normal used in Example 7 will only work if the three points $P_0$, $P_1$, and $P_2$ do not lie on a line.)

## Parallel Planes

As we indicated earlier, parallel planes have the same normals. This observation leads to a formal definition. Let $\Pi_1$ and $\Pi_2$ be planes in space with normals $\mathbf{n}_1$ and $\mathbf{n}_2$, respectively. We say that $\Pi_1$ and $\Pi_2$ are **parallel** if the normal $\mathbf{n}_1$ is parallel to the normal $\mathbf{n}_2$.

EXAMPLE 8    Let $\Pi_1$, $\Pi_2$, and $\Pi_3$ be planes having the following equations:

$$\textit{Equation of } \Pi_1\text{:} \quad 6x + 4y + 8z = 2$$
$$\textit{Equation of } \Pi_2\text{:} \quad x + 5y + 3z = 4$$
$$\textit{Equation of } \Pi_3\text{:} \quad 3x + 2y + 4z = 9$$

(a)   Determine if any two of these three planes are parallel.

(b)   Find the equation of the plane parallel to $\Pi_1$ passing through $P_0 = (1, 2, 1)$.

***Solution***

**(a)** Let $n_1$, $n_2$, and $n_3$ denote the normals for $\Pi_1$, $\Pi_2$, and $\Pi_3$, respectively. Then

$$
n_1 = \begin{bmatrix} 6 \\ 4 \\ 8 \end{bmatrix}, \qquad n_2 = \begin{bmatrix} 1 \\ 5 \\ 3 \end{bmatrix}, \qquad n_3 = \begin{bmatrix} 3 \\ 2 \\ 4 \end{bmatrix}.
$$

Clearly, $n_1 = 2n_3$, and so $n_1$ and $n_3$ are parallel vectors. Therefore, $\Pi_1$ and $\Pi_3$ are parallel planes.

**(b)** Any plane parallel to $\Pi_1$ has a normal equal to $n_1$. Thus, using Eq. (1), we find the equation of the plane parallel to $\Pi_1$ and containing $P_0 = (1, 2, 1)$ has equation

$$6x + 4y + 8z = 22$$

or, after canceling a common factor of 2,

$$3x + 2y + 4z = 11.$$

---

## 2.4   EXERCISES

In Exercises 1–2, give parametric equations for the line $L$ through $P_0$ in the direction $u$.

**1.** $P_0 = (2, 4, -3)$,   $u = \begin{bmatrix} 3 \\ 2 \\ 4 \end{bmatrix}$

**2.** $P_0 = (1, 1, -1)$,   $u = \begin{bmatrix} 2 \\ 0 \\ 3 \end{bmatrix}$

In Exercises 3–4, give parametric equations for the line $L$ through the two points.

**3.** $P_0 = (0, 4, 1)$,   $P_1 = (1, 2, 4)$

**4.** $P_0 = (5, 1, -3)$,   $P_1 = (6, 6, 4)$

In Exercises 5–8, determine whether the given lines are parallel.

**5.** $x = 3 + 2t$    $x = 5 - 4t$
$y = 2 - t$    $y = 6 + 2t$
$z = 1 + 3t$    $z = 2 - 6t$

**6.** $x = \phantom{0}2 + 6t$    $x = 4 + 3t$
$y = \phantom{0}2 + 4t$    $y = 7 + 2t$
$z = -1 + 3t$    $z = 2 + 3t$

**7.** $x = 1 - 2t$    $x = 7 + 2t$
$y = 5 + 3t$    $y = 2 - 3t$
$z = 4 - 2t$    $z = 3 + 4t$

**8.** $x = 5 - \phantom{0}t$    $x = 4 + 3t$
$y = 3 + 2t$    $y = 6 - 6t$
$z = 2 - 3t$    $z = 8 + 9t$

In Exercises 9–10, find parametric equations for the line $L$ through the point $P_0$ and normal to the given plane.

**9.** $P_0 = (1, 2, 1)$,   $3x + 4y - z = 9$

**10.** $P_0 = (2, 0, -3)$,   $x - y + 2z = 8$

In Exercises 11–14, find a point $P$ where the line intersects the given plane or decide that the line does not intersect the plane.

**11.** $x = 1 + 2t$
$y = 3 - \phantom{0}t,$    $x + y - z = 2$
$z = 5 + 4t$

**12.** $x = 4 + 2t$
$y = 7 + 2t,$    $x + y - z = 2$
$z = 5 + 4t$

**13.** $x = 8 + 4t$
$y = 3 + 4t,$    $x + 2y + z = 2$
$z = 4 - 8t$

**14.**  $x = 1 + 2t$
$y = 3 - t,$      $x + 2y + z = 4$
$z = 5 + 4t$

In Exercises 15–16, find the equation of the plane through $P_0$ with the given normal $\mathbf{n}$.

**15.** $P_0 = (3, 1, 3),$      $\mathbf{n} = \begin{bmatrix} 6 \\ 1 \\ -1 \end{bmatrix}$

**16.** $P_0 = (4, -2, 3),$      $\mathbf{n} = \begin{bmatrix} 1 \\ -2 \\ 3 \end{bmatrix}$

In Exercises 17–20, find the equation of the plane through the given (noncollinear) points $P$, $Q$, and $R$.

**17.**  $P = (1, 0, 3)$
$Q = (2, 1, 5)$
$R = (1, 4, 4)$

**18.**  $P = (5, 1, 7)$
$Q = (6, 9, 2)$
$R = (7, 2, 9)$

**19.**  $P = (3, 2, 3)$
$Q = (1, 1, 4)$
$R = (6, 2, 5)$

**20.**  $P = (4, 1, 0)$
$Q = (3, 2, 1)$
$R = (5, 1, 1)$

In Exercises 21–22, find a unit normal for the given plane.

**21.** $2x + y - 2z = 6$

**22.** $4x - 4y + 2z = 10$

In Exercises 23–24, find the equation of the plane through the point $P_0$ and parallel to the given plane.

**23.** $P_0 = (3, 8, 1),$     $x + 2y - 2z = 4$

**24.** $P_0 = (1, 1, 3),$     $2x - 3y + 2z = 6$

In Exercises 25–26, the given planes intersect in a line. Find parametric equations for the line of intersection. [*Hint:* The line of intersection consists of all points $(x, y, z)$ that satisfy both equations. Solve the system and designate the unconstrained variable as $t$.]

**25.** $x + z = 4,$     $2x - y + 3z = 3$

**26.** $x + 2y + z = 1,$     $2x + 5y + 3z = 4$

# SUPPLEMENTARY EXERCISES

**1.** Let $\mathbf{u} = \begin{bmatrix} 5 \\ 2 \end{bmatrix}$,   $\mathbf{v} = \begin{bmatrix} 7 \\ 1 \end{bmatrix}$,   $\mathbf{x} = \begin{bmatrix} 1 \\ 4 \end{bmatrix}$.

Write $\mathbf{x}$ in the form $\mathbf{x} = \mathbf{x}_1 + \mathbf{x}_2$ where $\mathbf{x}_1$ is parallel to $\mathbf{u}$ and $\mathbf{x}_2$ is parallel to $\mathbf{v}$.

**2.** A boat leaves its mainland dock and sails 10 miles in the direction 60° north of east, to an island dock. The boat then leaves the island, sailing 10 miles due northwest, to a buoy. Place an $xy$-coordinate system so that its origin is at the mainland dock and so that the $y$-axis points north. Give the coordinates of the island dock and the buoy. How far is the buoy from the mainland dock?

**3.** Let $P = (16, 20)$ and $Q = (12, -8)$. Find the co-ordinates of the point $R$ that is halfway between the midpoint of the segment $PQ$ and the point $Q$.

**4.** Let $\mathbf{u}$ and $\mathbf{v}$ be orthogonal unit vectors and let $\mathbf{a} = 2\mathbf{u} + 3\mathbf{v}$. Find $\|\mathbf{a}\|$.

**5.** Let $\mathbf{u}$, $\mathbf{v}$, and $\mathbf{w}$ be mutually orthogonal vectors such that $\|\mathbf{u}\| = 2$, $\|\mathbf{v}\| = 1$, and $\|\mathbf{w}\| = 2$. Let $\mathbf{a} = \mathbf{u} + \mathbf{v} + \mathbf{w}$. What is $\|\mathbf{a}\|$?

**6.** Let $\mathbf{u}$ and $\mathbf{v}$ be orthogonal vectors such that $\|\mathbf{u}\| = 2$ and $\|\mathbf{v}\| = 3$. Calculate the dot product $(\mathbf{u} - \mathbf{v}) \cdot (\mathbf{u} + \mathbf{v})$.

**7.** Let $\mathbf{u}$ and $\mathbf{v}$ be as in Exercise 6. Calculate $\|\mathbf{u} \times \mathbf{v}\|$.

**8.** Let $\mathbf{u}$ and $\mathbf{v}$ be as in Exercise 6. Calculate $\|(\mathbf{u} - \mathbf{v}) \times (\mathbf{u} + \mathbf{v})\|$.

**9.** Find all unit vectors in $R^3$ parallel to the $xz$-plane and orthogonal to $\begin{bmatrix} 3 \\ -2 \\ 4 \end{bmatrix}$.

**10.** A plane intersects the $x$-axis at the point $(a, 0, 0)$, the $y$-axis at $(0, b, 0)$ and the $z$-axis at $(0, 0, c)$, where $a$, $b$, and $c$ are nonzero. Find the equation of the plane and express it in the form $\alpha x + \beta y + \gamma z = 1$.

**11.** Do the four points $(1, 1, 2)$, $(2, 3, 9)$, $(-2, 1, -1)$, and $(1, 2, 5)$ all lie on the same plane?

**12.** Let $A$, $B$, and $C$ be distinct points on a circle of radius $r$ in the plane where $A$ and $B$ are endpoints of a diameter of the circle. Show that the triangle $ABC$ is a right triangle. [*Hint:* Set up a coordinate system in the plane with the origin at the center of the circle and such that $A = (-r, 0)$, $B = (r, 0)$.]

**13.** Let $A$, $B$, $C$, and $D$ be verticles, not endpoints of a quadrilateral in the plane. Show that the line segments joining the midpoints of opposite sides of $ABCD$ bisect each other. [*Hint:* Set up a coordinate system in the plane with $A = (a_1, a_2)$, $B = (b_1, b_2)$, $C = (c_1, c_2)$, $D = (d_1, d_2)$.]

# CONCEPTUAL EXERCISES

**1.** True or False: If $\mathbf{u} \cdot \mathbf{v} = 0$, then either $\mathbf{u} = \mathbf{0}$ or $\mathbf{v} = \mathbf{0}$.

**2.** True or False: If $\mathbf{u} \times \mathbf{v} = \mathbf{0}$, then either $\mathbf{u} = \mathbf{0}$ or $\mathbf{v} = \mathbf{0}$.

**3.** Prove the Parallelogram Law: $\|\mathbf{u}+\mathbf{v}\|^2 + \|\mathbf{u}-\mathbf{v}\|^2 = 2\|\mathbf{u}\|^2 + 2\|\mathbf{v}\|^2$.

**4.** Let $\mathbf{u}$ and $\mathbf{v}$ be nonzero vectors in the plane. Assume that $\mathbf{u}$ and $\mathbf{v}$ are not parallel vectors and that they have the same initial point. Draw the vectors $\mathbf{u} - \mathbf{v}$ and $\mathbf{u} + \mathbf{v}$. Use your sketch to explain why the result of Exercise 3 is called the Parallelogram Law.

**5.** Give an example of three distinct vectors $\mathbf{u}$, $\mathbf{v}$, and $\mathbf{w}$ such that $\mathbf{u} \times (\mathbf{v} \times \mathbf{w}) \neq (\mathbf{u} \times \mathbf{v}) \times \mathbf{w}$.

**6.** Let $A$ be a $(3 \times 3)$ matrix, given in column form as $A = [\mathbf{A}_1, \mathbf{A}_2, \mathbf{A}_3]$. Suppose each column vector is nonzero and that $\mathbf{A}_1 \cdot \mathbf{A}_2 = 0$, $\mathbf{A}_1 \cdot \mathbf{A}_3 = 0$, and $\mathbf{A}_2 \cdot \mathbf{A}_3 = 0$. Recall, for $\mathbf{b}$ a $(3 \times 1)$ vector, that the equation $A\mathbf{x} = \mathbf{b}$ can be written in the form

$$x_1\mathbf{A}_1 + x_2\mathbf{A}_2 + x_3\mathbf{A}_3 = \mathbf{b}. \qquad (1)$$

Use the orthogonality of the columns of $A$ to give a formula for $x_1$, $x_2$, $x_3$. [*Hint:* Form the dot product of $\mathbf{A}_i$ with both sides of (1).]

**7.** Let $A$ be as in Exercise 6. Show that $A$ is nonsingular.

**8.** Let $A$ be as in Exercise 6, along with the additional conditions that the columns of $A$ are unit vectors. That is, $\mathbf{A}_1 \cdot \mathbf{A}_1 = 1$, $\mathbf{A}_2 \cdot \mathbf{A}_2 = 1$, and $\mathbf{A}_3 \cdot \mathbf{A}_3 = 1$. Use the formula developed in Exercise 6 to show that $A^{-1} = A^T$. [*Hint:* Recall Eq. (7c) in Section 1.9.]

**9.** Let $A$ be as in Exercise 8; that is, $A^TA = I$. Show that the function $\mathbf{y} = A\mathbf{x}$ preserves lengths; that is, show that if $\mathbf{x}$ is $(3 \times 1)$, then $\|A\mathbf{x}\| = \|\mathbf{x}\|$.

**10.** Let $A$ be as in Exercise 8; that is, $A^TA = I$. Show that the function $\mathbf{y} = A\mathbf{x}$ preserves dot products; that is, show that if $\mathbf{u}$ and $\mathbf{v}$ are $(3 \times 1)$, then $(A\mathbf{u}) \cdot (A\mathbf{v}) = \mathbf{u} \cdot \mathbf{v}$.

**11.** Let $A$ be as in Exercise 8; that is, $A^TA = I$. Use the results of Exercises 9 and 10 to show that the function $\mathbf{y} = A\mathbf{x}$ preserves angles between vectors; that is, show that if the angle between $\mathbf{u}$ and $\mathbf{v}$ is $\theta$, then the angle between $A\mathbf{u}$ and $A\mathbf{v}$ is also $\theta$.

**12.** Let $\mathbf{u}$ and $\mathbf{v}$ be nonzero vectors such that $\|\mathbf{u}\| = \|\mathbf{v}\|$. Show that $\mathbf{u} - \mathbf{v}$ and $\mathbf{u} + \mathbf{v}$ are orthogonal.

# MATLAB EXERCISES

Exercises 1–4 are introductory exercises in programming. Each exercise asks you to write a MATLAB function (that is, a function M-file) that calculates the given quantity. If you are not familiar with MATLAB scripts and functions, you can read Section A-11 in the Appendix.

1. Recall that we can use Theorem 11 to find the area of a triangle whose vertices are $A = (a_1, a_2, a_3)$, $B = (b_1, b_2, b_3)$, and $C = (c_1, c_2, c_3)$ (see Example 8 in Section 2.3). Write a function M-file that calculates the area of a triangle having three given vertices. The function M-file should have the form

```
area = triangle(a,b,c)
```

where $a$, $b$, and $c$ are MATLAB row vectors representing the vertices of the triangle; that is, $a = [a_1, a_2, a_3]$, $b = [b_1, b_2, b_3]$, and $c = [c_1, c_2, c_3]$. As an option, you might want your function to issue a warning if the three vertices $a$, $b$, and $c$ are collinear. (See Exercise 4 where we discuss such a feature.)

2. Write a function M-file that calculates the volume of a parallelepiped whose sides are determined by given vectors

$$\mathbf{u} = \begin{bmatrix} u_1 \\ u_2 \\ u_3 \end{bmatrix}, \qquad \mathbf{v} = \begin{bmatrix} v_1 \\ v_2 \\ v_3 \end{bmatrix}, \qquad \mathbf{w} = \begin{bmatrix} w_1 \\ w_2 \\ w_3 \end{bmatrix}.$$

The function M-file should have the form

```
volume = parallelepiped(u,v,w).
```

3. Write a function M-file that calculates the area of a parallelogram having given vertices $a = [a_1, a_2, a_3]$, $b = [b_1, b_2, b_3]$, $c = [c_1, c_2, c_3]$, and $d = [d_1, d_2, d_3]$. The function M-file should have the form

```
area = parallelogram(a,b,c,d).
```

4. Write a function M-file that calculates the equation of the plane that passes through three given points $a = [a_1, a_2, a_3]$, $b = [b_1, b_2, b_3]$, and $c = [c_1, c_2, c_3]$. The equation of the plane should be given in the form

$$Ax + By + Cz = D.$$

Your function program should check to see if the given points $a$, $b$, and $c$ are collinear. To determine collinearity, you can calculate the cross product of $\mathbf{u}$ and $\mathbf{v}$ where

$$\mathbf{u} = \overrightarrow{ab} \text{ and } \mathbf{v} = \overrightarrow{ac}$$

(recall Theorem 12 in Section 2.3). If $a$, $b$, and $c$ are collinear, there is not a unique plane containing the three points and your program should communicate this fact to the user. The normal method of communicating whether or not a function encounters an abnormal situation is by "setting a flag." That is, a variable (a flag) is given one of several values in the function, depending on the circumstances encountered when the function is invoked. The flag is returned by the function and the user can tell what happened in the function by evaluating the flag.

To illustrate the ideas, we list the first few lines of one possible program for this exercise.

```
function [coefficients,ier]=plane(a,b,c)
%
%  This function calculates the equation of the plane
%     that passes through the points a, b and c.  The
%     flag ier is set to -1 if a, b and c are collinear
%     and is set to 1 otherwise.  When ier = 1, the
%     equation of the plane is Ax+By+Cz=D and this is
%     returned in the vector coefficients, where
%
             coefficients = [A, B, C, D].
%
%
ier = 1;
coefficients = [0,0,0,0];
u=b-a;
v=c-a;
w = cross(u,v);
normw = norm(w);
if normw == 0
   ier = -1;
   return
end
```

$$\vdots$$

$$\begin{bmatrix} \text{The rest of the program goes here, lines that} \\ \text{calculate the coefficients A, B, C, and D.} \end{bmatrix}$$

$$\vdots$$

The return statement in the lines above returns control to the calling program (the program that invoked the function "plane"). If $\mathbf{w} = \mathbf{u} \times \mathbf{v}$ is not the zero vector, then the return is not executed because $a$, $b$, and $c$ are not collinear. We leave it for you to complete this program. Test your function using the three points in Example 7 of Section 2.4. Also, test your function using the three collinear points

$$a = (2, 1, 5), \quad b = (6, 3, 15), \quad c = (-4, -2, -10).$$

# THE VECTOR SPACE $R^n$

3

OVERVIEW
In Chapter 2 we discussed geometric vector concepts in the familiar setting of two-space and three-space. In this chapter, we extend these concepts to $n$-dimensional space. For instance, we will see that lines and planes in three-space give rise to the idea of a subspace of $R^n$.

Many of the results in this chapter are grounded in the basic idea of linear independence that was introduced in Chapter 1. Linear independence is key, for example, to defining the concept of the dimension of a subspace or a basis for a subspace.

In turn, ideas such as subspace and basis are fundamental to modern mathematics and applications. We will see how these ideas are used to solve applied problems involving least-squares fits to data, Fourier series approximations of functions, systems of differential equations, and so forth.

In this chapter, for example, Sections 3.8 and 3.9 deal with least-squares fits to data. As we see in these two sections, methods for determining a least-squares fit (and a framework for interpreting the results of a least-squares fit) cannot be understood without a thorough appreciation of the basic topics in this chapter—subspace, basis, and dimension.

## 3.1    INTRODUCTION

In mathematics and the physical sciences, the term *vector* is applied to a wide variety of objects. Perhaps the most familiar application of the term is to quantities, such as force and velocity, that have both magnitude and direction. Such vectors can be represented in two-space or in three-space as directed line segments or arrows. (A review of geometric vectors is given in Chapter 2.) As we will see in Chapter 5, the term *vector* may also be used to describe objects such as matrices, polynomials, and continuous real-valued functions. In this section we demonstrate that $R^n$, the set of $n$-dimensional vectors, provides a natural bridge between the intuitive and natural concept of a geometric vector and that of an abstract vector in a general vector space. The remainder of the chapter is concerned with the algebraic and geometric structure of $R^n$ and subsets of $R^n$. Some of the concepts fundamental to describing this structure are subspace, basis, and dimension. These concepts are introduced and discussed in the first few sections. Although these ideas are relatively abstract, they are easy to understand in $R^n$, and they also have application to concrete problems. Thus $R^n$ will serve as an example and as a model for the study in Chapter 5 of general vector spaces.

To make the transition from geometric vectors in two-space and three-space to two-dimensional and three-dimensional vectors in $R^2$ and $R^3$, recall that the geometric vector, **v**, can be uniquely represented as a directed line segment $OP$, with initial point at the origin, $O$, and with terminal point $P$. If **v** is in two-space and point $P$ has coordinates $(a, b)$, then it is natural to represent **v** in $R^2$ as the vector

$$\mathbf{x} = \begin{bmatrix} a \\ b \end{bmatrix}.$$

Similarly, if **v** is in three-space and point $P$ has coordinates $(a, b, c)$, then **v** can be represented by the vector

$$\mathbf{x} = \begin{bmatrix} a \\ b \\ c \end{bmatrix}$$

 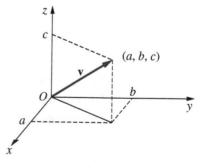

*Figure 3.1*    Geometric vectors

in $R^3$ (see Fig. 3.1). Under the correspondence $\mathbf{v} \rightarrow \mathbf{x}$ described above, the usual geometric addition of vectors translates to the standard algebraic addition in $R^2$ and $R^3$. Similarly, geometric multiplication by a scalar corresponds precisely to the standard algebraic scalar multiplication (see Fig. 3.2). Thus the study of $R^2$ and $R^3$ allows us to translate the geometric properties of vectors to algebraic properties. As we consider vectors from the algebraic viewpoint, it becomes natural to extend the concept of a vector to other objects that satisfy the same algebraic properties but for which there is no geometric representation. The elements of $R^n$, $n \geq 4$, are an immediate example.

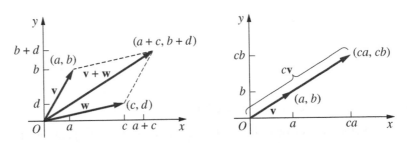

**Figure 3.2**    Addition and scalar multiplication of vectors

We conclude this section by noting a useful geometric interpretation for vectors in $R^2$ and $R^3$. A vector

$$\mathbf{x} = \left[ \begin{array}{c} a \\ b \end{array} \right]$$

in $R^2$ can be represented geometrically as the point in the plane that has coordinates $(a, b)$. Similarly, the vector

$$\mathbf{x} = \left[ \begin{array}{c} a \\ b \\ c \end{array} \right]$$

in $R^3$ corresponds to the point in three-space that has coordinates $(a, b, c)$. As the next two examples illustrate, this correspondence allows us to interpret subsets of $R^2$ and $R^3$ geometrically.

EXAMPLE 1    Give a geometric interpretation of the subset $W$ of $R^2$ defined by

$$W = \{\mathbf{x}: \mathbf{x} = \left[ \begin{array}{c} x_1 \\ x_2 \end{array} \right], \quad x_1 + x_2 = 2\}.$$

*Solution*    Geometrically, $W$ is the line in the plane with equation $x + y = 2$ (see Fig. 3.3).    ◼

**Figure 3.3**    The line $x + y = 2$

| | | EXAMPLE 2    Let $W$ be the subset of $R^3$ defined by

$$W = \{\mathbf{x} \colon \mathbf{x} = \begin{bmatrix} x_1 \\ x_2 \\ 1 \end{bmatrix}, \quad x_1 \text{ and } x_2 \text{ any real numbers}\}.$$

Give a geometric interpretation of $W$.

*Solution*    Geometrically, $W$ can be viewed as the plane in three-space with equation $z = 1$ (see Fig. 3.4).

**Figure 3.4**    The plane $z = 1$

## 3.1    EXERCISES

Exercises 1–11 refer to the vectors given in (1).

$$\mathbf{u} = \begin{bmatrix} 3 \\ 1 \end{bmatrix}, \quad \mathbf{v} = \begin{bmatrix} 1 \\ 2 \end{bmatrix},$$
$$\mathbf{x} = \begin{bmatrix} 0 \\ 1 \\ 3 \end{bmatrix}, \quad \mathbf{y} = \begin{bmatrix} 2 \\ 1 \\ 0 \end{bmatrix}, \tag{1}$$

In Exercises 1–11, sketch the geometric vector (with initial point at the origin) corresponding to each of the vectors given.

**1. u** and $-\mathbf{u}$

**2. v** and **2v**

**3. u** and $-3\mathbf{u}$

**4. v** and $-2\mathbf{v}$

**5. u, v,** and $\mathbf{u} + \mathbf{v}$

**6. u, 2v,** and $\mathbf{u} + 2\mathbf{v}$

**7. u, v,** and $\mathbf{u} - \mathbf{v}$

**8. u, v,** and $\mathbf{v} - \mathbf{u}$

**9. x** and **2x**

**10. y** and $-\mathbf{y}$

**11. x, y,** and $\mathbf{x} + \mathbf{y}$

In Exercises 12–17, interpret the subset $W$ of $R^2$ geometrically by sketching a graph for $W$.

**12.** $W = \{\mathbf{x} \colon \mathbf{x} = \begin{bmatrix} a \\ b \end{bmatrix}, \quad a + b = 1\}$

**13.** $W = \{ \mathbf{x} \colon \mathbf{x} = \begin{bmatrix} x_1 \\ x_2 \end{bmatrix}, \quad x_1 = -3x_2,$

   $x_2$ any real number$\}$

**14.** $W = \{ \mathbf{w} \colon \mathbf{w} = \begin{bmatrix} 0 \\ b \end{bmatrix}, \quad b$ any real number$\}$

**15.** $W = \{ \mathbf{u} \colon \mathbf{u} = \begin{bmatrix} c \\ d \end{bmatrix}, \quad c + d \geq 0 \}$

**16.** $W = \{ \mathbf{x} \colon \mathbf{x} = t \begin{bmatrix} 1 \\ 3 \end{bmatrix}, \quad t$ any real number$\}$

**17.** $W = \{ \mathbf{x} \colon \mathbf{x} = \begin{bmatrix} a \\ b \end{bmatrix}, \quad a^2 + b^2 = 4 \}$

In Exercises 18–21, interpret the subset $W$ of $R^3$ geometrically by sketching a graph for $W$.

**18.** $W = \{ \mathbf{x} \colon \mathbf{x} = \begin{bmatrix} a \\ 0 \\ 0 \end{bmatrix}, \quad a > 0 \}$

**19.** $W = \{ \mathbf{x} \colon \mathbf{x} = \begin{bmatrix} x_1 \\ x_2 \\ x_3 \end{bmatrix}, \quad x_1 = -x_2 - 2x_3 \}$

**20.** $W = \{ \mathbf{w} \colon \mathbf{w} = r \begin{bmatrix} 2 \\ 0 \\ 1 \end{bmatrix}, \quad r$ any real number$\}$

**21.** $W = \{ \mathbf{u} \colon \mathbf{u} = \begin{bmatrix} a \\ b \\ c \end{bmatrix}, \quad a^2 + b^2 + c^2 = 1$ and

   $c \geq 0 \}$

In Exercises 22–26, give a set-theoretic description of the given points as a subset $W$ of $R^2$.

**22.** The points on the line $x - 2y = 1$

**23.** The points on the $x$-axis

**24.** The points in the upper half-plane

**25.** The points on the line $y = 2$

**26.** The points on the parabola $y = x^2$

In Exercises 27–30, give a set-theoretic description of the given points as a subset $W$ of $R^3$.

**27.** The points on the plane $x + y - 2z = 0$

**28.** The points on the line with parametric equations
   $x = 2t, y = -3t$, and $z = t$

**29.** The points in the $yz$-plane

**30.** The points in the plane $y = 2$

# 3.2 VECTOR SPACE PROPERTIES OF $R^n$

Recall that $R^n$ is the set of all $n$-dimensional vectors with real components:

$$R^n = \{ \mathbf{x} \colon \mathbf{x} = \begin{bmatrix} x_1 \\ x_2 \\ \vdots \\ x_n \end{bmatrix}, \quad x_1, x_2, \ldots, x_n \text{ real numbers} \}.$$

If $\mathbf{x}$ and $\mathbf{y}$ are elements of $R^n$ with

$$\mathbf{x} = \begin{bmatrix} x_1 \\ x_2 \\ \vdots \\ x_n \end{bmatrix} \quad \text{and} \quad \mathbf{y} = \begin{bmatrix} y_1 \\ y_2 \\ \vdots \\ y_n \end{bmatrix},$$

then (see Section 1.5) the vector $\mathbf{x} + \mathbf{y}$ is defined by

$$\mathbf{x} + \mathbf{y} = \begin{bmatrix} x_1 + y_1 \\ x_2 + y_2 \\ \vdots \\ x_n + y_n \end{bmatrix},$$

and if $a$ is a real number, then the vector $a\mathbf{x}$ is defined to be

$$a\mathbf{x} = \begin{bmatrix} ax_1 \\ ax_2 \\ \vdots \\ ax_n \end{bmatrix}.$$

In the context of $R^n$, scalars are always real numbers. In particular, throughout this chapter, the term *scalar* always means a real number.

The following theorem gives the arithmetic properties of vector addition and scalar multiplication. Note that the statements in this theorem are already familiar from Section 1.6, which discusses the arithmetic properties of matrix operations (a vector in $R^n$ is an $(n \times 1)$ matrix, and hence the properties of matrix addition and scalar multiplication listed in Section 1.6 are inherited by vectors in $R^n$).

As we will see in Chapter 5, any set that satisfies the properties of Theorem 1 is called a ***vector space***; thus for each positive integer $n$, $R^n$ is an example of a vector space.

**THEOREM 1** If $\mathbf{x}$, $\mathbf{y}$, and $\mathbf{z}$ are vectors in $R^n$ and $a$ and $b$ are scalars, then the following properties hold:

**Closure properties:**

(c1) $\mathbf{x} + \mathbf{y}$ is in $R^n$.
(c2) $a\mathbf{x}$ is in $R^n$.

**Properties of addition:**

(a1) $\mathbf{x} + \mathbf{y} = \mathbf{y} + \mathbf{x}$.
(a2) $\mathbf{x} + (\mathbf{y} + \mathbf{z}) = (\mathbf{x} + \mathbf{y}) + \mathbf{z}$.
(a3) $R^n$ contains the zero vector, $\boldsymbol{\theta}$, and $\mathbf{x} + \boldsymbol{\theta} = \mathbf{x}$ for all $\mathbf{x}$ in $R^n$.
(a4) For each vector $\mathbf{x}$ in $R^n$, there is a vector $-\mathbf{x}$ in $R^n$ such that $\mathbf{x} + (-\mathbf{x}) = \boldsymbol{\theta}$.

**Properties of scalar multiplication:**

(m1) $a(b\mathbf{x}) = (ab)\mathbf{x}$.
(m2) $a(\mathbf{x} + \mathbf{y}) = a\mathbf{x} + a\mathbf{y}$.
(m3) $(a + b)\mathbf{x} = a\mathbf{x} + b\mathbf{x}$.
(m4) $1\mathbf{x} = \mathbf{x}$ for all $\mathbf{x}$ in $R^n$.

## Subspaces of $R^n$

In this chapter we are interested in subsets, $W$, of $R^n$ that satisfy all the properties of Theorem 1 (with $R^n$ replaced by $W$ throughout). Such a subset $W$ is called a ***subspace***

ORIGINƒ OF HIGHER-DIMENƒIONAL ƒPACEƒ   In addition to Grassmann (see Section 1.7), Sir William Hamilton (1805–1865) also envisioned algebras of $n$-tuples (which he called *polyplets*). In 1833, Hamilton gave rules for the addition and multiplication of ordered pairs, $(a, b)$, which became the algebra of complex numbers, $z = a + bi$. He searched for years for an extension to 3-tuples. He finally discovered, in a flash of inspiration while crossing a bridge, that the extension was possible if he used 4-tuples $(a, b, c, d) = a + bi + cj + dk$. In this algebra of quaternions, however, multiplication is not commutative; for example, $ij = k$, but $ji = -k$. Hamilton stopped and carved the basic formula, $i^2 = j^2 = k^2 = ijk$, on the bridge. He considered the quaternions his greatest achievement, even though his so-called Hamiltonian principle is considered fundamental to modern physics.

**Figure 3.5**
$W$ as a subset of $R^3$

of $R^n$. For example, consider the subset $W$ of $R^3$ defined by

$$W = \left\{ \mathbf{x} \colon \mathbf{x} = \begin{bmatrix} x_1 \\ x_2 \\ 0 \end{bmatrix}, \quad x_1 \text{ and } x_2 \text{ real numbers} \right\}.$$

Viewed geometrically, $W$ is the $xy$-plane (see Fig. 3.5), so it can be represented by $R^2$. Therefore, as can be easily shown, $W$ is a subspace of $R^3$.

The following theorem provides a convenient way of determining when a subset $W$ of $R^n$ is a subspace of $R^n$.

**THEOREM 2**   A subset $W$ of $R^n$ is a subspace of $R^n$ if and only if the following conditions are met:

**(s1)*** The zero vector, $\boldsymbol{\theta}$, is in $W$.

**(s2)**  $\mathbf{x} + \mathbf{y}$ is in $W$ whenever $\mathbf{x}$ and $\mathbf{y}$ are in $W$.

**(s3)**  $a\mathbf{x}$ is in $W$ whenever $\mathbf{x}$ is in $W$ and $a$ is any scalar.

**Proof**   Suppose that $W$ is a subset of $R^n$ that satisfies conditions (s1)–(s3). To show that $W$ is a subspace of $R^n$, we must show that the 10 properties of Theorem 1 (with $R^n$ replaced by $W$ throughout) are satisfied. But properties (a1), (a2), (m1), (m2), (m3), and (m4) are satisfied by every subset of $R^n$ and so hold in $W$. Condition (a3) is satisfied by $W$ because the hypothesis (s1) guarantees that $\boldsymbol{\theta}$ is in $W$. Similarly, (c1) and (c2) are given by the hypotheses (s2) and (s3), respectively. The only remaining condition is (a4), and we can easily see that $-\mathbf{x} = (-1)\mathbf{x}$. Thus if $\mathbf{x}$ is in $W$, then, by (s3), $-\mathbf{x}$ is also in $W$. Therefore, all the conditions of Theorem 1 are satisfied by $W$, and $W$ is a subspace of $R^n$.

For the converse, suppose $W$ is a subspace of $R^n$. The conditions (a3), (c1), and (c2) of Theorem 1 imply that properties (s1), (s2), and (s3) hold in $W$.  ■

The next example illustrates the use of Theorem 2 to verify that a subset $W$ of $R^n$ is a subspace of $R^n$.

---

*The usual statement of Theorem 2 lists only conditions (s2) and (s3) but assumes that the subset $W$ is nonempty. Thus (s1) replaces the assumption that $W$ is nonempty. The two versions are equivalent (see Exercise 34).

EXAMPLE 1    Let $W$ be the subset of $R^3$ defined by

$$W = \{x: x = \begin{bmatrix} x_1 \\ x_2 \\ x_3 \end{bmatrix}, \quad x_1 = x_2 - x_3, \quad x_2 \text{ and } x_3 \text{ any real numbers}\}.$$

Verify that $W$ is a subspace of $R^3$ and give a geometric interpretation of $W$.

*Solution*    To show that $W$ is a subspace of $R^3$, we must check that properties (s1)–(s3) of Theorem 2 are satisfied by $W$. Clearly the zero vector, $\boldsymbol{\theta}$, satisfies the condition $x_1 = x_2 - x_3$. Therefore, $\boldsymbol{\theta}$ is in $W$, showing that (s1) holds. Now let $\mathbf{u}$ and $\mathbf{v}$ be in $W$, where

$$\mathbf{u} = \begin{bmatrix} u_1 \\ u_2 \\ u_3 \end{bmatrix} \quad \text{and} \quad \mathbf{v} = \begin{bmatrix} v_1 \\ v_2 \\ v_3 \end{bmatrix},$$

and let $a$ be an arbitrary scalar. Since $\mathbf{u}$ and $\mathbf{v}$ are in $W$,

$$u_1 = u_2 - u_3 \quad \text{and} \quad v_1 = v_2 - v_3. \tag{1}$$

The sum $\mathbf{u} + \mathbf{v}$ and the scalar product $a\mathbf{u}$ are given by

$$\mathbf{u} + \mathbf{v} = \begin{bmatrix} u_1 + v_1 \\ u_2 + v_2 \\ u_3 + v_3 \end{bmatrix} \quad \text{and} \quad a\mathbf{u} = \begin{bmatrix} au_1 \\ au_2 \\ au_3 \end{bmatrix}.$$

To see that $\mathbf{u} + \mathbf{v}$ is in $W$, note that (1) gives

$$u_1 + v_1 = (u_2 - u_3) + (v_2 - v_3) = (u_2 + v_2) - (u_3 + v_3). \tag{2}$$

Thus if the components of $\mathbf{u}$ and $\mathbf{v}$ satisfy the condition $x_1 = x_2 - x_3$, then so do the components of the sum $\mathbf{u} + \mathbf{v}$. This argument shows that condition (s2) is met by $W$. Similarly, from (1),

$$au_1 = a(u_2 - u_3) = au_2 - au_3, \tag{3}$$

so $a\mathbf{u}$ is in $W$. Therefore, $W$ is a subspace of $R^3$.

Geometrically, $W$ is the plane whose equation is $x - y + z = 0$ (see Fig. 3.6). ■

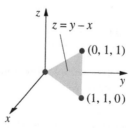

*Figure 3.6*    A portion of the plane $x - y + z = 0$

## Verifying that Subsets are Subspaces

Example 1 illustrates the typical procedure for verifying that a subset $W$ of $R^n$ is a subspace of $R^n$. In general such a verification proceeds along the following lines:

---

### Verifying that $W$ Is a Subspace of $R^n$

**Step 1.** An algebraic specification for the subset $W$ is given, and this specification serves as a test for determining whether a vector in $R^n$ is or is not in $W$.

**Step 2.** Test the zero vector, $\boldsymbol{\theta}$, of $R^n$ to see whether it satisfies the algebraic specification required to be in $W$. (This shows that $W$ is nonempty.)

**Step 3.** Choose two arbitrary vectors $\mathbf{x}$ and $\mathbf{y}$ from $W$. Thus $\mathbf{x}$ and $\mathbf{y}$ are in $R^n$, and both vectors satisfy the algebraic specification of $W$.

**Step 4.** Test the sum $\mathbf{x} + \mathbf{y}$ to see whether it meets the specification of $W$.

**Step 5.** For an arbitrary scalar, $a$, test the scalar multiple $a\mathbf{x}$ to see whether it meets the specification of $W$.

---

The next example illustrates again the use of the procedure described above to verify that a subset $W$ of $R^n$ is a subspace.

**EXAMPLE 2**  Let $W$ be the subset of $R^3$ defined by

$$W = \left\{ \mathbf{x} : \mathbf{x} = \begin{bmatrix} x_1 \\ x_2 \\ x_3 \end{bmatrix}, \quad x_2 = 2x_1, \quad x_3 = 3x_1, \quad x_1 \text{ any real number} \right\}.$$

Verify that $W$ is a subspace of $R^3$ and give a geometric interpretation of $W$.

*Solution*  For clarity in this initial example, we explicitly number the five steps used to verify that $W$ is a subspace.

1. The algebraic condition for $\mathbf{x}$ to be in $W$ is

$$x_2 = 2x_1 \quad \text{and} \quad x_3 = 3x_1. \tag{4}$$

In words, $\mathbf{x}$ is in $W$ if and only if the second component of $\mathbf{x}$ is twice the first component and the third component of $\mathbf{x}$ is three times the first.

2. Note that the zero vector, $\boldsymbol{\theta}$, clearly satisfies (4). Therefore, $\boldsymbol{\theta}$ is in $W$.

3. Next, let $\mathbf{u}$ and $\mathbf{v}$ be two arbitrary vectors in $W$:

$$\mathbf{u} = \begin{bmatrix} u_1 \\ u_2 \\ u_3 \end{bmatrix} \quad \text{and} \quad \mathbf{v} = \begin{bmatrix} v_1 \\ v_2 \\ v_3 \end{bmatrix}.$$

Because **u** and **v** are in $W$, each must satisfy the algebraic specification of $W$. That is,

$$u_2 = 2u_1 \quad \text{and} \quad u_3 = 3u_1 \tag{5a}$$

$$v_2 = 2v_1 \quad \text{and} \quad v_3 = 3v_1. \tag{5b}$$

4. Next, check whether the sum, **u** + **v**, is in $W$. (That is, does the vector **u** + **v** satisfy Eq. (4)?) Now, the sum **u** + **v** is given by

$$\mathbf{u} + \mathbf{v} = \begin{bmatrix} u_1 + v_1 \\ u_2 + v_2 \\ u_3 + v_3 \end{bmatrix}.$$

By (5a) and (5b), we have

$$u_2 + v_2 = 2(u_1 + v_1) \quad \text{and} \quad (u_3 + v_3) = 3(u_1 + v_1).$$

Thus **u** + **v** is in $W$ whenever **u** and **v** are both in $W$ (see Eq. (4)).

5. Similarly, for any scalar $a$, the scalar multiple $a\mathbf{u}$ is given by

$$a\mathbf{u} = \begin{bmatrix} au_1 \\ au_2 \\ au_3 \end{bmatrix}.$$

Using (5a) gives $au_2 = a(2u_1) = 2(au_1)$ and $au_3 = a(3u_1) = 3(au_1)$. Therefore, $a\mathbf{u}$ is in $W$ whenever **u** is in $W$ (see Eq. (4)).

Thus, by Theorem 2, $W$ is a subspace of $R^3$. Geometrically, $W$ is a line through the origin with parametric equations

$$\begin{aligned} x &= x_1 \\ y &= 2x_1 \\ z &= 3x_1. \end{aligned}$$

The graph of the line is given in Fig. 3.7.    ◼

Exercise 29 shows that any line in three-space through the origin is a subspace of $R^3$, and Example 3 of Section 3.3 shows that in three-space any plane through the origin is a subspace. Also note that for each positive integer $n$, $R^n$ is a subspace of itself and $\{\boldsymbol{\theta}\}$ is a subspace of $R^n$. We conclude this section with examples of subsets that are not subspaces.

EXAMPLE 3    Let $W$ be the subset of $R^3$ defined by

$$W = \{\mathbf{x}\colon \mathbf{x} = \begin{bmatrix} x_1 \\ x_2 \\ 1 \end{bmatrix}, \quad x_1 \text{ and } x_2 \text{ any real numbers}\}.$$

Show that $W$ is not a subspace of $R^3$.

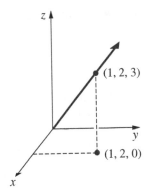

**Figure 3.7**    A geometric representation of the subspace $W$ (see Example 2)

**Solution**    To show that $W$ is not a subspace of $R^3$, we need only verify that at least one of the properties (s1)–(s3) of Theorem 2 fails. Note that geometrically $W$ can be interpreted as the plane $z = 1$, which does not contain the origin. In other words, the zero vector, $\boldsymbol{\theta}$, is not in $W$. Because condition (s1) of Theorem 2 is not met, $W$ is not a subspace of $R^3$. Although it is not necessary to do so, in this example we can also show that both conditions (s2) and (s3) of Theorem 2 fail. To see this, let $\mathbf{x}$ and $\mathbf{y}$ be in $W$, where

$$\mathbf{x} = \begin{bmatrix} x_1 \\ x_2 \\ 1 \end{bmatrix} \quad \text{and} \quad \mathbf{y} = \begin{bmatrix} y_1 \\ y_2 \\ 1 \end{bmatrix}.$$

Then $\mathbf{x} + \mathbf{y}$ is given by

$$\mathbf{x} + \mathbf{y} = \begin{bmatrix} x_1 + y_1 \\ x_2 + y_2 \\ 2 \end{bmatrix}.$$

In particular, $\mathbf{x} + \mathbf{y}$ is not in $W$, because the third component of $\mathbf{x} + \mathbf{y}$ does not have the value 1. Similarly,

$$a\mathbf{x} = \begin{bmatrix} ax_1 \\ ax_2 \\ a \end{bmatrix}.$$

So if $a \neq 1$, then $a\mathbf{x}$ is not in $W$.    ▬

EXAMPLE 4    Let $W$ be the subset of $R^2$ defined by

$$W = \{\mathbf{x}: \mathbf{x} = \begin{bmatrix} x_1 \\ x_2 \end{bmatrix}, \quad x_1 \text{ and } x_2 \text{ any integers}\}.$$

Demonstrate that $W$ is not a subspace of $R^2$.

*Solution*    In this case $\theta$ is in $W$, and it is easy to see that if $\mathbf{x}$ and $\mathbf{y}$ are in $W$, then so is $\mathbf{x} + \mathbf{y}$. If we set

$$\mathbf{x} = \begin{bmatrix} 1 \\ 1 \end{bmatrix}$$

and $a = 1/2$, then $\mathbf{x}$ is in $W$ but $a\mathbf{x}$ is not. Therefore, condition (s3) of Theorem 2 is not met by $W$, and hence $W$ is not a subspace of $R^2$. ◾

EXAMPLE 5    Let $W$ be the subspace of $R^2$ defined by

$$W = \{\mathbf{x}\colon \mathbf{x} = \begin{bmatrix} x_1 \\ x_2 \end{bmatrix}, \quad \text{where either } x_1 = 0 \text{ or } x_2 = 0\}.$$

Show that $W$ is not a subspace of $R^2$.

*Solution*    Let $\mathbf{x}$ and $\mathbf{y}$ be defined by

$$\mathbf{x} = \begin{bmatrix} 1 \\ 0 \end{bmatrix} \quad \text{and} \quad \mathbf{y} = \begin{bmatrix} 0 \\ 1 \end{bmatrix}.$$

Then $\mathbf{x}$ and $\mathbf{y}$ are in $W$. But

$$\mathbf{x} + \mathbf{y} = \begin{bmatrix} 1 \\ 1 \end{bmatrix}$$

is not in $W$, so $W$ is not a subspace of $R^2$. Note that $\theta$ is in $W$, and for any vector $\mathbf{x}$ in $W$ and any scalar $a$, $a\mathbf{x}$ is again in $W$. Geometrically, $W$ is the set of points in the plane that lie either on the $x$-axis or on the $y$-axis. Either of these axes alone is a subspace of $R^2$, but, as this example demonstrates, their union is not a subspace. ◾

## 3.2    EXERCISES

In Exercises 1–8, $W$ is a subset of $R^2$ consisting of vectors of the form

$$\mathbf{x} = \begin{bmatrix} x_1 \\ x_2 \end{bmatrix}.$$

In each case determine whether $W$ is a subspace of $R^2$. If $W$ is a subspace, then give a geometric description of $W$.

1. $W = \{\mathbf{x}\colon x_1 = 2x_2\}$
2. $W = \{\mathbf{x}\colon x_1 - x_2 = 2\}$
3. $W = \{\mathbf{x}\colon x_1 = x_2 \text{ or } x_1 = -x_2\}$
4. $W = \{\mathbf{x}\colon x_1 \text{ and } x_2 \text{ are rational numbers}\}$
5. $W = \{\mathbf{x}\colon x_1 = 0\}$
6. $W = \{\mathbf{x}\colon |x_1| + |x_2| = 0\}$

7. $W = \{\mathbf{x}\colon x_1^2 + x_2 = 1\}$
8. $W = \{\mathbf{x}\colon x_1 x_2 = 0\}$

In Exercises 9–17, $W$ is a subset of $R^3$ consisting of vectors of the form

$$\mathbf{x} = \begin{bmatrix} x_1 \\ x_2 \\ x_3 \end{bmatrix}.$$

In each case, determine whether $W$ is a subspace of $R^3$. If $W$ is a subspace, then give a geometric description of $W$.

9. $W = \{\mathbf{x}\colon x_3 = 2x_1 - x_2\}$
10. $W = \{\mathbf{x}\colon x_2 = x_3 + x_1\}$
11. $W = \{\mathbf{x}\colon x_1 x_2 = x_3\}$

12. $W = \{\mathbf{x}: x_1 = 2x_3\}$

13. $W = \{\mathbf{x}: x_1^2 = x_1 + x_2\}$

14. $W = \{\mathbf{x}: x_2 = 0\}$

15. $W = \{\mathbf{x}: x_1 = 2x_3, \quad x_2 = -x_3\}$

16. $W = \{\mathbf{x}: x_3 = x_2 = 2x_1\}$

17. $W = \{\mathbf{x}: x_2 = x_3 = 0\}$

18. Let $\mathbf{a}$ be a fixed vector in $R^3$, and define $W$ to be the subset of $R^3$ given by

$$W = \{\mathbf{x}: \mathbf{a}^T \mathbf{x} = 0\}.$$

Prove that $W$ is a subspace of $R^3$.

19. Let $W$ be the subspace defined in Exercise 18, where

$$\mathbf{a} = \begin{bmatrix} 1 \\ 2 \\ 3 \end{bmatrix}.$$

Give a geometric description for $W$.

20. Let $W$ be the subspace defined in Exercise 18, where

$$\mathbf{a} = \begin{bmatrix} 1 \\ 0 \\ 0 \end{bmatrix}.$$

Give a geometric description of $W$.

21. Let $\mathbf{a}$ and $\mathbf{b}$ be fixed vectors in $R^3$, and let $W$ be the subset of $R^3$ defined by

$$W = \{\mathbf{x}: \mathbf{a}^T \mathbf{x} = 0 \quad \text{and} \quad \mathbf{b}^T \mathbf{x} = 0\}.$$

Prove that $W$ is a subspace of $R^3$.

In Exercises 22–25, $W$ is the subspace of $R^3$ defined in Exercise 21. For each choice of $\mathbf{a}$ and $\mathbf{b}$, give a geometric description of $W$.

22. $\mathbf{a} = \begin{bmatrix} 1 \\ -1 \\ 2 \end{bmatrix}, \quad \mathbf{b} = \begin{bmatrix} 2 \\ -1 \\ 3 \end{bmatrix}$

23. $\mathbf{a} = \begin{bmatrix} 1 \\ 2 \\ 2 \end{bmatrix}, \quad \mathbf{b} = \begin{bmatrix} 1 \\ 3 \\ 0 \end{bmatrix}$

24. $\mathbf{a} = \begin{bmatrix} 1 \\ 1 \\ 1 \end{bmatrix}, \quad \mathbf{b} = \begin{bmatrix} 2 \\ 2 \\ 2 \end{bmatrix}$

25. $\mathbf{a} = \begin{bmatrix} 1 \\ 0 \\ -1 \end{bmatrix}, \quad \mathbf{b} = \begin{bmatrix} -2 \\ 0 \\ 2 \end{bmatrix}$

26. In $R^4$, let $\mathbf{x} = [1, -3, 2, 1]^T$, $\mathbf{y} = [2, 1, 3, 2]^T$, and $\mathbf{z} = [-3, 2, -1, 4]^T$. Set $a = 2$ and $b = -3$. Illustrate that the ten properties of Theorem 1 are satisfied by $\mathbf{x}$, $\mathbf{y}$, $\mathbf{z}$, $a$, and $b$.

27. In $R^2$, suppose that scalar multiplication were defined by

$$a\mathbf{x} = a \begin{bmatrix} x_1 \\ x_2 \end{bmatrix} = \begin{bmatrix} 2ax_1 \\ 2ax_2 \end{bmatrix}$$

for every scalar $a$. Illustrate with specific examples those properties of Theorem 1 that are not satisfied.

28. Let

$$W = \{\mathbf{x}: \mathbf{x} = \begin{bmatrix} x_1 \\ x_2 \end{bmatrix}, \quad x_2 \geq 0\}.$$

In the statement of Theorem 1, replace each occurrence of $R^n$ with $W$. Illustrate with specific examples each of the ten properties of Theorem 1 that are not satisfied.

29. In $R^3$, a line through the origin is the set of all points in $R^3$ whose coordinates satisfy $x_1 = at$, $x_2 = bt$, and $x_3 = ct$, where $t$ is a variable and $a$, $b$, and $c$ are not all zero. Show that a line through the origin is a subspace of $R^3$.

30. If $U$ and $V$ are subsets of $R^n$, then the set $U + V$ is defined by

$$U + V = \{\mathbf{x}: \mathbf{x} = \mathbf{u} + \mathbf{v}, \quad \mathbf{u} \text{ in } U \quad \text{and} \quad \mathbf{v} \text{ in } V\}.$$

Prove that if $U$ and $V$ are subspaces of $R^n$, then $U + V$ is a subspace of $R^n$.

31. Let $U$ and $V$ be subspaces of $R^n$. Prove that the intersection, $U \cap V$, is also a subspace of $R^n$.

32. Let $U$ and $V$ be the subspaces of $R^3$ defined by

$$U = \{\mathbf{x}: \mathbf{a}^T \mathbf{x} = 0\} \quad \text{and} \quad V = \{\mathbf{x}: \mathbf{b}^T \mathbf{x} = 0\},$$

where

$$\mathbf{a} = \begin{bmatrix} 1 \\ 1 \\ 0 \end{bmatrix} \quad \text{and} \quad \mathbf{b} = \begin{bmatrix} 0 \\ 1 \\ -1 \end{bmatrix}.$$

Demonstrate that the union, $U \cup V$, is not a subspace of $R^3$ (see Exercise 18).

33. Let $U$ and $V$ be subspaces of $R^n$.

    a) Show that the union, $U \cup V$, satisfies properties (s1) and (s3) of Theorem 2.

    b) If neither $U$ nor $V$ is a subset of the other, show that $U \cup V$ does not satisfy condition (s2) of

Theorem 2. [*Hint*: Choose vectors **u** and **v** such that **u** is in $U$ but not in $V$ and **v** is in $V$ but not in $U$. Assume that $\mathbf{u} + \mathbf{v}$ is in either $U$ or $V$ and reach a contradiction.]

**34.** Let $W$ be a nonempty subset of $R^n$ that satisfies conditions (s2) and (s3) of Theorem 2. Prove that $\boldsymbol{\theta}$ is in $W$ and conclude that $W$ is a subspace of $R^n$. (Thus property (s1) of Theorem 2 can be replaced with the assumption that $W$ is nonempty.)

## 3.3    EXAMPLES OF SUBSPACES

In this section we introduce several important and particularly useful examples of subspaces of $R^n$.

### The Span of a Subset

To begin, recall that if $\mathbf{v}_1, \ldots, \mathbf{v}_r$ are vectors in $R^n$, then a vector **y** in $R^n$ is a linear combination of $\mathbf{v}_1, \ldots, \mathbf{v}_r$, provided that there exist scalars $a_1, \ldots, a_r$ such that

$$\mathbf{y} = a_1\mathbf{v}_1 + \cdots + a_r\mathbf{v}_r.$$

The next theorem shows that the set of all linear combinations of $\mathbf{v}_1, \ldots, \mathbf{v}_r$ is a subspace of $R^n$.

**THEOREM 3**    If $\mathbf{v}_1, \ldots, \mathbf{v}_r$ are vectors in $R^n$, then the set $W$ consisting of all linear combinations of $\mathbf{v}_1, \ldots, \mathbf{v}_r$ is a subspace of $R^n$.

**Proof**    To show that $W$ is a subspace of $R^n$, we must verify that the three conditions of Theorem 2 are satisfied. Now $\boldsymbol{\theta}$ is in $W$ because

$$\boldsymbol{\theta} = 0\mathbf{v}_1 + \cdots + 0\mathbf{v}_r.$$

Next, suppose that **y** and **z** are in $W$. Then there exist scalars $a_1, \ldots, a_r, b_1, \ldots, b_r$ such that

$$\mathbf{y} = a_1\mathbf{v}_1 + \cdots + a_r\mathbf{v}_r$$

and

$$\mathbf{z} = b_1\mathbf{v}_1 + \cdots + b_r\mathbf{v}_r.$$

Thus,

$$\mathbf{y} + \mathbf{z} = (a_1 + b_1)\mathbf{v}_1 + \cdots + (a_r + b_r)\mathbf{v}_r,$$

so $\mathbf{y} + \mathbf{z}$ is a linear combination of $\mathbf{v}_1, \ldots, \mathbf{v}_r$; that is, $\mathbf{y} + \mathbf{z}$ is in $W$. Also, for any scalar $c$,

$$c\mathbf{y} = (ca_1)\mathbf{v}_1 + \cdots + (ca_r)\mathbf{v}_r.$$

In particular, $c\mathbf{y}$ is in $W$. It follows from Theorem 2 that $W$ is a subspace of $R^n$. ◼

If $S = \{\mathbf{v}_1, \ldots, \mathbf{v}_r\}$ is a subset of $R^n$, then the subspace $W$ consisting of all linear combinations of $\mathbf{v}_1, \ldots, \mathbf{v}_r$ is called the ***subspace spanned by S*** and will be denoted by

$$\text{Sp}(S) \quad \text{or} \quad \text{Sp}\{\mathbf{v}_1, \ldots, \mathbf{v}_r\}.$$

*Figure 3.8*
Sp{v}

For a single vector **v** in $R^n$, Sp{**v**} is the subspace

$$Sp\{\mathbf{v}\} = \{a\mathbf{v}: a \text{ is any real number}\}.$$

If **v** is a nonzero vector in $R^2$ or $R^3$, then Sp{**v**} can be interpreted as the line determined by **v** (see Fig. 3.8). As a specific example, consider

$$\mathbf{v} = \begin{bmatrix} 1 \\ 2 \\ 3 \end{bmatrix}.$$

Then

$$Sp\{\mathbf{v}\} = \{t \begin{bmatrix} 1 \\ 2 \\ 3 \end{bmatrix} : t \text{ is any real number}\}.$$

Thus Sp{**v**} is the line with parametric equations

$$x = t$$
$$y = 2t$$
$$z = 3t.$$

Equivalently, Sp{**v**} is the line that passes through the origin and through the point with coordinates 1, 2, and 3 (see Fig. 3.9).

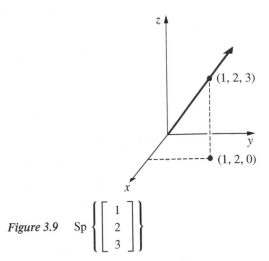

*Figure 3.9*   $Sp \left\{ \begin{bmatrix} 1 \\ 2 \\ 3 \end{bmatrix} \right\}$

If **u** and **v** are noncollinear geometric vectors, then

$$Sp\{\mathbf{u}, \mathbf{v}\} = \{a\mathbf{u} + b\mathbf{v}: a, b \text{ any real numbers}\}$$

is the plane containing **u** and **v** (see Fig. 3.10). The following example illustrates this case with a subspace of $R^3$.

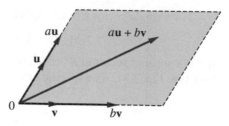

*Figure 3.10*    Sp{$\mathbf{u}$, $\mathbf{v}$}

EXAMPLE 1    Let $\mathbf{u}$ and $\mathbf{v}$ be the three-dimensional vectors

$$\mathbf{u} = \begin{bmatrix} 2 \\ 1 \\ 0 \end{bmatrix} \quad \text{and} \quad \mathbf{v} = \begin{bmatrix} 0 \\ 1 \\ 2 \end{bmatrix}.$$

Determine $W = \text{Sp}\{\mathbf{u}, \mathbf{v}\}$ and give a geometric interpretation of $W$.

*Solution*    Let $\mathbf{y}$ be an arbitrary vector in $R^3$, where

$$\mathbf{y} = \begin{bmatrix} y_1 \\ y_2 \\ y_3 \end{bmatrix}.$$

Then $\mathbf{y}$ is in $W$ if and only if there exist scalars $x_1$ and $x_2$ such that

$$\mathbf{y} = x_1\mathbf{u} + x_2\mathbf{v}. \tag{1}$$

That is, $\mathbf{y}$ is in $W$ if and only if there exist scalars $x_1$ and $x_2$ such that

$$\begin{aligned} y_1 &= 2x_1 \\ y_2 &= x_1 + x_2 \\ y_3 &= \phantom{x_1 +} 2x_2. \end{aligned} \tag{2}$$

The augmented matrix for linear system (2) is

$$\begin{bmatrix} 2 & 0 & y_1 \\ 1 & 1 & y_2 \\ 0 & 2 & y_3 \end{bmatrix},$$

PHY∫ICAL REPRE∫ENTATION∫ OF VECTOR∫    The vector space work of Grassmann and Hamilton was distilled and popularized for the case of $R^3$ by a Yale University physicist, Josiah Willard Gibbs (1839–1903). Gibbs produced a pamphlet, "Elements of Vector Analysis," mainly for the use of his students. In it, and subsequent articles, Gibbs simplified and improved Hamilton's work in multiple algebras with regard to three-dimensional space. This led to the familiar geometrical representation of vector algebra in terms of operations on directed line segments.

and this matrix is row equivalent to the matrix

$$\begin{bmatrix} 1 & 0 & (1/2)y_1 \\ 0 & 1 & y_2 - (1/2)y_1 \\ 0 & 0 & (1/2)y_3 + (1/2)y_1 - y_2 \end{bmatrix} \tag{3}$$

in echelon form. Therefore, linear system (2) is consistent if and only if $(1/2)y_1 - y_2 + (1/2)y_3 = 0$, or equivalently, if and only if

$$y_1 - 2y_2 + y_3 = 0. \tag{4}$$

Thus $W$ is the subspace given by

$$W = \{ \mathbf{y} = \begin{bmatrix} y_1 \\ y_2 \\ y_3 \end{bmatrix} : y_1 - 2y_2 + y_3 = 0 \}. \tag{5}$$

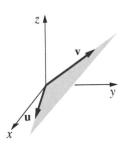

**Figure 3.11**
A portion of the plane
$x - 2y + z = 0$

It also follows from Eq. (5) that geometrically $W$ is the plane in three-space with equation $x - 2y + z = 0$ (see Fig. 3.11).

## The Null Space of a Matrix

We now introduce two subspaces that have particular relevance to the linear system of equations $A\mathbf{x} = \mathbf{b}$, where $A$ is an $(m \times n)$ matrix. The first of these subspaces is called the *null space* of $A$ (or the *kernel* of $A$) and consists of all solutions of $A\mathbf{x} = \boldsymbol{\theta}$.

DEFINITION 1

Let $A$ be an $(m \times n)$ matrix. The *null space* of $A$ [denoted $\mathcal{N}(A)$] is the set of vectors in $R^n$ defined by

$$\mathcal{N}(A) = \{\mathbf{x}: A\mathbf{x} = \boldsymbol{\theta}, \quad \mathbf{x} \text{ in } R^n\}.$$

In words, the null space consists of all those vectors $\mathbf{x}$ such that $A\mathbf{x}$ is the zero vector. The next theorem shows that the null space of an $(m \times n)$ matrix $A$ is a subspace of $R^n$.

THEOREM 4    If $A$ is an $(m \times n)$ matrix, then $\mathcal{N}(A)$ is a subspace of $R^n$.

*Proof*    To show that $\mathcal{N}(A)$ is a subspace of $R^n$, we must verify that the three conditions of Theorem 2 hold. Let $\boldsymbol{\theta}$ be the zero vector in $R^n$. Then

$$A\boldsymbol{\theta} = \boldsymbol{\theta}, \tag{6}$$

and so $\boldsymbol{\theta}$ is in $\mathcal{N}(A)$. (*Note*: In Eq. (6), the left $\boldsymbol{\theta}$ is in $R^n$ but the right $\boldsymbol{\theta}$ is in $R^m$.) Now let $\mathbf{u}$ and $\mathbf{v}$ be vectors in $\mathcal{N}(A)$. Then $\mathbf{u}$ and $\mathbf{v}$ are in $R^n$ and

$$A\mathbf{u} = \boldsymbol{\theta} \quad \text{and} \quad A\mathbf{v} = \boldsymbol{\theta}. \tag{7}$$

To see that $\mathbf{u} + \mathbf{v}$ is in $\mathcal{N}(A)$, we must test $\mathbf{u} + \mathbf{v}$ against the algebraic specification of $\mathcal{N}(A)$; that is, we must show that $A(\mathbf{u} + \mathbf{v}) = \boldsymbol{\theta}$. But it follows from Eq. (7) that

$$A(\mathbf{u} + \mathbf{v}) = A\mathbf{u} + A\mathbf{v} = \boldsymbol{\theta} + \boldsymbol{\theta} = \boldsymbol{\theta},$$

and therefore $\mathbf{u} + \mathbf{v}$ is in $\mathcal{N}(A)$. Similarly, for any scalar $a$, it follows from Eq. (7) that

$$A(a\mathbf{u}) = aA\mathbf{u} = a\boldsymbol{\theta} = \boldsymbol{\theta}.$$

Therefore, $a\mathbf{u}$ is in $\mathcal{N}(A)$. By Theorem 2, $\mathcal{N}(A)$ is a subspace of $R^n$. ◼

EXAMPLE 2    Describe $\mathcal{N}(A)$, where $A$ is the $(3 \times 4)$ matrix

$$A = \begin{bmatrix} 1 & 1 & 3 & 1 \\ 2 & 1 & 5 & 4 \\ 1 & 2 & 4 & -1 \end{bmatrix}.$$

**Solution**    $\mathcal{N}(A)$ is determined by solving the homogeneous system

$$A\mathbf{x} = \boldsymbol{\theta}. \tag{8}$$

This is accomplished by reducing the augmented matrix $[A \,|\, \boldsymbol{\theta}]$ to echelon form. It is easy to verify that $[A \,|\, \boldsymbol{\theta}]$ is row equivalent to

$$\begin{bmatrix} 1 & 0 & 2 & 3 & 0 \\ 0 & 1 & 1 & -2 & 0 \\ 0 & 0 & 0 & 0 & 0 \end{bmatrix}.$$

Solving the corresponding reduced system yields

$$x_1 = -2x_3 - 3x_4$$
$$x_2 = -\;x_3 + 2x_4$$

as the solution to Eq. (8). Thus a vector $\mathbf{x}$ in $R^4$,

$$\mathbf{x} = \begin{bmatrix} x_1 \\ x_2 \\ x_3 \\ x_4 \end{bmatrix},$$

is in $\mathcal{N}(A)$ if and only if $\mathbf{x}$ can be written in the form

$$\mathbf{x} = \begin{bmatrix} -2x_3 - 3x_4 \\ -x_3 + 2x_4 \\ x_3 \\ x_4 \end{bmatrix} = x_3 \begin{bmatrix} -2 \\ -1 \\ 1 \\ 0 \end{bmatrix} + x_4 \begin{bmatrix} -3 \\ 2 \\ 0 \\ 1 \end{bmatrix},$$

where $x_3$ and $x_4$ are arbitrary; that is,

$$\mathcal{N}(A) = \{\mathbf{x}: \mathbf{x} = x_3 \begin{bmatrix} -2 \\ -1 \\ 1 \\ 0 \end{bmatrix} + x_4 \begin{bmatrix} -3 \\ 2 \\ 0 \\ 1 \end{bmatrix}, \quad x_3 \text{ and } x_4 \text{ any real numbers}\}. \quad ◼$$

As the next example demonstrates, the fact that $\mathcal{N}(A)$ is a subspace can be used to show that in three-space every plane through the origin is a subspace.

**EXAMPLE 3**   Verify that any plane through the origin in $R^3$ is a subspace of $R^3$.

**Solution**   The equation of a plane in three-space through the origin is

$$ax + by + cz = 0, \tag{9}$$

where $a$, $b$, and $c$ are specified constants not all of which are zero. Now, Eq. (9) can be written as

$$A\mathbf{x} = \boldsymbol{\theta},$$

where $A$ is a $(1 \times 3)$ matrix and $\mathbf{x}$ is in $R^3$:

$$A = [a \quad b \quad c] \quad \text{and} \quad \mathbf{x} = \begin{bmatrix} x \\ y \\ z \end{bmatrix}.$$

Thus $\mathbf{x}$ is on the plane defined by Eq. (9) if and only if $\mathbf{x}$ is in $\mathcal{N}(A)$. Since $\mathcal{N}(A)$ is a subspace of $R^3$ by Theorem 4, any plane through the origin is a subspace of $R^3$. ◢

## The Range of a Matrix

Another important subspace associated with an $(m \times n)$ matrix $A$ is the **range** of $A$, defined as follows.

**DEFINITION 2**   Let $A$ be an $(m \times n)$ matrix. The **range** of $A$ [denoted $\mathcal{R}(A)$] is the set of vectors in $R^m$ defined by

$$\mathcal{R}(A) = \{\mathbf{y}: \mathbf{y} = A\mathbf{x} \text{ for some } \mathbf{x} \text{ in } R^n\}.$$

In words, the range of $A$ consists of the set of all vectors $\mathbf{y}$ in $R^m$ such that the linear system

$$A\mathbf{x} = \mathbf{y}$$

is consistent. As another way to view $\mathcal{R}(A)$, suppose that $A$ is an $(m \times n)$ matrix. We can regard multiplication by $A$ as defining a function from $R^n$ to $R^m$. In this sense, as $\mathbf{x}$ varies through $R^n$, the set of all vectors

$$\mathbf{y} = A\mathbf{x}$$

produced in $R^m$ constitutes the "range" of the function.

We saw in Section 1.5 (see Theorem 5) that if the $(m \times n)$ matrix $A$ has columns $\mathbf{A}_1, \mathbf{A}_2, \ldots, \mathbf{A}_n$ and if

$$\mathbf{x} = \begin{bmatrix} x_1 \\ x_2 \\ \vdots \\ x_n \end{bmatrix},$$

then the matrix equation

$$A\mathbf{x} = \mathbf{y}$$

is equivalent to the vector equation

$$x_1\mathbf{A}_1 + x_2\mathbf{A}_2 + \cdots + x_n\mathbf{A}_n = \mathbf{y}.$$

Therefore, it follows that

$$\mathcal{R}(A) = \text{Sp}\{\mathbf{A}_1, \mathbf{A}_2, \ldots, \mathbf{A}_n\}.$$

By Theorem 3, $\text{Sp}\{\mathbf{A}_1, \mathbf{A}_2, \ldots, \mathbf{A}_n\}$ is a subspace of $R^m$. (This subspace is also called the **column space** of matrix $A$.) Consequently, $\mathcal{R}(A)$ is a subspace of $R^m$, and we have proved the following theorem.

THEOREM 5    If $A$ is an $(m \times n)$ matrix and if $\mathcal{R}(A)$ is the range of $A$, then $\mathcal{R}(A)$ is a subspace of $R^m$.

The next example illustrates a way to give an algebraic specification for $\mathcal{R}(A)$.

EXAMPLE 4    Describe the range of $A$, where $A$ is the $(3 \times 4)$ matrix

$$A = \begin{bmatrix} 1 & 1 & 3 & 1 \\ 2 & 1 & 5 & 4 \\ 1 & 2 & 4 & -1 \end{bmatrix}.$$

*Solution*    Let $\mathbf{b}$ be an arbitrary vector in $R^3$,

$$\mathbf{b} = \begin{bmatrix} b_1 \\ b_2 \\ b_3 \end{bmatrix}.$$

Then $\mathbf{b}$ is in $\mathcal{R}(A)$ if and only if the system of equations

$$A\mathbf{x} = \mathbf{b}$$

is consistent. The augmented matrix for the system is

$$[A \mid \mathbf{b}] = \begin{bmatrix} 1 & 1 & 3 & 1 & b_1 \\ 2 & 1 & 5 & 4 & b_2 \\ 1 & 2 & 4 & -1 & b_3 \end{bmatrix},$$

which is equivalent to

$$\begin{bmatrix} 1 & 0 & 2 & 3 & b_2 - b_1 \\ 0 & 1 & 1 & -2 & 2b_1 - b_2 \\ 0 & 0 & 0 & 0 & -3b_1 + b_2 + b_3 \end{bmatrix}.$$

It follows that $A\mathbf{x} = \mathbf{b}$ has a solution [or equivalently, $\mathbf{b}$ is in $\mathcal{R}(A)$] if and only if $-3b_1 + b_2 + b_3 = 0$, or $b_3 = 3b_1 - b_2$, where $b_1$ and $b_2$ are arbitrary. Thus

$$\mathcal{R}(A) = \{\mathbf{b}: \mathbf{b} = \begin{bmatrix} b_1 \\ b_2 \\ 3b_1 - b_2 \end{bmatrix}$$

$$= b_1 \begin{bmatrix} 1 \\ 0 \\ 3 \end{bmatrix} + b_2 \begin{bmatrix} 0 \\ 1 \\ -1 \end{bmatrix}, \quad b_1 \text{ and } b_2 \text{ any real numbers}\}. \quad \blacksquare$$

### The Row Space of a Matrix

If $A$ is an $(m \times n)$ matrix with columns $\mathbf{A}_1, \mathbf{A}_2, \ldots, \mathbf{A}_n$, then we have already defined the *column space* of $A$ to be

$$\text{Sp}\{\mathbf{A}_1, \mathbf{A}_2, \ldots, \mathbf{A}_n\}.$$

In a similar fashion, the rows of $A$ can be regarded as vectors $\mathbf{a}_1, \mathbf{a}_2, \ldots, \mathbf{a}_m$ in $R^n$, and the *row space* of $A$ is defined to be

$$\text{Sp}\{\mathbf{a}_1, \mathbf{a}_2, \ldots, \mathbf{a}_m\}.$$

For example, if

$$A = \begin{bmatrix} 1 & 2 & 3 \\ 1 & 0 & 1 \end{bmatrix},$$

then the row space of $A$ is $\text{Sp}\{\mathbf{a}_1, \mathbf{a}_2\}$, where

$$\mathbf{a}_1 = [1 \quad 2 \quad 3] \quad \text{and} \quad \mathbf{a}_2 = [1 \quad 0 \quad 1].$$

The following theorem shows that row-equivalent matrices have the same row space.

**THEOREM 6**  Let $A$ be an $(m \times n)$ matrix, and suppose that $A$ is row equivalent to the $(m \times n)$ matrix $B$. Then $A$ and $B$ have the same row space. $\blacksquare$

The proof of Theorem 6 is given at the end of this section. To illustrate Theorem 6, let $A$ be the $(3 \times 3)$ matrix

$$A = \begin{bmatrix} 1 & -1 & 1 \\ 2 & -1 & 4 \\ 1 & 1 & 5 \end{bmatrix}.$$

By performing the elementary row operations $R_2 - 2R_1$, $R_3 - R_1$, $R_1 + R_2$, and $R_3 - 2R_2$, we obtain the matrix

$$B = \begin{bmatrix} 1 & 0 & 3 \\ 0 & 1 & 2 \\ 0 & 0 & 0 \end{bmatrix}.$$

By Theorem 6, matrices $A$ and $B$ have the same row space. Clearly the zero row of $B$ contributes nothing as an element of the spanning set, so the row space of $B$ is $\mathrm{Sp}\{\mathbf{b}_1, \mathbf{b}_2\}$, where

$$\mathbf{b}_1 = [1 \ \ 0 \ \ 3] \quad \text{and} \quad \mathbf{b}_2 = [0 \ \ 1 \ \ 2].$$

If the rows of $A$ are denoted by $\mathbf{a}_1$, $\mathbf{a}_2$, and $\mathbf{a}_3$, then

$$\mathrm{Sp}\{\mathbf{a}_1, \mathbf{a}_2, \mathbf{a}_3\} = \mathrm{Sp}\{\mathbf{b}_1, \mathbf{b}_2\}.$$

More generally, given a subset $S = \{\mathbf{v}_1, \ldots, \mathbf{v}_m\}$ of $R^n$, Theorem 6 allows us to obtain a "nicer" subset $T = \{\mathbf{w}_1, \ldots, \mathbf{w}_k\}$ of $R^n$ such that $\mathrm{Sp}(S) = \mathrm{Sp}(T)$. The next example illustrates this.

**EXAMPLE 5**   Let $S = \{\mathbf{v}_1, \mathbf{v}_2, \mathbf{v}_3, \mathbf{v}_4\}$ be a subset of $R^3$, where

$$\mathbf{v}_1 = \begin{bmatrix} 1 \\ 2 \\ 1 \end{bmatrix}, \quad \mathbf{v}_2 = \begin{bmatrix} 2 \\ 3 \\ 5 \end{bmatrix}, \quad \mathbf{v}_3 = \begin{bmatrix} 1 \\ 4 \\ -5 \end{bmatrix}, \quad \text{and} \quad \mathbf{v}_4 = \begin{bmatrix} 2 \\ 5 \\ -1 \end{bmatrix}.$$

Show that there exists a set $T = \{\mathbf{w}_1, \mathbf{w}_2\}$ consisting of two vectors in $R^3$ such that $\mathrm{Sp}(S) = \mathrm{Sp}(T)$.

**Solution**   Let $A$ be the $(3 \times 4)$ matrix

$$A = [\mathbf{v}_1, \mathbf{v}_2, \mathbf{v}_3, \mathbf{v}_4];$$

that is,

$$A = \begin{bmatrix} 1 & 2 & 1 & 2 \\ 2 & 3 & 4 & 5 \\ 1 & 5 & -5 & -1 \end{bmatrix}.$$

The matrix $A^T$ is the $(4 \times 3)$ matrix

$$A^T = \begin{bmatrix} 1 & 2 & 1 \\ 2 & 3 & 5 \\ 1 & 4 & -5 \\ 2 & 5 & -1 \end{bmatrix},$$

and the row vectors of $A^T$ are precisely the vectors $\mathbf{v}_1^T$, $\mathbf{v}_2^T$, $\mathbf{v}_3^T$, and $\mathbf{v}_4^T$. It is straightforward to see that $A^T$ reduces to the matrix

$$B^T = \begin{bmatrix} 1 & 0 & 7 \\ 0 & 1 & -3 \\ 0 & 0 & 0 \\ 0 & 0 & 0 \end{bmatrix}.$$

So, by Theorem 6, $A^T$ and $B^T$ have the same row space. Thus $A$ and $B$ have the same column space, where

$$B = \begin{bmatrix} 1 & 0 & 0 & 0 \\ 0 & 1 & 0 & 0 \\ 7 & -3 & 0 & 0 \end{bmatrix}.$$

In particular, $\text{Sp}(S) = \text{Sp}(T)$, where $T = \{\mathbf{w}_1, \mathbf{w}_2\}$,

$$\mathbf{w}_1 = \begin{bmatrix} 1 \\ 0 \\ 7 \end{bmatrix} \quad \text{and} \quad \mathbf{w}_2 = \begin{bmatrix} 0 \\ -1 \\ 3 \end{bmatrix}. \qquad \blacksquare$$

## Proof of Theorem 6 (Optional)

Assume that $A$ and $B$ are row-equivalent $(m \times n)$ matrices. Then there is a sequence of matrices

$$A = A_1, A_2, \ldots, A_{k-1}, A_k = B$$

such that for $2 \le j \le k$, $A_j$ is obtained by performing a single elementary row operation on $A_{j-1}$. It suffices, then, to show that $A_{j-1}$ and $A_j$ have the same row space for each $j, 2 \le j \le k$. This means that it is sufficient to consider only the case in which $B$ is obtained from $A$ by a single elementary row operation.

Let $A$ have rows $\mathbf{a}_1, \ldots, \mathbf{a}_m$; that is, $A$ is the $(m \times n)$ matrix

$$A = \begin{bmatrix} \mathbf{a}_1 \\ \vdots \\ \mathbf{a}_j \\ \vdots \\ \mathbf{a}_k \\ \vdots \\ \mathbf{a}_m \end{bmatrix},$$

where each $\mathbf{a}_i$ is a $(1 \times n)$ row vector;

$$\mathbf{a}_i = [a_{i1} \quad a_{i2} \quad \cdots \quad a_{in}].$$

Clearly the order of the rows is immaterial; that is, if $B$ is obtained by interchanging the $j$th and $k$th rows of $A$,

$$B = \begin{bmatrix} \mathbf{a}_1 \\ \vdots \\ \mathbf{a}_k \\ \vdots \\ \mathbf{a}_j \\ \vdots \\ \mathbf{a}_m \end{bmatrix},$$

then $A$ and $B$ have the same row space because

$$\text{Sp}\{\mathbf{a}_1, \ldots, \mathbf{a}_j, \ldots, \mathbf{a}_k, \ldots, \mathbf{a}_m\} = \text{Sp}\{\mathbf{a}_1, \ldots, \mathbf{a}_k, \ldots, \mathbf{a}_j, \ldots, \mathbf{a}_m\}.$$

Next, suppose that $B$ is obtained by performing the row operation $R_k + cR_j$ on $A$; thus,

$$B = \begin{bmatrix} \mathbf{a}_1 \\ \vdots \\ \mathbf{a}_j \\ \vdots \\ \mathbf{a}_k + c\mathbf{a}_j \\ \vdots \\ \mathbf{a}_m \end{bmatrix}.$$

If the vector $\mathbf{x}$ is in the row space of $A$, then there exist scalars $b_1, \ldots, b_m$ such that

$$\mathbf{x} = b_1\mathbf{a}_1 + \cdots + b_j\mathbf{a}_j + \cdots + b_k\mathbf{a}_k + \cdots + b_m\mathbf{a}_m. \tag{10}$$

The vector equation (10) can be rewritten as

$$\mathbf{x} = b_1\mathbf{a}_1 + \cdots + (b_j - cb_k)\mathbf{a}_j + \cdots + b_k(\mathbf{a}_k + c\mathbf{a}_j) + \cdots + b_m\mathbf{a}_m, \tag{11}$$

and hence $\mathbf{x}$ is in the row space of $B$. Conversely, if the vector $\mathbf{y}$ is in the row space of $B$, then there exist scalars $d_1, \ldots, d_m$ such that

$$\mathbf{y} = d_1\mathbf{a}_1 + \cdots + d_j\mathbf{a}_j + \cdots + d_k(\mathbf{a}_k + c\mathbf{a}_j) + \cdots + d_m\mathbf{a}_m. \tag{12}$$

But Eq. (12) can be rearranged as

$$\mathbf{y} = d_1\mathbf{a}_1 + \cdots + (d_j + cd_k)\mathbf{a}_j + \cdots + d_k\mathbf{a}_k + \cdots + d_m\mathbf{a}_m, \tag{13}$$

so $\mathbf{y}$ is in the row space of $A$. Therefore, $A$ and $B$ have the same row space.

The remaining case is the one in which $B$ is obtained from $A$ by multiplying the $j$th row by the nonzero scalar $c$. This case is left as Exercise 54 at the end of this section.

## 3.3    EXERCISES

Exercises 1–11 refer to the vectors in Eq. (14).

$$\mathbf{a} = \begin{bmatrix} 1 \\ -1 \end{bmatrix}, \quad \mathbf{b} = \begin{bmatrix} 2 \\ -3 \end{bmatrix}, \quad \mathbf{c} = \begin{bmatrix} -2 \\ 2 \end{bmatrix},$$

$$\mathbf{d} = \begin{bmatrix} 1 \\ 0 \end{bmatrix}, \quad \mathbf{e} = \begin{bmatrix} 0 \\ 0 \end{bmatrix}. \tag{14}$$

In Exercises 1–11, either show that $\text{Sp}(S) = R^2$ or give an algebraic specification for $\text{Sp}(S)$. If $\text{Sp}(S) \neq R^2$, then give a geometric description of $\text{Sp}(S)$.

1. $S = \{\mathbf{a}\}$    2. $S = \{\mathbf{b}\}$    3. $S = \{\mathbf{e}\}$
4. $S = \{\mathbf{a}, \mathbf{b}\}$    5. $S = \{\mathbf{a}, \mathbf{d}\}$    6. $S = \{\mathbf{a}, \mathbf{c}\}$

7. $S = \{\mathbf{b}, \mathbf{e}\}$    8. $S = \{\mathbf{a}, \mathbf{b}, \mathbf{d}\}$
9. $S = \{\mathbf{b}, \mathbf{c}, \mathbf{d}\}$    10. $S = \{\mathbf{a}, \mathbf{b}, \mathbf{e}\}$
11. $S = \{\mathbf{a}, \mathbf{c}, \mathbf{e}\}$

Exercises 12–19 refer to the vectors in Eq. (15).

$$\mathbf{v} = \begin{bmatrix} 1 \\ 2 \\ 0 \end{bmatrix}, \quad \mathbf{w} = \begin{bmatrix} 0 \\ -1 \\ 1 \end{bmatrix}, \quad \mathbf{x} = \begin{bmatrix} 1 \\ 1 \\ -1 \end{bmatrix},$$

$$\mathbf{y} = \begin{bmatrix} -2 \\ -2 \\ 2 \end{bmatrix}, \quad \mathbf{z} = \begin{bmatrix} 1 \\ 0 \\ 2 \end{bmatrix} \tag{15}$$

In Exercises 12–19, either show that $Sp(S) = R^3$ or give an algebraic specification for $Sp(S)$. If $Sp(S) \neq R^3$, then give a geometric description of $Sp(S)$.

**12.** $S = \{\mathbf{v}\}$

**13.** $S = \{\mathbf{w}\}$

**14.** $S = \{\mathbf{v}, \mathbf{w}\}$

**15.** $S = \{\mathbf{v}, \mathbf{x}\}$

**16.** $S = \{\mathbf{v}, \mathbf{w}, \mathbf{x}\}$

**17.** $S = \{\mathbf{w}, \mathbf{x}, \mathbf{z}\}$

**18.** $S = \{\mathbf{v}, \mathbf{w}, \mathbf{z}\}$

**19.** $S = \{\mathbf{w}, \mathbf{x}, \mathbf{y}\}$

**20.** Let $S$ be the set given in Exercise 14. For each vector given below, determine whether the vector is in $Sp(S)$. Express those vectors that are in $Sp(S)$ as a linear combination of $\mathbf{v}$ and $\mathbf{w}$.

a) $\begin{bmatrix} 1 \\ 1 \\ 1 \end{bmatrix}$     b) $\begin{bmatrix} 1 \\ 1 \\ -1 \end{bmatrix}$     c) $\begin{bmatrix} 1 \\ 2 \\ 0 \end{bmatrix}$

d) $\begin{bmatrix} 2 \\ 3 \\ 1 \end{bmatrix}$     e) $\begin{bmatrix} -1 \\ 2 \\ 4 \end{bmatrix}$     f) $\begin{bmatrix} 1 \\ 1 \\ 3 \end{bmatrix}$

**21.** Repeat Exercise 20 for the set $S$ given in Exercise 15.

**22.** Determine which of the vectors listed in Eq. (14) is in the null space of the matrix

$$A = \begin{bmatrix} 2 & 2 \\ 3 & 3 \end{bmatrix}.$$

**23.** Determine which of the vectors listed in Eq. (14) is in the null space of the matrix

$$A = \begin{bmatrix} 0 & 1 \\ 0 & 2 \\ 0 & 3 \end{bmatrix}.$$

**24.** Determine which of the vectors listed in Eq. (15) is in the null space of the matrix

$$A = [-2 \ \ 1 \ \ 1].$$

**25.** Determine which of the vectors listed in Eq. (15) is in the null space of the matrix

$$A = \begin{bmatrix} 1 & -1 & 0 \\ 2 & -1 & 1 \\ 3 & -5 & -2 \end{bmatrix}.$$

In Exercises 26–37, give an algebraic specification for the null space and the range of the given matrix $A$.

**26.** $A = \begin{bmatrix} 1 & -2 \\ -3 & 6 \end{bmatrix}$     **27.** $A = \begin{bmatrix} -1 & 3 \\ 2 & -6 \end{bmatrix}$

**28.** $A = \begin{bmatrix} 1 & 1 \\ 1 & 2 \end{bmatrix}$     **29.** $A = \begin{bmatrix} 1 & 1 \\ 2 & 5 \end{bmatrix}$

**30.** $A = \begin{bmatrix} 1 & -1 & 2 \\ 2 & -1 & 5 \end{bmatrix}$     **31.** $A = \begin{bmatrix} 1 & 2 & 1 \\ 3 & 6 & 4 \end{bmatrix}$

**32.** $A = \begin{bmatrix} 1 & 3 \\ 2 & 7 \\ 1 & 5 \end{bmatrix}$     **33.** $A = \begin{bmatrix} 0 & 1 \\ 0 & 2 \\ 0 & 3 \end{bmatrix}$

**34.** $A = \begin{bmatrix} 1 & -2 & 1 \\ 2 & -3 & 5 \\ 1 & 0 & 7 \end{bmatrix}$     **35.** $A = \begin{bmatrix} 1 & 2 & 3 \\ 1 & 3 & 1 \\ 2 & 2 & 10 \end{bmatrix}$

**36.** $A = \begin{bmatrix} 1 & 0 & -1 \\ -1 & 1 & 2 \\ 1 & 2 & 2 \end{bmatrix}$

**37.** $A = \begin{bmatrix} 1 & 2 & 1 \\ 2 & 5 & 4 \\ 1 & 3 & 4 \end{bmatrix}$

**38.** Let $A$ be the matrix given in Exercise 26.

a) For each vector $\mathbf{b}$ that follows, determine whether $\mathbf{b}$ is in $\mathcal{R}(A)$.

b) If $\mathbf{b}$ is in $\mathcal{R}(A)$, then exhibit a vector $\mathbf{x}$ in $R^2$ such that $A\mathbf{x} = \mathbf{b}$.

c) If $\mathbf{b}$ is in $\mathcal{R}(A)$, then write $\mathbf{b}$ as a linear combination of the columns of $A$.

i) $\mathbf{b} = \begin{bmatrix} 1 \\ -3 \end{bmatrix}$     ii) $\mathbf{b} = \begin{bmatrix} -1 \\ 2 \end{bmatrix}$

iii) $\mathbf{b} = \begin{bmatrix} 1 \\ 1 \end{bmatrix}$     iv) $\mathbf{b} = \begin{bmatrix} -2 \\ 6 \end{bmatrix}$

v) $\mathbf{b} = \begin{bmatrix} 3 \\ -6 \end{bmatrix}$     vi) $\mathbf{b} = \begin{bmatrix} 0 \\ 0 \end{bmatrix}$

**39.** Repeat Exercise 38 for the matrix $A$ given in Exercise 27.

**40.** Let $A$ be the matrix given in Exercise 34.

   **a)** For each vector $\mathbf{b}$ that follows, determine whether $\mathbf{b}$ is in $\mathcal{R}(A)$.

   **b)** If $\mathbf{b}$ is in $\mathcal{R}(A)$, then exhibit a vector $\mathbf{x}$ in $R^3$ such that $A\mathbf{x} = \mathbf{b}$.

   **c)** If $\mathbf{b}$ is in $\mathcal{R}(A)$, then write $\mathbf{b}$ as a linear combination of the columns of $A$.

$$\text{i) } \mathbf{b} = \begin{bmatrix} 1 \\ 2 \\ 0 \end{bmatrix} \qquad \text{ii) } \mathbf{b} = \begin{bmatrix} 1 \\ 1 \\ -1 \end{bmatrix}$$

$$\text{iii) } \mathbf{b} = \begin{bmatrix} 4 \\ 7 \\ 2 \end{bmatrix} \qquad \text{iv) } \mathbf{b} = \begin{bmatrix} 0 \\ 1 \\ 2 \end{bmatrix}$$

$$\text{v) } \mathbf{b} = \begin{bmatrix} 0 \\ 1 \\ -2 \end{bmatrix} \qquad \text{vi) } \mathbf{b} = \begin{bmatrix} 0 \\ 0 \\ 0 \end{bmatrix}$$

**41.** Repeat Exercise 40 for the matrix $A$ given in Exercise 35.

**42.** Let

$$W = \{\mathbf{y} = \begin{bmatrix} 2x_1 - 3x_2 + x_3 \\ -x_1 + 4x_2 - 2x_3 \\ 2x_1 + x_2 + 4x_3 \end{bmatrix} : x_1, x_2, x_3 \text{ real}\}.$$

Exhibit a $(3 \times 3)$ matrix $A$ such that $W = \mathcal{R}(A)$. Conclude that $W$ is a subspace of $R^3$.

**43.** Let

$$W = \{\mathbf{x} = \begin{bmatrix} x_1 \\ x_2 \\ x_3 \end{bmatrix} : 3x_1 - 4x_2 + 2x_3 = 0\}.$$

Exhibit a $(1 \times 3)$ matrix $A$ such that $W = \mathcal{N}(A)$. Conclude that $W$ is a subspace of $R^3$.

**44.** Let $S$ be the set of vectors given in Exercise 16. Exhibit a matrix $A$ such that $\text{Sp}(S) = \mathcal{R}(A)$.

**45.** Let $S$ be the set of vectors given in Exercise 17. Exhibit a matrix $A$ such that $\text{Sp}(S) = \mathcal{R}(A)$.

In Exercises 46–49, use the technique illustrated in Example 5 to find a set $T = \{\mathbf{w}_1, \mathbf{w}_2\}$ consisting of two vectors such that $\text{Sp}(S) = \text{Sp}(T)$.

$$\textbf{46. } S = \left\{ \begin{bmatrix} 1 \\ 0 \\ -1 \end{bmatrix}, \begin{bmatrix} 2 \\ 2 \\ 1 \end{bmatrix}, \begin{bmatrix} 1 \\ 2 \\ 2 \end{bmatrix} \right\}$$

$$\textbf{47. } S = \left\{ \begin{bmatrix} -2 \\ 1 \\ 3 \end{bmatrix}, \begin{bmatrix} 2 \\ 2 \\ -1 \end{bmatrix}, \begin{bmatrix} -2 \\ 7 \\ 7 \end{bmatrix} \right\}$$

$$\textbf{48. } S = \left\{ \begin{bmatrix} 1 \\ 0 \\ 1 \end{bmatrix}, \begin{bmatrix} -2 \\ 0 \\ -2 \end{bmatrix}, \begin{bmatrix} 1 \\ 1 \\ 2 \end{bmatrix}, \begin{bmatrix} -2 \\ 3 \\ 1 \end{bmatrix} \right\}$$

$$\textbf{49. } S = \left\{ \begin{bmatrix} 1 \\ 2 \\ 2 \end{bmatrix}, \begin{bmatrix} 1 \\ 5 \\ 3 \end{bmatrix}, \begin{bmatrix} 0 \\ 6 \\ 2 \end{bmatrix}, \begin{bmatrix} 1 \\ -1 \\ 1 \end{bmatrix} \right\}$$

**50.** Identify the range and the null space for each of the following.

   **a)** The $(n \times n)$ identity matrix

   **b)** The $(n \times n)$ zero matrix

   **c)** Any $(n \times n)$ nonsingular matrix $A$

**51.** Let $A$ and $B$ be $(n \times n)$ matrices. Verify that $\mathcal{N}(A) \cap \mathcal{N}(B) \subseteq \mathcal{N}(A + B)$.

**52.** Let $A$ be an $(m \times r)$ matrix and $B$ an $(r \times n)$ matrix.

   **a)** Show that $\mathcal{N}(B) \subseteq \mathcal{N}(AB)$.

   **b)** Show that $\mathcal{R}(AB) \subseteq \mathcal{R}(A)$.

**53.** Let $W$ be a subspace of $R^n$, and let $A$ be an $(m \times n)$ matrix. Let $V$ be the subset of $R^m$ defined by

$$V = \{\mathbf{y}: \mathbf{y} = A\mathbf{x} \text{ for some } \mathbf{x} \text{ in } W\}.$$

Prove that $V$ is a subspace of $R^m$.

**54.** Let $A$ be an $(m \times n)$ matrix, and let $B$ be obtained by multiplying the $k$th row of $A$ by the nonzero scalar $c$. Prove that $A$ and $B$ have the same row space.

## 3.4    BASES FOR SUBSPACES

Two of the most fundamental concepts of geometry are those of dimension and the use of coordinates to locate a point in space. In this section and the next, we extend these notions to an arbitrary subspace of $R^n$ by introducing the idea of a basis for a subspace. The first part of this section is devoted to developing the definition of a basis, and in the latter part of the section, we present techniques for obtaining bases for the subspaces introduced in Section 3.3. We will consider the concept of dimension in Section 3.5.

An example from $R^2$ will serve to illustrate the transition from geometry to algebra. We have already seen that each vector $\mathbf{v}$ in $R^2$,

$$\mathbf{v} = \begin{bmatrix} a \\ b \end{bmatrix}, \tag{1}$$

can be interpreted geometrically as the point with coordinates $a$ and $b$. Recall that in $R^2$ the vectors $\mathbf{e}_1$ and $\mathbf{e}_2$ are defined by

$$\mathbf{e}_1 = \begin{bmatrix} 1 \\ 0 \end{bmatrix} \quad \text{and} \quad \mathbf{e}_2 = \begin{bmatrix} 0 \\ 1 \end{bmatrix}.$$

Clearly the vector $\mathbf{v}$ in (1) can be expressed uniquely as a linear combination of $\mathbf{e}_1$ and $\mathbf{e}_2$:

$$\mathbf{v} = a\mathbf{e}_1 + b\mathbf{e}_2. \tag{2}$$

As we will see later, the set $\{\mathbf{e}_1, \mathbf{e}_2\}$ is an example of a *basis* for $R^2$ (indeed, it is called the *natural basis* for $R^2$). In Eq. (2), the vector $\mathbf{v}$ is determined by the coefficients $a$ and $b$ (see Fig. 3.12). Thus the geometric concept of characterizing a point by its coordinates can be interpreted algebraically as determining a vector by its coefficients when the vector is expressed as a linear combination of "basis" vectors. (In fact, the coefficients obtained are often referred to as the coordinates of the vector. This idea will be developed further in Chapter 5.) We turn now to the task of making these ideas precise in the context of an arbitrary subspace $W$ of $R^n$.

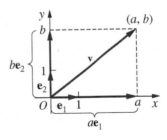

*Figure 3.12* $\quad \mathbf{v} = a\mathbf{e}_1 + b\mathbf{e}_2$

## Spanning Sets

Let $W$ be a subspace of $R^n$, and let $S$ be a subset of $W$. The discussion above suggests that the first requirement for $S$ to be a basis for $W$ is that each vector in $W$ be expressible as a linear combination of the vectors in $S$. This leads to the following definition.

**DEFINITION 3**

Let $W$ be a subspace of $R^n$, and let $S = \{\mathbf{w}_1, \ldots, \mathbf{w}_m\}$ be a subset of $W$. We say that $S$ is a *spanning set* for $W$, or simply that $S$ *spans* $W$, if every vector $\mathbf{w}$ in $W$ can be expressed as a linear combination of vectors in $S$;

$$\mathbf{w} = a_1\mathbf{w}_1 + \cdots + a_m\mathbf{w}_m.$$

A restatement of Definition 3 in the notation of the previous section is that $S$ is a spanning set of $W$ provided that $\text{Sp}(S) = W$. It is evident that the set $S = \{\mathbf{e}_1, \mathbf{e}_2, \mathbf{e}_3\}$, consisting of the unit vectors in $R^3$, is a spanning set for $R^3$. Specifically, if $\mathbf{v}$ is in $R^3$,

$$\mathbf{v} = \begin{bmatrix} a \\ b \\ c \end{bmatrix}, \tag{3}$$

then $\mathbf{v} = a\mathbf{e}_1 + b\mathbf{e}_2 + c\mathbf{e}_3$. The next two examples consider other subsets of $R^3$.

**EXAMPLE 1**   In $R^3$, let $S = \{\mathbf{u}_1, \mathbf{u}_2, \mathbf{u}_3\}$, where

$$\mathbf{u}_1 = \begin{bmatrix} 1 \\ -1 \\ 0 \end{bmatrix}, \quad \mathbf{u}_2 = \begin{bmatrix} -2 \\ 3 \\ 1 \end{bmatrix}, \quad \text{and} \quad \mathbf{u}_3 = \begin{bmatrix} 1 \\ 2 \\ 4 \end{bmatrix}.$$

Determine whether $S$ is a spanning set for $R^3$.

*Solution*   We must determine whether an arbitrary vector $\mathbf{v}$ in $R^3$ can be expressed as a linear combination of $\mathbf{u}_1$, $\mathbf{u}_2$, and $\mathbf{u}_3$. In other words, we must decide whether the vector equation

$$x_1\mathbf{u}_1 + x_2\mathbf{u}_2 + x_3\mathbf{u}_3 = \mathbf{v}, \tag{4}$$

where $\mathbf{v}$ is the vector in (3), always has a solution. The vector equation (4) is equivalent to the $(3 \times 3)$ linear system with the matrix equation

$$A\mathbf{x} = \mathbf{v}, \tag{5}$$

where $A$ is the $(3 \times 3)$ matrix $A = [\mathbf{u}_1, \mathbf{u}_2, \mathbf{u}_3]$. The augmented matrix for Eq. (5) is

$$[A \mid \mathbf{v}] = \begin{bmatrix} 1 & -2 & 1 & a \\ -1 & 3 & 2 & b \\ 0 & 1 & 4 & c \end{bmatrix},$$

and this matrix is row equivalent to

$$\begin{bmatrix} 1 & 0 & 0 & 10a + 9b - 7c \\ 0 & 1 & 0 & 4a + 4b - 3c \\ 0 & 0 & 1 & -a - b + c \end{bmatrix}.$$

Therefore,

$$x_1 = 10a + 9b - 7c$$
$$x_2 = \phantom{-}4a + 4b - 3c$$
$$x_3 = -a - \phantom{4}b + \phantom{3}c$$

is the solution of Eq. (4). In particular, Eq. (4) always has a solution, so $S$ is a spanning set for $R^3$. ◼

EXAMPLE 2    Let $S = \{\mathbf{v}_1, \mathbf{v}_2, \mathbf{v}_3\}$ be the subset of $R^3$ defined by

$$\mathbf{v}_1 = \begin{bmatrix} 1 \\ 2 \\ 3 \end{bmatrix}, \quad \mathbf{v}_2 = \begin{bmatrix} -1 \\ 0 \\ -7 \end{bmatrix}, \quad \text{and} \quad \mathbf{v}_3 = \begin{bmatrix} 2 \\ 7 \\ 0 \end{bmatrix}.$$

Does $S$ span $R^3$?

*Solution*    Let $\mathbf{v}$ be the vector given in Eq. (3). As before, the vector equation

$$x_1\mathbf{v}_1 + x_2\mathbf{v}_2 + x_3\mathbf{v}_3 = \mathbf{v} \tag{6}$$

is equivalent to the $(3 \times 3)$ system of equations

$$A\mathbf{x} = \mathbf{v}, \tag{7}$$

where $A = [\mathbf{v}_1, \mathbf{v}_2, \mathbf{v}_3]$. The augmented matrix for Eq. (7) is

$$[A \mid \mathbf{v}] = \begin{bmatrix} 1 & -1 & 2 & a \\ 2 & 0 & 7 & b \\ 3 & -7 & 0 & c \end{bmatrix},$$

and the matrix $[A \mid \mathbf{v}]$ is row equivalent to

$$\begin{bmatrix} 1 & 0 & 7/2 & b/2 \\ 0 & 1 & 3/2 & -a + (1/2)b \\ 0 & 0 & 0 & -7a + 2b + c \end{bmatrix}.$$

It follows that Eq. (6) has a solution if and only if $-7a + 2b + c = 0$. In particular, $S$ does not span $R^3$. Indeed,

$$\text{Sp}(S) = \{\mathbf{v}: \mathbf{v} = \begin{bmatrix} a \\ b \\ c \end{bmatrix}, \quad \text{where} -7a + 2b + c = 0\}.$$

For example, the vector

$$\mathbf{w} = \begin{bmatrix} 1 \\ 1 \\ 1 \end{bmatrix}$$

is in $R^3$ but is not in $\text{Sp}(S)$; that is, $\mathbf{w}$ cannot be expressed as a linear combination of $\mathbf{v}_1$, $\mathbf{v}_2$, and $\mathbf{v}_3$. ◼

The next example illustrates a procedure for constructing a spanning set for the null space, $\mathcal{N}(A)$, of a matrix $A$.

EXAMPLE 3    Let $A$ be the $(3 \times 4)$ matrix

$$A = \begin{bmatrix} 1 & 1 & 3 & 1 \\ 2 & 1 & 5 & 4 \\ 1 & 2 & 4 & -1 \end{bmatrix}.$$

Exhibit a spanning set for $\mathcal{N}(A)$, the null space of $A$.

Solution    The first step toward obtaining a spanning set for $\mathcal{N}(A)$ is to obtain an algebraic specification for $\mathcal{N}(A)$ by solving the homogeneous system $A\mathbf{x} = \boldsymbol{\theta}$. For the given matrix $A$, this was done in Example 2 of Section 3.3. Specifically,

$$\mathcal{N}(A) = \left\{ \mathbf{x} \colon \mathbf{x} = \begin{bmatrix} -2x_3 - 3x_4 \\ -x_3 + 2x_4 \\ x_3 \\ x_4 \end{bmatrix}, \quad x_3 \text{ and } x_4 \text{ any real numbers} \right\}.$$

Thus a vector $\mathbf{x}$ in $\mathcal{N}(A)$ is totally determined by the unconstrained parameters $x_3$ and $x_4$. Separating those parameters gives a decomposition of $\mathbf{x}$:

$$\mathbf{x} = \begin{bmatrix} -2x_3 - 3x_4 \\ -x_3 + 2x_4 \\ x_3 \\ x_4 \end{bmatrix} = \begin{bmatrix} -2x_3 \\ -x_3 \\ x_3 \\ 0 \end{bmatrix} + \begin{bmatrix} -3x_4 \\ 2x_4 \\ 0 \\ x_4 \end{bmatrix} = x_3 \begin{bmatrix} -2 \\ -1 \\ 1 \\ 0 \end{bmatrix} + x_4 \begin{bmatrix} -3 \\ 2 \\ 0 \\ 1 \end{bmatrix}. \quad (8)$$

Let $\mathbf{u}_1$ and $\mathbf{u}_2$ be the vectors

$$\mathbf{u}_1 = \begin{bmatrix} -2 \\ -1 \\ 1 \\ 0 \end{bmatrix} \quad \text{and} \quad \mathbf{u}_2 = \begin{bmatrix} -3 \\ 2 \\ 0 \\ 1 \end{bmatrix}.$$

By setting $x_3 = 1$ and $x_4 = 0$ in Eq. (8), we obtain $\mathbf{u}_1$, so $\mathbf{u}_1$ is in $\mathcal{N}(A)$. Similarly, $\mathbf{u}_2$ can be obtained by setting $x_3 = 0$ and $x_4 = 1$, so $\mathbf{u}_2$ is in $\mathcal{N}(A)$. Moreover, it is an immediate consequence of Eq. (8) that each vector $\mathbf{x}$ in $\mathcal{N}(A)$ is a linear combination of $\mathbf{u}_1$ and $\mathbf{u}_2$. Therefore, $\mathcal{N}(A) = \mathrm{Sp}\{\mathbf{u}_1, \mathbf{u}_2\}$; that is, $\{\mathbf{u}_1, \mathbf{u}_2\}$ is a spanning set for $\mathcal{N}(A)$. ■

The remaining subspaces introduced in Section 3.3 were either defined or characterized by a spanning set. If $S = \{\mathbf{v}_1, \ldots, \mathbf{v}_r\}$ is a subset of $R^n$, for instance, then obviously $S$ is a spanning set for $\mathrm{Sp}(S)$. If $A$ is an $(m \times n)$ matrix,

$$A = [\mathbf{A}_1, \ldots, \mathbf{A}_n],$$

then, as we saw in Section 3.3, $\{\mathbf{A}_1, \ldots, \mathbf{A}_n\}$ is a spanning set for $\mathcal{R}(A)$, the range of $A$. Finally, if

$$A = \begin{bmatrix} \mathbf{a}_1 \\ \mathbf{a}_2 \\ \vdots \\ \mathbf{a}_m \end{bmatrix},$$

where $\mathbf{a}_i$ is the $i$th-row vector of $A$, then, by definition, $\{\mathbf{a}_1, \ldots, \mathbf{a}_m\}$ is a spanning set for the row space of $A$.

## Minimal Spanning Sets

If $W$ is a subspace of $R^n$, $W \neq \{\boldsymbol{\theta}\}$, then spanning sets for $W$ abound. For example, a vector $\mathbf{v}$ in a spanning set can always be replaced by $a\mathbf{v}$, where $a$ is any nonzero scalar. It is easy to demonstrate, however, that not all spanning sets are equally desirable. For example, define $\mathbf{u}$ in $R^2$ by

$$\mathbf{u} = \begin{bmatrix} 1 \\ 1 \end{bmatrix}.$$

The set $S = \{\mathbf{e}_1, \mathbf{e}_2, \mathbf{u}\}$ is a spanning set for $R^2$. Indeed, for an arbitrary vector $\mathbf{v}$ in $R^2$,

$$\mathbf{v} = \begin{bmatrix} a \\ b \end{bmatrix},$$

$\mathbf{v} = (a - c)\mathbf{e}_1 + (b - c)\mathbf{e}_2 + c\mathbf{u}$, where $c$ is any real number whatsoever. But the subset $\{\mathbf{e}_1, \mathbf{e}_2\}$ already spans $R^2$, so the vector $\mathbf{u}$ is unnecessary.

Recall that a set $\{\mathbf{v}_1, \ldots, \mathbf{v}_m\}$ of vectors in $R^n$ is linearly independent if the vector equation

$$x_1\mathbf{v}_1 + \cdots + x_m\mathbf{v}_m = \boldsymbol{\theta} \tag{9}$$

has only the trivial solution $x_1 = \cdots = x_m = 0$; if Eq. (9) has a nontrivial solution, then the set is linearly dependent. The set $S = \{\mathbf{e}_1, \mathbf{e}_2, \mathbf{u}\}$ is linearly dependent because

$$\mathbf{e}_1 + \mathbf{e}_2 - \mathbf{u} = \boldsymbol{\theta}.$$

Our next example illustrates that a linearly dependent set is not an efficient spanning set; that is, fewer vectors will span the same space.

EXAMPLE 4    Let $S = \{\mathbf{v}_1, \mathbf{v}_2, \mathbf{v}_3\}$ be the subset of $R^3$, where

$$\mathbf{v}_1 = \begin{bmatrix} 1 \\ 1 \\ 1 \end{bmatrix}, \quad \mathbf{v}_2 = \begin{bmatrix} 2 \\ 3 \\ 1 \end{bmatrix}, \quad \text{and} \quad \mathbf{v}_3 = \begin{bmatrix} 3 \\ 5 \\ 1 \end{bmatrix}.$$

Show that $S$ is a linearly dependent set, and exhibit a subset $T$ of $S$ such that $T$ contains only two vectors but $\text{Sp}(T) = \text{Sp}(S)$.

*Solution*    The vector equation

$$x_1\mathbf{v}_1 + x_2\mathbf{v}_2 + x_3\mathbf{v}_3 = \boldsymbol{\theta} \tag{10}$$

is equivalent to the $(3 \times 3)$ homogeneous system of equations with augmented matrix

$$A = \begin{bmatrix} 1 & 2 & 3 & 0 \\ 1 & 3 & 5 & 0 \\ 1 & 1 & 1 & 0 \end{bmatrix}.$$

Matrix $A$ is row equivalent to

$$B = \begin{bmatrix} 1 & 0 & -1 & 0 \\ 0 & 1 & 2 & 0 \\ 0 & 0 & 0 & 0 \end{bmatrix}$$

in echelon form. Solving the system with augmented matrix $B$ gives

$$x_1 = \quad x_3$$
$$x_2 = -2x_3.$$

Because Eq. (10) has nontrivial solutions, the set $S$ is linearly dependent. Taking $x_3 = 1$, for example, gives $x_1 = 1$, $x_2 = -2$. Therefore,

$$\mathbf{v}_1 - 2\mathbf{v}_2 + \mathbf{v}_3 = \boldsymbol{\theta}. \tag{11}$$

Equation (11) allows us to express $\mathbf{v}_3$ as a linear combination of $\mathbf{v}_1$ and $\mathbf{v}_2$:

$$\mathbf{v}_3 = -\mathbf{v}_1 + 2\mathbf{v}_2.$$

(Note that we could just as easily have solved Eq. (11) for either $\mathbf{v}_1$ or $\mathbf{v}_2$.) It now follows that

$$\mathrm{Sp}\{\mathbf{v}_1, \mathbf{v}_2\} = \mathrm{Sp}\{\mathbf{v}_1, \mathbf{v}_2, \mathbf{v}_3\}.$$

To illustrate, let $\mathbf{v}$ be in the subspace $\mathrm{Sp}\{\mathbf{v}_1, \mathbf{v}_2, \mathbf{v}_3\}$:

$$\mathbf{v} = a_1\mathbf{v}_1 + a_2\mathbf{v}_2 + a_3\mathbf{v}_3.$$

Making the substitution $\mathbf{v}_3 = -\mathbf{v}_1 + 2\mathbf{v}_2$, yields

$$\mathbf{v} = a_1\mathbf{v}_1 + a_2\mathbf{v}_2 + a_3(-\mathbf{v}_1 + 2\mathbf{v}_2).$$

This expression simplifies to

$$\mathbf{v} = (a_1 - a_3)\mathbf{v}_1 + (a_2 + 2a_3)\mathbf{v}_2;$$

in particular, $\mathbf{v}$ is in $\mathrm{Sp}\{\mathbf{v}_1, \mathbf{v}_2\}$. Clearly any linear combination of $\mathbf{v}_1$ and $\mathbf{v}_2$ is in $\mathrm{Sp}(S)$ because

$$b_1\mathbf{v}_1 + b_2\mathbf{v}_2 = b_1\mathbf{v}_1 + b_2\mathbf{v}_2 + 0\mathbf{v}_3.$$

Thus if $T = \{\mathbf{v}_1, \mathbf{v}_2\}$, then $\mathrm{Sp}(T) = \mathrm{Sp}(S)$. ◾

The lesson to be drawn from Example 4 is that a linearly dependent spanning set contains redundant information. That is, if $S = \{\mathbf{w}_1, \ldots, \mathbf{w}_r\}$ is a linearly dependent spanning set for a subspace $W$, then at least one vector from $S$ is a linear combination of the other $r - 1$ vectors and can be discarded from $S$ to produce a smaller spanning set. On the other hand, if $B = \{\mathbf{v}_1, \ldots, \mathbf{v}_m\}$ is a linearly independent spanning set for $W$, then no vector in $B$ is a linear combination of the other $m - 1$ vectors in $B$. Hence if a vector is removed from $B$, this smaller set cannot be a spanning set for $W$ (in particular, the vector removed from $B$ is in $W$ but cannot be expressed as a linear combination of the vectors retained). In this sense a linearly independent spanning set is a minimal spanning set and hence represents the most efficient way of characterizing the subspace. This idea leads to the following definition.

| | |
|---|---|
| Definition 4 | Let $W$ be a nonzero subspace of $R^n$. A **basis** for $W$ is a linearly independent spanning set for $W$. |

Note that the zero subspace of $R^n$, $W = \{\theta\}$, contains only the vector $\theta$. Although it is the case that $\{\theta\}$ is a spanning set for $W$, the set $\{\theta\}$ is linearly dependent. Thus the concept of a basis is not meaningful for $W = \{\theta\}$.

## Uniqueness of Representation

Let $B = \{\mathbf{v}_1, \mathbf{v}_2, \ldots, \mathbf{v}_p\}$ be a basis for a subspace $W$ of $R^n$, and let $\mathbf{x}$ be a vector in $W$. Because $B$ is a spanning set, we know that there are scalars $a_1, a_2, \ldots, a_p$ such that

$$\mathbf{x} = a_1\mathbf{v}_1 + a_2\mathbf{v}_2 + \cdots + a_p\mathbf{v}_p. \tag{12}$$

Because $B$ is also a linearly independent set, we can show that the representation of $\mathbf{x}$ in Eq. (12) is unique. That is, if we have any representation of the form $\mathbf{x} = b_1\mathbf{v}_1 + b_2\mathbf{v}_2 + \cdots + b_p\mathbf{v}_p$, then $a_1 = b_1, a_2 = b_2, \ldots, a_p = b_p$. To establish this uniqueness, suppose that $b_1, b_2, \ldots, b_p$ are any scalars such that

$$\mathbf{x} = b_1\mathbf{v}_1 + b_2\mathbf{v}_2 + \cdots + b_p\mathbf{v}_p.$$

Subtracting the preceding equation from Eq. (12), we obtain

$$\theta = (a_1 - b_1)\mathbf{v}_1 + (a_2 - b_2)\mathbf{v}_2 + \cdots + (a_p - b_p)\mathbf{v}_p.$$

Then, using the fact that $\{\mathbf{v}_1, \mathbf{v}_2, \ldots, \mathbf{v}_p\}$ is linearly independent, we see that $a_1 - b_1 = 0$, $a_2 - b_2 = 0, \ldots, a_p - b_p = 0$. This discussion of uniqueness leads to the following remark.

***Remark*** Let $B = \{\mathbf{v}_1, \mathbf{v}_2, \ldots, \mathbf{v}_p\}$ be a basis for $W$, where $W$ is a subspace of $R^n$. If $\mathbf{x}$ is in $W$, then $\mathbf{x}$ can be represented uniquely in terms of the basis $B$. That is, there are unique scalars $a_1, a_2, \ldots, a_p$ such that

$$\mathbf{x} = a_1\mathbf{v}_1 + a_2\mathbf{v}_2 + \cdots + a_p\mathbf{v}_p.$$

As we see later, these scalars are called the **coordinates** of $x$ with respect to the basis.

## Examples of Bases

It is easy to show that the unit vectors

$$\mathbf{e}_1 = \begin{bmatrix} 1 \\ 0 \\ 0 \end{bmatrix}, \quad \mathbf{e}_2 = \begin{bmatrix} 0 \\ 1 \\ 0 \end{bmatrix}, \quad \text{and} \quad \mathbf{e}_3 = \begin{bmatrix} 0 \\ 0 \\ 1 \end{bmatrix}$$

constitute a basis for $R^3$. In general, the $n$-dimensional vectors $\mathbf{e}_1, \mathbf{e}_2, \ldots, \mathbf{e}_n$ form a basis for $R^n$, frequently called the natural basis.

In Exercise 30, the reader is asked to use Theorem 13 of Section 1.7 to prove that any linearly independent subset $B = \{\mathbf{v}_1, \mathbf{v}_2, \mathbf{v}_3\}$ of $R^3$ is actually a basis for $R^3$. Thus, for example, the vectors

$$\mathbf{v}_1 = \begin{bmatrix} 1 \\ 0 \\ 0 \end{bmatrix}, \quad \mathbf{v}_2 = \begin{bmatrix} 1 \\ 1 \\ 0 \end{bmatrix}, \quad \text{and} \quad \mathbf{v}_3 = \begin{bmatrix} 1 \\ 1 \\ 1 \end{bmatrix}$$

provide another basis for $R^3$.

In Example 3, a procedure for determining a spanning set for $\mathcal{N}(A)$, the null space of a matrix $A$, was illustrated. Note in Example 3 that the spanning set $\{\mathbf{u}_1, \mathbf{u}_2\}$ obtained is linearly independent, so it is a basis for $\mathcal{N}(A)$. Oftentimes, if a subspace $W$ of $R^n$ has an algebraic specification in terms of unconstrained variables, the procedure illustrated in Example 3 yields a basis for $W$. The next example provides another illustration.

**EXAMPLE 5**   Let $A$ be the $(3 \times 4)$ matrix given in Example 4 of Section 3.3. Use the algebraic specification of $\mathcal{R}(A)$ derived in that example to obtain a basis for $\mathcal{R}(A)$.

*Solution*   In Example 4 of Section 3.3, the range of $A$ was determined to be

$$\mathcal{R}(A) = \{\mathbf{b} \colon \mathbf{b} = \begin{bmatrix} b_1 \\ b_2 \\ 3b_1 - b_2 \end{bmatrix}, \quad b_1 \text{ and } b_2 \text{ any real numbers}\}.$$

Thus $b_1$ and $b_2$ are unconstrained variables, and a vector $\mathbf{b}$ in $\mathcal{R}(A)$ can be decomposed as

$$\mathbf{b} = \begin{bmatrix} b_1 \\ b_2 \\ 3b_1 - b_2 \end{bmatrix} = \begin{bmatrix} b_1 \\ 0 \\ 3b_1 \end{bmatrix} + \begin{bmatrix} 0 \\ b_2 \\ -b_2 \end{bmatrix} = b_1 \begin{bmatrix} 1 \\ 0 \\ 3 \end{bmatrix} + b_2 \begin{bmatrix} 0 \\ 1 \\ -1 \end{bmatrix}. \quad (13)$$

If $\mathbf{u}_1$ and $\mathbf{u}_2$ are defined by

$$\mathbf{u}_1 = \begin{bmatrix} 1 \\ 0 \\ 3 \end{bmatrix} \quad \text{and} \quad \mathbf{u} = \begin{bmatrix} 0 \\ 1 \\ -1 \end{bmatrix},$$

then $\mathbf{u}_1$ and $\mathbf{u}_2$ are in $\mathcal{R}(A)$. One can easily check that $\{\mathbf{u}_1, \mathbf{u}_2\}$ is a linearly independent set, and it is evident from Eq. (13) that $\mathcal{R}(A)$ is spanned by $\mathbf{u}_1$ and $\mathbf{u}_2$. Therefore, $\{\mathbf{u}_1, \mathbf{u}_2\}$ is a basis for $\mathcal{R}(A)$. ∎

The previous example illustrates how to obtain a basis for a subspace $W$, given an algebraic specification for $W$. The last two examples of this section illustrate two different techniques for constructing a basis for $W$ from a spanning set.

||| EXAMPLE 6   Let $W$ be the subspace of $R^4$ spanned by the set $S = \{\mathbf{v}_1, \mathbf{v}_2, \mathbf{v}_3, \mathbf{v}_4, \mathbf{v}_5\}$, where

$$\mathbf{v}_1 = \begin{bmatrix} 1 \\ 1 \\ 2 \\ -1 \end{bmatrix}, \quad \mathbf{v}_2 = \begin{bmatrix} 1 \\ 2 \\ 1 \\ 1 \end{bmatrix}, \quad \mathbf{v}_3 = \begin{bmatrix} 1 \\ 4 \\ -1 \\ 5 \end{bmatrix},$$

$$\mathbf{v}_4 = \begin{bmatrix} 1 \\ 0 \\ 4 \\ -1 \end{bmatrix}, \quad \text{and} \quad \mathbf{v}_5 = \begin{bmatrix} 2 \\ 5 \\ 0 \\ 2 \end{bmatrix}.$$

Find a subset of $S$ that is a basis for $W$.

*Solution*   The procedure is suggested by Example 4. The idea is to solve the dependence relation

$$x_1\mathbf{v}_1 + x_2\mathbf{v}_2 + x_3\mathbf{v}_3 + x_4\mathbf{v}_4 + x_5\mathbf{v}_5 = \boldsymbol{\theta} \tag{14}$$

and then determine which of the $\mathbf{v}_j$'s can be eliminated. If $V$ is the $(4 \times 5)$ matrix

$$V = [\mathbf{v}_1, \mathbf{v}_2, \mathbf{v}_3, \mathbf{v}_4, \mathbf{v}_5],$$

then the augmented matrix $[V \mid \boldsymbol{\theta}]$ reduces to

$$\begin{bmatrix} 1 & 0 & -2 & 0 & 1 & 0 \\ 0 & 1 & 3 & 0 & 2 & 0 \\ 0 & 0 & 0 & 1 & -1 & 0 \\ 0 & 0 & 0 & 0 & 0 & 0 \end{bmatrix}. \tag{15}$$

The system of equations with augmented matrix (15) has solution

$$\begin{aligned} x_1 &= 2x_3 - x_5 \\ x_2 &= -3x_3 - 2x_5 \\ x_4 &= x_5, \end{aligned} \tag{16}$$

where $x_3$ and $x_5$ are unconstrained variables. In particular, the set $S$ is linearly dependent. Moreover, taking $x_3 = 1$ and $x_5 = 0$ yields $x_1 = 2$, $x_2 = -3$, and $x_4 = 0$. Thus Eq. (14) becomes

$$2\mathbf{v}_1 - 3\mathbf{v}_2 + \mathbf{v}_3 = \boldsymbol{\theta}. \tag{17}$$

Since Eq. (17) can be solved for $\mathbf{v}_3$,

$$\mathbf{v}_3 = -2\mathbf{v}_1 + 3\mathbf{v}_2,$$

it follows that $\mathbf{v}_3$ is redundant and can be removed from the spanning set. Similarly, setting $x_3 = 0$ and $x_5 = 1$ gives $x_1 = -1$, $x_2 = -2$, and $x_4 = 1$. In this case, Eq. (14) becomes

$$-\mathbf{v}_1 - 2\mathbf{v}_2 + \mathbf{v}_4 + \mathbf{v}_5 = \boldsymbol{\theta},$$

and hence

$$\mathbf{v}_5 = \mathbf{v}_1 + 2\mathbf{v}_2 - \mathbf{v}_4.$$

Since both $\mathbf{v}_3$ and $\mathbf{v}_5$ are in $\mathrm{Sp}\{\mathbf{v}_1, \mathbf{v}_2, \mathbf{v}_4\}$, it follows (as in Example 4) that $\mathbf{v}_1$, $\mathbf{v}_2$, and $\mathbf{v}_4$ span $W$.

To see that the set $\{\mathbf{v}_1, \mathbf{v}_2, \mathbf{v}_4\}$ is linearly independent, note that the dependence relation

$$x_1\mathbf{v}_1 + x_2\mathbf{v}_2 + x_4\mathbf{v}_4 = \boldsymbol{\theta} \tag{18}$$

is just Eq. (14) with $\mathbf{v}_3$ and $\mathbf{v}_5$ removed. Thus the augmented matrix $[\mathbf{v}_1, \mathbf{v}_2, \mathbf{v}_4 \mid \boldsymbol{\theta}]$, for Eq. (18) reduces to

$$\begin{bmatrix} 1 & 0 & 0 & 0 \\ 0 & 1 & 0 & 0 \\ 0 & 0 & 1 & 0 \\ 0 & 0 & 0 & 0 \end{bmatrix}, \tag{19}$$

which is matrix (15) with the third and fifth columns removed. From matrix (19), it is clear that Eq. (18) has only the trivial solution; so $\{\mathbf{v}_1, \mathbf{v}_2, \mathbf{v}_4\}$ is a linearly independent set and therefore a basis for $W$. ◼

The procedure demonstrated in the preceding example can be outlined as follows:

1. A spanning set $S\{\mathbf{v}_1, \ldots, \mathbf{v}_m\}$ for a subspace $W$ is given.
2. Solve the vector equation

$$x_1\mathbf{v}_1 + \cdots + x_m\mathbf{v}_m = \boldsymbol{\theta}. \tag{20}$$

3. If Eq. (20) has only the trivial solution $x_1 = \cdots = x_m = 0$, then $S$ is a linearly independent set and hence is a basis for $W$.
4. If Eq. (20) has nontrivial solutions, then there are unconstrained variables. For each $x_j$ that is designated as an unconstrained variable, delete the vector $\mathbf{v}_j$ from the set $S$. The remaining vectors constitute a basis for $W$.

Our final technique for constructing a basis uses Theorem 7.

**THEOREM 7** If the nonzero matrix $A$ is row equivalent to the matrix $B$ in echelon form, then the nonzero rows of $B$ form a basis for the row space of $A$.

*Proof* By Theorem 6, $A$ and $B$ have the same row space. It follows that the nonzero rows of $B$ span the row space of $A$. Since the nonzero rows of an echelon matrix are linearly independent vectors, it follows that the nonzero rows of $B$ form a basis for the row space of $A$. ◼

**EXAMPLE 7** Let $W$ be the subspace of $R^4$ given in Example 6. Use Theorem 7 to construct a basis for $W$.

*Solution*    As in Example 6, let $V$ be the $(4 \times 5)$ matrix

$$V = [\mathbf{v}_1, \mathbf{v}_2, \mathbf{v}_3, \mathbf{v}_4, \mathbf{v}_5].$$

Thus $W$ can be viewed as the row space of the matrix $V^T$, where

$$V^T = \begin{bmatrix} 1 & 1 & 2 & -1 \\ 1 & 2 & 1 & 1 \\ 1 & 4 & -1 & 5 \\ 1 & 0 & 4 & -1 \\ 2 & 5 & 0 & 2 \end{bmatrix}.$$

Since $V^T$ is row equivalent to the matrix

$$B^T = \begin{bmatrix} 1 & 0 & 0 & -9 \\ 0 & 1 & 0 & 4 \\ 0 & 0 & 1 & 2 \\ 0 & 0 & 0 & 0 \\ 0 & 0 & 0 & 0 \end{bmatrix}$$

in echelon form, it follows from Theorem 7 that the nonzero rows of $B^T$ form a basis for the row space of $V^T$. Consequently the nonzero columns of

$$B = \begin{bmatrix} 1 & 0 & 0 & 0 & 0 \\ 0 & 1 & 0 & 0 & 0 \\ 0 & 0 & 1 & 0 & 0 \\ -9 & 4 & 2 & 0 & 0 \end{bmatrix}$$

are a basis for $W$. Specifically, the set $\{\mathbf{u}_1, \mathbf{u}_2, \mathbf{u}_3\}$ is a basis of $W$, where

$$\mathbf{u}_1 = \begin{bmatrix} 1 \\ 0 \\ 0 \\ -9 \end{bmatrix}, \quad \mathbf{u}_2 = \begin{bmatrix} 0 \\ 1 \\ 0 \\ 4 \end{bmatrix}, \quad \text{and} \quad \mathbf{u}_3 = \begin{bmatrix} 0 \\ 0 \\ 1 \\ 2 \end{bmatrix}.$$

The procedure used in the preceding example can be summarized as follows:

1. A spanning set $S = \{\mathbf{v}_1, \ldots, \mathbf{v}_m\}$ for a subspace $W$ of $R^n$ is given.
2. Let $V$ be the $(n \times m)$ matrix $V = [\mathbf{v}_1, \ldots \mathbf{v}_m]$. Use elementary row operations to transform $V^T$ to a matrix $B^T$ in echelon form.
3. The nonzero columns of $B$ are a basis for $W$.

## 3.4    EXERCISES

In Exercises 1–8, let $W$ be the subspace of $R^4$ consisting of vectors of the form

$$\mathbf{x} = \begin{bmatrix} x_1 \\ x_2 \\ x_3 \\ x_4 \end{bmatrix}.$$

Find a basis for $W$ when the components of $\mathbf{x}$ satisfy the given conditions.

**1.** $\begin{aligned} x_1 + x_2 - x_3 \quad\;\; &= 0 \\ x_2 \quad\;\; - x_4 &= 0 \end{aligned}$

**2.** $\begin{aligned} x_1 + x_2 - \;\; x_3 + x_4 &= 0 \\ x_2 - 2x_3 - x_4 &= 0 \end{aligned}$

**3.** $x_1 - x_2 + x_3 - 3x_4 = 0$

**4.** $x_1 - x_2 + x_3 = 0$

**5.** $x_1 + x_2 = 0$

**6.** $\begin{aligned} x_1 - x_2 \qquad\quad &= 0 \\ x_2 - 2x_3 \quad\;\; &= 0 \\ x_3 - x_4 &= 0 \end{aligned}$

**7.** $\begin{aligned} -x_1 + 2x_2 \qquad - x_4 &= 0 \\ x_2 + x_3 \quad\;\; &= 0 \end{aligned}$

**8.** $\begin{aligned} x_1 - x_2 - x_3 + x_4 &= 0 \\ x_2 + x_3 \quad\;\; &= 0 \end{aligned}$

**9.** Let $W$ be the subspace described in Exercise 1. For each vector $\mathbf{x}$ that follows, determine if $\mathbf{x}$ is in $W$. If $\mathbf{x}$ is in $W$, then express $\mathbf{x}$ as a linear combination of the basis vectors found in Exercise 1.

**a)** $\mathbf{x} = \begin{bmatrix} 1 \\ 1 \\ 2 \\ 1 \end{bmatrix}$    **b)** $\mathbf{x} = \begin{bmatrix} -1 \\ 2 \\ 3 \\ 2 \end{bmatrix}$

**c)** $\mathbf{x} = \begin{bmatrix} 3 \\ -3 \\ 0 \\ -3 \end{bmatrix}$    **d)** $\mathbf{x} = \begin{bmatrix} 2 \\ 0 \\ 2 \\ 0 \end{bmatrix}$

**10.** Let $W$ be the subspace described in Exercise 2. For each vector $\mathbf{x}$ that follows, determine if $\mathbf{x}$ is in $W$. If $\mathbf{x}$ is in $W$, then express $\mathbf{x}$ as a linear combination of the basis vectors found in Exercise 2.

**a)** $\mathbf{x} = \begin{bmatrix} -3 \\ 3 \\ 1 \\ 1 \end{bmatrix}$    **b)** $\mathbf{x} = \begin{bmatrix} 0 \\ 3 \\ 2 \\ -1 \end{bmatrix}$

**c)** $\mathbf{x} = \begin{bmatrix} 7 \\ 8 \\ 3 \\ 2 \end{bmatrix}$    **d)** $\mathbf{x} = \begin{bmatrix} 4 \\ -2 \\ 0 \\ -2 \end{bmatrix}$

In Exercises 11–16:

**a)** Find a matrix $B$ in reduced echelon form such that $B$ is row equivalent to the given matrix $A$.

**b)** Find a basis for the null space of $A$.

**c)** As in Example 6, find a basis for the range of $A$ that consists of columns of $A$. For each column, $\mathbf{A}_j$, of $A$ that does not appear in the basis, express $\mathbf{A}_j$ as a linear combination of the basis vectors.

**d)** Exhibit a basis for the row space of $A$.

**11.** $A = \begin{bmatrix} 1 & 2 & 3 & -1 \\ 3 & 5 & 8 & -2 \\ 1 & 1 & 2 & 0 \end{bmatrix}$

**12.** $A = \begin{bmatrix} 1 & 1 & 2 \\ 1 & 1 & 2 \\ 2 & 3 & 5 \end{bmatrix}$

**13.** $A = \begin{bmatrix} 1 & 2 & 1 & 0 \\ 2 & 5 & 3 & -1 \\ 2 & 2 & 0 & 2 \\ 0 & 1 & 1 & -1 \end{bmatrix}$

**14.** $A = \begin{bmatrix} 2 & 2 & 0 \\ 2 & 1 & 1 \\ 2 & 3 & 0 \end{bmatrix}$

**15.** $A = \begin{bmatrix} 1 & 2 & 1 \\ 2 & 4 & 1 \\ 3 & 6 & 2 \end{bmatrix}$

**16.** $A = \begin{bmatrix} 2 & 1 & 2 \\ 2 & 2 & 1 \\ 2 & 3 & 0 \end{bmatrix}$

**17.** Use the technique illustrated in Example 7 to obtain a basis for the range of $A$, where $A$ is the matrix given in Exercise 11.

**18.** Repeat Exercise 17 for the matrix given in Exercise 12.

**19.** Repeat Exercise 17 for the matrix given in Exercise 13.

**20.** Repeat Exercise 17 for the matrix given in Exercise 14.

In Exercises 21–24 for the given set $S$:

**a)** Find a subset of $S$ that is a basis for $\text{Sp}(S)$ using the technique illustrated in Example 6.

**b)** Find a basis for $\text{Sp}(S)$ using the technique illustrated in Example 7.

**21.** $S = \left\{ \begin{bmatrix} 1 \\ 2 \end{bmatrix}, \begin{bmatrix} 2 \\ 4 \end{bmatrix} \right\}$

**22.** $S = \left\{ \begin{bmatrix} 1 \\ 2 \end{bmatrix}, \begin{bmatrix} 2 \\ 1 \end{bmatrix}, \begin{bmatrix} 3 \\ 2 \end{bmatrix} \right\}$

**23.** $S = \left\{ \begin{bmatrix} 1 \\ 2 \\ 1 \end{bmatrix}, \begin{bmatrix} 2 \\ 5 \\ 0 \end{bmatrix}, \begin{bmatrix} 3 \\ 7 \\ 1 \end{bmatrix}, \begin{bmatrix} 1 \\ 1 \\ 3 \end{bmatrix} \right\}$

**24.** $S = \left\{ \begin{bmatrix} 1 \\ 2 \\ -1 \\ 3 \end{bmatrix}, \begin{bmatrix} -2 \\ 1 \\ 2 \\ -1 \end{bmatrix}, \begin{bmatrix} -1 \\ -1 \\ 1 \\ -3 \end{bmatrix}, \begin{bmatrix} -2 \\ 2 \\ 2 \\ 0 \end{bmatrix} \right\}$

**25.** Find a basis for the null space of each of the following matrices.

**a)** $\begin{bmatrix} 1 & 0 & 0 \\ 1 & 0 & 1 \end{bmatrix}$  **b)** $\begin{bmatrix} 1 & 1 & 0 \\ 1 & 1 & 0 \end{bmatrix}$

**c)** $\begin{bmatrix} 1 & 1 & 0 \\ 1 & 1 & 1 \end{bmatrix}$

**26.** Find a basis for the range of each matrix in Exercise 25.

**27.** Let $S = \{\mathbf{v}_1, \mathbf{v}_2, \mathbf{v}_3\}$, where

$$\mathbf{v}_1 = \begin{bmatrix} 1 \\ 2 \\ 1 \end{bmatrix}, \quad \mathbf{v}_2 = \begin{bmatrix} -1 \\ -1 \\ 1 \end{bmatrix}, \quad \text{and}$$

$$\mathbf{v}_3 = \begin{bmatrix} -1 \\ 1 \\ 5 \end{bmatrix}.$$

Show that $S$ is a linearly dependent set, and verify that $\text{Sp}\{\mathbf{v}_1, \mathbf{v}_2, \mathbf{v}_3\} = \text{Sp}\{\mathbf{v}_1, \mathbf{v}_2\}$.

**28.** Let $S = \{\mathbf{v}_1, \mathbf{v}_2, \mathbf{v}_3\}$, where

$$\mathbf{v}_1 = \begin{bmatrix} 1 \\ 0 \end{bmatrix}, \quad \mathbf{v}_2 = \begin{bmatrix} 0 \\ 1 \end{bmatrix}, \quad \text{and}$$

$$\mathbf{v}_3 = \begin{bmatrix} -1 \\ 1 \end{bmatrix}.$$

Find every subset of $S$ that is a basis for $R^2$.

**29.** Let $S = \{\mathbf{v}_1, \mathbf{v}_2, \mathbf{v}_3, \mathbf{v}_4\}$, where

$$\mathbf{v}_1 = \begin{bmatrix} 1 \\ 2 \\ 1 \end{bmatrix}, \quad \mathbf{v}_2 = \begin{bmatrix} -1 \\ -1 \\ 1 \end{bmatrix},$$

$$\mathbf{v}_3 = \begin{bmatrix} -1 \\ 1 \\ 7 \end{bmatrix}, \quad \text{and} \quad \mathbf{v}_4 = \begin{bmatrix} -2 \\ -4 \\ -4 \end{bmatrix}.$$

Find every subset of $S$ that is a basis for $R^3$.

**30.** Let $B = \{\mathbf{v}_1, \mathbf{v}_2, \mathbf{v}_3\}$ be a set of linearly independent vectors in $R^3$. Prove that $B$ is a basis for $R^3$. [*Hint:* Use Theorem 13 of Section 1.7 to show that $B$ is a spanning set for $R^3$.]

**31.** Let $B = \{\mathbf{v}_1, \mathbf{v}_2, \mathbf{v}_3\}$ be a subset of $R^3$ such that $\text{Sp}(B) = R^3$. Prove that $B$ is a basis for $R^3$. [*Hint:* Use Theorem 13 of Section 1.7 to show that $B$ is a linearly independent set.]

In Exercises 32–35, determine whether the given set $S$ is a basis for $R^3$.

**32.** $S = \left\{ \begin{bmatrix} 1 \\ -1 \\ -2 \end{bmatrix}, \begin{bmatrix} 1 \\ 1 \\ 2 \end{bmatrix}, \begin{bmatrix} 2 \\ -3 \\ -3 \end{bmatrix} \right\}$

**33.** $S = \left\{ \begin{bmatrix} 1 \\ 1 \\ -2 \end{bmatrix}, \begin{bmatrix} 2 \\ 5 \\ 2 \end{bmatrix}, \begin{bmatrix} 1 \\ 3 \\ 2 \end{bmatrix} \right\}$

**34.** $S = \left\{ \begin{bmatrix} 1 \\ -1 \\ -2 \end{bmatrix}, \begin{bmatrix} 1 \\ 1 \\ 2 \end{bmatrix}, \begin{bmatrix} 2 \\ -3 \\ -3 \end{bmatrix}, \begin{bmatrix} 1 \\ 4 \\ 5 \end{bmatrix} \right\}$

**35.** $S = \left\{ \begin{bmatrix} 1 \\ 1 \\ -2 \end{bmatrix}, \begin{bmatrix} 2 \\ 5 \\ 2 \end{bmatrix} \right\}$

**36.** Find a vector $\mathbf{w}$ in $R^3$ such that $\mathbf{w}$ is not a linear combination of $\mathbf{v}_1$ and $\mathbf{v}_2$:

$$\mathbf{v}_1 = \begin{bmatrix} 1 \\ 2 \\ -1 \end{bmatrix}, \quad \text{and} \quad \mathbf{v}_2 = \begin{bmatrix} 2 \\ -1 \\ -2 \end{bmatrix}.$$

**37.** Prove that every basis for $R^2$ contains exactly two vectors. Proceed by showing the following:

a) A basis for $R^2$ cannot have more than two vectors.

b) A basis for $R^2$ cannot have one vector. [*Hint:* Suppose that a basis for $R^2$ could contain one vector. Represent $\mathbf{e}_1$ and $\mathbf{e}_2$ in terms of the basis and obtain a contradiction.]

**38.** Show that any spanning set for $R^n$ must contain at least $n$ vectors. Proceed by showing that if $\mathbf{u}_1, \mathbf{u}_2, \ldots, \mathbf{u}_p$ are vectors in $R^n$, and if $p < n$, then there is a nonzero vector $\mathbf{v}$ in $R^n$ such that $\mathbf{v}^T \mathbf{u}_i = 0, 1 \leq i \leq p$. [*Hint:* Write the constraints as a $(p \times n)$ system and use Theorem 4 of Section 1.3.] Given $\mathbf{v}$ as above, can $\mathbf{v}$ be a linear combination of $\mathbf{u}_1, \mathbf{u}_2, \ldots, \mathbf{u}_p$?

**39.** Recalling Exercise 38, prove that every basis for $R^n$ contains exactly $n$ vectors.

## 3.5   DIMENSION

In this section we translate the geometric concept of dimension into algebraic terms. Clearly $R^2$ and $R^3$ have dimension 2 and 3, respectively, since these vector spaces are simply algebraic interpretations of two-space and three-space. It would be natural to extrapolate from these two cases and declare that $R^n$ has dimension $n$ for each positive integer $n$; indeed, we have earlier referred to elements of $R^n$ as $n$-dimensional vectors. But if $W$ is a subspace of $R^n$, how is the dimension of $W$ to be determined? An examination of the subspace, $W$, of $R^3$ defined by

$$W = \{\mathbf{x}: \mathbf{x} = \begin{bmatrix} x_2 - 2x_3 \\ x_2 \\ x_3 \end{bmatrix}, \quad x_2 \text{ and } x_3 \text{ any real numbers}\}$$

suggests a possibility. Geometrically, $W$ is the plane with equation $x = y - 2z$, so naturally the dimension of $W$ is 2. The techniques of the previous section show that $W$ has a basis $\{\mathbf{v}_1, \mathbf{v}_2\}$ consisting of the two vectors

$$\mathbf{v}_1 = \begin{bmatrix} 1 \\ 1 \\ 0 \end{bmatrix} \quad \text{and} \quad \mathbf{v}_2 = \begin{bmatrix} -2 \\ 0 \\ 1 \end{bmatrix}.$$

Thus in this case the dimension of $W$ is equal to the number of vectors in a basis for $W$.

### The Definition of Dimension

More generally, for any subspace $W$ of $R^n$, we wish to define the dimension of $W$ to be the number of vectors in a basis for $W$. We have seen, however, that a subspace $W$

may have many different bases. In fact, Exercise 30 of Section 3.4 shows that any set of three linearly independent vectors in $R^3$ is a basis for $R^3$. Therefore, for the concept of dimension to make sense, we must show that all bases for a given subspace $W$ contain the same number of vectors. This fact will be an easy consequence of the following theorem.

THEOREM 8    Let $W$ be a subspace of $R^n$, and let $B = \{\mathbf{w}_1, \mathbf{w}_2, \ldots, \mathbf{w}_p\}$ be a spanning set for $W$ containing $p$ vectors. Then any set of $p + 1$ or more vectors in $W$ is linearly dependent.

*Proof*    Let $\{\mathbf{s}_1, \mathbf{s}_2, \ldots, \mathbf{s}_m\}$ be any set of $m$ vectors in $W$, where $m > p$. To show that this set is linearly dependent, we first express each $\mathbf{s}_i$ in terms of the spanning set $B$:

$$
\begin{aligned}
\mathbf{s}_1 &= a_{11}\mathbf{w}_1 + a_{21}\mathbf{w}_2 + \cdots + a_{p1}\mathbf{w}_p \\
\mathbf{s}_2 &= a_{12}\mathbf{w}_1 + a_{22}\mathbf{w}_2 + \cdots + a_{p2}\mathbf{w}_p \\
&\ \vdots \qquad\qquad \vdots \qquad\qquad\qquad \vdots \\
\mathbf{s}_m &= a_{1m}\mathbf{w}_1 + a_{2m}\mathbf{w}_2 + \cdots + a_{pm}\mathbf{w}_p.
\end{aligned}
\tag{1}
$$

To show that $\{\mathbf{s}_1, \mathbf{s}_2, \ldots, \mathbf{s}_m\}$ is linearly dependent, we must show that there is a nontrivial solution of

$$
c_1\mathbf{s}_1 + c_2\mathbf{s}_2 + \cdots + c_m\mathbf{s}_m = \boldsymbol{\theta}.
\tag{2}
$$

Now using system (1), we can rewrite Eq. (2) in terms of the vectors in $B$ as

$$
\begin{aligned}
&c_1(a_{11}\mathbf{w}_1 + a_{21}\mathbf{w}_2 + \cdots + a_{p1}\mathbf{w}_p) + \\
&c_2(a_{12}\mathbf{w}_1 + a_{22}\mathbf{w}_2 + \cdots + a_{p2}\mathbf{w}_p) + \\
&\cdots + c_m(a_{1m}\mathbf{w}_1 + a_{2m}\mathbf{w}_2 + \cdots + a_{pm}\mathbf{w}_p) = \boldsymbol{\theta}.
\end{aligned}
\tag{3a}
$$

Equation (3a) can be regrouped as

$$
\begin{aligned}
&(c_1a_{11} + c_2a_{12} + \cdots + c_ma_{1m})\mathbf{w}_1 + \\
&(c_1a_{21} + c_2a_{22} + \cdots + c_ma_{2m})\mathbf{w}_2 + \\
&\cdots + (c_1a_{p1} + c_2a_{p2} + \cdots + c_ma_{pm})\mathbf{w}_p = \boldsymbol{\theta}.
\end{aligned}
\tag{3b}
$$

Now finding $c_1, c_2, \ldots, c_m$ to satisfy Eq. (2) is the same as finding $c_1, c_2, \ldots, c_m$ to satisfy Eq. (3b). Furthermore, we can clearly satisfy Eq. (3b) if we can choose zero for each coefficient of each $\mathbf{w}_i$. Therefore, to obtain one solution of Eq. (3b), it suffices to solve the system

$$
\begin{aligned}
a_{11}c_1 + a_{12}c_2 + \cdots + a_{1m}c_m &= 0 \\
a_{21}c_1 + a_{22}c_2 + \cdots + a_{2m}c_m &= 0 \\
\ \vdots \qquad\qquad \vdots \qquad\quad \vdots \\
a_{p1}c_1 + a_{p2}c_2 + \cdots + a_{pm}c_m &= 0.
\end{aligned}
\tag{4}
$$

[Recall that each $a_{ij}$ is a specified constant determined by system (1), whereas each $c_i$ is an unknown parameter of Eq. (2).] The homogeneous system in (4) has more unknowns than equations, so by Theorem 4 of Section 1.3 there is a nontrivial solution to system (4). But a solution to system (4) is also a solution to Eq. (2), so Eq. (2) has a nontrivial solution, and the theorem is established. ∎

As an immediate corollary of Theorem 8, we can show that all bases for a subspace contain the same number of vectors.

COROLLARY Let $W$ be a subspace of $R^n$, and let $B = \{\mathbf{w}_1, \mathbf{w}_2, \ldots, \mathbf{w}_p\}$ be a basis for $W$ containing $p$ vectors. Then every basis for $W$ contains $p$ vectors.

*Proof* Let $Q = \{\mathbf{u}_1, \mathbf{u}_2, \ldots, \mathbf{u}_r\}$ be any basis for $W$. Since $Q$ is a spanning set for $W$, by Theorem 8 any set of $r + 1$ or more vectors in $W$ is linearly dependent. Since $B$ is a linearly independent set of $p$ vectors in $W$, we know that $p \le r$. Similarly, since $B$ is a spanning set of $p$ vectors for $W$, any set of $p + 1$ or more vectors in $W$ is linearly dependent. By assumption, $Q$ is a set of $r$ linearly independent vectors in $W$; so $r \le p$. Now, since we have $p \le r$ and $r \le p$, it must be that $r = p$. ∎

Given that every basis for a subspace contains the same number of vectors, we can make the following definition without any possibility of ambiguity.

DEFINITION 5 Let $W$ be a subspace of $R^n$. If $W$ has a basis $B = \{\mathbf{w}_1, \mathbf{w}_2, \ldots, \mathbf{w}_p\}$ of $p$ vectors, then we say that $W$ is a subspace of **dimension $p$**, and we write $\dim(W) = p$.

In Exercise 30, the reader is asked to show that every nonzero subspace of $R^n$ does have a basis. Thus a value for dimension can be assigned to any subspace of $R^n$, where for completeness we define $\dim(W) = 0$ if $W$ is the zero subspace.

Since $R^3$ has a basis $\{\mathbf{e}_1, \mathbf{e}_2, \mathbf{e}_3\}$ containing three vectors, we see that $\dim(R^3) = 3$. In general, $R^n$ has a basis $\{\mathbf{e}_1, \mathbf{e}_2, \ldots, \mathbf{e}_n\}$ that contains $n$ vectors; so $\dim(R^n) = n$. Thus the definition of dimension—the number of vectors in a basis—agrees with the usual terminology; $R^3$ is three-dimensional, and in general, $R^n$ is $n$-dimensional.

EXAMPLE 1 Let $W$ be the subspace of $R^3$ defined by

$$W = \{\mathbf{x} \colon \mathbf{x} = \begin{bmatrix} x_1 \\ x_2 \\ x_3 \end{bmatrix}, \quad x_1 = -2x_3, x_2 = x_3, x_3 \text{ arbitrary}\}.$$

Exhibit a basis for $W$ and determine $\dim(W)$.

*Solution* A vector $\mathbf{x}$ in $W$ can be written in the form

$$\mathbf{x} = \begin{bmatrix} -2x_3 \\ x_3 \\ x_3 \end{bmatrix} = x_3 \begin{bmatrix} -2 \\ 1 \\ 1 \end{bmatrix}.$$

Therefore, the set $\{\mathbf{u}\}$ is a basis for $W$, where

$$\mathbf{u} = \begin{bmatrix} -2 \\ 1 \\ 1 \end{bmatrix}.$$

It follows that $\dim(W) = 1$. Geometrically, $W$ is the line through the origin and through the point with coordinates $(-2, 1, 1)$, so again the definition of dimension coincides with our geometric intuition.

The next example illustrates the importance of the corollary to Theorem 8.

EXAMPLE 2  Let $W$ be the subspace of $R^3$, $W = \text{span}\{\mathbf{u}_1, \mathbf{u}_2, \mathbf{u}_3, \mathbf{u}_4\}$, where

$$\mathbf{u}_1 = \begin{bmatrix} 1 \\ 1 \\ 2 \end{bmatrix}, \quad \mathbf{u}_2 = \begin{bmatrix} 2 \\ 4 \\ 0 \end{bmatrix}, \quad \mathbf{u}_3 = \begin{bmatrix} 3 \\ 5 \\ 2 \end{bmatrix}, \quad \text{and} \quad \mathbf{u}_4 = \begin{bmatrix} 2 \\ 5 \\ -2 \end{bmatrix}.$$

Use the techniques illustrated in Examples 5, 6, and 7 of Section 3.4 to find three different bases for $W$. Give the dimension of $W$.

*Solution*

(a)  The technique used in Example 5 consisted of finding a basis for $W$ by using the algebraic specification for $W$. In particular, let $\mathbf{b}$ be a vector in $R^3$:

$$\mathbf{b} = \begin{bmatrix} a \\ b \\ c \end{bmatrix}.$$

Then $\mathbf{b}$ is in $W$ if and only if the vector equation

$$x_1\mathbf{u}_1 + x_2\mathbf{u}_2 + x_3\mathbf{u}_3 + x_4\mathbf{u}_4 = \mathbf{b} \tag{5a}$$

is consistent. The matrix equation for (5a) is $U\mathbf{x} = \mathbf{b}$, where $U$ is the $(3 \times 4)$ matrix $U = [\mathbf{u}_1, \mathbf{u}_2, \mathbf{u}_3, \mathbf{u}_4]$. Now, the augmented matrix $[U \mid \mathbf{b}]$ is row equivalent to the matrix

$$\begin{bmatrix} 1 & 0 & 1 & -1 & 2a - b \\ 0 & 1 & 1 & 3/2 & -a/2 + b/2 \\ 0 & 0 & 0 & 0 & -4a + 2b + c \end{bmatrix}. \tag{5b}$$

Thus $\mathbf{b}$ is in $W$ if and only if $-4a + 2b + c = 0$ or, equivalently, $c = 4a - 2b$. The subspace $W$ can then be described by

$$W = \{\mathbf{b}: \mathbf{b} = \begin{bmatrix} a \\ b \\ 4a - 2b \end{bmatrix}, \quad a \text{ and } b \text{ any real numbers}\}.$$

From this description it follows that $W$ has a basis $\{\mathbf{v}_1, \mathbf{v}_2\}$, where

$$\mathbf{v}_1 = \begin{bmatrix} 1 \\ 0 \\ 4 \end{bmatrix} \quad \text{and} \quad \mathbf{v}_2 = \begin{bmatrix} 0 \\ 1 \\ -2 \end{bmatrix}.$$

**(b)** The technique used in Example 6 consisted of discarding redundant vectors from a spanning set for $W$. In particular since $\{\mathbf{u}_1, \mathbf{u}_2, \mathbf{u}_3, \mathbf{u}_4\}$ spans $W$, this technique gives a basis for $W$ that is a subset of $\{\mathbf{u}_1, \mathbf{u}_2, \mathbf{u}_3, \mathbf{u}_4\}$. To obtain such a subset, solve the dependence relation

$$x_1\mathbf{u}_1 + x_2\mathbf{u}_2 + x_3\mathbf{u}_3 + x_4\mathbf{u}_4 = \boldsymbol{\theta}. \tag{5c}$$

Note that Eq. (5c) is just Eq. (5a) with $\mathbf{b} = \boldsymbol{\theta}$. It is easily seen from matrix (5b) that Eq. (5c) is equivalent to the reduced system

$$\begin{aligned}
x_1 \quad &+ x_3 \quad - \quad x_4 = 0 \\
x_2 &+ x_3 + (3/2)x_4 = 0.
\end{aligned} \tag{5d}$$

Backsolving (5d) yields

$$\begin{aligned}
x_1 &= -x_3 + \quad x_4 \\
x_2 &= -x_3 - (3/2)x_4,
\end{aligned}$$

where $x_3$ and $x_4$ are arbitrary. Therefore, the vectors $\mathbf{u}_3$ and $\mathbf{u}_4$ can be deleted from the spanning set for $W$, leaving $\{\mathbf{u}_1, \mathbf{u}_2\}$ as a basis for $W$.

**(c)** Let $U$ be the $(3 \times 4)$ matrix whose columns span $W$, $U = [\mathbf{u}_1, \mathbf{u}_2, \mathbf{u}_3, \mathbf{u}_4]$. Following the technique of Example 7, reduce $U^T$ to the matrix

$$C^T = \begin{bmatrix} 1 & 0 & 4 \\ 0 & 1 & -2 \\ 0 & 0 & 0 \\ 0 & 0 & 0 \end{bmatrix}$$

in echelon form. In this case the nonzero columns of

$$C = \begin{bmatrix} 1 & 0 & 0 & 0 \\ 0 & 1 & 0 & 0 \\ 4 & -2 & 0 & 0 \end{bmatrix}$$

form a basis for $W$; that is, $\{\mathbf{w}_1, \mathbf{w}_2\}$ is a basis for $W$, where

$$\mathbf{w}_1 = \begin{bmatrix} 1 \\ 0 \\ 4 \end{bmatrix} \quad \text{and} \quad \mathbf{w}_2 = \begin{bmatrix} 0 \\ 1 \\ -2 \end{bmatrix}.$$

In each case the basis obtained for $W$ contains two vectors, so $\dim(W) = 2$. Indeed, viewed geometrically, $W$ is the plane with equation $-4x + 2y + z = 0$. ◼

## Properties of a $p$-Dimensional Subspace

An important feature of dimension is that a $p$-dimensional subspace $W$ has many of the same properties as $R^p$. For example, Theorem 11 of Section 1.7 shows that any set of $p + 1$ or more vectors in $R^p$ is linearly dependent. The following theorem shows that this same property and others hold in $W$ when $\dim(W) = p$.

THEOREM 9    Let $W$ be a subspace of $R^n$ with $\dim(W) = p$.

1.  Any set of $p + 1$ or more vectors in $W$ is linearly dependent.
2.  Any set of fewer than $p$ vectors in $W$ does not span $W$.
3.  Any set of $p$ linearly independent vectors in $W$ is a basis for $W$.
4.  Any set of $p$ vectors that spans $W$ is a basis for $W$.

*Proof*    Property 1 follows immediately from Theorem 8, because $\dim(W) = p$ means that $W$ has a basis (and hence a spanning set) of $p$ vectors.

Property 2 is equivalent to the statement that a spanning set for $W$ must contain at least $p$ vectors. Again, this is an immediate consequence of Theorem 8.

To establish property 3, let $\{\mathbf{u}_1, \mathbf{u}_2, \ldots, \mathbf{u}_p\}$ be a set of $p$ linearly independent vectors in $W$. To see that the given set spans $W$, let $\mathbf{v}$ be any vector in $W$. By property 1, the set $\{\mathbf{v}, \mathbf{u}_1, \mathbf{u}_2, \ldots, \mathbf{u}_p\}$ is a linearly dependent set of vectors because the set contains $p + 1$ vectors. Thus there are scalars $a_0, a_1, \ldots, a_p$ (not all of which are zero) such that

$$a_0\mathbf{v} + a_1\mathbf{u}_1 + a_2\mathbf{u}_2 + \cdots + a_p\mathbf{u}_p = \boldsymbol{\theta}. \tag{6}$$

In addition, in Eq. (6), $a_0$ cannot be zero because $\{\mathbf{u}_1, \mathbf{u}_2, \ldots, \mathbf{u}_p\}$ is a linearly independent set. Therefore, Eq. (6) can be rewritten as

$$\mathbf{v} = (-1/a_0)[a_1\mathbf{u}_1 + a_2\mathbf{u}_2 + \cdots + a_p\mathbf{u}_p]. \tag{7}$$

It is clear from Eq. (7) that any vector in $W$ can be expressed as a linear combination of $\mathbf{u}_1, \mathbf{u}_2, \ldots, \mathbf{u}_p$, so the given linearly independent set also spans $W$. Therefore, the set is a basis.

The proof of property 4 is left as an exercise.

EXAMPLE 3    Let $W$ be the subspace of $R^3$ given in Example 2, and let $\{\mathbf{v}_1, \mathbf{v}_2, \mathbf{v}_3\}$ be the subset of $W$ defined by

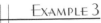

$$\mathbf{v}_1 = \begin{bmatrix} 1 \\ -1 \\ 6 \end{bmatrix}, \qquad \mathbf{v}_2 = \begin{bmatrix} 1 \\ 2 \\ 0 \end{bmatrix}, \quad \text{and} \quad \mathbf{v}_3 = \begin{bmatrix} 2 \\ 1 \\ 6 \end{bmatrix}.$$

Determine which of the subsets $\{\mathbf{v}_1\}$, $\{\mathbf{v}_2\}$, $\{\mathbf{v}_1, \mathbf{v}_2\}$, $\{\mathbf{v}_1, \mathbf{v}_3\}$, $\{\mathbf{v}_2, \mathbf{v}_3\}$, and $\{\mathbf{v}_1, \mathbf{v}_2, \mathbf{v}_3\}$ is a basis for $W$.

*Solution*    In Example 2, the subspace $W$ was described as

$$W = \{\mathbf{b}: \mathbf{b} = \begin{bmatrix} a \\ b \\ 4a - 2b \end{bmatrix}, \quad a \text{ and } b \text{ any real numbers}\}. \tag{8}$$

Using Eq. (8), we can easily check that $\mathbf{v}_1$, $\mathbf{v}_2$, and $\mathbf{v}_3$ are in $W$. We saw further in Example 2 that $\dim(W) = 2$. By Theorem 9, property 2, neither of the sets $\{\mathbf{v}_1\}$ or $\{\mathbf{v}_2\}$ spans $W$. By Theorem 9, property 1, the set $\{\mathbf{v}_1, \mathbf{v}_2, \mathbf{v}_3\}$ is linearly dependent. We can easily check that each of the sets $\{\mathbf{v}_1, \mathbf{v}_2\}$, $\{\mathbf{v}_1, \mathbf{v}_3\}$, and $\{\mathbf{v}_2, \mathbf{v}_3\}$, is linearly independent, so by Theorem 9, property 3, each is a basis for $W$.

## The Rank of a Matrix

In this subsection we use the concept of dimension to characterize nonsingular matrices and to determine precisely when a system of linear equations $A\mathbf{x} = \mathbf{b}$ is consistent. For an $(m \times n)$ matrix $A$, the dimension of the null space is called the **nullity of $A$**, and the dimension of the range of $A$ is called the **rank of $A$**. The following example will illustrate the relationship between the rank of $A$ and the nullity of $A$, as well as the relationship between the rank of $A$ and the dimension of the row space of $A$.

EXAMPLE 4   Find the rank, nullity, and dimension of the row space for the matrix $A$, where

$$A = \begin{bmatrix} 1 & 1 & 1 & 2 \\ -1 & 0 & 2 & -3 \\ 2 & 4 & 8 & 5 \end{bmatrix}.$$

*Solution*   To find the dimension of the row space of $A$, observe that $A$ is row equivalent to the matrix

$$B = \begin{bmatrix} 1 & 0 & -2 & 0 \\ 0 & 1 & 3 & 0 \\ 0 & 0 & 0 & 1 \end{bmatrix},$$

and $B$ is in echelon form. Since the nonzero rows of $B$ form a basis for the row space of $A$, the row space of $A$ has dimension 3.

   To find the nullity of $A$, we must determine the dimension of the null space. Since the homogeneous system $A\mathbf{x} = \boldsymbol{\theta}$ is equivalent to $B\mathbf{x} = \boldsymbol{\theta}$, the null space of $A$ can be determined by solving $B\mathbf{x} = \boldsymbol{\theta}$. This gives

$$\begin{aligned} x_1 &= 2x_3 \\ x_2 &= -3x_3 \\ x_4 &= 0. \end{aligned}$$

Thus $\mathcal{N}(A)$ can be described by

$$\mathcal{N}(A) = \{\mathbf{x}: \mathbf{x} = \begin{bmatrix} 2x_3 \\ -3x_3 \\ x_3 \\ 0 \end{bmatrix}, \quad x_3 \text{ any real number}\}.$$

It now follows that the nullity of $A$ is 1 because the vector

$$\mathbf{v} = \begin{bmatrix} 2 \\ -3 \\ 1 \\ 0 \end{bmatrix}$$

forms a basis for $\mathcal{N}(A)$.

   To find the rank of $A$, we must determine the dimension of the range of $A$. Recall that $\mathcal{R}(A)$, the range of $A$, equals the column space of $A$, so a basis for $\mathcal{R}(A)$ can be found by reducing $A^T$ to echelon form. It is straightforward to show that $A^T$ is row equivalent to the matrix $C^T$, where

$$C^T = \begin{bmatrix} 1 & 0 & 0 \\ 0 & 1 & 0 \\ 0 & 0 & 1 \\ 0 & 0 & 0 \end{bmatrix}.$$

The nonzero columns of the matrix $C$,

$$C = \begin{bmatrix} 1 & 0 & 0 & 0 \\ 0 & 1 & 0 & 0 \\ 0 & 0 & 1 & 0 \end{bmatrix},$$

form a basis for $\mathcal{R}(A)$. Thus the rank of $A$ is 3.     ◼

Note in the previous example that the row space of $A$ is a subspace of $R^4$, whereas the column space (or range) of $A$ is a subspace of $R^3$. Thus they are entirely different subspaces; even so, the dimensions are the same, and the next theorem states that this is always the case.

**THEOREM 10**     If $A$ is an $(m \times n)$ matrix, then the rank of $A$ is equal to the rank of $A^T$.     ◼

The proof of Theorem 10 will be given at the end of this section. Note that the range of $A^T$ is equal to the column space of $A^T$. But the column space of $A^T$ is precisely the row space of $A$, so the following corollary is actually a restatement of Theorem 10.

**COROLLARY**     If $A$ is an $(m \times n)$ matrix, then the row space and the column space of $A$ have the same dimension.     ◼

This corollary provides a useful way to determine the rank of a matrix $A$. Specifically, if $A$ is row equivalent to a matrix $B$ in echelon form, then the number, $r$, of nonzero rows in $B$ equals the rank of $A$.

The null space of an $(m \times n)$ matrix $A$ is determined by solving the homogeneous system of equations $A\mathbf{x} = \boldsymbol{\theta}$. Suppose the augmented matrix $[A \,|\, \boldsymbol{\theta}]$ for the system is row equivalent to the matrix $[B \,|\, \boldsymbol{\theta}]$, which is in echelon form. Then clearly $A$ is row equivalent to $B$, and the number, $r$, of nonzero rows of $B$ equals the rank of $A$. But $r$ is also the number of nonzero rows of $[B \,|\, \boldsymbol{\theta}]$. It follows from Theorem 3 of Section 1.3 that there are $n - r$ free variables in a solution for $A\mathbf{x} = \boldsymbol{\theta}$. But the number of vectors in a basis for $\mathcal{N}(A)$ equals the number of free variables in the solution for $A\mathbf{x} = \boldsymbol{\theta}$ (see Example 3 of Section 3.4); that is, the nullity of $A$ is $n - r$. Thus we have shown, informally, that the following formula holds.

***Remark***     If $A$ is an $(m \times n)$ matrix, then

$$n = \text{rank}(A) + \text{nullity}(A).$$

This remark will be proved formally in a more general context in Chapter 5.

Example 4 illustrates the argument preceding the remark. If $A$ is the matrix given in Example 4,

$$A = \begin{bmatrix} 1 & 1 & 1 & 2 \\ -1 & 0 & 2 & -3 \\ 2 & 4 & 8 & 5 \end{bmatrix}.$$

then the augmented matrix $[A \mid \theta]$ is row equivalent to

$$[B \mid \theta] = \begin{bmatrix} 1 & 0 & -2 & 0 & 0 \\ 0 & 1 & 3 & 0 & 0 \\ 0 & 0 & 0 & 1 & 0 \end{bmatrix}.$$

Since $A$ is row equivalent to $B$, the corollary to Theorem 10 implies that $A$ has rank 3. Further, in the notation of Theorem 3 of Section 1.3, the system $A\mathbf{x} = \theta$ has $n = 4$ unknowns, and the reduced matrix $[B \mid \theta]$ has $r = 3$ nonzero rows. Therefore, the solution for $A\mathbf{x} = \theta$ has $n - r = 4 - 3 = 1$ independent variables, and it follows that the nullity of $A$ is 1. In particular,

$$\text{rank}(A) + \text{nullity}(A) = 3 + 1 = 4,$$

as is guaranteed by the remark.

The following theorem uses the concept of the rank of a matrix to establish necessary and sufficient conditions for a system of equations, $A\mathbf{x} = \mathbf{b}$, to be consistent.

**THEOREM 11**    An $(m \times n)$ system of linear equations, $A\mathbf{x} = \mathbf{b}$, is consistent if and only if

$$\text{rank}(A) = \text{rank}([A \mid \mathbf{b}]).$$

*Proof*    Suppose that $A = [\mathbf{A}_1, \mathbf{A}_2, \ldots, \mathbf{A}_n]$. Then the rank of $A$ is the dimension of the column space of $A$, that is, the subspace

$$\text{Sp}\{\mathbf{A}_1, \mathbf{A}_2, \ldots, \mathbf{A}_n\}. \tag{9}$$

Similarly, the rank of $[A \mid \mathbf{b}]$ is the dimension of the subspace

$$\text{Sp}\{\mathbf{A}_1, \mathbf{A}_2, \ldots, \mathbf{A}_n, \mathbf{b}\}. \tag{10}$$

But we already know that $A\mathbf{x} = \mathbf{b}$ is consistent if and only if $\mathbf{b}$ is in the column space of $A$. It follows that $A\mathbf{x} = \mathbf{b}$ is consistent if and only if the subspaces given in Eq. (9) and Eq. (10) are equal and consequently have the same dimension.    ■

Our final theorem in this section shows that rank can be used to determine nonsingular matrices.

**THEOREM 12**    An $(n \times n)$ matrix $A$ is nonsingular if and only if the rank of $A$ is $n$.

*Proof*    Suppose that $A = [\mathbf{A}_1, \mathbf{A}_2, \ldots, \mathbf{A}_n]$. The proof of Theorem 12 rests on the observation that the range of $A$ is given by

$$\mathcal{R}(A) = \text{Sp}\{\mathbf{A}_1, \mathbf{A}_2, \ldots, \mathbf{A}_n\}. \tag{11}$$

If $A$ is nonsingular then, by Theorem 12 of Section 1.7, the columns of $A$ are linearly independent. Thus $\{\mathbf{A}_1, \mathbf{A}_2, \ldots, \mathbf{A}_n\}$ is a basis for $\mathcal{R}(A)$, and the rank of $A$ is $n$.

Conversely, suppose that $A$ has rank $n$; that is, $\mathcal{R}(A)$ has dimension $n$. It is an immediate consequence of Eq. (11) and Theorem 9, property 4, that $\{\mathbf{A}_1, \mathbf{A}_2, \ldots, \mathbf{A}_n\}$ is a basis for $\mathcal{R}(A)$. In particular, the columns of $A$ are linearly independent, so, by Theorem 12 of Section 1.7, $A$ is nonsingular. ◼

## Proof of Theorem 10 (Optional)

To prove Theorem 10, let $A = (a_{ij})$ be an $(m \times n)$ matrix. Denote the rows of $A$ by $\mathbf{a}_1, \mathbf{a}_2, \ldots, \mathbf{a}_m$. Thus,

$$\mathbf{a}_i = [a_{i1}, a_{i2}, \ldots, a_{in}].$$

Similarly, let $\mathbf{A}_1, \mathbf{A}_2, \ldots, \mathbf{A}_n$ be the columns of $A$, where

$$\mathbf{A}_j = \begin{bmatrix} a_{1j} \\ a_{2j} \\ \vdots \\ a_{mj} \end{bmatrix}.$$

Suppose that $A^T$ has rank $k$. Since the columns of $A^T$ are $\mathbf{a}_1^T, \mathbf{a}_2^T, \ldots, \mathbf{a}_m^T$, it follows that if

$$W = \text{Sp}\{\mathbf{a}_1, \mathbf{a}_2, \ldots, \mathbf{a}_m\},$$

then $\dim(W) = k$. Therefore, $W$ has a basis $\{\mathbf{w}_1, \mathbf{w}_2, \ldots, \mathbf{w}_k\}$, and, by Theorem 9, property 2, $m \geq k$. For $1 \leq j \leq k$, suppose that $\mathbf{w}_j$ is the $(1 \times n)$ vector

$$\mathbf{w}_j = [w_{j1}, w_{j2}, \ldots, w_{jn}].$$

Writing each $\mathbf{a}_i$ in terms of the basis yields

$$\begin{aligned}
[a_{11}, a_{12}, \ldots, a_{1n}] = \mathbf{a}_1 &= c_{11}\mathbf{w}_1 + c_{12}\mathbf{w}_2 + \cdots + c_{1k}\mathbf{w}_k \\
[a_{21}, a_{22}, \ldots, a_{2n}] = \mathbf{a}_2 &= c_{21}\mathbf{w}_1 + c_{22}\mathbf{w}_2 + \cdots + c_{2k}\mathbf{w}_k \\
\vdots \qquad\qquad &\qquad \vdots \quad\ \vdots \qquad\qquad\qquad \vdots \\
[a_{m1}, a_{m2}, \ldots, a_{mn}] = \mathbf{a}_m &= c_{m1}\mathbf{w}_1 + c_{m2}\mathbf{w}_2 + \cdots + c_{mk}\mathbf{w}_k.
\end{aligned} \tag{12}$$

Equating the $j$th component of the left side of system (12) with the $j$th component of the right side yields

$$\begin{bmatrix} a_{1j} \\ a_{2j} \\ \vdots \\ a_{mj} \end{bmatrix} = w_{1j}\begin{bmatrix} c_{11} \\ c_{21} \\ \vdots \\ c_{m1} \end{bmatrix} + w_{2j}\begin{bmatrix} c_{12} \\ c_{22} \\ \vdots \\ c_{m2} \end{bmatrix} + \cdots + w_{kj}\begin{bmatrix} c_{1k} \\ c_{2k} \\ \vdots \\ c_{mk} \end{bmatrix} \tag{13}$$

for $1 \leq j \leq n$. For $1 \leq i \leq k$, define $\mathbf{c}_i$ to be the $(m \times 1)$ column vector

$$\mathbf{c}_i = \begin{bmatrix} c_{1i} \\ c_{2i} \\ \vdots \\ c_{mi} \end{bmatrix}.$$

Then system (13) becomes

$$\mathbf{A}_j = w_{1j}\mathbf{c}_1 + w_{2j}\mathbf{c}_2 + \cdots + w_{kj}\mathbf{c}_k, \quad 1 \le j \le n. \tag{14}$$

It follows from the equations in (14) that

$$\mathcal{R}(A) = \text{Sp}\{\mathbf{A}_1, \mathbf{A}_2, \ldots \mathbf{A}_n\} \subseteq \text{Sp}\{\mathbf{c}_1, \mathbf{c}_2, \ldots, \mathbf{c}_k\}.$$

It follows from Theorem 8 that the subspace

$$V = \text{Sp}\{\mathbf{c}_1, \mathbf{c}_2, \ldots, \mathbf{c}_k\}$$

has dimension $k$, at most. By Exercise 32, $\dim[\mathcal{R}(A)] \le \dim(V) \le k$; that is, $\text{rank}(A) \le \text{rank}(A^T)$.

Since $(A^T)^T = A$, the same argument implies that $\text{rank}(A^T) \le \text{rank}(A)$. Thus $\text{rank}(A) = \text{rank}(A^T)$. ∎

## 3.5    EXERCISES

Exercises 1–14 refer to the vectors in (15).

$$\mathbf{u}_1 = \begin{bmatrix} 1 \\ 1 \end{bmatrix}, \quad \mathbf{u}_2 = \begin{bmatrix} 1 \\ 2 \end{bmatrix}, \quad \mathbf{u}_3 = \begin{bmatrix} -1 \\ 1 \end{bmatrix},$$

$$\mathbf{u}_4 = \begin{bmatrix} 0 \\ 0 \end{bmatrix}, \quad \mathbf{u}_5 = \begin{bmatrix} 3 \\ 3 \end{bmatrix}, \quad \mathbf{v}_1 = \begin{bmatrix} 1 \\ -1 \\ 1 \end{bmatrix},$$

$$\mathbf{v}_2 = \begin{bmatrix} 0 \\ 1 \\ 2 \end{bmatrix}, \quad \mathbf{v}_3 = \begin{bmatrix} 1 \\ -1 \\ 0 \end{bmatrix}, \quad \mathbf{v}_4 = \begin{bmatrix} -1 \\ 3 \\ 3 \end{bmatrix}$$

$$\tag{15}$$

In Exercises 1–6, determine by inspection why the given set $S$ is not a basis for $R^2$. (That is, either $S$ is linearly dependent or $S$ does not span $R^2$.)

**1.** $S = \{\mathbf{u}_1\}$      **2.** $S = \{\mathbf{u}_2\}$

**3.** $S = \{\mathbf{u}_1, \mathbf{u}_2, \mathbf{u}_3\}$      **4.** $S = \{\mathbf{u}_2, \mathbf{u}_3, \mathbf{u}_5\}$

**5.** $S = \{\mathbf{u}_1, \mathbf{u}_4\}$      **6.** $S = \{\mathbf{u}_1, \mathbf{u}_5\}$

In Exercises 7–9, determine by inspection why the given set $S$ is not a basis for $R^3$. (That is, either $S$ is linearly dependent or $S$ does not span $R^3$.)

**7.** $S = \{\mathbf{v}_1, \mathbf{v}_2\}$      **8.** $S = \{\mathbf{v}_1, \mathbf{v}_3\}$

**9.** $S = \{\mathbf{v}_1, \mathbf{v}_2, \mathbf{v}_3, \mathbf{v}_4\}$

In Exercises 10–14, use Theorem 9, property 3, to determine whether the given set is a basis for the indicated vector space.

**10.** $S = \{\mathbf{u}_1, \mathbf{u}_2\}$ for $R^2$

**11.** $S = \{\mathbf{u}_2, \mathbf{u}_3\}$ for $R^2$

**12.** $S = \{\mathbf{v}_1, \mathbf{v}_2, \mathbf{v}_3\}$ for $R^3$

**13.** $S = \{\mathbf{v}_1, \mathbf{v}_2, \mathbf{v}_4\}$ for $R^3$

**14.** $S = \{\mathbf{v}_2, \mathbf{v}_3, \mathbf{v}_4\}$ for $R^3$

In Exercises 15–20, $W$ is a subspace of $R^4$ consisting of vectors of the form

$$\mathbf{x} = \begin{bmatrix} x_1 \\ x_2 \\ x_3 \\ x_4 \end{bmatrix}.$$

Determine $\dim(W)$ when the components of $\mathbf{x}$ satisfy the given conditions.

**15.** $x_1 - 2x_2 + x_3 - x_4 = 0$

**16.** $x_1 - 2x_3 = 0$

**17.** $x_1 = -x_2 + 2x_4$
   $x_3 = \phantom{-x_2} - x_4$

**18.** $x_1 \phantom{+x_2} + x_3 - 2x_4 = 0$
   $x_2 + 2x_3 - 3x_4 = 0$

**19.** $x_1 = -x_4$
   $x_2 = \phantom{-}3x_4$
   $x_3 = \phantom{-}2x_4$

**20.** $x_1 - x_2 \phantom{- 2x_3} = 0$
   $x_2 - 2x_3 \phantom{x_4} = 0$
   $x_3 - x_4 = 0$

In Exercises 21–24, find a basis for $\mathcal{N}(A)$ and give the nullity and the rank of $A$.

**21.** $A = \begin{bmatrix} 1 & 2 \\ -2 & -4 \end{bmatrix}$      **22.** $A = \begin{bmatrix} -1 & 2 & 0 \\ 2 & -5 & 1 \end{bmatrix}$

**23.** $A = \begin{bmatrix} 1 & -1 & 3 \\ 2 & -1 & 8 \\ -1 & 4 & 3 \end{bmatrix}$

**24.** $A = \begin{bmatrix} 1 & 2 & 0 & 5 \\ 1 & 3 & 1 & 7 \\ 2 & 3 & -1 & 9 \end{bmatrix}$

In Exercises 25 and 26, find a basis for $\mathcal{R}(A)$ and give the nullity and the rank of $A$.

**25.** $A = \begin{bmatrix} 1 & 2 & 1 \\ -1 & 0 & 3 \\ 1 & 5 & 7 \end{bmatrix}$

**26.** $A = \begin{bmatrix} 1 & 1 & 2 & 0 \\ 2 & 4 & 2 & 4 \\ 2 & 1 & 5 & -2 \end{bmatrix}$

**27.** Let $W$ be a subspace, and let $S$ be a spanning set for $W$. Find a basis for $W$, and calculate $\dim(W)$ for each set $S$.

**a)** $S = \left\{ \begin{bmatrix} 1 \\ 1 \\ -2 \end{bmatrix}, \begin{bmatrix} -1 \\ -2 \\ 3 \end{bmatrix}, \begin{bmatrix} 1 \\ 0 \\ -1 \end{bmatrix}, \begin{bmatrix} 2 \\ -1 \\ 0 \end{bmatrix} \right\}$

**b)** $S = \left\{ \begin{bmatrix} 1 \\ 2 \\ -1 \\ 1 \end{bmatrix}, \begin{bmatrix} 3 \\ 1 \\ 1 \\ 2 \end{bmatrix}, \begin{bmatrix} -1 \\ 1 \\ -2 \\ 2 \end{bmatrix}, \begin{bmatrix} 0 \\ -2 \\ 1 \\ 2 \end{bmatrix} \right\}$

**28.** Let $W$ be the subspace of $R^4$ defined by $W = \{\mathbf{x}: \mathbf{v}^T\mathbf{x} = 0\}$. Calculate $\dim(W)$, where

$$\mathbf{v} = \begin{bmatrix} 1 \\ 2 \\ -3 \\ -1 \end{bmatrix}.$$

**29.** Let $W$ be the subspace of $R^4$ defined by $W = \{\mathbf{x}: \mathbf{a}^T\mathbf{x} = 0 \text{ and } \mathbf{b}^T\mathbf{x} = 0 \text{ and } \mathbf{c}^T\mathbf{x} = 0\}$. Calculate $\dim(W)$ for

$$\mathbf{a} = \begin{bmatrix} 1 \\ -1 \\ 0 \\ 0 \end{bmatrix}, \quad \mathbf{b} = \begin{bmatrix} 1 \\ 0 \\ -1 \\ 0 \end{bmatrix}, \quad \text{and}$$

$$\mathbf{c} = \begin{bmatrix} 0 \\ 1 \\ -1 \\ 0 \end{bmatrix}.$$

**30.** Let $W$ be a nonzero subspace of $R^n$. Show that $W$ has a basis. [*Hint:* Let $\mathbf{w}_1$ be any nonzero vector in $W$. If $\{\mathbf{w}_1\}$ is a spanning set for $W$, then we are done. If not, there is a vector $\mathbf{w}_2$ in $W$ such that $\{\mathbf{w}_1, \mathbf{w}_2\}$ is linearly independent. Why? Continue by asking whether this is a spanning set for $W$. Why must this process eventually stop?]

**31.** Suppose that $\{\mathbf{u}_1, \mathbf{u}_2, \dots, \mathbf{u}_p\}$ is a basis for a subspace $W$, and suppose that $\mathbf{x}$ is in $W$ with $\mathbf{x} = a_1\mathbf{u}_1 + a_2\mathbf{u}_2 + \cdots + a_p\mathbf{u}_p$. Show that this representation for $\mathbf{x}$ in terms of the basis is unique—that is, if $\mathbf{x} = b_1\mathbf{u}_1 + b_2\mathbf{u}_2 + \cdots + b_p\mathbf{u}_p$, then $b_1 = a_1, b_2 = a_2, \dots, b_p = a_p$.

**32.** Let $U$ and $V$ be subspaces of $R^n$, and suppose that $U$ is a subset of $V$. Prove that $\dim(U) \leq \dim(V)$. If $\dim(U) = \dim(V)$, prove that $V$ is contained in $U$, and thus conclude that $U = V$.

**33.** For each of the following, determine the largest possible value for the rank of $A$ and the smallest possible value for the nullity of $A$.

**a)** $A$ is $(3 \times 3)$
**b)** $A$ is $(3 \times 4)$
**c)** $A$ is $(5 \times 4)$

**34.** If $A$ is a $(3 \times 4)$ matrix, prove that the columns of $A$ are linearly dependent.

**35.** If $A$ is a $(4 \times 3)$ matrix, prove that the rows of $A$ are linearly dependent.

**36.** Let $A$ be an $(m \times n)$ matrix. Prove that $\text{rank}(A) \leq m$ and $\text{rank}(A) \leq n$.

**37.** Let $A$ be a $(2 \times 3)$ matrix with rank 2. Show that the $(2 \times 3)$ system of equations $A\mathbf{x} = \mathbf{b}$ is consistent for every choice of $\mathbf{b}$ in $R^2$.

**38.** Let $A$ be a $(3 \times 4)$ matrix with nullity 1. Prove that the $(3 \times 4)$ system of equations $A\mathbf{x} = \mathbf{b}$ is consistent for every choice of $\mathbf{b}$ in $R^3$.

**39.** Prove that an $(n \times n)$ matrix $A$ is nonsingular if and only if the nullity of $A$ is zero.

**40.** Let $A$ be an $(m \times m)$ nonsingular matrix, and let $B$ be an $(m \times n)$ matrix. Prove that $\mathcal{N}(AB) = \mathcal{N}(B)$ and conclude that rank $(AB) = $ rank $(B)$.

**41.** Prove property 4 of Theorem 9 as follows: Assume that $\dim(W) = p$ and let $S = \{\mathbf{w}_1, \ldots, \mathbf{w}_p\}$ be a set of $p$ vectors that spans $W$. To see that $S$ is linearly independent, suppose that $c_1\mathbf{w}_1 + \cdots + c_p\mathbf{w}_p = \boldsymbol{\theta}$. If $c_i \neq 0$, show that $W = \text{Sp}\{\mathbf{w}_1, \ldots, \mathbf{w}_{i-1},$

$\mathbf{w}_{i+1}, \ldots, \mathbf{w}_p\}$. Finally, use Theorem 8 to reach a contradiction.

**42.** Suppose that $S = \{\mathbf{u}_1, \mathbf{u}_2, \ldots, \mathbf{u}_p\}$ is a set of linearly independent vectors in a subspace $W$, where $\dim(W) = m$ and $m > p$. Prove that there is a vector $\mathbf{u}_{p+1}$ in $W$ such that $\{\mathbf{u}_1, \mathbf{u}_2, \ldots, \mathbf{u}_p, \mathbf{u}_{p+1}\}$ is linearly independent. Use this proof to show that a basis including all the vectors in $S$ can be constructed for $W$.

## 3.6 ORTHOGONAL BASES FOR SUBSPACES

We have seen that a basis provides a very efficient way to characterize a subspace. Also, given a subspace $W$, we know that there are many different ways to construct a basis for $W$. In this section we focus on a particular type of basis called an *orthogonal basis*.

### Orthogonal Bases

The idea of orthogonality is a generalization of the vector geometry concept of perpendicularity. If $\mathbf{u}$ and $\mathbf{v}$ are two vectors in $R^2$ or $R^3$, then we know that $\mathbf{u}$ and $\mathbf{v}$ are perpendicular if $\mathbf{u}^T\mathbf{v} = 0$ (see Theorem 7 in Section 2.3). For example, consider the vectors $\mathbf{u}$ and $\mathbf{v}$ given by

$$\mathbf{u} = \begin{bmatrix} 1 \\ -2 \end{bmatrix} \quad \text{and} \quad \mathbf{v} = \begin{bmatrix} 6 \\ 3 \end{bmatrix}.$$

Clearly $\mathbf{u}^T\mathbf{v} = 0$, and these two vectors are perpendicular when viewed as directed line segments in the plane (see Fig. 3.13).

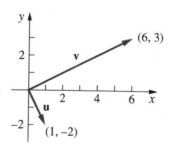

*Figure 3.13* In $R^2$, nonzero vectors $\mathbf{u}$ and $\mathbf{v}$ are perpendicular if and only if $\mathbf{u}^T\mathbf{v} = 0$.

In general, for vectors in $R^n$, we use the term *orthogonal* rather than the term *perpendicular*. Specifically, if $\mathbf{u}$ and $\mathbf{v}$ are vectors in $R^n$, we say that $\mathbf{u}$ and $\mathbf{v}$ are **orthogonal** if

$$\mathbf{u}^T\mathbf{v} = 0.$$

We will also find the concept of an orthogonal set of vectors to be useful.

DEFINITION 6 | Let $S = \{\mathbf{u}_1, \mathbf{u}_2, \ldots, \mathbf{u}_p\}$ be a set of vectors in $R^n$. The set $S$ is said to be an ***orthogonal set*** if each pair of distinct vectors from $S$ is orthogonal; that is, $\mathbf{u}_i^T \mathbf{u}_j = 0$ when $i \neq j$.

EXAMPLE 1     Verify that $S$ is an orthogonal set of vectors, where

$$S = \left\{ \begin{bmatrix} 1 \\ 0 \\ 1 \\ 2 \end{bmatrix}, \begin{bmatrix} 1 \\ 1 \\ -1 \\ 0 \end{bmatrix}, \begin{bmatrix} 1 \\ -2 \\ -1 \\ 0 \end{bmatrix} \right\},$$

***Solution***     If we use the notation $S = \{\mathbf{u}_1, \mathbf{u}_2, \mathbf{u}_3\}$, then

$$\mathbf{u}_1^T \mathbf{u}_2 = \begin{bmatrix} 1 & 0 & 1 & 2 \end{bmatrix} \begin{bmatrix} 1 \\ 1 \\ -1 \\ 0 \end{bmatrix} = 1 + 0 - 1 + 0 = 0$$

$$\mathbf{u}_1^T \mathbf{u}_3 = \begin{bmatrix} 1 & 0 & 1 & 2 \end{bmatrix} \begin{bmatrix} 1 \\ -2 \\ -1 \\ 0 \end{bmatrix} = 1 + 0 - 1 + 0 = 0$$

$$\mathbf{u}_2^T \mathbf{u}_3 = \begin{bmatrix} 1 & 1 & -1 & 0 \end{bmatrix} \begin{bmatrix} 1 \\ -2 \\ -1 \\ 0 \end{bmatrix} = 1 - 2 + 1 + 0 = 0.$$

Therefore, $S = \{\mathbf{u}_1, \mathbf{u}_2, \mathbf{u}_3\}$ is an orthogonal set of vectors in $R^4$.     ◼

An important property of an orthogonal set $S$ is that $S$ is necessarily linearly independent (so long as $S$ does not contain the zero vector).

THEOREM 13     Let $S = \{\mathbf{u}_1, \mathbf{u}_2, \ldots, \mathbf{u}_p\}$ be a set of nonzero vectors in $R^n$. If $S$ is an orthogonal set of vectors, then $S$ is a linearly independent set of vectors.

***Proof***     Let $c_1, c_2, \ldots, c_p$ be any scalars that satisfy

$$c_1 \mathbf{u}_1 + c_2 \mathbf{u}_2 + \cdots + c_p \mathbf{u}_p = \boldsymbol{\theta}. \tag{1}$$

Form the scalar product

$$\mathbf{u}_1^T (c_1 \mathbf{u}_1 + c_2 \mathbf{u}_2 + \cdots + c_p \mathbf{u}_p) = \mathbf{u}_1^T \boldsymbol{\theta}$$

or

$$c_1(\mathbf{u}_1^T\mathbf{u}_1) + c_2(\mathbf{u}_1^T\mathbf{u}_2) + \cdots + c_p(\mathbf{u}_1^T\mathbf{u}_p) = 0.$$

Since $\mathbf{u}_1^T\mathbf{u}_j = 0$ for $2 \le j \le p$, the expression above reduces to

$$c_1(\mathbf{u}_1^T\mathbf{u}_1) = 0. \tag{2}$$

Next, because $\mathbf{u}_1^T\mathbf{u}_1 > 0$ when $\mathbf{u}_1$ is nonzero, we see from Eq. (2) that $c_1 = 0$.

Similarly, forming the scalar product of both sides of Eq. (1) with $\mathbf{u}_i$, we see that $c_i(\mathbf{u}_i^T\mathbf{u}_i) = 0$ or $c_i = 0$ for $1 \le i \le p$. Thus $S$ is a linearly independent set of vectors.    ◼

By Theorem 13, any orthogonal set $S$ containing $p$ nonzero vectors from a $p$-dimensional subspace $W$ will be a basis for $W$ (since $S$ is a linearly independent subset of $p$ vectors from $W$, where $\dim(W) = p$). Such a basis is called an orthogonal basis. In the following definition, recall that the symbol $\|\mathbf{v}\|$ denotes the length of $\mathbf{v}$, $\|\mathbf{v}\| = \sqrt{\mathbf{v}^T\mathbf{v}}$.

---

**DEFINITION 7**

Let $W$ be a subspace of $R^n$, and let $B = \{\mathbf{u}_1, \mathbf{u}_2, \ldots, \mathbf{u}_p\}$ be a basis for $W$. If $B$ is an orthogonal set of vectors, then $B$ is called an ***orthogonal basis*** for $W$.

Furthermore, if $\|\mathbf{u}_i\| = 1$ for $1 \le i \le p$, then $B$ is said to be an ***orthonormal basis*** for $W$.

---

The word *orthonormal* suggests both *ortho*gonal and *normal*ized. Thus an orthonormal basis is an orthogonal basis consisting of vectors having length 1, where a vector of length 1 is a unit vector or a normalized vector. Observe that the unit vectors $\mathbf{e}_1, \mathbf{e}_2, \ldots, \mathbf{e}_n$ form an orthonormal basis for $R^n$.

**EXAMPLE 2**    Verify that the set $B = \{\mathbf{v}_1, \mathbf{v}_2, \mathbf{v}_3\}$ is an orthogonal basis for $R^3$, where

$$\mathbf{v}_1 = \begin{bmatrix} 1 \\ 2 \\ 1 \end{bmatrix}, \quad \mathbf{v}_2 = \begin{bmatrix} 3 \\ -1 \\ -1 \end{bmatrix}, \quad \text{and} \quad \mathbf{v}_3 = \begin{bmatrix} 1 \\ -4 \\ 7 \end{bmatrix}.$$

*Solution*    We first verify that $B$ is an orthogonal set by calculating

$$\mathbf{v}_1^T\mathbf{v}_2 = 3 - 2 - 1 = 0$$
$$\mathbf{v}_1^T\mathbf{v}_3 = 1 - 8 + 7 = 0$$
$$\mathbf{v}_2^T\mathbf{v}_3 = 3 + 4 - 7 = 0.$$

Now, $R^3$ has dimension 3. Thus, since $B$ is a set of three vectors and is also a linearly independent set (see Theorem 13), it follows that $B$ is an orthogonal basis for $R^3$.    ◼

These observations are stated formally in the following corollary of Theorem 13.

| | | COROLLARY | Let $W$ be a subspace of $R^n$, where $\dim(W) = p$. If $S$ is an orthogonal set of $p$ nonzero vectors and is also a subset of $W$, then $S$ is an orthogonal basis for $W$. ∎

## Orthonormal Bases

If $B = \{\mathbf{u}_1, \mathbf{u}_2, \ldots, \mathbf{u}_p\}$ is an orthogonal set, then $C = \{a_1\mathbf{u}_1, a_2\mathbf{u}_2, \ldots, a_p\mathbf{u}_p\}$ is also an orthogonal set for any scalars $a_1, a_2, \ldots, a_p$. If $B$ contains only nonzero vectors and if we define the scalars $a_i$ by

$$a_i = \frac{1}{\sqrt{\mathbf{u}_i^T \mathbf{u}_i}},$$

then $C$ is an ***orthonormal*** set. That is, we can convert an orthogonal set of nonzero vectors into an orthonormal set by dividing each vector by its length.

EXAMPLE 3    Recall that the set $B$ in Example 2 is an orthogonal basis for $R^3$. Modify $B$ so that it is an orthonormal basis.

*Solution*    Given that $B = \{\mathbf{v}_1, \mathbf{v}_2, \mathbf{v}_3\}$ is an orthogonal basis for $R^3$, we can modify $B$ to be an orthonormal basis by dividing each vector by its length. In particular (see Example 2), the lengths of $\mathbf{v}_1$, $\mathbf{v}_2$, and $\mathbf{v}_3$ are

$$\|\mathbf{v}_1\| = \sqrt{6}, \quad \|\mathbf{v}_2\| = \sqrt{11}, \quad \text{and} \quad \|\mathbf{v}_3\| = \sqrt{66}.$$

Therefore, the set $C = \{\mathbf{w}_1, \mathbf{w}_2, \mathbf{w}_3\}$ is an orthonormal basis for $R^3$, where

$$\mathbf{w}_1 = \frac{1}{\sqrt{6}}\mathbf{v}_1 = \begin{bmatrix} 1/\sqrt{6} \\ 2/\sqrt{6} \\ 1/\sqrt{6} \end{bmatrix}, \quad \mathbf{w}_2 = \frac{1}{\sqrt{11}}\mathbf{v}_2 = \begin{bmatrix} 3/\sqrt{11} \\ -1/\sqrt{11} \\ -1/\sqrt{11} \end{bmatrix}, \quad \text{and}$$

$$\mathbf{w}_3 = \frac{1}{\sqrt{66}}\mathbf{v}_3 = \begin{bmatrix} 1/\sqrt{66} \\ -4/\sqrt{66} \\ 7/\sqrt{66} \end{bmatrix}.$$
∎

## Determining Coordinates

Suppose that $W$ is a $p$-dimensional subspace of $R^n$, and $B = \{\mathbf{w}_1, \mathbf{w}_2, \ldots, \mathbf{w}_p\}$ is a basis for $W$. If $\mathbf{v}$ is any vector in $W$, then $\mathbf{v}$ can be written uniquely in the form

$$\mathbf{v} = a_1\mathbf{w}_1 + a_2\mathbf{w}_2 + \cdots + a_p\mathbf{w}_p. \tag{3}$$

(In Eq. (3), the fact that the scalars $a_1, a_2, \ldots, a_p$ are unique is proved in Exercise 31 of Section 3.5.) The scalars $a_1, a_2, \ldots, a_p$ in Eq. (3) are called the ***coordinates of v*** with respect to the basis $B$.

As we will see, it is fairly easy to determine the coordinates of a vector with respect to an orthogonal basis. To appreciate the savings in computation, consider how coordinates are found when the basis is not orthogonal. For instance, the set $B_1 = \{\mathbf{v}_1, \mathbf{v}_2, \mathbf{v}_3\}$ is a basis for $R^3$, where

$$\mathbf{v}_1 = \begin{bmatrix} 1 \\ 1 \\ -1 \end{bmatrix}, \quad \mathbf{v}_2 = \begin{bmatrix} -1 \\ 2 \\ 1 \end{bmatrix}, \quad \text{and} \quad \mathbf{v}_3 = \begin{bmatrix} 2 \\ -2 \\ 1 \end{bmatrix}.$$

As can be seen, $\mathbf{v}_1^T \mathbf{v}_3 \neq 0$, and so $B_1$ is not an orthogonal basis. Next, suppose we wish to express some vector $\mathbf{v}$ in $R^3$, say $\mathbf{v} = [5, -5, -2]^T$, in terms of $B_1$. We must solve the $(3 \times 3)$ system: $a_1\mathbf{v}_1 + a_2\mathbf{v}_2 + a_3\mathbf{v}_3 = \mathbf{v}$. In matrix terms the coordinates $a_1$, $a_2$, and $a_3$ are found by solving the equation

$$\begin{bmatrix} 1 & -1 & 2 \\ 1 & 2 & -2 \\ -1 & 1 & 1 \end{bmatrix} \begin{bmatrix} a_1 \\ a_2 \\ a_3 \end{bmatrix} = \begin{bmatrix} 5 \\ -5 \\ -2 \end{bmatrix}.$$

(By Gaussian elimination, the solution is $a_1 = 1$, $a_2 = -2$, $a_3 = 1$.)

By contrast, if $B_2 = \{\mathbf{w}_1, \mathbf{w}_2, \mathbf{w}_3\}$ is an orthogonal basis for $R^3$, it is easy to determine $a_1$, $a_2$, and $a_3$ so that

$$\mathbf{v} = a_1\mathbf{w}_1 + a_2\mathbf{w}_2 + a_3\mathbf{w}_3. \tag{4}$$

To find the coordinate $a_1$ in Eq. (4), we form the scalar product

$$\begin{aligned} \mathbf{w}_1^T \mathbf{v} &= \mathbf{w}_1^T (a_1\mathbf{w}_1 + a_2\mathbf{w}_2 + a_3\mathbf{w}_3) \\ &= a_1(\mathbf{w}_1^T \mathbf{w}_1) + a_2(\mathbf{w}_1^T \mathbf{w}_2) + a_3(\mathbf{w}_1^T \mathbf{w}_3) \\ &= a_1(\mathbf{w}_1^T \mathbf{w}_1). \end{aligned}$$

The last equality follows because $\mathbf{w}_1^T \mathbf{w}_2 = 0$ and $\mathbf{w}_1^T \mathbf{w}_3 = 0$. Therefore, from above

$$a_1 = \frac{\mathbf{w}_1^T \mathbf{v}}{\mathbf{w}_1^T \mathbf{w}_1}.$$

Similarly,

$$a_2 = \frac{\mathbf{w}_2^T \mathbf{v}}{\mathbf{w}_2^T \mathbf{w}_2} \quad \text{and} \quad a_3 = \frac{\mathbf{w}_3^T \mathbf{v}}{\mathbf{w}_3^T \mathbf{w}_3}.$$

(*Note:* Since $B_2$ is a basis, $\mathbf{w}_i^T \mathbf{w}_i > 0$, $1 \leq i \leq 3$.)

EXAMPLE 4    Express the vector $\mathbf{v}$ in terms of the orthogonal basis $B = \{\mathbf{w}_1, \mathbf{w}_2, \mathbf{w}_3\}$, where

$$\mathbf{v} = \begin{bmatrix} 12 \\ -3 \\ 6 \end{bmatrix}, \quad \mathbf{w}_1 = \begin{bmatrix} 1 \\ 2 \\ 1 \end{bmatrix}, \quad \mathbf{w}_2 = \begin{bmatrix} 3 \\ -1 \\ -1 \end{bmatrix}, \quad \text{and} \quad \mathbf{w}_3 = \begin{bmatrix} 1 \\ -4 \\ 7 \end{bmatrix}.$$

**Solution**    Beginning with the equation

$$\mathbf{v} = a_1\mathbf{w}_1 + a_2\mathbf{w}_2 + a_3\mathbf{w}_3,$$

we form scalar products to obtain

$$\mathbf{w}_1^T \mathbf{v} = a_1(\mathbf{w}_1^T \mathbf{w}_1), \quad \text{or} \quad 12 = 6a_1$$
$$\mathbf{w}_2^T \mathbf{v} = a_2(\mathbf{w}_2^T \mathbf{w}_2), \quad \text{or} \quad 33 = 11a_2$$
$$\mathbf{w}_3^T \mathbf{v} = a_3(\mathbf{w}_3^T \mathbf{w}_3), \quad \text{or} \quad 66 = 66a_3.$$

Thus $a_1 = 2$, $a_2 = 3$, and $a_3 = 1$. Therefore, as can be verified directly, $\mathbf{v} = 2\mathbf{w}_1 + 3\mathbf{w}_2 + \mathbf{w}_3$. ∎

In general, let $W$ be a subspace of $R^n$, and let $B = \{\mathbf{w}_1, \mathbf{w}_2, \ldots, \mathbf{w}_p\}$ be an orthogonal basis for $W$. If $\mathbf{v}$ is any vector in $W$, then $\mathbf{v}$ can be expressed uniquely in the form

$$\mathbf{v} = a_1\mathbf{w}_1 + a_2\mathbf{w}_2 + \cdots + a_p\mathbf{w}_p, \tag{5a}$$

where

$$a_i = \frac{\mathbf{w}_i^T \mathbf{v}}{\mathbf{w}_i^T \mathbf{w}_i}, \quad 1 \le i \le p. \tag{5b}$$

## Constructing an Orthogonal Basis

The next theorem gives a procedure that can be used to generate an orthogonal basis from any given basis. This procedure, called the Gram–Schmidt process, is quite practical from a computational standpoint (although some care must be exercised when programming the procedure for the computer). Generating an orthogonal basis is often the first step in solving problems in least-squares approximation; so Gram–Schmidt orthogonalization is of more than theoretical interest.

 THEOREM 14     **Gram–Schmidt**     Let $W$ be a $p$-dimensional subspace of $R^n$, and let $\{\mathbf{w}_1, \mathbf{w}_2, \ldots, \mathbf{w}_p\}$ be any basis for $W$. Then the set of vectors $\{\mathbf{u}_1, \mathbf{u}_2, \ldots, \mathbf{u}_p\}$ is an orthogonal basis for $W$, where

$$\mathbf{u}_1 = \mathbf{w}_1$$

$$\mathbf{u}_2 = \mathbf{w}_2 - \frac{\mathbf{u}_1^T \mathbf{w}_2}{\mathbf{u}_1^T \mathbf{u}_1}\mathbf{u}_1$$

$$\mathbf{u}_3 = \mathbf{w}_3 - \frac{\mathbf{u}_1^T \mathbf{w}_3}{\mathbf{u}_1^T \mathbf{u}_1}\mathbf{u}_1 - \frac{\mathbf{u}_2^T \mathbf{w}_3}{\mathbf{u}_2^T \mathbf{u}_2}\mathbf{u}_2,$$

and where, in general,

$$\mathbf{u}_i = \mathbf{w}_i - \sum_{k=1}^{i-1} \frac{\mathbf{u}_k^T \mathbf{w}_i}{\mathbf{u}_k^T \mathbf{u}_k}\mathbf{u}_k, \quad 2 \le i \le p. \tag{6}$$

∎

The proof of Theorem 14 is somewhat technical, and we defer it to the end of this section.

In Eq. (6) we have explicit expressions that can be used to generate an orthogonal set of vectors $\{\mathbf{u}_1, \mathbf{u}_2, \ldots, \mathbf{u}_p\}$ from a given set of linearly independent vectors. These explicit expressions are especially useful if we have reason to implement the Gram–Schmidt process on a computer.

However, for hand calculations, it is not necessary to memorize formula (6). All we need to remember is the form or the general pattern of the Gram–Schmidt process. In particular, the Gram–Schmidt process starts with a basis $\{\mathbf{w}_1, \mathbf{w}_2, \ldots, \mathbf{w}_p\}$ and generates new vectors $\mathbf{u}_1, \mathbf{u}_2, \mathbf{u}_3, \ldots$ according to the following pattern:

$$\mathbf{u}_1 = \mathbf{w}_1$$
$$\mathbf{u}_2 = \mathbf{w}_2 + a\mathbf{u}_1$$
$$\mathbf{u}_3 = \mathbf{w}_3 + b\mathbf{u}_1 + c\mathbf{u}_2$$
$$\mathbf{u}_4 = \mathbf{w}_4 + d\mathbf{u}_1 + e\mathbf{u}_2 + f\mathbf{u}_3$$
$$\vdots$$
$$\mathbf{u}_i = \mathbf{w}_i + \alpha_1\mathbf{u}_1 + \alpha_2\mathbf{u}_2 + \cdots + \alpha_{i-1}\mathbf{u}_{i-1}$$
$$\vdots$$

In this sequence, the scalars can be determined in a step-by-step fashion from the orthogonality conditions.

For instance, to determine the scalar $a$ in the definition of $\mathbf{u}_2$, we use the condition $\mathbf{u}_1^T\mathbf{u}_2 = 0$:

$$0 = \mathbf{u}_1^T\mathbf{u}_2 = \mathbf{u}_1^T\mathbf{w}_2 + a\mathbf{u}_1^T\mathbf{u}_1;$$
$$\textit{Therefore:} \quad a = -(\mathbf{u}_1^T\mathbf{w}_2)/(\mathbf{u}_1^T\mathbf{u}_1). \tag{7}$$

To determine the two scalars $b$ and $c$ in the definition of $\mathbf{u}_3$, we use the two conditions $\mathbf{u}_1^T\mathbf{u}_3 = 0$ and $\mathbf{u}_2^T\mathbf{u}_3 = 0$. In particular,

$$0 = \mathbf{u}_1^T\mathbf{u}_3 = \mathbf{u}_1^T\mathbf{w}_3 + b\mathbf{u}_1^T\mathbf{u}_1 + c\mathbf{u}_1^T\mathbf{u}_2$$
$$= \mathbf{u}_1^T\mathbf{w}_3 + b\mathbf{u}_1^T\mathbf{u}_1 \quad (\text{since } \mathbf{u}_1^T\mathbf{u}_2 = 0 \text{ by Eq. (7)})$$
$$\textit{Therefore:} \quad b = -(\mathbf{u}_1^T\mathbf{w}_3)/(\mathbf{u}_1^T\mathbf{u}_1).$$

Similarly,

$$0 = \mathbf{u}_2^T\mathbf{u}_3 = \mathbf{u}_2^T\mathbf{w}_3 + b\mathbf{u}_2^T\mathbf{u}_1 + c\mathbf{u}_2^T\mathbf{u}_2$$
$$= \mathbf{u}_2^T\mathbf{w}_3 + c\mathbf{u}_2^T\mathbf{u}_2 \quad (\text{since } \mathbf{u}_2^T\mathbf{u}_1 = 0 \text{ by Eq. (7)})$$
$$\textit{Therefore:} \quad c = -(\mathbf{u}_2^T\mathbf{w}_3)/(\mathbf{u}_2^T\mathbf{u}_2).$$

The examples that follow illustrate the previous calculations.

Finally, to use the Gram–Schmidt orthogonalization process to find an orthogonal basis for $W$, we need some basis for $W$ as a starting point. In many of the applications that require an orthogonal basis for a subspace $W$, it is relatively easy to produce this initial basis—we will give some examples in a later section. Given a basis for $W$, the Gram–Schmidt process proceeds in a mechanical fashion using Eq. (6). (*Note:* It was shown in Exercise 30 of Section 3.5 that every nonzero subspace of $R^n$ has a basis. Therefore, by Theorem 14, every nonzero subspace of $R^n$ has an orthogonal basis.)

| | | EXAMPLE 5   Let $W$ be the subspace of $R^3$ defined by $W = \text{Sp}\{\mathbf{w}_1, \mathbf{w}_2\}$, where

$$\mathbf{w}_1 = \begin{bmatrix} 1 \\ 1 \\ 2 \end{bmatrix} \quad \text{and} \quad \mathbf{w}_2 = \begin{bmatrix} 0 \\ 2 \\ -4 \end{bmatrix}.$$

Use the Gram–Schmidt process to construct an orthogonal basis for $W$.

**Solution**   We define vectors $\mathbf{u}_1$ and $\mathbf{u}_2$ of the form

$$\mathbf{u}_1 = \mathbf{w}_1$$
$$\mathbf{u}_2 = \mathbf{w}_2 + a\mathbf{u}_1,$$

where the scalar $a$ is found from the condition $\mathbf{u}_1^T \mathbf{u}_2 = 0$. Now, $\mathbf{u}_1 = [1, 1, 2]^T$ and thus $\mathbf{u}_1^T \mathbf{u}_2$ is given by

$$\mathbf{u}_1^T \mathbf{u}_2 = \mathbf{u}_1^T(\mathbf{w}_2 + a\mathbf{u}_1) = \mathbf{u}_1^T \mathbf{w}_2 + a\mathbf{u}_1^T \mathbf{u}_1 = -6 + 6a.$$

Therefore, to have $\mathbf{u}_1^T \mathbf{u}_2 = 0$, we need $a = 1$. With $a = 1$, $\mathbf{u}_2$ is given by $\mathbf{u}_2 = \mathbf{w}_2 + \mathbf{u}_1 = [1, 3, -2]^T$.

In detail, an orthogonal basis for $W$ is $B = \{\mathbf{u}_1, \mathbf{u}_2\}$, where

$$\mathbf{u}_1 = \begin{bmatrix} 1 \\ 1 \\ 2 \end{bmatrix} \quad \text{and} \quad \mathbf{u}_2 = \begin{bmatrix} 1 \\ 3 \\ -2 \end{bmatrix}. \qquad \blacksquare$$

For convenience in hand calculations, we can always eliminate fractional components in a set of orthogonal vectors. Specifically, if $\mathbf{x}$ and $\mathbf{y}$ are orthogonal, then so are $a\mathbf{x}$ and $\mathbf{y}$ for any scalar $a$:

$$\text{If} \quad \mathbf{x}^T \mathbf{y} = 0, \quad \text{then} \quad (a\mathbf{x})^T \mathbf{y} = a(\mathbf{x}^T \mathbf{y}) = 0.$$

We will make use of this observation in the following example.

| | | EXAMPLE 6   Use the Gram–Schmidt orthogonalization process to generate an orthogonal basis for $W = \text{Sp}\{\mathbf{w}_1, \mathbf{w}_2, \mathbf{w}_3\}$, where

$$\mathbf{w}_1 = \begin{bmatrix} 0 \\ 1 \\ 2 \\ 1 \end{bmatrix}, \quad \mathbf{w}_2 = \begin{bmatrix} 0 \\ 1 \\ 3 \\ 1 \end{bmatrix}, \quad \text{and} \quad \mathbf{w}_3 = \begin{bmatrix} 1 \\ 1 \\ 1 \\ 0 \end{bmatrix}.$$

**Solution**   First we should check to be sure that $\{\mathbf{w}_1, \mathbf{w}_2, \mathbf{w}_3\}$ is a linearly independent set. A calculation shows that the vectors are linearly independent. (Exercise 27 illustrates what happens when the Gram–Schmidt algorithm is applied to a linearly dependent set.)

To generate an orthogonal basis $\{\mathbf{u}_1, \mathbf{u}_2, \mathbf{u}_3\}$ from $\{\mathbf{w}_1, \mathbf{w}_2, \mathbf{w}_3\}$, we first set

$$\mathbf{u}_1 = \mathbf{w}_1$$
$$\mathbf{u}_2 = \mathbf{w}_2 + a\mathbf{u}_1$$
$$\mathbf{u}_3 = \mathbf{w}_3 + b\mathbf{u}_1 + c\mathbf{u}_2.$$

With $\mathbf{u}_1 = [0, 1, 2, 1]^T$, the orthogonality condition $\mathbf{u}_1^T \mathbf{u}_2 = 0$ leads to $\mathbf{u}_1^T \mathbf{w}_2 + a\mathbf{u}_1^T \mathbf{u}_1 = 0$, or $8 + 6a = 0$. Therefore, $a = -4/3$ and hence

$$\mathbf{u}_2 = \mathbf{w}_2 - (4/3)\mathbf{u}_1 = [0, -1/3, 1/3, -1/3]^T.$$

Next, the conditions $\mathbf{u}_1^T \mathbf{u}_3 = 0$ and $\mathbf{u}_2^T \mathbf{u}_3 = 0$ lead to

$$0 = \mathbf{u}_1^T (\mathbf{w}_3 + b\mathbf{u}_1 + c\mathbf{u}_2) = 3 + 6b$$
$$0 = \mathbf{u}_2^T (\mathbf{w}_3 + b\mathbf{u}_1 + c\mathbf{u}_2) = 0 + (1/3)c.$$

Therefore, $b = -1/2$ and $c = 0$. Having the scalars $b$ and $c$,

$$\mathbf{u}_3 = \mathbf{w}_3 - (1/2)\mathbf{u}_1 - (0)\mathbf{u}_2 = [1, 1/2, 0, -1/2]^T.$$

For convenience, we can eliminate the fractional components in $\mathbf{u}_2$ and $\mathbf{u}_3$ and obtain an orthogonal basis $\{\mathbf{v}_1, \mathbf{v}_2, \mathbf{v}_3\}$, where

$$\mathbf{v}_1 = \begin{bmatrix} 0 \\ 1 \\ 2 \\ 1 \end{bmatrix}, \quad \mathbf{v}_2 = \begin{bmatrix} 0 \\ -1 \\ 1 \\ -1 \end{bmatrix}, \quad \text{and} \quad \mathbf{v}_3 = \begin{bmatrix} 2 \\ 1 \\ 0 \\ -1 \end{bmatrix}. \quad \blacksquare$$

(*Note:* In Example 6, we could have also eliminated fractional components in the middle of the Gram–Schmidt process. That is, we could have redefined $\mathbf{u}_2$ to be the vector $\mathbf{u}_2 = [0, -1, 1, -1]^T$ and then calculated $\mathbf{u}_3$ with this new, redefined multiple of $\mathbf{u}_2$.)

As a final example, we use MATLAB to construct orthogonal bases.

EXAMPLE 7    Let $A$ be the $(3 \times 5)$ matrix

$$A = \begin{bmatrix} 1 & 2 & 1 & 3 & 2 \\ 4 & 1 & 0 & 6 & 1 \\ 1 & 1 & 2 & 4 & 5 \end{bmatrix}.$$

Find an orthogonal basis for $\mathcal{R}(A)$ and an orthogonal basis for $\mathcal{N}(A)$.

*Solution*    The MATLAB command `orth(A)` gives an orthonormal basis for the range of $A$. The command `null(A)` gives an orthonormal basis for the null space of $A$. The results are shown in Fig. 3.14. Observe that the basis for $\mathcal{R}(A)$ has three vectors; that is, the dimension of $\mathcal{R}(A)$ is three or, equivalently, $A$ has rank three. The basis for $\mathcal{N}(A)$ has two vectors; that is, the dimension of $\mathcal{N}(A)$ is two, or equivalently, $A$ has nullity two. $\blacksquare$

## Proof of Theorem 14 (Optional)

We first show that the expression given in Eq. (6) is always defined and that the vectors $\mathbf{u}_1, \mathbf{u}_2, \ldots, \mathbf{u}_p$ are all nonzero. To begin, $\mathbf{u}_1$ is a nonzero vector since $\mathbf{u}_1 = \mathbf{w}_1$. Thus $\mathbf{u}_1^T \mathbf{u}_1 > 0$, and so we can define $\mathbf{u}_2$. Furthermore, we observe that $\mathbf{u}_2$ has the form $\mathbf{u}_2 = \mathbf{w}_2 - b\mathbf{u}_1 = \mathbf{w}_2 - b_1\mathbf{w}_1$; so $\mathbf{u}_2$ is nonzero since it is a nontrivial linear combination

```
A=
     1      2      1      3      2
     4      1      0      6      1
     1      1      2      4      5

>>orth(A)

ans=
     0.3841        -0.1173       -0.9158
     0.7682         0.5908        0.2466
     0.5121        -0.7983        0.3170

>>null(A)

ans=
    -0.7528        -0.0690
    -0.2063         0.1800
    -0.1069        -0.9047
     0.5736        -0.0469
    -0.2243         0.3772
```

*Figure 3.14*  The MATLAB command `orth(A)` produces an orthonormal basis for the range of $A$. The command `null(A)` gives an orthonormal basis for the null space of $A$.

of $\mathbf{w}_1$ and $\mathbf{w}_2$. Proceeding inductively, suppose that $\mathbf{u}_1, \mathbf{u}_2, \ldots, \mathbf{u}_{i-1}$ have been generated by Eq. (6); and suppose that each $\mathbf{u}_k$ has the form

$$\mathbf{u}_k = \mathbf{w}_k - c_1\mathbf{w}_1 - c_2\mathbf{w}_2 - \cdots - c_{k-1}\mathbf{w}_{k-1}.$$

From this equation, each $\mathbf{u}_k$ is nonzero; and it follows that Eq. (6) is a well-defined expression [since $\mathbf{u}_k^T\mathbf{u}_k > 0$ for $1 \le k \le (i-1)$]. Finally, since each $\mathbf{u}_k$ in Eq. (6) is a linear combination of $\mathbf{w}_1, \mathbf{w}_2, \ldots, \mathbf{w}_k$, we see that $\mathbf{u}_i$ is a nontrivial linear combination of $\mathbf{w}_1, \mathbf{w}_2, \ldots, \mathbf{w}_i$; and therefore $\mathbf{u}_i$ is nonzero.

All that remains to be proved is that the vectors generated by Eq. (6) are orthogonal. Clearly $\mathbf{u}_1^T\mathbf{u}_2 = 0$. Proceeding inductively again, suppose that $\mathbf{u}_j^T\mathbf{u}_k = 0$ for any $j$ and $k$, where $j \ne k$ and $1 \le j, k \le i - 1$. From (6) we have

$$\mathbf{u}_j^T\mathbf{u}_i = \mathbf{u}_j^T\left(\mathbf{w}_i - \sum_{k=1}^{i-1}\frac{\mathbf{u}_k^T\mathbf{w}_i}{\mathbf{u}_k^T\mathbf{u}_k}\mathbf{u}_k\right) = \mathbf{u}_j^T\mathbf{w}_i - \sum_{k=1}^{i-1}\left(\frac{\mathbf{u}_k^T\mathbf{w}_i}{\mathbf{u}_k^T\mathbf{u}_k}\right)(\mathbf{u}_j^T\mathbf{u}_k)$$

$$= \mathbf{u}_j^T\mathbf{w}_i - \left(\frac{\mathbf{u}_j^T\mathbf{w}_i}{\mathbf{u}_j^T\mathbf{u}_j}\right)(\mathbf{u}_j^T\mathbf{u}_j) = 0.$$

Thus $\mathbf{u}_i$ is orthogonal to $\mathbf{u}_j$ for $1 \le j \le i - 1$. Having this result, we have shown that $\{\mathbf{u}_1, \mathbf{u}_2, \ldots, \mathbf{u}_p\}$ is an orthogonal set of $p$ nonzero vectors. So, by the corollary of Theorem 13, the vectors $\mathbf{u}_1, \mathbf{u}_2, \ldots, \mathbf{u}_p$ are an orthogonal basis for $W$.

## 3.6    EXERCISES

In Exercises 1–4, verify that $\{\mathbf{u}_1, \mathbf{u}_2, \mathbf{u}_3\}$ is an orthogonal set for the given vectors.

**1.** $\mathbf{u}_1 = \begin{bmatrix} 1 \\ 1 \\ 1 \end{bmatrix}$, $\mathbf{u}_2 = \begin{bmatrix} -1 \\ 0 \\ 1 \end{bmatrix}$, $\mathbf{u}_3 = \begin{bmatrix} -1 \\ 2 \\ -1 \end{bmatrix}$

**2.** $\mathbf{u}_1 = \begin{bmatrix} 1 \\ 0 \\ 1 \end{bmatrix}$, $\mathbf{u}_2 = \begin{bmatrix} -1 \\ 0 \\ 1 \end{bmatrix}$, $\mathbf{u}_3 = \begin{bmatrix} 0 \\ 1 \\ 0 \end{bmatrix}$

**3.** $\mathbf{u}_1 = \begin{bmatrix} 1 \\ 1 \\ 2 \end{bmatrix}$, $\mathbf{u}_2 = \begin{bmatrix} 2 \\ 0 \\ -1 \end{bmatrix}$, $\mathbf{u}_3 = \begin{bmatrix} 1 \\ -5 \\ 2 \end{bmatrix}$

**4.** $\mathbf{u}_1 = \begin{bmatrix} 2 \\ 1 \\ 2 \end{bmatrix}$, $\mathbf{u}_2 = \begin{bmatrix} 1 \\ 2 \\ -2 \end{bmatrix}$, $\mathbf{u}_3 = \begin{bmatrix} -2 \\ 2 \\ 1 \end{bmatrix}$

In Exercises 5–8, find values $a$, $b$, and $c$ such that $\{\mathbf{u}_1, \mathbf{u}_2, \mathbf{u}_3\}$ is an orthogonal set.

**5.** $\mathbf{u}_1 = \begin{bmatrix} 1 \\ 1 \\ 1 \end{bmatrix}$, $\mathbf{u}_2 = \begin{bmatrix} 2 \\ 2 \\ -4 \end{bmatrix}$, $\mathbf{u}_3 = \begin{bmatrix} a \\ b \\ c \end{bmatrix}$

**6.** $\mathbf{u}_1 = \begin{bmatrix} 2 \\ 0 \\ 1 \end{bmatrix}$, $\mathbf{u}_2 = \begin{bmatrix} 1 \\ 1 \\ -2 \end{bmatrix}$, $\mathbf{u}_3 = \begin{bmatrix} a \\ b \\ c \end{bmatrix}$

**7.** $\mathbf{u}_1 = \begin{bmatrix} 1 \\ 1 \\ 1 \end{bmatrix}$, $\mathbf{u}_2 = \begin{bmatrix} -2 \\ -1 \\ a \end{bmatrix}$, $\mathbf{u}_3 = \begin{bmatrix} 4 \\ b \\ c \end{bmatrix}$

**8.** $\mathbf{u}_1 = \begin{bmatrix} 2 \\ 1 \\ -1 \end{bmatrix}$, $\mathbf{u}_2 = \begin{bmatrix} a \\ 1 \\ -1 \end{bmatrix}$, $\mathbf{u}_3 = \begin{bmatrix} b \\ 3 \\ c \end{bmatrix}$

In Exercises 9–12, express the given vector $\mathbf{v}$ in terms of the orthogonal basis $B = \{\mathbf{u}_1, \mathbf{u}_2, \mathbf{u}_3\}$, where $\mathbf{u}_1, \mathbf{u}_2$, and $\mathbf{u}_3$ are as in Exercise 1.

**9.** $\mathbf{v} = \begin{bmatrix} 1 \\ 1 \\ 0 \end{bmatrix}$

**10.** $\mathbf{v} = \begin{bmatrix} 0 \\ 1 \\ 2 \end{bmatrix}$

**11.** $\mathbf{v} = \begin{bmatrix} 3 \\ 3 \\ 3 \end{bmatrix}$

**12.** $\mathbf{v} = \begin{bmatrix} 1 \\ 2 \\ 1 \end{bmatrix}$

In Exercises 13–18, use the Gram–Schmidt process to generate an orthogonal set from the given linearly independent vectors.

**13.** $\begin{bmatrix} 0 \\ 0 \\ 1 \\ 0 \end{bmatrix}$, $\begin{bmatrix} 1 \\ 1 \\ 2 \\ 1 \end{bmatrix}$, $\begin{bmatrix} 1 \\ 0 \\ 1 \\ 1 \end{bmatrix}$

**14.** $\begin{bmatrix} 1 \\ 0 \\ 1 \\ 2 \end{bmatrix}$, $\begin{bmatrix} 2 \\ 1 \\ 0 \\ 2 \end{bmatrix}$, $\begin{bmatrix} 1 \\ -1 \\ 0 \\ 1 \end{bmatrix}$

**15.** $\begin{bmatrix} 1 \\ 1 \\ 0 \end{bmatrix}$, $\begin{bmatrix} 0 \\ 2 \\ 1 \end{bmatrix}$, $\begin{bmatrix} 1 \\ 1 \\ 6 \end{bmatrix}$

**16.** $\begin{bmatrix} 0 \\ 1 \\ 2 \end{bmatrix}$, $\begin{bmatrix} 3 \\ 6 \\ 2 \end{bmatrix}$, $\begin{bmatrix} 10 \\ -5 \\ 5 \end{bmatrix}$

**17.** $\begin{bmatrix} 0 \\ 1 \\ 0 \\ 1 \end{bmatrix}$, $\begin{bmatrix} 1 \\ 2 \\ 0 \\ 0 \end{bmatrix}$, $\begin{bmatrix} 0 \\ 2 \\ 1 \\ 0 \end{bmatrix}$

**18.** $\begin{bmatrix} 1 \\ 1 \\ 0 \\ 2 \end{bmatrix}$, $\begin{bmatrix} 0 \\ 2 \\ 1 \\ 2 \end{bmatrix}$, $\begin{bmatrix} 0 \\ 1 \\ 0 \\ 2 \end{bmatrix}$

In Exercises 19 and 20, find a basis for the null space and the range of the given matrix. Then use Gram–Schmidt to obtain orthogonal bases.

**19.** $\begin{bmatrix} 1 & -2 & 1 & -5 \\ 2 & 1 & 7 & 5 \\ 1 & -1 & 2 & -2 \end{bmatrix}$

**20.** $\begin{bmatrix} 1 & 3 & 10 & 11 & 9 \\ -1 & 2 & 5 & 4 & 1 \\ 2 & -1 & -1 & 1 & 4 \end{bmatrix}$

**21.** Argue that any set of four or more nonzero vectors in $R^3$ cannot be an orthogonal set.

**22.** Let $S = \{\mathbf{u}_1, \mathbf{u}_2, \mathbf{u}_3\}$ be an orthogonal set of nonzero vectors in $R^3$. Define the $(3 \times 3)$ matrix $A$ by $A = [\mathbf{u}_1, \mathbf{u}_2, \mathbf{u}_3]$. Show that $A$ is nonsingular and $A^T A = D$, where $D$ is a diagonal matrix. Calculate the diagonal matrix $D$ when $A$ is created from the orthogonal vectors in Exercise 1.

**23.** Let $W$ be a $p$-dimensional subspace of $R^n$. If $\mathbf{v}$ is a vector in $W$ such that $\mathbf{v}^T \mathbf{w} = 0$ for every $\mathbf{w}$ in $W$, show that $\mathbf{v} = \boldsymbol{\theta}$. [*Hint:* Consider $\mathbf{w} = \mathbf{v}$.]

**24.** *The Cauchy–Schwarz inequality.* Let $\mathbf{x}$ and $\mathbf{y}$ be vectors in $R^n$. Prove that $|\mathbf{x}^T \mathbf{y}| \leq \|\mathbf{x}\| \|\mathbf{y}\|$. [*Hint:* Observe that $\|\mathbf{x} - c\mathbf{y}\|^2 \geq 0$ for any scalar $c$. If $\mathbf{y} \neq \boldsymbol{\theta}$,

let $c = \mathbf{x}^T \mathbf{y}/\mathbf{y}^T \mathbf{y}$ and expand $(\mathbf{x} - c\mathbf{y})^T (\mathbf{x} - c\mathbf{y}) \geq 0$. Also treat the case $\mathbf{y} = \boldsymbol{\theta}$.]

**25.** *The triangle inequality.* Let $\mathbf{x}$ and $\mathbf{y}$ be vectors in $R^n$. Prove that $\|\mathbf{x} + \mathbf{y}\| \leq \|\mathbf{x}\| + \|\mathbf{y}\|$. [*Hint:* Expand $\|\mathbf{x} + \mathbf{y}\|^2$ and use Exercise 24.]

**26.** Let $\mathbf{x}$ and $\mathbf{y}$ be vectors in $R^n$. Prove that $|\|\mathbf{x}\| - \|\mathbf{y}\|| \leq \|\mathbf{x} - \mathbf{y}\|$. [*Hint:* For one part consider $\|\mathbf{x} + (\mathbf{y} - \mathbf{x})\|$ and Exercise 25.]

**27.** If the hypotheses for Theorem 14 were altered so that $\{\mathbf{w}_i\}_{i=1}^{p-1}$ is linearly independent and $\{\mathbf{w}_i\}_{i=1}^{p}$ is linearly dependent, use Exercise 23 to show that Eq. (6) yields $\mathbf{u}_p = \boldsymbol{\theta}$.

**28.** Let $B = \{\mathbf{u}_1, \mathbf{u}_2, \ldots, \mathbf{u}_p\}$ be an *orthonormal* basis for a subspace $W$. Let $\mathbf{v}$ be any vector in $W$, where $\mathbf{v} = a_1 \mathbf{u}_1 + a_2 \mathbf{u}_2 + \cdots + a_p \mathbf{u}_p$. Show that
$$\|\mathbf{v}\|^2 = a_1^2 + a_2^2 + \cdots + a_p^2.$$

## LINEAR TRANSFORMATIONS FROM $R^n$ TO $R^m$

In this section we consider a special class of functions, called *linear transformations*, that map vectors to vectors. As we will presently observe, linear transformations arise naturally as a generalization of matrices. Moreover, linear transformations have important applications in engineering science, the social sciences, and various branches of mathematics.

The notation for linear transformations follows the usual notation for functions. If $V$ is a subspace of $R^n$ and $W$ is a subspace of $R^m$, then the notation

$$F: V \rightarrow W$$

will denote a function, $F$, whose domain is the subspace $V$ and whose range is contained in $W$. Furthermore, for $\mathbf{v}$ in $V$ we write

$$\mathbf{w} = F(\mathbf{v})$$

to indicate that $F$ maps $\mathbf{v}$ to $\mathbf{w}$. To illustrate, let $F: R^3 \rightarrow R^2$ be defined by

$$F(\mathbf{x}) = \begin{bmatrix} x_1 - x_2 \\ x_2 + x_3 \end{bmatrix},$$

where

$$\mathbf{x} = \begin{bmatrix} x_1 \\ x_2 \\ x_3 \end{bmatrix}.$$

In this case if, for example, $\mathbf{v}$ is the vector

$$\mathbf{v} = \begin{bmatrix} 1 \\ 2 \\ 3 \end{bmatrix},$$

then $F(\mathbf{v}) = \mathbf{w}$, where

$$\mathbf{w} = \begin{bmatrix} -1 \\ 5 \end{bmatrix}.$$

In earlier sections we have seen that an $(m \times n)$ matrix $A$ determines a function from $R^n$ to $R^m$. Specifically for $\mathbf{x}$ in $R^n$, the formula

$$T(\mathbf{x}) = A\mathbf{x} \tag{1}$$

defines a function $T: R^n \to R^m$. To illustrate, let $A$ be the $(3 \times 2)$ matrix

$$A = \begin{bmatrix} 1 & -1 \\ 0 & 2 \\ 3 & 1 \end{bmatrix}.$$

In this case Eq. (1) defines a function $T: R^2 \to R^3$, and the formula for $T$ is

$$T(\mathbf{x}) = T\left(\begin{bmatrix} x_1 \\ x_2 \end{bmatrix}\right) = \begin{bmatrix} 1 & -1 \\ 0 & 2 \\ 3 & 1 \end{bmatrix} \begin{bmatrix} x_1 \\ x_2 \end{bmatrix} = \begin{bmatrix} x_1 - x_2 \\ 2x_2 \\ 3x_1 + x_2 \end{bmatrix};$$

for instance,

$$T\left(\begin{bmatrix} 1 \\ 1 \end{bmatrix}\right) = \begin{bmatrix} 0 \\ 2 \\ 4 \end{bmatrix}.$$

Returning to the general case in which $A$ is an $(m \times n)$ matrix, note that the function $T$ defined by Eq. (1) satisfies the following linearity properties:

$$T(\mathbf{v} + \mathbf{w}) = A(\mathbf{v} + \mathbf{w}) = A\mathbf{v} + A\mathbf{w} = T(\mathbf{v}) + T(\mathbf{w})$$
$$T(c\mathbf{v}) = A(c\mathbf{v}) = cA\mathbf{v} = cT(\mathbf{v}), \tag{2}$$

where $\mathbf{v}$ and $\mathbf{w}$ are any vectors in $R^n$ and $c$ is an arbitrary scalar. We next define a linear transformation to be a function that satisfies the two linearity properties given in Eq. (2).

---

**DEFINITION 8**    Let $V$ and $W$ be subspaces of $R^n$ and $R^m$, respectively, and let $T$ be a function from $V$ to $W$, $T: V \to W$. We say that $T$ is a *linear transformation* if for all $\mathbf{u}$ and $\mathbf{v}$ in $V$ and for all scalars $a$

$$T(\mathbf{u} + \mathbf{v}) = T(\mathbf{u}) + T\mathbf{v})$$

and

$$T(a\mathbf{u}) = aT(\mathbf{u}). \tag{3}$$

It is apparent from Eq. (2) that the function $T$ defined in Eq. (1) by matrix multiplication is a linear transformation. Conversely, if $T: R^n \to R^m$ is a linear transformation, then (see Theorem 15 on page 232) there is an $(m \times n)$ matrix $A$ such that $T$ is defined by Eq. (1). Thus linear transformations from $R^n$ to $R^m$ are precisely those functions that can be defined by matrix multiplication as in Eq. (1). The situation is not so simple for linear transformations on arbitrary vector spaces or even for linear transformations on subspaces of $R^n$. Thus the concept of a linear transformation is a convenient and useful generalization to arbitrary subspaces of matrix functions defined as in Eq. (1).

## Examples of Linear Transformations

Most of the familiar functions from the reals to the reals are not linear transformations. For example, none of the functions

$$f(x) = x + 1, \qquad g(x) = x^2, \qquad h(x) = \sin x, \qquad k(x) = e^x$$

is a linear transformation. Indeed, it will follow from the exercises that a function $f: R \to R$ is a linear transformation if and only if $f$ is defined by $f(x) = ax$ for some scalar $a$.

We now give several examples to illustrate the use of Definition 8 in verifying whether a function is or is not a linear transformation.

EXAMPLE 1    Let $F: R^3 \to R^2$ be the function defined by

$$F(\mathbf{x}) = \begin{bmatrix} x_1 - x_2 \\ x_2 + x_3 \end{bmatrix}, \quad \text{where } \mathbf{x} = \begin{bmatrix} x_1 \\ x_2 \\ x_3 \end{bmatrix}.$$

Determine whether $F$ is a linear transformation.

*Solution*    We must determine whether the two linearity properties in Eq. (3) are satisfied by $F$. Thus let $\mathbf{u}$ and $\mathbf{v}$ be in $R^3$,

$$\mathbf{u} = \begin{bmatrix} u_1 \\ u_2 \\ u_3 \end{bmatrix} \quad \text{and} \quad \mathbf{v} = \begin{bmatrix} v_1 \\ v_2 \\ v_3 \end{bmatrix},$$

and let $c$ be a scalar. Then

$$\mathbf{u} + \mathbf{v} = \begin{bmatrix} u_1 + v_1 \\ u_2 + v_2 \\ u_3 + v_3 \end{bmatrix}.$$

Therefore, from the rule defining $F$,

$$F(\mathbf{u} + \mathbf{v}) = \begin{bmatrix} (u_1 + v_1) - (u_2 + v_2) \\ (u_2 + v_2) + (u_3 + v_3) \end{bmatrix}$$

$$= \begin{bmatrix} u_1 - u_2 \\ u_2 + u_3 \end{bmatrix} + \begin{bmatrix} v_1 - v_2 \\ v_2 + v_3 \end{bmatrix}$$

$$= F(\mathbf{u}) + F(\mathbf{v}).$$

Similarly,

$$F(c\mathbf{u}) = \begin{bmatrix} cu_1 - cu_2 \\ cu_2 + cu_3 \end{bmatrix} = c \begin{bmatrix} u_1 - u_2 \\ u_2 + u_3 \end{bmatrix} = cF(\mathbf{u}),$$

so $F$ is a linear transformation.

Note that $F$ can also be defined as $F(\mathbf{x}) = A\mathbf{x}$, where $A$ is the $(2 \times 3)$ matrix

$$A = \begin{bmatrix} 1 & -1 & 0 \\ 0 & 1 & 1 \end{bmatrix}.$$

**EXAMPLE 2**    Define $H: R^2 \to R^2$ by

$$H(\mathbf{x}) = \begin{bmatrix} x_1 - x_2 + 1 \\ 3x_2 \end{bmatrix}, \quad \text{where } \mathbf{x} = \begin{bmatrix} x_1 \\ x_2 \end{bmatrix}.$$

Determine whether $H$ is a linear transformation.

*Solution*    Let $\mathbf{u}$ and $\mathbf{v}$ be in $R^2$:

$$\mathbf{u} = \begin{bmatrix} u_1 \\ u_2 \end{bmatrix} \quad \text{and} \quad \mathbf{v} = \begin{bmatrix} v_1 \\ v_2 \end{bmatrix}.$$

Then

$$H(\mathbf{u} + \mathbf{v}) = \begin{bmatrix} (u_1 + v_1) - (u_2 + v_2) + 1 \\ 3(u_2 + v_2) \end{bmatrix},$$

while

$$H(\mathbf{u}) + H(\mathbf{v}) = \begin{bmatrix} u_1 - u_2 + 1 \\ 3u_2 \end{bmatrix} + \begin{bmatrix} v_1 - v_2 + 1 \\ 3v_2 \end{bmatrix}$$

$$= \begin{bmatrix} (u_1 + v_1) - (u_2 + v_2) + 2 \\ 3(u_2 + v_2) \end{bmatrix}.$$

Thus we see that $H(\mathbf{u} + \mathbf{v}) \neq H(\mathbf{u}) + H(\mathbf{v})$. Therefore, $H$ is not a linear transformation. Although it is not necessary, it can also be verified easily that if $c \neq 1$, then $H(c\mathbf{u}) \neq cH(\mathbf{u})$.

**EXAMPLE 3**    Let $W$ be a subspace of $R^n$ such that $\dim(W) = p$, and let $S = \{\mathbf{w}_1, \mathbf{w}_2, \ldots, \mathbf{w}_p\}$ be an orthonormal basis for $W$. Define $T: R^n \to W$ by

$$T(\mathbf{v}) = (\mathbf{v}^T \mathbf{w}_1)\mathbf{w}_1 + (\mathbf{v}^T \mathbf{w}_2)\mathbf{w}_2 + \cdots + (\mathbf{v}^T \mathbf{w}_p)\mathbf{w}_p. \tag{4}$$

Prove that $T$ is a linear transformation.

*Solution*    If $\mathbf{u}$ and $\mathbf{v}$ are in $R^n$, then

$$T(\mathbf{u} + \mathbf{v}) = [(\mathbf{u} + \mathbf{v})^T \mathbf{w}_1]\mathbf{w}_1 + [(\mathbf{u} + \mathbf{v})^T \mathbf{w}_2]\mathbf{w}_2 + \cdots + [(\mathbf{u} + \mathbf{v})^T \mathbf{w}_p]\mathbf{w}_p$$

$$= [(\mathbf{u}^T + \mathbf{v}^T)\mathbf{w}_1]\mathbf{w}_1 + [(\mathbf{u}^T + \mathbf{v}^T)\mathbf{w}_2]\mathbf{w}_2 + \cdots + [(\mathbf{u}^T + \mathbf{v}^T)\mathbf{w}_p]\mathbf{w}_p$$

$$= (\mathbf{u}^T \mathbf{w}_1)\mathbf{w}_1 + (\mathbf{u}^T \mathbf{w}_2)\mathbf{w}_2 + \cdots + (\mathbf{u}^T \mathbf{w}_p)\mathbf{w}_p$$

$$\quad + (\mathbf{v}^T \mathbf{w}_1)\mathbf{w}_1 + (\mathbf{v}^T \mathbf{w}_2)\mathbf{w}_2 + \cdots + (\mathbf{v}^T \mathbf{w}_p)\mathbf{w}_p$$

$$= T(\mathbf{u}) + T(\mathbf{v}).$$

It can be shown similarly that $T(c\mathbf{u}) = cT(\mathbf{u})$ for each scalar $c$, so $T$ is a linear transformation. ◼

The vector $T(\mathbf{v})$ defined by Eq. (4) is called the orthogonal projection of $\mathbf{v}$ onto $W$ and will be considered further in Sections 3.8 and 3.9. As a specific illustration of Example 3, let $W$ be the subspace of $R^3$ consisting of all vectors of the form

$$\mathbf{x} = \begin{bmatrix} x_1 \\ x_2 \\ 0 \end{bmatrix}.$$

Thus $W$ is the $xy$-plane, and the set $\{\mathbf{e}_1, \mathbf{e}_2\}$ is an orthonormal basis for $W$. For $\mathbf{x}$ in $R^3$,

$$\mathbf{x} = \begin{bmatrix} x_1 \\ x_2 \\ x_3 \end{bmatrix},$$

the formula in Eq. (4) yields

$$T(\mathbf{x}) = (\mathbf{x}^T \mathbf{e}_1)\mathbf{e}_1 + (\mathbf{x}^T \mathbf{e}_2)\mathbf{e}_2 = x_1\mathbf{e}_1 + x_2\mathbf{e}_2.$$

Thus,

$$T(\mathbf{x}) = \begin{bmatrix} x_1 \\ x_2 \\ 0 \end{bmatrix}.$$

This transformation is illustrated geometrically by Fig. 3.15.

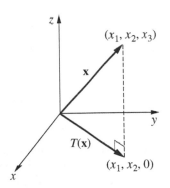

**Figure 3.15**    Orthogonal projection onto the $xy$-plane

EXAMPLE 4    Let $W$ be a subspace of $R^n$, and let $a$ be a scalar. Define $T \colon W \to W$ by $T(\mathbf{w}) = a\mathbf{w}$. Demonstrate that $T$ is a linear transformation.

*Solution*    If $\mathbf{v}$ and $\mathbf{w}$ are in $W$, then

$$T(\mathbf{v} + \mathbf{w}) = a(\mathbf{v} + \mathbf{w}) = a\mathbf{v} + a\mathbf{w} = T(\mathbf{v}) + T(\mathbf{w}).$$

Likewise, if $c$ is a scalar, then

$$T(c\mathbf{w}) = a(c\mathbf{w}) = c(a\mathbf{w}) = cT(\mathbf{w}).$$

It follows that $T$ is a linear transformation. ◾

The linear transformation defined in Example 4 is called a *dilation* when $a > 1$ and a *contraction* when $0 < a < 1$. These cases are illustrated geometrically in Fig. 3.16.

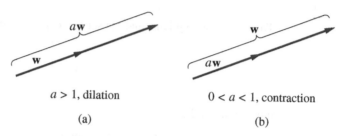

$a > 1$, dilation          $0 < a < 1$, contraction

(a)                              (b)

*Figure 3.16*    Dilations and contractions

The mapping $I: W \to W$ defined by $I(\mathbf{w}) = \mathbf{w}$ is the special case of Example 4 in which $a = 1$. The linear transformation $I$ is called the *identity transformation*.

EXAMPLE 5    Let $W$ be a subspace of $R^n$, and let $\theta$ be the zero vector in $R^m$. Define $T: W \to R^m$ by $T(\mathbf{w}) = \theta$ for each $\mathbf{w}$ in $W$. Show that $T$ is a linear transformation.

*Solution*    Let $\mathbf{v}$ and $\mathbf{w}$ be vectors in $W$, and let $c$ be a scalar. Then

$$T(\mathbf{v} + \mathbf{w}) = \theta = \theta + \theta = T(\mathbf{v}) + T(\mathbf{w})$$

and

$$T(c\mathbf{v}) = \theta = c\theta = cT(\mathbf{v}),$$

so $T$ is a linear transformation. ◾

The linear transformation $T$ defined in Example 5 is called the *zero transformation*.
Later in this section we will consider other examples when we study a particular class of linear transformations from $R^2$ to $R^2$. For the present, we turn to further properties of linear transformations.

## The Matrix of a Transformation

Let $V$ and $W$ be subspaces, and let $T: V \to W$ be a linear transformation. If $\mathbf{u}$ and $\mathbf{v}$ are vectors in $V$ and if $a$ and $b$ are scalars, then the linearity properties (3) yield

$$T(a\mathbf{u} + b\mathbf{v}) = T(a\mathbf{u}) + T(b\mathbf{v}) = aT(\mathbf{u}) + bT(\mathbf{v}). \tag{5}$$

Inductively we can extend Eq. (5) to any finite subset of $V$. That is, if $\mathbf{v}_1, \mathbf{v}_2, \ldots, \mathbf{v}_r$ are vectors in $V$ and if $c_1, c_2, \ldots, c_r$ are scalars, then

$$T(c_1\mathbf{v}_1 + c_2\mathbf{v}_2 + \cdots + c_r\mathbf{v}_r) = c_1 T(\mathbf{v}_1) + c_2 T(\mathbf{v}_2) + \cdots + c_r T(\mathbf{v}_r). \tag{6}$$

The following example illustrates an application of Eq. (6).

EXAMPLE 6　Let $W$ be the subspace of $R^3$ defined by

$$W = \left\{ \mathbf{x}: \mathbf{x} = \begin{bmatrix} x_2 + 2x_3 \\ x_2 \\ x_3 \end{bmatrix}, \quad x_2 \text{ and } x_3 \text{ any real numbers} \right\}.$$

Then $\{\mathbf{w}_1, \mathbf{w}_2\}$ is a basis for $W$, where

$$\mathbf{w}_1 = \begin{bmatrix} 1 \\ 1 \\ 0 \end{bmatrix} \quad \text{and} \quad \mathbf{w}_2 = \begin{bmatrix} 2 \\ 0 \\ 1 \end{bmatrix}.$$

Suppose that $T: W \rightarrow R^2$ is a linear transformation such that $T(\mathbf{w}_1) = \mathbf{u}_1$ and $T(\mathbf{w}_2) = \mathbf{u}_2$, where

$$\mathbf{u}_1 = \begin{bmatrix} 1 \\ 1 \end{bmatrix} \quad \text{and} \quad \mathbf{u}_2 = \begin{bmatrix} 1 \\ -1 \end{bmatrix}.$$

Let the vector $\mathbf{w}$ be given by

$$\mathbf{w} = \begin{bmatrix} -1 \\ 3 \\ -2 \end{bmatrix}.$$

Show that $\mathbf{w}$ is in $W$, express $\mathbf{w}$ as a linear combination of $\mathbf{w}_1$ and $\mathbf{w}_2$, and use Eq. (6) to determine $T(\mathbf{w})$.

Solution　It follows from the description of $W$ that $\mathbf{w}$ is in $W$. Furthermore, it is easy to see that

$$\mathbf{w} = 3\mathbf{w}_1 - 2\mathbf{w}_2.$$

By Eq. (6),

$$T(\mathbf{w}) = 3T(\mathbf{w}_1) - 2T(\mathbf{w}_2) = 3\mathbf{u}_1 - 2\mathbf{u}_2 = 3\begin{bmatrix} 1 \\ 1 \end{bmatrix} - 2\begin{bmatrix} 1 \\ -1 \end{bmatrix}.$$

Thus,

$$T(\mathbf{w}) = \begin{bmatrix} 1 \\ 5 \end{bmatrix}. \qquad \blacksquare$$

Example 6 illustrates that the action of a linear transformation $T$ on a subspace $W$ is completely determined once the action of $T$ on a basis for $W$ is known. Our next example provides yet another illustration of this fact.

EXAMPLE 7     Let $T: R^3 \to R^2$ be a linear transformation such that

$$T(\mathbf{e}_1) = \begin{bmatrix} 1 \\ 2 \end{bmatrix}, \qquad T(\mathbf{e}_2) = \begin{bmatrix} -1 \\ 1 \end{bmatrix}, \quad \text{and} \quad T(\mathbf{e}_3) = \begin{bmatrix} 2 \\ 3 \end{bmatrix}.$$

For an arbitrary vector $\mathbf{x}$ in $R^3$,

$$\mathbf{x} = \begin{bmatrix} x_1 \\ x_2 \\ x_3 \end{bmatrix},$$

give a formula for $T(\mathbf{x})$.

**Solution**     The vector $\mathbf{x}$ can be written in the form

$$\mathbf{x} = x_1\mathbf{e}_1 + x_2\mathbf{e}_2 + x_3\mathbf{e}_3,$$

so by Eq. (6),

$$T(\mathbf{x}) = x_1T(\mathbf{e}_1) + x_2T(\mathbf{e}_2) + x_3T(\mathbf{e}_3). \tag{7}$$

Thus,

$$T(\mathbf{x}) = x_1\begin{bmatrix} 1 \\ 2 \end{bmatrix} + x_2\begin{bmatrix} -1 \\ 1 \end{bmatrix} + x_3\begin{bmatrix} 2 \\ 3 \end{bmatrix} = \begin{bmatrix} x_1 - x_2 + 2x_3 \\ 2x_1 + x_2 + 3x_3 \end{bmatrix}. \qquad \blacksquare$$

Continuing with the notation of the preceding example, let $A$ be the $(2 \times 3)$ matrix with columns $T(\mathbf{e}_1)$, $T(\mathbf{e}_2)$, $T(\mathbf{e}_3)$; thus,

$$A = [T(\mathbf{e}_1), T(\mathbf{e}_2), T(\mathbf{e}_3)] = \begin{bmatrix} 1 & -1 & 2 \\ 2 & 1 & 3 \end{bmatrix}.$$

It is an immediate consequence of Eq. (7) and Theorem 5 of Section 1.5 that $T(\mathbf{x}) = A\mathbf{x}$. Thus Example 7 illustrates the following theorem.

THEOREM 15     Let $T: R^n \to R^m$ be a linear transformation, and let $\mathbf{e}_1, \mathbf{e}_2, \ldots, \mathbf{e}_n$ be the unit vectors in $R^n$. If $A$ is the $(m \times n)$ matrix defined by

$$A = [T(\mathbf{e}_1), T(\mathbf{e}_2), \ldots, T(\mathbf{e}_n)],$$

then $T(\mathbf{x}) = A\mathbf{x}$ for all $\mathbf{x}$ in $R^n$.

**Proof**     If $\mathbf{x}$ is a vector in $R^n$,

$$\mathbf{x} = \begin{bmatrix} x_1 \\ x_2 \\ \vdots \\ x_n \end{bmatrix},$$

then $\mathbf{x}$ can be expressed in the form

$$\mathbf{x} = x_1\mathbf{e}_1 + x_2\mathbf{e}_2 + \cdots + x_n\mathbf{e}_n.$$

It now follows from Eq. (6) that

$$T(\mathbf{x}) = x_1 T(\mathbf{e}_1) + x_2 T(\mathbf{e}_2) + \cdots + x_n T(\mathbf{e}_n). \tag{8}$$

If $A = [T(\mathbf{e}_1), T(\mathbf{e}_2), \ldots, T(\mathbf{e}_n)]$, then by Theorem 5 of Section 1.5, the right-hand side of Eq. (8) is simply $A\mathbf{x}$. Thus Eq. (8) is equivalent to $T(\mathbf{x}) = A\mathbf{x}$. ◼

EXAMPLE 8   Let $T: R^2 \to R^3$ be the linear transformation defined by the formula

$$T\left(\begin{bmatrix} x_1 \\ x_2 \end{bmatrix}\right) = \begin{bmatrix} x_1 + 2x_2 \\ -x_1 + x_2 \\ 2x_1 - x_2 \end{bmatrix}.$$

Find a matrix $A$ such that $T(\mathbf{x}) = A\mathbf{x}$ for each $\mathbf{x}$ in $R^2$.

**Solution**   By Theorem 15, $A$ is the $(3 \times 2)$ matrix

$$A = [T(\mathbf{e}_1), T(\mathbf{e}_2)].$$

It is an easy calculation that

$$T(\mathbf{e}_1) = \begin{bmatrix} 1 \\ -1 \\ 2 \end{bmatrix} \quad \text{and} \quad T(\mathbf{e}_2) = \begin{bmatrix} 2 \\ 1 \\ -1 \end{bmatrix}.$$

Therefore,

$$A = \begin{bmatrix} 1 & 2 \\ -1 & 1 \\ 2 & -1 \end{bmatrix}.$$

One can easily verify that $T(\mathbf{x}) = A\mathbf{x}$ for each $\mathbf{x}$ in $R^2$. ◼

## Null Space and Range

Associated with a linear transformation, $T$, are two important and useful subspaces called the null space and the range of $T$. These are defined as follows.

DEFINITION 9   Let $V$ and $W$ be subspaces, and let $T: V \to W$ be a linear transformation. The **null space** of $T$, denoted by $\mathcal{N}(T)$, is the subset of $V$ given by

$$\mathcal{N}(T) = \{\mathbf{v}: \mathbf{v} \text{ is in } V \text{ and } T(\mathbf{v}) = \boldsymbol{\theta}\}.$$

The **range** of $T$, denoted by $\mathcal{R}(T)$, is the subset of $W$ defined by

$$\mathcal{R}(T) = \{\mathbf{w}: \mathbf{w} \text{ is in } W \text{ and } \mathbf{w} = T(\mathbf{v}) \text{ for some } \mathbf{v} \text{ in } V\}.$$

That $\mathcal{N}(T)$ and $\mathcal{R}(T)$ are subspaces will be proved in the more general context of Chapter 5. If $T$ maps $R^n$ into $R^m$, then by Theorem 15 there exists an $(m \times n)$ matrix

$A$ such that $T(\mathbf{x}) = A\mathbf{x}$. In this case it is clear that the null space of $T$ is the null space of $A$ and the range of $T$ coincides with the range of $A$.

As with matrices, the dimension of the null space of a linear transformation $T$ is called the **nullity** of $T$, and the dimension of the range of $T$ is called the **rank** of $T$. If $T$ is defined by matrix multiplication, $T(\mathbf{x}) = A\mathbf{x}$, then the transformation $T$ and the matrix $A$ have the same nullity and the same rank. Moreover, if $T: R^n \rightarrow R^m$, then $A$ is an $(m \times n)$ matrix, so it follows from the remark in Section 3.5 that

$$\text{rank}(T) + \text{nullity}(T) = n. \tag{9}$$

Formula (9) will be proved in a more general setting in Chapter 5.

The next two examples illustrate the use of the matrix of $T$ to determine the null space and the range of $T$.

**EXAMPLE 9**   Let $F$ be the linear transformation given in Example 1, $F: R^3 \rightarrow R^2$. Describe the null space and the range of $F$, and determine the nullity and the rank of $F$.

*Solution*   It follows from Theorem 15 that $F(\mathbf{x}) = A\mathbf{x}$, where $A$ is the $(2 \times 3)$ matrix

$$A = [F(\mathbf{e}_1), F(\mathbf{e}_2), F(\mathbf{e}_3)] = \begin{bmatrix} 1 & -1 & 0 \\ 0 & 1 & 1 \end{bmatrix}.$$

Thus the null space and the range of $F$ coincide, respectively, with the null space and the range of $A$. The null space of $A$ is determined by backsolving the homogeneous system $A\mathbf{x} = \boldsymbol{\theta}$, where $\mathbf{x}$ is in $R^3$:

$$\mathbf{x} = \begin{bmatrix} x_1 \\ x_2 \\ x_3 \end{bmatrix}.$$

This gives

$$\mathcal{N}(F) = \mathcal{N}(A) = \{\mathbf{x} : x_1 = -x_3 \quad \text{and} \quad x_2 = -x_3\}.$$

Using the techniques of Section 3.4, we can easily see that the vector

$$\mathbf{u} = \begin{bmatrix} -1 \\ -1 \\ 1 \end{bmatrix}$$

is a basis for $\mathcal{N}(F)$, so $F$ has nullity 1. By Eq. (9),

$$\text{rank}(F) = n - \text{nullity}(F) = 3 - 1 = 2.$$

Thus $\mathcal{R}(F)$ is a two-dimensional subspace of $R^2$, and hence $\mathcal{R}(F) = R^2$.

Alternatively, note that the system of equations $A\mathbf{x} = \mathbf{b}$ has a solution for each $\mathbf{b}$ in $R^2$, so $\mathcal{R}(F) = \mathcal{R}(A) = R^2$.

**EXAMPLE 10**   Let $T: R^2 \rightarrow R^3$ be the linear transformation given in Example 8. Describe the null space and the range of $T$, and determine the nullity and the rank of $T$.

*Solution*    In Example 8 it was shown that $T(\mathbf{x}) = A\mathbf{x}$, where $A$ is the $(3 \times 2)$ matrix

$$A = \begin{bmatrix} 1 & 2 \\ -1 & 1 \\ 2 & -1 \end{bmatrix}.$$

If $\mathbf{b}$ is the $(3 \times 1)$ vector,

$$\mathbf{b} = \begin{bmatrix} b_1 \\ b_2 \\ b_3 \end{bmatrix},$$

then the augmented matrix $[A \mid \mathbf{b}]$ for the linear system $A\mathbf{x} = \mathbf{b}$ is row equivalent to

$$\begin{bmatrix} 1 & 0 & (1/3)b_1 - (2/3)b_2 \\ 0 & 1 & (1/3)b_1 + (1/3)b_2 \\ 0 & 0 & (-1/3)b_1 + (5/3)b_2 + b_3 \end{bmatrix} \tag{10}$$

Therefore, $T(\mathbf{x}) = A\mathbf{x} = \mathbf{b}$ can be solved if and only if $0 = (-1/3)b_1 + (5/3)b_2 + b_3$. The range of $T$ can thus be described as

$$\mathcal{R}(T) = \mathcal{R}(A)$$

$$= \{\mathbf{b}: \mathbf{b} = \begin{bmatrix} b_1 \\ b_2 \\ (1/3)b_1 - (5/3)b_2 \end{bmatrix}, \quad b_1 \text{ and } b_2 \text{ any real numbers}\}.$$

A basis for $\mathcal{R}(T)$ is $\{\mathbf{u}_1, \mathbf{u}_2\}$ where

$$\mathbf{u}_1 = \begin{bmatrix} 1 \\ 0 \\ 1/3 \end{bmatrix} \quad \text{and} \quad \mathbf{u}_2 = \begin{bmatrix} 0 \\ 1 \\ -5/3 \end{bmatrix}.$$

Thus $T$ has rank 2, and by Eq. (9),

$$\text{nullity}(T) = n - \text{rank}(T) = 2 - 2 = 0.$$

It follows that $T$ has null space $\{\boldsymbol{\theta}\}$. Alternatively, it is clear from matrix (10), with $\mathbf{b} = \boldsymbol{\theta}$, that the homogeneous system of equations $A\mathbf{x} = \boldsymbol{\theta}$ has only the trivial solution. Therefore, $\mathcal{N}(T) = \mathcal{N}(A) = \{\boldsymbol{\theta}\}$. ◼

## Orthogonal Transformations on $R^2$ (Optional)

It is often informative and useful to view linear transformations on either $R^2$ or $R^3$ from a geometric point of view. To illustrate this general notion, the remainder of this section is devoted to determining those linear transformations $T: R^2 \rightarrow R^2$ that preserve the length of a vector; that is, we are interested in linear transformations $T$ such that

$$\|T(\mathbf{v})\| = \|\mathbf{v}\| \tag{11}$$

for all $\mathbf{v}$ in $R^2$. Transformations that satisfy Eq. (11) are called ***orthogonal transformations***. We begin by giving some examples of orthogonal transformations.

EXAMPLE 11    Let $\theta$ be a fixed angle, and let $T\colon R^2 \to R^2$ be the linear transformation defined by $T(\mathbf{v}) = A\mathbf{v}$, where $A$ is the $(2 \times 2)$ matrix

$$A = \begin{bmatrix} \cos\theta & -\sin\theta \\ \sin\theta & \cos\theta \end{bmatrix}.$$

Give a geometric interpretation of $T$, and show that $T$ is an orthogonal transformation.

**Solution**    Suppose that $\mathbf{v}$ and $T(\mathbf{v})$ are given by

$$\mathbf{v} = \begin{bmatrix} a \\ b \end{bmatrix} \quad \text{and} \quad T(\mathbf{v}) = \begin{bmatrix} c \\ d \end{bmatrix}.$$

Then $T(\mathbf{v}) = A\mathbf{v}$, so

$$\begin{bmatrix} c \\ d \end{bmatrix} = \begin{bmatrix} \cos\theta & -\sin\theta \\ \sin\theta & \cos\theta \end{bmatrix} \begin{bmatrix} a \\ b \end{bmatrix} = \begin{bmatrix} a\cos\theta - b\sin\theta \\ a\sin\theta + b\cos\theta \end{bmatrix}. \tag{12}$$

We proceed now to show that $T(\mathbf{v})$ is obtained geometrically by rotating the vector $\mathbf{v}$ through the angle $\theta$. To see this, let $\phi$ be the angle between $\mathbf{v}$ and the positive $x$-axis (see Fig. 3.17), and set $r = \|\mathbf{v}\|$. Then the coordinates $a$ and $b$ can be written as

$$a = r\cos\phi, \qquad b = r\sin\phi. \tag{13}$$

Making the substitution (13) for $a$ and $b$ in (12) yields

$$c = r\cos\phi\cos\theta - r\sin\phi\sin\theta = r\cos(\phi + \theta)$$

and

$$d = r\cos\phi\sin\theta + r\sin\phi\cos\theta = r\sin(\phi + \theta).$$

Therefore, $c$ and $d$ are the coordinates of the point obtained by rotating the point $(a, b)$ through the angle $\theta$. Clearly then, $\|T(\mathbf{v})\| = \|\mathbf{v}\|$, and $T$ is an orthogonal linear transformation.

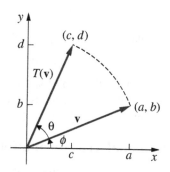

**Figure 3.17**    Rotation through the angle $\theta$

The linear transformation $T$ defined in Example 11 is called a **rotation**. Thus if $A$ is a $(2 \times 2)$ matrix,

$$A = \begin{bmatrix} a & -b \\ b & a \end{bmatrix},$$

where $a^2 + b^2 = 1$, then the linear transformation $T(\mathbf{v}) = A\mathbf{v}$ is the rotation through the angle $\theta$, $0 \leq \theta < 2\pi$, where $\cos\theta = a$ and $\sin\theta = b$.

|||
EXAMPLE 12    Define $T: R^2 \rightarrow R^2$ by $T(\mathbf{v}) = A\mathbf{v}$, where

$$A = \begin{bmatrix} -1/2 & \sqrt{3}/2 \\ -\sqrt{3}/2 & -1/2 \end{bmatrix}.$$

Give a geometric interpretation of $T$.

*Solution*    Since $\cos(4\pi/3) = -1/2$ and $\sin(4\pi/3) = -\sqrt{3}/2$, $T$ is the rotation through the angle $4\pi/3$. ∎

Now let $l$ be a line in the plane that passes through the origin, and let $\mathbf{v}$ be a vector in the plane. If we define $T(\mathbf{v})$ to be the symmetric image of $\mathbf{v}$ relative to $l$ (see Fig. 3.18), then clearly $T$ preserves the length of $\mathbf{v}$. It can be shown that $T$ is multiplication by the matrix

$$A = \begin{bmatrix} \cos\theta & \sin\theta \\ \sin\theta & -\cos\theta \end{bmatrix},$$

**Figure 3.18**
Reflection about a line

where $(1/2)\theta$ is the angle between $l$ and the positive $x$-axis. Any such transformation is called a ***reflection***. Note that a reflection $T$ is also an orthogonal linear transformation.

|||
EXAMPLE 13    Let $T: R^2 \rightarrow R^2$ be defined by $T(\mathbf{v}) = A\mathbf{v}$, where $A$ is the $(2 \times 2)$ matrix

$$A = \begin{bmatrix} 1/2 & \sqrt{3}/2 \\ \sqrt{3}/2 & -1/2 \end{bmatrix}.$$

Give a geometric interpretation of $T$.

*Solution*    Since $\cos(\pi/3) = 1/2$ and $\sin(\pi/3) = \sqrt{3}/2$, $T$ is the reflection about the line $l$, where $l$ is the line that passes through the origin at an angle of 30 degrees. ∎

The next theorem gives a characterization of orthogonal transformations on $R^2$. A consequence of this theorem will be that every orthogonal transformation is either a rotation or a reflection.

|||
THEOREM 16    Let $T: R^2 \rightarrow R^2$ be a linear transformation. Then $T$ is an orthogonal transformation if and only if $\|T(\mathbf{e}_1)\| = \|T(\mathbf{e}_2)\| = 1$ and $T(\mathbf{e}_1)$ is perpendicular to $T(\mathbf{e}_2)$.

*Proof*    If $T$ is an orthogonal transformation, then $\|T(\mathbf{v})\| = \|\mathbf{v}\|$ for every vector $\mathbf{v}$ in $R^2$. In particular, $\|T(\mathbf{e}_1)\| = \|\mathbf{e}_1\| = 1$, and similarly $\|T(\mathbf{e}_2)\| = 1$. Set $\mathbf{u}_1 = T(\mathbf{e}_1)$, $\mathbf{u}_2 = T(\mathbf{e}_2)$, and $\mathbf{v} = [1, 1]^T = \mathbf{e}_1 + \mathbf{e}_2$. Then

$$2 = \|\mathbf{v}\|^2 = \|T(\mathbf{v})\|^2 = \|T(\mathbf{e}_1 + \mathbf{e}_2)\|^2 = \|T(\mathbf{e}_1) + T(\mathbf{e}_2)\|^2.$$

Thus,

$$
\begin{aligned}
2 &= \|\mathbf{u}_1 + \mathbf{u}_2\|^2 \\
&= (\mathbf{u}_1 + \mathbf{u}_2)^T (\mathbf{u}_1 + \mathbf{u}_2) \\
&= (\mathbf{u}_1^T + \mathbf{u}_2^T)(\mathbf{u}_1 + \mathbf{u}_2) \\
&= \mathbf{u}_1^T \mathbf{u}_1 + \mathbf{u}_1^T \mathbf{u}_2 + \mathbf{u}_2^T \mathbf{u}_1 + \mathbf{u}_2^T \mathbf{u}_2 \\
&= \|\mathbf{u}_1\|^2 + 2\mathbf{u}_1^T \mathbf{u}_2 + \|\mathbf{u}_2\|^2 \\
&= 2 + 2\mathbf{u}_1^T \mathbf{u}_2.
\end{aligned}
$$

It follows that $\mathbf{u}_1^T \mathbf{u}_2 = 0$, so $\mathbf{u}_1$ is perpendicular to $\mathbf{u}_2$.

The proof of the converse is Exercise 47.

We can now use Theorem 16 to give a geometric description for any orthogonal linear transformation, $T$, on $R^2$. First, suppose that $T(\mathbf{e}_1) = \mathbf{u}_1$ and $T(\mathbf{e}_2) = \mathbf{u}_2$. If

$$
\mathbf{u}_1 = \left[ \begin{array}{c} a \\ b \end{array} \right],
$$

then $1 = \|\mathbf{u}_1\|^2 = a^2 + b^2$. Since $\|\mathbf{u}_2\| = 1$ and $\mathbf{u}_2$ is perpendicular to $\mathbf{u}_1$, there are two choices for $\mathbf{u}_2$ (see Fig. 3.19): either

$$
\mathbf{u}_2 = \left[ \begin{array}{c} -b \\ a \end{array} \right] \quad \text{or} \quad \mathbf{u}_2 = \left[ \begin{array}{c} b \\ -a \end{array} \right].
$$

In either case, it follows from Theorem 15 that $T$ is defined by $T(\mathbf{v}) = A\mathbf{v}$, where $A$ is the $(2 \times 2)$ matrix $A = [\mathbf{u}_1, \mathbf{u}_2]$. Thus if

$$
\mathbf{u}_2 = \left[ \begin{array}{c} -b \\ a \end{array} \right],
$$

then

$$
A = \left[ \begin{array}{cc} a & -b \\ b & a \end{array} \right],
$$

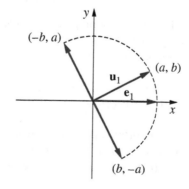

*Figure 3.19*    Choices for $\mathbf{u}_2$

so $T$ is a rotation. If

$$\mathbf{u}_2 = \begin{bmatrix} b \\ -a \end{bmatrix},$$

then

$$A = \begin{bmatrix} a & b \\ b & -a \end{bmatrix},$$

and $T$ is a reflection. In either case note that $A^T A = I$, so $A^T = A^{-1}$ (see Exercise 48). An $(n \times n)$ real matrix with the property that $A^T A = I$ is called an **orthogonal matrix**. Thus we have shown that an orthogonal transformation on $R^2$ is defined by

$$T(\mathbf{x}) = A\mathbf{x},$$

where $A$ is an orthogonal matrix.

---

## 3.7 EXERCISES

**1.** Define $T: R^2 \rightarrow R^2$ by

$$T\left(\begin{bmatrix} x_1 \\ x_2 \end{bmatrix}\right) = \begin{bmatrix} 2x_1 - 3x_2 \\ -x_1 + x_2 \end{bmatrix}.$$

Find each of the following.

**a)** $T\left(\begin{bmatrix} 0 \\ 0 \end{bmatrix}\right)$  **b)** $T\left(\begin{bmatrix} 1 \\ 1 \end{bmatrix}\right)$

**c)** $T\left(\begin{bmatrix} 2 \\ 1 \end{bmatrix}\right)$  **d)** $T\left(\begin{bmatrix} -1 \\ 0 \end{bmatrix}\right)$

**2.** Define $T: R^2 \rightarrow R^2$ by $T(\mathbf{x}) = A\mathbf{x}$, where

$$A = \begin{bmatrix} 1 & -1 \\ -3 & 3 \end{bmatrix}.$$

Find each of the following.

**a)** $T\left(\begin{bmatrix} 2 \\ 2 \end{bmatrix}\right)$  **b)** $T\left(\begin{bmatrix} 3 \\ 1 \end{bmatrix}\right)$

**c)** $T\left(\begin{bmatrix} 2 \\ 0 \end{bmatrix}\right)$  **d)** $T\left(\begin{bmatrix} 0 \\ 0 \end{bmatrix}\right)$

**3.** Let $T: R^3 \rightarrow R^2$ be the linear transformation defined by

$$T\left(\begin{bmatrix} x_1 \\ x_2 \\ x_3 \end{bmatrix}\right) = \begin{bmatrix} x_1 + 2x_2 + 4x_3 \\ 2x_1 + 3x_2 + 5x_3 \end{bmatrix}.$$

Which of the following vectors are in the null space of $T$?

**a)** $\begin{bmatrix} 0 \\ 0 \\ 0 \end{bmatrix}$  **b)** $\begin{bmatrix} 2 \\ -3 \\ 1 \end{bmatrix}$

**c)** $\begin{bmatrix} 1 \\ 2 \\ 1 \end{bmatrix}$  **d)** $\begin{bmatrix} -1 \\ 3/2 \\ -1/2 \end{bmatrix}$

**4.** Let $T: R^2 \rightarrow R^2$ be the function defined in Exercise 1. Find $\mathbf{x}$ in $R^2$ such that $T(\mathbf{x}) = \mathbf{b}$, where

$$\mathbf{b} = \begin{bmatrix} 2 \\ -2 \end{bmatrix}.$$

**5.** Let $T: R^2 \rightarrow R^2$ be the function given in Exercise 1. Show that for each $\mathbf{b}$ in $R^2$, there is an $\mathbf{x}$ in $R^2$ such that $T(\mathbf{x}) = \mathbf{b}$.

**6.** Let $T$ be the linear transformation given in Exercise 2. Find $\mathbf{x}$ in $R^2$ such that $T(\mathbf{x}) = \mathbf{b}$, where

$$\mathbf{b} = \begin{bmatrix} -2 \\ 6 \end{bmatrix}.$$

**7.** Let $T$ be the linear transformation given in Exercise 2. Show that there is no $\mathbf{x}$ in $R^2$ such that

$T(\mathbf{x}) = \mathbf{b}$ for

$$\mathbf{b} = \begin{bmatrix} 1 \\ 1 \end{bmatrix}.$$

In Exercises 8–17, determine whether the function $F$ is a linear transformation.

**8.** $F: R^2 \rightarrow R^2$ defined by

$$F\left(\begin{bmatrix} x_1 \\ x_2 \end{bmatrix}\right) = \begin{bmatrix} 2x_1 - x_2 \\ x_1 + 3x_2 \end{bmatrix}$$

**9.** $F: R^2 \rightarrow R^2$ defined by

$$F\left(\begin{bmatrix} x_1 \\ x_2 \end{bmatrix}\right) = \begin{bmatrix} x_2 \\ x_1 \end{bmatrix}$$

**10.** $F: R^2 \rightarrow R^2$ defined by

$$F\left(\begin{bmatrix} x_1 \\ x_2 \end{bmatrix}\right) = \begin{bmatrix} x_1 + x_2 \\ 1 \end{bmatrix}$$

**11.** $F: R^2 \rightarrow R^2$ defined by

$$F\left(\begin{bmatrix} x_1 \\ x_2 \end{bmatrix}\right) = \begin{bmatrix} x_1^2 \\ x_1 x_2 \end{bmatrix}$$

**12.** $F: R^3 \rightarrow R^2$ defined by

$$F\left(\begin{bmatrix} x_1 \\ x_2 \\ x_3 \end{bmatrix}\right) = \begin{bmatrix} x_1 - x_2 + x_3 \\ -x_1 + 3x_2 - 2x_3 \end{bmatrix}$$

**13.** $F: R^3 \rightarrow R^2$ defined by

$$F\left(\begin{bmatrix} x_1 \\ x_2 \\ x_3 \end{bmatrix}\right) = \begin{bmatrix} x_1 \\ x_2 \end{bmatrix}$$

**14.** $F: R^2 \rightarrow R^3$ defined by

$$F\left(\begin{bmatrix} x_1 \\ x_2 \end{bmatrix}\right) = \begin{bmatrix} x_1 - x_2 \\ -x_1 + x_2 \\ x_2 \end{bmatrix}$$

**15.** $F: R^2 \rightarrow R^3$ defined by

$$F\left(\begin{bmatrix} x_1 \\ x_2 \end{bmatrix}\right) = \begin{bmatrix} x_1 \\ x_2 \\ 0 \end{bmatrix}$$

**16.** $F: R^2 \rightarrow R$ defined by

$$F\left(\begin{bmatrix} x_1 \\ x_2 \end{bmatrix}\right) = 2x_1 + 3x_2$$

**17.** $F: R^2 \rightarrow R$ defined by

$$F\left(\begin{bmatrix} x_1 \\ x_2 \end{bmatrix}\right) = |x_1| + |x_2|$$

**18.** Let $W$ be the subspace of $R^3$ defined by

$$W = \{\mathbf{x}: \mathbf{x} = \begin{bmatrix} x_1 \\ x_2 \\ x_3 \end{bmatrix}, \quad x_2 = x_3 = 0\}.$$

Find an orthonormal basis for $W$, and use Eq. (4) of Example 3 to give a formula for the orthogonal projection $T: R^3 \rightarrow W$; that is, determine $T(\mathbf{v})$ for arbitrary $\mathbf{v}$ in $R^3$:

$$\mathbf{v} = \begin{bmatrix} a \\ b \\ c \end{bmatrix}.$$

Give a geometric interpretation of $W$, $\mathbf{v}$, and $T(\mathbf{v})$.

**19.** Let $T: R^2 \rightarrow R^3$ be a linear transformation such that $T(\mathbf{e}_1) = \mathbf{u}_1$ and $T(\mathbf{e}_2) = \mathbf{u}_2$, where

$$\mathbf{u}_1 = \begin{bmatrix} 1 \\ 0 \\ -1 \end{bmatrix} \quad \text{and} \quad \mathbf{u}_2 = \begin{bmatrix} 2 \\ 1 \\ 0 \end{bmatrix}.$$

Find each of the following.

**a)** $T\left(\begin{bmatrix} 1 \\ 1 \end{bmatrix}\right)$

**b)** $T\left(\begin{bmatrix} 2 \\ -1 \end{bmatrix}\right)$

**c)** $T\left(\begin{bmatrix} 3 \\ 2 \end{bmatrix}\right)$

**20.** Let $T: R^2 \rightarrow R^2$ be a linear transformation such that $T(\mathbf{v}_1) = \mathbf{u}_1$ and $T(\mathbf{v}_2) = \mathbf{u}_2$, where

$$\mathbf{v}_1 = \begin{bmatrix} 0 \\ 1 \end{bmatrix}, \quad \mathbf{v}_2 = \begin{bmatrix} -1 \\ 1 \end{bmatrix},$$

$$\mathbf{u}_1 = \begin{bmatrix} 0 \\ 2 \end{bmatrix}, \quad \text{and} \quad \mathbf{u}_2 = \begin{bmatrix} 3 \\ 1 \end{bmatrix}.$$

Find each of the following.

**a)** $T\left(\begin{bmatrix} 1 \\ 1 \end{bmatrix}\right)$

**b)** $T\left(\begin{bmatrix} 2 \\ -1 \end{bmatrix}\right)$

**c)** $T\left(\begin{bmatrix} 3 \\ 2 \end{bmatrix}\right)$

In Exercises 21–24, the action of a linear transformation $T$ on a basis for either $R^2$ or $R^3$ is given. In each case use Eq. (6) to derive a formula for $T$.

**21.** $T\left(\begin{bmatrix} 1 \\ 1 \end{bmatrix}\right) = \begin{bmatrix} 2 \\ -1 \end{bmatrix}$ and

$T\left(\begin{bmatrix} 1 \\ -1 \end{bmatrix}\right) = \begin{bmatrix} 0 \\ 3 \end{bmatrix}$

**22.** $T\left(\begin{bmatrix} 1 \\ 1 \end{bmatrix}\right) = \begin{bmatrix} 1 \\ 2 \\ 1 \end{bmatrix}$ and

$T\left(\begin{bmatrix} 1 \\ -1 \end{bmatrix}\right) = \begin{bmatrix} 0 \\ 2 \\ 2 \end{bmatrix}$

**23.** $T\left(\begin{bmatrix} 1 \\ 0 \\ 1 \end{bmatrix}\right) = \begin{bmatrix} 0 \\ 1 \end{bmatrix}$,

$T\left(\begin{bmatrix} 0 \\ -1 \\ 1 \end{bmatrix}\right) = \begin{bmatrix} 1 \\ 0 \end{bmatrix}$,

$T\left(\begin{bmatrix} 1 \\ -1 \\ 0 \end{bmatrix}\right) = \begin{bmatrix} 0 \\ 0 \end{bmatrix}$

**24.** $T\left(\begin{bmatrix} 1 \\ 0 \\ 1 \end{bmatrix}\right) = \begin{bmatrix} 0 \\ -1 \\ 1 \end{bmatrix}$,

$T\left(\begin{bmatrix} 0 \\ -1 \\ 1 \end{bmatrix}\right) = \begin{bmatrix} 2 \\ 1 \\ 0 \end{bmatrix}$,

$T\left(\begin{bmatrix} 1 \\ -1 \\ 0 \end{bmatrix}\right) = \begin{bmatrix} 0 \\ 0 \\ 1 \end{bmatrix}$

In Exercises 25–30, a linear transformation $T$ is given. In each case find a matrix $A$ such that $T(\mathbf{x}) = A\mathbf{x}$. Also describe the null space and the range of $T$ and give the rank and the nullity of $T$.

**25.** $T: R^2 \rightarrow R^2$ defined by

$T\left(\begin{bmatrix} x_1 \\ x_2 \end{bmatrix}\right) = \begin{bmatrix} x_1 + 3x_2 \\ 2x_1 + x_2 \end{bmatrix}$

**26.** $T: R^2 \rightarrow R^3$ defined by

$T\left(\begin{bmatrix} x_1 \\ x_2 \end{bmatrix}\right) = \begin{bmatrix} x_1 - x_2 \\ x_1 + x_2 \\ x_2 \end{bmatrix}$

**27.** $T: R^2 \rightarrow R$ defined by

$T\left(\begin{bmatrix} x_1 \\ x_2 \end{bmatrix}\right) = 3x_1 + 2x_2$

**28.** $T: R^3 \rightarrow R^3$ defined by

$T\left(\begin{bmatrix} x_1 \\ x_2 \\ x_3 \end{bmatrix}\right) = \begin{bmatrix} x_1 + x_2 \\ x_3 \\ x_2 \end{bmatrix}$

**29.** $T: R^3 \rightarrow R^2$ defined by

$T\left(\begin{bmatrix} x_1 \\ x_2 \\ x_3 \end{bmatrix}\right) = \begin{bmatrix} x_1 - x_2 \\ x_2 - x_3 \end{bmatrix}$

**30.** $T: R^3 \rightarrow R$ defined by

$T\left(\begin{bmatrix} x_1 \\ x_2 \\ x_3 \end{bmatrix}\right) = 2x_1 - x_2 + 4x_3$

**31.** Let $a$ be a real number, and define $f: R \rightarrow R$ by $f(x) = ax$ for each $x$ in $R$. Show that $f$ is a linear transformation.

**32.** Let $T: R \to R$ be a linear transformation, and suppose that $T(1) = a$. Show that $T(x) = ax$ for each $x$ in $R$.

**33.** Let $T: R^2 \to R^2$ be the function that maps each point in $R^2$ to its reflection with respect to the $x$-axis. Give a formula for $T$ and show that $T$ is a linear transformation.

**34.** Let $T: R^2 \to R^2$ be the function that maps each point in $R^2$ to its reflection with respect to the line $y = x$. Give a formula for $T$ and show that $T$ is a linear transformation.

**35.** Let $V$ and $W$ be subspaces, and let $F: V \to W$ and $G: V \to W$ be linear transformations. Define $F + G: V \to W$ by $[F + G](\mathbf{v}) = F(\mathbf{v}) + G(\mathbf{v})$ for each $\mathbf{v}$ in $V$. Prove that $F + G$ is a linear transformation.

**36.** Let $F: R^3 \to R^2$ and $G: R^3 \to R^2$ be defined by

$$F\left(\begin{bmatrix} x_1 \\ x_2 \\ x_3 \end{bmatrix}\right) = \begin{bmatrix} 2x_1 - 3x_2 + x_3 \\ 4x_1 + 2x_2 - 5x_3 \end{bmatrix}$$

and

$$G\left(\begin{bmatrix} x_1 \\ x_2 \\ x_3 \end{bmatrix}\right) = \begin{bmatrix} -x_1 + 4x_2 + 2x_3 \\ -2x_1 + 3x_2 + 3x_3 \end{bmatrix}.$$

a) Give a formula for the linear transformation $F + G$ (see Exercise 35).

b) Find matrices $A$, $B$, and $C$ such that $F(\mathbf{x}) = A\mathbf{x}$, $G(\mathbf{x}) = B\mathbf{x}$, and $(F + G)(\mathbf{x}) = C\mathbf{x}$.

c) Verify that $C = A + B$.

**37.** Let $V$ and $W$ be subspaces, and let $T: V \to W$ be a linear transformation. If $a$ is a scalar, define $aT: V \to W$ by $[aT](\mathbf{v}) = a[T(\mathbf{v})]$ for each $\mathbf{v}$ in $V$. Show that $aT$ is a linear transformation.

**38.** Let $T: R^3 \to R^2$ be the linear transformation defined in Exercise 29. The linear transformation $[3T]: R^3 \to R^2$ is defined in Exercise 37.

a) Give a formula for the transformation $3T$.

b) Find matrices $A$ and $B$ such that $T(\mathbf{x}) = A\mathbf{x}$ and $[3T](\mathbf{x}) = B\mathbf{x}$.

c) Verify that $B = 3A$.

**39.** Let $U$, $V$, and $W$ be subspaces, and let $F: U \to V$ and $G: V \to W$ be linear transformations. Prove that the composition $G \circ F: U \to W$ of $F$ and $G$,

defining by $[G \circ F](\mathbf{u}) = G(F(\mathbf{u}))$ for each $\mathbf{u}$ in $U$, is a linear transformation.

**40.** Let $F: R^3 \to R^2$ and $G: R^2 \to R^3$ be linear transformations defined by

$$F\left(\begin{bmatrix} x_1 \\ x_2 \\ x_3 \end{bmatrix}\right) = \begin{bmatrix} -x_1 + 2x_2 - 4x_3 \\ 2x_1 + 5x_2 + x_3 \end{bmatrix}$$

and

$$G\left(\begin{bmatrix} x_1 \\ x_2 \end{bmatrix}\right) = \begin{bmatrix} x_1 - 2x_2 \\ 3x_1 + 2x_2 \\ -x_1 + x_2 \end{bmatrix}.$$

a) By Exercise 39, $G \circ F: R^3 \to R^3$ is a linear transformation. Give a formula for $G \circ F$.

b) Find matrices $A$, $B$, and $C$ such that $F(\mathbf{x}) = A\mathbf{x}$, $G(\mathbf{x}) = B\mathbf{x}$, and $[G \circ F](\mathbf{x}) = C\mathbf{x}$.

c) Verify that $C = BA$.

**41.** Let $B$ be an $(m \times n)$ matrix, and let $T: R^n \to R^m$ be defined by $T(\mathbf{x}) = B\mathbf{x}$ for each $\mathbf{x}$ in $R^n$. If $A$ is the matrix for $T$ given by Theorem 15, show that $A = B$.

**42.** Let $F: R^n \to R^p$ and $G: R^p \to R^m$ be linear transformations, and assume that Theorem 15 yields matrices $A$ and $B$, respectively, for $F$ and $G$. Show that the matrix for the composition $G \circ F$ (see Exercise 39) is $BA$. [*Hint:* Show that $(G \circ F)(\mathbf{x}) = BA\mathbf{x}$ for $\mathbf{x}$ in $R^n$ and then apply Exercise 41.]

**43.** Let $I: R^n \to R^n$ be the identity transformation. Determine the matrix $A$ such that $I(\mathbf{x}) = A\mathbf{x}$ for each $\mathbf{x}$ in $R^n$.

**44.** Let $a$ be a real number and define $T: R^n \to R^n$ by $T(\mathbf{x}) = a\mathbf{x}$ (see Example 4). Determine the matrix $A$ such that $T(\mathbf{x}) = A\mathbf{x}$ for each $\mathbf{x}$ in $R^n$.

Exercises 45–49 are based on the optional material.

**45.** Let $T: R^2 \to R^2$ be a rotation through the angle $\theta$. In each of the following cases, exhibit the matrix for $T$. Also represent $\mathbf{v}$ and $T(\mathbf{v})$ geometrically, where

$$\mathbf{v} = \begin{bmatrix} 1 \\ 1 \end{bmatrix}.$$

a) $\theta = \pi/2$   b) $\theta = \pi/3$   c) $\theta = 2\pi/3$

**46.** Let $T: R^2 \to R^2$ be the reflection with respect to the line $l$. In each of the following cases, exhibit the matrix for $T$. Also represent $\mathbf{e}_1, \mathbf{e}_2, T(\mathbf{e}_1)$, and $T(\mathbf{e}_2)$ geometrically.

a) $l$ is the $x$-axis.    b) $l$ is the $y$-axis.
c) $l$ is the line with equation $y = x$.
d) $l$ is the line with equation $y = \sqrt{3}x$.

47. Let $T: R^2 \to R^2$ be a linear transformation that satisfies the conditions of Theorem 16. Show that $T$ is orthogonal. [*Hint:* If $\mathbf{v} = [a, b]^T$, then $\mathbf{v} = a\mathbf{e}_1 + b\mathbf{e}_2$. Now use Eq. (6).]

48. Let $T: R^2 \to R^2$ be an orthogonal linear transformation, and let $A$ be the corresponding $(2 \times 2)$ matrix. Show that $A^TA = I$. [*Hint:* Use Theorem 16.]

49. Let $A = [\mathbf{A}_1, \mathbf{A}_2]$ be a $(2 \times 2)$ matrix such that $A^TA = I$, and define $T: R^2 \to R^2$ by $T(\mathbf{x}) = A\mathbf{x}$.

a) Show that $\{\mathbf{A}_1, \mathbf{A}_2\}$ is an orthonormal set.

b) Use Theorem 16 to show that $T$ is an orthogonal transformation.

# 3.8 LEAST-SQUARES SOLUTIONS TO INCONSISTENT SYSTEMS, WITH APPLICATIONS TO DATA FITTING

When faced with solving a linear system of the form $A\mathbf{x} = \mathbf{b}$, our procedure has been to describe all solutions if the system is consistent but merely to say "there are no solutions" if the system is inconsistent. We now want to go a step further with regard to inconsistent systems. If a given linear system $A\mathbf{x} = \mathbf{b}$ has no solution, then we would like to do the next best thing—find a vector $\mathbf{x}^*$ such that the residual vector, $\mathbf{r} = A\mathbf{x}^* - \mathbf{b}$, is as small as possible. In terms of practical applications, we shall see that any technique for minimizing the residual vector can also be used to find best least-squares fits to data.

A common source of inconsistent systems are **overdetermined systems** (that is, systems with more equations than unknowns). The system that follows is an example of an overdetermined system:

$$
\begin{aligned}
x_1 + 4x_2 &= -2 \\
x_1 + 2x_2 &= \phantom{-}6 \\
2x_1 + 3x_2 &= \phantom{-}1.
\end{aligned}
$$

Overdetermined systems are often inconsistent, and the preceding example is no exception. Given that the above system has no solution, a reasonable goal is to find values for $x_1$ and $x_2$ that come as close as possible to satisfying all three equations. Methods for achieving that goal are the subject of this section.

## Least-Squares Solutions to $A\mathbf{x} = \mathbf{b}$

Consider the linear system $A\mathbf{x} = \mathbf{b}$ where $A$ is $(m \times n)$. If $\mathbf{x}$ is a vector in $R^n$, then the vector $\mathbf{r} = A\mathbf{x} - \mathbf{b}$ is called a **residual vector**. A vector $\mathbf{x}^*$ in $R^n$ that yields the smallest possible residual vector is called a least-squares solution to $A\mathbf{x} = \mathbf{b}$. More precisely, $\mathbf{x}^*$ is a **least-squares solution** to $A\mathbf{x} = \mathbf{b}$ if

$$\|A\mathbf{x}^* - \mathbf{b}\| \leq \|A\mathbf{x} - \mathbf{b}\|, \quad \text{for all } \mathbf{x} \text{ in } R^n.$$

(If $A\mathbf{x} = \mathbf{b}$ happens to be consistent, then a least-squares solution $\mathbf{x}^*$ is also a solution in the usual sense since $\|A\mathbf{x}^* - \mathbf{b}\| = 0$.)

The special case of an inconsistent $(3 \times 2)$ system $A\mathbf{x} = \mathbf{b}$ suggests how we can calculate least-squares solutions. In particular, consider Fig. 3.20 which illustrates a vector $\mathbf{b}$ that is not in $\mathcal{R}(A)$; that is, $A\mathbf{x} = \mathbf{b}$ is inconsistent.

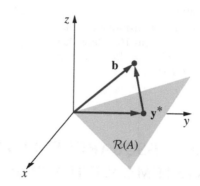

*Figure 3.20* $\mathbf{y}^*$ is the closest vector in $\mathcal{R}(A)$ to $\mathbf{b}$

Let the vector $\mathbf{y}^*$ in $\mathcal{R}(A)$ be the closest vector in $\mathcal{R}(A)$ to $\mathbf{b}$; that is

$$\|\mathbf{y}^* - \mathbf{b}\| \leq \|\mathbf{y} - \mathbf{b}\|, \quad \text{for all } \mathbf{y} \text{ in } \mathcal{R}(A).$$

Geometry suggests (see Fig. 3.20) that the vector $\mathbf{y}^* - \mathbf{b}$ is orthogonal to every vector in $\mathcal{R}(A)$. Since the columns of $A$ form a spanning set for $\mathcal{R}(A)$, this orthogonality condition leads to

$$\mathbf{A}_1^T(\mathbf{y}^* - \mathbf{b}) = 0$$
$$\mathbf{A}_2^T(\mathbf{y}^* - \mathbf{b}) = 0$$

or, in matrix-vector terms,

$$A^T(\mathbf{y}^* - \mathbf{b}) = \boldsymbol{\theta}.$$

Since $\mathbf{y}^* = A\mathbf{x}^*$ for some $\mathbf{x}^*$ in $R^2$, the preceding equation becomes $A^T(A\mathbf{x}^* - \mathbf{b}) = \boldsymbol{\theta}$, or

$$A^TA\mathbf{x}^* = A^T\mathbf{b}.$$

Thus, the geometry of the $(3 \times 2)$ system, as illustrated in Fig. 3.20, suggests that we can find least-squares solutions by solving the associated system (1):

$$A^TA\mathbf{x} = A^T\mathbf{b}. \tag{1}$$

As the following theorem asserts, this solution procedure is indeed valid.

**THEOREM 17** Consider the $(m \times n)$ system $A\mathbf{x} = \mathbf{b}$.

(a) The associated system $A^TA\mathbf{x} = A^T\mathbf{b}$ is always consistent.

(b) The least-squares solutions of $A\mathbf{x} = \mathbf{b}$ are precisely the solutions of $A^TA\mathbf{x} = A^T\mathbf{b}$.

(c) The least-squares solution is unique if and only if $A$ has rank $n$.

We will give the proof of Theorem 17 in the next section. For now, we will illustrate the use of Theorem 17 and also give some examples showing the connections between data-fitting problems and least-squares solutions of inconsistent systems. (In parts (a) and (b) of Theorem 17, the associated equations $A^TA\mathbf{x} = A^T\mathbf{b}$ are called the *normal equations*.)

**EXAMPLE 1**      Find the least-squares solutions to the inconsistent system

$$x_1 + 4x_2 = -2$$
$$x_1 + 2x_2 = 6$$
$$2x_1 + 3x_2 = 1.$$

**Solution**      By Theorem 17, we can find the least-squares solutions by solving the normal equations, $A^TA\mathbf{x} = A^T\mathbf{b}$, where

$$A = \begin{bmatrix} 1 & 4 \\ 1 & 2 \\ 2 & 3 \end{bmatrix} \quad \text{and} \quad \mathbf{b} = \begin{bmatrix} -2 \\ 6 \\ 1 \end{bmatrix}.$$

Forming $A^TA$ and $A^T\mathbf{b}$, we obtain

$$A^TA = \begin{bmatrix} 6 & 12 \\ 12 & 29 \end{bmatrix} \quad \text{and} \quad A^T\mathbf{b} = \begin{bmatrix} 6 \\ 7 \end{bmatrix}.$$

Solving the system $A^TA\mathbf{x} = A^T\mathbf{b}$, we find the least-squares solution

$$\mathbf{x}^* = \begin{bmatrix} 3 \\ -1 \end{bmatrix}.$$

## Least-Squares Fits to Data

One of the major applications for least-squares solutions is to the problem of determining best least-squares fits to data. To introduce this important topic, consider a table of data such as the one displayed next.

**Table 3.1**

| $t$ | $t_0$ | $t_1$ | $t_2$ | $\cdots$ | $t_n$ |
|---|---|---|---|---|---|
| $y$ | $y_0$ | $y_1$ | $y_2$ | $\cdots$ | $y_n$ |

Suppose, when we plot the data in Table 3.1, that it has a distribution such as the one shown in Fig. 3.21. When we examine Fig. 3.21, it appears that the data points nearly fall along a line of the form $y = mt + c$. A logical question is: "What is the best line that we can draw through the data, one that comes closest to representing the data?"

*Figure 3.21* A nearly linear distribution of data points

In order to answer this question, we need a way to quantify the terms *best* and *closest*. There are many different methods we might use to measure best, but one of the most useful is the **least-squares criterion**:

$$\text{Find } m \text{ and } c \text{ to minimize } \sum_{i=0}^{n} [(mt_i + c) - y_i]^2 \tag{2}$$

The particular linear polynomial $y = mt + c$ that minimizes the sum of squares in Eq. (2) is called the **best least-squares linear fit** to the data in Table 3.1. (We see in the next section that best least-squares linear fits always exist and are unique.)

Similarly, suppose the set of data points from Table 1 has a distribution such as the one displayed in Fig. 3.22. In this case, it appears that the data might nearly fall along the graph of a quadratic polynomial $y = at^2 + bt + c$. As in Eq. (2), we can use a least-squares criterion to choose the *best least-squares quadratic fit*:

$$\text{Find } a, b, \text{ and } c \text{ to minimize } \sum_{i=0}^{n} [(at_i^2 + bt_i + c) - y_i]^2.$$

In a like manner, we can consider fitting data in a least-squares sense with polynomials of any appropriate degree.

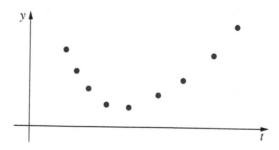

*Figure 3.22* A nearly parabolic distribution of data points

In the next several subsections, we examine the connection between least-squares fits to data and least-squares solutions to $A\mathbf{x} = \mathbf{b}$.

## Least-Squares Linear Fits to Data

Suppose the laws of physics tell us that two measurable quantities, $t$ and $y$, are related in a linear fashion:

$$y = mt + c. \tag{3}$$

Suppose also that we wish to determine experimentally the values of $m$ and $c$. If we know that Eq. (3) models the phenomena exactly and that we have made no experimental error, then we can determine $m$ and $c$ with only two experimental observations. For instance, if $y = y_0$ when $t = t_0$ and if $y = y_1$ when $t = t_1$, we can solve for $m$ and $c$ from

$$
\begin{array}{cc}
\begin{array}{l} mt_0 + c = y_0 \\ mt_1 + c = y_1 \end{array}
& \text{or} \quad
\begin{bmatrix} t_0 & 1 \\ t_1 & 1 \end{bmatrix}
\begin{bmatrix} m \\ c \end{bmatrix}
=
\begin{bmatrix} y_0 \\ y_1 \end{bmatrix}.
\end{array}
$$

Usually we must be resigned to experimental errors or to imperfections in the model given by Eq. (3). In this case, we would probably make a number of experimental observations, $(t_i, y_i)$ for $i = 0, 1, \ldots, k$. Using these observed values in Eq. (3) leads to an overdetermined system of the form

$$mt_0 + c = y_0$$
$$mt_1 + c = y_1$$
$$\vdots$$
$$mt_k + c = y_k.$$

In matrix terms, this overdetermined system can be expressed as $Ax = b$, where

$$
A = \begin{bmatrix} t_0 & 1 \\ t_1 & 1 \\ \vdots & \vdots \\ t_k & 1 \end{bmatrix}, \quad
\mathbf{x} = \begin{bmatrix} m \\ c \end{bmatrix}, \quad \text{and} \quad
\mathbf{b} = \begin{bmatrix} y_0 \\ y_1 \\ \vdots \\ y_k \end{bmatrix}.
$$

In this context, a least-squares solution to $Ax = b$ is a vector $\mathbf{x}^* = [m^*, c^*]^T$ that minimizes $\|Ax - b\|$, where

$$\|Ax - b\|^2 = \sum_{i=0}^{k} [(mt_i + c) - y_i]^2.$$

Comparing the equation above with the least-squares criterion (2), we see that the best least-squares linear fit, $y = m^*t + c^*$, can be determined by finding the least-squares solution of $Ax = b$.

EXAMPLE 2    Consider the experimental observations given in the following table:

| $t$ | 1 | 4 | 8 | 11 |
|---|---|---|---|---|
| $y$ | 1 | 2 | 4 | 5 |

Find the least-squares linear fit to the data.

*Solution*    For the function defined by $y = mt + c$, the data lead to the overdetermined system

$$m + c = 1$$
$$4m + c = 2$$
$$8m + c = 4$$
$$11m + c = 5.$$

In matrix terms, the system is $A\mathbf{x} = \mathbf{b}$, where

$$A = \begin{bmatrix} 1 & 1 \\ 4 & 1 \\ 8 & 1 \\ 11 & 1 \end{bmatrix}, \quad \mathbf{x} = \begin{bmatrix} m \\ c \end{bmatrix}, \quad \text{and} \quad \mathbf{b} = \begin{bmatrix} 1 \\ 2 \\ 4 \\ 5 \end{bmatrix}.$$

The least-squares solution, $\mathbf{x}^*$, is found by solving $A^T A\mathbf{x} = A^T\mathbf{b}$, where

$$A^T A = \begin{bmatrix} 202 & 24 \\ 24 & 4 \end{bmatrix} \quad \text{and} \quad A^T\mathbf{b} = \begin{bmatrix} 96 \\ 12 \end{bmatrix}.$$

There is a unique solution to $A^T A\mathbf{x} = A^T\mathbf{b}$ because $A$ has rank 2. The solution is

$$\mathbf{x}^* = \begin{bmatrix} 12/29 \\ 15/29 \end{bmatrix}.$$

Thus the least-squares linear fit is defined by

$$y = \frac{12}{29}t + \frac{15}{29}.$$

The data points and the linear fit are sketched in Fig. 3.23.

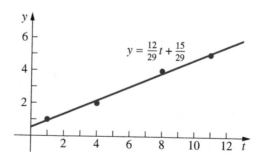

*Figure 3.23*    The least-squares linear fit to the data in Example 2

## Using MATLAB to Find Least-Squares Solutions

Up to now we have been finding least-squares solutions to inconsistent systems by solving the normal equations $A^T A\mathbf{x} = A^T\mathbf{b}$. This method is fine in theory but (because of roundoff error) it is not reliable for machine calculations—especially for large systems

$A\mathbf{x} = \mathbf{b}$. MATLAB has several reliable alternatives for finding least-squares solutions to inconsistent systems; these methods do not depend on solving the normal equations.

If $A$ is not square, the simple MATLAB command $\mathtt{x} = \mathtt{A \backslash b}$ produces a least-squares solution to $A\mathbf{x} = \mathbf{b}$ using a QR-factorization of $A$. (In Chapter 7, we give a thorough discussion of how to find least-squares solutions using QR-factorizations and Householder transformations.) If $A$ is square but inconsistent, then the command $\mathtt{x} = \mathtt{A \backslash b}$ results in a warning but does not return a least-squares solution. If $A$ is not square, a warning is also issued when $A$ does not have full rank. In the next section we will give more details about these matters and about using MATLAB to find least-squares solutions.

EXAMPLE 3 Lubricating characteristics of oils deteriorate at elevated temperatures, and the amount of bearing wear, $y$, is normally a linear function of the operating temperature, $t$. That is, $y = mt + b$. By weighing bearings before and after operation at various temperatures, the following table was constructed:

| Operating temperature, °C | 120 | 148 | 175 | 204 | 232 | 260 | 288 | 316 | 343 | 371 |
|---|---|---|---|---|---|---|---|---|---|---|
| Amount of wear, gm/10,000 hr | 3 | 4 | 5 | 5.5 | 6 | 7.5 | 8.8 | 10 | 11.1 | 12 |

Determine the least-squares linear fit from these readings and use it to determine an operating temperature that should limit bearing wear to 7 gm/10,000 hr of operation.

*Solution* For the system $A\mathbf{x} = \mathbf{b}$, we see that $A$ and $\mathbf{b}$ are given by

$$A = \begin{bmatrix} 120 & 148 & 175 & 204 & 232 & 260 & 288 & 316 & 343 & 371 \\ 1 & 1 & 1 & 1 & 1 & 1 & 1 & 1 & 1 & 1 \end{bmatrix}^T$$

$$\mathbf{b} = [3, \quad 4, \quad 5, \quad 5.5, \quad 6, \quad 7.5, \quad 8.8, \quad 10, \quad 11.1, \quad 12]^T.$$

The least-squares solution to $A\mathbf{x} = \mathbf{b}$ is found from the MATLAB commands in Fig. 3.24.

```
>>A=[120 148 175 204 232 260 288 316 343 371;
       1   1   1   1   1   1   1   1   1   1]';
>>b=[3 4 5 5.5 6 7.5 8.8 10 11.1 12]';
>>x=A\b

x=

    0.0362
   -1.6151
```

*Figure 3.24*   The MATLAB commands for Example 3

From Fig. 3.24 we see that the least-squares linear fit is

$$y = (0.0362)t - 1.6151.$$

Setting $y = 7$ yields $t = 237.986$. Hence an operating temperature of about 238°C should limit bearing wear to 7 gm/10,000 hr.  ◼

## General Least-Squares Fits

Consider the following table of data:

| $t$ | $t_0$ | $t_1$ | $t_2$ | $\cdots$ | $t_m$ |
|---|---|---|---|---|---|
| $y$ | $y_0$ | $y_1$ | $y_2$ | $\cdots$ | $y_m$ |

When the data points $(t_i, y_i)$ are plotted in the $ty$-plane, the plot may reveal a trend that is nonlinear (see Fig. 3.25). For a set of data such as that sketched in Fig. 3.25, a linear fit would not be appropriate. However, we might choose a polynomial function, $y = p(t)$, where

$$p(t_i) \simeq y_i, \quad 0 \le i \le m.$$

In particular, suppose we decide to fit the data with an $n$th-degree polynomial:

$$p(t) = a_n t^n + a_{n-1} t^{n-1} + \cdots + a_1 t + a_0, \quad m \ge n.$$

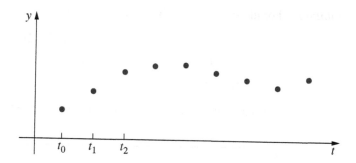

**Figure 3.25**     Nonlinear data

As a measure for goodness of fit, we can ask for coefficients $a_0, a_1, \ldots, a_n$ that minimize the quantity $Q(a_0, a_1, \ldots, a_n)$, where

$$Q(a_0, a_1, \ldots, a_n) = \sum_{i=0}^{m} [p(t_i) - y_i]^2$$

$$= \sum_{i=0}^{m} [(a_0 + a_1 t_i + \cdots + a_n t_i^n) - y_i]^2. \tag{4}$$

As can be seen by inspection, minimizing $Q(a_0, a_1, \ldots, a_n)$ is the same as minimizing $\|A\mathbf{x} - \mathbf{b}\|^2$, where

$$A = \begin{bmatrix} 1 & t_0 & t_0^2 & \cdots & t_0^n \\ 1 & t_1 & t_1^2 & \cdots & t_1^n \\ \vdots & & & & \vdots \\ 1 & t_m & t_m^2 & \cdots & t_m^n \end{bmatrix}, \quad \mathbf{x} = \begin{bmatrix} a_0 \\ a_1 \\ \vdots \\ a_n \end{bmatrix}, \quad \text{and} \quad \mathbf{b} = \begin{bmatrix} y_0 \\ y_1 \\ \vdots \\ y_m \end{bmatrix}. \quad (5)$$

As before, we can minimize $\|A\mathbf{x} - \mathbf{b}\|^2 = Q(a_0, a_1, \ldots, a_n)$ by solving $A^T A\mathbf{x} = A^T\mathbf{b}$. The $n$th-degree polynomial $p^*$ that minimizes Eq. (4) is called the least-squares $n$th-degree fit.

**EXAMPLE 4**  Consider the data from the following table:

| $t$ | $-2$ | $-1$ | $0$ | $1$ | $2$ |
|---|---|---|---|---|---|
| $y$ | $12$ | $5$ | $3$ | $2$ | $4$ |

Find the least-squares quadratic fit to the data.

***Solution***  Since we want a quadratic fit, we are trying to match the form $y = a_0 + a_1 t + a_2 t^2$ to the data. The equations are

$$a_0 - 2a_1 + 4a_2 = 12$$
$$a_0 - \phantom{2}a_1 + \phantom{4}a_2 = \phantom{1}5$$
$$a_0 \phantom{- 2a_1 + 4a_2} = \phantom{1}3$$
$$a_0 + \phantom{2}a_1 + \phantom{4}a_2 = \phantom{1}2$$
$$a_0 + 2a_1 + 4a_2 = \phantom{1}4.$$

This overdetermined system can be shown to be inconsistent. Therefore, we look for a least-squares solution to $A\mathbf{x} = \mathbf{b}$, where $A$ and $\mathbf{b}$ are as in system (5), with $n = 2$ and $m = 4$.

The matrix $A$ and the vectors $\mathbf{x}$ and $\mathbf{b}$ are

$$A = \begin{bmatrix} 1 & -2 & 4 \\ 1 & -1 & 1 \\ 1 & 0 & 0 \\ 1 & 1 & 1 \\ 1 & 2 & 4 \end{bmatrix}, \quad \mathbf{x} = \begin{bmatrix} a_0 \\ a_1 \\ a_2 \end{bmatrix}, \quad \text{and} \quad \mathbf{b} = \begin{bmatrix} 12 \\ 5 \\ 3 \\ 2 \\ 4 \end{bmatrix}.$$

The least-squares solution of $A\mathbf{x} = \mathbf{b}$ is found by solving $A^T A\mathbf{x} = A^T\mathbf{b}$, where

$$A^T A = \begin{bmatrix} 5 & 0 & 10 \\ 0 & 10 & 0 \\ 10 & 0 & 34 \end{bmatrix} \quad \text{and} \quad A^T\mathbf{b} = \begin{bmatrix} 26 \\ -19 \\ 71 \end{bmatrix}.$$

The solution is $\mathbf{x}^* = [87/35, -19/10, 19/14]$, and hence the least-squares quadratic fit is

$$p(t) = \frac{19}{14}t^2 - \frac{19}{10}t + \frac{87}{35}.$$

A graph of $y = p(t)$ and the data points are sketched in Fig. 3.26.

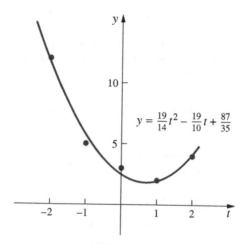

*Figure 3.26*    Least-squares quadratic fit for the data in Example 4

The same principles apply when we decide to fit data with any linear combination of functions. For example, suppose $y = f(t)$ is defined by

$$f(t) = a_1 g_1(t) + a_2 g_2(t) + \cdots + a_n g_n(t),$$

where $g_1, g_2, \ldots, g_n$ are given functions. We can use the method of least squares to determine scalars $a_1, a_2, \ldots, a_n$ that will minimize

$$Q(a_1, a_2, \ldots, a_n) = \sum_{i=1}^{m} [f(t_i) - y_i]^2$$

$$= \sum_{i=1}^{m} \{[a_1 g_1(t_i) + a_2 g_2(t_i) + \cdots + a_n g_n(t_i)] - y_i\}^2. \tag{6}$$

The ideas associated with minimizing $Q(a_1, a_2, \ldots, a_n)$ are explored in the exercises.

## Rank Deficient Matrices

In each of Examples 1–4, the least-squares solution to $A\mathbf{x} = \mathbf{b}$ was unique. Indeed, if $A$ is $(m \times n)$, then part (c) of Theorem 17 states that least-squares solutions are unique if and only if the rank of $A$ is equal to $n$. If the rank of $A$ is less than $n$, then we say that $A$ is **rank deficient**, or $A$ does not have **full rank**.

Therefore, when $A$ is rank deficient, there is an infinite family of least-squares solutions to $A\mathbf{x} = \mathbf{b}$. Such an example is given next. This example is worked using MATLAB, and we note that MATLAB produces only a single least-squares solution but does give a warning that $A$ is rank deficient. In Section 3.9 we will discuss this topic in more detail.

EXAMPLE 5    For $A$ and $\mathbf{b}$ as given, the system $A\mathbf{x} = \mathbf{b}$ has no solution. Find all the least-squares solutions

$$A = \begin{bmatrix} 1 & 0 & 2 \\ 0 & 2 & 2 \\ -1 & 1 & -1 \\ -1 & 2 & 0 \end{bmatrix}, \quad \mathbf{b} = \begin{bmatrix} 3 \\ -3 \\ 0 \\ -3 \end{bmatrix}.$$

*Solution*    The MATLAB calculation is displayed in Fig. 3.27(a). Notice that MATLAB warns us that $A$ is rank deficient, having rank two. In Exercise 18 we ask you to verify that $A$ does indeed have rank two.

```
>>A=[1 0 2;0 2 2;-1 1 -1;-1 2 0];
>>b=[3 -3 0 -3]';
>>x=A\b

Warning: Rank deficient, rank = 2  tol =    2.6645e-15


x=

        0
  -1.5000
   0.5000
```

*Figure 3.27(a)*    The MATLAB commands for Example 5

Since $A$ is rank deficient, there are infinitely many least-squares solutions to the inconsistent system $A\mathbf{x} = \mathbf{b}$. MATLAB returned just one of these solutions, namely $\mathbf{x} = [0, -1.5, 0.5]^T$. We can find all the solutions by solving the normal equations $A^T A\mathbf{x} = A^T\mathbf{b}$.

Fig. 3.27(b) shows the result of using MATLAB to solve the normal equations for the original system (since $A$ and $\mathbf{b}$ have already been defined, in Fig. 3.27(a), MATLAB

```
>>NormEqn=[A'*A,A'*b]

NormEqn =

     3   -3    3    6
    -3    9    3  -12
     3    3    9    0

>>rref(NormEqn)

ans =

     1    0    2    1
     0    1    1   -1
     0    0    0    0
```

*Figure 3.27(b)*    Setting up and solving the normal equations for
Example 5

makes it very easy to define the augmented matrix for $A^TA\mathbf{x} = A^T\mathbf{b}$). The complete
solution is $x_1 = 1 - 2x_3$, $x_2 = -1 - x_3$, or in vector form:

$$\mathbf{x}^* = \begin{bmatrix} 1 - 2x_3 \\ -1 - x_3 \\ x_3 \end{bmatrix} = \begin{bmatrix} 1 \\ -1 \\ 0 \end{bmatrix} + x_3 \begin{bmatrix} -2 \\ -1 \\ 1 \end{bmatrix}.$$

As can be seen from the complete solution just displayed, the particular MATLAB least-
squares solution can be recovered by setting $x_3 = 0.5$.

## 3.8    EXERCISES

In Exercises 1–6, find all vectors $\mathbf{x}^*$ that minimize
$\|A\mathbf{x}-\mathbf{b}\|$, where $A$ and $\mathbf{b}$ are as given. Use the procedure
suggested by Theorem 17, as illustrated in Examples 1
and 5.

**1.** $A = \begin{bmatrix} 1 & 2 \\ -1 & 1 \\ 1 & 3 \end{bmatrix}$, $\mathbf{b} = \begin{bmatrix} 1 \\ 1 \\ 1 \end{bmatrix}$

**2.** $A = \begin{bmatrix} 1 & 2 & 4 \\ -2 & -3 & -7 \\ 1 & 3 & 5 \end{bmatrix}$, $\mathbf{b} = \begin{bmatrix} 1 \\ 1 \\ 2 \end{bmatrix}$

**3.** $A = \begin{bmatrix} 1 & 2 & 1 \\ 3 & 5 & 4 \\ -1 & 1 & -4 \end{bmatrix}$, $\mathbf{b} = \begin{bmatrix} 1 \\ 3 \\ 0 \end{bmatrix}$

**4.** $A = \begin{bmatrix} 1 & 2 & -1 \\ 2 & 3 & 1 \\ -1 & -1 & -2 \\ 3 & 5 & 0 \end{bmatrix}$, $\mathbf{b} = \begin{bmatrix} 1 \\ 0 \\ 1 \\ 0 \end{bmatrix}$

**5.** $A = \begin{bmatrix} 1 & 2 \\ 2 & 4 \\ 3 & 6 \end{bmatrix}$, $\mathbf{b} = \begin{bmatrix} 0 \\ 2 \\ 16 \end{bmatrix}$

**6.** $A = \begin{bmatrix} 1 & 0 & 0 \\ 3 & 0 & 0 \\ 1 & 1 & 1 \end{bmatrix}$, $\quad \mathbf{b} = \begin{bmatrix} 11 \\ 3 \\ 1 \end{bmatrix}$

In Exercises 7–10, find the least-squares linear fit to the given data. In each exercise, plot the data points and the linear approximation.

**7.**

| $t$ | −1 | 0 | 1 | 2 |
|---|---|---|---|---|
| $y$ | 0 | 1 | 2 | 4 |

**8.**

| $t$ | −2 | 0 | 1 | 2 |
|---|---|---|---|---|
| $y$ | 2 | 1 | 0 | 0 |

**9.**

| $t$ | −1 | 0 | 1 | 2 |
|---|---|---|---|---|
| $y$ | −1 | 1 | 2 | 3 |

**10.**

| $t$ | 0 | 1 | 2 | 3 |
|---|---|---|---|---|
| $y$ | −2 | 3 | 7 | 10 |

In Exercises 11–14, find the least-squares quadratic fit to the given data. In each exercise, plot the data points and the quadratic approximation.

**11.**

| $t$ | −2 | −1 | 1 | 2 |
|---|---|---|---|---|
| $y$ | 2 | 0 | 1 | 2 |

**12.**

| $t$ | 0 | 1 | 2 | 3 |
|---|---|---|---|---|
| $y$ | 0 | 0 | 1 | 2 |

**13.**

| $t$ | −2 | −1 | 0 | 1 |
|---|---|---|---|---|
| $y$ | −3 | −1 | 0 | 3 |

**14.**

| $t$ | −2 | 0 | 1 | 2 |
|---|---|---|---|---|
| $y$ | 5 | 1 | 1 | 5 |

**15.** Consider the following table of data:

| $t$ | $t_1$ | $t_2$ | $\cdots$ | $t_m$ |
|---|---|---|---|---|
| $y$ | $y_1$ | $y_2$ | $\cdots$ | $y_m$ |

For given functions $g_1$ and $g_2$, consider a function $f$ defined by $f(t) = a_1 g_1(t) + a_2 g_2(t)$. Show that

$$\sum_{i=1}^{m} [f(t_i) - y_i]^2 = \|A\mathbf{x} - \mathbf{b}\|^2,$$

where

$$A = \begin{bmatrix} g_1(t_1) & g_2(t_1) \\ g_1(t_2) & g_2(t_2) \\ \vdots & \\ g_1(t_m) & g_2(t_m) \end{bmatrix}, \quad \mathbf{x} = \begin{bmatrix} a_1 \\ a_2 \end{bmatrix}, \quad \text{and}$$

$$\mathbf{b} = \begin{bmatrix} y_1 \\ y_2 \\ \vdots \\ y_m \end{bmatrix}.$$

**16.** Let $g_1(t) = \sqrt{t}$ and $g_2(t) = \cos \pi t$, and consider the data points $(t_i, y_i)$, $1 \le i \le 4$, defined by

| $t$ | 1 | 4 | 9 | 16 |
|---|---|---|---|---|
| $y$ | 0 | 2 | 4 | 5 |

As in Eq. (6), let $Q(a_1, a_2) = \sum_{i=1}^{4} [a_1 g_1(t_i) + a_2 g_2(t_i) - y_i]^2$, where $g_1(t_i) = \sqrt{t_i}$ and $g_2(t_i) = \cos \pi t_i$.

a) Use the result of Exercise 15 to determine $A$, $\mathbf{x}$, and $\mathbf{b}$ so that $Q(a_1, a_2) = \|A\mathbf{x} - \mathbf{b}\|^2$.

b) Find the coefficients for $f(t) = a_1 \sqrt{t} + a_2 \cos \pi t$ that minimize $Q(a_1, a_2)$.

**17.** Consider the $[(m+1) \times (n+1)]$ matrix $A$ in Eq. (5), where $m \ge n$. Show that $A$ has rank $n + 1$. [*Hint:* Suppose that $A\mathbf{x} = \boldsymbol{\theta}$, where $\mathbf{x} = [a_0, a_1, \ldots, a_n]^T$. What can you say about the polynomial $p(t) = a_0 + a_1 t + \cdots + a_n t^n$?]

**18.** Find the rank of the matrix $A$ in Example 5.

# THEORY AND PRACTICE OF LEAST SQUARES

**3.9**

In the previous section, we discussed least-squares solutions to $A\mathbf{x} = \mathbf{b}$ and the closely related idea of best least-squares fits to data. In this section, we have two major objectives:

(a) Develop the theory for the least-squares problem in $R^n$

**(b)** Use the theory to explain some of the technical language associated with least squares so that we can become comfortable using computational packages such as MATLAB for least-squares problems.

## The Least-Squares Problem in $R^n$

The theory necessary for a complete understanding of least squares is fairly concise and geometric. To ensure our development is completely unambiguous, we begin by reviewing some familiar terminology and notation. In particular, let $\mathbf{x}$ be a vector in $R^n$,

$$\mathbf{x} = \begin{bmatrix} x_1 \\ x_2 \\ \vdots \\ x_n \end{bmatrix}.$$

We define the **distance** between two vectors $\mathbf{x}$ and $\mathbf{y}$ to be the length of the vector $\mathbf{x} - \mathbf{y}$; recall that the length of $\mathbf{x} - \mathbf{y}$ is the number $\|\mathbf{x} - \mathbf{y}\|$ where

$$\|\mathbf{x} - \mathbf{y}\| = \sqrt{(\mathbf{x} - \mathbf{y})^T (\mathbf{x} - \mathbf{y})}$$
$$= \sqrt{(x_1 - y_1)^2 + (x_2 - y_2)^2 + \cdots + (x_n - y_n)^2}.$$

The problem we wish to consider is stated next.

---

**The Least-Squares Problem in $R^n$**

Let $W$ be a $p$-dimensional subspace of $R^n$. Given a vector $\mathbf{v}$ in $R^n$, find a vector $\mathbf{w}^*$ in $W$ such that

$$\|\mathbf{v} - \mathbf{w}^*\| \le \|\mathbf{v} - \mathbf{w}\|, \quad \text{for all } \mathbf{w} \text{ in } W.$$

The vector $\mathbf{w}^*$ is called the **best least-squares approximation to $v$**.

---

That is, among all vectors $\mathbf{w}$ in $W$, we want to find the special vector $\mathbf{w}^*$ in $W$ that is closest to $\mathbf{v}$. Although this problem can be extended to some very complicated and abstract settings, examination of the geometry of a simple special case will exhibit a fundamental principle that extends to all such problems.

Consider the special case where $W$ is a two-dimensional subspace of $R^3$. Geometrically, we can visualize $W$ as a plane through the origin (see Fig. 3.28). Given a point $\mathbf{v}$ not on $W$, we wish to find the point in the plane, $\mathbf{w}^*$, that is closest to $\mathbf{v}$. The geometry of this problem seems to insist (see Fig. 3.28) that $\mathbf{w}^*$ is characterized by the fact that the vector $\mathbf{v} - \mathbf{w}^*$ is perpendicular to the plane $W$.

The next theorem shows that Fig. 3.28 is not misleading. That is, if $\mathbf{v} - \mathbf{w}^*$ is orthogonal to every vector in $W$, then $\mathbf{w}^*$ is the best least-squares approximation to $\mathbf{v}$.

**THEOREM 18**     Let $W$ be a $p$-dimensional subspace of $R^n$, and let $\mathbf{v}$ be a vector in $R^n$. Suppose there is a vector $\mathbf{w}^*$ in $W$ such that $(\mathbf{v} - \mathbf{w}^*)^T \mathbf{w} = 0$ for every vector $\mathbf{w}$ in $W$. Then $\mathbf{w}^*$ is the best least-squares approximation to $\mathbf{v}$.

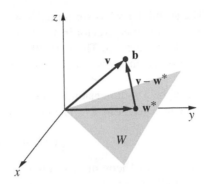

*Figure 3.28*  $\mathbf{w}^*$ is the closest point in the plane $W$ to $\mathbf{v}$

*Proof*  Let $\mathbf{w}$ be any vector in $W$ and consider the following calculation for the distance from $\mathbf{v}$ to $\mathbf{w}$:

$$\|\mathbf{v} - \mathbf{w}\|^2 = \|(\mathbf{v} - \mathbf{w}^*) + (\mathbf{w}^* - \mathbf{w})\|^2$$
$$= (\mathbf{v} - \mathbf{w}^*)^T (\mathbf{v} - \mathbf{w}^*) + 2(\mathbf{v} - \mathbf{w}^*)^T (\mathbf{w}^* - \mathbf{w})$$
$$+ (\mathbf{w}^* - \mathbf{w})^T (\mathbf{w}^* - \mathbf{w}) \tag{1}$$
$$= \|\mathbf{v} - \mathbf{w}^*\|^2 + \|\mathbf{w}^* - \mathbf{w}\|^2.$$

(The last equality follows because $\mathbf{w}^* - \mathbf{w}$ is a vector in $W$, and therefore $(\mathbf{v} - \mathbf{w}^*)^T (\mathbf{w}^* - \mathbf{w}) = 0$.) Since $\|\mathbf{w}^* - \mathbf{w}\|^2 \geq 0$, it follows from Eq. (1) that $\|\mathbf{v} - \mathbf{w}\|^2 \geq \|\mathbf{v} - \mathbf{w}^*\|^2$. Therefore, $\mathbf{w}^*$ is the best approximation to $\mathbf{v}$.  ■

The equality in calculation (1), $\|\mathbf{v} - \mathbf{w}\|^2 = \|\mathbf{v} - \mathbf{w}^*\|^2 + \|\mathbf{w}^* - \mathbf{w}\|^2$, is reminiscent of the Pythagorean theorem. A schematic view of this connection is sketched in Fig. 3.29.

*Figure 3.29*  A geometric interpretation of the vector $\mathbf{w}^*$ in $W$ closest to $\mathbf{v}$

In a later theorem, we will show that there is always one, and only one, vector $\mathbf{w}^*$ in $W$ such that $\mathbf{v} - \mathbf{w}^*$ is orthogonal to every vector in $W$. Thus it will be established that the best approximation always exists and is always unique. The proof of this fact will be constructive, so we now concentrate on methods for finding $\mathbf{w}^*$.

## Finding Best Approximations

Theorem 18 suggests a procedure for finding the best approximation $\mathbf{w}^*$. In particular, we should search for a vector $\mathbf{w}^*$ in $W$ that satisfies the following condition:

If $\mathbf{w}$ is any vector in $W$,  then $(\mathbf{v} - \mathbf{w}^*)^T \mathbf{w} = 0.$

The search for $\mathbf{w}^*$ is simplified if we make the following observation: If $\mathbf{v} - \mathbf{w}^*$ is orthogonal to every vector in $W$, then $\mathbf{v} - \mathbf{w}^*$ is also orthogonal to every vector in a basis for $W$. In fact, see Theorem 19, the condition that $\mathbf{v} - \mathbf{w}^*$ be orthogonal to the basis vectors is both necessary and sufficient for $\mathbf{v} - \mathbf{w}^*$ to be orthogonal to every vector in $W$.

**THEOREM 19**    Let $W$ be a $p$-dimensional subspace of $R^n$, and let $\{\mathbf{u}_1, \mathbf{u}_2, \ldots, \mathbf{u}_p\}$ be a basis for $W$. Let $\mathbf{v}$ be a vector in $R^n$. Then $(\mathbf{v} - \mathbf{w}^*)^T \mathbf{w} = 0$ for all $\mathbf{w}$ in $W$ if and only if

$$(\mathbf{v} - \mathbf{w}^*)^T \mathbf{u}_i = 0, \quad 1 \leq i \leq p.$$

The proof of Theorem 19 is left as Exercise 17.

As Theorem 19 states, the best approximation $\mathbf{w}^*$ can be found by solving the $p$ equations:

$$(\mathbf{v} - \mathbf{w}^*)^T \mathbf{u}_1 = 0$$
$$(\mathbf{v} - \mathbf{w}^*)^T \mathbf{u}_2 = 0$$
$$\vdots$$
$$(\mathbf{v} - \mathbf{w}^*)^T \mathbf{u}_p = 0$$

(2)

Suppose we can show that these $p$ equations always have a unique solution. Then, by Theorem 18, it will follow that the best approximation exists and is unique.

## Existence and Uniqueness of Best Approximations

We saw above that $\mathbf{w}^*$ is a best least-squares approximation to $\mathbf{v}$ if the vector $\mathbf{v} - \mathbf{w}^*$ satisfies system (2). We now use this result to prove that best approximations always exist and are always unique. In addition, we will give a formula for the best approximation.

**THEOREM 20**    Let $W$ be a $p$-dimensional subspace of $R^n$ and let $\mathbf{v}$ be a vector in $R^n$. Then there is one and only one best least-squares approximation in $W$ to $\mathbf{v}$.

*Proof*    The proof of existence is based on finding a solution to the system of Eq. (2). Now, system (2) is easiest to analyze and solve if we assume the basis vectors are orthogonal.

In particular, let $\{\mathbf{u}_1, \mathbf{u}_2, \ldots, \mathbf{u}_p\}$ be an orthogonal basis for $W$ (in Section 3.6 we observed that every subspace of $R^n$ has an orthogonal basis). Let $\mathbf{w}^*$ be a vector in $W$ where

$$\mathbf{w}^* = a_1 \mathbf{u}_1 + a_2 \mathbf{u}_2 + \cdots + a_p \mathbf{u}_p.$$

(3)

Using Eq. (3), the equations in system (2) become

$$(\mathbf{v} - (a_1 \mathbf{u}_1 + a_2 \mathbf{u}_2 + \cdots + a_p \mathbf{u}_p))^T \mathbf{u}_i = 0, \quad \text{for } i = 1, 2, \ldots, p.$$

Then, because the basis vectors are orthogonal, the preceding equations simplify considerably:

$$\mathbf{v}^T \mathbf{u}_i - a_i \mathbf{u}_i^T \mathbf{u}_i = 0, \quad \text{for } i = 1, 2, \ldots, p.$$

Solving for the coefficients $a_i$, we obtain

$$a_i = \frac{\mathbf{v}^T \mathbf{u}_i}{\mathbf{u}_i^T \mathbf{u}_i}.$$

Note that the preceding expression for $a_i$ is well defined since $\mathbf{u}_i$ is a basis vector, and hence the denominator $\mathbf{u}_i^T \mathbf{u}_i$ cannot be zero.

Having solved the system (2), we can write down an expression for a vector $\mathbf{w}^*$ such that $(\mathbf{v} - \mathbf{w}^*)^T \mathbf{w} = 0$ for all $\mathbf{w}$ in $W$. By Theorem 18, this vector $\mathbf{w}^*$ is a best approximation to $\mathbf{v}$:

$$\mathbf{w}^* = \sum_{i=1}^{p} \frac{\mathbf{v}^T \mathbf{u}_i}{\mathbf{u}_i^T \mathbf{u}_i} \mathbf{u}_i. \tag{4}$$

Having established the existence of best approximations with formula (4), we turn now to the question of uniqueness. To begin, suppose $\mathbf{w}$ is any best approximation to $\mathbf{v}$, and $\mathbf{w}^*$ is the best approximation defined by Eq. (4). Since the vector $\mathbf{v} - \mathbf{w}^*$ was constructed so as to be orthogonal to every vector in $W$, we can make a calculation similar to the one in Eq. (1) and conclude the following:

$$\|\mathbf{v} - \mathbf{w}\|^2 = \|\mathbf{v} - \mathbf{w}^*\|^2 + \|\mathbf{w}^* - \mathbf{w}\|^2.$$

But, if $\mathbf{w}$ and $\mathbf{w}^*$ are both best approximations to $\mathbf{v}$, then it follows from the equation above that $\|\mathbf{w}^* - \mathbf{w}\|^2 = 0$. This equality implies that $\mathbf{w}^* - \mathbf{w} = \boldsymbol{\theta}$ or $\mathbf{w}^* = \mathbf{w}$. Therefore, uniqueness of best approximations is established. ◼

The following example illustrates how a best approximation can be found from Eq. (4).

EXAMPLE 1  Let $W$ be the subspace of $R^3$ defined by

$$W = \left\{ \mathbf{x} : \mathbf{x} = \begin{bmatrix} x_1 \\ x_2 \\ x_3 \end{bmatrix}, \quad x_1 + x_2 - 3x_3 = 0 \right\}.$$

Let $\mathbf{v}$ be the vector $\mathbf{v} = [1, -2, -4]^T$. Use Eq. (4) to find the best least-squares approximation to $\mathbf{v}$.

*Solution*  Our first task is to find an orthogonal basis for $W$. We will use the Gram–Schmidt process to find such a basis.

To begin, $\mathbf{x}$ is in $W$ if and only if $x_1 = -x_2 + 3x_3$. That is, if and only if $\mathbf{x}$ has the form

$$\mathbf{x} = \begin{bmatrix} -x_2 + 3x_3 \\ x_2 \\ x_3 \end{bmatrix} = x_2 \begin{bmatrix} -1 \\ 1 \\ 0 \end{bmatrix} + x_3 \begin{bmatrix} 3 \\ 0 \\ 1 \end{bmatrix}.$$

Therefore, a natural basis for $W$ consists of the two vectors $\mathbf{w}_1 = [-1, 1, 0]^T$ and $\mathbf{w}_2 = [3, 0, 1]^T$.

We now use the Gram–Schmidt process to derive an orthogonal basis $\{\mathbf{u}_1, \mathbf{u}_2\}$ from the natural basis $\{\mathbf{w}_1, \mathbf{w}_2\}$. In particular,

**(a)**  Let $\mathbf{u}_1 = \mathbf{w}_1$.

**(b)**  Choose a scalar $a$ so that $\mathbf{u}_2 = \mathbf{w}_2 + a\mathbf{u}_1$ is orthogonal to $\mathbf{u}_1$.

To find the scalar $a$ in (b), consider

$$\mathbf{u}_1^T \mathbf{u}_2 = \mathbf{u}_1^T (\mathbf{w}_2 + a\mathbf{u}_1)$$
$$= \mathbf{u}_1^T \mathbf{w}_2 + a\mathbf{u}_1^T \mathbf{u}_1.$$

Thus, to have $\mathbf{u}_1^T \mathbf{u}_2 = 0$, we need $\mathbf{u}_1^T \mathbf{w}_2 + a\mathbf{u}_1^T \mathbf{u}_1 = 0$, or

$$a = -\frac{\mathbf{u}_1^T \mathbf{w}_2}{\mathbf{u}_1^T \mathbf{u}_1}$$
$$= -\frac{-3}{2}$$
$$= 1.5.$$

Having found $a$, we calculate the second vector in the orthogonal basis for $W$, finding
$\mathbf{u}_2 = \mathbf{w}_2 + 1.5\mathbf{u}_1 = [3, 0, 1]^T + 1.5[-1, 1, 0]^T = [1.5, 1.5, 1]^T$.

Next, let $\mathbf{w}^* = a_1\mathbf{u}_1 + a_2\mathbf{u}_2$ denote the best approximation, and determine the coefficients of $\mathbf{w}^*$ using Eq. (4):

$$a_1 = \frac{\mathbf{v}^T \mathbf{u}_1}{\mathbf{u}_1^T \mathbf{u}_1} = \frac{-3}{2} = -1.5$$

$$a_2 = \frac{\mathbf{v}^T \mathbf{u}_2}{\mathbf{u}_2^T \mathbf{u}_2} = \frac{-5.5}{5.5} = -1.$$

Therefore, the best approximation is given by

$$\mathbf{w}^* = -1.5\mathbf{u}_1 - \mathbf{u}_2 = -1.5[-1, 1, 0]^T - [1.5, 1.5, 1]^T = [0, -3, -1]^T.$$

(As a check for the calculations, we can form $\mathbf{v} - \mathbf{w}^* = [1, 1, -3]^T$ and verify that $\mathbf{v} - \mathbf{w}^*$ is orthogonal to each of the original basis vectors, $\mathbf{w}_1 = [-1, 1, 0]^T$ and $\mathbf{w}_2 = [3, 0, 1]^T$.)    ∎

## Least-Squares Solutions to Inconsistent Systems $A\mathbf{x} = \mathbf{b}$

In Section 3.8 we were interested in a special case of least-squares approximations—finding least-squares solutions to inconsistent systems $A\mathbf{x} = \mathbf{b}$. Recall that our method for finding least-squares solutions consisted of solving the normal equations $A^T A\mathbf{x} = A^T\mathbf{b}$. In turn, the validity of the normal equations approach was based on Theorem 17, which said:

(a)  The normal equations are always consistent.

(b)  The solutions of the normal equations are precisely the least-squares solutions of $A\mathbf{x} = \mathbf{b}$.

(c)  If $A$ is $(m \times n)$, then least-squares solutions of $A\mathbf{x} = \mathbf{b}$ are unique if and only if $A$ has rank $n$.

We are now in a position to sketch a proof of Theorem 17. The basic ideas supporting Theorem 17 are very important to a complete understanding of least-squares solutions of inconsistent systems. These ideas are easy to explain and are illustrated in Fig. 3.30.

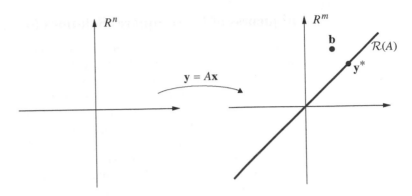

***Figure 3.30*** A geometric visualization of Theorem 17

In Fig. 3.30, we think of the $(m \times n)$ matrix $A$ as defining a function of the form $\mathbf{y} = A\mathbf{x}$ from $R^n$ to $R^m$. The subspace $\mathcal{R}(A)$ represents the range of $A$; it is a $p$-dimensional subspace of $R^m$. We have drawn the vector $\mathbf{b}$ so that it is not in $\mathcal{R}(A)$, illustrating the case where the system $A\mathbf{x} = \mathbf{b}$ is inconsistent. The vector $\mathbf{y}^*$ represents the (unique) best approximation in $\mathcal{R}(A)$ to $\mathbf{b}$.

***Proof of Theorem 17*** Because $\mathbf{y}^*$ is in $\mathcal{R}(A)$, there must be vectors $\mathbf{x}$ in $R^n$ such that $A\mathbf{x} = \mathbf{y}^*$. In addition, because $\mathbf{y}^*$ is the closest point in $\mathcal{R}(A)$ to $\mathbf{b}$, we can say:

A vector $\mathbf{x}$ in $\mathcal{R}^n$ is a best least-squares solution to $A\mathbf{x} = \mathbf{b}$ if and only if $A\mathbf{x} = \mathbf{y}^*$. $\hspace{2cm}$ (5)

In order to locate $\mathbf{y}^*$ in $W$, we note that $\mathbf{y}^*$ is characterized by $\mathbf{w}^T(\mathbf{y}^* - \mathbf{b}) = 0$ for any vector $\mathbf{w}$ in $\mathcal{R}(A)$. Then, since the columns of $A$ form a spanning set for $\mathcal{R}(A)$, $\mathbf{y}^*$ can be characterized by the conditions:

$$\mathbf{A}_i^T(\mathbf{y}^* - \mathbf{b}) = 0, \quad \text{for } i = 1, 2, \ldots, n. \hspace{2cm} (6)$$

The orthogonality conditions above can be rewritten in matrix/vector terms as

$$A^T(\mathbf{y}^* - \mathbf{b}) = \boldsymbol{\theta}. \hspace{2cm} (7)$$

Finally, since $\mathbf{y}^*$ is in $\mathcal{R}(A)$, finding $\mathbf{y}^*$ to solve Eq. (7) is the same as finding vectors $\mathbf{x}$ in $R^n$ that satisfy the normal equations:

$$A^T(A\mathbf{x} - \mathbf{b}) = \boldsymbol{\theta}. \hspace{2cm} (8)$$

We can now complete the proof of Theorem 17 by making the observation that Eq. (6) and Eq. (8) are equivalent in the following sense: A vector $\mathbf{x}$ in $R^n$ satisfies Eq. (8) if and only if the vector $\mathbf{y}^*$ satisfies Eq. (6), where $\mathbf{y}^* = A\mathbf{x}$.

To establish part (a) of Theorem 17, we note that Eq. (6) is consistent, and hence the normal equations given in Eq. (8) are consistent as well. Part (b) of Theorem 17 follows from rule (5) and the equivalence of equations (6) and (8). Part (c) of Theorem 17 follows because $A\mathbf{x} = \mathbf{y}^*$ has a unique solution if and only if the columns of $A$ are linearly independent. ∎

## Uniqueness of Least-Squares Solutions to $A\mathbf{x} = \mathbf{b}$

Best least-squares approximations are always unique but least-squares solutions to $A\mathbf{x} = \mathbf{b}$ might or might not be unique. The preceding statement is somewhat confusing because the term least-squares is being used in two different contexts. To clarify this widely accepted, but somewhat unfortunate, choice of terms, we can refer to Fig. 3.30.

In Fig. 3.30, the best least-squares approximation, $\mathbf{y}^*$, is unique (uniqueness was proved in Theorem 20). A best least-squares solution to $A\mathbf{x} = \mathbf{b}$, however, is a vector $\mathbf{x}$ such that $A\mathbf{x} = \mathbf{y}^*$, and there might or might not be infinitely many solutions to $A\mathbf{x} = \mathbf{y}^*$. (The equation $A\mathbf{x} = \mathbf{y}^*$ is always consistent because $\mathbf{y}^*$ is in $\mathcal{R}(A)$; the equation has a unique solution if and only if the columns of $A$ are linearly independent.)

Recall from the previous section that an $(m \times n)$ matrix $A$ is called **rank deficient** if it has rank less than $n$ (that is, if the columns of $A$ are linearly dependent). When $A$ is rank deficient, there are infinitely many least-squares solutions to $A\mathbf{x} = \mathbf{b}$. In this instance, we might want to select the minimum norm solution as the least-squares solution we use in our application. To explain, we say $\mathbf{x}^*$ is the **minimum norm** least-squares solution to $A\mathbf{x} = \mathbf{b}$ if $\|\mathbf{x}^*\|$ minimizes $\|\mathbf{x}\|$ among all least-squares solutions. That is,

$$\|\mathbf{x}^*\| = \min\{\|\mathbf{x}\| : A\mathbf{x} = \mathbf{y}^*\}.$$

It can be shown that the minimum norm solution always exists and is always unique.

The minimum norm solution is associated with another least-squares concept, that of the pseudoinverse of $A$. The pseudoinverse of $A$ is, in a sense, the closest thing to an inverse that a rectangular matrix can have. To explain the idea, we first introduce the **Frobenius norm** for an $(m \times n)$ matrix $A$. The Frobenius norm, denoted $\|A\|_F$, is defined by the following:

$$\|A\|_F = \sqrt{\sum_{i=1}^{m} \sum_{j=1}^{n} a_{ij}^2}.$$

Just as $\|\mathbf{x}\|$ measures the size of a vector $\mathbf{x}$, $\|A\|_F$ measures the size of a matrix $A$.

Now, let $A$ be an $(m \times n)$ matrix. The **pseudoinverse** of $A$, denoted $A^+$, is the $(n \times m)$ matrix that minimizes $\|AX - I\|_F$ where $I$ denotes the $(m \times m)$ identity matrix. It can be shown that such a minimizing matrix always exists and is always unique. As can be seen from the definition of the pseudoinverse, it is the closest thing (in a least-squares sense) to an inverse for a rectangular matrix. In the event that $A$ is square and invertible, then the pseudoinverse coincides with the usual inverse, $A^{-1}$. It can be shown that the minimum norm least-squares solution of $A\mathbf{x} = \mathbf{b}$ can be found from

$$\mathbf{x}^* = A^+\mathbf{b}.$$

An actual calculation of the pseudoinverse is usually made with the aid of another type of decomposition, the singular-value decomposition. A discussion of the singular-value decomposition would lead us too far afield, and so we ask the interested reader to consult a reference, such as Golub and Van Loan, *Matrix Computations*.

## MATLAB and Least-Squares Solutions

As we noted in the previous section, there are several ways to solve least-squares problems using MATLAB.

(a) If $A$ is $(m \times n)$ with $m \neq n$, then the MATLAB command A\b returns a least-squares solution to $A\mathbf{x} = \mathbf{b}$. If $A$ happens to be rank deficient, then MATLAB selects a least-squares solution with no more than $p$ nonzero entries (where $p$ denotes the rank of $A$). The least-squares solution is calculated using a QR-factorization for $A$ (see Chapter 7).

(b) If $A$ is square and inconsistent, then the MATLAB command A\b will produce a warning that $A$ is singular or nearly singular, but will not give a least-squares solution. One way to use MATLAB to find a least-squares solution for a square but inconsistent system is to set up and solve the normal equations.

(c) Whether $A$ is square or rectangular, the MATLAB command x = pinv(A)*b will give the minimum norm least-squares solution; the command pinv(A) generates the pseudoinverse $A^+$.

EXAMPLE 2   The following sample values from the function $z = f(x, y)$ were obtained from experimental observations:

$$f(1, 1) = -1.1 \qquad f(1, 2) = 0.9$$
$$f(2, 1) = \phantom{-}0.2 \qquad f(2, 2) = 2.0$$
$$f(3, 1) = \phantom{-}0.9 \qquad f(3, 2) = 3.1$$

We would like to approximate the surface $z = f(x, y)$ by a plane of the form $z = ax + by + c$. Use a least-squares criterion to choose the parameters $a$, $b$, and $c$.

**Solution**   The conditions implied by the experimental observations are

$$\begin{aligned} a + \phantom{2}b + c &= -1.1 \\ 2a + \phantom{2}b + c &= \phantom{-}0.2 \\ 3a + \phantom{2}b + c &= \phantom{-}0.9 \\ a + 2b + c &= \phantom{-}0.9 \\ 2a + 2b + c &= \phantom{-}2.0 \\ 3a + 2b + c &= \phantom{-}3.1. \end{aligned}$$

A least-squares solution,

$$a = 1.05, b = 2.00, c = -4.10,$$

to this overdetermined system $A\mathbf{x} = \mathbf{b}$ was found using MATLAB, see Fig. 3.31. Since MATLAB did not issue a rank deficient warning, we can assume that $A$ has full rank (rank equal to 3) and therefore that the least-squares solution is unique.

EXAMPLE 3   Find a least-squares solution to the equation $A\mathbf{x} = \mathbf{b}$ where

$$A = \begin{bmatrix} 1 & 1 & 2 \\ 1 & 2 & 3 \\ 1 & 3 & 4 \\ 1 & 4 & 5 \end{bmatrix}, \qquad \mathbf{b} = \begin{bmatrix} 1 \\ 2 \\ 1 \\ 2 \end{bmatrix}.$$

```
>>A=[1,1,1;2,1,1;3,1,1;1,2,1;2,2,1;3,2,1];
>>b=[-1.1,.2,.9,.9,2.,3.1]';
>>x=A\b

  x =

        1.0500
        2.0000
       -4.1000
```

*Figure 3.31*    The results of Example 2

*Solution*    The results are shown in Fig. 3.32(a). Note that MATLAB has issued a rank deficient warning and concluded that $A$ has rank 2. Because $A$ is not full rank, least-squares solutions to $A\mathbf{x} = \mathbf{b}$ are not unique. Since $A$ has rank 2, the MATLAB command A\b selects a solution with no more than 2 nonzero components, namely $\mathbf{x}_1 = [0.0, -0.8, 1.1]^T$.

As an alternative, we can use the pseudoinverse to calculate the minimum-norm least-squares solution (see Fig. 3.32(b)). As can be seen from Fig. 3.32(b), the MATLAB command pinv(A)*b has produced the least-squares solution $\mathbf{x}_2 = [0.6, -0.2, 0.4]^T$. A calculation shows that $\|\mathbf{x}_1\| = 1.2806$, while the minimum norm solution in Fig. 3.32(b) has $\|\mathbf{x}_2\| = 0.7483$.

Finally, to complete this example, we can find all possible least-squares solutions by solving the normal equations. We find, using the MATLAB command rref(B),

```
>>x=A\b

Warning: Rank deficient, rank = 2

x =

         0
   -0.8000
    1.1000
```

```
x=pinv(A)*b

  x =

         0.6000
        -0.2000
         0.4000
```

(a)                                          (b)

*Figure 3.32*    (a) Using the command A\b to find a least-squares solution for Example 3. (b) Using the pseudoinverse to find a least-squares solution for Example 3.

that the augmented matrix $B = [A^T A \mid A^T \mathbf{b}]$ is row equivalent to

$$\begin{bmatrix} 1 & 0 & 1 & 1 \\ 0 & 1 & 1 & .2 \\ 0 & 0 & 0 & 0 \end{bmatrix}.$$

Thus, the set of all least-squares solutions are found from $\mathbf{x} = [1 - x_3, 0.2 - x_3, x_3]^T = [1, 0.2, 0]^T + x_3[-1, -1, 1]^T.$ ◼

EXAMPLE 4 As a final example to illustrate how MATLAB treats inconsistent square systems, find a least-squares solution to $A\mathbf{x} = \mathbf{b}$ where

$$A = \begin{bmatrix} 2 & 3 & 5 \\ 1 & 0 & 3 \\ 3 & 3 & 8 \end{bmatrix}, \qquad \mathbf{b} = \begin{bmatrix} 1 \\ 1 \\ 1 \end{bmatrix}.$$

*Solution* The results are given in Fig. 3.33 where, for clarity, we used the rational format to display the calculations. As can be seen, the MATLAB command A\b results in a warning that $A$ may be ill conditioned and may have a solution vector with very large components.

Then, a least-squares solution is calculated using the pseudoinverse. The least-squares solution found is $\mathbf{x} = [2/39, -2/13, 8/39]^T$. ◼

```
>>A=[2,3,5;1,0,3;3,3,8];
>>b=[1,1,1]';
>>x=A\b

Warning: Matrix is close to singular or badly scaled.
        Results may be inaccurate. RCOND = 6.405133e-18

x =

-6755399441055744
750599937895082
2251799813685248

>>x=pinv(A)*b

x =

      2/39
     -2/13
      8/39
```

*Figure 3.33* The results from Example 4

## 3.9    EXERCISES

Exercises 1–16 refer to the following subspaces:

**a)** $W =$

$$\left\{ \mathbf{x}: \mathbf{x} = \begin{bmatrix} x_1 \\ x_2 \\ x_3 \end{bmatrix}, \quad x_1 - 2x_2 + x_3 = 0 \right\}$$

**b)** $W = \mathcal{R}(B), \quad B = \begin{bmatrix} 1 & 2 \\ 1 & 1 \\ 0 & 1 \end{bmatrix}$

**c)** $W = \mathcal{R}(B), \quad B = \begin{bmatrix} 1 & 2 & 4 \\ -1 & 0 & -2 \\ 1 & 1 & 3 \end{bmatrix}$

**d)** $W =$

$$\left\{ \mathbf{x}: \mathbf{x} = \begin{bmatrix} x_1 \\ x_2 \\ x_3 \end{bmatrix}, \quad \begin{matrix} x_1 + x_2 + x_3 = 0 \\ x_1 - x_2 - x_3 = 0 \end{matrix} \right\}$$

In Exercises 1–10, find a basis for the indicated subspace $W$. For the given vector $\mathbf{v}$, solve the normal equations (2) and determine the best approximation $\mathbf{w}^*$. Verify that $\mathbf{v} - \mathbf{w}^*$ is orthogonal to the basis vectors.

**1.** $W$ given by (a), $\mathbf{v} = [1, 2, 6]^T$

**2.** $W$ given by (a), $\mathbf{v} = [3, 0, 3]^T$

**3.** $W$ given by (a), $\mathbf{v} = [1, 1, 1]^T$

**4.** $W$ given by (b), $\mathbf{v} = [1, 1, 6]^T$

**5.** $W$ given by (b), $\mathbf{v} = [3, 3, 3]^T$

**6.** $W$ given by (b), $\mathbf{v} = [3, 0, 3]^T$

**7.** $W$ given by (c), $\mathbf{v} = [2, 0, 4]^T$

**8.** $W$ given by (c), $\mathbf{v} = [4, 0, -1]^T$

**9.** $W$ given by (d), $\mathbf{v} = [1, 3, 1]^T$

**10.** $W$ given by (d), $\mathbf{v} = [3, 4, 0]^T$

In Exercises 11–16, find an orthogonal basis for the indicated subspace $W$. Use Eq. (4) to determine the best approximation $\mathbf{w}^*$ for the given vector $\mathbf{v}$.

**11.** $W$ and $\mathbf{v}$ as in Exercise 1

**12.** $W$ and $\mathbf{v}$ as in Exercise 2

**13.** $W$ and $\mathbf{v}$ as in Exercise 4

**14.** $W$ and $\mathbf{v}$ as in Exercise 5

**15.** $W$ and $\mathbf{v}$ as in Exercise 7

**16.** $W$ and $\mathbf{v}$ as in Exercise 8

**17.** Prove Theorem 19.

## SUPPLEMENTARY EXERCISES

**1.** Let

$$W = \{\mathbf{x}: \mathbf{x} = \begin{bmatrix} x_1 \\ x_2 \end{bmatrix}, \quad x_1 x_2 = 0\}.$$

Verify that $W$ satisfies properties (s1) and (s3) of Theorem 2. Illustrate by example that $W$ does not satisfy (s2).

**2.** Let

$$W = \{\mathbf{x}: \mathbf{x} = \begin{bmatrix} x_1 \\ x_2 \end{bmatrix}, \quad x_1 \geq 0, \quad x_2 \geq 0\}.$$

Verify that $W$ satisfies properties (s1) and (s2) of Theorem 2. Illustrate by example that $W$ does not satisfy (s3).

**3.** Let

$$A = \begin{bmatrix} 2 & -1 & 1 \\ 1 & 4 & -1 \\ 2 & 2 & 1 \end{bmatrix}$$

and

$$W = \{\mathbf{x}: \mathbf{x} = \begin{bmatrix} x_1 \\ x_2 \\ x_3 \end{bmatrix}, \quad A\mathbf{x} = 3\mathbf{x}\}.$$

**a)** Show that $W$ is a subspace of $R^3$.

**b)** Find a basis for $W$ and determine $\dim(W)$.

**4.** If

$$S = \left\{ \begin{bmatrix} 1 \\ 1 \\ -2 \end{bmatrix}, \begin{bmatrix} 2 \\ 1 \\ 3 \end{bmatrix} \right\}$$

and

$$T = \left\{ \begin{bmatrix} 1 \\ 0 \\ 5 \end{bmatrix}, \begin{bmatrix} 0 \\ 1 \\ -7 \end{bmatrix}, \begin{bmatrix} 3 \\ 2 \\ 1 \end{bmatrix} \right\},$$

then show that $\text{Sp}(S) = \text{Sp}(T)$. [*Hint:* Obtain an algebraic specification for each of $\text{Sp}(S)$ and $\text{Sp}(T)$.]

**5.** Let

$$A = \begin{bmatrix} 1 & -1 & 2 & 3 \\ 2 & -2 & 5 & 4 \\ 1 & -1 & 0 & 7 \end{bmatrix}.$$

a) Reduce the matrix $A$ to echelon form, and determine the rank and the nullity of $A$.

b) Exhibit a basis for the row space of $A$.

c) Find a basis for the column space of $A$ (that is, for $\mathcal{R}(A)$) consisting of columns of $A$.

d) Use the answers obtained in parts b) and c) to exhibit bases for the row space and the column space of $A^T$.

e) Find a basis for $\mathcal{N}(A)$.

**6.** Let $S = \{\mathbf{v}_1, \mathbf{v}_2, \mathbf{v}_3\}$, where

$$\mathbf{v}_1 = \begin{bmatrix} 1 \\ -1 \\ 1 \end{bmatrix}, \quad \mathbf{v}_2 = \begin{bmatrix} 1 \\ 2 \\ -1 \end{bmatrix}, \quad \text{and}$$

$$\mathbf{v}_3 = \begin{bmatrix} 3 \\ 3 \\ -1 \end{bmatrix}.$$

a) Find a subset of $S$ that is a basis for $\text{Sp}(S)$.

b) Find a basis for $\text{Sp}(S)$ by setting $A = [\mathbf{v}_1, \mathbf{v}_2, \mathbf{v}_3]$ and reducing $A^T$ to echelon form.

c) Give an algebraic specification for $\text{Sp}(S)$, and use that specification to obtain a basis for $\text{Sp}(S)$.

**7.** Let $A$ be the $(m \times n)$ matrix defined by

$$A = \begin{bmatrix} n+1 & n+2 & \cdots & 2n-1 & 2n \\ 2n+1 & 2n+2 & \cdots & 3n-1 & 3n \\ \vdots & \vdots & & & \\ mn+1 & mn+2 & \cdots & (m+1)n-1 & (m+1)n \end{bmatrix}.$$

Find a basis for the row space of $A$, and determine the rank and the nullity of $A$.

**8.** In a)–c), use the given information to determine the nullity of $T$.

a) $T: R^3 \to R^2$ and the rank of $T$ is 2.

b) $T: R^3 \to R^3$ and the rank of $T$ is 2.

c) $T: R^3 \to R^3$ and the rank of $T$ is 3.

**9.** In a)–c), use the given information to determine the rank of $T$.

a) $T: R^3 \to R^2$ and the nullity of $T$ is 2.

b) $T: R^3 \to R^3$ and the nullity of $T$ is 1.

c) $T: R^2 \to R^3$ and the nullity of $T$ is 0.

**10.** Let $B = \{\mathbf{x}_1, \mathbf{x}_2\}$ be a basis for $R^2$, and let $T: R^2 \to R^2$ be a linear transformation such that

$$T(\mathbf{x}_1) = \begin{bmatrix} 1 \\ 1 \end{bmatrix} \quad \text{and} \quad T(\mathbf{x}_2) = \begin{bmatrix} 2 \\ -1 \end{bmatrix}.$$

If $\mathbf{e}_1 = \mathbf{x}_1 - 2\mathbf{x}_2$ and $\mathbf{e}_2 = 2\mathbf{x}_1 + \mathbf{x}_2$, where $\mathbf{e}_1$ and $\mathbf{e}_2$ are the unit vectors in $R^2$, then find the matrix of $T$.

**11.** Let

$$\mathbf{b} = \begin{bmatrix} a \\ b \end{bmatrix},$$

and suppose that $T: R^3 \to R^2$ is a linear transformation defined by $T(\mathbf{x}) = A\mathbf{x}$, where $A$ is a $(2 \times 3)$ matrix such that the augmented matrix $[A \mid \mathbf{b}]$ reduces to

$$\begin{bmatrix} 1 & 0 & 8 & -5a + 3b \\ 0 & 1 & -3 & 2a - b \end{bmatrix}.$$

a) Find vectors $\mathbf{x}_1$ and $\mathbf{x}_2$ in $R^3$ such that $T(\mathbf{x}_1) = \mathbf{e}_1$ and $T(\mathbf{x}_2) = \mathbf{e}_2$, where $\mathbf{e}_1$ and $\mathbf{e}_2$ are the unit vectors in $R^2$.

b) Exhibit a nonzero vector $\mathbf{x}_3$ in $R^3$ such that $\mathbf{x}_3$ is in $\mathcal{N}(T)$.

c) Show that $B = \{\mathbf{x}_1, \mathbf{x}_2, \mathbf{x}_3\}$ is a basis for $R^3$.

d) Express each of the unit vectors $\mathbf{e}_1, \mathbf{e}_2, \mathbf{e}_3$ of $R^3$ as a linear combination of the vectors in $B$. Now calculate $T(\mathbf{e}_i)$, $i = 1, 2, 3$, and determine the matrix $A$.

In Exercises 12–18, $\mathbf{b} = [a, b, c, d]^T$, $T: R^6 \to R^4$ is a linear transformation defined by $T(\mathbf{x}) = A\mathbf{x}$, and $A$ is a $(4 \times 6)$ matrix such that the augmented matrix $[A \mid \mathbf{b}]$ reduces to

$$\begin{bmatrix} 1 & 0 & 2 & 0 & -3 & 1 & \vline & 4a + b - 2c \\ 0 & 1 & -1 & 0 & 2 & 2 & \vline & 12a + 5b - 7c \\ 0 & 0 & 0 & 1 & -1 & -2 & \vline & -5a - 2b + 3c \\ 0 & 0 & 0 & 0 & 0 & 0 & \vline & -16a - 7b + 9c + d \end{bmatrix}.$$

**12.** Exhibit a basis for the row space of $A$, and determine the rank and the nullity of $A$.

**13.** Determine which of the following vectors are in $\mathcal{R}(T)$. Explain how you can tell.

$$\mathbf{w}_1 = \begin{bmatrix} 1 \\ -1 \\ 1 \\ 0 \end{bmatrix}, \quad \mathbf{w}_2 = \begin{bmatrix} 1 \\ 1 \\ 3 \\ 2 \end{bmatrix},$$

$$\mathbf{w}_3 = \begin{bmatrix} 2 \\ -2 \\ 1 \\ 9 \end{bmatrix}, \quad \mathbf{w}_4 = \begin{bmatrix} 2 \\ 1 \\ 4 \\ 3 \end{bmatrix}.$$

**14.** For each vector $\mathbf{w}_i$, $i = 1, 2, 3, 4$ listed in Exercise 13, if the system of equations $A\mathbf{x} = \mathbf{w}_i$ is consistent, then exhibit a solution.

**15.** For each vector $\mathbf{w}_i$, $i = 1, 2, 3, 4$ listed in Exercise 13, if $\mathbf{w}_i$ is in $\mathcal{R}(T)$, then find a vector $\mathbf{x}$ in $R^6$ such that $T(\mathbf{x}) = \mathbf{w}_i$.

**16.** Suppose that $A = [\mathbf{A}_1, \mathbf{A}_2, \mathbf{A}_3, \mathbf{A}_4, \mathbf{A}_5, \mathbf{A}_6]$.

**a)** For each vector $\mathbf{w}_i$, $i = 1, 2, 3, 4$, listed in Exercise 13, if $\mathbf{w}_i$ is in the column space of $A$, then express $\mathbf{w}_i$ as a linear combination of the columns of $A$.

**b)** Find a subset of $\{\mathbf{A}_1, \mathbf{A}_2, \mathbf{A}_3, \mathbf{A}_4, \mathbf{A}_5, \mathbf{A}_6\}$ that is a basis for the column space of $A$.

**c)** For each column, $\mathbf{A}_j$, of $A$ that does not appear in the basis obtained in part b), express $\mathbf{A}_j$ as a linear combination of the basis vectors.

**d)** Let $\mathbf{b} = [1, -2, 1, -7]^T$. Show that $\mathbf{b}$ is in the column space of $A$, and express $\mathbf{b}$ as a linear combination of the basis vectors found in part b).

**e)** If $\mathbf{x} = [2, 3, 1, -1, 1, 1]^T$, then express $A\mathbf{x}$ as a linear combination of the basis vectors found in part b).

**17. a)** Give an algebraic specification for $\mathcal{R}(T)$, and use that specification to determine a basis for $\mathcal{R}(T)$.

**b)** Show that $\mathbf{b} = [1, 2, 3, 3]^T$ is in $\mathcal{R}(T)$, and express $\mathbf{b}$ as a linear combination of the basis vectors found in part a).

**18. a)** Exhibit a basis for $\mathcal{N}(T)$.

**b)** Show that $\mathbf{x} = [6, 1, 1, -2, 2, -2]^T$ is in $\mathcal{N}(T)$, and express $\mathbf{x}$ as a linear combination of the basis vectors found in part a).

## CONCEPTUAL EXERCISES

In Exercises 1–12, answer true or false. Justify your answer by providing a counterexample if the statement is false or an outline of a proof if the statement is true.

**1.** If $W$ is a subspace of $R^n$ and $\mathbf{x}$ and $\mathbf{y}$ are vectors in $R^n$ such that $\mathbf{x} + \mathbf{y}$ is in $W$, then $\mathbf{x}$ is in $W$ and $\mathbf{y}$ is in $W$.

**2.** If $W$ is a subspace of $R^n$ and $a\mathbf{x}$ is in $W$, where $a$ is a nonzero scalar and $\mathbf{x}$ is in $R^n$, then $\mathbf{x}$ is in $W$.

**3.** If $S = \{\mathbf{x}_1, \ldots, \mathbf{x}_k\}$ is a subset of $R^n$ and $k \leq n$, then $S$ is a linearly independent set.

**4.** If $S = \{\mathbf{x}_1, \ldots, \mathbf{x}_k\}$ is a subset of $R^n$ and $k > n$, then $S$ is a linearly dependent set.

**5.** If $S = \{\mathbf{x}_1, \ldots, \mathbf{x}_k\}$ is a subset of $R^n$ and $k < n$, then $S$ is not a spanning set for $R^n$.

**6.** If $S = \{\mathbf{x}_1, \ldots, \mathbf{x}_k\}$ is a subset of $R^n$ and $k \geq n$, then $S$ is a spanning set for $R^n$.

**7.** If $S_1$ and $S_2$ are linearly independent subsets of $R^n$, then the set $S_1 \cup S_2$ is also linearly independent.

**8.** If $W$ is a subspace of $R^n$, then $W$ has exactly one basis.

9. If $W$ is a subspace of $R^n$, and $\dim(W) = k$, then $W$ contains exactly $k$ vectors.

10. If $B$ is a basis for $R^n$ and $W$ is a subspace of $R^n$, then some subset of $B$ is a basis for $W$.

11. If $W$ is a subspace of $R^n$, and $\dim(W) = n$, then $W = R^n$.

12. Let $W_1$ and $W_2$ be subspaces of $R^n$ with bases $B_1$ and $B_2$, respectively. Then $B_1 \cap B_2$ is a basis for $W_1 \cap W_2$.

In Exercises 13–23, give a brief answer.

13. Let $W$ be a subspace of $R^n$, and set $V = \{\mathbf{x}: \mathbf{x}$ is in $R^n$ but $\mathbf{x}$ is not in $W\}$. Determine if $V$ is a subspace of $R^n$.

14. Explain what is wrong with the following argument: Let $W$ be a subspace of $R^n$, and let $B = \{\mathbf{e}_1, \ldots, \mathbf{e}_n\}$ be the basis of $R^n$ consisting of the unit vectors. Since $B$ is linearly independent and since every vector $\mathbf{w}$ in $W$ can be written as a linear combination of the vectors in $B$, it follows that $B$ is a basis for $W$.

15. If $B = \{\mathbf{x}_1, \mathbf{x}_2, \mathbf{x}_3\}$ is a basis for $R^3$, show that $B' = \{\mathbf{x}_1, \mathbf{x}_1 + \mathbf{x}_2, \mathbf{x}_1 + \mathbf{x}_2 + \mathbf{x}_3\}$ is also a basis for $R^3$.

16. Let $W$ be a subspace of $R^n$, and let $S = \{\mathbf{w}_1, \ldots, \mathbf{w}_k\}$ be a linearly independent subset of $W$ such that $\{\mathbf{w}_1, \ldots, \mathbf{w}_k, \mathbf{w}\}$ is linearly dependent for every $\mathbf{w}$ in $W$. Prove that $S$ is a basis for $W$.

17. Let $\{\mathbf{u}_1, \ldots, \mathbf{u}_n\}$ be a linearly independent subset of $R^n$, and let $\mathbf{x}$ in $R^n$ be such that $\mathbf{u}_1^T \mathbf{x} = \cdots = \mathbf{u}_n^T \mathbf{x} = 0$. Show that $\mathbf{x} = \boldsymbol{\theta}$.

18. Let $\mathbf{u}$ be a nonzero vector in $R^n$, and let $W$ be the subset of $R^n$ defined by $W = \{\mathbf{x}: \mathbf{u}^T \mathbf{x} = 0\}$.

   a) Prove that $W$ is a subspace of $R^n$.

   b) Show that $\dim(W) = n - 1$.

   c) If $\boldsymbol{\theta} = \mathbf{w} + c\mathbf{u}$, where $\mathbf{w}$ is in $W$ and $c$ is a scalar, show that $\mathbf{w} = \boldsymbol{\theta}$ and $c = 0$. [*Hint:* Consider $\mathbf{u}^T(\mathbf{w} + c\mathbf{u})$.]

   d) If $\{\mathbf{w}_1, \ldots, \mathbf{w}_{n-1}\}$ is a basis for $W$, show that $\{\mathbf{w}_1, \ldots, \mathbf{w}_{n-1}, \mathbf{u}\}$ is a basis for $R^n$. [*Hint:* Suppose that $c_1\mathbf{w}_1 + \cdots + c_{n-1}\mathbf{w}_{n-1} + c\mathbf{u} = \boldsymbol{\theta}$.

Now set $\mathbf{w} = c_1\mathbf{w}_1 + \cdots + c_{n-1}\mathbf{w}_{n-1}$ and use part c).]

19. Let $V$ and $W$ be subspaces of $R^n$ such that $V \cap W = \{\boldsymbol{\theta}\}$ and $\dim(V) + \dim(W) = n$.

   a) If $\mathbf{v} + \mathbf{w} = \boldsymbol{\theta}$, where $\mathbf{v}$ is in $V$ and $\mathbf{w}$ is in $W$, show that $\mathbf{v} = \boldsymbol{\theta}$ and $\mathbf{w} = \boldsymbol{\theta}$.

   b) If $B_1$ is a basis for $V$ and $B_2$ is a basis for $W$, show that $B_1 \cup B_2$ is a basis for $R^n$. [*Hint:* Use part a) to show that $B_1 \cup B_2$ is linearly independent.]

   c) If $\mathbf{x}$ is in $R^n$, show that $\mathbf{x}$ can be written in the form $\mathbf{x} = \mathbf{v} + \mathbf{w}$, where $\mathbf{v}$ is in $V$ and $\mathbf{w}$ is in $W$. [*Hint:* First note that $\mathbf{x}$ can be written as a linear combination of the vectors in $B_1 \cup B_2$.]

   d) Show that the representation obtained in part c) is unique; that is, if $\mathbf{x} = \mathbf{v}_1 + \mathbf{w}_1$, where $\mathbf{v}_1$ is in $V$ and $\mathbf{w}_1$ is in $W$, then $\mathbf{v} = \mathbf{v}_1$ and $\mathbf{w} = \mathbf{w}_1$.

20. A linear transformation $T: R^n \to R^n$ is **onto** provided that $\mathcal{R}(T) = R^n$. Prove each of the following.

   a) If the rank of $T$ is $n$, then $T$ is onto.

   b) If the nullity of $T$ is zero, then $T$ is onto.

   c) If $T$ is onto, then the rank of $T$ is $n$ and the nullity of $T$ is zero.

21. If $T: R^n \to R^m$ is a linear transformation, then show that $T(\boldsymbol{\theta}_n) = \boldsymbol{\theta}_m$, where $\boldsymbol{\theta}_n$ and $\boldsymbol{\theta}_m$ are the zero vectors in $R^n$ and $R^m$, respectively.

22. Let $T: R^n \to R^m$ be a linear transformation, and suppose that $S = \{\mathbf{x}_1, \ldots, \mathbf{x}_k\}$ is a subset of $R^n$ such that $\{T(\mathbf{x}_1), \ldots, T(\mathbf{x}_k)\}$ is a linearly independent subset of $R^m$. Show that the set $S$ is linearly independent.

23. Let $T: R^n \to R^m$ be a linear transformation with nullity zero. If $S = \{\mathbf{x}_1, \ldots, \mathbf{x}_k\}$ is a linearly independent subset of $R^n$, then show that $\{T(\mathbf{x}_1), \ldots, T(\mathbf{x}_k)\}$ is a linearly independent subset of $R^m$.

## MATLAB EXERCISES

A continuing problem for university administrations is managing admissions so that the freshman class entering in the fall is neither too large nor too small. As you know, most high school seniors apply simultaneously for admission to several different universities. Therefore, a university must accept more applicants than it can handle in order to compensate for the expected number who decline an offer of admission.

Least-squares fits to historical data is often used for forecasting, whether it be forecasting university enrollments, or for business applications such as inventory control, or for technical applications such as modeling drag based on wind-tunnel data. In this exercise, we use a linear least-squares fit to model enrollment data.

1. **Forecasting enrollments**   The following enrollment data is from Virginia Tech. It lists the total number of students, both undergraduate and graduate.

### Total enrollment at Virginia Tech, 1979–1996

| Year | Number | Year | Number | Year | Number |
|------|--------|------|--------|------|--------|
| 1979 | 20414  | 1985 | 22044  | 1991 | 23912  |
| 1980 | 21071  | 1986 | 22345  | 1992 | 23637  |
| 1981 | 21586  | 1987 | 22702  | 1993 | 23865  |
| 1982 | 21510  | 1988 | 22361  | 1994 | 23873  |
| 1983 | 21356  | 1989 | 22922  | 1995 | 23674  |
| 1984 | 22454  | 1990 | 23365  | 1996 | 24812  |

a) To get a feeling for the data, enter the numbers of students in a vector called TOTAL. Then, issue the MATLAB command plot(TOTAL,'o'). This command will give a scatterplot of the sixteen data points. If you want the years listed on the horizontal axis, you can define the vector YEAR with the command YEAR = 1979:1996 and then use the plot command plot(YEAR, TOTAL,'o'). Note that the scatterplot indicates a general trend of increasing enrollments, but with enrollments that decrease from time to time.

b) Because it is such a common but important problem, MATLAB has commands that can be used to generate best least-squares polynomial approximations. In particular, given data vectors X and Y, the command A = polyfit(X, Y, n) gives the vector of coefficients for the best least-squares polynomial of degree $n$ to the data. Given a vector of evaluation points T, the command POFT = polyval(A, T) will evaluate (at each point of T) the polynomial having a vector of coefficients given by A. Use the polyfit command A = polyfit(YEAR,TOTAL,1) to generate the coefficients for a linear fit of the data graphed in part a). Issue the hold command to hold the graph from part a). Generate the vector Y from Y=polyval(A,YEAR) and note that Y is the vector of values of the linear fit. Issue the command plot(YEAR,Y) to superimpose the graph of the linear fit on the scatterplot from part a).

c) In order to gain a feeling for how well the linear fit works as a forecasting tool, imagine that you do not know the enrollments for 1996 and 1995. Calculate the linear fit for the smaller set of data, the years 1979–1994, a set of 16 points. How well does the linear fit over these sixteen points predict the actual enrollment numbers for 1995 and 1996?

**d)** Use the linear fit calculated in part b) to estimate the year when enrollment can be expected to reach 30,000 and the year when enrollment should reach 35,000.

How does a computer evaluate functions such as $y = \cos x$ or $y = e^x$? Exercises 2–5 illustrate how mathematical functions such as $y = \tan x$ are evaluated on a computer or calculator. By way of introduction, note that the only operations a computer can actually perform are addition, subtraction, multiplication, and division. A computer cannot actually evaluate functions such as $y = \sqrt{x}$ or $y = \sin x$; instead, whenever a number such as $y = \sqrt{2.7}$ or $y = \sin 2.7$ is requested, the computer executes an algorithm that yields an *approximation* of the requested number. We now consider some computer algorithms for approximating mathematical functions.

**2.** We begin by formulating a method for estimating the function $y = \cos x$. Recall that $y = \cos x$ is periodic with period $2\pi$. Therefore, if we can find a polynomial $y = g(x)$ that is a good approximation when $x$ is $[-\pi, \pi]$, then we can also use it to approximate $y = \cos a$ for any real number $a$. To illustrate this point, consider the value $a = 17.3$ and note that $5\pi < 17.3 < 7\pi$. Now, let $x = 17.3 - 6\pi$ and note:

$$x = 17.3 - 6\pi \text{ is in the interval } [-\pi, \pi]. \tag{1}$$

$$\cos 17.3 = \cos(17.3 - 6\pi) = \cos x \approx g(x). \tag{2}$$

In general, if $a$ is any real number, then we can always locate $a$ between two successive odd multiples of $\pi$, $(2k-1)\pi \le a \le (2k+1)\pi$. Having located $a$, we see that $x = a - 2k\pi$ is in the interval $[-\pi, \pi]$ and therefore we have a good approximation for the value $\cos(a - 2k\pi)$, namely $g(a - 2k\pi)$. But, because of periodicity, $\cos(a - 2k\pi) = \cos a$, and so $g(a - 2k\pi)$ is also a good approximation for $\cos a$.

In light of the preceding observations, we turn our attention to the problem of approximating $y = \cos x$, for $x$ in the interval $[-\pi, \pi]$. First, note that the approximation interval can be further reduced from $[-\pi, \pi]$ to $[0, \pi/2]$. In particular, if we have an approximation to $y = \cos x$ that is good in $[0, \pi/2]$, then we can use it to give a good approximation in $[-\pi, \pi]$. We ask you to establish this fact in part a).

**a)** Suppose $y = g(x)$ is a good approximation to $y = \cos x$ whenever $x$ is in the interval $[0, \pi/2]$. Now, let $a$ be in the interval $[\pi/2, \pi]$. Use inequalities to show that $\pi - a$ is in the interval $[0, \pi/2]$. Next, use trigonometric identities to show that $\cos a = -\cos(\pi - a)$. Thus, for $a$ in $[\pi/2, \pi]$, we can use the approximation:

$$\cos a = -\cos(\pi - a) \approx -g(\pi - a).$$

Finally, since $\cos -x = \cos x$, the approximation $\cos x \approx g(x)$ can be extended to the interval $[-\pi, \pi]$.

**b)** In part a) we saw that if we had an approximation for $y = \cos x$ that is a good one in $[0, \pi/2]$, then we could use it to approximate $y = \cos a$ for any real value $a$. In this part, we see how a least-squares approximation $y = g(x)$ will serve as a good way to estimate $y = \cos x$ in $[0, \pi/2]$.

If we want to generate a least-squares approximation to $y = \cos x$, we need a collection of data points $(x_i, \cos x_i)$, $i = 1, 2, \ldots, m$. Given these $m$ data points, we can choose $y = g(x)$ to be the best least-squares polynomial approximation of degree $n$ for the data. In order to carry out this project, however, we need to select appropriate values for both $m$ and $n$. There is a rule of thumb that is well known among people who need to analyze data:

*The degree of the least-squares fit should be about half the number of data points.*

So, when we have $m = 10$ data points, we might guess that a polynomial of degree $n = 5$ will provide a reasonable least-squares fit. (By increasing the degree of the fitting polynomial, we can drive the error at the data points to zero; in fact, when $n = m - 1$, the fitting polynomial becomes an *interpolating polynomial*, matching the data points exactly. However, the graph of a high-degree interpolating polynomial often oscillates wildly and leads to a poor approximation between the data points. This deficiency of interpolating polynomials is one of the main reasons for using least-squares fits—we are looking for an approximation that behaves smoothly over the entire interval and the choice $n \approx m/2$ seems to work well in practice. In a later MATLAB exercise (see Chapter 4) we will explore some of the problems associated with polynomial interpolation.)

So, for $m = 10$, 12, 14, 16, 18, and 20, let us choose $y = g(x)$ to be the least-squares polynomial approximation of degree $n = 5, 6, 7, 8, 9$, and 10 respectively. As data values $x_i$, let us choose $m$ points equally spaced in $[0, \pi/2]$. We also need a measure of goodness for the approximation $\cos x \approx g(x)$. Let $t_1, t_2, \ldots, t_{100}$ denote 100 points, equally spaced in $[0, \pi/2]$ and let $D$ denote the maximum value of $|\cos t_i - g(t_i)|$, $i = 1, 2, \ldots, 100$. The size of $D$ will serve as a measure of how well $g(x)$ approximates $\cos x$.

For each value of $m$, find the least-squares polynomial approximation of degree $n$ and list the coefficients of the polynomial, using long format. Next, calculate the number $D$ defined in the previous paragraph. Finally, list in column form and in long format, the 100 values $(\cos t_i, g(t_i))$. Write a brief report summarizing your conclusions.

*Note:* MATLAB provides a number of computational tools (see Appendix A) that make it very easy to carry out the investigations in Exercise 1. In particular, the command `linspace` generates vectors with equally-spaced components (the data values $x_i$ and $t_i$). If $X$ denotes the vector of data values $x_i$, then the command $Y$ = `cos(X)` generates a vector of data values $x_i$, $y_i = \cos x_i$. In MATLAB, the number $\pi$ can be entered by typing `pi`. Recall from part b) of Exercise 1 that the MATLAB function *polyfit* will calculate the coefficients for a best least-squares approximation and the function *polyval* will evaluate the approximation at a given set of points. Finally, to calculate the largest entry in absolute value of a vector **v**, use the command `maximum(abs(v))`.

*Note:* Exercise 1 illustrates the basic ideas underlying computer evaluation of mathematical functions. For obvious competitive reasons, computer and calculator manufacturers generally will not reveal the details of how their particular machine evaluates mathematical functions. If you are interested in knowing more about this topic, you might consult the *Computer Evaluation of Mathematical Functions* by C. T. Fike. In addition, the now outdated line of IBM 360 and 370 mainframe computers provided a manual giving the exact description of how each FORTRAN command was implemented by their compiler (for instance, the FORTRAN command $y$ = `sqrt`($\alpha$) was executed by carrying out two steps of Newton's method for the equation $x^2 = \alpha$, starting with an initial guess generated from the value $\alpha$).

3. If you enjoy programming, write a MATLAB function that calculates $y = \cos x$ for any real input value $x$. You could draw on the ideas in Exercise 1.

4. Repeat Exercise 1 for the function $y = e^x$. Consider choosing a least-squares polynomial approximation $y = g(x)$ that is good on the interval $[0, 1]$ and then using the fact that $e^{a+b} = e^a e^b$. For example, suppose $x = 4.19$. You could approximate $e^{4.19}$ as follows:

$$e^{4.19} = e^4 e^{0.19} \approx e^4 g(0.19).$$

For the preceding approximation, we would have the constant $e$ precalculated and stored. Then, the evaluation of $e^4$ just requires multiplication.

**5.** Repeat Exercise 1 for the function $y = \tan x$. This time, a polynomial approximation will not be effective since the tangent has vertical asymptotes at $x = -\pi/2$ and $x = \pi/2$ and polynomial functions cannot imitate such behavior. For functions having either vertical or horizontal asymptotes, you can try approximating by a ***rational function*** (that is, by a quotient of polynomials).

In particular, let $y = f(x)$ denote the function that we wish to approximate. A rational function approximation for $f$ will typically take the following form:

$$f(x) \approx \frac{a_0 + a_1 x + \cdots + a_m x^m}{b_0 + b_1 x + \cdots + b_n x^n}.$$

The preceding approximation actually has $m + n + 1$ parameters because we can divide numerator and denominator by a constant. For example, we can assume that $b_0 = 1$ if we want an approximation that is valid for $x = 0$.

An example should clarify the ideas. Suppose for $0 \le x < \pi/2$, we want to approximate $y = \tan x$ by a rational function of the form

$$g(x) = \frac{a_0 + a_1 x + a_2 x^2}{1 + b_1 x + b_2 x^2}.$$

Since $g$ is a five parameter function, we will use a least-squares criterion involving ten data values to determine $a_0$, $a_1$, $a_2$, $b_1$, and $b_2$. Since we want $g(x)$ to approximate $\tan x$, the ten data values will be $y_i = \tan x_i$ for $i = 1, 2, \ldots, 10$. In particular, the ten conditions $y_i = g(x_i)$ lead to the system:

$$y_1(1 + b_1 x_1 + b_2 x_1^2) = a_0 + a_1 x_1 + a_2 x_1^2$$
$$y_2(1 + b_1 x_2 + b_2 x_2^2) = a_0 + a_1 x_2 + a_2 x_2^2$$
$$\vdots$$
$$y_{10}(1 + b_1 x_{10} + b_2 x_{10}^2) = a_0 + a_1 x_{10} + a_2 x_{10}^2$$

In matrix terms, this system is

$$\begin{bmatrix} 1 & x_1 & x_1^2 & -x_1 y_1 & -x_1^2 y_1 \\ 1 & x_2 & x_2^2 & -x_2 y_2 & -x_2^2 y_2 \\ \vdots & & & & \vdots \\ 1 & x_{10} & x_{10}^2 & -x_{10} y_{10} & -x_{10}^2 y_{10} \end{bmatrix} \begin{bmatrix} a_0 \\ a_1 \\ a_2 \\ b_1 \\ b_2 \end{bmatrix} = \begin{bmatrix} y_1 \\ y_2 \\ \vdots \\ y_{10} \end{bmatrix}.$$

As in Exercise 1, try various choices for $m$ and $n$ until you obtain a good approximation $g(x)$ for $\tan x$. Since the tangent function is odd, you might want to select $m$ to be an odd integer and $n$ to be an even integer.

There are other ways you might think of to approximate $y = \tan x$. For instance, if you have separate polynomial approximations for $y = \sin x$ and $y = \cos x$, then it also makes sense to use the quotient of these two approximations; you will find, however, that the choice of a rational function determined as above will be better.

# THE EIGENVALUE
# PROBLEM

An understanding of the eigenvalue problem requires several results about determinants.
We review the necessary results in Section 4.2.

Readers familiar with determinants may omit Sections 4.2 and 4.3 with no loss of continuity.

A thorough treatment of determinants is given in Chapter 6. Chapter 6 is designed so that it can
be covered now (before eigenvalues) or later (after eigenvalues).

OVERVIEW        As we shall see, the eigenvalue problem is of great practical importance in mathematics
and applications. In Section 4.1 we introduce the eigenvalue problem for the special case
of $(2 \times 2)$ matrices; this special case can be handled using ideas developed in Chapter 1.
In Section 4.4 we move on to the general case, the eigenvalue problem for $(n \times n)$
matrices. The general case requires several results from determinant theory, and these
are summarized in Section 4.2. If you are familiar with these results, you can proceed
directly to the general $(n \times n)$ case in Section 4.4.

If you have time and if you want a thorough discussion of determinants, you might
want to cover Chapter 6 (Determinants) before Chapter 4 (The Eigenvalue Problem).
Chapters 4 and 6 are independent, and they are designed to be read in any order.

# THE EIGENVALUE PROBLEM FOR (2 × 2) MATRICES

The *eigenvalue problem*, the topic of this chapter, is a problem of considerable theoretical interest and wide-ranging application. For instance, applications found in Sections 4.8 and 5.10 and Chapter 7 include procedures for:

(a)  solving systems of differential equations;

(b)  analyzing population growth models;

(c)  calculating powers of matrices;

(d)  diagonalizing linear transformations; and

(e)  simplifying and describing the graphs of quadratic forms in two and three variables.

The eigenvalue problem is formulated as follows.

---

**The Eigenvalue Problem**

For an $(n \times n)$ matrix $A$, find all scalars $\lambda$ such that the equation

$$A\mathbf{x} = \lambda\mathbf{x} \tag{1}$$

has a nonzero solution, $\mathbf{x}$. Such a scalar $\lambda$ is called an *eigenvalue* of $A$, and any nonzero $(n \times 1)$ vector $\mathbf{x}$ satisfying Eq. (1) is called an *eigenvector* corresponding to $\lambda$.

---

Let $\mathbf{x}$ be an eigenvector of $A$ corresponding to an eigenvalue $\lambda$. Then the vector $A\mathbf{x}$ is a scalar multiple of $\mathbf{x}$ (see Eq. (1)). Represented as geometric vectors, $\mathbf{x}$ and $A\mathbf{x}$ have the same direction if $\lambda$ is positive and the opposite direction if $\lambda$ is negative (see Fig. 4.1).

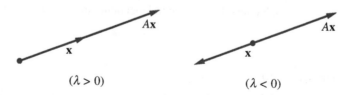

$(\lambda > 0)$ $\qquad\qquad\qquad$ $(\lambda < 0)$

*Figure 4.1*    Let $A\mathbf{x} = \lambda\mathbf{x}$, where $\mathbf{x}$ is a nonzero vector. Then $\mathbf{x}$ and $A\mathbf{x}$ are parallel vectors.

Now, we can rewrite Eq. (1) as

$$A\mathbf{x} - \lambda\mathbf{x} = \boldsymbol{\theta},$$

or

$$(A - \lambda I)\mathbf{x} = \boldsymbol{\theta}, \quad \mathbf{x} \neq \boldsymbol{\theta}, \tag{2}$$

where $I$ is the $(n \times n)$ identity matrix. If Eq. (2) is to have nonzero solutions, then $\lambda$ must be chosen so that the $(n \times n)$ matrix $A - \lambda I$ is singular. Therefore, the eigenvalue problem consists of two parts:

**1.** Find all scalars $\lambda$ such that $A - \lambda I$ is singular.

**2.** Given a scalar $\lambda$ such that $A - \lambda I$ is singular, find all nonzero vectors $\mathbf{x}$ such that $(A - \lambda I)\mathbf{x} = \boldsymbol{\theta}$.

If we know an eigenvalue of $A$, then the variable-elimination techniques described in Chapter 1 provide an efficient way to find the eigenvectors. The new feature of the eigenvalue problem is in part 1, determining all scalars $\lambda$ such that the matrix $A - \lambda I$ is singular. In the next subsection, we discuss how such values $\lambda$ are found.

## Eigenvalues for (2 × 2) Matrices

Before discussing how the eigenvalue problem is solved for a general $(n \times n)$ matrix $A$, we first consider the special case where $A$ is a $(2 \times 2)$ matrix. In particular, suppose we want to solve the eigenvalue problem for a matrix $A$ of the form

$$A = \begin{bmatrix} a & b \\ c & d \end{bmatrix}.$$

As we noted above, the first step is to find all scalars $\lambda$ such that $A - \lambda I$ is singular. The matrix $A - \lambda I$ is given by

$$A - \lambda I = \begin{bmatrix} a & b \\ c & d \end{bmatrix} - \begin{bmatrix} \lambda & 0 \\ 0 & \lambda \end{bmatrix},$$

or

$$A - \lambda I = \begin{bmatrix} a - \lambda & b \\ c & d - \lambda \end{bmatrix}.$$

Next we recall (see Exercise 68 in Section 1.9) that a $(2 \times 2)$ matrix is singular if and only if the product of the diagonal entries is equal to the product of the off-diagonal entries. That is, if $B$ is the $(2 \times 2)$ matrix

$$B = \begin{bmatrix} r & s \\ t & u \end{bmatrix}, \tag{3a}$$

then

$$B \text{ is singular} \Leftrightarrow ru - st = 0. \tag{3b}$$

If we apply the result in (3b) to the matrix $A - \lambda I$, it follows that $A - \lambda I$ is singular if and only if $\lambda$ is a value such that

$$(a - \lambda)(d - \lambda) - bc = 0. \tag{4}$$

Expanding the equation for $\lambda$ given above, we obtain the following condition on $\lambda$:

$$\lambda^2 - (a + d)\lambda + (ad - bc) = 0.$$

Equivalently, $A - \lambda I$ is singular if and only if $\lambda$ is a root of the polynomial equation

$$t^2 - (a+d)t + (ad - bc) = 0. \tag{5}$$

An example will serve to illustrate this idea.

**EXAMPLE 1**  Find all scalars $\lambda$ such that $A - \lambda I$ is singular, where

$$A = \begin{bmatrix} 5 & -2 \\ 6 & -2 \end{bmatrix}.$$

*Solution*  The matrix $A - \lambda I$ has the form

$$A - \lambda I = \begin{bmatrix} 5 - \lambda & -2 \\ 6 & -2 - \lambda \end{bmatrix}.$$

As in Eq. (4), $A - \lambda I$ is singular if and only if

$$-(5 - \lambda)(2 + \lambda) + 12 = 0,$$

or $\lambda^2 - 3\lambda + 2 = 0$. Since $\lambda^2 - 3\lambda + 2 = (\lambda - 2)(\lambda - 1)$, it follows that $A - \lambda I$ is singular if and only if $\lambda = 2$ or $\lambda = 1$.   ■

As a check for the calculations in Example 1, we list the matrices $A - \lambda I$ for $\lambda = 2$ and $\lambda = 1$:

$$A - 2I = \begin{bmatrix} 3 & -2 \\ 6 & -4 \end{bmatrix}, \qquad A - I = \begin{bmatrix} 4 & -2 \\ 6 & -3 \end{bmatrix}. \tag{6}$$

Note that these matrices, $A - 2I$ and $A - I$, are singular.

## Eigenvectors for (2 × 2) Matrices

As we observed earlier, the eigenvalue problem consists of two steps: First find the eigenvalues (the scalars $\lambda$ such that $A - \lambda I$ is singular). Next find the eigenvectors (the nonzero vectors $\mathbf{x}$ such that $(A - \lambda I)\mathbf{x} = \boldsymbol{\theta}$).

In the following example, we find the eigenvectors for matrix $A$ in Example 1.

**EXAMPLE 2**  For matrix $A$ in Example 1, determine the eigenvectors corresponding to $\lambda = 2$ and to $\lambda = 1$.

*Solution*  According to Eq. (2), the eigenvectors corresponding to $\lambda = 2$ are the nonzero solutions of $(A - 2I)\mathbf{x} = \boldsymbol{\theta}$. Thus, for the singular matrix $A - 2I$ listed in (6), we need to solve the homogeneous system

$$3x_1 - 2x_2 = 0$$
$$6x_1 - 4x_2 = 0.$$

The solution of this system is given by $3x_1 = 2x_2$, or $x_1 = (2/3)x_2$. Thus all the nonzero solutions of $(A - 2I)\mathbf{x} = \boldsymbol{\theta}$ are of the form

$$\mathbf{x} = \begin{bmatrix} (2/3)x_2 \\ x_2 \end{bmatrix} = x_2 \begin{bmatrix} 2/3 \\ 1 \end{bmatrix}, \quad x_2 \neq 0.$$

For $\lambda = 1$, the solutions of $(A - I)\mathbf{x} = \boldsymbol{\theta}$ are found by solving

$$4x_1 - 2x_2 = 0$$
$$6x_1 - 3x_2 = 0.$$

The nonzero solutions of this system are all of the form

$$\mathbf{x} = \begin{bmatrix} (1/2)x_2 \\ x_2 \end{bmatrix} = x_2 \begin{bmatrix} 1/2 \\ 1 \end{bmatrix}, \quad x_2 \neq 0.$$

The results of Examples 1 and 2 provide the solution to the eigenvalue problem for the matrix $A$, where $A$ is given by

$$A = \begin{bmatrix} 5 & -2 \\ 6 & -2 \end{bmatrix}.$$

In a summary form, the eigenvalues and corresponding eigenvectors are as listed below:

*Eigenvalue:* $\lambda = 2$; *Eigenvectors:* $\mathbf{x} = a \begin{bmatrix} 2/3 \\ 1 \end{bmatrix}$, $a \neq 0$.

*Eigenvalue:* $\lambda = 1$; *Eigenvectors:* $\mathbf{x} = a \begin{bmatrix} 1/2 \\ 1 \end{bmatrix}$, $a \neq 0$.

Note that for a given eigenvalue $\lambda$, there are infinitely many eigenvectors corresponding to $\lambda$. Since Eq. (2) is a homogeneous system, it follows that if $\mathbf{x}$ is an eigenvector corresponding to $\lambda$, then so is $a\mathbf{x}$ for any nonzero scalar $a$.

Finally, we make the following observation: If $A$ is a $(2 \times 2)$ matrix, then we have a simple test for determining those values $\lambda$ such that $A - \lambda I$ is singular. But if $A$ is an $(n \times n)$ matrix with $n > 2$, we do not (as yet) have a test for determining whether $A - \lambda I$ is singular. In the next section a singularity test based on the theory of determinants will be developed.

## 4.1 EXERCISES

In Exercises 1–12, find the eigenvalues and the eigenvectors for the given matrix.

1. $A = \begin{bmatrix} 1 & 0 \\ 2 & 3 \end{bmatrix}$

2. $A = \begin{bmatrix} 2 & 1 \\ 0 & -1 \end{bmatrix}$

3. $A = \begin{bmatrix} 2 & -1 \\ -1 & 2 \end{bmatrix}$

4. $A = \begin{bmatrix} 1 & -2 \\ 1 & 4 \end{bmatrix}$

5. $A = \begin{bmatrix} 2 & 1 \\ 1 & 2 \end{bmatrix}$

6. $A = \begin{bmatrix} 3 & -1 \\ 5 & -3 \end{bmatrix}$

7. $A = \begin{bmatrix} 1 & 0 \\ 2 & 1 \end{bmatrix}$

8. $A = \begin{bmatrix} 2 & 3 \\ 0 & 2 \end{bmatrix}$

9. $A = \begin{bmatrix} 2 & 2 \\ 3 & 3 \end{bmatrix}$

10. $A = \begin{bmatrix} 1 & 2 \\ 4 & 8 \end{bmatrix}$

11. $A = \begin{bmatrix} 1 & -1 \\ 1 & 3 \end{bmatrix}$

12. $A = \begin{bmatrix} 2 & -1 \\ 1 & 4 \end{bmatrix}$

Using Eq. (4), apply the singularity test to the matrices in Exercises 13–16. Show that there is no *real* scalar $\lambda$ such that $A - \lambda I$ is singular. [*Note:* Complex eigenvalues are discussed in Section 4.6.]

**13.** $A = \begin{bmatrix} -2 & -1 \\ 5 & 2 \end{bmatrix}$    **14.** $A = \begin{bmatrix} 3 & -2 \\ 5 & -3 \end{bmatrix}$

**15.** $A = \begin{bmatrix} 2 & -1 \\ 1 & 2 \end{bmatrix}$    **16.** $A = \begin{bmatrix} 1 & -1 \\ 1 & 1 \end{bmatrix}$

**17.** Consider the $(2 \times 2)$ *symmetric* matrix

$$A = \begin{bmatrix} a & b \\ b & d \end{bmatrix}.$$

Show that there are always real scalars $\lambda$ such that $A - \lambda I$ is singular. [*Hint:* Use the quadratic formula for the roots of Eq. (5).]

**18.** Consider the $(2 \times 2)$ matrix $A$ given by

$$A = \begin{bmatrix} a & b \\ -b & a \end{bmatrix}, \quad b \neq 0.$$

Show that there are no real scalars $\lambda$ such that $A - \lambda I$ is singular.

**19.** Let $A$ be a $(2 \times 2)$ matrix. Show that $A$ and $A^T$ have the same set of eigenvalues by considering the polynomial equation (5).

## 4.2    DETERMINANTS AND THE EIGENVALUE PROBLEM

Now we turn our attention to the eigenvalue problem for a general $(n \times n)$ matrix $A$. As we observed in the last section, the first task is to determine all scalars $\lambda$ such that the matrix $A - \lambda I$ given by

$$A - \lambda I = \begin{bmatrix} a - \lambda & b \\ c & d - \lambda \end{bmatrix},$$

we have a simple test for singularity:

$$A - \lambda I \text{ is singular} \Leftrightarrow (a - \lambda)(d - \lambda) - bc = 0.$$

For a general $(n \times n)$ matrix $A$, the theory of determinants can be used to discover those values $\lambda$ such that $A - \lambda I$ is singular.

Determinant theory has long intrigued mathematicians. The reader has probably learned how to calculate determinants, at least for $(2 \times 2)$ and $(3 \times 3)$ matrices. The purpose of this section is to briefly review those aspects of determinant theory that can be used in the eigenvalue problem. A formal development of determinants, including proofs, definitions, and the important properties of determinants, can be found in Chapter 6. In this section we present three basic results: an algorithm for evaluating determinants, a characterization of singular matrices in terms of determinants, and a result concerning determinants of matrix products.

### Determinants of $(2 \times 2)$ Matrices

We begin with the definition for the determinant of a $(2 \times 2)$ matrix.

DEFINITION 1    Let $A$ be the $(2 \times 2)$ matrix

$$A = \begin{bmatrix} a_{11} & a_{12} \\ a_{21} & a_{22} \end{bmatrix}.$$

The **determinant** of $A$, denoted by $\det(A)$, is the number

$$\det(A) = \begin{vmatrix} a_{11} & a_{12} \\ a_{21} & a_{22} \end{vmatrix} = a_{11}a_{22} - a_{21}a_{12}.$$

(*Note:* As Definition 1 indicates, the determinant of a $(2 \times 2)$ matrix is simply the difference of the products of the diagonal entries and the off-diagonal entries. Thus, in the context of the singularity test displayed in Eqs. (3a) and (3b) in the previous section, a $(2 \times 2)$ matrix $A$ is singular if and only if $\det(A) = 0$. Also note that we designate the determinant of $A$ by vertical bars when we wish to exhibit the entries of $A$.)

EXAMPLE 1    Find $\det(A)$, where

$$A = \begin{bmatrix} 2 & 4 \\ 1 & 3 \end{bmatrix}.$$

*Solution*    By Definition 1,

$$\det(A) = \begin{vmatrix} 2 & 4 \\ 1 & 3 \end{vmatrix} = 2 \cdot 3 - 1 \cdot 4 = 2.$$

EXAMPLE 2    Find $\det(A)$, where

$$A = \begin{bmatrix} 2 & 4 \\ 3 & 6 \end{bmatrix}.$$

DETERMINANTS   Determinants were studied and extensively used long before matrix algebra was developed. In 1693, the co-founder of calculus, Gottfried Wilhelm Leibniz (1646–1716), essentially used determinants to determine if a $(3 \times 3)$ linear system was consistent. (Similar work was done ten years earlier in Japan by Seki-Kowa.) Cramer's Rule (see Section 6.4), which uses determinants to solve linear systems, was developed in 1729 by Colin Maclaurin (1698–1746). Joseph Louis Lagrange (1736–1813) used determinants to express the area of a triangle and the volume of a tetrahedron.

It was Augustin-Louis Cauchy (1789–1857) who first coined the term "determinant" and in 1812 published a unification of the theory of determinants. In subsequent publications Cauchy used determinants in a variety of ways such as the development of the functional determinant commonly called the *Jacobian*.

*Solution*   By Definition 1,

$$\det(A) = \begin{vmatrix} 2 & 4 \\ 3 & 6 \end{vmatrix} = 2 \cdot 6 - 3 \cdot 4 = 0.$$

Again, Examples 1 and 2 are special instances that reaffirm our earlier observation about the singularity of a $(2 \times 2)$ matrix $A$. That is, $A$ is singular if and only if $\det(A) = 0$.

## Determinants of $(3 \times 3)$ Matrices

In Definition 1, we associated a number, $\det(A)$, with a $(2 \times 2)$ matrix $A$. This number assignment had the property that $\det(A) = 0$ if and only if $A$ is singular. We now develop a similar association of a number, $\det(A)$, with an $(n \times n)$ matrix $A$.

We first consider the case in which $n = 3$.

**DEFINITION 2**   Let $A$ be the $(3 \times 3)$ matrix

$$A = \begin{bmatrix} a_{11} & a_{12} & a_{13} \\ a_{21} & a_{22} & a_{23} \\ a_{31} & a_{32} & a_{33} \end{bmatrix}.$$

The **determinant of** $A$ is the number $\det(A)$, where

$$\det(A) = a_{11} \begin{vmatrix} a_{22} & a_{23} \\ a_{32} & a_{33} \end{vmatrix} - a_{12} \begin{vmatrix} a_{21} & a_{23} \\ a_{31} & a_{33} \end{vmatrix} + a_{13} \begin{vmatrix} a_{21} & a_{22} \\ a_{31} & a_{32} \end{vmatrix}. \qquad (1)$$

(*Note:* The determinant of a $(3 \times 3)$ matrix is defined to be the *weighted sum* of three $(2 \times 2)$ determinants. Similarly, the determinant of an $(n \times n)$ matrix will be defined as the weighted sum of $n$ determinants each of order $[(n-1) \times (n-1)]$.)

**EXAMPLE 3**   Find $\det(A)$, where

$$A = \begin{bmatrix} 1 & 2 & -1 \\ 5 & 3 & 4 \\ -2 & 0 & 1 \end{bmatrix}.$$

*Solution*   From Definition 2,

$$\det(A) = (1) \begin{vmatrix} 3 & 4 \\ 0 & 1 \end{vmatrix} - (2) \begin{vmatrix} 5 & 4 \\ -2 & 1 \end{vmatrix} + (-1) \begin{vmatrix} 5 & 3 \\ -2 & 0 \end{vmatrix}$$

$$= 1(3 \cdot 1 - 4 \cdot 0) - 2[5 \cdot 1 - 4(-2)] - 1[5 \cdot 0 - 3(-2)]$$

$$= 3 - 26 - 6 = -29.$$

## Minors and Cofactors

If we examine the three $(2 \times 2)$ determinants that appear in Eq. (1), we can see a pattern. In particular, the entries in the first $(2 \times 2)$ determinant can be obtained from the matrix $A$ by striking out the first row and column of $A$. Similarly, the entries in the second $(2 \times 2)$ determinant can be obtained by striking out the first row and second column of $A$. Finally, striking out the first row and third column yields the third $(2 \times 2)$ determinant.

The process of generating submatrices by striking out rows and columns is fundamental to the definition of a general $(n \times n)$ determinant. For a general $(n \times n)$ matrix $A$, we will use the notation $M_{rs}$ to designate the $[(n-1) \times (n-1)]$ matrix generated by removing row $r$ and column $s$ from $A$ (see Definition 3).

DEFINITION 3

Let $A = (a_{ij})$ be an $(n \times n)$ matrix. The $[(n-1) \times (n-1)]$ matrix that results from removing the $r$th row and $s$th column from $A$ is called a **minor matrix of $A$** and is designated by $M_{rs}$.

Example 4 illustrates the idea in Definition 3.

EXAMPLE 4    List the minor matrices $M_{21}$, $M_{23}$, $M_{42}$, and $M_{11}$ for the $(4 \times 4)$ matrix $A$ given by

$$
A = \begin{bmatrix} 1 & 2 & 1 & 3 \\ 0 & 1 & 2 & 0 \\ 4 & 2 & 0 & -1 \\ -2 & 3 & 1 & 1 \end{bmatrix}.
$$

*Solution*    The minor matrix $M_{21}$ is obtained from $A$ by removing the second row and the first column from $A$:

$$
M_{21} = \begin{bmatrix} 2 & 1 & 3 \\ 2 & 0 & -1 \\ 3 & 1 & 1 \end{bmatrix}.
$$

Similarly, we have

$$
M_{23} = \begin{bmatrix} 1 & 2 & 3 \\ 4 & 2 & -1 \\ -2 & 3 & 1 \end{bmatrix}, \qquad M_{42} = \begin{bmatrix} 1 & 1 & 3 \\ 0 & 2 & 0 \\ 4 & 0 & -1 \end{bmatrix}, \quad \text{and}
$$

$$
M_{11} = \begin{bmatrix} 1 & 2 & 0 \\ 2 & 0 & -1 \\ 3 & 1 & 1 \end{bmatrix}.
$$

Using the notation for a minor matrix, we can reinterpret the definition of a $(3 \times 3)$ determinant as follows: If $A = (a_{ij})$ is a $(3 \times 3)$ matrix, then from Eq. (1) and Definition 3,

$$\det(A) = a_{11} \det(M_{11}) - a_{12} \det(M_{12}) + a_{13} \det(M_{13}). \tag{2}$$

In determinant theory, the number $\det(M_{ij})$ is called a minor. Precisely, if $A = (a_{ij})$ is an $(n \times n)$ matrix, then the number $\det(M_{ij})$ is the **minor of the $(i, j)$th entry, $a_{ij}$.** In addition, the numbers $A_{ij}$ defined by

$$A_{ij} = (-1)^{i+j} \det(M_{ij})$$

are known as **cofactors** (or **signed minors**). Thus the expression for $\det(A)$ in Eq. (2) is known as a **cofactor expansion** corresponding to the first row.

It is natural, then, to wonder about other cofactor expansions of $A$ that parallel the one given in Eq. (2). For instance, what is the cofactor expansion of $A$ corresponding to the second row or even, perhaps, corresponding to the third column?

By analogy, a cofactor expansion along the second row would have the form

$$-a_{21} \det(M_{21}) + a_{22} \det(M_{22}) - a_{23} \det(M_{23}). \tag{3}$$

An expansion along the third column would take the form

$$a_{13} \det(M_{13}) - a_{23} \det(M_{23}) + a_{33} \det(M_{33}). \tag{4}$$

**EXAMPLE 5**   Let $A$ denote the $(3 \times 3)$ matrix from Example 3,

$$A = \begin{bmatrix} 1 & 2 & -1 \\ 5 & 3 & 4 \\ -2 & 0 & 1 \end{bmatrix}.$$

Calculate the second-row and third-column cofactor expansions defined by Eqs. (3) and (4), respectively.

**Solution**   According to the pattern in Eq. (3), a second-row expansion has the value

$$-5 \begin{vmatrix} 2 & -1 \\ 0 & 1 \end{vmatrix} + 3 \begin{vmatrix} 1 & -1 \\ -2 & 1 \end{vmatrix} - 4 \begin{vmatrix} 1 & 2 \\ -2 & 0 \end{vmatrix} = -10 - 3 - 16 = -29.$$

Using Eq. (4), we obtain a third-column expansion given by

$$- \begin{vmatrix} 5 & 3 \\ -2 & 0 \end{vmatrix} - 4 \begin{vmatrix} 1 & 2 \\ -2 & 0 \end{vmatrix} + \begin{vmatrix} 1 & 2 \\ 5 & 3 \end{vmatrix} = -6 - 16 - 7 = -29.$$

(*Note:* For the $(3 \times 3)$ matrix $A$ in Example 5, there are three possible row expansions and three possible column expansions. It can be shown that each of these six expansions yields exactly the same value, namely, $-29$. In general, as we observe in the next subsection, all row expansions and all column expansions produce the same value for any $(n \times n)$ matrix.)

## The Determinant of an $(n \times n)$ Matrix

We now give an inductive definition for det$(A)$, the determinant of an $(n \times n)$ matrix. That is, det$(A)$ is defined in terms of determinants of $[(n - 1) \times (n - 1)]$ matrices. The natural extension of Definition 2 is the following.

DEFINITION 4

Let $A = (a_{ij})$ be an $(n \times n)$ matrix. The ***determinant of*** $A$ is the number det$(A)$, where

$$\det(A) = a_{11} \det(M_{11}) - a_{12} \det(M_{12}) + \cdots + (-1)^{n+1} a_{1n} \det(M_{1n})$$

$$= \sum_{j=1}^{n} (-1)^{j+1} a_{1j} \det(M_{1j}). \tag{5}$$

The definition for det$(A)$ can be stated in a briefer form if we recall the notation $A_{ij}$ for a cofactor. That is, $A_{ij} = (-1)^{i+j} \det(M_{ij})$. Using the cofactor notation, we can rephrase Definition 4 as

$$\det(A) = \sum_{j=1}^{n} a_{1j} A_{1j}. \tag{6}$$

In the following example we see how Eq. (5) gives the determinant of a $(4 \times 4)$ matrix as the sum of four $(3 \times 3)$ determinants, where each $(3 \times 3)$ determinant is the sum of three $(2 \times 2)$ determinants.

EXAMPLE 6 Use Definition 4 to calculate the det$(A)$, where

$$A = \begin{bmatrix} 1 & 2 & -1 & 1 \\ -1 & 0 & 2 & -2 \\ 3 & -1 & 1 & 1 \\ 2 & 0 & -1 & 2 \end{bmatrix}.$$

*Solution*    The determinants of the minor matrices $M_{11}$, $M_{12}$, $M_{13}$, and $M_{14}$ are $(3 \times 3)$ determinants and are calculated as before with Definition 2:

$$\det(M_{11}) = \begin{vmatrix} 0 & 2 & -2 \\ -1 & 1 & 1 \\ 0 & -1 & 2 \end{vmatrix} = 0 \begin{vmatrix} 1 & 1 \\ -1 & 2 \end{vmatrix} - 2 \begin{vmatrix} -1 & 1 \\ 0 & 2 \end{vmatrix} + (-2) \begin{vmatrix} -1 & 1 \\ 0 & -1 \end{vmatrix} = 2$$

$$\det(M_{12}) = \begin{vmatrix} -1 & 2 & -2 \\ 3 & 1 & 1 \\ 2 & -1 & 2 \end{vmatrix} = (-1) \begin{vmatrix} 1 & 1 \\ -1 & 2 \end{vmatrix} - 2 \begin{vmatrix} 3 & 1 \\ 2 & 2 \end{vmatrix} + (-2) \begin{vmatrix} 3 & 1 \\ 2 & -1 \end{vmatrix} = -1$$

$$\det(M_{13}) = \begin{vmatrix} -1 & 0 & -2 \\ 3 & -1 & 1 \\ 2 & 0 & 2 \end{vmatrix} = (-1) \begin{vmatrix} -1 & 1 \\ 0 & 2 \end{vmatrix} - 0 \begin{vmatrix} 3 & 1 \\ 2 & 2 \end{vmatrix} + (-2) \begin{vmatrix} 3 & -1 \\ 2 & 0 \end{vmatrix} = -2$$

$$\det(M_{14}) = \begin{vmatrix} -1 & 0 & 2 \\ 3 & -1 & 1 \\ 2 & 0 & -1 \end{vmatrix} = (-1) \begin{vmatrix} -1 & 1 \\ 0 & -1 \end{vmatrix} - 0 \begin{vmatrix} 3 & 1 \\ 2 & -1 \end{vmatrix} + 2 \begin{vmatrix} 3 & -1 \\ 2 & 0 \end{vmatrix} = 3.$$

Hence, from Eq. (5) with $n = 4$,

$$\det(A) = 1(2) - 2(-1) + (-1)(-2) - 1(3) = 3.$$    ◼

**EXAMPLE 7**    For the $(4 \times 4)$ matrix $A$ in Example 6, calculate the second-column cofactor expansion given by

$$-a_{12} \det(M_{12}) + a_{22} \det(M_{22}) - a_{32} \det(M_{32}) + a_{42} \det(M_{42}).$$

*Solution*    From Example 6, $\det(M_{12}) = -1$. Since $a_{22} = 0$ and $a_{42} = 0$, we need not calculate $\det(M_{22})$ and $\det(M_{42})$. The only other value needed is $\det(M_{32})$, where

$$\det(M_{32}) = \begin{vmatrix} 1 & -1 & 1 \\ -1 & 2 & -2 \\ 2 & -1 & 2 \end{vmatrix} = 1 \begin{vmatrix} 2 & -2 \\ -1 & 2 \end{vmatrix} - (-1) \begin{vmatrix} -1 & -2 \\ 2 & 2 \end{vmatrix} + 1 \begin{vmatrix} -1 & 2 \\ 2 & -1 \end{vmatrix} = 1.$$

Thus the second-column expansion gives the value

$$-2(-1) + 0 \det(M_{22}) - (-1)(1) + 0 \det(M_{42}) = 3.$$    ◼

From Example 6, $\det(A) = 3$. From Example 7, a second-column expansion also produces the same value, 3. The next theorem states that a cofactor expansion along any row or any column always produces the same number, $\det(A)$. The expansions in the theorem are phrased in the same brief notation as in Eq. (6). The proof of Theorem 1 is given in Chapter 6.

**THEOREM 1**    Let $A = (a_{ij})$ be an $(n \times n)$ matrix with minor matrices $M_{ij}$ and cofactors $A_{ij} = (-1)^{i+j} \det(M_{ij})$. Then

$$\det(A) = \sum_{j=1}^{n} a_{ij} A_{ij} \quad (i\text{th-row expansion})$$

$$= \sum_{i=1}^{n} a_{ij} A_{ij} \quad (j\text{th-column expansion}) \quad \blacksquare$$

Because of Theorem 1, we can always find $\det(A)$ by choosing the row or column of $A$ with the most zeros for the cofactor expansion. (If $a_{ij} = 0$, then $a_{ij} A_{ij} = 0$, and we need not compute $A_{ij}$.) In the next section we consider how to use elementary row or column operations to create zeros and hence simplify determinant calculations.

## Determinants and Singular Matrices

Theorems 2 and 3, which follow, are fundamental to our study of eigenvalues. These theorems are stated here and their proofs are given in Chapter 6.

THEOREM 2  Let $A$ and $B$ be $(n \times n)$ matrices. Then

$$\det(AB) = \det(A) \det(B). \quad \blacksquare$$

The following example illustrates Theorem 2.

EXAMPLE 8  Calculate $\det(A)$, $\det(B)$, and $\det(AB)$ for the matrices

$$A = \begin{bmatrix} 1 & 2 \\ -1 & 1 \end{bmatrix} \quad \text{and} \quad B = \begin{bmatrix} 2 & 3 \\ 1 & -1 \end{bmatrix}.$$

**Solution**  The product, $AB$, is given by

$$AB = \begin{bmatrix} 4 & 1 \\ -1 & -4 \end{bmatrix}.$$

Clearly $\det(AB) = -15$. We also see that $\det(A) = 3$ and $\det(B) = -5$. Observe, for this special case, that $\det(A) \det(B) = \det(AB)$. $\quad \blacksquare$

To study the eigenvalue problem for an $(n \times n)$ matrix, we need a test for singularity. The following theorem shows that determinant theory provides a simple and elegant test.

THEOREM 3  Let $A$ be an $(n \times n)$ matrix. Then

$$A \text{ is singular if and only if } \det(A) = 0. \quad \blacksquare$$

Theorem 3 is already familiar for the case in which $A$ is a $(2 \times 2)$ matrix (recall Definition 1 and Examples 1 and 2). An outline for the proof of Theorem 3 is given in the next section. Finally, in Section 4.4 we will be able to use Theorem 3 to devise a procedure for solving the eigenvalue problem.

We conclude this brief introduction to determinants by observing that it is easy to calculate the determinant of a triangular matrix.

| | | THEOREM 4    Let $T = (t_{ij})$ be an $(n \times n)$ triangular matrix. Then

$$\det(T) = t_{11}t_{22}\ldots t_{nn}.$$ ◼

The proof of Theorem 4 is left to the exercises. The next example illustrates how a proof for Theorem 4 might be constructed.

| | | EXAMPLE 9    Use a cofactor expansion (as in Definition 4 or Theorem 1) to calculate $\det(T)$:

$$T = \begin{bmatrix} 2 & 1 & 3 & 7 \\ 0 & 4 & 8 & 1 \\ 0 & 0 & 1 & 5 \\ 0 & 0 & 0 & 3 \end{bmatrix}.$$

*Solution*    By Theorem 1, we can use a cofactor expansion along any row or column to calculate $\det(T)$. Because of the structure of $T$, an expansion along the first column or the fourth row will be easiest.

Expanding along the first column, we find

$$\det(T) = \begin{vmatrix} 2 & 1 & 3 & 7 \\ 0 & 4 & 8 & 1 \\ 0 & 0 & 1 & 5 \\ 0 & 0 & 0 & 3 \end{vmatrix} = 2 \begin{vmatrix} 4 & 8 & 1 \\ 0 & 1 & 5 \\ 0 & 0 & 3 \end{vmatrix}$$

$$= (2)(4) \begin{vmatrix} 1 & 5 \\ 0 & 3 \end{vmatrix} = 24.$$

This example provides a special case of Theorem 4. ◼

(*Note:* An easy corollary to Theorem 4 is the following: If $I$ is the $(n \times n)$ identity matrix, then $\det(I) = 1$. In the exercises that follow, some additional results are derived from the theorems in this section and from the fact that $\det(I) = 1$.)

## 4.2    EXERCISES

In Exercises 1–6, list the minor matrix $M_{ij}$, and calculate the cofactor $A_{ij} = (-1)^{i+j} \det(M_{ij})$ for the matrix $A$ given by

$$A = \begin{bmatrix} 2 & -1 & 3 & 1 \\ 4 & 1 & 3 & -1 \\ 6 & 2 & 4 & 1 \\ 2 & 2 & 0 & -2 \end{bmatrix} \qquad (7)$$

**1.** $M_{11}$    **2.** $M_{21}$    **3.** $M_{31}$

**4.** $M_{41}$    **5.** $M_{34}$    **6.** $M_{43}$

**7.** Use the results of Exercises 1–4 to calculate $\det(A)$ for the matrix $A$ given in (7).

In Exercises 8–19, calculate the determinant of the given matrix. Use Theorem 3 to state whether the matrix is singular or nonsingular.

**8.** $A = \begin{bmatrix} 2 & 1 \\ -1 & 2 \end{bmatrix}$    **9.** $A = \begin{bmatrix} 1 & -1 \\ -2 & 2 \end{bmatrix}$

**10.** $A = \begin{bmatrix} 2 & 3 \\ 4 & 6 \end{bmatrix}$    **11.** $A = \begin{bmatrix} 1 & 1 \\ 2 & 1 \end{bmatrix}$

**12.** $A = \begin{bmatrix} 1 & 2 & 4 \\ 2 & 3 & 7 \\ 4 & 2 & 10 \end{bmatrix}$    **13.** $A = \begin{bmatrix} 2 & -3 & 2 \\ -1 & -2 & 1 \\ 3 & 1 & -1 \end{bmatrix}$

**14.** $A = \begin{bmatrix} 1 & 2 & 1 \\ 0 & 3 & 2 \\ -1 & 1 & 1 \end{bmatrix}$    **15.** $A = \begin{bmatrix} 2 & 0 & 0 \\ 1 & 3 & 2 \\ 2 & 1 & 4 \end{bmatrix}$

**16.** $A = \begin{bmatrix} 2 & 0 & 0 \\ 3 & 1 & 0 \\ 2 & 4 & 2 \end{bmatrix}$    **17.** $A = \begin{bmatrix} 1 & 2 & 1 & 5 \\ 0 & 3 & 0 & 0 \\ 0 & 4 & 1 & 2 \\ 0 & 3 & 1 & 4 \end{bmatrix}$

**18.** $A = \begin{bmatrix} 0 & 1 & 0 & 0 \\ 0 & 0 & 1 & 0 \\ 1 & 0 & 0 & 0 \\ 0 & 0 & 0 & 1 \end{bmatrix}$

**19.** $A = \begin{bmatrix} 0 & 0 & 0 & 2 \\ 0 & 0 & 3 & 1 \\ 0 & 2 & 1 & 2 \\ 3 & 4 & 1 & 4 \end{bmatrix}$

**20.** Let $A = (a_{ij})$ be a given $(3 \times 3)$ matrix. Form the associated $(3 \times 5)$ matrix $B$ shown next:

$$B = \begin{bmatrix} a_{11} & a_{12} & a_{13} & a_{11} & a_{12} \\ a_{21} & a_{22} & a_{23} & a_{21} & a_{22} \\ a_{31} & a_{32} & a_{33} & a_{31} & a_{32} \end{bmatrix}$$

a) Subtract the sum of the three upward diagonal products from the sum of the three downward diagonal products and argue that your result is equal to det($A$).

b) Show, by example, that a similar basketweave algorithm cannot be used to calculate the determinant of a $(4 \times 4)$ matrix.

In Exercises 21 and 22, find all ordered pairs $(x, y)$ such that $A$ is singular.

**21.** $A = \begin{bmatrix} x & y & 1 \\ 2 & 3 & 1 \\ 0 & -1 & 1 \end{bmatrix}$    **22.** $A = \begin{bmatrix} x & 1 & 1 \\ 2 & 1 & 1 \\ 0 & -1 & y \end{bmatrix}$

**23.** Let $A = (a_{ij})$ be the $(n \times n)$ matrix specified thus: $a_{ij} = d$ for $i = j$ and $a_{ij} = 1$ for $i \neq j$. For $n = 2$, 3, and 4, show that

$$\det(A) = (d - 1)^{n-1}(d - 1 + n).$$

**24.** Let $A$ and $B$ be $(n \times n)$ matrices. Use Theorems 2 and 3 to give a quick proof of each of the following.

a) If either $A$ or $B$ is singular, then $AB$ is singular.

b) If $AB$ is singular, then either $A$ or $B$ is singular.

**25.** Suppose that $A$ is an $(n \times n)$ nonsingular matrix, and recall that $\det(I) = 1$, where $I$ is the $(n \times n)$ identity matrix. Show that $\det(A^{-1}) = 1/\det(A)$.

**26.** If $A$ and $B$ are $(n \times n)$ matrices, then usually $AB \neq BA$. Nonetheless, argue that always $\det(AB) = \det(BA)$.

In Exercises 27–30, use Theorem 2 and Exercise 25 to evaluate the given determinant, where $A$ and $B$ are $(n \times n)$ matrices with $\det(A) = 3$ and $\det(B) = 5$.

**27.** $\det(ABA^{-1})$    **28.** $\det(A^2 B)$

**29.** $\det(A^{-1}B^{-1}A^2)$    **30.** $\det(AB^{-1}A^{-1}B)$

**31. a)** Let $A$ be an $(n \times n)$ matrix. If $n = 3$, $\det(A)$ can be found by evaluating three $(2 \times 2)$ determinants. If $n = 4$, $\det(A)$ can be found by evaluating twelve $(2 \times 2)$ determinants. Give a formula, $H(n)$, for the number of $(2 \times 2)$ determinants necessary to find $\det(A)$ for an arbitrary $n$.

b) Suppose you can perform additions, subtractions, multiplications, and divisions each at a rate of one per second. How long does it take to evaluate $H(n)$ $(2 \times 2)$ determinants when $n = 2$, $n = 5$, and $n = 10$?

**32.** Let $U$ and $V$ be $(n \times n)$ upper-triangular matrices. Prove a special case of Theorem 2: $\det(UV) = \det(U)\det(V)$. [*Hint:* Use the definition for matrix multiplication to calculate the diagonal entries of the product $UV$, and then apply Theorem 4. You will also need to recall from Exercise 67 in Section 1.5 that $UV$ is an upper-triangular matrix.]

**33.** Let $V$ be an $(n \times n)$ triangular matrix. Use Theorem 4 to prove that $\det(V^T) = \det(V)$.

**34.** Let $T = (t_{ij})$ be an $(n \times n)$ upper-triangular matrix. Prove that $\det(T) = t_{11}t_{22}\ldots t_{nn}$. [*Hint:* Use mathematical induction, beginning with a $(2 \times 2)$ upper-triangular determinant.]

## ELEMENTARY OPERATIONS AND DETERMINANTS (OPTIONAL)*

We saw in Section 4.2 that having many zero entries in a matrix simplifies the calculation of its determinant. The ultimate case is given in Theorem 4. If $T = (t_{ij})$ is an $(n \times n)$ triangular matrix, then it is very easy to calculate $\det(T)$:

$$\det(T) = t_{11}t_{22} \ldots t_{nn}.$$

In Chapter 1, we used elementary row operations to create zero entries. We now consider these row operations (along with similar column operations) and describe their effect on the value of the determinant. For instance, consider the $(2 \times 2)$ matrices

$$A = \begin{bmatrix} 1 & 2 \\ 3 & 4 \end{bmatrix} \quad \text{and} \quad B = \begin{bmatrix} 3 & 4 \\ 1 & 2 \end{bmatrix}.$$

Clearly $B$ is the result of interchanging the first and second rows of $A$ (an elementary row operation). Also, we see that $\det(A) = -2$, whereas $\det(B) = 2$. This computation demonstrates that performing an elementary operation may change the value of the determinant. As we will see, however, it is possible to predict in advance the nature of any changes that might be produced by an elementary operation. For example, we will see that a row interchange always reverses the sign of the determinant.

Before studying the effects of elementary row operations on determinants, we consider the following theorem, which is an immediate consequence of Theorem 1.

 **THEOREM 5**    If $A$ is an $(n \times n)$ matrix, then

$$\det(A) = \det(A^T).$$

***Proof***    The proof is by induction, and we begin with the case $n = 2$. Let $A = (a_{ij})$ be a $(2 \times 2)$ matrix:

$$A = \begin{bmatrix} a_{11} & a_{12} \\ a_{21} & a_{22} \end{bmatrix}, \quad A^T = \begin{bmatrix} a_{11} & a_{21} \\ a_{12} & a_{22} \end{bmatrix}.$$

Hence it is clear that $\det(A) = \det(A^T)$ when $A$ is a $(2 \times 2)$ matrix.

The inductive step hinges on the following observation about minor matrices: Suppose that $B$ is a square matrix, and let $C = B^T$. Next, let $M_{rs}$ and $N_{rs}$ denote minor matrices of $B$ and $C$, respectively. Then these minor matrices are related by

$$N_{ij} = (M_{ji})^T. \tag{1}$$

(In words, the $ij$th minor matrix of $B^T$ is equal to the transpose of the $ji$th minor matrix of $B$.)

To proceed with the induction, suppose that Theorem 5 is valid for all $(k \times k)$ matrices, $2 \le k \le n - 1$. Let $A$ be an $(n \times n)$ matrix, where $n > 2$. Let $M_{rs}$ denote the

---

*The results in this section are not required for a study of the eigenvalue problem. They are included here for the convenience of the reader and because they follow naturally from definitions and theorems in the previous section. See Chapter 6 for proofs.

minor matrices of $A$, and let $N_{rs}$ denote the minor matrices of $A^T$. Consider an expansion of $\det(A)$ along the first row and an expansion of $\det(A^T)$ along the first column:

$$\det(A) = a_{11}\det(M_{11}) - a_{12}\det(M_{12}) + \cdots + (-1)^{n+1}a_{1n}\det(M_{1n})$$

$$\det(A^T) = a_{11}\det(N_{11}) - a_{12}\det(N_{21}) + \cdots + (-1)^{n+1}a_{1n}\det(N_{n1}).$$

(2)

(The expansion for $\det(A^T)$ in Eq. (2) incorporates the fact that the first-column entries for $A^T$ are the same as the first-row entries of $A$.)

By Eq. (1), the minor matrices $N_{j1}$ in Eq. (2) satisfy $N_{j1} = (M_{1j})^T$, $1 \leq j \leq n$. By the inductive hypotheses, $\det(M_{1j}^T) = \det(M_{1j})$, since $M_{1j}$ is a matrix of order $n-1$. Therefore, both expansions in Eq. (2) have the same value, showing that $\det(A^T) = \det(A)$. ◼

One valuable aspect of Theorem 5 is that it tells us an elementary column operation applied to a square matrix A will affect $\det(A)$ in precisely the same way as the corresponding elementary row operation.

## Effects of Elementary Operations

We first consider how the determinant changes when rows of a matrix are interchanged.

**THEOREM 6**  Let $A$ be an $(n \times n)$ matrix, and let $B$ be formed by interchanging any two rows (or columns) of $A$. Then

$$\det(B) = -\det(A).$$

***Proof***  First we consider the case where the two rows to be interchanged are adjacent, say, the $i$th and $(i+1)$st rows. Let $M_{ij}$, $1 \leq j \leq n$, be the minor matrices of $A$ from the $i$th row, and let $N_{i+1,j}$, $1 \leq j \leq n$, be the minor matrices of $B$ from the $(i+1)$st row. A bit of reflection will reveal that $N_{i+1,j} = M_{ij}$. Since $a_{i1}, a_{i2}, \ldots, a_{in}$ are the elements of the $(i+1)$st row of $B$, we have

$$\det(B) = \sum_{j=1}^{n}(-1)^{i+1+j}a_{ij}\det(N_{i+1,j})$$

$$= -\sum_{j=1}^{n}(-1)^{i+j}a_{ij}\det(N_{i+1,j})$$

$$= -\sum_{j=1}^{n}(-1)^{i+j}a_{ij}\det(M_{ij}), \quad \text{since } N_{i+1,j} = M_{ij}$$

$$= -\det(A).$$

Thus far we know that interchanging any two *adjacent* rows changes the sign of the determinant. Now suppose that $B$ is formed by interchanging the $i$th and $k$th rows of $A$, where $k \geq i+1$. The $i$th row can be moved to the $k$th row by $(k-i)$ successive interchanges of adjacent rows. The original $k$th row at this point is now the $(k-1)$st row. This row can be moved to the $i$th row by $(k-1-i)$ successive interchanges of adjacent rows. At this point all other rows are in their original positions. Hence, we have formed $B$ with $2k - 1 - 2i$ successive interchanges of adjacent rows. Thus,

$$\det(B) = (-1)^{(2k-1-2i)}\det(A) = -\det(A). \quad ◼$$

COROLLARY    If $A$ is an $(n \times n)$ matrix with two identical rows (columns), then $\det(A) = 0$. ▬

We leave the proof of the corollary as an exercise.

EXAMPLE 1    Find $\det(A)$, where

$$A = \begin{bmatrix} 0 & 0 & 0 & 4 \\ 0 & 0 & 3 & 2 \\ 0 & 1 & 2 & 5 \\ 2 & 3 & 1 & 3 \end{bmatrix}.$$

*Solution*    We could calculate $\det(A)$ by using a cofactor expansion, but we also see that we can rearrange the rows of $A$ to produce a triangular matrix.

Adopting the latter course of action, we have

$$\det(A) = \begin{vmatrix} 0 & 0 & 0 & 4 \\ 0 & 0 & 3 & 2 \\ 0 & 1 & 2 & 5 \\ 2 & 3 & 1 & 3 \end{vmatrix} = - \begin{vmatrix} 2 & 3 & 1 & 3 \\ 0 & 0 & 3 & 2 \\ 0 & 1 & 2 & 5 \\ 0 & 0 & 0 & 4 \end{vmatrix} = \begin{vmatrix} 2 & 3 & 1 & 3 \\ 0 & 1 & 2 & 5 \\ 0 & 0 & 3 & 2 \\ 0 & 0 & 0 & 4 \end{vmatrix} = 24. \quad ▬$$

Next we consider the effect of another elementary operation.

THEOREM 7    Suppose that $B$ is obtained from the $(n \times n)$ matrix $A$ by multiplying one row (or column) of $A$ by a nonzero scalar $c$ and leaving the other rows (or columns) unchanged. Then

$$\det(B) = c \det(A).$$

*Proof*    Suppose that $[ca_{i1}, ca_{i2}, \ldots, ca_{in}]$ is the $i$th row of $B$. Since the other rows of $B$ are unchanged from $A$, the minor matrices of $B$ from the $i$th row are the same as $M_{ij}$, the minor matrices of $A$ from the $i$th row. Using a cofactor expansion from the $i$th row of $B$ to calculate $\det(B)$ gives

$$\det(B) = \sum_{j=1}^{n} (ca_{ij})(-1)^{i+j} \det(M_{ij})$$

$$= c \sum_{j=1}^{n} a_{ij}(-1)^{i+j} \det(M_{ij})$$

$$= c \det(A). \quad ▬$$

As we see in the next theorem, the third elementary operation leaves the determinant unchanged. (*Note:* Theorem 8 is also valid when the word *column* is substituted for the word *row*.)

THEOREM 8    Let $A$ be an $(n \times n)$ matrix. Suppose that $B$ is the matrix obtained from $A$ by replacing the $i$th row of $A$ by the $i$th row of $A$ plus a constant multiple of the $k$th row of $A$, $k \neq i$. Then

$$\det(B) = \det(A).$$

***Proof***  Note that the $i$th row of $B$ has the form

$$[a_{i1} + ca_{k1}, a_{i2} + ca_{k2}, \ldots, a_{in} + ca_{kn}].$$

Since the other rows of $B$ are unchanged from $A$, the minor matrices taken with respect to the $i$th row of $B$ are the same as the minor matrices $M_{ij}$ of $A$.

Using a cofactor expansion of $\det(B)$ from the $i$th row, we have

$$\det(B) = \sum_{j=1}^{n} (a_{ij} + ca_{kj})(-1)^{i+j} \det(M_{ij})$$

$$= \sum_{j=1}^{n} a_{ij}(-1)^{i+j} \det(M_{ij}) + c \sum_{j=1}^{n} a_{kj}(-1)^{i+j} \det(M_{ij}) \qquad (3)$$

$$= \det(A) + c \sum_{j=1}^{n} a_{kj}(-1)^{i+j} \det(M_{ij}).$$

Theorem 8 will be proved if we can show that the last summation on the right-hand side of Eq. (3) has the value zero. In order to prove that the summation has the value zero, construct a matrix $Q$ by replacing the $i$th row of $A$ by the $k$th row of $A$. The matrix $Q$ so constructed has two identical rows (the $k$th row of $A$ appears both as the $k$th row and the $i$th row of $Q$). Therefore, by the corollary to Theorem 6, $\det(Q) = 0$. Next, expanding $\det(Q)$ along the $i$th row of $Q$, we obtain (since the $i$th-row minors of $Q$ are the same as those of $A$ and since the $ij$th entry of $Q$ is $a_{kj}$)

$$0 = \det(Q) = \sum_{j=1}^{n} a_{kj}(-1)^{i+j} \det(M_{ij}). \qquad (4)$$

Substituting Eq. (4) into Eq. (3) establishes the theorem.    ◼

EXAMPLE 2    Evaluate $\det(A)$, where

$$A = \begin{bmatrix} 1 & 2 & 1 \\ 0 & 3 & 2 \\ -2 & 1 & 1 \end{bmatrix}.$$

***Solution***  The value of $\det(A)$ is unchanged if we add a multiple of 2 times row 1 to row 3. The effect of this row operation will be to introduce another zero entry in the first column. Specifically,

$$\det(A) = \begin{vmatrix} 1 & 2 & 1 \\ 0 & 3 & 2 \\ -2 & 1 & 1 \end{vmatrix} \xrightarrow[=]{(R_3 + 2R_1)} \begin{vmatrix} 1 & 2 & 1 \\ 0 & 3 & 2 \\ 0 & 5 & 3 \end{vmatrix} = -1. \qquad ◼$$

## Using Elementary Operations to Simplify Determinants

Clearly it is usually easier to calculate the determinant of a matrix with several zero entries than to calculate one with no zero entries. Therefore, a common strategy in determinant evaluation is to mimic the steps of Gaussian elimination—that is, to use elementary row or column operations to reduce the matrix to triangular form.

**EXAMPLE 3**    Evaluate $\det(A)$, where

$$A = \begin{bmatrix} 1 & 2 & -1 \\ 5 & 3 & 4 \\ -2 & 0 & 1 \end{bmatrix}.$$

*Solution*    With Gaussian elimination, we would first form the matrix $B$ by the following operations: Replace $R_2$ by $R_2 - 5R_1$ and replace $R_3$ by $R_3 + 2R_1$. From Theorem 8, the matrix $B$ produced by these two row operations has the same determinant as the original matrix $A$. In detail:

$$\det(A) = \begin{vmatrix} 1 & 2 & -1 \\ 5 & 3 & 4 \\ -2 & 0 & 1 \end{vmatrix} = \begin{vmatrix} 1 & 2 & -1 \\ 0 & -7 & 9 \\ 0 & 4 & -1 \end{vmatrix} = 1 \begin{vmatrix} -7 & 9 \\ 4 & -1 \end{vmatrix} = 7 - 36 = -29. \quad \blacksquare$$

We could have created a zero in the (2, 1) position of the last (2 × 2) determinant. The formula for (2 × 2) determinants is so simple, however, that it is customary to evaluate a (2 × 2) determinant directly. The next example illustrates that we need not always attempt to go to a triangular form in order to simplify a determinant.

**EXAMPLE 4**    Evaluate $\det(A)$, where

$$A = \begin{bmatrix} 1 & 2 & -1 & 1 \\ -1 & 0 & 2 & -2 \\ 3 & -1 & 1 & 1 \\ 2 & 0 & -1 & 2 \end{bmatrix}.$$

*Solution*    We can introduce a third zero in the second column if we replace $R_1$ by $R_1 + 2R_3$:

$$\det(A) = \begin{vmatrix} 1 & 2 & -1 & 1 \\ -1 & 0 & 2 & -2 \\ 3 & -1 & 1 & 1 \\ 2 & 0 & -1 & 2 \end{vmatrix} = \begin{vmatrix} 7 & 0 & 1 & 3 \\ -1 & 0 & 2 & -2 \\ 3 & -1 & 1 & 1 \\ 2 & 0 & -1 & 2 \end{vmatrix}$$

$$= -(-1) \begin{vmatrix} 7 & 1 & 3 \\ -1 & 2 & -2 \\ 2 & -1 & 2 \end{vmatrix}.$$

(The second equality is from Theorem 8. The third equality is from an expansion along the second column.) Next we replace $R_2$ by $R_2 - 2R_1$ and $R_3$ by $R_1 + R_3$.

The details are

$$\det(A) = \begin{vmatrix} 7 & 1 & 3 \\ -1 & 2 & -2 \\ 2 & -1 & 2 \end{vmatrix} = \begin{vmatrix} 7 & 1 & 3 \\ -15 & 0 & -8 \\ 9 & 0 & 5 \end{vmatrix}$$

$$= -1 \begin{vmatrix} -15 & -8 \\ 9 & 5 \end{vmatrix} = (75 - 72) = 3.$$

The next example illustrates that if the entries in a determinant are integers, then we can avoid working with fractions until the last step. The technique involves multiplying various rows by constants to make each entry in a column divisible by the pivot entry in the column.

EXAMPLE 5   Find $\det(A)$, where

$$A = \begin{bmatrix} 2 & 3 & -2 & 4 \\ 3 & -3 & 5 & 2 \\ 5 & 2 & 4 & 3 \\ -3 & 4 & -3 & 2 \end{bmatrix}.$$

*Solution*   We first multiply rows 2, 3, and 4 by 2 to make them divisible by 2. The row reduction operations to create zeros in the first column can then proceed without using fractions. The row operations are $R_2 - 3R_1$, $R_3 - 5R_1$, and $R_4 + 3R_1$:

$$\det(A) = \begin{vmatrix} 2 & 3 & -2 & 4 \\ 3 & -3 & 5 & 2 \\ 5 & 2 & 4 & 3 \\ -3 & 4 & -3 & 2 \end{vmatrix} = \frac{1}{8} \begin{vmatrix} 2 & 3 & -2 & 4 \\ 6 & -6 & 10 & 4 \\ 10 & 4 & 8 & 6 \\ -6 & 8 & -6 & 4 \end{vmatrix}$$

$$= \frac{1}{8} \begin{vmatrix} 2 & 3 & -2 & 4 \\ 0 & -15 & 16 & -8 \\ 0 & -11 & 18 & -14 \\ 0 & 17 & -12 & 16 \end{vmatrix} = \frac{2}{8} \begin{vmatrix} -15 & 16 & -8 \\ -11 & 18 & -14 \\ 17 & -12 & 16 \end{vmatrix}$$

$$= \frac{1}{4} \begin{vmatrix} -15 & 2(8) & 2(-4) \\ -11 & 2(9) & 2(-7) \\ 17 & 2(-6) & 2(8) \end{vmatrix} = \frac{2(2)}{4} \begin{vmatrix} -15 & 8 & -4 \\ -11 & 9 & -7 \\ 17 & -6 & 8 \end{vmatrix}.$$

We now multiply the second row by 4 and use $R_2 - 7R_1$ and $R_3 + 2R_1$:

$$\det(A) = \frac{1}{4} \begin{vmatrix} -15 & 8 & -4 \\ -44 & 36 & -28 \\ 17 & -6 & 8 \end{vmatrix} = \frac{1}{4} \begin{vmatrix} -15 & 8 & -4 \\ 61 & -20 & 0 \\ -13 & 10 & 0 \end{vmatrix}$$

$$= \frac{-4}{4}(610 - 260) = -350.$$

The preceding examples illustrate that there are many strategies that will lead to a simpler determinant calculation. Exactly which choices are made are determined by experience and personal preference.

## Proof of Theorem 3

In the last section we stated Theorem 3: An $(n \times n)$ matrix $A$ is singular if and only if $\det(A) = 0$. The results of this section enable us to sketch a proof for Theorem 3.

If $A$ is an $(n \times n)$ matrix, then we know from Chapter 1 that we can use Gaussian elimination to produce a row-equivalent upper-triangular matrix $T$. This matrix $T$ can be formed by using row interchanges and adding multiples of one row to other rows. Thus, by Theorems 6 and 8,

$$\det(A) = \pm \det(T). \tag{5}$$

An outline for the proof of Theorem 3 is given below. We use $t_{ij}$ to denote the entries of the upper-triangular matrix $T$:

1. $\det(A) = 0 \Leftrightarrow \det(T) = 0$,  by Eq. (5);
2. $\det(T) = 0 \Leftrightarrow t_{ii} = 0$ for some $i$,  by Theorem 4;
3. $t_{ii} = 0$ for some $i \Leftrightarrow T$ singular   (see Exercise 56 of Section 1.7);
4. $T$ singular $\Leftrightarrow A$ singular,   since $T$ and $A$ are row equivalent.

## 4.3   EXERCISES

In Exercises 1–6, evaluate $\det(A)$ by using row operations to introduce zeros into the second and third entries of the first column.

1. $A = \begin{bmatrix} 1 & 2 & 1 \\ 3 & 0 & 2 \\ -1 & 1 & 3 \end{bmatrix}$

2. $A = \begin{bmatrix} 2 & 4 & 6 \\ 3 & 1 & 2 \\ 1 & 2 & 1 \end{bmatrix}$

3. $A = \begin{bmatrix} 3 & 6 & 9 \\ 2 & 0 & 2 \\ 1 & 2 & 0 \end{bmatrix}$

4. $A = \begin{bmatrix} 1 & 1 & 2 \\ -2 & 1 & 3 \\ 1 & 4 & 1 \end{bmatrix}$

5. $A = \begin{bmatrix} 2 & 4 & -3 \\ 3 & 2 & 5 \\ 2 & 3 & 4 \end{bmatrix}$

6. $A = \begin{bmatrix} 3 & 4 & -2 \\ 2 & 3 & 5 \\ 2 & 4 & 3 \end{bmatrix}$

In Exercises 7–12, use only column interchanges or row interchanges to produce a triangular determinant and then find the value of the original determinant.

7. $\begin{vmatrix} 1 & 0 & 0 & 0 \\ 2 & 0 & 0 & 3 \\ 1 & 1 & 0 & 1 \\ 1 & 4 & 2 & 2 \end{vmatrix}$

8. $\begin{vmatrix} 0 & 0 & 3 & 1 \\ 2 & 1 & 0 & 1 \\ 0 & 0 & 0 & 2 \\ 0 & 2 & 2 & 1 \end{vmatrix}$

**9.** $\begin{vmatrix} 0 & 0 & 2 & 0 \\ 0 & 0 & 1 & 3 \\ 0 & 4 & 1 & 3 \\ 2 & 1 & 5 & 6 \end{vmatrix}$
  **10.** $\begin{vmatrix} 0 & 0 & 1 & 0 \\ 1 & 2 & 1 & 3 \\ 0 & 0 & 0 & 5 \\ 0 & 3 & 1 & 2 \end{vmatrix}$

**11.** $\begin{vmatrix} 0 & 0 & 1 & 0 \\ 0 & 2 & 6 & 3 \\ 2 & 4 & 1 & 5 \\ 0 & 0 & 0 & 4 \end{vmatrix}$
  **12.** $\begin{vmatrix} 0 & 1 & 0 & 0 \\ 0 & 2 & 0 & 3 \\ 2 & 1 & 0 & 6 \\ 3 & 2 & 2 & 4 \end{vmatrix}$

In Exercises 13–18, assume that the $(3 \times 3)$ matrix $A$ satisfies $\det(A) = 2$, where $A$ is given by

$$A = \begin{bmatrix} a & b & c \\ d & e & f \\ g & h & i \end{bmatrix}.$$

Calculate $\det(B)$ in each case.

**13.** $B = \begin{bmatrix} a & b & 3c \\ d & e & 3f \\ g & h & 3i \end{bmatrix}$
 **14.** $B = \begin{bmatrix} d & e & f \\ g & h & i \\ a & b & c \end{bmatrix}$

**15.** $B = \begin{bmatrix} b & a & c \\ e & d & f \\ h & g & i \end{bmatrix}$

**16.** $B = \begin{bmatrix} a & b & c \\ a+d & b+e & c+f \\ g & h & i \end{bmatrix}$

**17.** $B = \begin{bmatrix} d & e & f \\ 2a & 2b & 2c \\ g & h & i \end{bmatrix}$

**18.** $B = \begin{bmatrix} d & f & e \\ a & c & b \\ g & i & h \end{bmatrix}$

In Exercises 19–22, evaluate the $(4 \times 4)$ determinants. Theorems 6–8 can be used to simplify the calculations.

**19.** $\begin{vmatrix} 2 & 4 & 2 & 6 \\ 1 & 3 & 2 & 1 \\ 2 & 1 & 2 & 3 \\ 1 & 2 & 1 & 1 \end{vmatrix}$
  **20.** $\begin{vmatrix} 0 & 2 & 1 & 3 \\ 1 & 2 & 1 & 0 \\ 0 & 1 & 1 & 3 \\ 2 & 2 & 1 & 2 \end{vmatrix}$

**21.** $\begin{vmatrix} 0 & 4 & 1 & 3 \\ 0 & 2 & 2 & 1 \\ 1 & 3 & 1 & 2 \\ 2 & 2 & 1 & 4 \end{vmatrix}$
  **22.** $\begin{vmatrix} 2 & 2 & 4 & 4 \\ 1 & 1 & 3 & 3 \\ 1 & 0 & 2 & 1 \\ 4 & 1 & 3 & 2 \end{vmatrix}$

In Exercises 23 and 24, use row operations to obtain a triangular determinant and find the value of the original Vandermonde determinant.

**23.** $\begin{vmatrix} 1 & a & a^2 \\ 1 & b & b^2 \\ 1 & c & c^2 \end{vmatrix}$
  **24.** $\begin{vmatrix} 1 & a & a^2 & a^3 \\ 1 & b & b^2 & b^3 \\ 1 & c & c^2 & c^3 \\ 1 & d & d^2 & d^3 \end{vmatrix}$

**25.** Let $A$ be an $(n \times n)$ matrix. Use Theorem 7 to argue that $\det(cA) = c^n \det(A)$.

**26.** Prove the corollary to Theorem 6. [*Hint:* Suppose that the $i$th and $j$th rows of $A$ are identical. Interchange these two rows and let $B$ denote the matrix that results. How are $\det(A)$ and $\det(B)$ related?]

**27.** Find examples of $(2 \times 2)$ matrices $A$ and $B$ such that $\det(A + B) \neq \det(A) + \det(B)$.

**28.** An $(n \times n)$ matrix $A$ is called *skew symmetric* if $A^T = -A$. Show that if $A$ is skew symmetric, then $\det(A) = (-1)^n \det(A)$. [*Hint:* Use Theorem 5 and Exercise 25.] Now, argue that an $(n \times n)$ skew-symmetric matrix is singular when $n$ is an odd integer.

# 4.4    EIGENVALUES AND THE CHARACTERISTIC POLYNOMIAL

Having given the brief introduction to determinant theory presented in Section 4.2, we return to the central topic of this chapter, the eigenvalue problem. For reference, recall that the eigenvalue problem for an $(n \times n)$ matrix $A$ has two parts:

1. Find all scalars $\lambda$ such that $A - \lambda I$ is singular. (Such scalars are the **eigenvalues** of $A$.)
2. Given an eigenvalue $\lambda$, find all nonzero vectors $\mathbf{x}$ such that $(A - \lambda I)\mathbf{x} = \boldsymbol{\theta}$. (Such vectors are the **eigenvectors** corresponding to the eigenvalue $\lambda$.)

In this section we focus on part 1, finding the eigenvalues. In the next section we discuss eigenvectors.

In Section 4.1, we were able to determine the eigenvalues of a $(2 \times 2)$ matrix by using a test for singularity given by Eq. (4) in Section 4.1. Knowing Theorem 3 from Section 4.2, we now have a test for singularity that is applicable to any $(n \times n)$ matrix. As applied to the eigenvalue problem, Theorem 3 can be used as follows:

$$A - \lambda I \text{ is singular} \Leftrightarrow \det(A - \lambda I) = 0. \tag{1}$$

An example will illustrate how the singularity test given in Eq. (1) is used in practice.

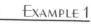 **EXAMPLE 1**    Use the singularity test given in Eq. (1) to determine the eigenvalues of the $(3 \times 3)$ matrix $A$, where

$$A = \begin{bmatrix} 1 & 1 & 1 \\ 0 & 3 & 3 \\ -2 & 1 & 1 \end{bmatrix}.$$

**Solution**    A scalar $\lambda$ is an eigenvalue of $A$ if and only if $A - \lambda I$ is singular. According to the singularity test in Eq. (1), $\lambda$ is an eigenvalue of $A$ if and only if $\lambda$ is a scalar such that

$$\det(A - \lambda I) = 0.$$

Thus we focus on $\det(A - \lambda I)$, where $A - \lambda I$ is the matrix given by

$$A - \lambda I = \begin{bmatrix} 1 & 1 & 1 \\ 0 & 3 & 3 \\ -2 & 1 & 1 \end{bmatrix} - \begin{bmatrix} \lambda & 0 & 0 \\ 0 & \lambda & 0 \\ 0 & 0 & \lambda \end{bmatrix}$$

$$= \begin{bmatrix} 1 - \lambda & 1 & 1 \\ 0 & 3 - \lambda & 3 \\ -2 & 1 & 1 - \lambda \end{bmatrix}.$$

Expanding $\det(A - \lambda I)$ along the first column, we have

$$\det(A - \lambda I) = \begin{vmatrix} 1-\lambda & 1 & 1 \\ 0 & 3-\lambda & 3 \\ -2 & 1 & 1-\lambda \end{vmatrix}$$

$$= (1-\lambda)\begin{vmatrix} 3-\lambda & 3 \\ 1 & 1-\lambda \end{vmatrix} - (0)\begin{vmatrix} 1 & 1 \\ 1 & 1-\lambda \end{vmatrix}$$

$$+ (-2)\begin{vmatrix} 1 & 1 \\ 3-\lambda & 3 \end{vmatrix}$$

$$= (1-\lambda)[(3-\lambda)(1-\lambda) - 3] - 2[3 - (3-\lambda)]$$
$$= (1-\lambda)[\lambda^2 - 4\lambda] - 2[\lambda]$$
$$= [-\lambda^3 + 5\lambda^2 - 4\lambda] - [2\lambda]$$
$$= -\lambda^3 + 5\lambda^2 - 6\lambda$$
$$= -\lambda(\lambda^2 - 5\lambda + 6)$$
$$= -\lambda(\lambda - 3)(\lambda - 2).$$

From the singularity test in Eq. (1), we see that $A - \lambda I$ is singular if and only if $\lambda = 0$, $\lambda = 3$, or $\lambda = 2$.

The ideas developed in Example 1 will be formalized in the next subsection.

## The Characteristic Polynomial

From the singularity condition given in Eq. (1), we know that $A - \lambda I$ is singular if and only if $\det(A - \lambda I) = 0$. In Example 1, for a $(3 \times 3)$ matrix $A$, we saw that the expression $\det(A - \lambda I)$ was a polynomial of degree 3 in $\lambda$. In general, it can be shown that $\det(A - \lambda I)$ is a polynomial of degree $n$ in $\lambda$ when $A$ is $(n \times n)$. Then, since $A - \lambda I$ is singular if and only if $\det(A - \lambda I) = 0$, it follows that the eigenvalues of $A$ are precisely the zeros of the polynomial $\det(A - \lambda I)$.

To avoid any possible confusion between the eigenvalues $\lambda$ of $A$ and the problem of finding the zeros of this associated polynomial (called the characteristic polynomial of $A$), we will use the variable $t$ instead of $\lambda$ in the characteristic polynomial and write $p(t) = \det(A - tI)$. To summarize this discussion, we give Theorems 9 and 10.

THEOREM 9   Let $A$ be an $(n \times n)$ matrix. Then $\det(A - tI)$ is a polynomial of degree $n$ in $t$.

The proof of Theorem 9 is somewhat tedious, and we omit it. The fact that $\det(A - tI)$ is a polynomial leads us to the next definition.

Let $A$ be an $(n \times n)$ matrix. The $n$th-degree polynomial, $p(t)$, given by

$$p(t) = \det(A - tI)$$

is called the **characteristic polynomial** for $A$.

Again, in the context of the singularity test in Eq. (1), the roots of $p(t) = 0$ are the eigenvalues of $A$. This observation is stated formally in the next theorem.

**THEOREM 10** Let $A$ be an $(n \times n)$ matrix, and let $p$ be the characteristic polynomial for $A$. Then the eigenvalues of $A$ are precisely the roots of $p(t) = 0$. ◾

Theorem 10 has the effect of replacing the original problem—determining values $\lambda$ for which $A - \lambda I$ is singular—by an equivalent problem, finding the roots of a polynomial equation $p(t) = 0$. Since polynomials are familiar and an immense amount of theoretical and computational machinery has been developed for solving polynomial equations, we should feel more comfortable with the eigenvalue problem.

The equation $p(t) = 0$ that must be solved to find the eigenvalues of $A$ is called the **characteristic equation**. Suppose that $p(t)$ has degree $n$, where $n \geq 1$. Then the equation $p(t) = 0$ can have no more than $n$ distinct roots. From this fact, it follows that:

**(a)** An $(n \times n)$ matrix can have no more than $n$ distinct eigenvalues.

Also, by the fundamental theorem of algebra, the equation $p(t) = 0$ always has at least one root (possibly complex). Therefore:

**(b)** An $(n \times n)$ matrix always has at least one eigenvalue (possibly complex).

Finally, we recall that any $n$th-degree polynomial $p(t)$ can be written in the factored form

$$p(t) = a(t - r_1)(t - r_2) \cdots (t - r_n).$$

The zeros of $p, r_1, r_2, \ldots, r_n$, however, need not be distinct or real. The number of times the factor $(t - r)$ appears in the factorization of $p(t)$ given above is called the **algebraic multiplicity** of $r$.

**EXAMPLE 2** Find the characteristic polynomial and the eigenvalues for the $(2 \times 2)$ matrix

$$A = \begin{bmatrix} 1 & 5 \\ 3 & 3 \end{bmatrix}.$$

**Solution** By Definition 5, the characteristic polynomial is found by calculating $p(t) = \det(A - tI)$, or

$$p(t) = \begin{vmatrix} 1 - t & 5 \\ 3 & 3 - t \end{vmatrix} = (1 - t)(3 - t) - 15$$

$$= t^2 - 4t - 12 = (t - 6)(t + 2).$$

THE FUNDAMENTAL THEOREM OF ALGEBRA  The eigenvalues of an $(n \times n)$ matrix $A$ are the zeros of $p(t) = \det(A - tI)$, a polynomial of degree $n$. The fundamental theorem of algebra states that the equation $p(t) = 0$ has a solution, $r_1$, in the field of complex numbers. Since $q(t) = p(t)/(t - r_1)$ is a polynomial of degree $n - 1$, repeated use of this result allows us to write

$$p(t) = a(t - r_1)(t - r_2) \cdots (t - r_n).$$

A number of famous mathematicians (including Newton, Euler, d'Alembert, and Lagrange) attempted proofs of the fundamental theorem. In 1799, Gauss critiqued these attempts and presented a proof of his own. He admitted that his proof contained an unestablished assertion, but he stated that its validity could not be doubted. Gauss gave three more proofs in his lifetime, but all suffered from an imperfect understanding of the concept of continuity and the structure of the complex number system. These properties were established in 1874 by Weierstrass and not only made the proofs by Gauss rigorous, but a 1746 proof due to d'Alembert as well.

By Theorem 10, the eigenvalues of $A$ are the roots of $p(t) = 0$; thus the eigenvalues are $\lambda = 6$ and $\lambda = -2$. ◼

EXAMPLE 3  Find the characteristic polynomial and the eigenvalues for the $(2 \times 2)$ matrix

$$A = \begin{bmatrix} 2 & -1 \\ 1 & 2 \end{bmatrix}.$$

**Solution**  The characteristic polynomial is

$$p(t) = \begin{vmatrix} 2 - t & -1 \\ 1 & 2 - t \end{vmatrix} = t^2 - 4t + 5.$$

By the quadratic formula, the eigenvalues are $\lambda = 2 + i$ and $\lambda = 2 - i$. Therefore, this example illustrates that a matrix with real entries can have eigenvalues that are complex. In Section 4.6, we discuss complex eigenvalues and eigenvectors at length. ◼

EXAMPLE 4  Find the characteristic polynomial and the eigenvalues for the $(3 \times 3)$ matrix

$$A = \begin{bmatrix} 3 & -1 & -1 \\ -12 & 0 & 5 \\ 4 & -2 & -1 \end{bmatrix}.$$

**Solution**  By Definition 5, the characteristic polynomial is given by $p(t) = \det(A - tI)$, or

$$p(t) = \begin{vmatrix} 3 - t & -1 & -1 \\ -12 & -t & 5 \\ 4 & -2 & -1 - t \end{vmatrix}.$$

Expanding along the first column, we have

$$p(t) = (3-t) \begin{vmatrix} -t & 5 \\ -2 & -1-t \end{vmatrix} + 12 \begin{vmatrix} -1 & -1 \\ -2 & -1-t \end{vmatrix} + 4 \begin{vmatrix} -1 & -1 \\ -t & 5 \end{vmatrix}$$

$$= (3-t)[t(1+t)+10] + 12[(1+t)-2] + 4[-5-t]$$

$$= (3-t)[t^2+t+10] + 12[t-1] + 4[-t-5]$$

$$= [-t^3+2t^2-7t+30] + [12t-12] + [-4t-20]$$

$$= -t^3+2t^2+t-2.$$

By Theorem 10, the eigenvalues of $A$ are the roots of $p(t) = 0$. We can write $p(t)$ as

$$p(t) = -(t-2)(t-1)(t+1),$$

and thus the eigenvalues of $A$ are $\lambda = 2$, $\lambda = 1$, and $\lambda = -1$.    ◼

(*Note:* Finding or approximating the root of a polynomial equation is a task that is generally best left to the computer. Therefore, so that the theory associated with the eigenvalue problem is not hidden by a mass of computational details, the examples and exercises in this chapter will usually be constructed so that the characteristic equation has integer roots.)

## Special Results

If we know the eigenvalues of a matrix $A$, then we also know the eigenvalues of certain matrices associated with $A$. A list of such results is found in Theorems 11 and 12.

THEOREM 11    Let $A$ be an $(n \times n)$ matrix, and let $\lambda$ be an eigenvalue of $A$. Then:

(a)  $\lambda^k$ is an eigenvalue of $A^k$, $k = 2, 3, \ldots$.

(b)  If $A$ is nonsingular, then $1/\lambda$ is an eigenvalue of $A^{-1}$.

(c)  If $\alpha$ is any scalar, then $\lambda + \alpha$ is an eigenvalue of $A + \alpha I$.

*Proof*    Property (a) is proved by induction, and we begin with the case $k = 2$. Suppose that $\lambda$ is an eigenvalue of $A$ with an associated eigenvector, $\mathbf{x}$. That is,

$$A\mathbf{x} = \lambda\mathbf{x}, \quad \mathbf{x} \neq \boldsymbol{\theta}. \tag{2}$$

Multiplying both sides of Eq. (2) by the matrix $A$ gives

$$A(A\mathbf{x}) = A(\lambda\mathbf{x})$$

$$A^2\mathbf{x} = \lambda(A\mathbf{x})$$

$$A^2\mathbf{x} = \lambda(\lambda\mathbf{x})$$

$$A^2\mathbf{x} = \lambda^2\mathbf{x}, \quad \mathbf{x} \neq \boldsymbol{\theta}.$$

Thus $\lambda^2$ is an eigenvalue of $A^2$ with a corresponding eigenvector, $\mathbf{x}$.

In the exercises the reader is asked to finish the proof of property (a) and prove properties (b) and (c) of Theorem 11. (*Note:* As the proof of Theorem 11 will demonstrate, if $\mathbf{x}$ is any eigenvector of $A$, then $\mathbf{x}$ is also an eigenvector of $A^k$, $A^{-1}$, and $A + \alpha I$.)    ◼

| | | EXAMPLE 5 | Let $A$ be the $(3 \times 3)$ matrix in Example 4. Determine the eigenvalues of $A^5$, $A^{-1}$, and $A + 2I$.

**Solution**    From Example 4, the eigenvalues of $A$ are $\lambda = 2$, $\lambda = 1$, and $\lambda = -1$. By Theorem 11, $A^5$ has eigenvalues $\lambda = 2^5 = 32$, $\lambda = 1^5 = 1$, and $\lambda = (-1)^5 = -1$. Since $A^5$ is a $(3 \times 3)$ matrix and can have no more than three eigenvalues, those eigenvalues must be 32, 1, and $-1$.

Similarly, the eigenvalues of $A^{-1}$ are $\lambda = 1/2$, $\lambda = 1$, and $\lambda = -1$. The eigenvalues of $A + 2I$ are $\lambda = 4$, $\lambda = 3$, and $\lambda = 1$.    ∎

The proof of the next theorem rests on the following fact (see Section 1.7): If $B$ is a square matrix, then both $B$ and $B^T$ are nonsingular or both $B$ and $B^T$ are singular. (See also Exercise 30.)

| | | THEOREM 12 | Let $A$ be an $(n \times n)$ matrix. Then $A$ and $A^T$ have the same eigenvalues.

**Proof**    Observe that $(A - \lambda I)^T = A^T - \lambda I$. By our earlier remark, $A - \lambda I$ and $(A - \lambda I)^T$ are either both singular or both nonsingular. Thus $\lambda$ is an eigenvalue of $A$ if and only if $\lambda$ is an eigenvalue of $A^T$.    ∎

The next result follows immediately from the definition of an eigenvalue. We write the result as a theorem because it provides another important characterization of singularity.

| | | THEOREM 13 | Let $A$ be an $(n \times n)$ matrix. Then $A$ is singular if and only if $\lambda = 0$ is an eigenvalue of $A$.    ∎

(*Note:* If $A$ is singular, then the eigenvectors corresponding to $\lambda = 0$ are in the null space of $A$.)

Our final theorem treats a class of matrices for which eigenvalues can be determined by inspection.

| | | THEOREM 14 | Let $T = (t_{ij})$ be an $(n \times n)$ triangular matrix. Then the eigenvalues of $T$ are the diagonal entries, $t_{11}, t_{22}, \ldots, t_{nn}$.

**Proof**    Since $T$ is triangular, the matrix $T - tI$ is also triangular. The diagonal entries of $T - tI$ are $t_{11} - t$, $t_{22} - t, \ldots, t_{nn} - t$. Thus, by Theorem 4, the characteristic polynomial is given by

$$p(t) = \det(T - tI) = (t_{11} - t)(t_{22} - t) \cdots (t_{nn} - t).$$

By Theorem 10, the eigenvalues are $\lambda = t_{11}$, $\lambda = t_{22}, \ldots, \lambda = t_{nn}$.    ∎

| | | EXAMPLE 6 | Find the characteristic polynomial and the eigenvalues for the matrix $A$ given by

$$A = \begin{bmatrix} 1 & 2 & 1 & 0 \\ 0 & 3 & -1 & 1 \\ 0 & 0 & 2 & 1 \\ 0 & 0 & 0 & 3 \end{bmatrix}.$$

***Solution***   By Theorem 4, $p(t) = \det(A - tI)$ has the form

$$p(t) = (1 - t)(3 - t)^2(2 - t).$$

The eigenvalues are $\lambda = 1, \lambda = 2$, and $\lambda = 3$. The eigenvalues $\lambda = 1$ and $\lambda = 2$ have algebraic multiplicity 1, whereas the eigenvalue $\lambda = 3$ has algebraic multiplicity 2.   ◼

## Computational Considerations

In all the examples we have considered so far, it was possible to factor the characteristic polynomial and thus determine the eigenvalues by inspection. In reality we can rarely expect to be able to factor the characteristic polynomial; so we must solve the characteristic equation by using numerical root-finding methods. To be more specific about root finding, we recall that there are formulas for the roots of some polynomial equations. For instance, the solution of the linear equation

$$at + b = 0, \quad a \neq 0,$$

is given by

$$t = -\frac{b}{a};$$

and the roots of the quadratic equation

$$at^2 + bt + c = 0, \quad a \neq 0,$$

are given by the familiar quadratic formula

$$t = \frac{-b \pm \sqrt{b^2 - 4ac}}{2a}.$$

There are similar (although more complicated) formulas for the roots of third-degree and fourth-degree polynomial equations. Unfortunately there are no such formulas for polynomials of degree 5 or higher [that is, formulas that express the zeros of $p(t)$ as a simple function of the coefficients of $p(t)$]. Moreover, in the mid-nineteenth century Abel *proved* that such formulas cannot exist for polynomials of degree 5 or higher.[*] This means that in general we cannot expect to find the eigenvalues of a large matrix exactly—the best we can do is to find good approximations to the eigenvalues. The eigenvalue problem differs qualitatively from the problem of solving $A\mathbf{x} = \mathbf{b}$. For a system $A\mathbf{x} = \mathbf{b}$, if we are willing to invest the effort required to solve the system by hand, we can obtain the exact solution in a finite number of steps. On the other hand, we cannot in general expect to find roots of a polynomial equation in a finite number of steps.

Finding roots of the characteristic equation is not the only computational aspect of the eigenvalue problem that must be considered. In fact, it is not hard to see that special techniques must be developed even to find the characteristic polynomial. To see the dimensions of this problem, consider the characteristic polynomial of an $(n \times n)$ matrix $A$: $p(t) = \det(A - tI)$. The evaluation of $p(t)$ from a cofactor expansion of $\det(A - tI)$

---

[*]For a historical discussion, see J. E. Maxfield and M. W. Maxfield, *Abstract Algebra and Solution by Radicals* (Dover, 1992).

ultimately requires the evaluation of $n!/2$ determinants of order $(2 \times 2)$. Even for modest values of $n$, the number $n!/2$ is alarmingly large. For instance,

$$10!/2 = 1,814,400,$$

whereas

$$20!/2 > 1.2 \times 10^{18}.$$

The enormous number of calculations required to compute $\det(A - tI)$ means that we cannot find $p(t)$ in any practical sense by expanding $\det(A - tI)$. In Chapter 6, we note that there are relatively efficient ways of finding $\det(A)$, but these techniques (which amount to using elementary row operations to triangularize $A$) are not useful in our problem of computing $\det(A - tI)$ because of the variable $t$. In Section 7.3, we resolve this difficulty by using similarity transformations to transform $A$ to a matrix $H$, where $A$ and $H$ have the same characteristic polynomial, and where it is a trivial matter to calculate the characteristic polynomial for $H$. Moreover, these transformation methods will give us some other important results as a by-product, results such as the Cayley–Hamilton theorem, which have some practical computational significance.

## 4.4    EXERCISES

In Exercises 1–14, find the characteristic polynomial and the eigenvalues for the given matrix. Also, give the algebraic multiplicity of each eigenvalue. [*Note:* In each case the eigenvalues are integers.]

1. $\begin{bmatrix} 1 & 0 \\ 2 & 3 \end{bmatrix}$    2. $\begin{bmatrix} 2 & 1 \\ 0 & -1 \end{bmatrix}$

3. $\begin{bmatrix} 2 & -1 \\ -1 & 2 \end{bmatrix}$    4. $\begin{bmatrix} 13 & -16 \\ 9 & -11 \end{bmatrix}$

5. $\begin{bmatrix} 1 & -1 \\ 1 & 3 \end{bmatrix}$    6. $\begin{bmatrix} 2 & 2 \\ 3 & 3 \end{bmatrix}$

7. $\begin{bmatrix} -6 & -1 & 2 \\ 3 & 2 & 0 \\ -14 & -2 & 5 \end{bmatrix}$    8. $\begin{bmatrix} -2 & -1 & 0 \\ 0 & 1 & 1 \\ -2 & -2 & -1 \end{bmatrix}$

9. $\begin{bmatrix} 3 & -1 & -1 \\ -12 & 0 & 5 \\ 4 & -2 & -1 \end{bmatrix}$    10. $\begin{bmatrix} -7 & 4 & -3 \\ 8 & -3 & 3 \\ 32 & -16 & 13 \end{bmatrix}$

11. $\begin{bmatrix} 2 & 4 & 4 \\ 0 & 1 & -1 \\ 0 & 1 & 3 \end{bmatrix}$    12. $\begin{bmatrix} 6 & 4 & 4 & 1 \\ 4 & 6 & 1 & 4 \\ 4 & 1 & 6 & 4 \\ 1 & 4 & 4 & 6 \end{bmatrix}$

13. $\begin{bmatrix} 5 & 4 & 1 & 1 \\ 4 & 5 & 1 & 1 \\ 1 & 1 & 4 & 2 \\ 1 & 1 & 2 & 4 \end{bmatrix}$    14. $\begin{bmatrix} 1 & -1 & -1 & -1 \\ -1 & 1 & -1 & -1 \\ -1 & -1 & 1 & -1 \\ -1 & -1 & -1 & 1 \end{bmatrix}$

15. Prove property (b) of Theorem 11. [*Hint:* Begin with $A\mathbf{x} = \lambda\mathbf{x}$, $\mathbf{x} \neq \boldsymbol{\theta}$.]

16. Prove property (c) of Theorem 11.

17. Complete the proof of property (a) of Theorem 11.

18. Let $q(t) = t^3 - 2t^2 - t + 2$; and for any $(n \times n)$ matrix $H$, define the matrix polynomial $q(H)$ by

$$q(H) = H^3 - 2H^2 - H + 2I,$$

where $I$ is the $(n \times n)$ identity matrix.

a) Prove that if $\lambda$ is an eigenvalue of $H$, then the number $q(\lambda)$ is an eigenvalue of the matrix $q(H)$. [*Hint:* Suppose that $H\mathbf{x} = \lambda\mathbf{x}$, where $\mathbf{x} \neq \boldsymbol{\theta}$, and use Theorem 11 to evaluate $q(H)\mathbf{x}$.]

b) Use part a) to calculate the eigenvalues of $q(A)$ and $q(B)$, where $A$ and $B$ are from Exercises 7 and 8, respectively.

19. With $q(t)$ as in Exercise 18, verify that $q(C)$ is the zero matrix, where $C$ is from Exercise 9. (Note that $q(t)$ is the characteristic polynomial for $C$. See Exercises 20–23.)

Exercises 20–23 illustrate the **Cayley–Hamilton theorem**, which states that if $p(t)$ is the characteristic polynomial for $A$, then $p(A)$ is the zero matrix. (As in Exercise 18, $p(A)$ is the $(n \times n)$ matrix that comes from substituting $A$ for $t$ in $p(t)$.) In Exercises 20–23, verify that $p(A) = \mathcal{O}$ for the given matrix $A$.

**20.** $A$ in Exercise 3      **21.** $A$ in Exercise 4

**22.** $A$ in Exercise 9      **23.** $A$ in Exercise 13

**24.** This problem establishes a special case of the Cayley–Hamilton theorem.

  **a)** Prove that if $B$ is a $(3 \times 3)$ matrix, and if $B\mathbf{x} = \boldsymbol{\theta}$ for every $\mathbf{x}$ in $R^3$, then $B$ is the zero matrix. [*Hint:* Consider $B\mathbf{e}_1$, $B\mathbf{e}_2$, and $B\mathbf{e}_3$.]

  **b)** Suppose that $\lambda_1$, $\lambda_2$, and $\lambda_3$ are the eigenvalues of a $(3 \times 3)$ matrix $A$, and suppose that $\mathbf{u}_1$, $\mathbf{u}_2$, and $\mathbf{u}_3$ are corresponding eigenvectors. Prove that if $\{\mathbf{u}_1, \mathbf{u}_2, \mathbf{u}_3\}$ is a linearly independent set, and if $p(t)$ is the characteristic polynomial for $A$, then $p(A)$ is the zero matrix. [*Hint:* Any vector $\mathbf{x}$ in $R^3$ can be expressed as a linear combination of $\mathbf{u}_1$, $\mathbf{u}_2$, and $\mathbf{u}_3$.]

**25.** Consider the $(2 \times 2)$ matrix $A$ given by

$$A = \begin{bmatrix} a & b \\ c & d \end{bmatrix}.$$

The characteristic polynomial for $A$ is $p(t) = t^2 - (a+d)t + (ad - bc)$. Verify the Cayley–Hamilton theorem for $(2 \times 2)$ matrices by forming $A^2$ and showing that $p(A)$ is the zero matrix.

**26.** Let $A$ be the $(3 \times 3)$ upper-triangular matrix given by

$$A = \begin{bmatrix} a & d & f \\ 0 & b & e \\ 0 & 0 & c \end{bmatrix}.$$

The characteristic polynomial for $A$ is $p(t) = -(t-a)(t-b)(t-c)$. Verify that $p(A)$ has the form $p(A) = -(A - aI)(A - bI)(A - cI)$. [*Hint:* Expand $p(t)$ and $p(A)$; for instance, $(A - bI)(A - cI) = A^2 - (b+c)A + bcI$]. Next, show that $p(A)$ is the zero matrix by forming the product of the matrices $A - aI$, $A - bI$, and $A - cI$. [*Hint:* Form the product $(A - bI)(A - cI)$ first.]

**27.** Let $q(t) = t^n + a_{n-1}t^{n-1} + \cdots + a_1 t + a_0$, and define the $(n \times n)$ "companion" matrix by

$$A = \begin{bmatrix} -a_{n-1} & -a_{n-2} & \cdots & -a_1 & -a_0 \\ 1 & 0 & \cdots & 0 & 0 \\ 0 & 1 & \cdots & 0 & 0 \\ \vdots & & & & \vdots \\ 0 & 0 & \cdots & 1 & 0 \end{bmatrix}.$$

  **a)** For $n = 2$ and for $n = 3$, show that $\det(A - tI) = (-1)^n q(t)$.

  **b)** Give the companion matrix $A$ for the polynomial $q(t) = t^4 + 3t^3 - t^2 + 2t - 2$. Verify that $q(t)$ is the characteristic polynomial for $A$.

  **c)** Prove for all $n$ that $\det(A - tI) = (-1)^n q(t)$.

**28.** The power method is a numerical method used to estimate the dominant eigenvalue of a matrix A. (By the dominant eigenvalue, we mean the one that is largest in absolute value.) The algorithm proceeds as follows:

  **a)** Choose any starting vector $\mathbf{x}_0$, $\mathbf{x}_0 \neq \boldsymbol{\theta}$.

  **b)** Let $\mathbf{x}_{k+1} = A\mathbf{x}_k$, $k = 0, 1, 2, \ldots$.

  **c)** Let $\beta_k = \mathbf{x}_k^T \mathbf{x}_{k+1}/\mathbf{x}_k^T \mathbf{x}_k$, $k = 0, 1, 2, \ldots$.

    Under suitable conditions, it can be shown that $\{\beta_k\} \to \lambda_1$, where $\lambda_1$ is the dominant eigenvalue of $A$. Use the power method to estimate the dominant eigenvalue of the matrix in Exercise 9. Use the starting vector

$$\mathbf{x} = \begin{bmatrix} 1 \\ 1 \\ 1 \end{bmatrix}$$

and calculate $\beta_0$, $\beta_1$, $\beta_2$, $\beta_3$, and $\beta_4$.

**29.** This exercise gives a condition under which the power method (see Exercise 28) converges. Suppose that $A$ is an $(n \times n)$ matrix and has real eigenvalues $\lambda_1, \lambda_2, \ldots, \lambda_n$ with corresponding eigenvectors $\mathbf{u}_1, \mathbf{u}_2, \ldots, \mathbf{u}_n$. Furthermore, suppose that $|\lambda_1| > |\lambda_2| \geq \cdots \geq |\lambda_n|$, and the starting vector $\mathbf{x}_0$ satisfies $\mathbf{x}_0 = c_1\mathbf{u}_1 + c_2\mathbf{u}_2 + \cdots + c_n\mathbf{u}_n$, where $c_1 \neq 0$. Prove that

$$\lim_{k \to \infty} \beta_k = \lambda_1.$$

[*Hint:* Observe that $\mathbf{x}_j = A^j\mathbf{x}_0$, $j = 1, 2, \ldots$, and use Theorem 11 to calculate $\mathbf{x}_{k+1}$ and $\mathbf{x}_k$. Next, factor all powers of $\lambda_1$ from the numerator and denominator of $\beta_k = \mathbf{x}_k^T\mathbf{x}_{k+1}/\mathbf{x}_k^T\mathbf{x}_k$.]

**30.** Theorem 12 shows that $A$ and $A^T$ have the same eigenvalues. In Theorem 5 of Section 4.3, it was shown that $\det(A) = \det(A^T)$. Use this result to show that $A$ and $A^T$ have the same characteristic polynomial. [*Note:* Theorem 12 proves that $A - \lambda I$ and $A^T - \lambda I$ are singular or nonsingular together. This exercise shows that the eigenvalues of $A$ and $A^T$ have the same algebraic multiplicity.]

The characteristic polynomial $p(t) = \det(A - tI)$ has the form $p(t) = (-1)^n t^n + a_{n-1} t^{n-1} + \cdots + a_1 t + a_0$.

The coefficients of $p(t)$ can be found by evaluating $\det(A - tI)$ at $n$ distinct values of $t$ and solving the resulting Vandermonde system for $a_{n-1}, \ldots, a_1, a_0$. Employ this technique in Exercises 31–34 to find the characteristic polynomial for the indicated matrix $A$.

**31.** $A$ in Exercise 5      **32.** $A$ in Exercise 6

**33.** $A$ in Exercise 7      **34.** $A$ in Exercise 8

## EIGENVECTORS AND EIGENSPACES

As we saw in the previous section, we can find the eigenvalues of a matrix $A$ by solving the characteristic equation $\det(A - tI) = 0$. Once we know the eigenvalues, the familiar technique of Gaussian elimination can be employed to find the eigenvectors that correspond to the various eigenvalues.

In particular, the eigenvectors corresponding to an eigenvalue $\lambda$ of $A$ are the nonzero solutions of

$$(A - \lambda I)\mathbf{x} = \boldsymbol{\theta}. \tag{1}$$

Given a value for $\lambda$, the equations in (1) can be solved for $\mathbf{x}$ by using Gaussian elimination.

EXAMPLE 1    Find the eigenvectors that correspond to the eigenvalues of matrix $A$ in Example 1 of Section 4.4.

*Solution*    For matrix $A$ in Example 1, $A - \lambda I$ is the matrix

$$A - \lambda I = \begin{bmatrix} 1 - \lambda & 1 & 1 \\ 0 & 3 - \lambda & 3 \\ -2 & 1 & 1 - \lambda \end{bmatrix}.$$

Also, from Example 1 we know that the eigenvalues of $A$ are given by $\lambda = 0$, $\lambda = 2$, and $\lambda = 3$.

For each eigenvalue $\lambda$, we find the eigenvectors that correspond to $\lambda$ by solving the system $(A - \lambda I)\mathbf{x} = \boldsymbol{\theta}$. For the eigenvalue $\lambda = 0$, we have $(A - 0I)\mathbf{x} = \boldsymbol{\theta}$, or $A\mathbf{x} = \boldsymbol{\theta}$, to solve:

$$\begin{aligned} x_1 + x_2 + x_3 &= 0 \\ 3x_2 + 3x_3 &= 0 \\ -2x_1 + x_2 + x_3 &= 0. \end{aligned}$$

The solution of this system is $x_1 = 0$, $x_2 = -x_3$, with $x_3$ arbitrary. Thus the eigenvectors of $A$ corresponding to $\lambda = 0$ are given by

$$\mathbf{x} = \begin{bmatrix} 0 \\ -a \\ a \end{bmatrix} = a \begin{bmatrix} 0 \\ -1 \\ 1 \end{bmatrix}, \quad a \neq 0,$$

and any such vector $\mathbf{x}$ satisfies $A\mathbf{x} = 0 \cdot \mathbf{x}$. This equation illustrates that the definition of eigenvalues does allow the possibility that $\lambda = 0$ is an eigenvalue. We stress, however, that the zero vector is never considered an eigenvector (after all, $A\mathbf{x} = \lambda\mathbf{x}$ is always satisfied for $\mathbf{x} = \boldsymbol{\theta}$, no matter what value $\lambda$ has).

The eigenvectors corresponding to the eigenvalue $\lambda = 3$ are found by solving $(A - 3I)\mathbf{x} = \boldsymbol{\theta}$:

$$-2x_1 + x_2 + x_3 = 0$$
$$3x_3 = 0$$
$$-2x_1 + x_2 - 2x_3 = 0.$$

The solution of this system is $x_3 = 0$, $x_2 = 2x_1$, with $x_1$ arbitrary. Thus the nontrivial solutions of $(A - 3I)\mathbf{x} = \boldsymbol{\theta}$ (the eigenvectors of $A$ corresponding to $\lambda = 3$) all have the form

$$\mathbf{x} = \begin{bmatrix} a \\ 2a \\ 0 \end{bmatrix} = a \begin{bmatrix} 1 \\ 2 \\ 0 \end{bmatrix}, \quad a \neq 0.$$

Finally, the eigenvectors corresponding to $\lambda = 2$ are found from $(A - 2I)\mathbf{x} = \boldsymbol{\theta}$, and the solution is $x_1 = -2x_3$, $x_2 = -3x_3$, with $x_3$ arbitrary. So the eigenvectors corresponding to $\lambda = 2$ are of the form

$$\mathbf{x} = \begin{bmatrix} -2a \\ -3a \\ a \end{bmatrix} = a \begin{bmatrix} -2 \\ -3 \\ 1 \end{bmatrix}, \quad a \neq 0. \qquad \blacksquare$$

We pause here to make several comments. As Example 1 shows, there are infinitely many eigenvectors that correspond to a given eigenvalue. This comment should be obvious, for if $A - \lambda I$ is a singular matrix, there are infinitely many nontrivial solutions of $(A - \lambda I)\mathbf{x} = \boldsymbol{\theta}$. In particular, if $A\mathbf{x} = \lambda\mathbf{x}$ for some nonzero vector $\mathbf{x}$, then we also have $A\mathbf{y} = \lambda\mathbf{y}$ when $\mathbf{y} = a\mathbf{x}$, with $a$ being any scalar. Thus any nonzero multiple of an eigenvector is again an eigenvector.

Next, we again note that the scalar $\lambda = 0$ may be an eigenvalue of a matrix, as Example 1 showed. In fact, from Theorem 13 of Section 4.4 we know that $\lambda = 0$ is an eigenvalue of $A$ whenever $A$ is singular.

Last, we observe from Example 1 that finding all the eigenvectors corresponding to $\lambda = 0$ is precisely the same as finding the null space of $A$ and then deleting the zero vector, $\boldsymbol{\theta}$. Likewise, the eigenvectors of $A$ corresponding to $\lambda = 2$ and $\lambda = 3$ are the nonzero vectors in the null space of $A - 2I$ and $A - 3I$, respectively.

## Eigenspaces and Geometric Multiplicity

In the preceding discussion, we made the following observation: If $\lambda$ is an eigenvalue of $A$, then the eigenvectors corresponding to $\lambda$ are precisely the nonzero vectors in the null space of $A - \lambda I$. It is convenient to formalize this observation.

---

**DEFINITION 6**       Let $A$ be an $(n \times n)$ matrix. If $\lambda$ is an eigenvalue of $A$, then:

(a) The null space of $A - \lambda I$ is denoted by $E_\lambda$ and is called the ***eigenspace*** of $\lambda$.

(b) The dimension of $E_\lambda$ is called the ***geometric multiplicity*** of $\lambda$.

---

(*Note:* Since $A - \lambda I$ is singular, the dimension of $E_\lambda$, the geometric multiplicity of $\lambda$, is always at least 1 and may be larger. It can be shown that the geometric multiplicity of $\lambda$ is never larger than the algebraic multiplicity of $\lambda$. The next three examples illustrate some of the possibilities.)

**EXAMPLE 2**    Determine the algebraic and geometric multiplicities for the eigenvalues of $A$

$$A = \begin{bmatrix} 1 & 1 & 0 \\ 0 & 1 & 1 \\ 0 & 0 & 1 \end{bmatrix}.$$

*Solution*    The characteristic polynomial is $p(t) = (1 - t)^3$, and thus the only eigenvalue of $A$ is $\lambda = 1$. The eigenvalue $\lambda = 1$ has algebraic multiplicity 3.

The eigenspace is found by solving $(A - I)\mathbf{x} = \boldsymbol{\theta}$. The system $(A - I)\mathbf{x} = \boldsymbol{\theta}$ is

$$x_2 = 0$$
$$x_3 = 0.$$

Thus $\mathbf{x}$ is in the eigenspace $E_\lambda$ corresponding to $\lambda = 1$ if and only if $\mathbf{x}$ has the form

$$\mathbf{x} = \begin{bmatrix} x_1 \\ 0 \\ 0 \end{bmatrix} = x_1 \begin{bmatrix} 1 \\ 0 \\ 0 \end{bmatrix}. \tag{2}$$

The geometric multiplicity of the eigenvalue $\lambda = 1$ is 1, and $\mathbf{x}$ is an eigenvector if $\mathbf{x}$ has the form (2) with $x_1 \neq 0$.

**EXAMPLE 3**    Determine the algebraic and geometric multiplicities for the eigenvalues of $B$,

$$B = \begin{bmatrix} 1 & 1 & 0 \\ 0 & 1 & 0 \\ 0 & 0 & 1 \end{bmatrix}.$$

*Solution* The characteristic polynomial is $p(t) = (1 - t)^3$, so $\lambda = 1$ is the only eigenvalue, and it has algebraic multiplicity 3.

The corresponding eigenspace is found by solving $(B - I)\mathbf{x} = \boldsymbol{\theta}$. Now $(B - I)\mathbf{x} = \boldsymbol{\theta}$ if and only if $\mathbf{x}$ has the form

$$\mathbf{x} = \begin{bmatrix} x_1 \\ 0 \\ x_3 \end{bmatrix} = x_1 \begin{bmatrix} 1 \\ 0 \\ 0 \end{bmatrix} + x_3 \begin{bmatrix} 0 \\ 0 \\ 1 \end{bmatrix}. \tag{3}$$

By (3), the eigenspace has dimension 2, and so the eigenvalue $\lambda = 1$ has geometric multiplicity 2. The eigenvectors of $B$ are the nonzero vectors of the form (3). ◼

EXAMPLE 4 Determine the algebraic and geometric multiplicities for the eigenvalues of $C$,

$$C = \begin{bmatrix} 1 & 0 & 0 \\ 0 & 1 & 0 \\ 0 & 0 & 1 \end{bmatrix}.$$

*Solution* The characteristic polynomial is $p(t) = (1 - t)^3$, so $\lambda = 1$ has algebraic multiplicity 3.

The eigenspace is found by solving $(C - I)\mathbf{x} = \boldsymbol{\theta}$, and since $C - I$ is the zero matrix, every vector in $R^3$ is in the null space of $C - I$. The geometric multiplicity of the eigenvalue $\lambda = 1$ is equal to 3. ◼

(*Note:* The matrices in Examples 2, 3, and 4 all have the same characteristic polynomial, $p(t) = (1 - t)^3$. However, the respective eigenspaces are different.)

## Defective Matrices

For applications (such as diagonalization) it will be important to know whether an $(n \times n)$ matrix $A$ has a set of $n$ linearly independent eigenvectors. As we will see later, if $A$ is an $(n \times n)$ matrix and if some eigenvalue of $A$ has a geometric multiplicity that is less than its algebraic multiplicity, then $A$ will not have a set of $n$ linearly independent eigenvectors. Such a matrix is called defective.

DEFINITION 7 Let $A$ be an $(n \times n)$ matrix. If there is an eigenvalue $\lambda$ of $A$ such that the geometric multiplicity of $\lambda$ is less than the algebraic multiplicity of $\lambda$, then $A$ is called a *defective* matrix.

Note that the matrices in Examples 1 and 4 are not defective. The matrices in Examples 2 and 3 are defective. Example 5 provides another instance of a defective matrix.

| | | EXAMPLE 5     Find all the eigenvalues and eigenvectors of the matrix $A$:

$$A = \begin{bmatrix} -4 & 1 & 1 & 1 \\ -16 & 3 & 4 & 4 \\ -7 & 2 & 2 & 1 \\ -11 & 1 & 3 & 4 \end{bmatrix}.$$

Also, determine the algebraic and geometric multiplicities of the eigenvalues.

*Solution*     Omitting the details, a cofactor expansion yields

$$\det(A - tI) = t^4 - 5t^3 + 9t^2 - 7t + 2$$
$$= (t - 1)^3(t - 2).$$

Hence the eigenvalues are $\lambda = 1$ (algebraic multiplicity 3) and $\lambda = 2$ (algebraic multiplicity 1).

In solving $(A - 2I)\mathbf{x} = \boldsymbol{\theta}$, we reduce the augmented matrix $[A - 2I \,|\, \boldsymbol{\theta}]$ as follows, multiplying rows 2, 3, and 4 by constants to avoid working with fractions:

$$[A - 2I \,|\, \boldsymbol{\theta}] = \begin{bmatrix} -6 & 1 & 1 & 1 & 0 \\ -16 & 1 & 4 & 4 & 0 \\ -7 & 2 & 0 & 1 & 0 \\ -11 & 1 & 3 & 2 & 0 \end{bmatrix} \sim \begin{bmatrix} -6 & 1 & 1 & 1 & 0 \\ -48 & 3 & 12 & 12 & 0 \\ -42 & 12 & 0 & 6 & 0 \\ -66 & 6 & 18 & 12 & 0 \end{bmatrix}$$

$$\sim \begin{bmatrix} -6 & 1 & 1 & 1 & 0 \\ 0 & -5 & 4 & 4 & 0 \\ 0 & 5 & -7 & -1 & 0 \\ 0 & -5 & 7 & 1 & 0 \end{bmatrix} \sim \begin{bmatrix} -6 & 1 & 1 & 1 & 0 \\ 0 & -5 & 4 & 4 & 0 \\ 0 & 0 & -3 & 3 & 0 \\ 0 & 0 & 0 & 0 & 0 \end{bmatrix}.$$

Backsolving yields $x_1 = 3x_4/5$, $x_2 = 8x_4/5$, $x_3 = x_4$. Hence $\mathbf{x}$ is an eigenvector corresponding to $\lambda = 2$ only if

$$\mathbf{x} = \begin{bmatrix} x_1 \\ x_2 \\ x_3 \\ x_4 \end{bmatrix} = \begin{bmatrix} 3x_4/5 \\ 8x_4/5 \\ x_4 \\ x_4 \end{bmatrix} = \frac{x_4}{5} \begin{bmatrix} 3 \\ 8 \\ 5 \\ 5 \end{bmatrix}, \quad x_4 \neq 0.$$

Thus the algebraic and geometric multiplicities of the eigenvalue $\lambda = 2$ are equal to 1.

In solving $(A - I)\mathbf{x} = \mathbf{0}$, we reduce the augmented matrix $[A - I \mid \mathbf{0}]$:

$$[A - I \mid \mathbf{0}] = \begin{bmatrix} -5 & 1 & 1 & 1 & 0 \\ -16 & 2 & 4 & 4 & 0 \\ -7 & 2 & 1 & 1 & 0 \\ -11 & 1 & 3 & 3 & 0 \end{bmatrix} \sim \begin{bmatrix} -5 & 1 & 1 & 1 & 0 \\ -80 & 10 & 20 & 20 & 0 \\ -35 & 10 & 5 & 5 & 0 \\ -55 & 5 & 15 & 15 & 0 \end{bmatrix}$$

$$\sim \begin{bmatrix} -5 & 1 & 1 & 1 & 0 \\ 0 & -6 & 4 & 4 & 0 \\ 0 & 3 & -2 & -2 & 0 \\ 0 & -6 & 4 & 4 & 0 \end{bmatrix}$$

$$\sim \begin{bmatrix} -5 & 1 & 1 & 1 & 0 \\ 0 & 3 & -2 & -2 & 0 \\ 0 & 0 & 0 & 0 & 0 \\ 0 & 0 & 0 & 0 & 0 \end{bmatrix}.$$

Backsolving yields $x_1 = (x_3 + x_4)/3$ and $x_2 = 2(x_3 + x_4)/3$. Thus $\mathbf{x}$ is an eigenvector corresponding to $\lambda = 1$ only if $\mathbf{x}$ is a nonzero vector of the form

$$\mathbf{x} = \begin{bmatrix} x_1 \\ x_2 \\ x_3 \\ x_4 \end{bmatrix} = \begin{bmatrix} (x_3 + x_4)/3 \\ 2(x_3 + x_4)/3 \\ x_3 \\ x_4 \end{bmatrix} = \frac{x_3}{3}\begin{bmatrix} 1 \\ 2 \\ 3 \\ 0 \end{bmatrix} + \frac{x_4}{3}\begin{bmatrix} 1 \\ 2 \\ 0 \\ 3 \end{bmatrix}. \tag{4}$$

By (4), the eigenspace $E_\lambda$ corresponding to $\lambda = 1$ has a basis consisting of the vectors

$$\begin{bmatrix} 1 \\ 2 \\ 3 \\ 0 \end{bmatrix} \quad \text{and} \quad \begin{bmatrix} 1 \\ 2 \\ 0 \\ 3 \end{bmatrix}.$$

Since $E_\lambda$ has dimension 2, the eigenvalue $\lambda = 1$ has geometric multiplicity 2 and algebraic multiplicity 3. (Matrix $A$ is defective.) ◼

The next theorem shows that a matrix can be defective only if it has repeated eigenvalues. (As shown in Example 4, however, repeated eigenvalues do not necessarily mean that a matrix is defective.)

**THEOREM 15**    Let $\mathbf{u}_1, \mathbf{u}_2, \ldots, \mathbf{u}_k$ be eigenvectors of an $(n \times n)$ matrix $A$ corresponding to distinct eigenvalues $\lambda_1, \lambda_2, \ldots, \lambda_k$. That is,

$$A\mathbf{u}_j = \lambda_j \mathbf{u}_j \quad \text{for } j = 1, 2, \ldots, k; \quad k \leq n \tag{5}$$

$$\lambda_i \neq \lambda_j \quad \text{for } i \neq j; \quad 1 \leq i, j \leq k. \tag{6}$$

Then $\{\mathbf{u}_1, \mathbf{u}_2, \ldots, \mathbf{u}_k\}$ is a linearly independent set.

***Proof***   Since $\mathbf{u}_1 \neq \boldsymbol{\theta}$, the set $\{\mathbf{u}_1\}$ is trivially linearly independent. If the set $\{\mathbf{u}_1, \mathbf{u}_2, \ldots, \mathbf{u}_k\}$ were linearly dependent, then there would exist an integer $m$, $2 \leq m \leq k$, such that:

(a)   $S_1 = \{\mathbf{u}_1, \mathbf{u}_2, \ldots, \mathbf{u}_{m-1}\}$ is linearly independent.

(b)   $S_2 = \{\mathbf{u}_1, \mathbf{u}_2, \ldots, \mathbf{u}_{m-1}, \mathbf{u}_m\}$ is linearly dependent.

Now since $S_2$ is linearly dependent, there exist scalars $c_1, c_2, \ldots, c_m$ (not all zero) such that

$$c_1\mathbf{u}_1 + c_2\mathbf{u}_2 + \cdots + c_{m-1}\mathbf{u}_{m-1} + c_m\mathbf{u}_m = \boldsymbol{\theta}. \tag{7}$$

Furthermore, $c_m$ in Eq. (7) cannot be zero. (If $c_m = 0$, then Eq. (7) would imply that $S_1$ is linearly dependent, contradicting (a).)

Multiplying both sides of Eq. (7) by $A$ and using $A\mathbf{u}_j = \lambda_j\mathbf{u}_j$, we obtain

$$c_1\lambda_1\mathbf{u}_1 + c_2\lambda_2\mathbf{u}_2 + \cdots + c_{m-1}\lambda_{m-1}\mathbf{u}_{m-1} + c_m\lambda_m\mathbf{u}_m = \boldsymbol{\theta}. \tag{8}$$

Multiplying both sides of Eq. (7) by $\lambda_m$ yields

$$c_1\lambda_m\mathbf{u}_1 + c_2\lambda_m\mathbf{u}_2 + \cdots + c_{m-1}\lambda_m\mathbf{u}_{m-1} + c_m\lambda_m\mathbf{u}_m = \boldsymbol{\theta}. \tag{9}$$

Subtracting Eq. (8) from Eq. (9), we find that

$$c_1(\lambda_m - \lambda_1)\mathbf{u}_1 + c_2(\lambda_m - \lambda_2)\mathbf{u}_2 + \cdots + c_{m-1}(\lambda_m - \lambda_{m-1})\mathbf{u}_{m-1} = \boldsymbol{\theta}. \tag{10}$$

If we set $\beta_j = c_j(\lambda_m - \lambda_j)$, $1 \leq j \leq m - 1$, Eq. (10) becomes

$$\beta_1\mathbf{u}_1 + \beta_2\mathbf{u}_2 + \cdots + \beta_{m-1}\mathbf{u}_{m-1} = \boldsymbol{\theta}.$$

Since $S_1$ is linearly independent, it then follows that

$$\beta_1 = \beta_2 = \cdots = \beta_{m-1} = 0,$$

or

$$c_j(\lambda_m - \lambda_j) = 0, \quad \text{for } j = 1, 2, \ldots, m - 1.$$

Because $\lambda_m \neq \lambda_j$ for $j \neq m$, we must have $c_j = 0$ for $1 \leq j \leq m - 1$.

Finally (see Eq. 7), if $c_j = 0$ for $1 \leq j \leq m - 1$, then $c_m\mathbf{u}_m = \boldsymbol{\theta}$. Since $c_m \neq 0$, it follows that $\mathbf{u}_m = \boldsymbol{\theta}$. But $\mathbf{u}_m$ is an eigenvector, and so $\mathbf{u}_m \neq \boldsymbol{\theta}$. Hence we have contradicted the assumption that there is an $m$, $m \leq k$, such that $S_2$ is linearly dependent. Thus $\{\mathbf{u}_1, \mathbf{u}_2, \ldots, \mathbf{u}_k\}$ is linearly independent. ∎

An important and useful corollary to Theorem 15 is given next.

COROLLARY   Let $A$ be an $(n \times n)$ matrix. If $A$ has $n$ distinct eigenvalues, then $A$ has a set of $n$ linearly independent eigenvectors. ∎

## 4.5    EXERCISES

The following list of matrices and their respective characteristic polynomials is referred to in Exercises 1–11.

$$A = \begin{bmatrix} 2 & -1 \\ -1 & 2 \end{bmatrix},$$

$$p(t) = (t-3)(t-1),$$

$$B = \begin{bmatrix} 1 & -1 \\ 1 & 3 \end{bmatrix},$$

$$p(t) = (t-2)^2,$$

$$C = \begin{bmatrix} -6 & -1 & 2 \\ 3 & 2 & 0 \\ -14 & -2 & 5 \end{bmatrix},$$

$$p(t) = -(t-1)^2(t+1),$$

$$D = \begin{bmatrix} -7 & 4 & -3 \\ 8 & -3 & 3 \\ 32 & -16 & 13 \end{bmatrix},$$

$$p(t) = -(t-1)^3,$$

$$E = \begin{bmatrix} 6 & 4 & 4 & 1 \\ 4 & 6 & 1 & 4 \\ 4 & 1 & 6 & 4 \\ 1 & 4 & 4 & 6 \end{bmatrix},$$

$$p(t) = (t+1)(t+5)^2(t-15),$$

$$F = \begin{bmatrix} 1 & -1 & -1 & -1 \\ -1 & 1 & -1 & -1 \\ -1 & -1 & 1 & -1 \\ -1 & -1 & -1 & 1 \end{bmatrix},$$

$$p(t) = (t+2)(t-2)^3$$

In Exercises 1–11, find a basis for the eigenspace $E_\lambda$ for the given matrix and the value of $\lambda$. Determine the algebraic and geometric multiplicities of $\lambda$.

1. $A, \lambda = 3$    2. $A, \lambda = 1$    3. $B, \lambda = 2$
4. $C, \lambda = 1$    5. $C, \lambda = -1$    6. $D, \lambda = 1$
7. $E, \lambda = -1$    8. $E, \lambda = 5$    9. $E, \lambda = 15$
10. $F, \lambda = -2$    11. $F, \lambda = 2$

In Exercises 12–17, find the eigenvalues and the eigenvectors for the given matrix. Is the matrix defective?

12. $\begin{bmatrix} 1 & 1 & -1 \\ 0 & 2 & -1 \\ 0 & 0 & 1 \end{bmatrix}$    13. $\begin{bmatrix} 2 & 1 & 2 \\ 0 & 3 & 2 \\ 0 & 0 & 2 \end{bmatrix}$

14. $\begin{bmatrix} 1 & 2 & 1 \\ 0 & 1 & 2 \\ 0 & 0 & 1 \end{bmatrix}$    15. $\begin{bmatrix} 2 & 0 & 3 \\ 0 & 2 & 1 \\ 0 & 0 & 1 \end{bmatrix}$

16. $\begin{bmatrix} -1 & 6 & 2 \\ 0 & 5 & -6 \\ 1 & 0 & -2 \end{bmatrix}$    17. $\begin{bmatrix} 3 & -1 & -1 \\ -12 & 0 & 5 \\ 4 & -2 & -1 \end{bmatrix}$

18. If a vector $\mathbf{x}$ is a linear combination of eigenvectors of a matrix $A$, then it is easy to calculate the product $\mathbf{y} = A^k\mathbf{x}$ for any positive integer $k$. For instance, suppose that $A\mathbf{u}_1 = \lambda_1\mathbf{u}_1$ and $A\mathbf{u}_2 = \lambda_2\mathbf{u}_2$, where $\mathbf{u}_1$ and $\mathbf{u}_2$ are nonzero vectors. If $\mathbf{x} = a_1\mathbf{u}_1 + a_2\mathbf{u}_2$, then (see Theorem 11 of Section 4.4) $\mathbf{y} = A^k\mathbf{x} = A^k(a_1\mathbf{u}_1 + a_2\mathbf{u}_2) = a_1A^k\mathbf{u}_1 + a_2A^k\mathbf{u}_2 = a_1(\lambda_1)^k\mathbf{u}_1 + a_2(\lambda_2)^k\mathbf{u}_2$. Find $A^{10}\mathbf{x}$, where

$$A = \begin{bmatrix} 4 & -2 \\ 5 & -3 \end{bmatrix} \quad \text{and} \quad \mathbf{x} = \begin{bmatrix} 0 \\ 9 \end{bmatrix}.$$

19. As in Exercise 18, calculate $A^{10}\mathbf{x}$ for

$$A = \begin{bmatrix} 1 & 2 & -1 \\ 0 & 5 & -2 \\ 0 & 6 & -2 \end{bmatrix} \quad \text{and} \quad \mathbf{x} = \begin{bmatrix} 2 \\ 4 \\ 7 \end{bmatrix}.$$

20. Consider a $(4 \times 4)$ matrix $H$ of the form

$$H = \begin{bmatrix} \times & \times & \times & \times \\ a & \times & \times & \times \\ 0 & b & \times & \times \\ 0 & 0 & c & \times \end{bmatrix} \quad (11)$$

In matrix (11) the entries designated $\times$ may be zero or nonzero. Suppose, in matrix (11), that $a$, $b$, and $c$ are nonzero. Let $\lambda$ be any eigenvalue of $H$. Show that the geometric multiplicity of $\lambda$ is equal to 1. [*Hint:* Verify that the rank of $H - \lambda I$ is exactly equal to 3.]

21. An $(n \times n)$ matrix $P$ is called *idempotent* if $P^2 = P$. Show that if $P$ is an invertible idempotent matrix, then $P = I$.

22. Let $P$ be an idempotent matrix. Show that the only eigenvalues of $P$ are $\lambda = 0$ and $\lambda = 1$. [*Hint:* Suppose that $P\mathbf{x} = \lambda\mathbf{x}, \mathbf{x} \neq \boldsymbol{\theta}$.]

23. Let $\mathbf{u}$ be a vector in $R^n$ such that $\mathbf{u}^T\mathbf{u} = 1$. Show that the $(n \times n)$ matrix $P = \mathbf{u}\mathbf{u}^T$ is an idempotent matrix. [*Hint:* Use the associative properties of matrix multiplication.]

24. Verify that if $Q$ is idempotent, then so is $I - Q$. Also verify that $(I - 2Q)^{-1} = I - 2Q$.

25. Suppose that $\mathbf{u}$ and $\mathbf{v}$ are vectors in $R^n$ such that $\mathbf{u}^T\mathbf{u} = 1$, $\mathbf{v}^T\mathbf{v} = 1$, and $\mathbf{u}^T\mathbf{v} = 0$. Show that $P = \mathbf{u}\mathbf{u}^T + \mathbf{v}\mathbf{v}^T$ is idempotent.

26. Show that any nonzero vector of the form $a\mathbf{u} + b\mathbf{v}$ is an eigenvector corresponding to $\lambda = 1$ for the matrix $P$ in Exercise 25.

**27.** Let $A$ be an $(n \times n)$ symmetric matrix, with (real) distinct eigenvalues $\lambda_1, \lambda_2, \ldots, \lambda_n$. Let the corresponding eigenvectors $\mathbf{u}_1, \mathbf{u}_2, \ldots, \mathbf{u}_n$ be chosen so that $\|\mathbf{u}_i\| = 1$ (that is, $\mathbf{u}_i^T \mathbf{u}_i = 1$). Exercise 29 shows that $A$ can be decomposed as

$$A = \lambda_1 \mathbf{u}_1 \mathbf{u}_1^T + \lambda_2 \mathbf{u}_2 \mathbf{u}_2^T + \cdots + \lambda_n \mathbf{u}_n \mathbf{u}_n^T. \quad (12)$$

Verify decomposition (12) for each of the following matrices.

**a)** $B = \begin{bmatrix} 2 & -1 \\ -1 & 2 \end{bmatrix}$ **b)** $C = \begin{bmatrix} 1 & 2 \\ 2 & 1 \end{bmatrix}$

**c)** $D = \begin{bmatrix} 3 & 2 \\ 2 & 0 \end{bmatrix}$

**28.** Let $A$ be a symmetric matrix and suppose that $A\mathbf{u} = \lambda\mathbf{u}$, $\mathbf{u} \neq \boldsymbol{\theta}$ and $A\mathbf{v} = \beta\mathbf{v}$, $\mathbf{v} \neq \boldsymbol{\theta}$. Also suppose that $\lambda \neq \beta$. Show that $\mathbf{u}^T\mathbf{v} = 0$. [*Hint:* Since

$A\mathbf{v}$ and $\mathbf{u}$ are vectors, $(A\mathbf{v})^T\mathbf{u} = \mathbf{u}^T(A\mathbf{v})$. Rewrite the term $(A\mathbf{v})^T\mathbf{u}$ by using Theorem 10, property 2, of Section 1.6.]

**29.** Having $A$ as in Exercise 27, we see from Exercise 28 that $\mathbf{u}_i^T\mathbf{u}_j = 0$, $i \neq j$. By the corollary to Theorem 15, $\{\mathbf{u}_1, \mathbf{u}_2, \ldots, \mathbf{u}_n\}$ is an orthonormal basis for $R^n$. To show that decomposition (12) is valid, let $C$ denote the right-hand side of (12). Then show that $(A - C)\mathbf{u}_i = \boldsymbol{\theta}$ for $1 \leq i \leq n$. Finally, show that $A - C$ is the zero matrix. [*Hint:* Look at Exercise 24 in Section 4.4.]

(*Note:* We will see in the next section that a real symmetric matrix has only real eigenvalues. It can also be shown that the eigenvectors can be chosen to be orthonormal, even when the eigenvalues are not distinct. Thus decomposition (12) is valid for any real symmetric matrix $A$.)

# COMPLEX EIGENVALUES AND EIGENVECTORS

Up to now we have not examined in detail the case in which the characteristic equation has complex roots—that is, the case in which a matrix has complex eigenvalues. We will see that the possibility of complex eigenvalues does not pose any additional problems except that the eigenvectors corresponding to complex eigenvalues will have complex components, and complex arithmetic will be required to find these eigenvectors.

EXAMPLE 1 Find the eigenvalues and the eigenvectors for

$$A = \begin{bmatrix} 3 & 1 \\ -2 & 1 \end{bmatrix}.$$

*Solution* The characteristic polynomial for $A$ is $p(t) = t^2 - 4t + 5$. The eigenvalues of $A$ are the roots of $p(t) = 0$, which we can find from the quadratic formula,

$$\lambda = \frac{4 \pm \sqrt{-4}}{2} = 2 \pm i,$$

where $i = \sqrt{-1}$. Thus despite the fact that $A$ is a real matrix, the eigenvalues of $A$ are complex, $\lambda = 2 + i$ and $\lambda = 2 - i$. To find the eigenvectors of $A$ corresponding to $\lambda = 2 + i$, we must solve $[A - (2+i)I]\mathbf{x} = \boldsymbol{\theta}$, which leads to the $(2 \times 2)$ homogeneous system

$$\begin{aligned} (1-i)x_1 + \quad x_2 &= 0 \\ -2x_1 - (1+i)x_2 &= 0. \end{aligned} \quad (1)$$

COMPLEX NUMBERS   Ancient peoples knew that certain quadratic equations, such as $x^2 + 1 = 0$, had no real solutions. This posed no difficulty, however, because their particular problems (such as finding the intersections of a line and a circle) did not require complex solutions. Hence people paid complex numbers little attention and referred to them as *imaginary numbers*. In 1545, however, Cardano published a formula for finding the roots of a cubic equation that often required algebraic manipulation of $\sqrt{-1}$ in order to find certain real solutions. Guided by Cardano's formula, Bombelli, in 1572, is credited with working out the algebra of complex numbers. However, the important link to geometry, the association of $a + bi$ with the point $(a, b)$, was not developed for another hundred years.

Probably the two people most influential in developing complex numbers into their essential role in describing scientific phenomena were Leonhard Euler (1707–1783) and Augustin-Louis Cauchy (1789–1857). Besides introducing much of the mathematical notation used today, Euler used complex numbers to unify the study of exponential, logarithmic, and trigonometric functions. Cauchy is regarded as the founder of the field of functions of a complex variable. Many terms and results in the extension of calculus to complex variables are due to Cauchy and are named after him.

At the end of this section, we will discuss the details of how such a system is solved. For the moment, we merely note that if the first equation is multiplied by $1 + i$, then Eq. (1) is equivalent to

$$2x_1 + (1 + i)x_2 = 0$$
$$-2x_1 - (1 + i)x_2 = 0.$$

Thus the solutions of Eq. (1) are determined by $x_1 = -(1 + i)x_2/2$. The nonzero solutions of Eq. (1), the eigenvectors corresponding to $\lambda = 2 + i$, are of the form

$$\mathbf{x} = a \begin{bmatrix} 1 + i \\ -2 \end{bmatrix}, \quad a \neq 0.$$

Similar calculations show that the eigenvectors of $A$ corresponding to $\lambda = 2 - i$ are all of the form

$$\mathbf{x} = b \begin{bmatrix} 1 - i \\ -2 \end{bmatrix}, \quad b \neq 0. \qquad \blacksquare$$

## Complex Arithmetic and Complex Vectors

Before giving the major theoretical results of this section, we briefly review several of the details of complex arithmetic. We will usually represent a complex number $z$ in the form $z = a + ib$, where $a$ and $b$ are real numbers and $i^2 = -1$. In the representation $z = a + ib$, $a$ is called the *real part* of $z$, and $b$ is called the *imaginary part* of $z$. If $z = a + ib$ and $w = c + id$, then $z + w = (a + c) + i(b + d)$, whereas $zw = (ac - bd) + i(ad + bc)$. Thus, for example, if $z_1 = 2 + 3i$ and $z_2 = 1 - i$, then

$$z_1 + z_2 = 3 + 2i \quad \text{and} \quad z_1 z_2 = 5 + i.$$

If $z$ is the complex number $z = a + ib$, then the **conjugate** of $z$ (denoted by $\bar{z}$) is defined to be $\bar{z} = a - ib$. We list several properties of the conjugate operation:

$$\overline{(z + w)} = \bar{z} + \bar{w}$$
$$\overline{(zw)} = \bar{z}\bar{w}$$
$$z + \bar{z} = 2a \qquad\qquad (2)$$
$$z - \bar{z} = 2ib$$
$$z\bar{z} = a^2 + b^2.$$

From the last equality, we note that $z\bar{z}$ is a positive real quantity when $z \neq 0$. In fact, if we visualize $z$ as the point $(a, b)$ in the coordinate plane (called the **complex plane**), then $\sqrt{a^2 + b^2}$ is the distance from $(a, b)$ to the origin (see Fig. 4.2). Hence we define the **magnitude** of $z$ to be $|z|$, where

$$|z| = \sqrt{\bar{z}z} = \sqrt{a^2 + b^2}.$$

We also note from (2) that if $z = \bar{z}$, then $b = 0$ and so $z$ is a real number.

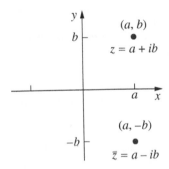

**Figure 4.2**    A complex number and its conjugate

---

|||  EXAMPLE 2   Let $z = 4 - 2i$ and $w = 3 + 5i$.

(a) Find the values of the real and imaginary parts of $w$.

(b) Calculate $\bar{z}$, $\bar{w}$, and $|z|$.

(c) Find $u = 2z + 3\bar{w}$ and $v = \bar{z}w$.

**Solution**

(a) Since $w = 3 + 5i$, the real part of $w$ is 3, and the imaginary part is 5.

(b) For $z = 4 - 2i$, $\bar{z} = 4 + 2i$. Similarly, since $w = 3 + 5i$, we have $\bar{w} = 3 - 5i$. Finally, $|z| = \sqrt{(4)^2 + (-2)^2} = \sqrt{20}$.

(c) Here, $2z = 2(4 - 2i) = 8 - 4i$, whereas $3\bar{w} = 3(3 - 5i) = 9 - 15i$. Therefore,

$$u = 2z + 3\bar{w} = (8 - 4i) + (9 - 15i) = 17 - 19i.$$

The product $v = \bar{z}w$ is calculated as follows:

$$v = \bar{z}w = (4 + 2i)(3 + 5i)$$
$$= 12 + 6i + 20i + 10i^2$$
$$= 2 + 26i.$$

The conjugate operation is useful when dealing with matrices and vectors that have complex components. We define the conjugate of a vector as follows: If $\mathbf{x} = [x_1, x_2, \ldots, x_n]^T$, then the **conjugate vector** (denoted by $\bar{\mathbf{x}}$) is given by

$$\bar{\mathbf{x}} = \begin{bmatrix} \bar{x}_1 \\ \bar{x}_2 \\ \vdots \\ \bar{x}_n \end{bmatrix}.$$

In (3), an example of a vector $\mathbf{x}$ and its conjugate, $\bar{\mathbf{x}}$, is given:

$$\mathbf{x} = \begin{bmatrix} 2 + 3i \\ 4 \\ 1 - 7i \end{bmatrix}, \qquad \bar{\mathbf{x}} = \begin{bmatrix} 2 - 3i \\ 4 \\ 1 + 7i \end{bmatrix}. \tag{3}$$

The **magnitude** or **norm** of a complex vector $\mathbf{x}$ (denoted by $\|\mathbf{x}\|$) is defined in terms of $\mathbf{x}$ and $\bar{\mathbf{x}}$:

$$\|\mathbf{x}\| = \sqrt{\bar{\mathbf{x}}^T \mathbf{x}}. \tag{4}$$

With respect to Eq. (4), note that

$$\bar{\mathbf{x}}^T \mathbf{x} = \bar{x}_1 x_1 + \bar{x}_2 x_2 + \cdots + \bar{x}_n x_n = |x_1|^2 + |x_2|^2 + \cdots + |x_n|^2.$$

(If $\mathbf{x}$ is a real vector, so that $\bar{\mathbf{x}} = \mathbf{x}$, then the definition for $\|\mathbf{x}\|$ in Eq. (4) agrees with our earlier definition in Section 1.6.)

As the next example illustrates, the scalar product $\mathbf{x}^T \mathbf{y}$ will usually be complex values if $\mathbf{x}$ and $\mathbf{y}$ are complex vectors.

EXAMPLE 3    Find $\mathbf{x}^T \mathbf{y}$, $\|\mathbf{x}\|$, and $\|\mathbf{y}\|$ for

$$\mathbf{x} = \begin{bmatrix} 2 \\ 1 - i \\ 3 + 2i \end{bmatrix} \quad \text{and} \quad \mathbf{y} = \begin{bmatrix} i \\ 1 + i \\ 2 - i \end{bmatrix}.$$

*Solution*    For $\mathbf{x}^T \mathbf{y}$, we find

$$\mathbf{x}^T \mathbf{y} = (2)(i) + (1 - i)(1 + i) + (3 + 2i)(2 - i)$$
$$= (2i) + (2) + (8 + i)$$
$$= 10 + 3i.$$

Similarly, $\|\mathbf{x}\| = \sqrt{\bar{\mathbf{x}}^T \mathbf{x}} = \sqrt{4 + 2 + 13} = \sqrt{19}$, whereas $\|\mathbf{y}\| = \sqrt{\bar{\mathbf{y}}^T \mathbf{y}} = \sqrt{1 + 2 + 5} = \sqrt{8}$.

## Eigenvalues of Real Matrices

In a situation where complex numbers might arise, it is conventional to refer to a vector **x** as a *real vector* if all the components of **x** are known to be real numbers. Similarly, we use the term *real matrix* to denote a matrix $A$, all of whose entries are real.

With these preliminaries, we can present two important results. The first result was illustrated in Example 1. We found $\lambda = 2 + i$ to be an eigenvalue with a corresponding eigenvector $\mathbf{x} = [1 + i, -2]^T$. We also found that the conjugates, $\bar{\lambda} = 2 - i$ and $\bar{\mathbf{x}} = [1 - i, -2]^T$, were the other eigenvalue/eigenvector pair. That is, the eigenvalues and eigenvectors occurred in conjugate pairs. The next theorem tells us that Example 1 is typical.

**THEOREM 16** Let $A$ be a real $(n \times n)$ matrix with an eigenvalue $\lambda$ and corresponding eigenvector **x**. Then $\bar{\lambda}$ is also an eigenvalue of $A$, and $\bar{\mathbf{x}}$ is an eigenvector corresponding to $\bar{\lambda}$.

**Proof** It can be shown (see Exercise 36) that $\overline{\lambda \mathbf{x}} = \bar{\lambda} \bar{\mathbf{x}}$. Furthermore, since $A$ is real, it can be shown (see Exercise 36) that

$$\overline{A\mathbf{x}} = \bar{A}\bar{\mathbf{x}} = A\bar{\mathbf{x}}.$$

Using these two results and the assumption $A\mathbf{x} = \lambda \mathbf{x}$, we obtain

$$A\mathbf{x} = \overline{A\mathbf{x}} = \overline{\lambda \mathbf{x}} = \bar{\lambda} \bar{\mathbf{x}}, \quad \mathbf{x} \neq \boldsymbol{\theta}.$$

Thus $\bar{\lambda}$ is an eigenvalue corresponding to the eigenvector $\bar{\mathbf{x}}$. ◼

Finally, as the next theorem shows, there is an important class of matrices for which the possibility of complex eigenvalues is precluded.

**THEOREM 17** If $A$ is an $(n \times n)$ real symmetric matrix, then all the eigenvalues of $A$ are real.

**Proof** Let $A$ by any $(n \times n)$ real symmetric matrix, and suppose that $A\mathbf{x} = \lambda \mathbf{x}$, where $\mathbf{x} \neq \boldsymbol{\theta}$ and where we allow the possibility that **x** is a complex vector. To isolate $\lambda$, we first note that

$$\bar{\mathbf{x}}^T (A\mathbf{x}) = \bar{\mathbf{x}}^T (\lambda \mathbf{x}) = \lambda (\bar{\mathbf{x}}^T \mathbf{x}). \tag{5}$$

Regarding $A\mathbf{x}$ as a vector, we see that $\bar{\mathbf{x}}^T (A\mathbf{x}) = (A\mathbf{x})^T \bar{\mathbf{x}}$ (since, in general, $\mathbf{u}^T \mathbf{v} = \mathbf{v}^T \mathbf{u}$ for complex vectors **u** and **v**). Using this observation in Eq. (5), we obtain

$$\lambda \bar{\mathbf{x}}^T \mathbf{x} = \bar{\mathbf{x}}^T (A\mathbf{x}) = (A\mathbf{x})^T \bar{\mathbf{x}} = \mathbf{x}^T A^T \bar{\mathbf{x}} = \mathbf{x}^T A\bar{\mathbf{x}}, \tag{6}$$

with the last equality holding because $A = A^T$. Since $A$ is real, we also know that $A\bar{\mathbf{x}} = \overline{\lambda \mathbf{x}}$; hence we deduce from Eq. (6) that

$$\lambda \bar{\mathbf{x}}^T \mathbf{x} = \mathbf{x}^T A\bar{\mathbf{x}} = \mathbf{x}^T (\bar{\lambda} \bar{\mathbf{x}}) = \bar{\lambda} \mathbf{x}^T \bar{\mathbf{x}},$$

or

$$\lambda \bar{\mathbf{x}}^T \mathbf{x} = \bar{\lambda} \mathbf{x}^T \bar{\mathbf{x}}. \tag{7}$$

Because $\mathbf{x} \neq \boldsymbol{\theta}$, $\bar{\mathbf{x}}^T\mathbf{x}$ is nonzero, and so from Eq. (7) we see that $\bar{\lambda} = \lambda$, which means that $\lambda$ is real. ◼

## Gaussian Elimination for Systems with Complex Coefficients (Optional)

The remainder of this section is concerned with the computational details of solving $(A - \lambda I)\mathbf{x} = \boldsymbol{\theta}$ when $\lambda$ is complex. We will see that although the arithmetic is tiresome, we can use Gaussian elimination to solve a system of linear equations that has some complex coefficients in exactly the same way that we solve systems of linear equations having real coefficients. For example, consider the $(2 \times 2)$ system

$$a_{11}x_1 + a_{12}x_2 = b_1$$
$$a_{21}x_1 + a_{22}x_2 = b_2,$$

where the coefficients $a_{ij}$ may be complex. Just as before, we can multiply the first equation by $-a_{21}/a_{11}$, add the result to the second equation to eliminate $x_1$ from the second equation, and then backsolve to find $x_2$ and $x_1$. For larger systems with complex coefficients, the principles of Gaussian elimination are exactly the same as they are for real systems; only the computational details are different.

One computational detail that might be unfamiliar is dividing one complex number by another (the first step of Gaussian elimination for the $(2 \times 2)$ system above is to form $a_{21}/a_{11}$). To see how a complex division is carried out, let $z = a + ib$ and $w = c + id$, where $w \neq 0$. To form the quotient $z/w$, we multiply numerator and denominator by $\bar{w}$:

$$\frac{z}{w} = \frac{z\bar{w}}{w\bar{w}}.$$

In detail, we have

$$\frac{z}{w} = \frac{z\bar{w}}{w\bar{w}} = \frac{(a+ib)(c-id)}{c^2+d^2} = \frac{(ac+bd)+i(bc-ad)}{c^2+d^2}. \tag{8}$$

Our objective is to express the quotient $z/w$ in the standard form $z/w = r + is$, where $r$ and $s$ are real numbers; from Eq. (8), $r$ and $s$ are given by

$$r = \frac{ac+bd}{c^2+d^2} \quad \text{and} \quad s = \frac{bc-ad}{c^2+d^2}.$$

For instance,

$$\frac{2+3i}{1+2i} = \frac{(2+3i)(1-2i)}{(1+2i)(1-2i)} = \frac{8-i}{5} = \frac{8}{5} - \frac{1}{5}i.$$

**EXAMPLE 4**    Use Gaussian elimination to solve the system in (1):

$$(1-i)x_1 + \qquad x_2 = 0$$
$$-2x_1 - (1+i)x_2 = 0.$$

*Solution*  The initial step in solving this system is to multiply the first equation by $2/(1-i)$ and then add the result to the second equation. Following the discussion above, we write $2/(1-i)$ as

$$\frac{2}{1-i} = \frac{2(1+i)}{(1-i)(1+i)} = \frac{2+2i}{2} = 1+i.$$

Multiplying the first equation by $1+i$ and adding the result to the second equation produces the equivalent system

$$(1-i)x_1 + x_2 = 0$$
$$0 = 0,$$

which leads to $x_1 = -x_2/(1-i)$. Simplifying, we obtain

$$x_1 = \frac{-x_2}{1-i} = \frac{-x_2(1+i)}{(1-i)(1+i)} = \frac{-(1+i)}{2}x_2.$$

With $x_2 = -2a$, the solutions are all of the form

$$\mathbf{x} = a \begin{bmatrix} 1+i \\ -2 \end{bmatrix}.$$

(*Note:* Since we are allowing the possibility of vectors with complex components, we will also allow the parameter $a$ in Example 4 to be complex. For example, with $a = i$ we see that

$$\mathbf{x} = \begin{bmatrix} -1+i \\ -2i \end{bmatrix}$$

is also a solution.)

EXAMPLE 5  Find the eigenvalues and the eigenvectors of $A$, where

$$A = \begin{bmatrix} -2 & -2 & -9 \\ -1 & 1 & -3 \\ 1 & 1 & 4 \end{bmatrix}.$$

*Solution*  The characteristic polynomial of $A$ is

$$p(t) = -(t-1)(t^2 - 2t + 2).$$

Thus the eigenvalues of $A$ are $\lambda = 1, \lambda = 1+i, \lambda = 1-i$.

As we noted earlier, the complex eigenvalues occur in conjugate pairs; and if we find an eigenvector $\mathbf{x}$ for $\lambda = 1+i$, then we immediately see that $\bar{\mathbf{x}}$ is an eigenvector for $\bar{\lambda} = 1-i$. In this example we find the eigenvectors for $\lambda = 1+i$ by reducing the augmented matrix $[A - \lambda I \mid \boldsymbol{\theta}]$ to echelon form. Now for $\lambda = 1+i$,

$$[A - \lambda I \mid \boldsymbol{\theta}] = \begin{bmatrix} -3-i & -2 & -9 & 0 \\ -1 & -i & -3 & 0 \\ 1 & 1 & 3-i & 0 \end{bmatrix}.$$

To introduce a zero into the (2, 1) position, we use the multiple $m$, where

$$m = \frac{1}{-3-i} = \frac{-1}{3+i} = \frac{-(3-i)}{(3+i)(3-i)} = \frac{-3+i}{10}.$$

Multiplying the first row by $m$ and adding the result to the second row, and then multiplying the first row by $-m$ and adding the result to the third row, we find that $[A - \lambda I \mid \theta]$ is row equivalent to

$$\begin{bmatrix} -3-i & -2 & -9 & 0 \\ 0 & \dfrac{6-12i}{10} & \dfrac{-3-9i}{10} & 0 \\ 0 & \dfrac{4+2i}{10} & \dfrac{3-i}{10} & 0 \end{bmatrix}.$$

Multiplying the second and third rows by 10 in the preceding matrix, we obtain a row-equivalent matrix:

$$\begin{bmatrix} -3-i & -2 & -9 & 0 \\ 0 & 6-12i & -3-9i & 0 \\ 0 & 4+2i & 3-i & 0 \end{bmatrix}.$$

Completing the reduction, we multiply the second row by $r$ and add the result to the third row, where $r$ is the multiple

$$r = \frac{-(4+2i)}{6-12i} = \frac{-(4+2i)(6+12i)}{(6-12i)(6+12i)} = \frac{-60i}{180} = \frac{-i}{3}.$$

We obtain the row-equivalent matrix

$$\begin{bmatrix} -3-i & -2 & -9 & 0 \\ 0 & 6-12i & -3-9i & 0 \\ 0 & 0 & 0 & 0 \end{bmatrix};$$

and the eigenvectors of $A$ corresponding to $\lambda = 1 + i$ are found by solving

$$\begin{aligned} -(3+i)x_1 - \quad 2x_2 &= \quad\quad 9x_3 \\ (6-12i)x_2 &= (3+9i)x_3, \end{aligned} \tag{9}$$

with $x_3$ arbitrary, $x_3 \neq 0$. We first find $x_2$ from

$$x_2 = \frac{3+9i}{6-12i}x_3 = \frac{(3+9i)(6+12i)}{180}x_3 = \frac{-90+90i}{180}x_3,$$

or

$$x_2 = \frac{-1+i}{2}x_3.$$

From the first equation in (9), we obtain

$$-(3+i)x_1 = 2x_2 + 9x_3 = (8+i)x_3,$$

or

$$x_1 = \frac{-(8+i)}{3+i} x_3 = \frac{-(8+i)(3-i)}{10} x_3 = \frac{-25+5i}{10} x_3 = \frac{-5+i}{2} x_3.$$

Setting $x_3 = 2a$, we have $x_2 = (-1+i)a$ and $x_1 = (-5+i)a$; so the eigenvectors of $A$ corresponding to $\lambda = 1 + i$ are all of the form

$$\mathbf{x} = \begin{bmatrix} (-5+i)a \\ (-1+i)a \\ 2a \end{bmatrix} = a \begin{bmatrix} -5+i \\ -1+i \\ 2 \end{bmatrix}, \quad a \neq 0.$$

Furthermore, we know that eigenvectors of $A$ corresponding to $\bar{\lambda} = 1 - i$ have the form

$$\bar{\mathbf{x}} = b \begin{bmatrix} -5-i \\ -1-i \\ 2 \end{bmatrix}, \quad b \neq 0. \quad ◼$$

If linear algebra software is available, then finding eigenvalues and eigenvectors is a simple matter.

EXAMPLE 6    Find the eigenvalues and the eigenvectors for the $(4 \times 4)$ matrix

$$A = \begin{bmatrix} 3 & 3 & 6 & 9 \\ 1 & 4 & 3 & 7 \\ 2 & -5 & 8 & 3 \\ 2 & -9 & 7 & 4 \end{bmatrix}.$$

*Solution*    We used MATLAB to solve this problem. The command [V, D] = eig(A) produces a diagonal matrix $D$ and a matrix of eigenvectors $V$. That is, $AV = DV$ or (if $A$ is not defective) $V^{-1}AV = D$. The results from MATLAB are shown in Fig. 4.3. As can be seen from the matrix $D$ in Fig. 4.3, $A$ has two complex eigenvalues, which are (to the places shown) $\lambda = 6.9014 + 5.3028i$ and $\lambda = 6.9014 - 5.3028i$. In addition, $A$ has two real eigenvalues $\lambda = 4.0945$ and $\lambda = 1.1027$. Eigenvectors are found in the corresponding columns of $V$. ◼

As the preceding examples indicate, finding eigenvectors that correspond to a complex eigenvalue proceeds exactly as for a real eigenvalue except for the additional details required by complex arithmetic.

Although complex eigenvalues and eigenvectors may seem an undue complication, they are in fact fairly important to applications. For instance, we note (without trying to be precise) that oscillatory and periodic solutions to first-order systems of differential equations correspond to complex eigenvalues; and since many physical systems exhibit such behavior, we need some way to model them.

```
A=
        3       3       6       9
        1       4       3       7
        2      -5       8       3
        2      -9       7       4

>>[V,D]=eig(A)

V =
    0.6897 + 0.2800i     0.6897 - 0.2800i     0.8216      0.9609
    0.4761 + 0.2051i     0.4761 - 0.2051i     0.4196     -0.0067
    0.1338 + 0.2255i     0.1338 - 0.2255i     0.3014     -0.2765
   -0.1139 + 0.3090i    -0.1139 - 0.3090i    -0.2409     -0.0160

D =
    6.9014 + 5.3028i            0                  0           0
           0            6.9014 - 5.3028i           0           0
           0                    0               4.0945         0
           0                    0                  0        1.1027
```

*Figure 4.3*    MATLAB was used to find the eigenvalues and eigenvectors of matrix $A$ in Example 6—that is, $AV = VD$ or $V^{-1}AV = D$, where $D$ is diagonal.

## 4.6    EXERCISES

In Exercises 1–18, $s = 1 + 2i$, $u = 3 - 2i$, $v = 4 + i$, $w = 2 - i$, and $z = 1 + i$. In each exercise, perform the indicated calculation and express the result in the form $a + ib$.

**1.** $\bar{u}$
**2.** $\bar{z}$
**3.** $u + \bar{v}$

**4.** $\bar{z} + w$
**5.** $u + \bar{u}$
**6.** $s - \bar{s}$

**7.** $v\bar{v}$
**8.** $u\bar{v}$
**9.** $s^2 - w$

**10.** $z^2 w$
**11.** $\bar{u}w^2$
**12.** $s(u^2 + v)$

**13.** $u/v$
**14.** $v/u^2$
**15.** $s/z$

**16.** $(w + \bar{v})/u$
**17.** $w + iz$
**18.** $s - iw$

Find the eigenvalues and the eigenvectors for the matrices in Exercises 19–24. (For the matrix in Exercise 24, one eigenvalue is $\lambda = 1 + 5i$.)

**19.** $\begin{bmatrix} 6 & 8 \\ -1 & 2 \end{bmatrix}$

**20.** $\begin{bmatrix} 2 & 4 \\ -2 & -2 \end{bmatrix}$

**21.** $\begin{bmatrix} -2 & -1 \\ 5 & 2 \end{bmatrix}$

**22.** $\begin{bmatrix} 5 & -5 & -5 \\ -1 & 4 & 2 \\ 3 & -5 & -3 \end{bmatrix}$

**23.** $\begin{bmatrix} 1 & -4 & -1 \\ 3 & 2 & 3 \\ 1 & 1 & 3 \end{bmatrix}$

**24.** $\begin{bmatrix} 1 & -5 & 0 & 0 \\ 5 & 1 & 0 & 0 \\ 0 & 0 & 1 & -2 \\ 0 & 0 & 2 & 1 \end{bmatrix}$

In Exercises 25 and 26, solve the linear system.

**25.** $(1 + i)x + iy = \quad 5 + 4i$
$(1 - i)x - 4y = -11 + 5i$

**26.** $(1 - i)x - (3 + i)y = -5 - i$
$(2 + i)x + (1 + 2i)y = \quad 1 + 6i$

In Exercises 27–30, calculate $\|\mathbf{x}\|$.

**27.** $\mathbf{x} = \begin{bmatrix} 1+i \\ 2 \end{bmatrix}$      **28.** $\mathbf{x} = \begin{bmatrix} 3+i \\ 2-i \end{bmatrix}$

**29.** $\mathbf{x} = \begin{bmatrix} 1-2i \\ i \\ 3+i \end{bmatrix}$      **30.** $\mathbf{x} = \begin{bmatrix} 2i \\ 1-i \\ 3 \end{bmatrix}$

In Exercises 31–34, use linear algebra software to find the eigenvalues and the eigenvectors.

**31.** $\begin{bmatrix} 2 & 2 & 5 \\ 5 & 3 & 7 \\ 1 & 5 & 3 \end{bmatrix}$      **32.** $\begin{bmatrix} 1 & 2 & 8 \\ 8 & 4 & 9 \\ 2 & 6 & 1 \end{bmatrix}$

**33.** $\begin{bmatrix} 5 & -1 & 0 & 8 \\ 3 & 6 & 8 & -3 \\ 1 & 1 & 4 & 2 \\ 9 & 7 & 6 & 9 \end{bmatrix}$      **34.** $\begin{bmatrix} 5 & 5 & 4 & 6 \\ 0 & 8 & 6 & 7 \\ 1 & 2 & 3 & 1 \\ 6 & 3 & 8 & 5 \end{bmatrix}$

**35.** Establish the five properties of the conjugate operation listed in (2).

**36.** Let $A$ be an $(m \times n)$ matrix, and let $B$ be an $(n \times p)$ matrix, where the entries of $A$ and $B$ may be complex. Use Exercise 35 and the definition of $AB$ to show that $\overline{AB} = \bar{A}\bar{B}$. (By $\bar{A}$, we mean the matrix whose $ij$th entry is the conjugate of the $ij$th entry of $A$.) If $A$ is a real matrix and $\mathbf{x}$ is an $(n \times 1)$ vector, show that $\overline{A\mathbf{x}} = A\bar{\mathbf{x}}$.

**37.** Let $A$ be an $(m \times n)$ matrix, where the entries of $A$ may be complex. It is customary to use the symbol $A^*$ to denote the matrix

$$A^* = (\bar{A})^T.$$

Suppose that $A$ is an $(m \times n)$ matrix and $B$ is an $(n \times p)$ matrix. Use Exercise 36 and the properties of the transpose operation to give a quick proof that $(AB)^* = B^*A^*$.

**38.** An $(n \times n)$ matrix $A$ is called **Hermitian** if $A^* = A$.

  **a)** Prove that a Hermitian matrix $A$ has only real eigenvalues. [*Hint:* Observing that $\bar{\mathbf{x}}^T\mathbf{x} = \mathbf{x}^*\mathbf{x}$, modify the proof of Theorem 17.]

  **b)** Let $A = (a_{ij})$ be an $(n \times n)$ Hermitian matrix. Show that $a_{ii}$ is real for $1 \leq i \leq n$.

**39.** Let $p(t) = a_0 + a_1 t + \cdots + a_n t^n$, where the coefficients $a_0, a_1, \ldots, a_n$ are all real.

  **a)** Prove that if $r$ is a complex root of $p(t) = 0$, then $\bar{r}$ is also a root of $p(t) = 0$.

  **b)** If $p(t)$ has degree 3, argue that $p(t)$ must have at least one real root.

  **c)** If $A$ is a $(3 \times 3)$ real matrix, argue that $A$ must have at least one real eigenvalue.

**40.** An $(n \times n)$ real matrix $A$ is called **orthogonal** if $A^TA = I$. Let $\lambda$ be an eigenvalue of an orthogonal matrix $A$, where $\lambda = r + is$. Prove that $\lambda\bar{\lambda} = r^2 + s^2 = 1$. [*Hint:* First show that $\|A\mathbf{x}\| = \|\mathbf{x}\|$ for any vector $\mathbf{x}$.]

**41.** A real symmetric $(n \times n)$ matrix $A$ is called **positive definite** if $\mathbf{x}^TA\mathbf{x} > 0$ for all $\mathbf{x}$ in $R^n$, $\mathbf{x} \neq \boldsymbol{\theta}$. Prove that the eigenvalues of a real symmetric positive-definite matrix $A$ are all positive.

**42.** An $(n \times n)$ matrix $A$ is called **unitary** if $A^*A = I$. (If $A$ is a real unitary matrix, then $A$ is orthogonal; see Exercise 40.) Show that if $A$ is unitary and $\lambda$ is an eigenvalue for $A$, then $|\lambda| = 1$.

# 4.7 SIMILARITY TRANSFORMATIONS AND DIAGONALIZATION

In Chapter 1, we saw that two linear systems of equations have the same solution if their augmented matrices are row equivalent. In this chapter, we are interested in identifying classes of matrices that have the same eigenvalues.

As we know, the eigenvalues of an $(n \times n)$ matrix $A$ are the zeros of its characteristic polynomial,

$$p(t) = \det(A - tI).$$

Thus if an $(n \times n)$ matrix $B$ has the same characteristic polynomial as $A$, then $A$ and $B$ have the same eigenvalues. As we will see, it is fairly simple to find such matrices $B$.

## Similarity

In particular, let $A$ be an $(n \times n)$ matrix, and let $S$ be a nonsingular $(n \times n)$ matrix. Then, as the following calculation shows, the matrices $A$ and $B = S^{-1}AS$ have the same characteristic polynomial. To establish this fact, observe that the characteristic polynomial for $S^{-1}AS$ is given by

$$
\begin{aligned}
p(t) &= \det(S^{-1}AS - tI) \\
&= \det(S^{-1}AS - tS^{-1}S) \\
&= \det[S^{-1}(A - tI)S] \\
&= \det(S^{-1})\det(A - tI)\det(S), \quad \text{by Theorem 2} \\
&= [\det(S^{-1})\det(S)]\det(A - tI) \\
&= \det(A - tI).
\end{aligned}
\tag{1}
$$

(The last equality given follows because $\det(S^{-1})\det(S) = \det(S^{-1}S) = \det(I) = 1$.)

Thus, by (1), the matrices $S^{-1}AS$ and $A$ have the same characteristic polynomial and hence the same set of eigenvalues. The discussion above leads to the next definition.

**DEFINITION 8**    The $(n \times n)$ matrices $A$ and $B$ are said to be *similar* if there is a nonsingular $(n \times n)$ matrix $S$ such that $B = S^{-1}AS$.

The calculations carried out in (1) show that similar matrices have the same characteristic polynomial. Consequently the following theorem is immediate.

**THEOREM 18**    If $A$ and $B$ are similar $(n \times n)$ matrices, then $A$ and $B$ have the same eigenvalues. Moreover, these eigenvalues have the same algebraic multiplicity. ◼

Although similar matrices always have the same characteristic polynomial, it is not true that two matrices with the same characteristic polynomial are necessarily similar. As a simple example, consider the two matrices

$$
A = \begin{bmatrix} 1 & 0 \\ 1 & 1 \end{bmatrix} \quad \text{and} \quad I = \begin{bmatrix} 1 & 0 \\ 0 & 1 \end{bmatrix}.
$$

Now $p(t) = (1 - t)^2$ is the characteristic polynomial for both $A$ and $I$; so $A$ and $I$ have the same set of eigenvalues. If $A$ and $I$ were similar, however, there would be a $(2 \times 2)$ matrix $S$ such that

$$
I = S^{-1}AS.
$$

But the equation $I = S^{-1}AS$ is equivalent to $S = AS$, which is in turn equivalent to $SS^{-1} = A$ or $I = A$. Thus $I$ and $A$ cannot be similar. (A repetition of this argument shows that the only matrix similar to the identity matrix is $I$ itself.) In this respect, similarity is a more fundamental concept for the eigenvalue problem than is the characteristic polynomial; two matrices can have exactly the same characteristic polynomial without being similar; so similarity leads to a more finely detailed way of distinguishing matrices.

Although similar matrices have the same eigenvalues, they do not generally have the same eigenvectors. For example, if $B = S^{-1}AS$ and if $B\mathbf{x} = \lambda\mathbf{x}$, then

$$S^{-1}AS\mathbf{x} = \lambda\mathbf{x} \quad \text{or} \quad A(S\mathbf{x}) = \lambda(S\mathbf{x}).$$

Thus if $\mathbf{x}$ is an eigenvector for $B$ corresponding to $\lambda$, then $S\mathbf{x}$ is an eigenvector for $A$ corresponding to $\lambda$.

## Diagonalization

Computations involving an $(n \times n)$ matrix $A$ can often be simplified if we know that $A$ is similar to a diagonal matrix. To illustrate, suppose $S^{-1}AS = D$, where $D$ is a diagonal matrix. Next, suppose we need to calculate the power $A^k$, here $k$ is a positive integer. Knowing that $D = S^{-1}AS$, we can proceed as follows:

$$\begin{aligned} D^k &= (S^{-1}AS)^k \\ &= S^{-1}A^kS. \end{aligned} \tag{2}$$

(The fact that $(S^{-1}AS)^k = S^{-1}A^kS$ is established in Exercise 25.) Note that because $D$ is a diagonal matrix, it is easy to form the power $D^k$.

Once the matrix $D^k$ is computed, the matrix $A^k$ can be recovered from Eq. (2) by forming $SD^kS^{-1}$:

$$SD^kS^{-1} = S(S^{-1}A^kS)S^{-1} = A^k.$$

Whenever an $(n \times n)$ matrix $A$ is similar to a diagonal matrix, we say that $A$ is *diagonalizable*. The next theorem gives a characterization of diagonalizable matrices.

**THEOREM 19** An $(n \times n)$ matrix $A$ is diagonalizable if and only if $A$ possesses a set of $n$ linearly independent eigenvectors.

*Proof* Suppose that $\{\mathbf{u}_1, \mathbf{u}_2, \ldots, \mathbf{u}_n\}$ is a set of $n$ linearly independent eigenvectors for $A$:

$$A\mathbf{u}_k = \lambda_k\mathbf{u}_k, \quad k = 1, 2, \ldots, n.$$

Let $S$ be the $(n \times n)$ matrix whose column vectors are the eigenvectors of $A$:

$$S = [\mathbf{u}_1, \mathbf{u}_2, \ldots, \mathbf{u}_n].$$

Now $S$ is a nonsingular matrix; so $S^{-1}$ exists where

$$S^{-1}S = [S^{-1}\mathbf{u}_1, S^{-1}\mathbf{u}_2, \ldots, S^{-1}\mathbf{u}_n] = [\mathbf{e}_1, \mathbf{e}_2, \ldots, \mathbf{e}_n] = I. \tag{3}$$

Furthermore, since $A\mathbf{u}_k = \lambda_k\mathbf{u}_k$, we obtain

$$AS = [A\mathbf{u}_1, A\mathbf{u}_2, \ldots, A\mathbf{u}_n] = [\lambda_1\mathbf{u}_1, \lambda_2\mathbf{u}_2, \ldots, \lambda_n\mathbf{u}_n];$$

and so from Eq. (3),

$$S^{-1}AS = [\lambda_1 S^{-1}\mathbf{u}_1, \lambda_2 S^{-1}\mathbf{u}_2, \ldots, \lambda_n S^{-1}\mathbf{u}_n] = [\lambda_1\mathbf{e}_1, \lambda_2\mathbf{e}_2, \ldots, \lambda_n\mathbf{e}_n].$$

Therefore, $S^{-1}AS$ has the form

$$S^{-1}AS = \begin{bmatrix} \lambda_1 & 0 & 0 & \cdots & 0 \\ 0 & \lambda_2 & 0 & \cdots & 0 \\ 0 & 0 & \lambda_3 & \cdots & 0 \\ \vdots & & & & \vdots \\ 0 & 0 & 0 & \cdots & \lambda_n \end{bmatrix} = D;$$

and we have shown that if $A$ has $n$ linearly independent eigenvectors, then $A$ is similar to a diagonal matrix.

Now suppose that $C^{-1}AC = D$, where $C$ is nonsingular and $D$ is a diagonal matrix. Let us write $C$ and $D$ in column form as

$$C = [\mathbf{C}_1, \mathbf{C}_2, \ldots, \mathbf{C}_n] \quad \text{and} \quad D = [d_1\mathbf{e}_1, d_2\mathbf{e}_2, \ldots, d_n\mathbf{e}_n].$$

From $C^{-1}AC = D$, we obtain $AC = CD$, and we write both of these in column form as

$$AC = [A\mathbf{C}_1, A\mathbf{C}_2, \ldots, A\mathbf{C}_n]$$
$$CD = [d_1C\mathbf{e}_1, d_2C\mathbf{e}_2, \ldots, d_nC\mathbf{e}_n].$$

But since $C\mathbf{e}_k = \mathbf{C}_k$ for $k = 1, 2, \ldots, n$, we see that $AC = CD$ implies

$$A\mathbf{C}_k = d_k\mathbf{C}_k, \quad k = 1, 2, \ldots, n.$$

Since $C$ is nonsingular, the vectors $\mathbf{C}_1, \mathbf{C}_2, \ldots, \mathbf{C}_n$ are linearly independent (and in particular, no $\mathbf{C}_k$ is the zero vector). Thus the diagonal entries of $D$ are the eigenvalues of $A$, and the column vectors of $C$ are a set of $n$ linearly independent eigenvectors. ■

Note that the proof of Theorem 19 gives a procedure for diagonalizing an $(n \times n)$ matrix $A$. That is, if $A$ has $n$ linearly independent eigenvectors $\mathbf{u}_1, \mathbf{u}_2, \ldots, \mathbf{u}_n$, then the matrix $S = [\mathbf{u}_1, \mathbf{u}_2, \ldots, \mathbf{u}_n]$ will diagonalize $A$.

EXAMPLE 1    Show that $A$ is diagonalizable by finding a matrix $S$ such that $S^{-1}AS = D$:

$$A = \begin{bmatrix} 5 & -6 \\ 3 & -4 \end{bmatrix}.$$

**Solution**    It is easy to verify that $A$ has eigenvalues $\lambda_1 = 2$ and $\lambda_2 = -1$ with corresponding eigenvectors

$$\mathbf{u}_1 = \begin{bmatrix} 2 \\ 1 \end{bmatrix} \quad \text{and} \quad \mathbf{u}_2 = \begin{bmatrix} 1 \\ 1 \end{bmatrix}.$$

Forming $S = [\mathbf{u}_1, \mathbf{u}_2]$, we obtain

$$S = \begin{bmatrix} 2 & 1 \\ 1 & 1 \end{bmatrix}, \quad S^{-1} = \begin{bmatrix} 1 & -1 \\ -1 & 2 \end{bmatrix}.$$

As a check on the calculations, we form $S^{-1}AS$. The matrix $AS$ is given by

$$AS = \begin{bmatrix} 5 & -6 \\ 3 & -4 \end{bmatrix} \begin{bmatrix} 2 & 1 \\ 1 & 1 \end{bmatrix} = \begin{bmatrix} 4 & -1 \\ 2 & -1 \end{bmatrix}.$$

Next, forming $S^{-1}(AS)$, we obtain

$$S^{-1}(AS) = \begin{bmatrix} 1 & -1 \\ -1 & 2 \end{bmatrix} \begin{bmatrix} 4 & -1 \\ 2 & -1 \end{bmatrix} = \begin{bmatrix} 2 & 0 \\ 0 & -1 \end{bmatrix} = D. \qquad \blacksquare$$

---

EXAMPLE 2    Use the result of Example 1 to calculate $A^{10}$, where

$$A = \begin{bmatrix} 5 & -6 \\ 3 & -4 \end{bmatrix}.$$

*Solution*    As was noted in Eq. (2), $D^{10} = S^{-1}A^{10}S$. Therefore, $A^{10} = SD^{10}S^{-1}$. Now by Example 1,

$$D^{10} = \begin{bmatrix} 2^{10} & 0 \\ 0 & (-1)^{10} \end{bmatrix} = \begin{bmatrix} 1024 & 0 \\ 0 & 1 \end{bmatrix}.$$

Hence $A^{10} = SD^{10}S^{-1}$ is given by

$$A^{10} = \begin{bmatrix} 2047 & -2046 \\ 1023 & -1022 \end{bmatrix}. \qquad \blacksquare$$

Sometimes complex arithmetic is necessary to diagonalize a real matrix.

---

EXAMPLE 3    Show that $A$ is diagonalizable by finding a matrix $S$ such that $S^{-1}AS = D$:

$$A = \begin{bmatrix} 1 & 1 \\ -1 & 1 \end{bmatrix}.$$

*Solution*    $A$ has eigenvalues $\lambda_1 = 1 + i$ and $\lambda_2 = 1 - i$, with corresponding eigenvectors

$$\mathbf{u}_1 = \begin{bmatrix} 1 \\ i \end{bmatrix} \quad \text{and} \quad \mathbf{u}_2 = \begin{bmatrix} 1 \\ -i \end{bmatrix}.$$

Forming the matrix $S = [\mathbf{u}_1, \mathbf{u}_2]$, we obtain

$$S = \begin{bmatrix} 1 & 1 \\ i & -i \end{bmatrix}, \quad S^{-1} = \begin{bmatrix} \dfrac{1}{2} & -\dfrac{i}{2} \\ \dfrac{1}{2} & \dfrac{i}{2} \end{bmatrix}.$$

As a check, note that $AS$ is given by

$$AS = \begin{bmatrix} 1 & 1 \\ -1 & 1 \end{bmatrix} \begin{bmatrix} 1 & 1 \\ i & -i \end{bmatrix} = \begin{bmatrix} 1+i & 1-i \\ -1+i & -1-i \end{bmatrix}.$$

Next, $S^{-1}(AS)$ is the matrix

$$S^{-1}(AS) = \frac{1}{2} \begin{bmatrix} 1 & -i \\ 1 & i \end{bmatrix} \begin{bmatrix} 1+i & 1-i \\ -1+i & -1-i \end{bmatrix} = \begin{bmatrix} 1+i & 0 \\ 0 & 1-i \end{bmatrix} = D. \quad \blacksquare$$

Some types of matrices are known to be diagonalizable. The next theorem lists one such condition. Then, in the last subsection, we prove the important theorem: If $A$ is a real symmetric matrix, then $A$ is diagonalizable.

**THEOREM 20**    Let $A$ be an $(n \times n)$ matrix with $n$ distinct eigenvalues. Then $A$ is diagonalizable.

*Proof*    By Theorem 15, if $A$ has $n$ distinct eigenvalues, then $A$ has a set of $n$ linearly independent eigenvectors. Thus by Theorem 19, $A$ is diagonalizable. ∎

As the next example shows, a matrix $A$ may be diagonalizable even though it has repeated eigenvalues.

**EXAMPLE 4**    Show that $A$ is diagonalizable, where

$$A = \begin{bmatrix} 25 & -8 & 30 \\ 24 & -7 & 30 \\ -12 & 4 & -14 \end{bmatrix}.$$

*Solution*    The eigenvalues of $A$ are $\lambda_1 = \lambda_2 = 1$ and $\lambda_3 = 2$. The eigenspace corresponding to $\lambda_1 = \lambda_2 = 1$ has dimension 2, with a basis $\{\mathbf{u}_1, \mathbf{u}_2\}$, where

$$\mathbf{u}_1 = \begin{bmatrix} 1 \\ 3 \\ 0 \end{bmatrix} \quad \text{and} \quad \mathbf{u}_2 = \begin{bmatrix} -4 \\ 3 \\ 4 \end{bmatrix}.$$

An eigenvector corresponding to $\lambda_3 = 2$ is

$$\mathbf{u}_3 = \begin{bmatrix} 4 \\ 4 \\ -2 \end{bmatrix}.$$

Defining $S$ by $S = [\mathbf{u}_1, \mathbf{u}_2, \mathbf{u}_3]$, we can verify that

$$S^{-1}AS = D = \begin{bmatrix} 1 & 0 & 0 \\ 0 & 1 & 0 \\ 0 & 0 & 2 \end{bmatrix}.$$ ∎

## Orthogonal Matrices

A remarkable and useful fact about symmetric matrices is that they are always diagonalizable. Moreover, the diagonalization of a symmetric matrix $A$ can be accomplished with a special type of matrix known as an orthogonal matrix.

**DEFINITION 9**    A real $(n \times n)$ matrix $Q$ is called an ***orthogonal*** matrix if $Q$ is invertible and $Q^{-1} = Q^T$.

Definition 9 can be rephrased as follows: A real square matrix $Q$ is orthogonal if and only if

$$Q^T Q = I. \tag{4}$$

Another useful description of orthogonal matrices can be obtained from Eq. (4). In particular, suppose that $Q = [\mathbf{q}_1, \mathbf{q}_2, \ldots, \mathbf{q}_n]$ is an $(n \times n)$ matrix. Since the $i$th row of $Q^T$ is equal to $\mathbf{q}_i^T$, the definition of matrix multiplication tells us:

The $ij$th entry of $Q^T Q$ is equal to $\mathbf{q}_i^T \mathbf{q}_j$.

Therefore, by Eq. (4), an $(n \times n)$ matrix $Q = [\mathbf{q}_1, \mathbf{q}_2, \ldots, \mathbf{q}_n]$ is orthogonal if and only if:

The columns of $Q$, $\{\mathbf{q}_1, \mathbf{q}_2, \ldots, \mathbf{q}_n\}$,   (5)
form an orthonormal set of vectors.

EXAMPLE 5    Verify that the matrices, $Q_1$ and $Q_2$ are orthogonal:

$$Q_1 = \frac{1}{\sqrt{2}} \begin{bmatrix} 1 & 0 & 1 \\ 0 & \sqrt{2} & 0 \\ -1 & 0 & 1 \end{bmatrix} \quad \text{and} \quad Q_2 = \begin{bmatrix} 0 & 0 & 1 \\ 1 & 0 & 0 \\ 0 & 1 & 0 \end{bmatrix}.$$

**Solution**    We use Eq. (4) to show that $Q_1$ is orthogonal. Specifically,

$$Q_1^T Q_1 = \frac{1}{2} \begin{bmatrix} 1 & 0 & -1 \\ 0 & \sqrt{2} & 0 \\ 1 & 0 & 1 \end{bmatrix} \begin{bmatrix} 1 & 0 & 1 \\ 0 & \sqrt{2} & 0 \\ -1 & 0 & 1 \end{bmatrix} = \frac{1}{2} \begin{bmatrix} 2 & 0 & 0 \\ 0 & 2 & 0 \\ 0 & 0 & 2 \end{bmatrix} = I.$$

We use condition Eq. (5) to show that $Q_2$ is orthogonal. The column vectors of $Q_2$ are, in the order they appear, $\{\mathbf{e}_2, \mathbf{e}_3, \mathbf{e}_1\}$. Since these vectors are orthonormal, it follows from Eq. (5) that $Q_2$ is orthogonal. ◼

From the characterization of orthogonal matrices given in condition Eq. (5), the following observation can be made: If $Q = [\mathbf{q}_1, \mathbf{q}_2, \ldots, \mathbf{q}_n]$ is an $(n \times n)$ orthogonal matrix and if $P = [\mathbf{p}_1, \mathbf{p}_2, \ldots, \mathbf{p}_n]$ is formed by rearranging the columns of $Q$, then $P$ is also an orthogonal matrix.

As a special case of this observation, suppose that $P$ is a matrix formed by rearranging the columns of the identity matrix, $I$. Then, since $I$ is an orthogonal matrix, it follows that $P$ is orthogonal as well. Such a matrix $P$, formed by rearranging the columns of $I$, is called a *permutation* matrix. The matrix $Q_2$ in Example 5 is a specific instance of a $(3 \times 3)$ permutation matrix.

Orthogonal matrices have some special properties that make them valuable tools for applications. These properties were mentioned in Section 3.7 with regard to $(2 \times 2)$ orthogonal matrices. Suppose we think of an $(n \times n)$ matrix $Q$ as defining a function (or linear transformation) from $R^n$ to $R^n$. That is, for $\mathbf{x}$ in $R^n$, consider the function defined by

$$\mathbf{y} = Q\mathbf{x}.$$

As the next theorem shows, if $Q$ is orthogonal, then the function $\mathbf{y} = Q\mathbf{x}$ preserves the lengths of vectors and the angles between pairs of vectors.

Let $Q$ be an $(n \times n)$ orthogonal matrix.

    **(a)** If $\mathbf{x}$ is in $R^n$, then $\|Q\mathbf{x}\| = \|\mathbf{x}\|$.

    **(b)** If $\mathbf{x}$ and $\mathbf{y}$ are in $R^n$, then $(Q\mathbf{x})^T(Q\mathbf{y}) = \mathbf{x}^T\mathbf{y}$.

    **(c)** $\text{Det}(Q) = \pm 1$.

*Proof* We will prove property (a) and leave properties (b) and (c) to the exercises. Let $\mathbf{x}$ be a vector in $R^n$. Then

$$\|Q\mathbf{x}\| = \sqrt{(Q\mathbf{x})^T(Q\mathbf{x})} = \sqrt{\mathbf{x}^T Q^T Q \mathbf{x}} = \sqrt{\mathbf{x}^T I \mathbf{x}} = \sqrt{\mathbf{x}^T \mathbf{x}} = \|\mathbf{x}\|.$$

The fact that $\mathbf{x}^T(Q^TQ)\mathbf{x} = \mathbf{x}^T I \mathbf{x}$ comes from Eq. (4). ◼

    Theorem 21 can be illustrated geometrically (see Figs. 4.4 and 4.5). In Fig. 4.4(a), a vector $\mathbf{x}$ in $R^2$ is shown, where $\|\mathbf{x}\| = 1$. The vector $Q\mathbf{x}$ is shown in Fig. 4.4(b), where, by Theorem 21, $Q\mathbf{x}$ also has length 1. In Fig. 4.5(a), vectors $\mathbf{x}$ and $\mathbf{y}$ are shown, where $\|\mathbf{x}\| = 1$ and $\|\mathbf{y}\| = 2$. From vector geometry, we know that the angle $\theta$ between $\mathbf{x}$ and $\mathbf{y}$ satisfies the condition

$$\mathbf{x}^T\mathbf{y} = \|\mathbf{x}\|\|\mathbf{y}\|\cos\theta, \quad 0 \le \theta \le \pi. \tag{6}$$

In Fig. 4.5(b), the vectors $Q\mathbf{x}$ and $Q\mathbf{y}$ are shown, where the angle between $Q\mathbf{x}$ and $Q\mathbf{y}$ is also equal to $\theta$. To establish that the angle between $\mathbf{x}$ and $\mathbf{y}$ is equal to the angle between $Q\mathbf{x}$ and $Q\mathbf{y}$, we can argue as follows: Let $\gamma$ denote the angle between $Q\mathbf{x}$ and $Q\mathbf{y}$, where $0 \le \gamma \le \pi$. As in Eq. (6), the angle $\gamma$ satisfies the condition

$$(Q\mathbf{x})^T(Q\mathbf{y}) = \|Q\mathbf{x}\|\|Q\mathbf{y}\|\cos\gamma, \quad 0 \le \gamma \le \pi. \tag{7}$$

By Theorem 21, $(Q\mathbf{x})^T(Q\mathbf{y}) = \mathbf{x}^T\mathbf{y}$ and $\|Q\mathbf{x}\|\|Q\mathbf{y}\| = \|\mathbf{x}\|\|\mathbf{y}\|$. Thus, from Eq. (6) and Eq. (7), $\cos\theta = \cos\gamma$. Since the cosine function is one-to-one on $[0, \pi]$, the condition $\cos\theta = \cos\gamma$ implies that $\theta = \gamma$.

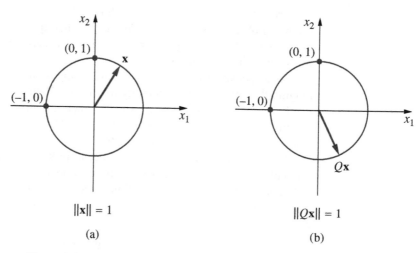

$\|\mathbf{x}\| = 1$            $\|Q\mathbf{x}\| = 1$

     (a)                   (b)

*Figure 4.4*    The length of $\mathbf{x}$ is equal to the length of $Q\mathbf{x}$

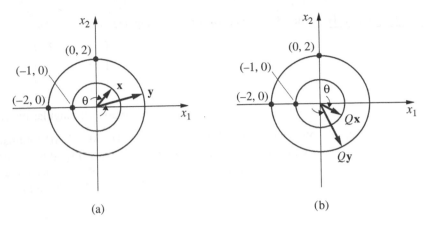

(a)    (b)

*Figure 4.5*    The angle between **x** and **y** is equal to the angle between $Q$**x** and $Q$**y**.

## Diagonalization of Symmetric Matrices

We conclude this section by showing that every symmetric matrix can be diagonalized by an orthogonal matrix. Several approaches can be used to establish this diagonalization result. We choose to demonstrate it by first stating a special case of a theorem known as Schur's theorem.

 THEOREM 22    Let $A$ be an $(n \times n)$ matrix, where $A$ has only real eigenvalues. Then there is an $(n \times n)$ orthogonal matrix $Q$ such that

$$Q^T A Q = T,$$

where $T$ is an $(n \times n)$ upper-triangular matrix.    ◼

We leave the proof of Theorem 22 as a series of somewhat challenging exercises. It is important to observe that the triangular matrix $T$ in Theorem 22 is similar to $A$. That is, since $Q^{-1} = Q^T$, it follows that $Q^T A Q$ is a similarity transformation.

Schur's theorem (of which Theorem 22 is a special case) states that any $(n \times n)$ matrix $A$ is unitarily similar to a triangular matrix $T$. The definition of a unitary matrix is given in the exercises of the previous section.

Linear algebra software can be used to find matrices $Q$ and $T$ that satisfy the conclusions of Schur's theorem: $Q^T A Q = T$. Note that we can rewrite $Q^T A Q = T$ as

$$A = Q T Q^T.$$

The decomposition $A = Q T Q^T$ is called a ***Schur decomposition*** or a ***Schur factorization*** of $A$.

EXAMPLE 6    The $(3 \times 3)$ matrix $A$ has real eigenvalues:

$$A = \begin{bmatrix} 2 & 4 & 3 \\ 7 & 5 & 9 \\ 1 & 3 & 1 \end{bmatrix}.$$

Find an orthogonal matrix $Q$ and an upper-triangular matrix $T$ such that $Q^T A Q = T$.

*Solution*    We used MATLAB in this example. The MATLAB command $[Q, T]$ = schur($A$) yields appropriate matrices $Q$ and $T$ (see Fig. 4.6). Since $A$ and $T$ are similar, the eigenvalues of $A$ are the diagonal entries of $T$. Thus, to the places shown in Fig. 4.6, the eigenvalues of $A$ are $\lambda = 11.6179$, $\lambda = -0.3125$, and $\lambda = -3.3055$. ◢

```
A=
        2       4       3
        7       5       9
        1       3       1

>>[Q,T]=schur(A)

Q=
     -0.4421    0.7193   -0.5359
     -0.8514   -0.1486    0.5030
     -0.2822   -0.6786   -0.6781

T=
     11.6179    2.1869    6.6488
          0   -0.3125    0.1033
          0        0   -3.3055
```

*Figure 4.6*    MATLAB was used in Example 6 to find matrices $Q$ and $T$ such that $Q^T A Q = T$.

With Theorem 22, it is a simple matter to show that any real symmetric matrix can be diagonalized by an orthogonal matrix. In fact, as the next theorem states, a matrix is orthogonally diagonalizable if and only if the matrix is symmetric. We will use this result in Section 7.1 when we discuss diagonalizing quadratic forms.

THEOREM 23    Let $A$ be a real $(n \times n)$ matrix.

(a) If $A$ is symmetric, then there is an orthogonal matrix $Q$ such that $Q^T A Q = D$, where $D$ is diagonal.

(b) If $Q^T A Q = D$, where $Q$ is orthogonal and $D$ is diagonal, then $A$ is a symmetric matrix.

***Proof*** To prove property (a), suppose $A$ is symmetric. Recall, by Theorem 17, that $A$ has only real eigenvalues. Thus, by Theorem 22, there is an orthogonal matrix $Q$ such that $Q^T A Q = M$, where $M$ is an upper-triangular matrix. Using the transpose operation on the equality $M = Q^T A Q$ and also using the fact that $A^T = A$, we obtain

$$M^T = (Q^T A Q)^T = Q^T A^T Q = Q^T A Q = M.$$

Thus, since $M$ is upper triangular and $M^T = M$, it follows that $M$ is a diagonal matrix.

To prove property (b), suppose that $Q^T A Q = D$, where $Q$ is orthogonal and $D$ is diagonal. Since $D$ is diagonal, we know that $D^T = D$. Thus, using the transpose operation on the equality $Q^T A Q = D$, we obtain

$$Q^T A Q = D = D^T = (Q^T A Q)^T = Q^T A^T Q.$$

From this result, we see that $Q^T A Q = Q^T A^T Q$. Multiplying by $Q$ and $Q^T$, we obtain

$$Q(Q^T A Q)Q^T = Q(Q^T A^T Q)Q^T$$
$$(QQ^T)A(QQ^T) = (QQ^T)A^T(QQ^T)$$
$$A = A^T.$$

Thus, since $A = A^T$, matrix $A$ is symmetric. ◼

Theorem 23 states that every real symmetric matrix $A$ is orthogonally diagonalizable; that is, $Q^T A Q = D$, where $Q$ is orthogonal and $D$ is diagonal. From the proof of Theorem 19 (also, see Examples 1, 3, and 4), the eigenvalues of $A$ are the diagonal entries of $D$, and eigenvectors of $A$ can be chosen as the columns of $Q$. Since the columns of $Q$ form an orthonormal set, the following result is a corollary of Theorem 23.

**COROLLARY** Let $A$ be a real $(n \times n)$ symmetric matrix. It is possible to choose eigenvectors $\mathbf{u}_1, \mathbf{u}_2, \ldots, \mathbf{u}_n$ for $A$ such that $\{\mathbf{u}_1, \mathbf{u}_2, \ldots, \mathbf{u}_n\}$ is an orthonormal basis for $R^n$. ◼

The corollary is illustrated in the next example. Before presenting the example, we note the following fact, which is established in Exercise 43:

> If $\mathbf{u}$ and $\mathbf{v}$ are eigenvectors of a symmetric matrix and if $\mathbf{u}$ and $\mathbf{v}$ belong to different eigenspaces, then $\mathbf{u}^T \mathbf{v} = 0$. $\qquad$ (8)

Note that if $A$ is not symmetric, then eigenvectors corresponding to different eigenvalues are not generally orthogonal.

**EXAMPLE 7** Find an orthonormal basis for $R^4$ consisting of eigenvectors of the matrix

$$A = \begin{bmatrix} 1 & -1 & -1 & -1 \\ -1 & 1 & -1 & -1 \\ -1 & -1 & 1 & -1 \\ -1 & -1 & -1 & 1 \end{bmatrix}.$$

*Solution*    Matrix $A$ is a special case of the Rodman matrix (see Exercise 42). The characteristic polynomial for $A$ is given by

$$p(t) = \det(A - tI) = (t - 2)^3(t + 2).$$

Thus the eigenvalues of $A$ are $\lambda_1 = \lambda_2 = \lambda_3 = 2$ and $\lambda_4 = -2$.

It is easy to verify that corresponding eigenvectors are given by

$$\mathbf{w}_1 = \begin{bmatrix} 1 \\ -1 \\ 0 \\ 0 \end{bmatrix}, \quad \mathbf{w}_2 = \begin{bmatrix} 1 \\ 0 \\ -1 \\ 0 \end{bmatrix}, \quad \mathbf{w}_3 = \begin{bmatrix} 1 \\ 0 \\ 0 \\ -1 \end{bmatrix}, \quad \text{and} \quad \mathbf{w}_4 = \begin{bmatrix} 1 \\ 1 \\ 1 \\ 1 \end{bmatrix}.$$

Note that $\mathbf{w}_1$, $\mathbf{w}_2$, and $\mathbf{w}_3$ belong to the eigenspace associated with $\lambda = 2$, whereas $\mathbf{w}_4$ is in the eigenspace associated with $\lambda = -2$. As is promised by condition (8), $\mathbf{w}_1^T \mathbf{w}_4 = \mathbf{w}_2^T \mathbf{w}_4 = \mathbf{w}_3^T \mathbf{w}_4 = 0$. Also note that the matrix $S$ defined by $S = [\mathbf{w}_1, \mathbf{w}_2, \mathbf{w}_3, \mathbf{w}_4]$ will diagonalize $A$. However, $S$ is not an orthogonal matrix.

To obtain an orthonormal basis for $R^4$ (and hence an orthogonal matrix $Q$ that diagonalizes $A$), we first find an orthogonal basis for the eigenspace associated with $\lambda = 2$. Applying the Gram–Schmidt process to the set $\{\mathbf{w}_1, \mathbf{w}_2, \mathbf{w}_3\}$, we produce orthogonal vectors

$$\mathbf{x}_1 = \begin{bmatrix} 1 \\ -1 \\ 0 \\ 0 \end{bmatrix}, \quad \mathbf{x}_2 = \begin{bmatrix} 1/2 \\ 1/2 \\ -1 \\ 0 \end{bmatrix}, \quad \text{and} \quad \mathbf{x}_3 = \begin{bmatrix} 1/3 \\ 1/3 \\ 1/3 \\ -1 \end{bmatrix}.$$

Thus the set $\{\mathbf{x}_1, \mathbf{x}_2, \mathbf{x}_3, \mathbf{w}_4\}$ is an orthogonal basis for $R^4$ consisting of eigenvectors of $A$. This set can then be normalized to determine an orthonormal basis for $R^4$ and an orthogonal matrix $Q$ that diagonalizes $A$.    ◼

We conclude by mentioning a result that is useful in applications. Let $A$ be an $(n \times n)$ symmetric matrix with eigenvalues $\lambda_1, \lambda_2, \ldots, \lambda_n$. Let $\mathbf{u}_1, \mathbf{u}_2, \ldots, \mathbf{u}_n$ be a corresponding set of orthonormal eigenvectors, where $A\mathbf{u}_i = \lambda_i \mathbf{u}_i$, $1 \leq i \leq n$. Matrix $A$ can be expressed in the form

$$A = \lambda_1 \mathbf{u}_1 \mathbf{u}_1^T + \lambda_2 \mathbf{u}_2 \mathbf{u}_2^T + \cdots + \lambda_n \mathbf{u}_n \mathbf{u}_n^T. \tag{9}$$

In Eq. (9), each $(n \times n)$ matrix $\mathbf{u}_i \mathbf{u}_i^T$ is a rank-one matrix. Expression (9) is called a ***spectral decomposition for*** $A$. A proof for Eq. (9) can be constructed along the lines of Exercise 29 of Section 4.5.

---

### 4.7    EXERCISES

In Exercises 1–12, determine whether the given matrix $A$ is diagonalizable. If $A$ is diagonalizable, calculate $A^5$ using the method of Example 2.

1. $A = \begin{bmatrix} 2 & -1 \\ -1 & 2 \end{bmatrix}$

2. $A = \begin{bmatrix} 1 & -1 \\ -1 & 1 \end{bmatrix}$

3. $A = \begin{bmatrix} -3 & 2 \\ -2 & 1 \end{bmatrix}$  4. $A = \begin{bmatrix} 1 & 3 \\ 0 & 1 \end{bmatrix}$

5. $A = \begin{bmatrix} 1 & 0 \\ 10 & 2 \end{bmatrix}$  6. $A = \begin{bmatrix} -1 & 7 \\ 0 & 1 \end{bmatrix}$

7. $A = \begin{bmatrix} 3 & -2 & -4 \\ 8 & -7 & -16 \\ -3 & 3 & 7 \end{bmatrix}$

8. $A = \begin{bmatrix} -1 & -1 & -4 \\ -8 & -3 & -16 \\ 1 & 2 & 7 \end{bmatrix}$

9. $A = \begin{bmatrix} 3 & -1 & -1 \\ -12 & 0 & 5 \\ 4 & -2 & -1 \end{bmatrix}$

10. $A = \begin{bmatrix} 1 & 1 & -1 \\ 0 & 2 & -1 \\ 0 & 0 & 1 \end{bmatrix}$  11. $A = \begin{bmatrix} 1 & 1 & -2 \\ 0 & 2 & -1 \\ 0 & 0 & 1 \end{bmatrix}$

12. $A = \begin{bmatrix} 1 & 3 & 3 \\ 0 & 5 & 4 \\ 0 & 0 & 1 \end{bmatrix}$

In Exercises 13–18, use condition (5) to determine whether the given matrix $Q$ is orthogonal.

13. $Q = \begin{bmatrix} 0 & 1 \\ 1 & 0 \end{bmatrix}$  14. $Q = \dfrac{1}{\sqrt{5}} \begin{bmatrix} 1 & -2 \\ 2 & 1 \end{bmatrix}$

15. $Q = \begin{bmatrix} 2 & -1 \\ 1 & 2 \end{bmatrix}$  16. $Q = \begin{bmatrix} 3 & 2 \\ -2 & 3 \end{bmatrix}$

17. $Q = \dfrac{1}{\sqrt{6}} \begin{bmatrix} \sqrt{3} & 1 & \sqrt{2} \\ 0 & -2 & \sqrt{2} \\ -\sqrt{3} & 1 & \sqrt{2} \end{bmatrix}$

18. $Q = \begin{bmatrix} 1 & 1 & -4 \\ 2 & -2 & 1 \\ 1 & 3 & 2 \end{bmatrix}$

In Exercises 19 and 20, find values $\alpha$, $\beta$, $a$, $b$, and $c$ such that matrix $Q$ is orthogonal. Choose positive values for $\alpha$ and $\beta$. [*Hint:* Use condition (5) to determine the values.]

19. $Q = \begin{bmatrix} \alpha & \beta & a \\ 0 & 2\beta & b \\ \alpha & -\beta & c \end{bmatrix}$  20. $Q = \begin{bmatrix} \alpha & -\beta & a \\ \alpha & 3\beta & b \\ \alpha & -2\beta & c \end{bmatrix}$

In Exercises 21–24, use linear algebra software to find an orthogonal matrix $Q$ and an upper-triangular matrix $T$ such that $Q^TAQ = T$. [*Note:* In each exercise, the matrix $A$ has only real eigenvalues.]

21. $\begin{bmatrix} 1 & 0 & 1 \\ 3 & 3 & 5 \\ 2 & 6 & 2 \end{bmatrix}$  22. $\begin{bmatrix} 3 & 0 & 7 \\ 9 & -6 & 4 \\ 1 & 1 & 4 \end{bmatrix}$

23. $\begin{bmatrix} 4 & 5 & 2 & 8 \\ 0 & 6 & 7 & 5 \\ 2 & 4 & 5 & 3 \\ 9 & 7 & 3 & 6 \end{bmatrix}$  24. $\begin{bmatrix} 4 & 7 & 3 & 5 \\ 8 & 5 & 7 & 8 \\ 2 & 4 & 3 & 5 \\ 0 & 5 & 7 & 4 \end{bmatrix}$

25. Let $A$ be an $(n \times n)$ matrix, and let $S$ be a nonsingular $(n \times n)$ matrix.

   a) Verify that $(S^{-1}AS)^2 = S^{-1}A^2S$ and that $(S^{-1}AS)^3 = S^{-1}A^3S$.

   b) Prove by induction that $(S^{-1}AS)^k = S^{-1}A^kS$ for any positive integer $k$.

26. Show that if $A$ is diagonalizable and if $B$ is similar to $A$, then $B$ is diagonalizable. [*Hint:* Suppose that $S^{-1}AS = D$ and $W^{-1}AW = B$.]

27. Suppose that $B$ is similar to $A$. Show each of the following.

   a) $B + \alpha I$ is similar to $A + \alpha I$.

   b) $B^T$ is similar to $A^T$.

   c) If $A$ is nonsingular, then $B$ is nonsingular and, moreover, $B^{-1}$ is similar to $A^{-1}$.

28. Prove properties (b) and (c) of Theorem 21. [*Hint:* For property (c), use the fact that $Q^TQ = I$.]

29. Let $\mathbf{u}$ be a vector in $R^n$ such that $\mathbf{u}^T\mathbf{u} = 1$. Let $Q = I - 2\mathbf{u}\mathbf{u}^T$. Show that $Q$ is an orthogonal matrix. Also, calculate the vector $Q\mathbf{u}$. Is $\mathbf{u}$ an eigenvector for $Q$?

30. Suppose that $A$ and $B$ are orthogonal $(n \times n)$ matrices. Show that $AB$ is an orthogonal matrix.

31. Let $\mathbf{x}$ be a nonzero vector in $R^2$, $\mathbf{x} = [a, b]^T$. Find a vector $\mathbf{y}$ in $R^2$ such that $\mathbf{x}^T\mathbf{y} = 0$ and $\mathbf{y}^T\mathbf{y} = 1$.

32. Let $A$ be a real $(2 \times 2)$ matrix with only real eigenvalues. Suppose that $A\mathbf{u} = \lambda\mathbf{u}$, where $\mathbf{u}^T\mathbf{u} = 1$. By Exercise 31, there is a vector $\mathbf{v}$ in $R^2$ such that

$\mathbf{u}^T\mathbf{v} = 0$ and $\mathbf{v}^T\mathbf{v} = 1$. Let $Q$ be the $(2 \times 2)$ matrix given by $Q = [\mathbf{u}, \mathbf{v}]$, and note that $Q$ is an orthogonal matrix. Verify that

$$Q^TAQ = \begin{bmatrix} \lambda & \mathbf{u}^TA\mathbf{v} \\ 0 & \mathbf{v}^TA\mathbf{v} \end{bmatrix}.$$

(Thus Theorem 22 is proved for a $(2 \times 2)$ matrix $A$.)

In Exercises 33–36, use the procedure outlined in Exercise 32 to find an orthogonal matrix $Q$ such that $Q^TAQ = T$, $T$ upper triangular.

**33.** $A = \begin{bmatrix} 1 & -1 \\ 1 & 3 \end{bmatrix}$     **34.** $A = \begin{bmatrix} 5 & -2 \\ 6 & -2 \end{bmatrix}$

**35.** $A = \begin{bmatrix} 2 & -1 \\ -1 & 2 \end{bmatrix}$     **36.** $A = \begin{bmatrix} 2 & 2 \\ 3 & 3 \end{bmatrix}$

**37.** Let $A$ and $R$ be $(n \times n)$ matrices. Show that the $ij$th entry of $R^TAR$ is given by $\mathbf{R}_i^T A\mathbf{R}_j$, where $R = [\mathbf{R}_1, \mathbf{R}_2, \ldots, \mathbf{R}_n]$.

**38.** Let $A$ be a real $(3 \times 3)$ matrix with only real eigenvalues. Suppose that $A\mathbf{u} = \lambda\mathbf{u}$, where $\mathbf{u}^T\mathbf{u} = 1$. By the Gram–Schmidt process, there are vectors $\mathbf{v}$ and $\mathbf{w}$ in $R^3$ such that $\{\mathbf{u}, \mathbf{v}, \mathbf{w}\}$ is an orthonormal set. Consider the orthogonal matrix $Q$ given by $Q = [\mathbf{u}, \mathbf{v}, \mathbf{w}]$. Verify that

$$Q^TAQ = \begin{bmatrix} \lambda & \mathbf{u}^TA\mathbf{v} & \mathbf{u}^TA\mathbf{w} \\ 0 & \mathbf{v}^TA\mathbf{v} & \mathbf{v}^TA\mathbf{w} \\ 0 & \mathbf{w}^TA\mathbf{v} & \mathbf{w}^TA\mathbf{w} \end{bmatrix}$$

$$= \begin{bmatrix} \lambda & \mathbf{u}^TA\mathbf{v} \;\; \mathbf{u}^TA\mathbf{w} \\ \hline 0 & \\ 0 & A_1 \end{bmatrix}.$$

**39.** Let $B = Q^TAQ$, where $Q$ and $A$ are as in Exercise 38. Consider the $(2 \times 2)$ submatrix of $B$ given

by $A_1$ in Exercise 38. Show that the eigenvalues of $A_1$ are real. [*Hint:* Calculate $\det(B - tI)$, and show that every eigenvalue of $A_1$ is an eigenvalue of $B$. Then make a statement showing that all the eigenvalues of $B$ are real.]

**40.** Let $B = Q^TAQ$, where $Q$ and $A$ are as in Exercise 38. By Exercises 32 and 39, there is a $(2 \times 2)$ matrix $S$ such that $S^TS = I$, $S^TA_1S = T_1$, where $T_1$ is upper triangular. Form the $(3 \times 3)$ matrix $R$:

$$R = \begin{bmatrix} 1 & 0 \;\; 0 \\ \hline 0 & \\ 0 & S \end{bmatrix}.$$

Verify each of the following.

a) $R^TR = I$.

b) $R^TQ^TAQR$ is an upper-triangular matrix.

(Note that this exercise verifies Theorem 22 for a $(3 \times 3)$ matrix $A$.)

**41.** Following the outline of Exercises 38–40, use induction to prove Theorem 22.

**42.** Consider the $(n \times n)$ symmetric matrix $A = (a_{ij})$ defined as follows:

a) $a_{ii} = 1, 1 \le i \le n$;

b) $a_{ij} = -1, i \ne j, 1 \le i, j \le n$.

(A $(4 \times 4)$ version of this matrix is given in Example 7.) Verify that the eigenvalues of $A$ are $\lambda = 2$ (geometric multiplicity $n - 1$) and $\lambda = 2 - n$ (geometric multiplicity 1). [*Hint:* Show that the following are eigenvectors: $\mathbf{u}_i = \mathbf{e}_1 - \mathbf{e}_i, 2 \le i \le n$ and $\mathbf{u}_1 = [1, 1, \ldots, 1]^T$.]

**43.** Suppose that $A$ is a real symmetric matrix and that $A\mathbf{u} = \lambda\mathbf{u}$, $A\mathbf{v} = \beta\mathbf{v}$, where $\lambda \ne \beta$, $\mathbf{u} \ne \boldsymbol{\theta}$, and $\mathbf{v} \ne \boldsymbol{\theta}$. Show that $\mathbf{u}^T\mathbf{v} = 0$. [*Hint:* Consider $\mathbf{u}^TA\mathbf{v}$.]

---

### 4.8    DIFFERENCE EQUATIONS; MARKOV CHAINS; SYSTEMS OF DIFFERENTIAL EQUATIONS (OPTIONAL)

In this section we examine how eigenvalues can be used to solve difference equations and systems of differential equations. In Chapter 7, we treat other applications of eigenvalues and also return to a deeper study of systems of differential equations.

Let $A$ be an $(n \times n)$ matrix, and let $\mathbf{x}_0$ be a vector in $R^n$. Consider the sequence of vectors $\{\mathbf{x}_k\}$ defined by

$$\mathbf{x}_1 = A\mathbf{x}_0$$
$$\mathbf{x}_2 = A\mathbf{x}_1$$
$$\mathbf{x}_3 = A\mathbf{x}_2$$
$$\vdots$$

In general, this sequence is given by

$$\mathbf{x}_k = A\mathbf{x}_{k-1}, \quad k = 1, 2, \ldots. \tag{1}$$

Vector sequences that are generated as in Eq. (1) occur in a variety of applications and serve as mathematical models to describe population growth, ecological systems, radar tracking of airborne objects, digital control of chemical processes, and the like. One of the objectives in such models is to describe the behavior of the sequence $\{\mathbf{x}_k\}$ in qualitative or quantitative terms. In this section we see that the behavior of the sequence $\{\mathbf{x}_k\}$ can be analyzed from the eigenvalues of $A$.

The following simple example illustrates a typical sequence of the form (1).

EXAMPLE 1    Let $\mathbf{x}_k = A\mathbf{x}_{k-1}, k = 1, 2, \ldots$. Calculate $\mathbf{x}_1, \mathbf{x}_2, \mathbf{x}_3, \mathbf{x}_4,$ and $\mathbf{x}_5$, where

$$A = \begin{bmatrix} .8 & .2 \\ .2 & .8 \end{bmatrix} \quad \text{and} \quad \mathbf{x}_0 = \begin{bmatrix} 1 \\ 2 \end{bmatrix}.$$

*Solution*    Some routine but tedious calculations show that

$$\mathbf{x}_1 = A\mathbf{x}_0 = \begin{bmatrix} 1.2 \\ 1.8 \end{bmatrix}, \quad \mathbf{x}_2 = A\mathbf{x}_1 = \begin{bmatrix} 1.32 \\ 1.68 \end{bmatrix}, \quad \mathbf{x}_3 = A\mathbf{x}_2 = \begin{bmatrix} 1.392 \\ 1.608 \end{bmatrix}$$

$$\mathbf{x}_4 = A\mathbf{x}_3 = \begin{bmatrix} 1.4352 \\ 1.5648 \end{bmatrix}, \quad \text{and} \quad \mathbf{x}_5 = A\mathbf{x}_4 = \begin{bmatrix} 1.46112 \\ 1.53888 \end{bmatrix}.$$

In Example 1, the first six terms of a vector sequence $\{\mathbf{x}_k\}$ are listed. An inspection of these first few terms suggests that the sequence might have some regular pattern of behavior. For instance, the first components of these vectors are steadily increasing, whereas the second components are steadily decreasing. In fact, as shown in Example 3, this monotonic behavior persists for all terms of the sequence $\{\mathbf{x}_k\}$. Moreover, it can be shown that

$$\lim_{k \to \infty} \mathbf{x}_k = \mathbf{x}^*,$$

where the limit vector $\mathbf{x}^*$ is given by

$$\mathbf{x}^* = \begin{bmatrix} 1.5 \\ 1.5 \end{bmatrix}.$$

## Difference Equations

Let $A$ be an $(n \times n)$ matrix. The equation

$$\mathbf{x}_k = A\mathbf{x}_{k-1} \tag{2}$$

is called a ***difference equation***. A ***solution*** to the difference equation is any sequence of vectors $\{\mathbf{x}_k\}$ that satisfies Eq. (2). That is, a solution is a sequence $\{\mathbf{x}_k\}$ whose successive terms are related by $\mathbf{x}_1 = A\mathbf{x}_0$, $\mathbf{x}_2 = A\mathbf{x}_1, \ldots, \mathbf{x}_k = A\mathbf{x}_{k-1}, \ldots$. (Equation 2 is not the most general form of a difference equation.)

The basic challenge posed by a difference equation is to describe the behavior of the sequence $\{\mathbf{x}_k\}$. Some specific questions are:

1.  For a given starting vector $\mathbf{x}_0$, is there a vector $\mathbf{x}^*$ such that

$$\lim_{k \to \infty} \mathbf{x}_k = \mathbf{x}^*?$$

2.  If the sequence $\{\mathbf{x}_k\}$ does have a limit, $\mathbf{x}^*$, what is the limit vector?
3.  Find a "formula" that can be used to calculate $\mathbf{x}_k$ in terms of the starting vector $\mathbf{x}_0$.
4.  Given a vector $\mathbf{b}$ and an integer $k$, determine $\mathbf{x}_0$ so that $\mathbf{x}_k = \mathbf{b}$.
5.  Given a vector $\mathbf{b}$, characterize the set of starting vectors $\mathbf{x}_0$ for which $\{\mathbf{x}_k\} \to \mathbf{b}$.

Unlike many equations, the Difference Eq. in (2) does not raise any interesting questions concerning the existence or uniqueness of solutions. For a given starting vector $\mathbf{x}_0$, we see that a solution to Eq. (2) always exists because it can be constructed. For instance, in Example 1 we found the first six terms of the solution to the given difference equation. In terms of uniqueness, suppose $\mathbf{x}_0$ is a given starting vector. It can be shown (see Exercise 21) that if $\{\mathbf{w}_k\}$ is any sequence satisfying Eq. (2) and if $\mathbf{w}_0 = \mathbf{x}_0$, then $\mathbf{w}_k = \mathbf{x}_k$, $k = 1, 2, \ldots$.

The next example shows how a difference equation might serve as a mathematical model for a physical process. The model is kept very simple so that the details do not obscure the ideas. Thus the example should be considered illustrative rather than realistic.

**EXAMPLE 2** Suppose that animals are being raised for market, and the grower wishes to determine how the annual rate of harvesting animals will affect the yearly size of the herd.

*Solution* To begin, let $x_1(k)$ and $x_2(k)$ be the state variables that measure the size of the herd in the $k$th year of operation, where

$$x_1(k) = \text{number of animals less than one year old at year } k$$

$$x_2(k) = \text{number of animals more than one year old at year } k.$$

We assume that animals less than one year old do not reproduce, and that animals more than one year old have a reproduction rate of $b$ per year. Thus if the herd has $x_2(k)$ mature animals at year $k$, we expect to have $x_1(k + 1)$ young animals at year $k + 1$, where

$$x_1(k + 1) = bx_2(k).$$

Next we assume that the young animals have a death rate of $d_1$ per year, and the mature animals have a death rate of $d_2$ per year. Furthermore, we assume that the mature animals are harvested at a rate of $h$ per year and that young animals are not harvested. Thus we expect to have $x_2(k+1)$ mature animals at year $k+1$, where

$$x_2(k+1) = x_1(k) + x_2(k) - d_1 x_1(k) - d_2 x_2(k) - h x_2(k).$$

This equation reflects the following facts: An animal that is young at year $k$ will mature by year $k+1$; an animal that is mature at year $k$ is still mature at year $k+1$; a certain percentage of young and mature animals will die during the year; and a certain percentage of mature animals will be harvested during the year. Collecting like terms in the second equation and combining the two equations, we obtain the state equations for the herd:

$$\begin{aligned} x_1(k+1) &= b x_2(k) \\ x_2(k+1) &= (1-d_1)x_1(k) + (1-d_2-h)x_2(k). \end{aligned} \tag{3}$$

The state equations give the size and composition of the herd at year $k+1$ in terms of the size and composition of the herd at year $k$. For example, if we know the initial composition of the herd at year zero, $x_1(0)$ and $x_2(0)$, we can use (3) to calculate the composition of the herd after one year, $x_1(1)$ and $x_2(1)$.

In matrix form, (3) becomes

$$\mathbf{x}(k) = A\mathbf{x}(k-1), \quad k = 1, 2, 3, \ldots,$$

where

$$\mathbf{x}(k) = \begin{bmatrix} x_1(k) \\ x_2(k) \end{bmatrix} \quad \text{and} \quad A = \begin{bmatrix} 0 & b \\ (1-d_1) & (1-d_2-h) \end{bmatrix}.$$

In the context of this example, the growth and composition of the herd are governed by the eigenvalues of $A$, and these can be controlled by varying the parameter $h$. ◼

## Solving Difference Equations

Consider the difference equation

$$\mathbf{x}_k = A\mathbf{x}_{k-1}, \tag{4}$$

where $A$ is an $(n \times n)$ matrix. The key to finding a useful form for solutions of Eq. (4) is to observe that the sequence $\{\mathbf{x}_k\}$ can be calculated by multiplying powers of $A$ by the starting vector $\mathbf{x}_0$. That is,

$$\begin{aligned} \mathbf{x}_1 &= A\mathbf{x}_0 \\ \mathbf{x}_2 &= A\mathbf{x}_1 = A(A\mathbf{x}_0) = A^2\mathbf{x}_0 \\ \mathbf{x}_3 &= A\mathbf{x}_2 = A(A^2\mathbf{x}_0) = A^3\mathbf{x}_0 \\ \mathbf{x}_4 &= A\mathbf{x}_3 = A(A^3\mathbf{x}_0) = A^4\mathbf{x}_0, \end{aligned}$$

and, in general,

$$\mathbf{x}_k = A^k\mathbf{x}_0, \quad k = 1, 2, \ldots. \tag{5}$$

Next, let $A$ have eigenvalues $\lambda_1, \lambda_2, \ldots, \lambda_n$ and corresponding eigenvectors $\mathbf{u}_1, \mathbf{u}_2, \ldots, \mathbf{u}_n$. We now make a critical assumption: Let us suppose that matrix $A$ is not defective. That is, let us suppose that the set of eigenvectors $\{\mathbf{u}_1, \mathbf{u}_2, \ldots, \mathbf{u}_n\}$ is linearly independent.

With the assumption that $A$ is not defective, we can use the set of eigenvectors as a basis for $R^n$. In particular, any starting vector $\mathbf{x}_0$ can be expressed as a linear combination of the eigenvectors:

$$\mathbf{x}_0 = a_1\mathbf{u}_1 + a_2\mathbf{u}_2 + \cdots + a_n\mathbf{u}_n.$$

Then, using Eq. (5), we can obtain the following expression for $\mathbf{x}_k$:

$$
\begin{aligned}
\mathbf{x}_k &= A^k\mathbf{x}_0 \\
&= A^k(a_1\mathbf{u}_1 + a_2\mathbf{u}_2 + \cdots + a_n\mathbf{u}_n) \\
&= a_1 A^k\mathbf{u}_1 + a_2 A^k\mathbf{u}_2 + \cdots + a_n A^k\mathbf{u}_n \\
&= a_1(\lambda_1)^k\mathbf{u}_1 + a_2(\lambda_2)^k\mathbf{u}_2 + \cdots + a_n(\lambda_n)^k\mathbf{u}_n.
\end{aligned}
\tag{6}
$$

(This last equality comes from Theorem 11 of Section 4.4: If $A\mathbf{u} = \lambda\mathbf{u}$, then $A^k\mathbf{u} = \lambda^k\mathbf{u}$.)

Note that if $A$ does not have a set of $n$ linearly independent eigenvectors, then the expression for $\mathbf{x}_k$ in Eq. (6) must be modified. The modification depends on the idea of a generalized eigenvector. It can be shown (see Section 7.8) that we can always choose a basis for $R^n$ consisting of eigenvectors and generalized eigenvectors of $A$.

EXAMPLE 3    Use Eq. (6) to find an expression for $\mathbf{x}_k$, where $\mathbf{x}_k$ is the $k$th term of the sequence in Example 1. Use your expression to calculate $\mathbf{x}_k$ for $k = 10$ and $k = 20$. Determine whether the sequence $\{\mathbf{x}_k\}$ converges.

*Solution*    The sequence $\{\mathbf{x}_k\}$ in Example 1 is generated by $\mathbf{x}_k = A\mathbf{x}_{k-1}, k = 1, 2, \ldots$, where

$$
A = \begin{bmatrix} .8 & .2 \\ .2 & .8 \end{bmatrix} \quad \text{and} \quad \mathbf{x}_0 = \begin{bmatrix} 1 \\ 2 \end{bmatrix}.
$$

Now the characteristic polynomial for $A$ is

$$p(t) = t^2 - 1.6t + 0.6 = (t - 1)(t - 0.6).$$

Therefore, the eigenvalues of $A$ are $\lambda_1 = 1$ and $\lambda_2 = 0.6$. Corresponding eigenvectors are

$$
\mathbf{u}_1 = \begin{bmatrix} 1 \\ 1 \end{bmatrix} \quad \text{and} \quad \mathbf{u}_2 = \begin{bmatrix} 1 \\ -1 \end{bmatrix}.
$$

The starting vector $\mathbf{x}_0$ can be expressed in terms of the eigenvectors as $\mathbf{x}_0 = 1.5\mathbf{u}_1 - 0.5\mathbf{u}_2$:

$$
\mathbf{x}_0 = \begin{bmatrix} 1 \\ 2 \end{bmatrix} = 1.5 \begin{bmatrix} 1 \\ 1 \end{bmatrix} - 0.5 \begin{bmatrix} 1 \\ -1 \end{bmatrix}.
$$

Therefore, the terms of the sequence $\{\mathbf{x}_k\}$ are given by

$$
\begin{aligned}
\mathbf{x}_k = A^k\mathbf{x}_0 &= A^k(1.5\mathbf{u}_1 - 0.5\mathbf{u}_2) \\
&= 1.5A^k\mathbf{u}_1 - 0.5A^k\mathbf{u}_2 \\
&= 1.5(1)^k\mathbf{u}_1 - 0.5(0.6)^k\mathbf{u}_2 \\
&= 1.5\mathbf{u}_1 - 0.5(0.6)^k\mathbf{u}_2.
\end{aligned}
$$

In detail, the components of $\mathbf{x}_k$ are

$$\mathbf{x}_k = \begin{bmatrix} 1.5 - 0.5(0.6)^k \\ 1.5 + 0.5(0.6)^k \end{bmatrix}, \quad k = 0, 1, 2, \ldots. \tag{7}$$

For $k = 10$ and $k = 20$, we calculate $\mathbf{x}_k$ from Eq. (7), finding

$$\mathbf{x}_{10} = \begin{bmatrix} 1.496976\ldots \\ 1.503023\ldots \end{bmatrix} \quad \text{and} \quad \mathbf{x}_{20} = \begin{bmatrix} 1.499981\ldots \\ 1.500018\ldots \end{bmatrix}.$$

Finally, since $\lim_{k \to \infty}(0.6)^k = 0$, we see from Eq. (7) that

$$\lim_{k \to \infty} \mathbf{x}_k = \mathbf{x}^* = \begin{bmatrix} 1.5 \\ 1.5 \end{bmatrix}.$$

## Types of Solutions to Difference Equations

If we reflect about the results of Example 3, the following observations emerge: Suppose a sequence $\{\mathbf{x}_k\}$ is generated by $\mathbf{x}_k = A\mathbf{x}_{k-1}, k = 1, 2, \ldots$, where $A$ is the $(2 \times 2)$ matrix

$$A = \begin{bmatrix} .8 & .2 \\ .2 & .8 \end{bmatrix}.$$

Then, no matter what starting vector $\mathbf{x}_0$ is selected, the sequence $\{\mathbf{x}_k\}$ will either converge to the zero vector, or the sequence will converge to a multiple of $\mathbf{u}_1 = [1, 1]^T$.

To verify this observation, let $\mathbf{x}_0$ be any given initial vector. We can express $\mathbf{x}_0$ in terms of the eigenvectors:

$$\mathbf{x}_0 = a_1\mathbf{u}_1 + a_2\mathbf{u}_2.$$

Since the eigenvalues of $A$ are $\lambda_1 = 1$ and $\lambda_2 = 0.6$, the vector $\mathbf{x}_k$ is given by

$$\mathbf{x}_k = A^k\mathbf{x}_0 = a_1(1)^k\mathbf{u}_1 + a_2(0.6)^k\mathbf{u}_2 = a_1\mathbf{u}_1 + a_2(0.6)^k\mathbf{u}_2.$$

Given this expression for $\mathbf{x}_k$, there are only two possibilities:

1. If $a_1 \neq 0$, then $\lim_{k \to \infty} \mathbf{x}_k = a_1\mathbf{u}_1$.
2. If $a_1 = 0$, then $\lim_{k \to \infty} \mathbf{x}_k = \boldsymbol{\theta}$.

In general, an analogous description can be given for the possible solutions of any difference equation. Specifically, let $A$ be a nondefective $(n \times n)$ matrix with eigenvalues $\lambda_1, \lambda_2, \ldots, \lambda_n$. For convenience, let us assume the eigenvalues are indexed according to their magnitude, where

$$|\lambda_1| \geq |\lambda_2| \geq \cdots \geq |\lambda_n|.$$

Let $\mathbf{x}_0$ be any initial vector, and consider the sequence $\{\mathbf{x}_k\}$, where $\mathbf{x}_k = A\mathbf{x}_{k-1}, k = 1, 2, \ldots$. Finally, suppose $\mathbf{x}_0$ is expressed as

$$\mathbf{x}_0 = a_1\mathbf{u}_1 + a_2\mathbf{u}_2 + \cdots + a_n\mathbf{u}_n,$$

where $a_1 \neq 0$.

From Eq. (6), we have the following possibilities for the sequence $\{\mathbf{x}_k\}$:

1. If $|\lambda_1| < 1$, then $\lim_{k \to \infty} \mathbf{x}_k = \boldsymbol{\theta}$.
2. If $|\lambda_1| = 1$, then there is a constant $M > 0$ such that $\|\mathbf{x}_k\| \leq M$, for all $k$.
3. If $\lambda_1 = 1$ and $|\lambda_2| < 1$, then $\lim_{k \to \infty} \mathbf{x}_k = a_1 \mathbf{u}_1$.
4. If $|\lambda_1| > 1$, then $\lim_{k \to \infty} \|\mathbf{x}_k\| = \infty$.

Other possibilities exist that are not listed. For example, if $\lambda_1 = 1$, $\lambda_2 = 1$, and $|\lambda_3| < 1$, then $\{\mathbf{x}_k\} \to a_1 \mathbf{u}_1 + a_2 \mathbf{u}_2$.

Also, in listing the possibilities we assumed that $A$ was not defective and that $a_1 \neq 0$. If $a_1 = 0$ but $a_2 \neq 0$, it should be clear that a similar list can be made by using $\lambda_2$ in place of $\lambda_1$. If matrix $A$ is defective, it can be shown (see Section 7.8) that the list above is still valid, with the following exception (see Exercise 19 for an example): If $|\lambda_1| = 1$ and if the geometric multiplicity of $\lambda_1$ is less than the algebraic multiplicity, then it will usually be the case that $\|\mathbf{x}_k\| \to \infty$ as $k \to \infty$.

### EXAMPLE 4

For the herd model described in Example 2, let the parameters be given by $b = 0.9$, $d_1 = 0.1$, and $d_2 = 0.2$. Thus $\mathbf{x}_k = A\mathbf{x}_{k-1}$, where

$$A = \begin{bmatrix} 0 & .9 \\ .9 & .8 - h \end{bmatrix}.$$

Determine a harvest rate $h$ so that the herd neither dies out nor grows without bound.

**Solution**    For any given harvest rate $h$, the matrix $A$ will have eigenvalues $\lambda_1$ and $\lambda_2$, where $|\lambda_1| \geq |\lambda_2|$. If $|\lambda_1| < 1$, then $\{\mathbf{x}_k\} \to \boldsymbol{\theta}$, and the herd is dying out. If $|\lambda_1| > 1$, then $\{\|\mathbf{x}_k\|\} \to \infty$, which indicates that the herd is increasing without bound.

Therefore, we want to select $h$ so that $\lambda_1 = 1$. For any given $h$, $\lambda_1$ and $\lambda_2$ are roots of the characteristic equation $p(t) = 0$, where

$$p(t) = \det(A - tI) = t^2 - (.8 - h)t - .81.$$

To have $\lambda_1 = 1$, we need $p(1) = 0$, or

$$(1)^2 - (.8 - h)(1) - .81 = 0,$$

or

$$h - .61 = 0.$$

Thus a harvest rate of $h = 0.61$ will lead to $\lambda_1 = 1$ and $\lambda_2 = -0.81$.    ■

Note that to the extent the herd model in Examples 2 and 4 is valid, a harvest rate of less than 0.61 will cause the herd to grow, whereas a rate greater than 0.61 will cause the herd to decrease. A harvest rate of 0.61 will cause the herd to approach a steady-state distribution of 9 young animals for every 10 mature animals. That is, for any initial vector $\mathbf{x}_0 = a_1 \mathbf{u}_1 + a_2 \mathbf{u}_2$, we have (with $h = 0.61$)

$$\mathbf{x}_k = a_1 \mathbf{u}_1 + a_2(-0.81)^k \mathbf{u}_2,$$

where the eigenvectors $\mathbf{u}_1$ and $\mathbf{u}_2$ are given by

$$\mathbf{u}_1 = \begin{bmatrix} 9 \\ 10 \end{bmatrix} \quad \text{and} \quad \mathbf{u}_2 = \begin{bmatrix} 10 \\ -9 \end{bmatrix}.$$

## Markov Chains

A special type of difference equation arises in the study of Markov chains or Markov processes. We cannot go into the interesting theory of Markov chains, but we will give an example that illustrates some of the ideas.

EXAMPLE 5   An automobile rental company has three locations, which we designate as $P$, $Q$, and $R$. When an automobile is rented at one of the locations, it may be returned to any of the three locations.

Suppose, at some specific time, that there are $p$ cars at location $P$, $q$ cars at $Q$, and $r$ cars at $R$. Experience has shown, in any given week, that the $p$ cars at location $P$ are distributed as follows: 10% are rented and returned to $Q$, 30% are rented and returned to $R$, and 60% remain at $P$ (these either are not rented or are rented and returned to $P$). Similar rental histories are known for locations $Q$ and $R$, as summarized below.

**Weekly Distribution History**

*Location* $P$:   60% stay at $P$, 10% go to $Q$, 30% go to $R$.

*Location* $Q$:   10% go to $P$, 80% stay at $Q$, 10% go to $R$.

*Location* $R$:   10% go to $P$, 20% go to $Q$, 70% stay at $R$.

**Solution**   Let $\mathbf{x}_k$ represent the state of the rental fleet at the beginning of week $k$:

$$\mathbf{x}_k = \begin{bmatrix} p(k) \\ q(k) \\ r(k) \end{bmatrix}.$$

For the state vector $\mathbf{x}_k$, $p(k)$ denotes the number of cars at location $P$, $q(k)$ the number at $Q$, and $r(k)$ the number at $R$.

From the weekly distribution history, we see that

$$p(k+1) = .6p(k) + .1q(k) + .1r(k)$$
$$q(k+1) = .1p(k) + .8q(k) + .2r(k)$$
$$r(k+1) = .3p(k) + .1q(k) + .7r(k).$$

(For instance, the number of cars at $P$ when week $k+1$ begins is determined by the 60% that remain at $P$, the 10% that arrive from $Q$, and the 10% that arrive from $R$.)

To the extent that the weekly distribution percentages do not change, the rental fleet is rearranged among locations $P$, $Q$, and $R$ according to the rule $\mathbf{x}_{k+1} = A\mathbf{x}_k$, $k = 0, 1, \ldots$, where $A$ is the $(3 \times 3)$ matrix

$$A = \begin{bmatrix} .6 & .1 & .1 \\ .1 & .8 & .2 \\ .3 & .1 & .7 \end{bmatrix}.$$

Example 5 represents a situation in which a fixed population (the rental fleet) is rearranged in stages (week by week) among a fixed number of categories (the locations $P$, $Q$, and $R$). Moreover, in Example 5 the rules governing the rearrangement remain fixed from stage to stage (the weekly distribution percentages stay constant). In general, such problems can be modeled by a difference equation of the form

$$\mathbf{x}_{k+1} = A\mathbf{x}_k, \quad k = 0, 1, \ldots.$$

For such problems the matrix $A$ is often called a **transition** matrix. Such a matrix has two special properties:

The entries of $A$ are all nonnegative. (8a)

In each column of $A$, the sum of the entries has the value 1. (8b)

It turns out that a matrix having properties (8a) and (8b) always has an eigenvalue of $\lambda = 1$. This fact is established in Exercise 26 and illustrated in the next example.

EXAMPLE 6    Suppose the automobile rental company described in Example 5 has a fleet of 600 cars. Initially an equal number of cars is based at each location, so that $p(0) = 200$, $q(0) = 200$, and $r(0) = 200$. As in Example 5, let the week-by-week distribution of cars be governed by $\mathbf{x}_{k+1} = A\mathbf{x}_k, k = 0, 1, \ldots$, where

$$\mathbf{x}_k = \begin{bmatrix} p(k) \\ q(k) \\ r(k) \end{bmatrix}, \quad A = \begin{bmatrix} .6 & .1 & .1 \\ .1 & .8 & .2 \\ .3 & .1 & .7 \end{bmatrix}, \quad \text{and} \quad \mathbf{x}_0 = \begin{bmatrix} 200 \\ 200 \\ 200 \end{bmatrix}.$$

Find $\lim_{k \to \infty} \mathbf{x}_k$. Determine the number of cars at each location in the $k$th week, for $k = 1, 5,$ and 10.

Solution    If $A$ is not defective, we can use Eq. (6) to express $\mathbf{x}_k$ as

$$\mathbf{x}_k = a_1(\lambda_1)^k \mathbf{u}_1 + a_2(\lambda_2)^k \mathbf{u}_2 + a_3(\lambda_3)^k \mathbf{u}_3,$$

where $\{\mathbf{u}_1, \mathbf{u}_2, \mathbf{u}_3\}$ is a basis for $R^3$, consisting of eigenvectors of $A$.

It can be shown that $A$ has eigenvalues $\lambda_1 = 1$, $\lambda_2 = .6$, and $\lambda_3 = .5$. Thus $A$ has three linearly independent eigenvectors:

$$\lambda_1 = 1, \quad \mathbf{u}_1 = \begin{bmatrix} 4 \\ 9 \\ 7 \end{bmatrix}; \quad \lambda_2 = .6 \quad \mathbf{u}_2 = \begin{bmatrix} 0 \\ 1 \\ -1 \end{bmatrix};$$

$$\lambda_3 = .5, \quad \mathbf{u}_3 = \begin{bmatrix} -1 \\ -1 \\ 2 \end{bmatrix}.$$

The initial vector, $\mathbf{x}_0 = [200, 200, 200]^T$, can be written as

$$\mathbf{x}_0 = 30\mathbf{u}_1 - 150\mathbf{u}_2 - 80\mathbf{u}_3.$$

Thus the vector $\mathbf{x}_k = [p(k), q(k), r(k)]^T$ is given by

$$\begin{aligned} \mathbf{x}_k &= A^k \mathbf{x}_0 \\ &= A^k(30\mathbf{u}_1 - 150\mathbf{u}_2 - 80\mathbf{u}_3) \\ &= 30(\lambda_1)^k \mathbf{u}_1 - 150(\lambda_2)^k \mathbf{u}_2 - 80(\lambda_3)^k \mathbf{u}_3 \\ &= 30\mathbf{u}_1 - 150(.6)^k \mathbf{u}_2 - 80(.5)^k \mathbf{u}_3. \end{aligned}$$

(9)

From the expression above, we see that

$$\lim_{k \to \infty} \mathbf{x}_k = 30\mathbf{u}_1 = \begin{bmatrix} 120 \\ 270 \\ 210 \end{bmatrix}.$$

Therefore, as the weeks proceed, the rental fleet will tend to an equilibrium state with 120 cars at $P$, 270 cars at $Q$, and 210 cars at $R$. To the extent that the model is valid, location $Q$ will require the largest facility for maintenance, parking, and the like.

Finally, using Eq. (9), we can calculate the state of the fleet for the $k$th week:

$$\mathbf{x}_1 = \begin{bmatrix} 160 \\ 220 \\ 220 \end{bmatrix}, \quad \mathbf{x}_5 = \begin{bmatrix} 122.500 \\ 260.836 \\ 216.664 \end{bmatrix}, \quad \text{and} \quad \mathbf{x}_{10} = \begin{bmatrix} 120.078 \\ 269.171 \\ 210.751 \end{bmatrix}. \quad \blacksquare$$

Note that the components of $\mathbf{x}_{10}$ are rounded to three places. Of course, for an actual fleet the state vectors $\mathbf{x}_k$ must have only integer components. The fact that the sequence defined in Eq. (9) need not have integer components represents a limitation of the assumed distribution model.

## Systems of Differential Equations

Difference equations are useful for describing the state of a physical system at discrete values of time. Mathematical models that describe the evolution of a physical system for all values of time are frequently expressed in terms of a differential equation or a system of differential equations. A simple example of a system of differential equations is

$$\begin{aligned} v'(t) &= av(t) + bw(t) \\ w'(t) &= cv(t) + dw(t). \end{aligned} \tag{10}$$

In Eq. (10), the problem is to find functions $v(t)$ and $w(t)$ that simultaneously satisfy these equations and in which initial conditions $v(0)$ and $w(0)$ may also be specified. We can express Eq. (10) in matrix terms if we let

$$\mathbf{x}(t) = \begin{bmatrix} v(t) \\ w(t) \end{bmatrix}.$$

Then Eq. (10) can be written as $\mathbf{x}'(t) = A\mathbf{x}(t)$, where

$$\mathbf{x}'(t) = \begin{bmatrix} v'(t) \\ w'(t) \end{bmatrix} \quad \text{and} \quad A = \begin{bmatrix} a & b \\ c & d \end{bmatrix}.$$

The equation $\mathbf{x}'(t) = A\mathbf{x}(t)$ is reminiscent of the simple scalar differential equation, $y'(t) = \alpha y(t)$, which is frequently used in calculus to model problems such as radioactive decay or bacterial growth. To find a function $y(t)$ that satisfies the identity $y'(t) = \alpha y(t)$, we rewrite the equation as $y'(t)/y(t) = \alpha$. Integrating both sides with respect to $t$ yields $\ln|y(t)| = \alpha t + \beta$, or equivalently $y(t) = y_0 e^{\alpha t}$, where $y_0 = y(0)$.

Using the scalar equation as a guide, we assume the vector equation $\mathbf{x}'(t) = A\mathbf{x}(t)$ has a solution of the form

$$\mathbf{x}(t) = e^{\lambda t}\mathbf{u}, \tag{11}$$

where **u** is a constant vector. To see if the function $\mathbf{x}(t)$ in Eq. (11) can be a solution, we differentiate and get $\mathbf{x}'(t) = \lambda e^{\lambda t}\mathbf{u}$. On the other hand, $A\mathbf{x}(t) = e^{\lambda t}A\mathbf{u}$; so Eq. (11) will be a solution of $\mathbf{x}'(t) = A\mathbf{x}(t)$ if and only if

$$e^{\lambda t}(A - \lambda I)\mathbf{u} = \boldsymbol{\theta}. \tag{12}$$

Now $e^{\lambda t} \neq 0$ for all values of $t$; so Eq. (12) will be satisfied only if $(A - \lambda I)\mathbf{u} = \boldsymbol{\theta}$. Therefore, if $\lambda$ is an eigenvalue of $A$ and **u** is a corresponding eigenvector, then $\mathbf{x}(t)$ given in Eq. (11) is a solution to $\mathbf{x}'(t) = A\mathbf{x}(t)$. (*Note:* The choice $\mathbf{u} = \boldsymbol{\theta}$ will also give a solution, but it is a trivial solution.)

If the $(2 \times 2)$ matrix $A$ has eigenvalues $\lambda_1$ and $\lambda_2$ with corresponding eigenvectors $\mathbf{u}_1$ and $\mathbf{u}_2$, then two solutions of $\mathbf{x}'(t) = A\mathbf{x}(t)$ are $\mathbf{x}_1(t) = e^{\lambda_1 t}\mathbf{u}_1$ and $\mathbf{x}_2(t) = e^{\lambda_2 t}\mathbf{u}_2$. It is easy to verify that any linear combination of $\mathbf{x}_1(t)$ and $\mathbf{x}_2(t)$ is also a solution; so

$$\mathbf{x}(t) = a_1\mathbf{x}_1(t) + a_2\mathbf{x}_2(t) \tag{13}$$

will solve $\mathbf{x}'(t) = A\mathbf{x}(t)$ for any choice of scalars $a_1$ and $a_2$. Finally, the initial-value problem consists of finding a solution to $\mathbf{x}'(t) = A\mathbf{x}(t)$ that satisfies an initial condition, $\mathbf{x}(0) = \mathbf{x}_0$, where $\mathbf{x}_0$ is some specified vector. Given the form of $\mathbf{x}_1(t)$ and $\mathbf{x}_2(t)$, it is clear from Eq. (13) that $\mathbf{x}(0) = a_1\mathbf{u}_1 + a_2\mathbf{u}_2$. If the eigenvectors $\mathbf{u}_1$ and $\mathbf{u}_2$ are linearly independent, we can always choose scalars $b_1$ and $b_2$ so that $\mathbf{x}_0 = b_1\mathbf{u}_1 + b_2\mathbf{u}_2$; and therefore $\mathbf{x}(t) = b_1\mathbf{x}_1(t) + b_2\mathbf{x}_2(t)$ is the solution of $\mathbf{x}'(t) = A\mathbf{x}(t)$, $\mathbf{x}(0) = \mathbf{x}_0$.

**EXAMPLE 7**    Solve the initial-value problem

$$v'(t) = v(t) - 2w(t), \quad v(0) = 4$$
$$w'(t) = v(t) + 4w(t), \quad w(0) = -3.$$

**Solution**    In vector form, the given equation can be expressed as $\mathbf{x}'(t) = A\mathbf{x}(t)$, $\mathbf{x}(0) = \mathbf{x}_0$, where

$$\mathbf{x}(t) = \begin{bmatrix} v(t) \\ w(t) \end{bmatrix}, \quad A = \begin{bmatrix} 1 & -2 \\ 1 & 4 \end{bmatrix}, \quad \text{and} \quad \mathbf{x}_0 = \begin{bmatrix} 4 \\ -3 \end{bmatrix}.$$

The eigenvalues of $A$ are $\lambda_1 = 2$ and $\lambda_2 = 3$, with corresponding eigenvectors

$$\mathbf{u}_1 = \begin{bmatrix} 2 \\ -1 \end{bmatrix} \quad \text{and} \quad \mathbf{u}_2 = \begin{bmatrix} 1 \\ -1 \end{bmatrix}.$$

As before, $\mathbf{x}_1(t) = e^{2t}\mathbf{u}_1$ and $\mathbf{x}_2(t) = e^{3t}\mathbf{u}_2$ are solutions of $\mathbf{x}'(t) = A\mathbf{x}(t)$, as is any linear combination, $\mathbf{x}(t) = b_1\mathbf{x}_1(t) + b_2\mathbf{x}_2(t)$. We now need only choose appropriate constants $b_1$ and $b_2$ so that $\mathbf{x}(0) = \mathbf{x}_0$, where we know $\mathbf{x}(0) = b_1\mathbf{u}_1 + b_2\mathbf{u}_2$. For $\mathbf{x}_0$ as given, it is routine to find $\mathbf{x}_0 = \mathbf{u}_1 + 2\mathbf{u}_2$. Thus the solution of $\mathbf{x}'(t) = A\mathbf{x}(t)$, $\mathbf{x}(0) = \mathbf{x}_0$ is $\mathbf{x}(t) = \mathbf{x}_1(t) + 2\mathbf{x}_2(t)$, or

$$\mathbf{x}(t) = e^{2t}\mathbf{u}_1 + 2e^{3t}\mathbf{u}_2.$$

In terms of the functions $v$ and $w$, we have

$$\mathbf{x}(t) = \begin{bmatrix} v(t) \\ w(t) \end{bmatrix} = e^{2t}\begin{bmatrix} 2 \\ -1 \end{bmatrix} + 2e^{3t}\begin{bmatrix} 1 \\ -1 \end{bmatrix} = \begin{bmatrix} 2e^{2t} + 2e^{3t} \\ -e^{2t} - 2e^{3t} \end{bmatrix}. \quad \blacksquare$$

In general, given the problem of solving

$$\mathbf{x}'(t) = A\mathbf{x}(t), \quad \mathbf{x}(0) = \mathbf{x}_0, \tag{14}$$

where $A$ is an $(n \times n)$ matrix, we can proceed just as above. We first find the eigenvalues $\lambda_1, \lambda_2, \ldots, \lambda_n$ of $A$ and corresponding eigenvectors $\mathbf{u}_1, \mathbf{u}_2, \ldots, \mathbf{u}_n$. For each $i$, $\mathbf{x}_i(t) = e^{\lambda_i t}\mathbf{u}_i$ is a solution of $\mathbf{x}'(t) = A\mathbf{x}(t)$, as is the general expression

$$\mathbf{x}(t) = b_1\mathbf{x}_1(t) + b_2\mathbf{x}_2(t) + \cdots + b_n\mathbf{x}_n(t). \tag{15}$$

As before, $\mathbf{x}(0) = b_1\mathbf{u}_1 + b_2\mathbf{u}_2 + \cdots + b_n\mathbf{u}_n$; so if $\mathbf{x}_0$ can be expressed as a linear combination of $\mathbf{u}_1, \mathbf{u}_2, \ldots, \mathbf{u}_n$, then we can construct a solution to Eq. (14) in the form of Eq. (15). If the eigenvectors of $A$ do not form a basis for $R^n$, we can still get a solution of the form Eq. (15); but a more detailed analysis is required. See Example 4, Section 7.8.

---

## 4.8   EXERCISES

In Exercises 1–6, consider the vector sequence $\{\mathbf{x}_k\}$, where $\mathbf{x}_k = A\mathbf{x}_{k-1}$, $k = 1, 2, \ldots$. For the given starting vector $\mathbf{x}_0$, calculate $\mathbf{x}_1$, $\mathbf{x}_2$, $\mathbf{x}_3$, and $\mathbf{x}_4$ by using direct multiplication, as in Example 1.

**1.** $A = \begin{bmatrix} 0 & 1 \\ 1 & 0 \end{bmatrix}$,   $\mathbf{x}_0 = \begin{bmatrix} 2 \\ 4 \end{bmatrix}$

**2.** $A = \begin{bmatrix} .5 & .5 \\ .5 & .5 \end{bmatrix}$,   $\mathbf{x}_0 = \begin{bmatrix} 16 \\ 8 \end{bmatrix}$

**3.** $A = \begin{bmatrix} .5 & .25 \\ .5 & .75 \end{bmatrix}$,   $\mathbf{x}_0 = \begin{bmatrix} 128 \\ 64 \end{bmatrix}$

**4.** $A = \begin{bmatrix} 2 & -1 \\ -1 & 2 \end{bmatrix}$,   $\mathbf{x}_0 = \begin{bmatrix} 3 \\ 1 \end{bmatrix}$

**5.** $A = \begin{bmatrix} 1 & 4 \\ 1 & 1 \end{bmatrix}$,   $\mathbf{x}_0 = \begin{bmatrix} -1 \\ 2 \end{bmatrix}$

**6.** $A = \begin{bmatrix} 3 & 1 \\ 4 & 3 \end{bmatrix}$,   $\mathbf{x}_0 = \begin{bmatrix} 2 \\ 0 \end{bmatrix}$

In Exercises 7–14, let $\mathbf{x}_k = A\mathbf{x}_{k-1}$, $k = 1, 2, \ldots$, for the given $A$ and $\mathbf{x}_0$. Find an expression for $\mathbf{x}_k$ by using Eq. (6), as in Example 3. With a calculator, compute $\mathbf{x}_4$ and $\mathbf{x}_{10}$ from the expression. Comment on $\lim_{k\to\infty} \mathbf{x}_k$.

**7.** $A$ and $\mathbf{x}_0$ in Exercise 1

**8.** $A$ and $\mathbf{x}_0$ in Exercise 2

**9.** $A$ and $\mathbf{x}_0$ in Exercise 3

**10.** $A$ and $\mathbf{x}_0$ in Exercise 4

**11.** $A$ and $\mathbf{x}_0$ in Exercise 5

**12.** $A$ and $\mathbf{x}_0$ in Exercise 6

**13.** $A = \begin{bmatrix} 3 & -1 & -1 \\ -12 & 0 & 5 \\ 4 & -2 & -1 \end{bmatrix}$,   $\mathbf{x}_0 = \begin{bmatrix} 3 \\ -14 \\ 8 \end{bmatrix}$

**14.** $A = \begin{bmatrix} -6 & 1 & 3 \\ -3 & 0 & 2 \\ -20 & 2 & 10 \end{bmatrix}$,   $\mathbf{x}_0 = \begin{bmatrix} 1 \\ 1 \\ -1 \end{bmatrix}$

In Exercises 15–18, solve the initial-value problem.

**15.** $u'(t) = 5u(t) - 6v(t), \quad u(0) = 4$
$v'(t) = 3u(t) - 4v(t), \quad v(0) = 1$

**16.** $u'(t) = u(t) + 2v(t), \quad u(0) = 1$
$v'(t) = 2u(t) + v(t), \quad v(0) = 5$

**17.** $u'(t) = u(t) + v(t) + w(t), \quad u(0) = 3$
$v'(t) = 3v(t) + 3w(t), \quad v(0) = 3$
$w'(t) = -2u(t) + v(t) + w(t), \quad w(0) = 1$

**18.** $u'(t) = -2u(t) + 2v(t) - 3w(t), \quad u(0) = 3$
$v'(t) = 2u(t) + v(t) - 6w(t), \quad v(0) = -1$
$w'(t) = -u(t) - 2v(t), \quad w(0) = 3$

**19.** Consider the matrix $A$ given by

$$A = \begin{bmatrix} 1 & 2 \\ 0 & 1 \end{bmatrix}.$$

Note that $\lambda = 1$ is the only eigenvalue of $A$.

a) Verify that $A$ is defective.

b) Consider the sequence $\{\mathbf{x}_k\}$ determined by $\mathbf{x}_k = A\mathbf{x}_{k-1}$, $k = 1, 2, \ldots$, where $\mathbf{x}_0 = [1, 1]^T$. Use induction to show that

$\mathbf{x}_k = [2k + 1, 1]^T$. (This exercise gives an example of a sequence $\mathbf{x}_k = A\mathbf{x}_{k-1}$, where $\lim_{k\to\infty} \|\mathbf{x}_k\| = \infty$, even though $A$ has no eigenvalue larger than 1 in magnitude.)

In Exercises 20 and 21, choose a value $\alpha$ so that the matrix $A$ has an eignevalue of $\lambda = 1$. Then, for $\mathbf{x}_0 = [1, 1]^T$, calculate $\lim_{k\to\infty} \mathbf{x}_k$, where $\mathbf{x}_k = A\mathbf{x}_{k-1}$, $k = 1, 2, \ldots$.

20. $A = \begin{bmatrix} .5 & .5 \\ .5 & 1 + \alpha \end{bmatrix}$

21. $A = \begin{bmatrix} 0 & .3 \\ .6 & 1 + \alpha \end{bmatrix}$

22. Suppose that $\{\mathbf{u}_k\}$ and $\{\mathbf{v}_k\}$ are sequences satisfying $\mathbf{u}_k = A\mathbf{u}_{k-1}$, $k = 1, 2, \ldots$, and $\mathbf{v}_k = A\mathbf{v}_{k-1}$, $k = 1, 2, \ldots$. Show that if $\mathbf{u}_0 = \mathbf{v}_0$, then $\mathbf{u}_i = \mathbf{v}_i$ for all $i$.

23. Let $B = (b_{ij})$ be an $(n \times n)$ matrix. Matrix $B$ is called a stochastic matrix if $B$ contains only nonnegative entries and if $b_{i1} + b_{i2} + \cdots + b_{in} = 1$, $1 \le i \le n$. (That is, $B$ is a stochastic matrix if $B^T$ satisfies conditions 8a and 8b.) Show that $\lambda = 1$ is an eigenvalue of $B$. [*Hint:* Consider the vector $\mathbf{w} = [1, 1, \ldots, 1]^T$.]

24. Suppose that $B$ is a stochastic matrix whose entries are all positive. By Exercise 23, $\lambda = 1$ is an eigenvalue of $B$. Show that if $B\mathbf{u} = \mathbf{u}$, $\mathbf{u} \ne \boldsymbol{\theta}$, then $\mathbf{u}$ is a multiple of the vector $\mathbf{w}$ defined in Exercise 23.

[*Hint:* Define $\mathbf{v} = \alpha\mathbf{u}$ so that $v_i = 1$ and $|v_j| \le 1$, $1 \le j \le n$. Consider the $i$th equations in $B\mathbf{w} = \mathbf{w}$ and $B\mathbf{v} = \mathbf{v}$.]

25. Let $B$ be a stochastic matrix, and let $\lambda$ by any eigenvalue of $B$. Show that $|\lambda| \le 1$. For simplicity, assume that $\lambda$ is real. [*Hint:* Suppose that $B\mathbf{u} = \lambda\mathbf{u}$, $\mathbf{u} \ne \boldsymbol{\theta}$. Define a vector $\mathbf{v}$ as in Exercise 24.]

26. Let $A$ be an $(n \times n)$ matrix satisfying conditions (8a) and (8b). Show that $\lambda = 1$ is an eigenvalue of $A$ and that if $A\mathbf{u} = \beta\mathbf{u}$, $\mathbf{u} \ne \boldsymbol{\theta}$, then $|\beta| \le 1$. [*Hint:* Matrix $A^T$ is stochastic.]

27. Suppose that $(A - \lambda I)\mathbf{u} = \boldsymbol{\theta}$, $\mathbf{u} \ne \boldsymbol{\theta}$, and there is a vector $\mathbf{v}$ such that $(A - \lambda I)\mathbf{v} = \mathbf{u}$. Then $\mathbf{v}$ is called a **generalized eigenvector**. Show that $\{\mathbf{u}, \mathbf{v}\}$ is a linearly independent set. [*Hint:* Note that $A\mathbf{v} = \lambda\mathbf{v} + \mathbf{u}$. Suppose that $a\mathbf{u} + b\mathbf{v} = \boldsymbol{\theta}$, and multiply this equation by $A$.]

28. Let $A$, $\mathbf{u}$, and $\mathbf{v}$ be as in Exercise 27. Show that $A^k\mathbf{v} = \lambda^k\mathbf{v} + k\lambda^{k-1}\mathbf{u}$, $k = 1, 2, \ldots$.

29. Consider matrix $A$ in Exercise 19.

a) Find an eigenvector $\mathbf{u}$ and a generalized eigenvector $\mathbf{v}$ for $A$.

b) Express $\mathbf{x}_0 = [1, 1]^T$ as $\mathbf{x}_0 = a\mathbf{u} + b\mathbf{v}$.

c) Using the result of Exercise 28, find an expression for $A^k\mathbf{x}_0 = A^k(a\mathbf{u} + b\mathbf{v})$.

d) Verify that $A^k\mathbf{x}_0 = [2k + 1, 1]^T$ as was shown by other means in Exercise 19.

---

# SUPPLEMENTARY EXERCISES

1. Find all values $x$ such that $A$ is singular, where

$$A = \begin{bmatrix} x & 1 & 2 \\ 3 & x & 0 \\ 0 & -1 & 1 \end{bmatrix}.$$

2. For what values $x$ does $A$ have only real eigenvalues, where

$$A = \begin{bmatrix} 2 & 1 \\ x & 3 \end{bmatrix}?$$

3. Let

$$A = \begin{bmatrix} a & b \\ c & d \end{bmatrix},$$

where $a + b = 2$ and $c + d = 2$. Show that $\lambda = 2$ is an eigenvalue for $A$. [*Hint:* Guess an eigenvector.]

4. Let $A$ and $B$ be $(3 \times 3)$ matrices such that $\det(A) = 2$ and $\det(B) = 9$. Find the values of each of the following.

a) $\det(A^{-1}B^2)$

b) $\det(3A)$

c) $\det(AB^2A^{-1})$

**5.** For what values $x$ is $A$ defective, where

$$A = \begin{bmatrix} 2 & x \\ 0 & 2 \end{bmatrix}.$$

In Exercises 6–9, $A$ is a $(2 \times 2)$ matrix such that $A^2 + 3A - I = \mathcal{O}$.

**6.** Suppose we know that

$$A\mathbf{u} = \begin{bmatrix} 2 \\ 1 \end{bmatrix}, \quad \text{where } \mathbf{u} = \begin{bmatrix} 1 \\ 3 \end{bmatrix}.$$

Find $A^2\mathbf{u}$ and $A^3\mathbf{u}$.

**7.** Show that $A$ is nonsingular. [*Hint:* Is there a nonzero vector $\mathbf{x}$ such that $A\mathbf{x} = \boldsymbol{\theta}$?]

**8.** Find $A^{-1}\mathbf{u}$, where $\mathbf{u}$ is as in Exercise 6.

**9.** Using the fact that $A^2 = I - 3A$, we can find scalars $a_k$ and $b_k$ such that $A^k = a_k A + b_k I$. Find these scalars for $k = 2, 3, 4$, and 5.

In Exercises 10 and 11, find the eigenvalues $\lambda_i$ given the corresponding eigenvector $\mathbf{u}_i$. Do not calculate the characteristic polynomial for $A$.

**10.** $A = \begin{bmatrix} 2 & -12 \\ 1 & -5 \end{bmatrix}$, $\quad \mathbf{u}_1 = \begin{bmatrix} 4 \\ 1 \end{bmatrix}$,

$\mathbf{u}_2 = \begin{bmatrix} 3 \\ 1 \end{bmatrix}$

**11.** $A = \begin{bmatrix} 1 & 2 \\ -1 & 4 \end{bmatrix}$, $\quad \mathbf{u}_1 = \begin{bmatrix} 2 \\ 1 \end{bmatrix}$,

$\mathbf{u}_2 = \begin{bmatrix} 1 \\ 1 \end{bmatrix}$

**12.** Find $x$ so that $\mathbf{u}$ is an eigenvector. What is the corresponding eigenvalue $\lambda$?

$$A = \begin{bmatrix} 2 & x \\ 1 & -5 \end{bmatrix}, \quad \mathbf{u} = \begin{bmatrix} 1 \\ -1 \end{bmatrix}$$

**13.** Find $x$ and $y$ so that $\mathbf{u}$ is an eigenvector corresponding to the eigenvalue $\lambda = 1$:

$$A = \begin{bmatrix} x & y \\ 2x & -y \end{bmatrix}, \quad \mathbf{u} = \begin{bmatrix} -1 \\ 1 \end{bmatrix}$$

**14.** Find $x$ and $y$ so that $\mathbf{u}$ is an eigenvector corresponding to the eigenvalue $\lambda = 4$:

$$A = \begin{bmatrix} x+y & y \\ x-3 & 1 \end{bmatrix}, \quad \mathbf{u} = \begin{bmatrix} -3 \\ 1 \end{bmatrix}$$

## CONCEPTUAL EXERCISES

In Exercises 1–8, answer true or false. Justify your answer by providing a counterexample if the statement is false or an outline of a proof if the statement is true. In each exercise, $A$ is a real $(n \times n)$ matrix.

**1.** If $A$ is nonsingular with $A^{-1} = A^T$, then $\det(A) = 1$.

**2.** If $\mathbf{x}$ is an eigenvector for $A$, where $A$ is nonsingular, then $\mathbf{x}$ is also an eigenvector for $A^{-1}$.

**3.** If $A$ is nonsingular, then $\det(A^4)$ is positive.

**4.** If $A$ is defective, then $A$ is singular.

**5.** If $A$ is an orthogonal matrix and if $\mathbf{x}$ is in $R^n$, then $\|A\mathbf{x}\| = \|\mathbf{x}\|$.

**6.** If $S$ is $(n \times n)$ and nonsingular, then $A$ and $S^{-1}AS$ have the same eigenvalues.

**7.** If $A$ and $B$ are diagonal $(n \times n)$ matrices, then $\det(A + B) = \det(A) + \det(B)$.

**8.** If $A$ is singular, then $A$ is defective.

In Exercises 9–14, give a brief answer.

**9.** Suppose that $A$ and $Q$ are $(n \times n)$ matrices where $Q$ is orthogonal. Then we know that $A$ and $B = Q^T A Q$ have the same eigenvalues.

**a)** If $\mathbf{x}$ is an eigenvector of $B$ corresponding to $\lambda$, give an eigenvector of $A$ corresponding to $\lambda$.

**b)** If $u$ is an eigenvector of $A$ corresponding to $\lambda$, give an eigenvector of $B$ corresponding to $\lambda$.

**10.** Suppose that $A$ is $(n \times n)$ and $A^3 = \mathcal{O}$. Show that 0 is the only eigenvalue of $A$.

**11.** Show that if $A$ is $(n \times n)$ and is similar to the $(n \times n)$ identity $I$, then $A = I$.

**12.** Let $A$ and $B$ be $(n \times n)$ with $A$ nonsingular. Show that $AB$ and $BA$ are similar. [*Hint:* Consider $S^{-1}ABS = BA$.]

**13.** Suppose that $A$ and $B$ are $(n \times n)$ and $A$ is similar to $B$. Show that $A^k$ is similar to $B^k$ for $k = 2, 3,$ and 4.

**14.** Let $u$ be a vector in $R^n$ such that $u^Tu = 1$, and let $A$ denote the $(n \times n)$ matrix $A = I - 2uu^T$.

**a)** Is $A$ symmetric?

**b)** Is $A$ orthogonal?

**c)** Calculate $Au$.

**d)** Suppose that $w$ is in $R^n$ and $u^Tw = 0$. What is $Aw$?

**e)** Give the eigenvalues of $A$ and give the geometric multiplicity for each eignevalue.

---

# MATLAB EXERCISES

**1. Recognizing eigenvectors geometrically**   Let $x = [x_1, x_2]^T$ and let $y = [y_1, y_2]^T$ be vectors in $R^2$. The following MATLAB command gives us a geometric representation of $x$ and $y$:

$$\texttt{plot([0, x(1)], [0, x(2)], [0, y(1)], [0, y(2)]).} \quad (1)$$

(In particular, the single command `plot([0, x(1)], [0, x(2)])` draws a line from the origin $(0, 0)$ to the point $(x(1), x(2))$; this line is a geometric representation of the vector $x$. The longer command (1) draws two lines, one representing $x$ and the other $y$.)

**a)** Let $A$ be the $(2 \times 2)$ matrix

$$A = \begin{bmatrix} 3 & 7 \\ 1 & 3 \end{bmatrix}.$$

For each of the following vectors $x$, use the command (1) to plot $x$ and $y = Ax$. Which of the vectors $x$ is an eigenvector for $A$? How can you tell from the geometric representation drawn by MATLAB?

**i)** $x = \begin{bmatrix} 0.3536 \\ 0.9354 \end{bmatrix}$     **ii)** $x = \begin{bmatrix} 0.9354 \\ 0.3536 \end{bmatrix}$

**iii)** $x = \begin{bmatrix} -0.3536 \\ 0.9354 \end{bmatrix}$     **iv)** $x = \begin{bmatrix} -0.9354 \\ 0.3536 \end{bmatrix}.$

**b)** Let $\lambda$ be an eigenvalue for $A$ with corresponding eigenvector $x$. Then:

$$\frac{(Ax)^Tx}{x^Tx} = \frac{(\lambda x)^Tx}{x^Tx} = \frac{\lambda x^Tx}{x^Tx} = \lambda.$$

The expression $(Au)^Tu/u^Tu$ is called a ***Rayleigh quotient***. Therefore, the preceding formula says that if $u$ is an eigenvector for $A$, then the value of the Rayleigh quotient is equal to an eigenvalue corresponding to $u$.

For each of the eigenvectors found in part a), use MATLAB to compute the Rayleigh quotient and hence determine the corresponding eigenvalue $\lambda$. Check your calculations by comparing $A\mathbf{x}$ and $\lambda\mathbf{x}$.

c) Repeat parts a) and b) for the following matrix $A$ and vectors given in i)–iv):

$$A = \begin{bmatrix} 1 & 3 \\ 1 & 1 \end{bmatrix}$$

and

i) $\mathbf{x} = \begin{bmatrix} -0,8660 \\ 0.5000 \end{bmatrix}$  ii) $\mathbf{x} = \begin{bmatrix} 0.5000 \\ 0.8660 \end{bmatrix}$

iii) $\mathbf{x} = \begin{bmatrix} -0.5000 \\ 0.8660 \end{bmatrix}$  iv) $\mathbf{x} = \begin{bmatrix} -0.8660 \\ 0.5000 \end{bmatrix}$.

2. **Determinants of block matrices** In the MATLAB exercises for Chapter 1, we discussed how block matrices could be multiplied by thinking of the blocks as numbers. In this exercise, we extend the ideas to include determinants of block matrices.

Consider a $(2 \times 2)$ block matrix $A$ of the form

$$A = \begin{bmatrix} A_1 & A_2 \\ A_3 & A_4 \end{bmatrix}. \tag{2}$$

We would like to be able to say that $\det(A) = \det(A_1)\det(A_4) - \det(A_3)\det(A_2)$ and, in fact, sometimes we can; but, sometimes we cannot.

a) Generate a random $(6 \times 6)$ matrix $A$ and partition it into four $(3 \times 3)$ blocks in order to create a $(2 \times 2)$ block matrix of the form displayed in Eq. (2). Use the MATLAB determinant command to calculate $\det(A)$—as you might expect, the command is det (A). Use MATLAB to calculate the determinant of each block and compare your result with the value: $\det(A_1)\det(A_4) - \det(A_3)\det(A_2)$. Is the formula $\det(A) = \det(A_1)\det(A_4) - \det(A_3)\det(A_2)$ valid in general?

b) Now, let us do part a) again. This time, however, we will choose $A_3$ to be the $(3 \times 3)$ zero matrix. That is, $A$ is a **block upper-triangular** matrix. Verify for your randomly chosen matrix that the expected result holds:

*If $A$ is block upper triangular, then $\det(A) = \det(A_1)\det(A_4)$.*

c) The result in part b) suggests the following theorem:

*The determinant of a block triangular matrix is equal to the product of the determinants of its diagonal blocks.*

This theorem is indeed true and it is valid for a matrix with any number of blocks, so long as the matrix is partitioned in such a way that the diagonal blocks are square. Illustrate this result by generating a random $(12 \times 12)$ matrix $A$ and partitioning it as follows:

$$A = \begin{bmatrix} A_{11} & A_{12} & A_{13} \\ 0 & A_{22} & A_{23} \\ 0 & 0 & A_{33} \end{bmatrix}.$$

Your $(3 \times 3)$ block upper-triangular matrix $A$ must have its diagonal blocks square, but there is no other requirement. For example, $A_{11}$ could be $(2 \times 2)$, $A_{22}$ could be $(7 \times 7)$, and $A_{33}$ could be $(3 \times 3)$. The proof of the theorem stated above can be established using techniques discussed in Chapter 6.

**3. Dominant eigenvalues** An eigenvalue $\lambda$ for a matrix $A$ is called a *dominant eigenvalue* if $|\lambda| > |\beta|$ for any other eigenvalue $\beta$ of $A$. This exercise will illustrate how powers of $A$ multiplying a starting vector $\mathbf{x}_0$ will line up along a *dominant eigenvector*. That is, given a starting vector $\mathbf{x}_0$, the following sequence of vectors will tend to become a multiple of an eigenvector associated with the dominant eigenvalue $\lambda$.

$$\mathbf{x}_1 = A\mathbf{x}_0, \mathbf{x}_2 = A\mathbf{x}_1, \ldots, \mathbf{x}_k = A\mathbf{x}_{k-1}, \ldots. \tag{3}$$

The sequence of vectors defined above was discussed in Section 4.8 under the topics of *difference equations* and *Markov chains*. In that section we saw how the dominant eigenvalue/eigenvector pair determined the steady-state solution of the difference equation. The sequence of vectors was also introduced in Exercise 28 in Section 4.4. In that exercise, we saw the converse; that estimates of the steady-state solution can be used to estimate a dominant eigenvalue and eigenvector (this procedure is the *power method*).

The point of this exercise is to illustrate numerically and graphically how the sequence (3) lines up in the direction of a dominant eigenvector. First, however, we want to recall why this sequence behaves in such a fashion.

As an example, suppose $A$ is a $(3 \times 3)$ matrix with eigenvalues $\lambda_1$, $\lambda_2$, $\lambda_3$ and eigenvectors $\mathbf{u}_1$, $\mathbf{u}_2$, $\mathbf{u}_3$. Further, suppose $\lambda_1$ is a dominant eigenvalue. Now we know that the $k$th term in sequence (3) can be expressed as $\mathbf{x}_k = A^k\mathbf{x}_0$ (see Eqs. (4) and (5) in Section 4.8). Finally, let us suppose that $\mathbf{x}_0$ can be expessed as a linear combination of the eigenvectors:

$$\mathbf{x}_0 = c_1\mathbf{u}_1 + c_2\mathbf{u}_2 + c_3\mathbf{u}_3.$$

Using the fact that $\mathbf{x}_k = A^k\mathbf{x}_0$, we see from the preceding representation for $\mathbf{x}_0$ that we have

$$\mathbf{x}_k = c_1(\lambda_1)^k\mathbf{u}_1 + c_2(\lambda_2)^k\mathbf{u}_2 + c_3(\lambda_3)^k\mathbf{u}_3$$

or

$$\mathbf{x}_k = c_1\lambda_1^k\left(\mathbf{u}_1 + \frac{c_2}{c_1}\left(\frac{\lambda_2}{\lambda_1}\right)^k\mathbf{u}_2 + \frac{c_3}{c_1}\left(\frac{\lambda_3}{\lambda_1}\right)^k\mathbf{u}_3\right). \tag{4}$$

Since $\lambda_1$ is a dominant eigenvalue, the reason that $\mathbf{x}_k$ lines up in the direction of the dominant eigenvector $\mathbf{u}_1$ is clear from formula (4) for $\mathbf{x}_k$.

We note that formula (4) can be used in two different ways. For a given starting vector $\mathbf{x}_0$, we can use (4) to estimate the steady-state vector $\mathbf{x}_k$ at some future time $t_k$ (this use is discussed in Section 4.8). Conversely, given a matrix $A$, we can calculate the sequence (3) and use formula (4) to estimate the dominant eigenvalue (this use is the power method).

**a)** Let the matrix $A$ and the starting vector $\mathbf{x}_0$ be as follows:

$$A = \begin{bmatrix} 3 & -1 & -1 \\ -12 & 0 & 5 \\ 4 & -2 & -1 \end{bmatrix}, \quad \mathbf{x}_0 = \begin{bmatrix} 1 \\ 1 \\ 1 \end{bmatrix}.$$

Use MATLAB to generate $\mathbf{x}_1, \mathbf{x}_2, \ldots, \mathbf{x}_{10}$. (You need not use subscripted vectors, you can simply repeat the following command ten times: $x = A*x$. This assignment statement replaces **x** by $A$**x** each time it is executed.) As you can see, the vectors $\mathbf{x}_k$ are lining up in a certain direction. To conveniently identify that direction, divide each component of $\mathbf{x}_{10}$ by the first component of $\mathbf{x}_{10}$. Calculate the next three vectors in the sequence (the vectors $\mathbf{x}_{11}$, $\mathbf{x}_{12}$, and $\mathbf{x}_{13}$) normalizing each one as you did for $\mathbf{x}_{10}$. What is your guess as to a dominant eigenvector for $A$?

**b)** From formula (4) we see that $\mathbf{x}_{k+1} \approx \lambda_1 \mathbf{x}_k$. Use this approximation and the results of part a) to estimate the dominant eigenvalue of $A$.

**c)** As you can see from part a), when we generate the sequence (3) we obtain vectors with larger and larger components when the dominant eigenvalue is larger than 1 in absolute value. To avoid vectors with large components, it is customary to normalize each vector in the sequence. Thus, rather than generating sequence (3), we instead generate the following sequence (5) of unit vectors:

$$\mathbf{x}_1 = \frac{A\mathbf{x}_0}{\|A\mathbf{x}_0\|}, \mathbf{x}_2 = \frac{A\mathbf{x}_1}{\|A\mathbf{x}_1\|}, \dots, \mathbf{x}_k = \frac{A\mathbf{x}_{k-1}}{A\mathbf{x}_{k-1}}, \dots \tag{5}$$

A slight modification of formula (4) shows that the normalized sequence (5) also lines up along the dominant eigenvector. Repeat part a) using the normalized sequence (5) and observe that you find the same dominant eigenvector. Try several different starting vectors, such as $\mathbf{x}_0 = [1, 2, 3]^T$.

**d)** This exercise illustrates graphically the ideas in parts a)–c). Consider the matrix $A$ and starting vector $\mathbf{x}_0$ given by

$$A = \begin{bmatrix} 2.8 & -1.6 \\ -1.6 & 5.2 \end{bmatrix}, \quad \mathbf{x}_0 = \begin{bmatrix} 1/\sqrt{2} \\ 1/\sqrt{2} \end{bmatrix}.$$

Use MATLAB to calculate the sequence of vectors defined by (5). In order to give a geometric representation of each term in the sequence, we can use the following MATLAB commands:

```
x=[1,1]'
x=x/norm(x)
plot([0, x(1)], [0, x(2)])
hold
x = A*x/norm(A*x)
plot([0, x(1)], [0, x(2)])
x = A*x/norm(A*x)
plot([0, x(1)], [0, x(2)])
   etc.
```

Continue until the sequences appear to be stabilizing.

**e)** Exercise 28 in Section 4.4 describes the power method, which is based on the ideas discussed so far in this exercise. Exercise 28 gives an easy way (based on Rayleigh quotients) to estimate the dominant eigenvalue that corresponds to the dominant eigenvectors generated by the sequence (5); see the definition of $\beta_k$ in part c) of Exercise 28. Use this idea to estimate the dominant eigenvalue for the matrix $A$ in part d) of this MATLAB exercise.

# Vector Spaces and Linear Transformations

**OVERVIEW**

In Chapter 3 we saw, by using an algebraic perspective, that we could extend geometric vector concepts to $R^n$. In this chapter, using $R^n$ as a model, we further extend the idea of a vector to include objects such as matrices, polynomials, functions, infinite sequences, and so forth.

As we will see in this chapter, concepts introduced in Chapter 3 (such as subspace, basis, and dimension) have natural extensions to the general vector space setting. In addition, applications treated in Chapter 3 (such as least squares fits to data) also have extensions to the general vector space setting.

**CORE SECTIONS**

## 5.1    INTRODUCTION

Chapter 3 illustrated that by passing from a purely geometric view of vectors to an algebraic perspective we could, in a natural way, extend the concept of a vector to include elements of $R^n$. Using $R^n$ as a model, this chapter extends the notion of a vector even further to include objects such as matrices, polynomials, functions continuous on a given interval, and solutions to certain differential equations. Most of the elementary concepts (such as subspace, basis, and dimension) that are important to understanding vector spaces are immediate generalizations of the same concepts in $R^n$.

Linear transformations were also introduced in Chapter 3, and we showed in Section 3.7 that a linear transformation, $T$, from $R^n$ to $R^m$ is always defined by matrix multiplication; that is,

$$T(\mathbf{x}) = A\mathbf{x} \tag{1}$$

for some $(m \times n)$ matrix $A$. In Sections 5.7–5.10, we will consider linear transformations on arbitrary vector spaces, thus extending the theory of mappings defined as in Eq. (1) to a more general setting. For example, differentiation and integration can be viewed as linear transformations.

Although the theory of vector spaces is relatively abstract, the vector-space structure provides a unifying framework of great flexibility, and many important practical problems fit naturally into a vector-space framework. As examples, the set of all solutions to a differential equation such as

$$a(x)y'' + b(x)y' + c(x)y = 0$$

can be shown to be a two-dimensional vector space. Thus if two *linearly independent* solutions are known, then all the solutions are determined. The previously defined notion of dot product can be extended to more general vector spaces and used to define the distance between two vectors. This notion is essential when one wishes to approximate one object with another (for example, to approximate a function with a polynomial). Linear transformations permit a natural extension of the important concepts of eigenvalues and eigenvectors to arbitrary vector spaces.

A basic feature of vector spaces is that they possess both an algebraic character and a geometric character. In this regard the geometric character frequently gives a pictorial insight into how a particular problem can be solved, whereas the algebraic character is used actually to calculate a solution.

As an example of how we can use this dual geometric/algebraic character of vector spaces, consider the following. In 1811 and 1822, Fourier, in his *Mathematical Theory of Heat*, made extremely important discoveries by using trigonometric series of the form

$$s(x) = \sum_{k=0}^{\infty}(a_k \cos kx + b_k \sin kx)$$

to represent functions, $f(x)$, $-\pi \leq x \leq \pi$. Today these representations can be visualized and utilized in a simple way using vector-space concepts.

For any positive integer $n$, let $\mathcal{S}_n$ represent the set of all trigonometric polynomials of degree at most $n$:

$$\mathcal{S}_n = \left\{ s_n(x) : s_n(x) = \sum_{k=0}^{n}(a_k \cos kx + b_k \sin kx), \quad a_k \text{ and } b_k \text{ real numbers} \right\}.$$

Now, if $s_n^*(x)$ is the best approximation in $\mathcal{S}_n$ to $f(x)$, then we might hope that $s(x) = \lim_{n \to \infty} s_n^*(x)$. A heuristic picture of this setting is shown in Fig. 5.1, where $\mathcal{F}[-\pi, \pi]$ denotes all functions defined on $[-\pi, \pi]$.

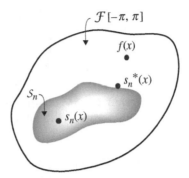

***Figure 5.1***    Among all $s_n(x)$ in $\mathcal{S}_n$, we are searching for $s^*(x)$, which best approximates $f(x)$, $-\pi \leq x \leq \pi$.

In Fig. 5.2, we have a vector approximation problem that we already know how to work from calculus. Here $\Pi$ is a plane through the origin, and we are searching for a point $y^*$ in $\Pi$ that is closer to the given point $b$ than any other point $y$ in $\Pi$. Using $\mathbf{b}$, $\mathbf{y}$, and $\mathbf{y}^*$ as the position vectors for the points $b$, $y$, and $y^*$, respectively, we know that $\mathbf{y}^*$ is characterized by the fact that the remainder vector, $\mathbf{b} - \mathbf{y}^*$, is perpendicular to every position vector $\mathbf{y}$ in $\Pi$. That is, we can find $\mathbf{y}^*$ by setting $(\mathbf{b} - \mathbf{y}^*)^T \mathbf{u}_1 = 0$ and $(\mathbf{b} - \mathbf{y}^*)^T \mathbf{u}_2 = 0$, where $\{\mathbf{u}_1, \mathbf{u}_2\}$ is any basis for $\Pi$.

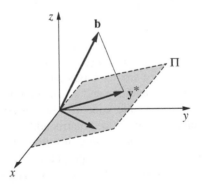

***Figure 5.2***    The vector $\mathbf{y}^*$ in $\Pi$ is closer to $\mathbf{b}$ than is any other vector $\mathbf{y}$ in $\Pi$ if and only if $\mathbf{b} - \mathbf{y}^*$ is perpendicular to all $\mathbf{y}$ in $\Pi$.

Figure 5.3 gives another way of visualizing this problem. We see a striking similarity between Figs. 5.1 and 5.3. It gives us the inspiration to ask if we can find $s_n^*(x)$ in Fig. 5.1 by choosing its coefficients, $a_k$ and $b_k$, so that the remainder function, $f(x) - s_n^*(x)$, is in some way "perpendicular" to every $s_n(x)$ in $\mathcal{S}_n$.

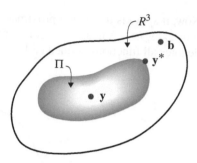

*Figure 5.3*    An abstract representation of the problem of finding the closest vector, $y^*$, in a subspace $\Pi$ to a vector $b$.

As we will show in Section 5.6, this is precisely the approach we use to compute $s_n^*(x)$. Thus the geometric character of the vector-space setting provides our intuition with a possible procedure for solution. We must then use the algebraic character to:

**(a)**   argue that our intuition is valid, and

**(b)**   perform the actual calculation of the coefficients $a_k$ and $b_k$ for $s_n^*(x)$.

# VECTOR SPACES

We begin our study of vector spaces by recalling the basic properties of $R^n$. First recall that there are two algebraic operations in $R^n$:

**1.**   Vectors in $R^n$ can be added.

**2.**   Any vector in $R^n$ can be multiplied by a scalar.

Furthermore, these two operations satisfy the 10 basic properties given in Theorem 1 of Section 3.2. For example, if $u$ and $v$ are in $R^n$, then $u + v$ is also in $R^n$. Moreover, $u + v = v + u$ and $(u + v) + w = u + (v + w)$ for all $u$, $v$, and $w$ in $R^n$.

There are numerous sets other than $R^n$ on which there are defined algebraic operations of addition and scalar multiplication. Moreover, in many cases these operations will satisfy the same 10 rules listed in Theorem 1 of Section 3.2. For example, we have already defined matrix addition and scalar multiplication on the set of all $(m \times n)$ matrices. Furthermore, it follows from Theorems 7, 8, and 9 of Section 1.6 that these operations satisfy the properties given in Theorem 1 of Section 3.2 (see Example 2 later in this section). Thus, with $R^n$ as a model, we could just as easily study the set of all $(m \times n)$ matrices and derive most of the properties and concepts given in Chapter 3, but in the context of matrices. Rather than study each such set individually, however, it is more efficient to define a *vector space* in the abstract as any set of objects that has algebraic operations that satisfy a given list of basic properties. Using only these assumed properties, we can prove other properties and develop further concepts. The results obtained in this manner then apply to any specific vector space. For example, later in this chapter the term *linearly independent* will be applied to a set of matrices, a set of polynomials, or a set of continuous functions.

Drawing on this discussion, we see that a general vector space should consist of a set of elements (or vectors), $V$, and a set of scalars, $S$, together with two algebraic operations:

1. An addition, which is defined between any two elements of $V$ and which produces a sum that is in $V$;

2. A scalar multiplication, which defines how to multiply any element of $V$ by a scalar from $S$.

In practice the set $V$ can consist of any collection of objects for which meaningful operations of addition and scalar multiplication can be defined. For example, $V$ might be the set of all $(2 \times 3)$ matrices, the set $R^4$ of all four-dimensional vectors, a set of functions, a set of polynomials, or the set of all solutions to a linear homogeneous differential equation. We will take the set $S$ of scalars to be the set of real numbers, although for added flexibility other sets of scalars may be used (for example, $S$ could be the set of complex numbers). Throughout this chapter the term *scalar* will always denote a real number.

Using $R^n$ as a model and the properties of $R^n$ listed in Theorem 1 of Section 3.2 as a guide, we now define a general vector space. Note that the definition says nothing about the set $V$ but rather specifies rules that the algebraic operations must satisfy.

---

DEFINITION 1

A set of elements $V$ is said to be a **vector space** over a scalar field $S$ if an addition operation is defined between any two elements of $V$ and a scalar multiplication operation is defined between any element of $S$ and any vector in $V$. Moreover, if $\mathbf{u}$, $\mathbf{v}$, and $\mathbf{w}$ are vectors in $V$, and if $a$ and $b$ are any two scalars, then these 10 properties must hold.

*Closure properties:*

(c1)    $\mathbf{u} + \mathbf{v}$ is a vector in $V$.
(c2)    $a\mathbf{v}$ is a vector in $V$.

*Properties of addition:*

(a1)    $\mathbf{u} + \mathbf{v} = \mathbf{v} + \mathbf{u}$.
(a2)    $\mathbf{u} + (\mathbf{v} + \mathbf{w}) = (\mathbf{u} + \mathbf{v}) + \mathbf{w}$.
(a3)    There is a vector $\boldsymbol{\theta}$ in $V$ such that $\mathbf{v} + \boldsymbol{\theta} = \mathbf{v}$ for all $\mathbf{v}$ in $V$.
(a4)    Given a vector $\mathbf{v}$ in $V$, there is a vector $-\mathbf{v}$ in $V$ such that $\mathbf{v} + (-\mathbf{v}) = \boldsymbol{\theta}$.

*Properties of scalar multiplication:*

(m1)    $a(b\mathbf{v}) = (ab)\mathbf{v}$.
(m2)    $a(\mathbf{u} + \mathbf{v}) = a\mathbf{u} + a\mathbf{v}$.
(m3)    $(a + b)\mathbf{v} = a\mathbf{v} + b\mathbf{v}$.
(m4)    $1\mathbf{v} = \mathbf{v}$ for all $\mathbf{v}$ in $V$.

---

The first two conditions, (c1) and (c2), in Definition 1, called **closure properties**, ensure that the sum of any two vectors in $V$ remains in $V$ and that any scalar multiple of a vector in $V$ remains in $V$. In condition (a3), $\boldsymbol{\theta}$ is naturally called the **zero vector** (or the **additive identity**). In (a4), the vector $-\mathbf{v}$ is called the **additive inverse** of $\mathbf{v}$, and (a4) asserts that the equation $\mathbf{v} + \mathbf{x} = \boldsymbol{\theta}$ has a solution in $V$. When the set of scalars $S$ is the set of real numbers, $V$ is called a **real vector space**; and as we have said, we will consider only real vector spaces.

## Example of Vector Spaces

We already have two familiar examples of vector spaces, namely, $R^n$ and the set of all $(m \times n)$ matrices. It is easy to verify that these are vector spaces, and the verification is sketched in the next two examples.

EXAMPLE 1     For any positive integer $n$, verify that $R^n$ is a real vector space.

*Solution*     Theorem 1 of Section 3.2 shows that $R^n$ satisfies the properties listed in Definition 1, so $R^n$ is a real vector space.

Example 2 may strike the reader as being a little unusual since we are considering matrices as elements in a vector space. The example, however, illustrates the flexibility of the vector-space concept; any set of entities that has addition and scalar multiplication operations can be a vector space, provided that addition and scalar multiplication satisfy the requirements of Definition 1.

EXAMPLE 2     Verify that the set of all $(2 \times 3)$ matrices with real entries is a real vector space.

*Solution*     Let $A$ and $B$ be any $(2 \times 3)$ matrices, and let addition and scalar multiplication be defined as in Definitions 6 and 7 of Section 1.5. Therefore, $A + B$ and $aA$ are defined by

$$A + B = \begin{bmatrix} a_{11} & a_{12} & a_{13} \\ a_{21} & a_{22} & a_{23} \end{bmatrix} + \begin{bmatrix} b_{11} & b_{12} & b_{13} \\ b_{21} & b_{22} & b_{23} \end{bmatrix}$$

$$= \begin{bmatrix} a_{11} + b_{11} & a_{12} + b_{12} & a_{13} + b_{13} \\ a_{21} + b_{21} & a_{22} + b_{22} & a_{23} + b_{23} \end{bmatrix}$$

$$aA = a \begin{bmatrix} a_{11} & a_{12} & a_{13} \\ a_{21} & a_{22} & a_{23} \end{bmatrix} = \begin{bmatrix} aa_{11} & aa_{12} & aa_{13} \\ aa_{21} & aa_{22} & aa_{23} \end{bmatrix}.$$

From these definitions it is obvious that both the sum $A + B$ and the scalar multiple $aA$ are again $(2 \times 3)$ matrices; so (c1) and (c2) of Definition 1 hold. Properties (a1), (a2), (a3), and (a4) follow from Theorem 7 of Section 1.6; and (m1), (m2), and (m3) are proved in Theorems 8 and 9 of Section 1.6. Property (m4) is immediate from the definition of scalar multiplication [clearly $1A = A$ for any $(2 \times 3)$ matrix $A$]. For emphasis we recall that the zero element in this vector space is the matrix

$$\mathcal{O} = \begin{bmatrix} 0 & 0 & 0 \\ 0 & 0 & 0 \end{bmatrix},$$

and clearly $A + \mathcal{O} = A$ for any $(2 \times 3)$ matrix $A$. We further observe that $(-1)A$ is the additive inverse for $A$ because

$$A + (-1)A = \mathcal{O}.$$

[That is, $(-1)A$ is a matrix we can add to $A$ to produce the zero element $\mathcal{O}$.] A duplication of these arguments shows that for any $m$ and $n$ the set of all $(m \times n)$ matrices with real entries is a real vector space. ∎

The next three examples show that certain sets of functions have a natural vector-space structure.

EXAMPLE 3   Let $\mathcal{P}_2$ denote the set of all real polynomials of degree 2 or less. Verify that $\mathcal{P}_2$ is a real vector space.

**Solution**   Note that a natural addition is associated with polynomials. For example, let $p(x)$ and $q(x)$ be the polynomials

$$p(x) = 2x^2 - x + 3 \text{ and } q(x) = x^2 + 2x - 1.$$

Then the sum $r(x) = p(x) + q(x)$ is the polynomial $r(x) = 3x^2 + x + 2$. Scalar multiplication is defined similarly; so if $s(x) = 2q(x)$, then

$$s(x) = 2x^2 + 4x - 2.$$

Given this natural addition and scalar multiplication associated with the set $\mathcal{P}_2$, it seems reasonable to expect that $\mathcal{P}_2$ is a real vector space.

To establish this conclusion rigorously, we must be a bit more careful. To begin, we define $\mathcal{P}_2$ to be the set of all expressions (or functions) of the form

$$p(x) = a_2x^2 + a_1x + a_0, \tag{1}$$

where $a_2$, $a_1$, and $a_0$ are any real constants. Thus the following polynomials are vectors in $\mathcal{P}_2$:

$$p_1(x) = x^2 - x + 3, \quad p_2(x) = x^2 + 1, \quad p_3(x) = x - 2,$$
$$p_4(x) = 2x, \quad p_5(x) = 7, \quad p_6(x) = 0.$$

For instance, we see that $p_2(x)$ has the form of Eq. (1), with $a_2 = 1$, $a_1 = 0$, and $a_0 = 1$. Similarly, $p_4(x)$ is in $\mathcal{P}_2$ because $p_4(x)$ is a function of the form (1), where $a_2 = 0$, $a_1 = 2$, and $a_0 = 0$. Finally, $p_6(x)$ has the form (1) with $a_2 = 0$, $a_1 = 0$, and $a_0 = 0$. To define addition precisely, let

$$p(x) = a_2x^2 + a_1x + a_0 \text{ and } q(x) = b_2x^2 + b_1x + b_0$$

be two vectors in $\mathcal{P}_2$. We define the sum $r(x) = p(x) + q(x)$ to be the polynomial

$$r(x) = (a_2 + b_2)x^2 + (a_1 + b_1)x + (a_0 + b_0);$$

and we define the scalar multiple $s(x) = cp(x)$ to be the polynomial

$$s(x) = (ca_2)x^2 + (ca_1)x + (ca_0).$$

We leave it to the reader to verify that these algebraic operations meet the requirements of Definition 1; we note only that we choose the zero vector to be the polynomial that is identically zero. That is, the zero element in $\mathcal{P}_2$ is the polynomial $\theta(x)$, where $\theta(x) = 0$; or in terms of Eq. (1), $\theta(x)$ is defined by

$$\theta(x) = 0x^2 + 0x + 0.$$ ∎

EXAMPLE 4    In this example we take $\mathcal{P}_n$ to be the set of all real polynomials of degree $n$ or less. That is, $\mathcal{P}_n$ consists of all functions $p(x)$ of the form

$$p(x) = a_n x^n + a_{n-1} x^{n-1} + \cdots + a_2 x^2 + a_1 x + a_0,$$

where $a_n, a_{n-1}, \ldots, a_2, a_1, a_0$ are any real constants. With addition and scalar multiplication defined as in Example 3, it is easy to show that $\mathcal{P}_n$ is a real vector space. ∎

The next example presents one of the more important vector spaces in applications.

EXAMPLE 5    Let $C[a, b]$ be the set of functions defined by

$$C[a, b] = \{f(x): f(x) \text{ is a real-valued continuous function, } a \leq x \leq b\}.$$

Verify that $C[a, b]$ is a real vector space.

*Solution*    $C[a, b]$ has a natural addition, just as $\mathcal{P}_n$. If $f$ and $g$ are vectors in $C[a, b]$, then we define the sum $h = f + g$ to be the function $h$ given by

$$h(x) = f(x) + g(x), \quad a \leq x \leq b.$$

Similarly, if $c$ is a scalar, then the scalar multiple $q = cf$ is the function

$$q(x) = cf(x), \quad a \leq x \leq b.$$

As a concrete example, if $f(x) = e^x$ and $g(x) = \sin x$, then $3f + g$ is the function $r$, where the action of $r$ is defined by $r(x) = 3e^x + \sin x$. Note that the closure properties, (c1) and (c2), follow from elementary results of calculus—sums and scalar multiples of continuous functions are again continuous functions. The remaining eight properties of Definition 1 are easily seen to hold in $C[a, b]$; the verification proceeds exactly as in $\mathcal{P}_n$. ∎

Note that any polynomial can be regarded as a continuous function on any interval $[a, b]$. Thus for any given positive integer $n$, $\mathcal{P}_n$ is not only a subset of $C[a, b]$ but also a vector space contained in the vector space $C[a, b]$. This concept of a vector space that contains a smaller vector space (or a vector subspace) is quite important and is one topic of the next section.

FUNCTION SPACES    The giant step of expanding vector spaces from $R^n$ to spaces of functions was a combined effort of many mathematicians. Probably foremost among them, however, was David Hilbert (1862–1943), for whom Hilbert spaces are named. Hilbert had great success in solving several important contemporary problems by emphasizing abstraction and an axiomatic approach. His ideas on abstract spaces came largely from his work on important integral equations in physics. Hilbert related integral equations to problems of infinitely-many equations in infinitely-many unknowns, a natural extension of a fundamental problem in the setting of $R^n$. Great credit for expansion of vector-space ideas is also given to the work of Riesz, Fischer, Fréchet, and Weyl. In particular, Hermann Weyl (1885–1955) was known for his stress on the rigorous application of axiomatic logic rather than visual plausibility, which was all too often accepted as proof.

## Further Vector-Space Properties

The algebraic operations in a vector space have additional properties that can be derived from the 10 fundamental properties listed in Definition 1. The first of these, the cancellation laws for vector addition, are straightforward to prove and will be left as exercises.

---

**Cancellation Laws for Vector Addition**

Let $V$ be a vector space, and let $\mathbf{u}$, $\mathbf{v}$, and $\mathbf{w}$ be vectors in $V$.

1. If $\mathbf{u} + \mathbf{v} = \mathbf{u} + \mathbf{w}$, then $\mathbf{v} = \mathbf{w}$.
2. If $\mathbf{v} + \mathbf{u} = \mathbf{w} + \mathbf{u}$, then $\mathbf{v} = \mathbf{w}$.

---

Some additional properties of vector spaces are summarized in Theorem 1.

**THEOREM 1**     If $V$ is a vector space, then:

1. The zero vector, $\boldsymbol{\theta}$, is unique.
2. For each $\mathbf{v}$, the additive inverse $-\mathbf{v}$ is unique.
3. $0\mathbf{v} = \boldsymbol{\theta}$ for every $\mathbf{v}$ in $V$, where 0 is the zero scalar.
4. $a\boldsymbol{\theta} = \boldsymbol{\theta}$ for every scalar $a$.
5. If $a\mathbf{v} = \boldsymbol{\theta}$, then $a = 0$ or $\mathbf{v} = \boldsymbol{\theta}$.
6. $(-1)\mathbf{v} = -\mathbf{v}$.

**Proof**     [We prove properties 1, 4, and 6 and leave the remaining properties as exercises.] We first prove property 1. Suppose that $\zeta$ is a vector in $V$ such that $\mathbf{v} + \zeta = \mathbf{v}$ for all $\mathbf{v}$ in $V$. Then setting $\mathbf{v} = \boldsymbol{\theta}$, we have

$$\boldsymbol{\theta} + \zeta = \boldsymbol{\theta}. \tag{2}$$

By property (a3) of Definition 1, we know also that

$$\zeta + \boldsymbol{\theta} = \zeta. \tag{3}$$

But from property (a1) of Definition 1, we know that $\zeta + \boldsymbol{\theta} = \boldsymbol{\theta} + \zeta$; so using Eq. (2), property (a1), and Eq. (3), we conclude that

$$\boldsymbol{\theta} = \boldsymbol{\theta} + \zeta = \zeta + \boldsymbol{\theta} = \zeta,$$

or $\boldsymbol{\theta} = \zeta$.

We next prove property 4 of Theorem 1. We do so by observing that $\boldsymbol{\theta} + \boldsymbol{\theta} = \boldsymbol{\theta}$, from property (a3) of Definition 1. Therefore if $a$ is any scalar, we see from property (m2) of Definition 1 that

$$a\boldsymbol{\theta} = a(\boldsymbol{\theta} + \boldsymbol{\theta}) = a\boldsymbol{\theta} + a\boldsymbol{\theta}. \tag{4}$$

Since $a\theta = a\theta + \theta$ by property (a3) of Definition 1, Eq. (4) becomes

$$a\theta + \theta = a\theta + a\theta.$$

The cancellation laws now yield $\theta = a\theta$.

Finally, we outline a proof for property 6 of Theorem 1 by displaying a sequence of equalities (the last equality is based on property 3, which is an exercise):

$$\mathbf{v} + (-1)\mathbf{v} = (1)\mathbf{v} + (-1)\mathbf{v} = [1 + (-1)]\mathbf{v} = 0\mathbf{v} = \boldsymbol{\theta}.$$

Thus $(-1)\mathbf{v}$ is a solution to the equation $\mathbf{v} + \mathbf{x} = \boldsymbol{\theta}$. But from property 2 of Theorem 1, the additive inverse $-\mathbf{v}$ is the only solution of $\mathbf{v} + \mathbf{x} = \boldsymbol{\theta}$; so we must have $(-1)\mathbf{v} = -\mathbf{v}$. Thus property 6 constitutes a formula for the additive inverse. This formula is not totally unexpected, but neither is it so obvious as it might seem, since a number of vector-space properties were required to prove it. ◼

EXAMPLE 6   We conclude this section by introducing the **zero vector space**. The zero vector space contains only one vector, $\boldsymbol{\theta}$; the arithmetic operations are defined by

$$\theta + \theta = \theta$$
$$k\theta = \theta.$$

It is easy to verify that the set $\{\theta\}$ with the operations just defined is a vector space. ◼

## 5.2   EXERCISES

For $\mathbf{u}$, $\mathbf{v}$, and $\mathbf{w}$ given in Exercises 1–3, calculate $\mathbf{u} - 2\mathbf{v}$, $\mathbf{u} - (2\mathbf{v} - 3\mathbf{w})$, and $-2\mathbf{u} - \mathbf{v} + 3\mathbf{w}$.

**1.** In the vector space of $(2 \times 3)$ matrices

$$\mathbf{u} = \begin{bmatrix} 2 & 1 & 3 \\ -1 & 1 & 2 \end{bmatrix}, \qquad \mathbf{v} = \begin{bmatrix} 1 & 4 & -1 \\ 5 & 2 & 7 \end{bmatrix},$$

$$\mathbf{w} = \begin{bmatrix} 4 & -5 & 11 \\ -13 & -1 & -1 \end{bmatrix}.$$

**2.** In the vector space $\mathcal{P}_2$

$$\mathbf{u} = x^2 - 2, \quad \mathbf{v} = x^2 + 2x - 1, \quad \mathbf{w} = 2x + 1.$$

**3.** In the vector space $C[0, 1]$

$$\mathbf{u} = e^x, \quad \mathbf{v} = \sin x, \quad \mathbf{w} = \sqrt{x^2 + 1}.$$

**4.** For $\mathbf{u}$, $\mathbf{v}$, and $\mathbf{w}$ in Exercise 2, find nonzero scalars $c_1, c_2, c_3$ such that $c_1\mathbf{u} + c_2\mathbf{v} + c_3\mathbf{w} = \boldsymbol{\theta}$. Are there nonzero scalars $c_1, c_2, c_3$ such that $c_1\mathbf{u} + c_2\mathbf{v} + c_3\mathbf{w} = \boldsymbol{\theta}$ for $\mathbf{u}$, $\mathbf{v}$, and $\mathbf{w}$ in Exercise 1?

**5.** For $\mathbf{u}$, $\mathbf{v}$, and $\mathbf{w}$ in Exercise 2, find scalars $c_1, c_2, c_3$ such that $c_1\mathbf{u} + c_2\mathbf{v} + c_3\mathbf{w} = x^2 + 6x + 1$. Show that there are no scalars $c_1, c_2, c_3$ such that $c_1\mathbf{u} + c_2\mathbf{v} + c_3\mathbf{w} = x^2$.

In Exercises 6–11, the given set is a subset of a vector space. Which of these subsets are also vector spaces in their own right? To answer this question, determine whether the subset satisfies the 10 properties of Definition 1. (*Note:* Because these sets are subsets of a vector space, properties (a1), (a2), (m1), (m2), (m3), and (m4) are automatically satisfied.)

**6.** $S = \{\mathbf{v} \text{ in } R^4: v_1 + v_4 = 0\}$

**7.** $S = \{\mathbf{v} \text{ in } R^4: v_1 + v_4 = 1\}$

**8.** $P = \{p(x) \text{ in } \mathcal{P}_2: p(0) = 0\}$

**9.** $P = \{p(x) \text{ in } \mathcal{P}_2: p''(0) \neq 0\}$

**10.** $P = \{p(x) \text{ in } \mathcal{P}_2: p(x) = p(-x) \text{ for all } x\}$

**11.** $P = \{p(x) \text{ in } \mathcal{P}_2: p(x) \text{ has degree } 2\}$

In Exercises 12–16, $V$ is the vector space of all real $(3 \times 4)$ matrices. Which of the given subsets of $V$ are also vector spaces?

**12.** $S = \{A \text{ in } V: a_{11} = 0\}$

**13.** $S = \{A \text{ in } V: a_{11} + a_{23} = 0\}$

**14.** $S = \{A \text{ in } V: |a_{11}| + |a_{21}| = 1\}$

**15.** $S = \{A \text{ in } V: a_{32} \neq 0\}$

**16.** $S = \{A \text{ in } V: \text{ each } a_{ij} \text{ is an integer}\}$

**17.** Let $Q$ denote the set of all $(2 \times 2)$ nonsingular matrices with the usual matrix addition and scalar multiplication. Show that $Q$ is not a vector space by exhibiting specific matrices in $Q$ that violate property (c1) of Definition 1. Also show that properties (c2) and (a3) are not met.

**18.** Let $Q$ denote the set of all $(2 \times 2)$ singular matrices with the usual matrix addition and scalar multiplication. Determine whether $Q$ is a vector space.

**19.** Let $Q$ denote the set of all $(2 \times 2)$ symmetric matrices with the usual matrix addition and scalar multiplication. Verify that $Q$ is a vector space.

**20.** Prove the cancellation laws for vector addition.

**21.** Prove property 2 of Theorem 1. [*Hint:* See the proof of Theorem 15 in Section 1.9.]

**22.** Prove property 3 of Theorem 1. [*Hint:* Note that $0\mathbf{v} = (0 + 0)\mathbf{v}$. Now mimic the proof given for property 4.]

**23.** Prove property 5 of Theorem 1. (If $a \neq 0$ then multiply both sides of $a\mathbf{v} = \boldsymbol{\theta}$ by $a^{-1}$. Use properties (m1) and (m4) of Definition 1 and use property 4 of Theorem 1.)

**24.** Prove that the zero vector space, defined in Example 6, is indeed a vector space.

In Exercises 25–29, the given set is a subset of $C[-1, 1]$. Which of these are also vector spaces?

**25.** $F = \{f(x) \text{ in } C[-1, 1]: f(-1) = f(1)\}$

**26.** $F = \{f(x) \text{ in } C[-1, 1]: f(x) = 0 \text{ for } -1/2 \leq x \leq 1/2\}$

**27.** $F = \{f(x) \text{ in } C[-1, 1]: f(1) = 1\}$

**28.** $F = \{f(x) \text{ in } C[-1, 1]: f(1) = 0\}$

**29.** $F = \left\{ f(x) \text{ in } C[-1, 1]: \int_{-1}^{1} f(x)\, dx = 0 \right\}$

**30.** The set $C^2[a, b]$ is defined to be the set of all real-valued functions $f(x)$ defined on $[a, b]$, where $f(x)$, $f'(x)$, and $f''(x)$ are continuous on $[a, b]$. Verify that $C^2[a, b]$ is a vector space by citing the appropriate theorems on continuity and differentiability from calculus.

**31.** The following are subsets of the vector space $C^2[-1, 1]$. Which of these are vector spaces?

  a) $F = \{f(x) \text{ in } C^2[-1, 1]: f''(x) + f(x) = 0, -1 \leq x \leq 1\}$

  b) $F = \{f(x) \text{ in } C^2[-1, 1]: f''(x) + f(x) = x^2, -1 \leq x \leq 1\}$

**32.** Show that the set $P$ of all real polynomials is a vector space.

**33.** Let $\mathcal{F}(R)$ denote the set of all real-valued functions defined on the reals. Thus

$$\mathcal{F}(R) = \{f: f \text{ is a function}, f: R \to R\}.$$

With addition of functions and scalar multiplication defined as in Example 5, show that $\mathcal{F}(R)$ is a vector space.

**34.** Let

$$V = \left\{ \mathbf{x}: \mathbf{x} = \begin{bmatrix} x_1 \\ x_2 \end{bmatrix}, \text{ where } x_1 \text{ and } x_2 \text{ are in } R \right\}.$$

For $\mathbf{u}$ and $\mathbf{v}$ in $V$ and $c$ in $R$, define the operations of addition and scalar multiplication on $V$ by

$$\mathbf{u} + \mathbf{v} = \begin{bmatrix} u_1 \\ u_2 \end{bmatrix} + \begin{bmatrix} v_1 \\ v_2 \end{bmatrix} = \begin{bmatrix} u_1 + v_1 + 1 \\ u_2 + v_2 - 1 \end{bmatrix} \text{ and}$$

$$c\mathbf{u} = \begin{bmatrix} cu_1 \\ cu_2 \end{bmatrix}. \tag{5}$$

  a) Show that the operations defined in (5) satisfy properties (c1), (c2), (a1)–(a4), (m1), and (m4) of Definition 1.

  b) Give examples to illustrate that properties (m2) and (m3) are not satisfied by the operations defined in (5).

**35.** Let

$$V = \left\{ \mathbf{x}: \mathbf{x} = \begin{bmatrix} x_1 \\ x_2 \end{bmatrix}, \text{ where } x_1 \text{ and } x_2 \text{ are in } R \right\}.$$

For $\mathbf{u}$ and $\mathbf{v}$ in $V$ and $c$ in $R$, define the operations of addition and scalar multiplication on $V$ by

$$\mathbf{u} + \mathbf{v} = \begin{bmatrix} u_1 \\ u_2 \end{bmatrix} + \begin{bmatrix} v_1 \\ v_2 \end{bmatrix} = \begin{bmatrix} u_1 + v_1 \\ u_2 + v_2 \end{bmatrix} \quad \text{and}$$

$$c\mathbf{u} = \begin{bmatrix} 0 \\ 0 \end{bmatrix}. \tag{6}$$

Show that the operations defined in (6) satisfy all the properties of Definition 1 except (m4). (Note that the addition given in (6) is the usual addition of $R^2$. Since $R^2$ is a vector space, all the additive properties of Definition 1 are satisfied.)

**36.** Let

$$V = \{\mathbf{x} \colon \mathbf{x} = \begin{bmatrix} x_1 \\ x_2 \end{bmatrix}, \quad \text{where } x_2 > 0\}.$$

For $\mathbf{u}$ and $\mathbf{v}$ in $V$ and $c$ in $R$, define addition and scalar multiplication by

$$\mathbf{u} + \mathbf{v} = \begin{bmatrix} u_1 \\ u_2 \end{bmatrix} + \begin{bmatrix} v_1 \\ v_2 \end{bmatrix} = \begin{bmatrix} u_1 + v_1 \\ u_2 v_2 \end{bmatrix} \quad \text{and}$$

$$c\mathbf{u} = \begin{bmatrix} cu_1 \\ u_2^c \end{bmatrix}. \tag{7}$$

With the operations defined in (7), show that $V$ is a vector space.

## SUBSPACES

Chapter 3 demonstrated that whenever $W$ is a $p$-dimensional subspace of $R^n$, then $W$ behaves essentially like $R^p$ (for instance, any set of $p + 1$ vectors in $W$ is linearly dependent). The situation is much the same in a general vector space $V$. In this setting, certain subsets of $V$ inherit the vector-space structure of $V$ and are vector spaces in their own right.

| DEFINITION 2 | If $V$ and $W$ are real vector spaces, and if $W$ is a nonempty subset of $V$, then $W$ is called a *subspace* of $V$. |
|---|---|

Subspaces have considerable practical importance and are useful in problems involving approximation, optimization, differential equations, and so on. The vector-space/subspace framework allows us to pose and rigorously answer questions such as, *How can we find good polynomial approximations to complicated functions?* and *How can we generate good approximate solutions to differential equations?* Questions such as these are at the heart of many technical problems; and vector-space techniques, together with the computational power of the computer, are useful in helping to answer them.

As was the case in $R^n$, it is fairly easy to recognize when a subset of a vector space $V$ is actually a subspace. Specifically, the following restatement of Theorem 2 of Section 3.2 holds in any vector space.

| THEOREM 2 | Let $W$ be a subset of a vector space $V$. Then $W$ is a subspace of $V$ if and only if the following conditions are met: |
|---|---|

(s1)   The zero vector, $\theta$, of $V$ is in $W$.

(s2)   $\mathbf{u} + \mathbf{v}$ is in $W$ whenever $\mathbf{u}$ and $\mathbf{v}$ are in $W$.

(s3)   $a\mathbf{u}$ is in $W$ whenever $\mathbf{u}$ is in $W$ and $a$ is any scalar.  ◼

The proof of Theorem 2 coincides with the proof given in Section 3.2 with one minor exception. In $R^n$ it is easily seen that $-\mathbf{v} = (-1)\mathbf{v}$ for any vector $\mathbf{v}$. In a general vector space $V$, this is a consequence of Theorem 1 of Section 5.2.

## Examples of Subspaces

If we are given that $W$ is a subset of a known vector space $V$, Theorem 2 simplifies the task of determining whether or not $W$ is itself a vector space. Instead of testing all 10 properties of Definition 1, Theorem 2 states that we need only verify that properties (s1)–(s3) hold. Furthermore, just as in Chapter 3, a subset $W$ of $V$ will be specified by certain defining relationships that tell whether a vector $\mathbf{u}$ is in $W$. Thus to verify that (s1) holds, it must be shown that the zero vector, $\theta$, of $V$ satisfies the specification given for $W$. To check (s2) and (s3), we select two arbitrary vectors, say $\mathbf{u}$ and $\mathbf{v}$, that satisfy the defining relationships of $W$ (that is, $\mathbf{u}$ and $\mathbf{v}$ are in $W$). We then test $\mathbf{u} + \mathbf{v}$ and $a\mathbf{u}$ to see whether they also satisfy the defining relationships of $W$. (That is, do $\mathbf{u} + \mathbf{v}$ and $a\mathbf{u}$ belong to $W$?) The next three examples illustrate the use of Theorem 2.

EXAMPLE 1     Let $V$ be the vector space of all real $(2 \times 2)$ matrices, and let $W$ be the subset of $V$ specified by

$$W = \{A: A = \begin{bmatrix} 0 & a_{12} \\ a_{21} & 0 \end{bmatrix}, \quad a_{12} \text{ and } a_{21} \text{ any real scalars}\}.$$

Verify that $W$ is a subspace of $V$.

Solution     The zero vector for $V$ is the $(2 \times 2)$ zero matrix $\mathcal{O}$, and $\mathcal{O}$ is in $W$ since it satisfies the defining relationships of $W$. If $A$ and $B$ are any two vectors in $W$, then $A$ and $B$ have the form

$$A = \begin{bmatrix} 0 & a_{12} \\ a_{21} & 0 \end{bmatrix}, \quad B = \begin{bmatrix} 0 & b_{12} \\ b_{21} & 0 \end{bmatrix}.$$

Thus $A + B$ and $aA$ have the form

$$A + B = \begin{bmatrix} 0 & a_{12} + b_{12} \\ a_{21} + b_{21} & 0 \end{bmatrix}, \quad aA = \begin{bmatrix} 0 & aa_{12} \\ aa_{21} & 0 \end{bmatrix}.$$

Therefore, $A + B$ and $aA$ are in $W$, and we conclude that $W$ is a subspace of the set of all real $(2 \times 2)$ matrices.  ◼

EXAMPLE 2     Let $W$ be the subset of $C[a, b]$ (see Example 5 of Section 5.2) defined by

$$W = \{f(x) \text{ in } C[a, b]: f(a) = f(b)\}.$$

Verify that $W$ is a subspace of $C[a, b]$.

*Solution*    The zero vector in $C[a, b]$ is the zero function, $\theta(x)$, defined by $\theta(x) = 0$ for all $x$ in the interval $[a, b]$. In particular, $\theta(a) = \theta(b)$ since $\theta(a) = 0$ and $\theta(b) = 0$. Therefore, $\theta(x)$ is in $W$. Now let $g(x)$ and $h(x)$ be any two functions that are in $W$, that is,

$$g(a) = g(b) \text{ and } h(a) = h(b). \tag{1}$$

The sum of $g(x)$ and $h(x)$ is the function $s(x)$ defined by $s(x) = g(x) + h(x)$. To see that $s(x)$ is in $W$, note that property (1) gives

$$s(a) = g(a) + h(a) = g(b) + h(b) = s(b).$$

Similarly, if $c$ is a scalar, then it is immediate from property (1) that $cg(a) = cg(b)$. It follows that $cg(x)$ is in $W$. Theorem 2 now implies that $W$ is a subspace of $C[a, b]$. ■

The next example illustrates how to use Theorem 2 to show that a subset of a vector space is not a vector space. Recall from Chapter 3 that if a subset fails to satisfy any one of the properties (s1), (s2), or (s3), then it is not a subspace.

EXAMPLE 3    Let $V$ be the vector space of all $(2 \times 2)$ matrices, and let $W$ be the subspace of $V$ specified by

$$W = \left\{A: A = \begin{bmatrix} a & b \\ c & d \end{bmatrix}, \quad ad = 0 \text{ and } bc = 0\right\}.$$

Show that $W$ is not a subspace of $V$.

*Solution*    It is straightforward to show that $W$ satisfies properties (s1) and (s3) of Theorem 2. Thus to demonstrate that $W$ is not a subspace of $V$, we must show that (s2) fails. It suffices to give a specific example that illustrates the failure of (s2). For example, define $A$ and $B$ by

$$A = \begin{bmatrix} 1 & 0 \\ 0 & 0 \end{bmatrix} \text{ and } B = \begin{bmatrix} 0 & 0 \\ 0 & 1 \end{bmatrix}.$$

Then $A$ and $B$ are in $W$, but $A + B$ is not, since

$$A + B = \begin{bmatrix} 1 & 0 \\ 0 & 1 \end{bmatrix}.$$

In particular, $ad = (1)(1) = 1$, so $ad \neq 0$. ■

If $n \leq m$, then $\mathcal{P}_n$ is a subspace of $\mathcal{P}_m$. We can verify this assertion directly from Definition 2 since we have already shown that $\mathcal{P}_n$ and $\mathcal{P}_m$ are each real vector spaces, and $\mathcal{P}_n$ is a subset of $\mathcal{P}_m$. Similarly, for any $n$, $\mathcal{P}_n$ is a subspace of $C[a, b]$. Again this assertion follows directly from Definition 2 since any polynomial is continuous on any interval $[a, b]$. Therefore, $\mathcal{P}_n$ can be considered a subspace of $C[a, b]$, as well as a vector space in its own right.

## Spanning Sets

The vector-space structure as given in Definition 1 guarantees that the notion of a linear combination makes sense in a general vector space. Specifically, the vector **v** is a *linear* *combination* of the vectors $\mathbf{v}_1$, $\mathbf{v}_2$, ..., $\mathbf{v}_m$ provided that there exist scalars $a_1, a_2, \ldots, a_m$ such that

$$\mathbf{v} = a_1\mathbf{v}_1 + a_2\mathbf{v}_2 + \cdots + a_m\mathbf{v}_m.$$

The next example illustrates this concept in the vector space $\mathcal{P}_2$.

**EXAMPLE 4**  In $\mathcal{P}_2$ let $p(x)$, $p_1(x)$, $p_2(x)$, and $p_3(x)$ be defined by $p(x) = -1 + 2x^2$, $p_1(x) = 1 + 2x - 2x^2$, $p_2(x) = -1 - x$, and $p_3(x) = -3 - 4x + 4x^2$. Express $p(x)$ as a linear combination of $p_1(x)$, $p_2(x)$, and $p_3(x)$.

**Solution**  Setting $p(x) = a_1 p_1(x) + a_2 p_2(x) + a_3 p_3(x)$ yields

$$-1 + 2x^2 = a_1(1 + 2x - 2x^2) + a_2(-1 - x) + a_3(-3 - 4x + 4x^2).$$

Equating coefficients yields the system of equations

$$
\begin{aligned}
a_1 - a_2 - 3a_3 &= -1 \\
2a_1 - a_2 - 4a_3 &= 0 \\
-2a_1 \quad\quad + 4a_3 &= 2.
\end{aligned}
$$

This system has the unique solution $a_1 = 3$, $a_2 = -2$, and $a_3 = 2$. We can easily check that

$$p(x) = 3p_1(x) - 2p_2(x) + 2p_3(x).$$ ◼

The very useful concept of a spanning set is suggested by the preceding discussion.

**DEFINITION 3**

Let $V$ be a vector space, and let $Q = \{\mathbf{v}_1, \mathbf{v}_2, \ldots, \mathbf{v}_m\}$ be a set of vectors in $V$. If every vector $\mathbf{v}$ in $V$ is a linear combination of vectors in $Q$,

$$\mathbf{v} = a_1\mathbf{v}_1 + a_2\mathbf{v}_2 + \cdots + a_m\mathbf{v}_m,$$

then we say that $Q$ is a *spanning set* for $V$.

For many vector spaces $V$, it is relatively easy to find a natural spanning set. For example, it is easily seen that $\{1, x, x^2\}$ is a spanning set for $\mathcal{P}_2$ and, in general, $\{1, x, \ldots, x^n\}$ is a spanning set for $\mathcal{P}_n$. The vector space of all $(2 \times 2)$ matrices is spanned by the set $\{E_{11}, E_{12}, E_{21}, E_{22}\}$, where

$$E_{11} = \begin{bmatrix} 1 & 0 \\ 0 & 0 \end{bmatrix}, \quad E_{12} = \begin{bmatrix} 0 & 1 \\ 0 & 0 \end{bmatrix}, \quad E_{21} = \begin{bmatrix} 0 & 0 \\ 1 & 0 \end{bmatrix}, \quad \text{and} \quad E_{22} = \begin{bmatrix} 0 & 0 \\ 0 & 1 \end{bmatrix}.$$

More generally, if the $(m \times n)$ matrix $E_{ij}$ is the matrix with 1 as the $ij$th entry and zeros elsewhere, then $\{E_{ij}: 1 \le i \le m, 1 \le j \le n\}$ is a spanning set for the vector space of $(m \times n)$ real matrices.

If $Q = \{\mathbf{v}_1, \mathbf{v}_2, \ldots, \mathbf{v}_k\}$ is a set of vectors in a vector space $V$, then, as in Section 3.3, the *span* of $Q$, denoted $\mathrm{Sp}(Q)$, is the set of all linear combinations of $\mathbf{v}_1, \mathbf{v}_2, \ldots, \mathbf{v}_k$:

$$\mathrm{Sp}(Q) = \{\mathbf{v}: \mathbf{v} = a_1\mathbf{v}_1 + a_2\mathbf{v}_2 + \cdots + a_k\mathbf{v}_k\}.$$

From closure properties (c1) and (c2) of Definition 1, it is obvious that $\text{Sp}(Q)$ is a subset of $V$. In fact, the proof of Theorem 3 in Section 3.3 is valid in a general vector space, so we have the following theorem.

**THEOREM 3** If $V$ is a vector space and $Q = \{v_1, v_2, \ldots, v_k\}$ is a set of vectors in $V$, then $\text{Sp}(Q)$ is a subspace of $V$. ∎

The connection between spanning sets and the span of a set is fairly obvious. If $W$ is a subspace of $V$ and $Q \subseteq W$, then $Q$ is a spanning set for $W$ if and only if $W = \text{Sp}(Q)$. As the next three examples illustrate, it is often easy to obtain a spanning set for a subspace $W$ when an algebraic specification for $W$ is given.

**EXAMPLE 5** Let $V$ be the vector space of all real ($2 \times 2$) matrices, and let $W$ be the subspace given in Example 1:

$$W = \left\{ A \colon A = \begin{bmatrix} 0 & a_{12} \\ a_{21} & 0 \end{bmatrix}, \quad a_{12} \text{ and } a_{21} \text{ any real scalars} \right\}.$$

Find a spanning set for $W$.

*Solution* One obvious spanning set for $W$ is seen to be the set of vectors $Q = \{A_1, A_2\}$, where

$$A_1 = \begin{bmatrix} 0 & 1 \\ 0 & 0 \end{bmatrix} \quad \text{and} \quad A_2 = \begin{bmatrix} 0 & 0 \\ 1 & 0 \end{bmatrix}.$$

To verify this assertion, suppose $A$ is in $W$, where

$$A = \begin{bmatrix} 0 & a_{12} \\ a_{21} & 0 \end{bmatrix}.$$

Then clearly $A = a_{12}A_1 + a_{21}A_2$, and therefore $Q$ is a spanning set for $W$. ∎

**EXAMPLE 6** Let $W$ be the subspace of $\mathcal{P}_2$ defined by

$$W = \{p(x) \colon p(x) = a_0 + a_1x + a_2x^2, \quad \text{where } a_2 = -a_1 + 2a_0\}.$$

Exhibit a spanning set for $W$.

*Solution* Let $p(x) = a_0 + a_1x + a_2x^2$ be a vector in $W$. From the specifications of $W$, we know that $a_2 = -a_1 + 2a_0$. That is,

$$\begin{aligned} p(x) &= a_0 + a_1x + a_2x^2 \\ &= a_0 + a_1x + (-a_1 + 2a_0)x^2 \\ &= a_0(1 + 2x^2) + a_1(x - x^2). \end{aligned}$$

Since every vector $p$ in $W$ is a linear combination of $p_1(x) = 1 + 2x^2$ and $p_2(x) = x - x^2$, we see that $\{p_1(x), p_2(x)\}$ is a spanning set for $W$. ∎

A square matrix, $A = (a_{ij})$, is called **skew symmetric** if $A^T = -A$. Recall that the $ij$th entry of $A^T$ is $a_{ji}$, the $ji$th entry of $A$. Thus the entries of $A$ must satisfy $a_{ji} = -a_{ij}$ in order for $A$ to be skew symmetric. In particular, each entry, $a_{ii}$, on the main diagonal must be zero since $a_{ii} = -a_{ii}$.

EXAMPLE 7    Let $W$ be the set of all $(3 \times 3)$ skew-symmetric matrices. Show that $W$ is a subspace of the vector space $V$ of all $(3 \times 3)$ matrices, and exhibit a spanning set for $W$.

*Solution*    Let $\mathcal{O}$ denote the $(3 \times 3)$ zero matrix. Clearly $\mathcal{O}^T = \mathcal{O} = -\mathcal{O}$, so $\mathcal{O}$ is in $W$. If $A$ and $B$ are in $W$, then $A^T = -A$ and $B^T = -B$. Therefore,

$$(A + B)^T = A^T + B^T = -A - B = -(A + B).$$

It follows that $A + B$ is skew symmetric; that is, $A + B$ is in $W$. Likewise, if $c$ is a scalar, then

$$(cA)^T = cA^T = c(-A) = -(cA),$$

so $cA$ is in $W$. By Theorem 2, $W$ is a subspace of $V$. Moreover, the remarks preceding the example imply that $W$ can be described by

$$W = \{A: A = \begin{bmatrix} 0 & a & b \\ -a & 0 & c \\ -b & -c & 0 \end{bmatrix}, \quad a, b, c \text{ any real numbers}\}.$$

From this description it is easily seen that a natural spanning set for $W$ is the set $Q = \{A_1, A_2, A_3\}$, where

$$A_1 = \begin{bmatrix} 0 & 1 & 0 \\ -1 & 0 & 0 \\ 0 & 0 & 0 \end{bmatrix}, \quad A_2 = \begin{bmatrix} 0 & 0 & 1 \\ 0 & 0 & 0 \\ -1 & 0 & 0 \end{bmatrix}, \quad \text{and} \quad A_3 = \begin{bmatrix} 0 & 0 & 0 \\ 0 & 0 & 1 \\ 0 & -1 & 0 \end{bmatrix}.$$

Finally, note that in Definition 3 we have implicitly assumed that spanning sets are finite. This is not a required assumption, and frequently $\mathrm{Sp}(Q)$ is defined as the set of all finite linear combinations of vectors from $Q$, where $Q$ may be either an infinite set or a finite set. We do not need this full generality, and we will explore this idea no further other than to note later that one contrast between the vector space $R^n$ and a general vector space $V$ is that $V$ might not possess a finite spanning set. An example of a vector space where the most natural spanning set is infinite is the vector space $\mathcal{P}$, consisting of all polynomials (we place no upper limit on the degree). Then, for instance, $\mathcal{P}_n$ is a subspace of $\mathcal{P}$ for each $n$, $n = 1, 2, 3, \ldots$. A natural spanning set for $\mathcal{P}$ (in the generalized sense described earlier) is the infinite set

$$Q = \{1, x, x^2, \ldots, x^k, \ldots\}.$$

---

## 5.3    EXERCISES

Let $V$ be the vector space of all $(2 \times 3)$ matrices. Which of the subsets in Exercises 1–4 are subspaces of $V$?

**1.** $W = \{A \text{ in } V: a_{11} + a_{13} = 1\}$

**2.** $W = \{A \text{ in } V: a_{11} - a_{12} + 2a_{13} = 0\}$

**3.** $W = \{A \text{ in } V: a_{11} - a_{12} = 0, a_{12} + a_{13} = 0,$ and $a_{23} = 0\}$

**4.** $W = \{A \text{ in } V: a_{11}a_{12}a_{13} = 0\}$

In Exercises 5–8, which of the given subsets of $\mathcal{P}_2$ are subspaces of $\mathcal{P}_2$?

**5.** $W = \{p(x) \text{ in } \mathcal{P}_2: p(0) + p(2) = 0\}$

**6.** $W = \{p(x) \text{ in } \mathcal{P}_2: p(1) = p(3)\}$

**7.** $W = \{p(x) \text{ in } \mathcal{P}_2: p(1)p(3) = 0\}$

**8.** $W = \{p(x) \text{ in } \mathcal{P}_2: p(1) = -p(-1)\}$

In Exercises 9–12, which of the given subsets of $C[1, -1]$ are subspaces of $C[-1, 1]$?

**9.** $F = \{f(x) \text{ in } C[-1, 1]: f(-1) = -f(1)\}$

**10.** $F = \{f(x) \text{ in } C[-1, 1]: f(x) \geq 0 \text{ for all } x \text{ in } [-1, 1]\}$

**11.** $F = \{f(x) \text{ in } C[-1, 1]: f(-1) = -2 \text{ and } f(1) = 2\}$

**12.** $F = \{f(x) \text{ in } C[-1, 1]: f(1/2) = 0\}$

In Exercises 13–16, which of the given subsets of $C^2[-1, 1]$ (see Exercise 30 of Section 5.2) are subspaces of $C^2[-1, 1]$?

**13.** $F = \{f(x) \text{ in } C^2[-1, 1]: f''(0) = 0\}$

**14.** $F = \{f(x) \text{ in } C^2[-1, 1]: f''(x) - e^x f'(x) + xf(x) = 0, -1 \leq x \leq 1\}$

**15.** $F = \{f(x) \text{ in } C^2[-1, 1]: f''(x) + f(x) = \sin x, -1 \leq x \leq 1\}$

**16.** $F = \{f(x) \text{ in } C^2[-1, 1]: f''(x) = 0, -1 \leq x \leq 1\}$

In Exercises 17–21, express the given vector as a linear combination of the vectors in the given set $Q$.

**17.** $p(x) = -1 - 3x + 3x^2$ and $Q = \{p_1(x), p_2(x), p_3(x)\}$, where $p_1(x) = 1 + 2x + x^2, p_2(x) = 2 + 5x$, and $p_3(x) = 3 + 8x - 2x^2$

**18.** $p(x) = -2 - 4x + x^2$ and

$$Q = \{p_1(x), p_2(x), p_3(x), p_4(x)\},$$

and where $p_1(x) = 1 + 2x^2 + x^3, p_2(x) = 1 + x + 2x^3, p_3(x) = -1 - 3x + 4x^2 - 4x^3$, and $p_4(x) = 1 + 2x - x^2 + x^3$

**19.** $A = \begin{bmatrix} -2 & -4 \\ 1 & 0 \end{bmatrix}$ and $Q = \{B_1, B_2, B_3, B_4\}$,

where $B_1 = \begin{bmatrix} 1 & 0 \\ 2 & 1 \end{bmatrix}$, $B_2 = \begin{bmatrix} 1 & 1 \\ 0 & 2 \end{bmatrix}$,

$B_3 = \begin{bmatrix} -1 & -3 \\ 4 & -4 \end{bmatrix}$, and $B_4 = \begin{bmatrix} 1 & 2 \\ -1 & 1 \end{bmatrix}$.

**20.** $f(x) = e^x$ and $Q = \{\sinh x, \cosh x\}$

**21.** $f(x) = \cos 2x$ and $Q = \{\sin^2 x, \cos^2 x\}$

**22.** Let $V$ be the vector space of all $(2 \times 2)$ matrices. The subset $W$ of $V$ defined by

$$W = \{A \text{ in } V: a_{11} - a_{12} = 0, \ a_{12} + a_{22} = 0\}$$

is a subspace of $V$. Find a spanning set for $W$. [*Hint:*

Observe that $A$ is in $W$ if and only if $A$ has the form

$$A = \begin{bmatrix} a_{11} & a_{11} \\ a_{21} & -a_{11} \end{bmatrix},$$

where $a_{11}$ and $a_{21}$ are arbitrary.]

**23.** Let $W$ be the subset of $P_3$ defined by

$$W = \{p(x) \text{ in } P_3: p(1) = p(-1) \text{ and } p(2) = p(-2)\}.$$

Show that $W$ is a subspace of $P_3$, and find a spanning set for $W$.

**24.** Let $W$ be the subset of $P_3$ defined by

$$W = \{p(x) \text{ in } P_3: p(1) = 0 \text{ and } p'(-1) = 0\}.$$

Show that $W$ is a subspace of $P_3$, and find a spanning set for $W$.

**25.** Find a spanning set for each of the subsets that is a subspace in Exercises 1–8.

**26.** Show that the set $W$ of all symmetric $(3 \times 3)$ matrices is a subspace of the vector space of all $(3 \times 3)$ matrices. Find a spanning set for $W$.

**27.** The trace of an $(n \times n)$ matrix $A = (a_{ij})$, denoted $\text{tr}(A)$, is defined to be the sum of the diagonal elements of $A$; that is, $\text{tr}(A) = a_{11} + a_{22} + \cdots + a_{nn}$. Let $V$ be the vector space of all $(3 \times 3)$ matrices, and let $W$ be defined by

$$W = \{A \text{ in } V: \text{tr}(A) = 0\}.$$

Show that $W$ is a subspace of $V$, and exhibit a spanning set for $W$.

**28.** Let $A$ be an $(n \times n)$ matrix. Show that $B = (A + A^T)/2$ is symmetric and that $C = (A - A^T)/2$ is skew symmetric.

**29.** Use Exercise 28 to show that every $(n \times n)$ matrix can be expressed as the sum of a symmetric matrix and a skew-symmetric matrix.

**30.** Use Exercises 26 and 29 and Example 7 to construct a spanning set for the vector space of all $(3 \times 3)$ matrices where the spanning set consists entirely of symmetric and skew-symmetric matrices. Specify how a $(3 \times 3)$ matrix $A = (a_{ij})$ can be expressed by using this spanning set.

**31.** Let $V$ be the set of all $(3 \times 3)$ upper-triangular matrices, and note that $V$ is a vector space. Each of the subsets $W$ is a subspace of $V$. Find a spanning set for $W$.

**a)** $W = \{A \text{ in } V: a_{11} = 0, a_{22} = 0, a_{33} = 0\}$

**b)** $W = \{A \text{ in } V: a_{11} + a_{22} + a_{33} = 0, a_{12} + a_{23} = 0\}$

**c)** $W = \{A \text{ in } V: a_{11} = a_{12}, a_{13} = a_{23}, a_{22} = a_{33}\}$

**d)** $W = \{A \text{ in } V: a_{11} = a_{22}, a_{22} - a_{33} = 0, a_{12} + a_{23} = 0\}$

**32.** Let $p(x) = a_0 + a_1 x + a_2 x^2$ be a vector in $\mathcal{P}_2$. Find $b_0, b_1$, and $b_2$ in terms of $a_0, a_1$, and $a_2$ so that $p(x) = b_0 + b_1(x + 1) + b_2(x + 1)^2$. [*Hint:* Equate the coefficients of like powers of $x$.] Represent $q(x) = 1 - x + 2x^2$ and $r(x) = 2 - 3x + x^2$ in terms of the spanning set $\{1, x + 1, (x + 1)^2\}$.

**33.** Let $A$ be an arbitrary matrix in the vector space of all $(2 \times 2)$ matrices:

$$A = \begin{bmatrix} a & b \\ c & d \end{bmatrix}.$$

Find scalars $x_1, x_2, x_3, x_4$ in terms of $a, b, c$, and $d$ such that $A = x_1 B_1 + x_2 B_2 + x_3 B_3 + x_4 B_4$, where

$$B_1 = \begin{bmatrix} 1 & 0 \\ 1 & -2 \end{bmatrix}, \quad B_2 = \begin{bmatrix} 2 & 1 \\ 1 & -2 \end{bmatrix},$$

$$B_3 = \begin{bmatrix} -1 & 3 \\ -3 & 6 \end{bmatrix}, \quad \text{and} \quad B_4 = \begin{bmatrix} 1 & 1 \\ -2 & 5 \end{bmatrix}.$$

Represent the matrices

$$C = \begin{bmatrix} 0 & 2 \\ -1 & 1 \end{bmatrix} \quad \text{and} \quad D = \begin{bmatrix} 2 & 1 \\ 0 & 1 \end{bmatrix}$$

in terms of the spanning set $\{B_1, B_2, B_3, B_4\}$.

## 5.4 LINEAR INDEPENDENCE, BASES, AND COORDINATES

One of the central ideas of Chapters 1 and 3 is linear independence. As we will see, this concept generalizes directly to vector spaces. With the concepts of linear independence and spanning sets, it is easy to extend the idea of a basis to our vector-space setting. The notion of a basis is one of the most fundamental concepts in the study of vector spaces. For example, in certain vector spaces a basis can be used to produce a coordinate system for the space. As a consequence, a real vector space with a basis of $n$ vectors behaves essentially like $R^n$. Moreover, this coordinate system sometimes permits a geometric perspective in an otherwise nongeometric setting.

### Linear Independence

We begin by restating Definition 11 of Section 1.7 in a general vector-space setting.

DEFINITION 4

Let $V$ be a vector space, and let $\{v_1, v_2, \ldots, v_p\}$ be a set of vectors in $V$. This set is *linearly dependent* if there are scalars $a_1, a_2, \ldots, a_p$, not all of which are zero, such that

$$a_1 v_1 + a_2 v_2 + \cdots + a_p v_p = \boldsymbol{\theta}. \tag{1}$$

The set $\{v_1, v_2, \ldots, v_p\}$ is *linearly independent* if it is not linearly dependent; that is, the only scalars for which Eq. (1) holds are the scalars $a_1 = a_2 = \cdots = a_p = 0$.

Note that as a consequence of property 3 of Theorem 1 in Section 5.2, the vector equation (1) in Definition 4 always has the trivial solution $a_1 = a_2 = \cdots = a_p = 0$. Thus the set $\{v_1, v_2, \ldots, v_p\}$ is linearly independent if the trivial solution is the only solution to Eq. (1). If another solution exists, then the set is linearly dependent.

As before, it is easy to prove that a set $\{v_1, v_2, \ldots, v_p\}$ is linearly dependent if and only if some $v_i$ is a linear combination of the other $p - 1$ vectors in the set. The only real distinction between linear independence/dependence in $R^n$ and in a general vector space is that we cannot always test for dependence by solving a homogeneous system of equations. That is, in a general vector space we may have to go directly to the defining equation

$$a_1 v_1 + a_2 v_2 + \cdots + a_p v_p = \theta$$

and attempt to determine whether there are nontrivial solutions. Examples 2 and 3 illustrate the point.

**EXAMPLE 1**     Let $V$ be the vector space of $(2 \times 2)$ matrices, and let $W$ be the subspace

$$W = \{A \colon A = \begin{bmatrix} 0 & a_{12} \\ a_{21} & 0 \end{bmatrix}, \quad a_{12} \text{ and } a_{21} \text{ any real scalars}\}.$$

Define matrices $B_1$, $B_2$, and $B_3$ in $W$ by

$$B_1 = \begin{bmatrix} 0 & 2 \\ 1 & 0 \end{bmatrix}, \quad B_2 = \begin{bmatrix} 0 & 1 \\ 0 & 0 \end{bmatrix}, \quad \text{and} \quad B_3 = \begin{bmatrix} 0 & 2 \\ 3 & 0 \end{bmatrix}.$$

Show that the set $\{B_1, B_2, B_3\}$ is linearly dependent, and express $B_3$ as a linear combination of $B_1$ and $B_2$. Show that $\{B_1, B_2\}$ is a linearly independent set.

**Solution**     According to Definition 4, the set $\{B_1, B_2, B_3\}$ is linearly dependent provided that there exist nontrivial solutions to the equation

$$a_1 B_1 + a_2 B_2 + a_3 B_3 = \mathcal{O}, \tag{2}$$

where $\mathcal{O}$ is the zero element in $V$ [that is, $\mathcal{O}$ is the $(2 \times 2)$ zero matrix]. Writing Eq. (2) in detail, we see that $a_1, a_2, a_3$ are solutions of Eq. (2) if

$$\begin{bmatrix} 0 & 2a_1 \\ a_1 & 0 \end{bmatrix} + \begin{bmatrix} 0 & a_2 \\ 0 & 0 \end{bmatrix} + \begin{bmatrix} 0 & 2a_3 \\ 3a_3 & 0 \end{bmatrix} = \begin{bmatrix} 0 & 0 \\ 0 & 0 \end{bmatrix}.$$

With corresponding entries equated, $a_1, a_2, a_3$ must satisfy

$$2a_1 + a_2 + 2a_3 = 0 \quad \text{and} \quad a_1 + 3a_3 = 0.$$

This $(2 \times 3)$ homogeneous system has nontrivial solutions by Theorem 4 of Section 1.3, and one such solution is $a_1 = -3$, $a_2 = 4$, $a_3 = 1$. In particular,

$$-3B_1 + 4B_2 + B_3 = \mathcal{O}; \tag{3}$$

so the set $\{B_1, B_2, B_3\}$ is a linearly dependent set of vectors in $W$. It is an immediate consequence of Eq. (3) that

$$B_3 = 3B_1 - 4B_2.$$

To see that the set $\{B_1, B_2\}$ is linearly independent, let $a_1$ and $a_2$ be scalars such that $a_1 B_1 + a_2 B_2 = \mathcal{O}$. Then we must have

$$2a_1 + a_2 = 0 \quad \text{and} \quad a_1 = 0.$$

Hence $a_1 = 0$ and $a_2 = 0$; so if $a_1 B_1 + a_2 B_2 = \mathcal{O}$, then $a_1 = a_2 = 0$. Thus $\{B_1, B_2\}$ is a linearly independent set of vectors in $W$. ◼

Establishing linear independence/dependence in a vector space of functions such as $\mathcal{P}_n$ or $C[a, b]$ may sometimes require techniques from calculus. We illustrate one such technique in the following example.

**EXAMPLE 2**   Show that $\{1, x, x^2\}$ is a linearly independent set in $\mathcal{P}_2$.

**Solution**   Suppose that $a_0, a_1, a_2$ are any scalars that satisfy the defining equation

$$a_0 + a_1 x + a_2 x^2 = \theta(x), \tag{4}$$

where $\theta(x)$ is the zero polynomial. If Eq. (4) is to be an identity holding for all values of $x$, then [since $\theta'(x) = \theta(x)$] we can differentiate both sides of Eq. (4) to obtain

$$a_1 + 2a_2 x = \theta(x). \tag{5}$$

Similarly, differentiating both sides of Eq. (5), we obtain

$$2a_2 = \theta(x). \tag{6}$$

From Eq. (6) we must have $a_2 = 0$. If $a_2 = 0$, then Eq. (5) requires $a_1 = 0$; hence in Eq. (4), $a_0 = 0$ as well. Therefore, the only scalars that satisfy Eq. (4) are $a_0 = a_1 = a_2 = 0$, and thus $\{1, x, x^2\}$ is linearly independent in $\mathcal{P}_2$. (Also see the material on Wronskians in Section 6.5.) ◼

The following example illustrates another procedure for showing that a set of functions is linearly independent.

**EXAMPLE 3**   Show that $\{\sqrt{x}, 1/x, x^2\}$ is a linearly independent subset of $C[1, 10]$.

**Solution**   If the equation

$$a_1 \sqrt{x} + a_2(1/x) + a_3 x^2 = 0 \tag{7}$$

holds for all $x$, $1 \leq x \leq 10$, then it must hold for any three values of $x$ in the interval. Successively letting $x = 1$, $x = 4$, and $x = 9$ in Eq. (7) yields the system of equations

$$\begin{aligned} a_1 + \quad a_2 + \quad a_3 &= 0 \\ 2a_1 + (1/4)a_2 + 16a_3 &= 0 \\ 3a_1 + (1/9)a_2 + 81a_3 &= 0. \end{aligned} \tag{8}$$

It is easily shown that the trivial solution $a_1 = a_2 = a_3 = 0$ is the unique solution for system (8). It follows that the set $\{\sqrt{x}, 1/x, x^2\}$ is linearly independent.

Note that a nontrivial solution for system (8) would have yielded no information regarding the linear independence/dependence of the given set of functions. We could have concluded only that Eq. (7) holds when $x = 1$, $x = 4$, or $x = 9$. ◼

## Vector-Space Bases

It is now straightforward to combine the concepts of linear independence and spanning sets to define a basis for a vector space.

| | |
|---|---|
| DEFINITION 5 | Let $V$ be a vector space, and let $B = \{v_1, v_2, \ldots, v_p\}$ be a spanning set for $V$. If $B$ is linearly independent, then $B$ is a **basis** for $V$. |

Thus as before, a basis for $V$ is a linearly independent spanning set for $V$. (Again we note the implicit assumption that a basis contains only a finite number of vectors.)

There is often a "natural" basis for a vector space. We have seen in Chapter 3 that the set of unit vectors $\{e_1, e_2, \ldots, e_n\}$ in $R^n$ is a basis for $R^n$. In the preceding section we noted that the set $\{1, x, x^2\}$ is a spanning set for $\mathcal{P}_2$. Example 2 showed further that $\{1, x, x^2\}$ is linearly independent and hence is a basis for $\mathcal{P}_2$. More generally, the set $\{1, x, \ldots, x^n\}$ is a natural basis for $\mathcal{P}_n$. Similarly, the matrices

$$E_{11} = \begin{bmatrix} 1 & 0 \\ 0 & 0 \end{bmatrix}, \quad E_{12} = \begin{bmatrix} 0 & 1 \\ 0 & 0 \end{bmatrix}, \quad E_{21} = \begin{bmatrix} 0 & 0 \\ 1 & 0 \end{bmatrix}, \quad \text{and} \quad E_{22} = \begin{bmatrix} 0 & 0 \\ 0 & 1 \end{bmatrix}$$

constitute a basis for the vector space of all $(2 \times 2)$ real matrices (see Exercise 11). In general, the set of $(m \times n)$ matrices $\{E_{ij} : 1 \le i \le m, 1 \le j \le n\}$ defined in Section 5.3 is a natural basis for the vector space of all $(m \times n)$ real matrices.

Examples 5, 6, and 7 in Section 5.3 demonstrated a procedure for obtaining a natural spanning set for a subspace $W$ when an algebraic specification for $W$ is given. The spanning set obtained in this manner is often a basis for $W$. The following example provides another illustration.

EXAMPLE 4    Let $V$ be the vector space of all $(2 \times 2)$ real matrices, and let $W$ be the subspace defined by

$$W = \{A : A = \begin{bmatrix} a & a+b \\ a-b & b \end{bmatrix}, \quad a \text{ and } b \text{ any real numbers}\}.$$

Exhibit a basis for $W$.

*Solution*    In the specification for $W$, $a$ and $b$ are unconstrained variables. Assigning values $a = 1, b = 0$ and then $a = 0, b = 1$ yields the matrices

$$B_1 = \begin{bmatrix} 1 & 1 \\ 1 & 0 \end{bmatrix} \quad \text{and} \quad B_2 = \begin{bmatrix} 0 & 1 \\ -1 & 1 \end{bmatrix}$$

in $W$. Since

$$\begin{bmatrix} a & a+b \\ a-b & b \end{bmatrix} = a \begin{bmatrix} 1 & 1 \\ 1 & 0 \end{bmatrix} + b \begin{bmatrix} 0 & 1 \\ -1 & 1 \end{bmatrix},$$

the set $\{B_1, B_2\}$ is clearly a spanning set for $W$. The equation

$$c_1 B_1 + c_2 B_2 = \mathcal{O}$$

(where $\mathcal{O}$ is the $(2 \times 2)$ zero matrix) is equivalent to

$$\begin{bmatrix} c_1 & c_1 + c_2 \\ c_1 - c_2 & c_2 \end{bmatrix} = \begin{bmatrix} 0 & 0 \\ 0 & 0 \end{bmatrix}.$$

Equating entries immediately yields $c_1 = c_2 = 0$; so the set $\{B_1, B_2\}$ is linearly independent and hence is a basis for $W$. ▰

## Coordinate Vectors

As we noted in Chapter 3 a basis is a minimal spanning set; as such, a basis contains no redundant information. This lack of redundance is an important feature of a basis in the general vector-space setting and allows every vector to be represented uniquely in terms of the basis (see Theorem 4). We cannot make such an assertion of unique representation about a spanning set that is linearly dependent; in fact, in this case, the representation is never unique.

 THEOREM 4     Let $V$ be a vector space, and let $B = \{\mathbf{v}_1, \mathbf{v}_2, \ldots, \mathbf{v}_p\}$ be a basis for $V$. For each vector $\mathbf{w}$ in $V$, there exists a unique set of scalars $w_1, w_2, \ldots, w_p$ such that

$$\mathbf{w} = w_1\mathbf{v}_1 + w_2\mathbf{v}_2 + \cdots + w_p\mathbf{v}_p.$$

*Proof*     Let $\mathbf{w}$ be a vector in $V$ and suppose that $\mathbf{w}$ is represented in two ways as

$$\mathbf{w} = w_1\mathbf{v}_1 + w_2\mathbf{v}_2 + \cdots + w_p\mathbf{v}_p$$
$$\mathbf{w} = u_1\mathbf{v}_1 + u_2\mathbf{v}_2 + \cdots + u_p\mathbf{v}_p.$$

Subtracting, we obtain

$$\boldsymbol{\theta} = (w_1 - u_1)\mathbf{v}_1 + (w_2 - u_2)\mathbf{v}_2 + \cdots + (w_p - u_p)\mathbf{v}_p.$$

Therefore, since $\{\mathbf{v}_1, \mathbf{v}_2, \ldots, \mathbf{v}_p\}$ is a linearly independent set, it follows that $w_1 - u_1 = 0$, $w_2 - u_2 = 0, \ldots, w_p - u_p = 0$. That is, a vector $\mathbf{w}$ cannot be represented in two different ways in terms of a basis $B$. ▰

Now, let $V$ be a vector space with a basis $B = \{\mathbf{v}_1, \mathbf{v}_2, \ldots, \mathbf{v}_p\}$. Given that each vector $\mathbf{w}$ in $V$ has a unique representation in terms of $B$ as

$$\mathbf{w} = w_1\mathbf{v}_1 + w_2\mathbf{v}_2 + \cdots + w_p\mathbf{v}_p, \tag{9}$$

it follows that the scalars $w_1, w_2, \ldots, w_p$ serve to characterize $\mathbf{w}$ completely in terms of the basis $B$. In particular, we can identify $\mathbf{w}$ unambiguously with the vector $[\mathbf{w}]_B$ in $R^p$, where

$$[\mathbf{w}]_B = \begin{bmatrix} w_1 \\ w_2 \\ \vdots \\ w_p \end{bmatrix}.$$

We will call the unique scalars $w_1, w_2, \ldots, w_p$ in Eq. (9) the ***coordinates of w*** with respect to the basis $B$, and we will call the vector $[\mathbf{w}]_B$ in $R_p$ the ***coordinate vector of w*** with respect to $B$. This idea is a useful one; for example, we will show that a set of vectors $\{\mathbf{u}_1, \mathbf{u}_2, \ldots, \mathbf{u}_r\}$ in $V$ is linearly independent if and only if the coordinate vectors $[\mathbf{u}_1]_B, [\mathbf{u}_2]_B, \ldots, [\mathbf{u}_r]_B$ are linearly independent in $R^n$. Since we know how to determine whether vectors in $R^p$ are linearly independent or not, we can use the idea of coordinates to reduce a problem of linear independence/dependence in a general vector space to an equivalent problem in $R^p$, which we can work. Finally, we note that the subscript $B$ is necessary when we write $[\mathbf{w}]_B$, since the coordinate vector for $\mathbf{w}$ changes when we change the basis.

EXAMPLE 5     Let $V$ be the vector space of all real $(2 \times 2)$ matrices. Let $B = \{E_{11}, E_{12}, E_{21}, E_{22}\}$ and $Q = \{E_{11}, E_{21}, E_{12}, E_{22}\}$, where

$$E_{11} = \begin{bmatrix} 1 & 0 \\ 0 & 0 \end{bmatrix}, \quad E_{12} = \begin{bmatrix} 0 & 1 \\ 0 & 0 \end{bmatrix}, \quad E_{21} = \begin{bmatrix} 0 & 0 \\ 1 & 0 \end{bmatrix}, \quad \text{and} \quad E_{22} = \begin{bmatrix} 0 & 0 \\ 0 & 1 \end{bmatrix}.$$

Let the matrix $A$ be defined by

$$A = \begin{bmatrix} 2 & -1 \\ -3 & 4 \end{bmatrix}.$$

Find $[A]_B$ and $[A]_Q$.

*Solution*     We have already noted that $B$ is the natural basis for $V$. Since $Q$ contains the same vectors as $B$, but in a different order, $Q$ is also a basis for $V$. It is easy to see that

$$A = 2E_{11} - E_{12} - 3E_{21} + 4E_{22},$$

so

$$[A]_B = \begin{bmatrix} 2 \\ -1 \\ -3 \\ 4 \end{bmatrix}.$$

Similarly,

$$A = 2E_{11} - 3E_{21} - E_{12} + 4E_{22},$$

so

$$[A]_Q = \begin{bmatrix} 2 \\ -3 \\ -1 \\ 4 \end{bmatrix}.$$

It is apparent in the preceding example that the ordering of the basis vectors determined the ordering of the components of the coordinate vectors. A basis with such an implicitly fixed ordering is usually called an ***ordered basis.*** Although we do not intend to dwell on this point, we do have to be careful to work with a fixed ordering in a basis.

If $V$ is a vector space with (ordered) basis $B = \{\mathbf{v}_1, \mathbf{v}_2, \ldots, \mathbf{v}_p\}$, then the correspondence

$$\mathbf{v} \rightarrow [\mathbf{v}]_B$$

provides an identification between vectors in $V$ and elements of $R^p$. For instance, the preceding example identified a $(2 \times 2)$ matrix with a vector in $R^4$. The following lemma lists some of the properties of this correspondence. (The lemma hints at the idea of an isomorphism that will be developed in detail later.)

LEMMA Let $V$ be a vector space that has a basis $B = \{\mathbf{v}_1, \mathbf{v}_2, \ldots, \mathbf{v}_p\}$. If $\mathbf{u}$ and $\mathbf{v}$ are vectors in $V$ and if $c$ is a scalar, then the following hold:

$$[\mathbf{u} + \mathbf{v}]_B = [\mathbf{u}]_B + [\mathbf{v}]_B$$

and

$$[c\mathbf{u}]_B = c[\mathbf{u}]_B.$$

**Proof** Suppose that $\mathbf{u}$ and $\mathbf{v}$ are expressed in terms of the basis vectors in $B$ as

$$\mathbf{u} = a_1\mathbf{v}_1 + a_2\mathbf{v}_2 + \cdots + a_p\mathbf{v}_p$$

and

$$\mathbf{v} = b_1\mathbf{v}_1 + b_2\mathbf{v}_2 + \cdots + b_p\mathbf{v}_p.$$

Then clearly

$$\mathbf{u} + \mathbf{v} = (a_1 + b_1)\mathbf{v}_1 + (a_2 + b_2)\mathbf{v}_2 + \cdots + (a_p + b_p)\mathbf{v}_p$$

and

$$c\mathbf{u} = (ca_1)\mathbf{v}_1 + (ca_2)\mathbf{v}_2 + \cdots + (ca_p)\mathbf{v}_p.$$

Therefore,

$$[\mathbf{u}]_B = \begin{bmatrix} a_1 \\ a_2 \\ \vdots \\ a_p \end{bmatrix}, \quad [\mathbf{v}]_B = \begin{bmatrix} b_1 \\ b_2 \\ \vdots \\ b_p \end{bmatrix},$$

$$[\mathbf{u} + \mathbf{v}]_B = \begin{bmatrix} a_1 + b_1 \\ a_2 + b_2 \\ \vdots \\ a_p + b_p \end{bmatrix}, \quad \text{and} \quad [c\mathbf{u}] = \begin{bmatrix} ca_1 \\ ca_2 \\ \vdots \\ ca_p \end{bmatrix}.$$

We can now easily see that $[\mathbf{u} + \mathbf{v}]_B = [\mathbf{u}]_B + [\mathbf{v}]_B$ and $[c\mathbf{u}]_B = c[\mathbf{u}]_B$. ◼

The following example illustrates the preceding lemma.

EXAMPLE 6 In $\mathcal{P}_2$, let $p(x) = 3 - 2x + x^2$ and $q(x) = -2 + 3x - 4x^2$. Show that

$$[p(x) + q(x)]_B = [p(x)]_B + [q(x)]_B \quad \text{and} \quad [2p(x)]_B = 2[p(x)]_B,$$

where $B$ is the natural basis for $\mathcal{P}_2$: $B = \{1, x, x^2\}$.

**Solution** The coordinate vectors for $p(x)$ and $q(x)$ are

$$[p(x)]_B = \begin{bmatrix} 3 \\ -2 \\ 1 \end{bmatrix} \quad \text{and} \quad [q(x)]_B = \begin{bmatrix} -2 \\ 3 \\ -4 \end{bmatrix}.$$

Furthermore, $p(x) + q(x) = 1 + x - 3x^2$ and $2p(x) = 6 - 4x + 2x^2$. Thus

$$[p(x) + q(x)]_B = \begin{bmatrix} 1 \\ 1 \\ -3 \end{bmatrix} \quad \text{and} \quad [2p(x)]_B = \begin{bmatrix} 6 \\ -4 \\ 2 \end{bmatrix}.$$

Therefore, $[p(x) + q(x)]_B = [p(x)]_B + [q(x)]_B$ and $[2p(x)]_B = 2[p(x)]_B$.  ■

Suppose that the vector space $V$ has basis $B = \{\mathbf{v}_1, \mathbf{v}_2, \ldots, \mathbf{v}_p\}$, and let $\{\mathbf{u}_1, \mathbf{u}_2, \ldots, \mathbf{u}_m\}$ be a subset of $V$. The two properties in the preceding lemma can easily be combined and extended to give

$$[c_1\mathbf{u}_1 + c_2\mathbf{u}_2 + \cdots + c_m\mathbf{u}_m]_B = c_1[\mathbf{u}_1]_B + c_2[\mathbf{u}_2]_B + \cdots + c_m[\mathbf{u}_m]_B. \quad (10)$$

This observation will be useful in proving the next theorem.

**THEOREM 5**    Suppose that $V$ is a vector space with a basis $B = \{\mathbf{v}_1, \mathbf{v}_2, \ldots, \mathbf{v}_p\}$. Let $S = \{\mathbf{u}_1, \mathbf{u}_2, \ldots, \mathbf{u}_m\}$ be a subset of $V$, let $T = \{[\mathbf{u}_1]_B, [\mathbf{u}_2]_B, \ldots, [\mathbf{u}_m]_B\}$.

1. A vector $\mathbf{u}$ in $V$ is in $\text{Sp}(S)$ if and only if $[\mathbf{u}]_B$ is in $\text{Sp}(T)$.
2. The set $S$ is linearly independent in $V$ if and only if the set $T$ is linearly independent in $R^p$.

*Proof*    The vector equation

$$\mathbf{u} = x_1\mathbf{u}_1 + x_2\mathbf{u}_2 + \cdots + x_m\mathbf{u}_m \quad (11)$$

in $V$ is equivalent to the equation

$$[\mathbf{u}]_B = [x_1\mathbf{u}_1 + x_2\mathbf{u}_2 + \cdots + x_m\mathbf{u}_m]_B \quad (12)$$

in $R^p$. It follows from Eq. (10) that Eq. (12) is equivalent to

$$[\mathbf{u}]_B = x_1[\mathbf{u}_1]_B + x_2[\mathbf{u}_2]_B + \cdots + x_m[\mathbf{u}_m]_B. \quad (13)$$

Therefore, the vector equation (11) in $V$ is equivalent to the vector equation (13) in $R^p$. In particular, Eq. (11) has a solution $x_1 = c_1, x_2 = c_2, \ldots, x_m = c_m$ if and only if Eq. (13) has the same solution. Thus $\mathbf{u}$ is in $\text{Sp}(S)$ if and only if $[\mathbf{u}]_B$ is in $\text{Sp}(T)$.

To avoid confusion in the proof of property 2, let $\theta_V$ denote the zero vector for $V$ and let $\theta_p$ denote the $p$-dimensional zero vector in $R^p$. Then $[\theta_V]_B = \theta_p$. Thus setting $\mathbf{u} = \theta_V$ in Eq. (11) and Eq. (13) implies that the vector equations

$$\theta_V = x_1\mathbf{u}_1 + x_2\mathbf{u}_2 + \cdots + x_m\mathbf{u}_m \quad (14)$$

and

$$\theta_p = x_1[\mathbf{u}_1]_B + x_2[\mathbf{u}_2]_B + \cdots + x_m[\mathbf{u}_m]_B \quad (15)$$

have the same solutions. In particular, Eq. (14) has *only* the trivial solution if and only if Eq. (15) has *only* the trivial solution; that is, $S$ is a linearly independent set in $V$ if and only if $T$ is linearly independent in $R^p$.  ◼

An immediate corollary to Theorem 5 is as follows.

| | | COROLLARY | Let $V$ be a vector space with a basis $B = \{\mathbf{v}_1, \mathbf{v}_2, \ldots, \mathbf{v}_p\}$. Let $S = \{\mathbf{u}_1, \mathbf{u}_2, \ldots, \mathbf{u}_m\}$ be a subset of $V$, and let $T = \{[\mathbf{u}_1]_B, [\mathbf{u}_2]_B, \ldots, [\mathbf{u}_m]_B\}$. Then $S$ is a basis for $V$ if and only if $T$ is a basis for $R^p$.

*Proof*   By Theorem 5, $S$ is both linearly independent and a spanning set for $V$ if and only if $T$ is both linearly independent and a spanning set for $R^p$.   ◼

Theorem 5 and its corollary allow us to use the techniques developed in Chapter 3 to solve analogous problems in vector spaces other than $R^p$. The next two examples provide illustrations.

| | | EXAMPLE 7   Use the corollary to Theorem 5 to show that the set $\{1, 1 + x, 1 + 2x + x^2\}$ is a basis for $\mathcal{P}_2$.

*Solution*   Let $B$ be the standard basis for $\mathcal{P}_2$: $B = \{1, x, x^2\}$. The coordinate vectors of $1$, $1 + x$, and $1 + 2x + x^2$ are

$$[1]_B = \begin{bmatrix} 1 \\ 0 \\ 0 \end{bmatrix}, \quad [1 + x]_B = \begin{bmatrix} 1 \\ 1 \\ 0 \end{bmatrix}, \quad \text{and} \quad [1 + 2x + x^2]_B = \begin{bmatrix} 1 \\ 2 \\ 1 \end{bmatrix}.$$

Clearly the coordinate vectors $[1]_B$, $[1+x]_B$, and $[1+2x+x^2]_B$ are linearly independent in $R^3$. Since $R^3$ has dimension 3, the coordinate vectors constitute a basis for $R^3$. It now follows that $\{1, 1 + x, 1 + 2x + x^2\}$ is a basis for $\mathcal{P}_2$.   ◼

| | | EXAMPLE 8   Let $V$ be the vector space of all $(2 \times 2)$ matrices, and let the subset $S$ of $V$ be defined by $S = \{A_1, A_2, A_3, A_4\}$, where

$$A_1 = \begin{bmatrix} 1 & 2 \\ -1 & 3 \end{bmatrix}, \quad A_2 = \begin{bmatrix} 0 & -1 \\ 1 & 4 \end{bmatrix},$$

$$A_3 = \begin{bmatrix} -1 & 0 \\ 1 & -10 \end{bmatrix}, \quad \text{and} \quad A_4 = \begin{bmatrix} 3 & 7 \\ -2 & 6 \end{bmatrix}.$$

Use the corollary to Theorem 5 and the techniques of Section 3.4 to obtain a basis for $\mathrm{Sp}(S)$.

*Solution*   If $B$ is the natural basis for $V$, $B = \{E_{11}, E_{12}, E_{21}, E_{22}\}$, then

$$[A_1]_B = \begin{bmatrix} 1 \\ 2 \\ -1 \\ 3 \end{bmatrix}, \quad [A_2]_B = \begin{bmatrix} 0 \\ -1 \\ 1 \\ 4 \end{bmatrix},$$

$$[A_3]_B = \begin{bmatrix} -1 \\ 0 \\ 1 \\ -10 \end{bmatrix}, \quad \text{and} \quad [A_4]_B = \begin{bmatrix} 3 \\ 7 \\ -2 \\ 6 \end{bmatrix}.$$

Let $T = \{[A_1]_B, [A_2]_B, [A_3]_B, [A_4]_B\}$. Several techniques for obtaining a basis for $\text{Sp}(T)$ were illustrated in Section 3.4. For example, using the method demonstrated in Example 7 of Section 3.4, we form the matrix

$$C = \begin{bmatrix} 1 & 0 & -1 & 3 \\ 2 & -1 & 0 & 7 \\ -1 & 1 & 1 & -2 \\ 3 & 4 & -10 & 6 \end{bmatrix}.$$

The matrix $C^T$ can be reduced to the matrix

$$D^T = \begin{bmatrix} 1 & 2 & -1 & 3 \\ 0 & -1 & 1 & 4 \\ 0 & 0 & 2 & 1 \\ 0 & 0 & 0 & 0 \end{bmatrix}.$$

Thus

$$D = \begin{bmatrix} 1 & 0 & 0 & 0 \\ 2 & -1 & 0 & 0 \\ -1 & 1 & 2 & 0 \\ 3 & 4 & 1 & 0 \end{bmatrix},$$

and the nonzero columns of $D$ constitute a basis for $\text{Sp}(T)$. Denote the nonzero columns of $D$ by $\mathbf{w}_1, \mathbf{w}_2,$ and $\mathbf{w}_3$, respectively. Thus

$$\mathbf{w}_1 = \begin{bmatrix} 1 \\ 2 \\ -1 \\ 3 \end{bmatrix}, \quad \mathbf{w}_2 = \begin{bmatrix} 0 \\ -1 \\ 1 \\ 4 \end{bmatrix}, \quad \text{and} \quad \mathbf{w}_3 = \begin{bmatrix} 0 \\ 0 \\ 2 \\ 1 \end{bmatrix},$$

and $\{\mathbf{w}_1, \mathbf{w}_2, \mathbf{w}_3\}$ is a basis for $\text{Sp}(T)$. If $B_1, B_2,$ and $B_3$ are $(2 \times 2)$ matrices such that $[B_1]_B = \mathbf{w}_1, [B_2]_B = \mathbf{w}_2,$ and $[B_3]_B = \mathbf{w}_3$, then it follows from Theorem 5 that $\{B_1, B_2, B_3\}$ is a basis for $\text{Sp}(S)$. If

$$B_1 = E_{11} + 2E_{12} - E_{21} + 3E_{22},$$

then clearly $[B_1]_B = \mathbf{w}_1$. $B_2$ and $B_3$ are obtained in the same fashion, and

$$B_1 = \begin{bmatrix} 1 & 2 \\ -1 & 3 \end{bmatrix}, \quad B_2 = \begin{bmatrix} 0 & -1 \\ 1 & 4 \end{bmatrix}, \quad \text{and} \quad B_3 = \begin{bmatrix} 0 & 0 \\ 2 & 1 \end{bmatrix}. \quad \blacksquare$$

Examples 7 and 8 illustrate an important point. Although Theorem 5 shows that questions regarding the span or the linear dependence/independence of a subset of $V$ can be translated to an equivalent problem in $R^p$, we do need one basis for $V$ as a point of reference. For example, in $\mathcal{P}_2$, once we know that $B = \{1, x, x^2\}$ is a basis, we can use Theorem 5 to pass from a problem in $\mathcal{P}_2$ to an analogous problem in $R^3$. In order to obtain the first basis $B$, however, we cannot use Theorem 5.

EXAMPLE 9   In $\mathcal{P}_4$, consider the set of vectors $S = \{p_1, p_2, p_3, p_4, p_5\}$, where $p_1(x) = x^4 + 3x^3 + 2x + 4$, $p_2(x) = x^3 - x^2 + 5x + 1$, $p_3(x) = x^4 + x + 3$, $p_4(x) = x^4 + x^3 - x + 2$, and $p_5(x) = x^4 + x^2$. Is $S$ a basis for $\mathcal{P}_4$?

*Solution*   Let $B$ denote the standard basis for $\mathcal{P}_4$, $B = \{1, x, x^2, x^3, x^4\}$. By the corollary to Theorem 5, $S$ is a basis for $\mathcal{P}_4$ if and only if $T$ is a basis for $R^5$, where $T = \{[p_1]_B, [p_2]_B, [p_3]_B, [p_4]_B, [p_5]_B\}$. In particular, the coordinate vectors in $T$ are

$$[p_1]_B = \begin{bmatrix} 4 \\ 2 \\ 0 \\ 3 \\ 1 \end{bmatrix}, \quad [p_2]_B = \begin{bmatrix} 1 \\ 5 \\ -1 \\ 1 \\ 0 \end{bmatrix}, \quad [p_3]_B = \begin{bmatrix} 3 \\ 1 \\ 0 \\ 0 \\ 1 \end{bmatrix},$$

$$[p_4]_B = \begin{bmatrix} 2 \\ -1 \\ 0 \\ 1 \\ 1 \end{bmatrix}, \quad \text{and} \quad [p_5]_B = \begin{bmatrix} 0 \\ 0 \\ 1 \\ 0 \\ 1 \end{bmatrix}.$$

Since $R^5$ has dimension 5 and $T$ contains 5 vectors, $T$ will be a basis for $R^5$ if $T$ is a linearly independent set. To check whether $T$ is linearly independent, we form the matrix $A$ whose columns are the vectors in $T$ and use MATLAB to reduce $A$ to echelon form. As can be seen from the results in Fig. 5.4, the columns of $A$ are linearly independent. Hence, $T$ is a basis for $R^5$. Therefore, $S$ is a basis for $\mathcal{P}_4$. ◾

```
A=
       4      1      3      2      0
       2      5      1     -1      0
       0     -1      0      0      1
       3      1      0      1      0
       1      0      1      1      1

>>rref(A)

ans=
       1      0      0      0      0
       0      1      0      0      0
       0      0      1      0      0
       0      0      0      1      0
       0      0      0      0      1
```

*Figure 5.4*   MATLAB was used for Example 9 to determine whether the columns of $A$ are linearly independent. Since $A$ is row equivalent to the identity, its columns are linearly independent.

## 5.4 EXERCISES

In Exercises 1–4, $W$ is a subspace of the vector space $V$ of all $(2 \times 2)$ matrices. A matrix $A$ in $W$ is written as

$$A = \begin{bmatrix} a & b \\ c & d \end{bmatrix}.$$

In each case exhibit a basis for $W$.

1. $W = \{A : a + b + c + d = 0\}$
2. $W = \{A : a = -d, \quad b = 2d, \quad c = -3d\}$
3. $W = \{A : a = 0\}$
4. $W = \{A : b = a - c, \quad d = 2a + c\}$

In Exercises 5–8, $W$ is a subspace of $\mathcal{P}_2$. In each case exhibit a basis for $W$.

5. $W = \{p(x) = a_0 + a_1 x + a_2 x^2 : a_2 = a_0 - 2a_1\}$
6. $W = \{p(x) = a_0 + a_1 x + a_2 x^2 : a_0 = 3a_2,$
   $a_1 = -a_2\}$
7. $W = \{p(x) = a_0 + a_1 x + a_2 x^2 : p(0) = 0\}$
8. $W = \{p(x) = a_0 + a_1 x + a_2 x^2 : p(1) = p'(1) = 0\}$
9. Find a basis for the subspace $V$ of $\mathcal{P}_4$, where $V = \{p(x) \text{ in } \mathcal{P}_4 : p(0) = 0, \ p'(1) = 0, \ p''(-1) = 0\}$.
10. Prove that the set of all real $(2 \times 2)$ symmetric matrices is a subspace of the vector space of all real $(2 \times 2)$ matrices. Find a basis for this subspace (see Exercise 26 of Section 5.3).
11. Let $V$ be the vector space of all $(2 \times 2)$ real matrices. Show that $B = \{E_{11}, E_{12}, E_{21}, E_{22}\}$ (see Example 5) is a basis for $V$.
12. With respect to the basis $B = \{1, x, x^2\}$ for $\mathcal{P}_2$, find the coordinate vector for each of the following.
    a) $p(x) = x^2 - x + 1$
    b) $p(x) = x^2 + 4x - 1$
    c) $p(x) = 2x + 5$
13. With respect to the basis $B = \{E_{11}, E_{12}, E_{21}, E_{22}\}$ for the vector space $V$ of all $(2 \times 2)$ matrices, find the coordinate vector for each of the following.
    a) $A_1 = \begin{bmatrix} 2 & -1 \\ 3 & 2 \end{bmatrix}$    b) $A_2 = \begin{bmatrix} 1 & 0 \\ -1 & 1 \end{bmatrix}$
    c) $A_3 = \begin{bmatrix} 2 & 3 \\ 0 & 0 \end{bmatrix}$
14. Prove that $\{1, x, x^2, \ldots, x^n\}$ is a linearly independent set in $\mathcal{P}_n$ by supposing that $p(x) = \theta(x)$, where

$p(x) = a_0 + a_1 x + \cdots + a_n x^n$. Next, take successive derivatives as in Example 2.

In Exercises 15–17, use the basis $B$ of Exercise 11 and property 2 of Theorem 5 to test for linear independence in the vector space of $(2 \times 2)$ matrices.

15. $A_1 = \begin{bmatrix} 2 & 1 \\ 2 & 1 \end{bmatrix}$, $A_2 = \begin{bmatrix} 3 & 0 \\ 0 & 2 \end{bmatrix}$,
    $A_3 = \begin{bmatrix} 1 & 1 \\ 2 & 1 \end{bmatrix}$

16. $A_1 = \begin{bmatrix} 1 & 3 \\ 2 & 1 \end{bmatrix}$, $A_2 = \begin{bmatrix} 4 & -2 \\ 0 & 6 \end{bmatrix}$,
    $A_3 = \begin{bmatrix} 6 & 4 \\ 4 & 8 \end{bmatrix}$

17. $A_1 = \begin{bmatrix} 2 & 2 \\ 1 & 3 \end{bmatrix}$, $A_2 = \begin{bmatrix} 1 & 4 \\ 0 & 5 \end{bmatrix}$,
    $A_3 = \begin{bmatrix} 4 & 10 \\ 1 & 13 \end{bmatrix}$

In Exercises 18–21, use Exercise 14 and property 2 of Theorem 5 to test for linear independence in $\mathcal{P}_3$.

18. $\{x^3 - x, x^2 - 1, x + 4\}$
19. $\{x^2 + 2x - 1, x^2 - 5x + 2, 3x^2 - x\}$
20. $\{x^3 - x^2, x^2 - x, x - 1, x^3 - 1\}$
21. $\{x^3 + 1, x^2 + 1, x + 1, 1\}$
22. In $\mathcal{P}_2$, let $S = \{p_1(x), p_2(x), p_3(x), p_4(x)\}$, where $p_1(x) = 1 + 2x + x^2, p_2(x) = 2 + 5x, p_3(x) = 3 + 7x + x^2$, and $p_4(x) = 1 + x + 3x^2$. Use the method illustrated in Example 8 to obtain a basis for $\text{Sp}(S)$. [*Hint:* Use the basis $B = \{1, x, x^2\}$ to obtain coordinate vectors for $p_1(x), p_2(x), p_3(x)$, and $p_4(x)$. Now use the method illustrated in Example 7 of Section 3.4.]
23. Let $S$ be the subset of $\mathcal{P}_2$ given in Exercise 22. Find a subset of $S$ that is a basis for $\text{Sp}(S)$. [*Hint:* Proceed as in Exercise 22, but use the technique illustrated in Example 6 of Section 3.4.]
24. Let $V$ be the vector space of all $(2 \times 2)$ matrices and let $S = \{A_1, A_2, A_3, A_4\}$, where

$$A_1 = \begin{bmatrix} 1 & 2 \\ -1 & 3 \end{bmatrix}, \quad A_2 = \begin{bmatrix} -2 & 1 \\ 2 & -1 \end{bmatrix},$$

$$A_3 = \begin{bmatrix} -1 & -1 \\ 1 & -3 \end{bmatrix}, \quad \text{and} \quad A_4 = \begin{bmatrix} -2 & 2 \\ 2 & 0 \end{bmatrix}.$$

As in Example 8, find a basis for $Sp(S)$.

**25.** Let $V$ and $S$ be as in Exercise 24. Find a subset of $S$ that is a basis for $Sp(S)$. [*Hint:* Use Theorem 5 and the technique illustrated in Example 6 of Section 3.4.]

**26.** In $\mathcal{P}_2$, let $Q = \{p_1(x), p_2(x), p_3(x)\}$, where $p_1(x) = -1 + x + 2x^2$, $p_2(x) = x + 3x^2$, and $p_3(x) = 1 + 2x + 8x^2$. Use the basis $B = \{1, x, x^2\}$ to show that $Q$ is a basis for $\mathcal{P}_2$.

**27.** Let $Q$ be the basis for $\mathcal{P}_2$ given in Exercise 26. Find $[p(x)]_Q$ for $p(x) = 1 + x + x^2$.

**28.** Let $Q$ be the basis for $\mathcal{P}_2$ given in Exercise 26. Find $[p(x)]_Q$ for $p(x) = a_0 + a_1x + a_2x^2$.

**29.** In the vector space $V$ of $(2 \times 2)$ matrices, let $Q = \{A_1, A_2, A_3, A_4\}$ where

$$A_1 = \begin{bmatrix} 1 & 0 \\ 0 & 0 \end{bmatrix}, \quad A_2 = \begin{bmatrix} 1 & -1 \\ 0 & 0 \end{bmatrix},$$

$$A_3 = \begin{bmatrix} 0 & 2 \\ 0 & 0 \end{bmatrix}, \quad \text{and} \quad A_4 = \begin{bmatrix} -3 & 0 \\ 2 & 1 \end{bmatrix}.$$

Use the corollary to Theorem 5 and the natural basis for $V$ to show that $Q$ is a basis for $V$.

**30.** With $V$ and $Q$ as in Exercise 29, find $[A]_Q$ for

$$A = \begin{bmatrix} 7 & 3 \\ -3 & -1 \end{bmatrix}.$$

**31.** With $V$ and $Q$ as in Exercise 29, find $[A]_Q$ for

$$A = \begin{bmatrix} a & b \\ c & d \end{bmatrix}.$$

**32.** Give an alternative proof that $\{1, x, x^2\}$ is a linearly independent set in $\mathcal{P}_2$ as follows: Let $p(x) = a_0 + a_1x + a_2x^2$, and suppose that $p(x) = \theta(x)$. Then $p(-1) = 0$, $p(0) = 0$, and $p(1) = 0$. These three equations can be used to show that $a_0 = a_1 = a_2 = 0$.

**33.** The set $\{\sin x, \cos x\}$ is a subset of the vector space $C[-\pi, \pi]$. Prove that the set is linearly independent. [*Hint:* Set $f(x) = c_1 \sin x + c_2 \cos x$, and assume that $f(x) = \theta(x)$. Then $f(0) = 0$ and $f(\pi/2) = 0$.]

In Exercises 34 and 35, $V$ is the set of functions

$$V = \{f(x): f(x) = ae^x + be^{2x} + ce^{3x} + de^{4x}$$
$$\text{for real numbers } a, b, c, d\}.$$

It can be shown that $V$ is a vector space.

**34.** Show that $B = \{e^x, e^{2x}, e^{3x}, e^{4x}\}$ is a basis for $V$. [*Hint:* To see that $B$ is a linearly independent set, let $h(x) = c_1e^x + c_2e^{2x} + c_3e^{3x} + c_4e^{4x}$ and assume that $h(x) = \theta(x)$. Then $h'(x) = \theta(x)$, $h''(x) = \theta(x)$, and $h'''(x) = \theta(x)$. Therefore, $h(0) = 0$, $h'(0) = 0$, $h''(0) = 0$, and $h'''(0) = 0$.]

**35.** Let $S = \{g_1(x), g_2(x), g_3(x)\}$ be the subset of $V$, where $g_1(x) = e^x - e^{4x}$, $g_2(x) = e^{2x} + e^{3x}$, and $g_3(x) = -e^x + e^{3x} + e^{4x}$. Use Theorem 5 and basis $B$ of Exercise 34 to show that $S$ is a linearly independent set.

**36.** Prove that if $Q = \{v_1, v_2, \ldots, v_m\}$ is a linearly independent subset of a vector space $V$, and if $w$ is a vector in $V$ such that $w$ is not in $Sp(Q)$, then $\{v_1, v_2, \ldots, v_m, w\}$ is also a linearly independent set in $V$. [*Note:* $\theta$ is always in $Sp(Q)$.]

**37.** Let $S = \{v_1, v_2, \ldots, v_n\}$ be a subset of a vector space $V$, where $n \geq 2$. Prove that set $S$ is linearly dependent if and only if at least one of the vectors, $v_j$, can be expressed as a linear combination of the remaining vectors.

**38.** Use Exercise 37 to obtain necessary and sufficient conditions for a set $\{u, v\}$ of two vectors to be linearly dependent. Determine by inspection whether each of the following sets is linearly dependent or linearly independent.

**a)** $\{1 + x, x^2\}$

**b)** $\{x, e^x\}$

**c)** $\{x, 3x\}$

**d)** $\left\{ \begin{bmatrix} -1 & 2 \\ 1 & 3 \end{bmatrix}, \begin{bmatrix} 2 & -4 \\ -2 & -6 \end{bmatrix} \right\}$

**e)** $\left\{ \begin{bmatrix} 0 & 0 \\ 0 & 0 \end{bmatrix}, \begin{bmatrix} 1 & 0 \\ 0 & 1 \end{bmatrix} \right\}$

## 5.5    DIMENSION

We now use Theorem 5 to generalize the idea of dimension to the general vector-space setting. We begin with two theorems that will be needed to show that dimension is a well-defined concept. These theorems are direct applications of the corollary to Theorem 5, and the proofs are left to the exercises because they are essentially the same as the proofs of the analogous theorems from Section 3.5.

**THEOREM 6**    If $V$ is a vector space and if $B = \{\mathbf{v}_1, \mathbf{v}_2, \ldots, \mathbf{v}_p\}$ is a basis of $V$, then any set of $p + 1$ vectors in $V$ is linearly dependent. ∎

**THEOREM 7**    Let $V$ be a vector space, and let $B = \{\mathbf{v}_1, \mathbf{v}_2, \ldots, \mathbf{v}_p\}$ be a basis for $V$. If $Q = \{\mathbf{u}_1, \mathbf{u}_2, \ldots, \mathbf{u}_m\}$ is also a basis for $V$, then $m = p$. ∎

If $V$ is a vector space that has a basis of $p$ vectors, then no ambiguity can arise if we define the dimension of $V$ to be $p$ (since the number of vectors in a basis for $V$ is an invariant property of $V$ by Theorem 7). There is, however, one extreme case, which is also included in Definition 6. That is, there may not be a finite set of vectors that spans $V$; in this case we call $V$ an infinite-dimensional vector space.

**DEFINITION 6**

Let $V$ be a vector space.

1. If $V$ has a basis $B = \{\mathbf{v}_1, \mathbf{v}_2, \ldots, \mathbf{v}_n\}$ of $n$ vectors, then $V$ has *dimension n*, and we write $\dim(V) = n$. [If $V = \{\boldsymbol{\theta}\}$, then $\dim(V) = 0$.]

2. If $V$ is nontrivial and does not have a basis containing a finite number of vectors, then $V$ is an *infinite-dimensional* vector space.

We already know from Chapter 3 that $R^n$ has dimension $n$. In the preceding section it was shown that $\{1, x, x^2\}$ is a basis for $\mathcal{P}_2$, so $\dim(\mathcal{P}_2) = 3$. Similarly, the set $\{1, x, \ldots, x^n\}$ is a basis for $\mathcal{P}_n$, so $\dim(\mathcal{P}_n) = n + 1$. The vector space $V$ consisting of all $(2 \times 2)$ real matrices has a basis with four vectors, namely, $B = \{E_{11}, E_{12}, E_{21}, E_{22}\}$. Therefore, $\dim(V) = 4$. More generally, the space of all $(m \times n)$ real matrices has dimension $mn$ because the $(m \times n)$ matrices $E_{ij}$, $1 \le i \le m, 1 \le j \le n$, constitute a basis for the space.

**EXAMPLE 1**    Let $W$ be the subspace of the set of all $(2 \times 2)$ matrices defined by

$$W = \{A = \begin{bmatrix} a & b \\ c & d \end{bmatrix} : 2a - b + 3c + d = 0\}.$$

Determine the dimension of $W$.

*Solution*    The algebraic specification for $W$ can be rewritten as $d = -2a + b - 3c$. Thus an element of $W$ is completely determined by the three independent variables $a$, $b$, and $c$.

In succession, let $a = 1, b = 0, c = 0$; $a = 0, b = 1, c = 0$; and $a = 0, b = 0, c = 1$. This yields three matrices

$$A_1 = \begin{bmatrix} 1 & 0 \\ 0 & -2 \end{bmatrix}, \quad A_2 = \begin{bmatrix} 0 & 1 \\ 0 & 1 \end{bmatrix}, \quad \text{and} \quad A_3 = \begin{bmatrix} 0 & 0 \\ 1 & -3 \end{bmatrix}$$

in $W$. The matrix $A$ is in $W$ if and only if $A = aA_1 + bA_2 + cA_3$, so $\{A_1, A_2, A_3\}$ is a spanning set for $W$. It is easy to show that the set $\{A_1, A_2, A_3\}$ is linearly independent, so it is a basis for $W$. It follows that $\dim(W) = 3$. ∎

An example of an infinite-dimensional vector space is given next, in Example 2. As Example 2 illustrates, we can show that a vector space $V$ is infinite dimensional if we can show that $V$ contains subspaces of dimension $k$ for $k = 1, 2, 3, \ldots$.

If $W$ is a subspace of a vector space $V$, and if $\dim(W) = k$, then it is almost obvious that $\dim(V) \geq \dim(W) = k$ (we leave the proof of this as an exercise). This observation can be used to show that $C[a, b]$ is an infinite-dimensional vector space.

**EXAMPLE 2** Show that $C[a, b]$ is an infinite-dimensional vector space.

**Solution** To show that $C[a, b]$ is not a finite-dimensional vector space, we merely note that $\mathcal{P}_n$ is a subspace of $C[a, b]$ for every $n$. But $\dim(\mathcal{P}_n) = n + 1$; and so $C[a, b]$ contains subspaces of arbitrarily large dimension. Thus $C[a, b]$ must be an infinite-dimensional vector space. ∎

## Properties of a $p$-Dimensional Vector Space

The next two theorems summarize some of the properties of a $p$-dimensional vector space $V$ and show how properties of $R^p$ carry over into $V$.

**THEOREM 8** Let $V$ be a finite-dimensional vector space with $\dim(V) = p$.

1.  Any set of $p + 1$ or more vectors in $V$ is linearly dependent.
2.  Any set of $p$ linearly independent vectors in $V$ is a basis for $V$. ∎

This theorem is a direct generalization from $R^p$ (Exercise 20). To complete our discussion of finite-dimensional vector spaces, we state the following lemma.

**LEMMA** Let $V$ be a vector space, and let $Q = \{\mathbf{u}_1, \mathbf{u}_2, \ldots, \mathbf{u}_p\}$ be a spanning set for $V$. Then there is a subset $Q'$ of $Q$ that is a basis for $V$.

**Proof** (We only sketch the proof of this lemma because the proof follows familiar lines.) If $Q$ is linearly independent, then $Q$ itself is a basis for $V$. If $Q$ is linearly dependent, we can express some vector from $Q$ in terms of the other $p - 1$ vectors in $Q$. Without loss of generality, let us suppose we can express $\mathbf{u}_1$ in terms of $\mathbf{u}_2, \mathbf{u}_3, \ldots, \mathbf{u}_p$. In that event we have

$$\text{Sp}\{\mathbf{u}_2, \mathbf{u}_3, \ldots, \mathbf{u}_p\} = \text{Sp}\{\mathbf{u}_1, \mathbf{u}_2, \mathbf{u}_3, \ldots, \mathbf{u}_p\} = V;$$

if $\{\mathbf{u}_2, \mathbf{u}_3, \ldots, \mathbf{u}_p\}$ is linearly independent, it is a basis for $V$. If $\{\mathbf{u}_2, \mathbf{u}_3, \ldots, \mathbf{u}_p\}$ is linearly dependent, we continue discarding redundant vectors until we obtain a linearly independent spanning set, $Q'$. ∎

The following theorem is a companion to Theorem 8.

**THEOREM 9**   Let $V$ be a finite-dimensional vector space with $\dim(V) = p$.

1. Any spanning set for $V$ must contain at least $p$ vectors.
2. Any set of $p$ vectors that spans $V$ is a basis for $V$.

*Proof*   Property 1 follows immediately from the preceding lemma, for if there were a spanning set $Q$ for $V$ that contained fewer than $p$ vectors, then we could find a subset $Q'$ of $Q$ that is a basis for $V$ containing fewer than $p$ vectors. This finding would contradict Theorem 7, so property 1 must be valid.

Property 2 also follows from the lemma, because we know there is a subset $Q'$ of $Q$ such that $Q'$ is a basis for $V$. Since $\dim(V) = p$, $Q'$ must have $p$ vectors, and since $Q' \subseteq Q$, where $Q$ has $p$ vectors, we must have $Q' = Q$.  ◼

**EXAMPLE 3**   Let $V$ be the vector space of all $(2 \times 2)$ real matrices. In $V$, set

$$A_1 = \begin{bmatrix} 1 & 0 \\ -1 & 0 \end{bmatrix}, \quad A_2 = \begin{bmatrix} 0 & 1 \\ 2 & 0 \end{bmatrix}, \quad A_3 = \begin{bmatrix} 0 & 0 \\ -1 & 3 \end{bmatrix},$$

$$A_4 = \begin{bmatrix} 1 & 0 \\ -1 & 1 \end{bmatrix}, \quad \text{and} \quad A_5 = \begin{bmatrix} 2 & 1 \\ 3 & 1 \end{bmatrix}.$$

For each of the sets $\{A_1, A_2, A_3\}$, $\{A_1, A_2, A_3, A_4\}$, and $\{A_1, A_2, A_3, A_4, A_5\}$, determine whether the set is a basis for $V$.

*Solution*   We have already noted that $\dim(V) = 4$ and that $B = \{E_{11}, E_{12}, E_{21}, E_{22}\}$ is a basis for $V$. It follows from property 1 of Theorem 9 that the set $\{A_1, A_2, A_3\}$ does not span $V$. Likewise, property 1 of Theorem 8 implies that $\{A_1, A_2, A_3, A_4, A_5\}$ is a linearly dependent set. By property 2 of Theorem 8, the set $\{A_1, A_2, A_3, A_4\}$ is a basis for $V$ if and only if it is a linearly independent set. It is straightforward to see that the set of coordinate vectors $\{[A_1]_B, [A_2]_B, [A_3]_B, [A_4]_B\}$ is a linearly independent set. By Theorem 5 of Section 5.4, the set $\{A_1, A_2, A_3, A_4\}$ is also linearly independent; thus the set is a basis for $V$.  ◼

## 5.5   EXERCISES

1. Let $V$ be the set of all real $(3 \times 3)$ matrices, and let $V_1$ and $V_2$ be subsets of $V$, where $V_1$ consists of all the $(3 \times 3)$ lower-triangular matrices and $V_2$ consists of all the $(3 \times 3)$ upper-triangular matrices.

   a) Show that $V_1$ and $V_2$ are subspaces of $V$.
   b) Find bases for $V_1$ and $V_2$.
   c) Calculate $\dim(V)$, $\dim(V_1)$, and $\dim(V_2)$.

2. Suppose that $V_1$ and $V_2$ are subspaces of a vector space $V$. Show that $V_1 \cap V_2$ is also a subspace of $V$.

It is not necessarily true that $V_1 \cup V_2$ is a subspace of $V$. Let $V = R^2$ and find two subspaces of $R^2$ whose union is not a subspace of $R^2$.

3. Let $V$, $V_1$, and $V_2$ be as in Exercise 1. By Exercise 2, $V_1 \cap V_2$ is a subspace of $V$. Describe $V_1 \cap V_2$ and calculate its dimension.

4. Let $V$ be as in Exercise 1, and let $W$ be the subset of all the $(3 \times 3)$ symmetric matrices in $V$. Clearly $W$ is a subspace of $V$. What is $\dim(W)$?

**5.** Recall that a square matrix $A$ is called skew symmetric if $A^T = -A$. Let $V$ be as in Exercise 1 and let $W$ be the subset of all the $(3 \times 3)$ skew-symmetric matrices in $V$. Calculate $\dim(W)$.

**6.** Let $W$ be the subspace of $\mathcal{P}_2$ consisting of polynomials $p(x) = a_0 + a_1 x + a_2 x^2$ such that $2a_0 - a_1 + 3a_2 = 0$. Determine $\dim(W)$.

**7.** Let $W$ be the subspace of $\mathcal{P}_4$ defined thus: $p(x)$ is in $W$ if and only if $p(1) + p(-1) = 0$ and $p(2) + p(-2) = 0$. What is $\dim(W)$?

In Exercises 8–13, a subset $S$ of a vector space $V$ is given. In each case choose one of the statements i), ii), or iii) that holds for $S$ and verify that this is the case.

**i)** $S$ is a basis for $V$.

**ii)** $S$ does not span $V$.

**iii)** $S$ is linearly dependent.

**8.** $S = \{1 + x - x^2, x + x^3, -x^2 + x^3\}$; $\quad V = \mathcal{P}_3$

**9.** $S = \{1 + x^2, x - x^2, 1 + x, 2 - x + x^2\}$; $\quad V = \mathcal{P}_2$

**10.** $S = \{1 + x + x^2, x + x^2, x^2\}$; $\quad V = \mathcal{P}_2$

**11.** $S = \left\{ \begin{bmatrix} 0 & 1 \\ 1 & 0 \end{bmatrix}, \begin{bmatrix} 1 & 0 \\ 0 & 1 \end{bmatrix} \right\}$;

$V$ is the set of all $(2 \times 2)$ real matrices.

**12.** $S = \left\{ \begin{bmatrix} 0 & 0 \\ 0 & 1 \end{bmatrix}, \begin{bmatrix} 0 & 1 \\ 0 & 1 \end{bmatrix}, \begin{bmatrix} 1 & 1 \\ 1 & 1 \end{bmatrix}, \begin{bmatrix} 0 & 1 \\ 1 & 1 \end{bmatrix} \right\}$;

$V$ is the set of all $(2 \times 2)$ real matrices.

**13.** $S = \left\{ \begin{bmatrix} 1 & 0 \\ -1 & 0 \end{bmatrix}, \begin{bmatrix} 1 & 2 \\ 1 & -2 \end{bmatrix}, \begin{bmatrix} 1 & -1 \\ 1 & 4 \end{bmatrix}, \right.$

$\left. \begin{bmatrix} 3 & 4 \\ 0 & 4 \end{bmatrix}, \begin{bmatrix} 0 & 1 \\ -1 & 3 \end{bmatrix} \right\}$;

$V$ is the set of all $(2 \times 2)$ real matrices.

**14.** Let $W$ be the subspace of $C[-\pi, \pi]$ consisting of functions of the form $f(x) = a \sin x + b \cos x$. Determine the dimension of $W$.

**15.** Let $V$ denote the set of all infinite sequences of real numbers:

$$V = \{\mathbf{x} : \mathbf{x} = \{x_i\}_{i=1}^{\infty}, \quad x_i \text{ in } R\}.$$

If $\mathbf{x} = \{x_i\}_{i=1}^{\infty}$ and $\mathbf{y} = \{y_i\}_{i=1}^{\infty}$ are in $V$, then $\mathbf{x} + \mathbf{y}$ is the sequence $\{x_i + y_i\}_{i=1}^{\infty}$. If $c$ is a real number, then $c\mathbf{x}$ is the sequence $\{cx_i\}_{i=1}^{\infty}$.

**a)** Prove that $V$ is a vector space.

**b)** Show that $V$ has infinite dimension. [*Hint:* For each positive integer, $k$, let $\mathbf{s}_k$ denote the

sequence $\mathbf{s}_k = \{e_{ki}\}_{i=1}^{\infty}$, where $e_{kk} = 1$, but $e_{ki} = 0$ for $i \neq k$. For each positive integer $n$, show that $\{\mathbf{s}_1, \mathbf{s}_2, \ldots, \mathbf{s}_n\}$ is a linearly independent subset of $V$.]

**16.** Let $V$ be a vector space, and let $W$ be a subspace of $V$, where $\dim(W) = k$. Prove that if $V$ is finite dimensional, then $\dim(V) \geq k$. [*Hint:* $W$ must contain a set of $k$ linearly independent vectors.]

**17.** Let $W$ be a subspace of a finite-dimensional vector space $V$, where $W$ contains at least one nonzero vector. Prove that $W$ has a basis and that $\dim(W) \leq \dim(V)$. [*Hint:* Use Exercise 36 of Section 5.4 to show that $W$ has a basis.]

**18.** Prove Theorem 6. [*Hint:* Let $\{\mathbf{u}_1, \mathbf{u}_2, \ldots, \mathbf{u}_k\}$ be a subset of $V$, where $k \geq p + 1$. Consider the vectors $[\mathbf{u}_1]_B, [\mathbf{u}_2]_B, \ldots, [\mathbf{u}_k]_B$ in $R^p$ and apply Theorem 5 of Section 5.4.]

**19.** Prove Theorem 7.

**20.** Prove Theorem 8.

**21.** (*Change of basis;* see also Section 5.10). Let $V$ be a vector space, where $\dim(V) = n$, and let $B = \{\mathbf{v}_1, \mathbf{v}_2, \ldots, \mathbf{v}_n\}$ and $C = \{\mathbf{u}_1, \mathbf{u}_2, \ldots, \mathbf{u}_n\}$ be two bases for $V$. Let $\mathbf{w}$ be any vector in $V$, and suppose that $\mathbf{w}$ has these representations in terms of the bases $B$ and $C$:

$$\mathbf{w} = d_1 \mathbf{v}_1 + d_2 \mathbf{v}_2 + \cdots + d_n \mathbf{v}_n$$
$$\mathbf{w} = c_1 \mathbf{u}_1 + c_2 \mathbf{u}_2 + \cdots + c_n \mathbf{u}_n.$$

By considering Eq. (10) of Section 5.4, convince yourself that the coordinate vectors for $\mathbf{w}$ satisfy

$$[\mathbf{w}]_B = A[\mathbf{w}]_C,$$

where $A$ is the $(n \times n)$ matrix whose $i$th column is equal to $[\mathbf{u}_i]_B$, $1 \leq i \leq n$. As an application, consider the two bases for $\mathcal{P}_2$: $C = \{1, x, x^2\}$ and $B = \{1, x + 1, (x + 1)^2\}$.

**a)** Calculate the $(3 \times 3)$ matrix $A$ just described.

**b)** Using the identity $[p]_B = A[p]_C$, calculate the coordinate vector of $p(x) = x^2 + 4x + 8$ with respect to $B$.

**22.** The matrix $A$ in Exercise 21 is called a transition matrix and shows how to transform a representation with respect to one basis into a representation with respect to another. Use the matrix in part a) of Exercise 21 to convert $p(x) = c_0 + c_1 x + c_2 x^2$ to the form $p(x) = a_0 + a_1(x + 1) + a_2(x + 1)^2$, where:

a) $p(x) = x^2 + 3x - 2$;

b) $p(x) = 2x^2 - 5x + 8$;

c) $p(x) = -x^2 - 2x + 3$;

d) $p(x) = x - 9$.

**23.** By Theorem 5 of Section 5.4, an $(n \times n)$ transition matrix (see Exercises 21 and 22) is always nonsingular. Thus if $[\mathbf{w}]_B = A[\mathbf{w}]_c$, then $[\mathbf{w}]_C = A^{-1}[\mathbf{w}]_B$. Calculate $A^{-1}$ for the matrix in part a) of Exercise 21 and use the result to transform each of the following polynomials to the form $a_0 + a_1 x + a_2 x^2$.

a) $p(x) = 2 - 3(x + 1) + 7(x + 1)^2$

b) $p(x) = 1 + 4(x + 1) - (x + 1)^2$

c) $p(x) = 4 + (x + 1)$

d) $p(x) = 9 - (x + 1)^2$

**24.** Find a matrix $A$ such that $[p]_B = A[p]_c$ for all $p(x)$ in $\mathcal{P}_3$, where $C = \{1, x, x^2, x^3\}$ and $B = \{1, x, x(x - 1), x(x - 1)(x - 2)\}$. Use $A$ to convert each of the following to the form $p(x) = a_0 + a_1 x + a_2 x(x - 1) + a_3 x(x - 1)(x - 2)$.

a) $p(x) = x^3 - 2x^2 + 5x - 9$

b) $p(x) = x^2 + 7x - 2$

c) $p(x) = x^3 + 1$

d) $p(x) = x^3 + 2x^2 + 2x + 3$

---

## 5.6    INNER-PRODUCT SPACES, ORTHOGONAL BASES, AND PROJECTIONS (OPTIONAL)

Up to now we have considered a vector space solely as an entity with an algebraic structure. We know, however, that $R^n$ possesses more than just an algebraic structure; in particular, we know that we can measure the size or length of a vector $\mathbf{x}$ in $R^n$ by the quantity $\|\mathbf{x}\| = \sqrt{\mathbf{x}^T \mathbf{x}}$. Similarly, we can define the distance from $\mathbf{x}$ to $\mathbf{y}$ as $\|\mathbf{x} - \mathbf{y}\|$. The ability to measure distances means that $R^n$ has a geometric structure, which supplements the algebraic structure. The geometric structure can be employed to study problems of convergence, continuity, and the like. In this section we briefly describe how a suitable measure of distance might be imposed on a general vector space. Our development will be brief, and we will leave most of the details to the reader; but the ideas parallel those in Sections 3.6 and 3.8–3.9.

### Inner-Product Spaces

To begin, we observe that the geometric structure for $R^n$ is based on the scalar product $\mathbf{x}^T \mathbf{y}$. Essentially the scalar product is a real-valued function of two vector variables: Given $\mathbf{x}$ and $\mathbf{y}$ in $R^n$, the scalar product produces a number $\mathbf{x}^T \mathbf{y}$. Thus to derive a geometric structure for a vector space $V$, we should look for a generalization of the scalar-product function. A consideration of the properties of the scalar-product function leads to the definition of an inner-product function for a vector space. (With reference to Definition 7, which follows, we note that the expression $\mathbf{u}^T \mathbf{v}$ does not make sense in a general vector space $V$. Thus not only does the nomenclature change—scalar product becomes inner product—but also the notation changes as well, with $\langle \mathbf{u}, \mathbf{v} \rangle$ denoting the inner product of $\mathbf{u}$ and $\mathbf{v}$.)

DEFINITION 7

An *inner product* on a real vector space $V$ is a function that assigns a real number, $\langle \mathbf{u}, \mathbf{v} \rangle$, to each pair of vectors $\mathbf{u}$ and $\mathbf{v}$ in $V$, and that satisfies these properties:

1. $\langle \mathbf{u}, \mathbf{u} \rangle \geq 0$ and $\langle \mathbf{u}, \mathbf{u} \rangle = 0$ if and only if $\mathbf{u} = \boldsymbol{\theta}$.
2. $\langle \mathbf{u}, \mathbf{v} \rangle = \langle \mathbf{v}, \mathbf{u} \rangle$.
3. $\langle a\mathbf{u}, \mathbf{v} \rangle = a\langle \mathbf{u}, \mathbf{v} \rangle$.
4. $\langle \mathbf{u}, \mathbf{v} + \mathbf{w} \rangle = \langle \mathbf{u}, \mathbf{v} \rangle + \langle \mathbf{u}, \mathbf{w} \rangle$.

The usual scalar product in $R^n$ is an inner product in the sense of Definition 7, where $\langle \mathbf{x}, \mathbf{y} \rangle = \mathbf{x}^T \mathbf{y}$. To illustrate the flexibility of Definition 7, we also note that there are other sorts of inner products for $R^n$. The following example gives another inner product for $R^2$.

EXAMPLE 1    Let $V$ be the vector space $R^2$, and let $A$ be the $(2 \times 2)$ matrix

$$A = \begin{bmatrix} 3 & 2 \\ 2 & 4 \end{bmatrix}.$$

Verify that the function $\langle \mathbf{u}, \mathbf{v} \rangle = \mathbf{u}^T A \mathbf{v}$ is an inner product for $R^2$.

*Solution*    Let $\mathbf{u}$ be a vector in $R^2$:

$$\mathbf{u} = \begin{bmatrix} u_1 \\ u_2 \end{bmatrix}.$$

Then

$$\langle \mathbf{u}, \mathbf{u} \rangle = \mathbf{u}^T A \mathbf{u} = [u_1, u_2] \begin{bmatrix} 3 & 2 \\ 2 & 4 \end{bmatrix} \begin{bmatrix} u_1 \\ u_2 \end{bmatrix},$$

so $\langle \mathbf{u}, \mathbf{u} \rangle = 3u_1^2 + 4u_1u_2 + 4u_2^2 = 2u_1^2 + (u_1 + 2u_2)^2$. Thus $\langle \mathbf{u}, \mathbf{u} \rangle \geq 0$ and $\langle \mathbf{u}, \mathbf{u} \rangle = 0$ if and only if $u_1 = u_2 = 0$. This shows that property 1 of Definition 7 is satisfied.

To see that property 2 of Definition 7 holds, note that $A$ is symmetric; that is, $A^T = A$. Also observe that if $\mathbf{u}$ and $\mathbf{v}$ are in $R^2$, then $\mathbf{u}^T A \mathbf{v}$ is a $(1 \times 1)$ matrix, so $(\mathbf{u}^T A \mathbf{v})^T = \mathbf{u}^T A \mathbf{v}$. It now follows that $\langle \mathbf{u}, \mathbf{v} \rangle = \mathbf{u}^T A \mathbf{v} = (\mathbf{u}^T A \mathbf{v})^T = \mathbf{v}^T A^T (\mathbf{u}^T)^T = \mathbf{v}^T A^T \mathbf{u} = \langle \mathbf{v}, \mathbf{u} \rangle$.

Properties 3 and 4 of Definition 7 follow easily from the properties of matrix multiplication, so $\langle \mathbf{u}, \mathbf{v} \rangle$ is an inner product for $R^2$. ■

In Example 1, an inner product for $R^2$ was defined in terms of a matrix $A$:

$$\langle \mathbf{u}, \mathbf{v} \rangle = \mathbf{u}^T A \mathbf{v}.$$

In general, we might ask the following question:

*"For what $(n \times n)$ matrices, A, does the operation $\mathbf{u}^T A \mathbf{v}$ define an inner product on $R^n$?"*

The answer to this question is suggested by the solution to Example 1. In particular (see Exercises 3 and 32), the operation $\langle \mathbf{u}, \mathbf{v} \rangle = \mathbf{u}^T A \mathbf{v}$ is an inner product for $R^n$ if and only if $A$ is a symmetric positive-definite matrix.

There are a number of ways in which inner products can be defined on spaces of functions. For example, Exercise 6 will show that

$$\langle p, q \rangle = p(0)q(0) + p(1)q(1) + p(2)q(2)$$

defines one inner product for $\mathcal{P}_2$. The following example gives yet another inner product for $\mathcal{P}_2$.

**EXAMPLE 2**    For $p(t)$ and $q(t)$ in $\mathcal{P}_2$, verify that

$$\langle p, q \rangle = \int_0^1 p(t)q(t)\, dt$$

is an inner product.

*Solution*    To check property 1 of Definition 7, note that

$$\langle p, p \rangle = \int_0^1 p(t)^2\, dt,$$

and $p(t)^2 \geq 0$ for $0 \leq t \leq 1$. Thus $\langle p, p \rangle$ is the area under the curve $p(t)^2, 0 \leq t \leq 1$. Hence $\langle p, p \rangle \geq 0$, and equality holds if and only if $p(t) = 0, 0 \leq t \leq 1$ (see Fig. 5.5).

Properties 2, 3, and 4 of Definition 7 are straightforward to verify, and we include here only the verification of property 4. If $p(t)$, $q(t)$, and $r(t)$ are in $\mathcal{P}_2$, then

$$\langle p, q + r \rangle = \int_0^1 p(t)[q(t) + r(t)]\, dt = \int_0^1 [p(t)q(t) + p(t)r(t)]\, dt$$

$$= \int_0^1 p(t)q(t)\, dt + \int_0^1 p(t)r(t)\, dt = \langle p, q \rangle + \langle p, r \rangle,$$

as required by property 4.

*Figure 5.5*
The value $\langle p, p \rangle$ is equal to the area under the graph of $y = p(t)^2$.

After the key step of defining a vector-space analog of the scalar product, the rest is routine. For purposes of reference we call a vector space with an inner product an ***inner-product space***. As in $R^n$, we can use the inner product as a measure of size: If $V$ is an inner-product space, then for each $\mathbf{v}$ in $V$ we define $\|\mathbf{v}\|$ (the ***norm*** of $\mathbf{v}$) as

$$\|\mathbf{v}\| = \sqrt{\langle \mathbf{v}, \mathbf{v} \rangle}.$$

Note that $\langle \mathbf{v}, \mathbf{v} \rangle \geq 0$ for all $\mathbf{v}$ in $V$, so the norm function is always defined.

**EXAMPLE 3**    Use the inner product for $\mathcal{P}_2$ defined in Example 2 to determine $\|t^2\|$.

*Solution*    By definition, $\|t^2\| = \sqrt{\langle t^2, t^2 \rangle}$. But $\langle t^2, t^2 \rangle = \int_0^1 t^2 t^2\, dt = \int_0^1 t^4\, dt = 1/5$, so $\|t^2\| = 1/\sqrt{5}$.

Before continuing, we pause to illustrate one way in which the inner-product space framework is used in practice. One of the many inner products for the vector space $C[0, 1]$ is

$$\langle f, g \rangle = \int_0^1 f(x)g(x)\, dx.$$

If $f$ is a relatively complicated function in $C[0, 1]$, we might wish to approximate $f$ by a simpler function, say a polynomial. For definiteness suppose we want to find a polynomial $p$ in $\mathcal{P}_2$ that is a good approximation to $f$. The phrase "good approximation" is too vague to be used in any calculation, but the inner-product space framework allows us to measure size and thus to pose some meaningful problems. In particular, we can ask for a polynomial $p^*$ in $\mathcal{P}_2$ such that

$$\|f - p^*\| \le \|f - p\|$$

for all $p$ in $\mathcal{P}_2$. Finding such a polynomial $p^*$ in this setting is equivalent to minimizing

$$\int_0^1 [f(x) - p(x)]^2 \, dx$$

among all $p$ in $\mathcal{P}_2$. We will present a procedure for doing this shortly.

## Orthogonal Bases

If $\mathbf{u}$ and $\mathbf{v}$ are vectors in an inner-product space $V$, we say that $\mathbf{u}$ and $\mathbf{v}$ are *orthogonal* if $\langle \mathbf{u}, \mathbf{v} \rangle = 0$. Similarly, $B = \{\mathbf{v}_1, \mathbf{v}_2, \ldots, \mathbf{v}_p\}$ is an *orthogonal set* in $V$ if $\langle \mathbf{v}_i, \mathbf{v}_j \rangle = 0$ when $i \ne j$. In addition, if an orthogonal set of vectors $B$ is a basis for $V$, we call $B$ an *orthogonal basis*. The next two theorems correspond to their analogs in $R^n$, and we leave the proofs to the exercises. [See Eq. (5a), Eq. (5b), and Theorem 14 of Section 3.6.]

**THEOREM 10** Let $B = \{\mathbf{v}_1, \mathbf{v}_2, \ldots, \mathbf{v}_n\}$ be an orthogonal basis for an inner-product space $V$. If $\mathbf{u}$ is any vector in $V$, then

$$\mathbf{u} = \frac{\langle \mathbf{v}_1, \mathbf{u} \rangle}{\langle \mathbf{v}_1, \mathbf{v}_1 \rangle} \mathbf{v}_1 + \frac{\langle \mathbf{v}_2, \mathbf{u} \rangle}{\langle \mathbf{v}_2, \mathbf{v}_2 \rangle} \mathbf{v}_2 + \cdots + \frac{\langle \mathbf{v}_n, \mathbf{u} \rangle}{\langle \mathbf{v}_n, \mathbf{v}_n \rangle} \mathbf{v}_n.$$

**THEOREM 11** **Gram–Schmidt Orthogonalization** Let $V$ be an inner-product space, and let $\{\mathbf{u}_1, \mathbf{u}_2, \ldots, \mathbf{u}_n\}$ be a basis for $V$. Let $\mathbf{v}_1 = \mathbf{u}_1$, and for $2 \le k \le n$ define $\mathbf{v}_k$ by

$$\mathbf{v}_k = \mathbf{u}_k - \sum_{j=1}^{k-1} \frac{\langle \mathbf{u}_k, \mathbf{v}_j \rangle}{\langle \mathbf{v}_j, \mathbf{v}_j \rangle} \mathbf{v}_j.$$

Then $\{\mathbf{v}_1, \mathbf{v}_2, \ldots, \mathbf{v}_n\}$ is an orthogonal basis for $V$.

**EXAMPLE 4** Let the inner product on $\mathcal{P}_2$ be the one given in Example 2. Starting with the natural basis $\{1, x, x^2\}$, use Gram–Schmidt orthogonalization to obtain an orthogonal basis for $\mathcal{P}_2$.

*Solution* If we let $\{p_0, p_1, p_2\}$ denote the orthogonal basis, we have $p_0(x) = 1$ and find $p_1(x)$ from

$$p_1(x) = x - \frac{\langle p_0, x \rangle}{\langle p_0, p_0 \rangle} p_0(x).$$

We calculate

$$\langle p_0, x \rangle = \int_0^1 x \, dx = 1/2 \text{ and } \langle p_0, p_0 \rangle = \int_0^1 dx = 1;$$

so $p_1(x) = x - 1/2$. The next step of the Gram–Schmidt orthogonalization process is to form

$$p_2(x) = x^2 - \frac{\langle p_1, x^2 \rangle}{\langle p_1, p_1 \rangle} p_1(x) - \frac{\langle p_0, x^2 \rangle}{\langle p_0, p_0 \rangle} p_0(x).$$

The required constants are

$$\langle p_1, x^2 \rangle = \int_0^1 (x^3 - x^2/2)\, dx = 1/12$$

$$\langle p_1, p_1 \rangle = \int_0^1 (x^2 - x + 1/4)\, dx = 1/12$$

$$\langle p_0, x^2 \rangle = \int_0^1 x^2\, dx = 1/3$$

$$\langle p_0, p_0 \rangle = \int_0^1 dx = 1.$$

Therefore, $p_2(x) = x^2 - p_1(x) - p_0(x)/3 = x^2 - x + 1/6$, and $\{p_0, p_1, p_2\}$ is an orthogonal basis for $\mathcal{P}_2$ with respect to the inner product. ∎

EXAMPLE 5    Let $B = \{p_0, p_1, p_2\}$ be the orthogonal basis for $\mathcal{P}_2$ obtained in Example 4. Find the coordinates of $x^2$ relative to $B$.

*Solution*    By Theorem 10, $x^2 = a_0 p_0(x) + a_1 p_1(x) + a_2 p_2(x)$, where

$$a_0 = \langle p_0, x^2 \rangle / \langle p_0, p_0 \rangle$$
$$a_1 = \langle p_1, x^2 \rangle / \langle p_1, p_1 \rangle$$
$$a_2 = \langle p_2, x^2 \rangle / \langle p_2, p_2 \rangle.$$

The necessary calculations are

$$\langle p_0, x^2 \rangle = \int_0^1 x^2\, dx = 1/3$$

$$\langle p_1, x^2 \rangle = \int_0^1 [x^3 - (1/2)x^2]\, dx = 1/12$$

$$\langle p_2, x^2 \rangle = \int_0^1 [x^4 - x^3 + (1/6)x^2]\, dx = 1/180$$

$$\langle p_0, p_0 \rangle = \int_0^1 dx = 1$$

$$\langle p_1, p_1 \rangle = \int_0^1 [x^2 - x + 1/4]\, dx = 1/12$$

$$\langle p_2, p_2 \rangle = \int_0^1 [x^2 - x + 1/6]^2\, dx = 1/180.$$

Thus $a_0 = 1/3$, $a_1 = 1$, and $a_2 = 1$. We can easily check that $x^2 = (1/3)p_0(x) + p_1(x) + p_2(x)$. ∎

## Orthogonal Projections

We return now to the previously discussed problem of finding a polynomial $p^*$ in $\mathcal{P}_2$ that is the best approximation of a function $f$ in $C[0, 1]$. Note that the problem amounts to determining a vector $p^*$ in a subspace of an inner-product space, where $p^*$ is closer to $f$ than any other vector in the subspace. The essential aspects of this problem can be stated formally as the following general problem:

Let $V$ be an inner-product space and let $W$ be a subspace of $V$. Given a vector $\mathbf{v}$ in $V$, find a vector $\mathbf{w}^*$ in $W$ such that

$$\|\mathbf{v} - \mathbf{w}^*\| \le \|\mathbf{v} - \mathbf{w}\| \quad \text{for all } \mathbf{w} \text{ in } W. \tag{1}$$

A vector $\mathbf{w}^*$ in $W$ satisfying inequality (1) is called the ***projection of v*** onto $W$, or (frequently) the ***best least-squares approximation*** to $\mathbf{v}$. Intuitively $\mathbf{w}^*$ is the nearest vector in $W$ to $\mathbf{v}$.

The solution process for this problem is almost exactly the same as that for the least-squares problem in $R^n$. One distinction in our general setting is that the subspace $W$ might not be finite dimensional. If $W$ is an infinite-dimensional subspace of $V$, then there may or may not be a projection of $\mathbf{v}$ onto $W$. If $W$ is finite dimensional, then a projection always exists, is unique, and can be found explicitly. The next two theorems outline this concept, and again we leave the proofs to the reader since they parallel the proof of Theorem 18 of Section 3.9.

**THEOREM 12**     Let $V$ be an inner-product space, and let $W$ be a subspace of $V$. Let $\mathbf{v}$ be a vector in $V$, and suppose $\mathbf{w}^*$ is a vector in $W$ such that

$$\langle \mathbf{v} - \mathbf{w}^*, \mathbf{w} \rangle = 0 \quad \text{for all } \mathbf{w} \text{ in } W.$$

Then $\|\mathbf{v} - \mathbf{w}^*\| \le \|\mathbf{v} - \mathbf{w}\|$ for all $\mathbf{w}$ in $W$ with equality holding only for $\mathbf{w} = \mathbf{w}^*$. ∎

**THEOREM 13**     Let $V$ be an inner-product space, and let $\mathbf{v}$ be a vector in $V$. Let $W$ be an $n$-dimensional subspace of $V$, and let $\{\mathbf{u}_1, \mathbf{u}_2, \ldots, \mathbf{u}_n\}$ be an orthogonal basis for $W$. Then

$$\|\mathbf{v} - \mathbf{w}^*\| \le \|\mathbf{v} - \mathbf{w}\| \text{ for all } \mathbf{w} \text{ in } W$$

if and only if

$$\mathbf{w}^* = \frac{\langle \mathbf{v}, \mathbf{u}_1 \rangle}{\langle \mathbf{u}_1, \mathbf{u}_1 \rangle} \mathbf{u}_1 + \frac{\langle \mathbf{v}, \mathbf{u}_2 \rangle}{\langle \mathbf{u}_2, \mathbf{u}_2 \rangle} \mathbf{u}_2 + \cdots + \frac{\langle \mathbf{v}, \mathbf{u}_n \rangle}{\langle \mathbf{u}_n, \mathbf{u}_n \rangle} \mathbf{u}_n. \tag{2}$$

∎

In view of Theorem 13, it follows that when $W$ is a finite-dimensional subspace of an inner-product space $V$, we can always find projections by first finding an orthogonal basis for $W$ (by using Theorem 11) and then calculating the projection $\mathbf{w}^*$ from Eq. (2).

To illustrate the process of finding a projection, we return to the inner-product space $C[0, 1]$ with the subspace $\mathcal{P}_2$. As a specific but rather unrealistic function, $f$, we choose $f(x) = \cos x$, $x$ in radians. The inner product is

$$\langle f, g \rangle = \int_0^1 f(x)g(x)\, dx.$$

| | | EXAMPLE 6    In the vector space $C[0, 1]$, let $f(x) = \cos x$. Find the projection of $f$ onto the subspace $\mathcal{P}_2$.

*Solution*    Let $\{p_0, p_1, p_2\}$ be the orthogonal basis for $\mathcal{P}_2$ found in Example 4. (Note that the inner product used in Example 4 coincides with the present inner product on $C[0, 1]$. By Theorem 13, the projection of $f$ onto $\mathcal{P}_2$ is the polynomial $p^*$ defined by

$$p^*(x) = \frac{\langle f, p_0 \rangle}{\langle p_0, p_0 \rangle} p_0(x) + \frac{\langle f, p_1 \rangle}{\langle p_1, p_1 \rangle} p_1(x) + \frac{\langle f, p_2 \rangle}{\langle p_2, p_2 \rangle} p_2(x),$$

where

$$\langle f, p_0 \rangle = \int_0^1 \cos(x)\, dx \simeq .841471$$

$$\langle f, p_1 \rangle = \int_0^1 (x - 1/2) \cos(x)\, dx \simeq .038962$$

$$\langle f, p_2 \rangle = \int_0^1 (x^2 - x + 1/6) \cos(x)\, dx \simeq -.002394.$$

From Example 5, we have $\langle p_0, p_0 \rangle = 1$, $\langle p_1, p_1 \rangle = 1/12$, and $\langle p_2, p_2 \rangle = 1/180$. Therefore, $p^*(x)$ is given by

$$p^*(x) = \langle f, p_0 \rangle p_0(x) + 12 \langle f, p_1 \rangle p_1(x) + 180 \langle f, p_2 \rangle p_2(x)$$
$$\simeq .841471 p_0(x) - .467544 p_1(x) - .430920 p_2(x).$$

In order to assess how well $p^*(x)$ approximates $\cos x$ in the interval $[0, 1]$, we can tabulate $p^*(x)$ and $\cos x$ at various values of $x$ (see Table 5.1). ∎

| | | EXAMPLE 7    The function $Si(x)$ (important in applications such as optics) is defined as follows:

$$Si(x) = \int_0^x \frac{\sin u}{u}\, du, \quad \text{for } x \neq 0. \tag{3}$$

The integral in (3) is not an elementary one and so, for a given value of $x$, $Si(x)$ must be evaluated using a numerical integration procedure. In this example, we approximate

**Table 5.1**

| $x$ | $p^*(x)$ | $\cos x$ | $p^*(x) - \cos x$ |
|-----|----------|----------|-------------------|
| 0.0 | 1.0034 | 1.000 | .0034 |
| 0.2 | .9789 | .9801 | −.0012 |
| 0.4 | .9198 | .9211 | −.0013 |
| 0.6 | .8263 | .8253 | .0010 |
| 0.8 | .6983 | .6967 | .0016 |
| 1.0 | .5359 | .5403 | −.0044 |

Si($x$) by a cubic polynomial for $0 \leq x \leq 1$. In particular, it can be shown that if we define Si($0$) $= 0$, then Si($x$) is continuous for all $x$. Thus we can ask:

*"What is the projection of Si($x$) onto the subspace $\mathcal{P}_3$ of $C[0, 1]$?"*

This projection will serve as an approximation to Si($x$) for $0 \leq x \leq 1$.

**Solution**   We used the computer algebra system Derive to carry out the calculations. Some of the steps are shown in Fig. 5.6. To begin, let $\{p_0, p_1, p_2, p_3\}$ be the orthogonal basis for $\mathcal{P}_3$ found by the Gram–Schmidt process. From Example 4, we already know that

6: $\quad \displaystyle\int_0^1 x^3 \; \text{P1 (x) dx}$

7: $\quad \dfrac{3}{40}$

8: $\quad \displaystyle\int_0^1 x^3 \; \text{P2 (x) dx}$

9: $\quad \dfrac{1}{120}$

15: $\quad \text{P3 (x)} := x^3 - \dfrac{1}{4} \; \text{P0 (x)} - \dfrac{9}{10} \; \text{P1 (x)} - \dfrac{3}{2} \; \text{P2 (x)}$

16: $\quad \text{P3 (x)} := x^3 - \dfrac{3x^2}{2} + \dfrac{3x}{5} - \dfrac{1}{20}$

17: $\quad \displaystyle\int_0^1 \text{P3 (x) P3 (x) dx}$

18: $\quad \dfrac{1}{2800}$

49: $\quad \displaystyle\int_0^1 180 \; \text{P2 (x)} \displaystyle\int_0^x \dfrac{\text{SIN (u)}}{u} \; \text{du dx}$

50: $\quad -0.0804033$

51: $\quad \displaystyle\int_0^1 2800 \; \text{P3 (x)} \displaystyle\int_0^x \dfrac{\text{SIN (u)}}{u} \; \text{du dx}$

52: $\quad -0.0510442$

*Figure 5.6*   Some of the steps used by Derive to generate the projection of Si($x$) onto $\mathcal{P}_3$ in Example 7

$p_0(x) = 1$, $p_1(x) = x - 1/2$, and $p_2(x) = x^2 - x + 1/6$. To find $p_3$, we first calculate the inner products

$$\langle p_0, x^3 \rangle, \langle p_1, x^3 \rangle, \langle p_2, x^3 \rangle$$

(see steps 6–9 in Fig. 5.6 for $\langle p_1, x^3 \rangle$ and $\langle p_2, x^3 \rangle$).

Using Theorem 11, we find $p_3$ and, for later use, $\langle p_3, p_3 \rangle$:

$$p_3(x) = x^3 - (3/2)x^2 + (3/5)x - 1/20$$
$$\langle p_3, p_3 \rangle = 1/2800$$

(see steps 15–18 in Fig. 5.6). Finally, by Theorem 13, the projection of $Si(x)$ onto $\mathcal{P}_3$ is the polynomial $p^*$ defined by

$$p^*(x) = \frac{\langle Si, p_0 \rangle}{\langle p_0, p_0 \rangle} p_0(x) + \frac{\langle Si, p_1 \rangle}{\langle p_1, p_1 \rangle} p_1(x) + \frac{\langle Si, p_2 \rangle}{\langle p_2, p_2 \rangle} p_2(x) + \frac{\langle Si, p_3 \rangle}{\langle p_3, p_3 \rangle} p_3(x)$$

$$= \langle Si, p_0 \rangle p_0(x) + 12\langle Si, p_1 \rangle p_1(x) + 180\langle Si, p_2 \rangle p_2(x) + 2800\langle Si, p_3 \rangle p_3(x).$$

In the expression above for $p^*$, the inner products $\langle Si, p_k \rangle$ for $k = 0, 1, 2$, and 3 are given by

$$\langle Si, p_k \rangle = \int_0^1 p_k(x)Si(x)\, dx = \int_0^1 p_k(x) \left\{ \int_0^x \frac{\sin u}{u}\, du \right\} dx$$

(see steps 49–52 in Fig. 5.6 for $180\langle Si, p_2 \rangle$ and $2800\langle Si, p_3 \rangle$).

Now, since $Si(x)$ must be estimated numerically, it follows that the inner products $\langle Si, p_k \rangle$ must be estimated as well. Using Derive to approximate the inner products, we obtain the projection (or best least-squares approximation)

$$p^*(x) = .486385 p_0(x) + .951172 p_1(x) - .0804033 p_2(x) - .0510442 p_3(x).$$

To assess how well $p^*(x)$ approximates $Si(x)$ in [0, 1], we tabulate each function at a few selected points (see Table 5.2). As can be seen from Table 5.2, it appears that $p^*(x)$ is a very good approximation to $Si(x)$. ◼

**Table 5.2**

| $x$ | $p^*(x)$ | $Si(x)$ | $p^*(x) - Si(x)$ |
|-----|----------|---------|------------------|
| 0.0 | .000049 | .000000 | .000049 |
| 0.2 | .199578 | .199556 | .000028 |
| 0.4 | .396449 | .396461 | −.000012 |
| 0.6 | .588113 | .588128 | −.000015 |
| 0.8 | .772119 | .772095 | .000024 |
| 1.0 | .946018 | .946083 | −.000065 |

## 5.6     EXERCISES

**1.** Prove that $\langle \mathbf{x}, \mathbf{y} \rangle = 4x_1y_1 + x_2y_2$ is an inner product on $R^2$, where

$$\mathbf{x} = \begin{bmatrix} x_1 \\ x_2 \end{bmatrix} \quad \text{and} \quad \mathbf{y} = \begin{bmatrix} y_1 \\ y_2 \end{bmatrix}.$$

**2.** Prove that $\langle \mathbf{x}, \mathbf{y} \rangle = a_1x_1y_1 + a_2x_2y_2 + \cdots + a_nx_ny_n$ is an inner product on $R^n$, where $a_1, a_2, \ldots, a_n$ are positive real numbers and where

$$\mathbf{x} = [x_1, x_2, \ldots, x_n]^T \quad \text{and}$$
$$\mathbf{y} = [y_1, y_2, \ldots, y_n]^T.$$

**3.** A real $(n \times n)$ symmetric matrix $A$ is called *positive definite* if $\mathbf{x}^T A \mathbf{x} > 0$ for all $\mathbf{x}$ in $R^n$, $\mathbf{x} \neq \theta$. Let $A$ be a symmetric positive-definite matrix, and verify that

$$\langle \mathbf{x}, \mathbf{y} \rangle = \mathbf{x}^T A \mathbf{y}$$

defines an inner product on $R^n$; that is, verify that the four properties of Definition 7 are satisfied.

**4.** Prove that the following symmetric matrix $A$ is positive definite. Prove this by choosing an arbitrary vector $\mathbf{x}$ in $R^2$, $\mathbf{x} \neq \theta$, and calculating $\mathbf{x}^T A \mathbf{x}$.

$$A = \begin{bmatrix} 1 & 1 \\ 1 & 2 \end{bmatrix}$$

**5.** In $P_2$ let $p(x) = a_0 + a_1x + a_2x^2$ and $q(x) = b_0 + b_1x + b_2x^2$. Prove that $\langle p, q \rangle = a_0b_0 + a_1b_1 + a_2b_2$ is an inner product on $P_2$.

**6.** Prove that $\langle p, q \rangle = p(0)q(0) + p(1)q(1) + p(2)q(2)$ is an inner product on $P_2$.

**7.** Let $A = (a_{ij})$ and $B = (b_{ij})$ be $(2 \times 2)$ matrices. Show that $\langle A, B \rangle = a_{11}b_{11} + a_{12}b_{12} + a_{21}b_{21} + a_{22}b_{22}$ is an inner product for the vector space of all $(2 \times 2)$ matrices.

**8.** For $\mathbf{x} = [1, -2]^T$ and $\mathbf{y} = [0, 1]^T$ in $R^2$, find $\langle \mathbf{x}, \mathbf{y} \rangle$, $\|\mathbf{x}\|$, $\|\mathbf{y}\|$, and $\|\mathbf{x} - \mathbf{y}\|$ using the inner product given in Exercise 1.

**9.** Repeat Exercise 8 with the inner product defined in Exercise 3 and the matrix $A$ given in Exercise 4.

**10.** In $P_2$ let $p(x) = -1 + 2x + x^2$ and $q(x) = 1 - x + 2x^2$. Using the inner product given in Exercise 5, find $\langle p, q \rangle$, $\|p\|$, $\|q\|$, and $\|p - q\|$.

**11.** Repeat Exercise 10 using the inner product defined in Exercise 6.

**12.** Show that $\{1, x, x^2\}$ is an orthogonal basis for $P_2$ with the inner product defined in Exercise 5 but not with the inner product in Exercise 6.

**13.** In $R^2$ let $S = \{\mathbf{x} : \|\mathbf{x}\| = 1\}$. Sketch a graph of $S$ if $\langle \mathbf{x}, \mathbf{y} \rangle = \mathbf{x}^T \mathbf{y}$. Now graph $S$ using the inner product given in Exercise 1.

**14.** Let $A$ be the matrix given in Exercise 4, and for $\mathbf{x}, \mathbf{y}$ in $R^2$ define $\langle \mathbf{x}, \mathbf{y} \rangle = \mathbf{x}^T A \mathbf{y}$ (see Exercise 3). Starting with the natural basis $\{\mathbf{e}_1, \mathbf{e}_2\}$, use Theorem 11 to obtain an orthogonal basis $\{\mathbf{u}_1, \mathbf{u}_2\}$ for $R^2$.

**15.** Let $\{\mathbf{u}_1, \mathbf{u}_2\}$ be the orthogonal basis for $R^2$ obtained in Exercise 14 and let $\mathbf{v} = [3, 4]^T$. Use Theorem 10 to find scalars $a_1, a_2$ such that $\mathbf{v} = a_1\mathbf{u}_1 + a_2\mathbf{u}_2$.

**16.** Use Theorem 11 to calculate an orthogonal basis $\{p_0, p_1, p_2\}$ for $P_2$ with respect to the inner product in Exercise 6. Start with the natural basis $\{1, x, x^2\}$ for $P_2$.

**17.** Use Theorem 10 to write $q(x) = 2 + 3x - 4x^2$ in terms of the orthogonal basis $\{p_0, p_1, p_2\}$ obtained in Exercise 16.

**18.** Show that the function defined in Exercise 6 is not an inner product for $P_3$. [*Hint:* Find $p(x)$ in $P_3$ such that $\langle p, p \rangle = 0$, but $p \neq \theta$.]

**19.** Starting with the natural basis $\{1, x, x^2, x^3, x^4\}$, generate an orthogonal basis for $P_4$ with respect to the inner product

$$\langle p, q \rangle = \sum_{i=-2}^{2} p(i)q(i).$$

**20.** If $V$ is an inner-product space, show that $\langle \mathbf{v}, \theta \rangle = 0$ for each vector $\mathbf{v}$ in $V$.

**21.** Let $V$ be an inner-product space, and let $\mathbf{u}$ be a vector in $V$ such that $\langle \mathbf{u}, \mathbf{v} \rangle = 0$ for every vector $\mathbf{v}$ in $V$. Show that $\mathbf{u} = \theta$.

**22.** Let $a$ be a scalar and $\mathbf{v}$ a vector in an inner-product space $V$. Prove that $\|a\mathbf{v}\| = |a|\|\mathbf{v}\|$.

**23.** Prove that if $\{\mathbf{v}_1, \mathbf{v}_2, \ldots, \mathbf{v}_k\}$ is an orthogonal set of nonzero vectors in an inner-product space, then this set is linearly independent.

**24.** Prove Theorem 10.

**25.** Approximate $x^3$ with a polynomial in $\mathcal{P}_2$. [*Hint:* Use the inner product

$$\langle p, q \rangle = \int_0^1 p(t)q(t)\, dt,$$

and let $\{p_0, p_1, p_2\}$ be the orthogonal basis for $\mathcal{P}_2$ obtained in Example 4. Now apply Theorem 13.]

**26.** In Examples 4 and 7 we found $p_0(x), \ldots, p_3(x)$, which are orthogonal with respect to

$$\langle f, g \rangle = \int_0^1 f(x)g(x)\, dx.$$

Continue the process, and find $p_4(x)$ so that $\{p_0, p_1, \ldots, p_4\}$ is an orthogonal basis for $\mathcal{P}_4$. (Clearly there is an infinite sequence of polynomials $p_0, p_1, \ldots, p_n, \ldots$ that satisfy

$$\int_0^1 p_i(x)p_j(x)\, dx = 0, \quad i \neq j.$$

These are called the ***Legendre polynomials***.)

**27.** With the orthogonal basis for $\mathcal{P}_3$ obtained in Example 7, use Theorem 13 to find the projection of $f(x) = \cos x$ in $\mathcal{P}_3$. Construct a table similar to Table 5.1 and note the improvement.

**28.** An inner product on $C[-1, 1]$ is

$$\langle f, g \rangle = \frac{2}{\pi} \int_{-1}^{1} \frac{f(x)g(x)}{\sqrt{1 - x^2}}\, dx.$$

Starting with the set $\{1, x, x^2, x^3, \ldots\}$, use the Gram–Schmidt process to find polynomials $T_0(x)$, $T_1(x)$, $T_2(x)$, and $T_3(x)$ such that $\langle T_i, T_j \rangle = 0$ when $i \neq j$. These polynomials are called the ***Chebyshev polynomials of the first kind***. [*Hint:* Make a change of variables $x = \cos\theta$.]

**29.** A sequence of orthogonal polynomials usually satisfies a three-term recurrence relation. For example, the Chebyshev polynomials are related by

$$T_{n+1}(x) = 2xT_n(x) - T_{n-1}(x), \quad n = 1, 2, \ldots,$$
$$\text{(R)}$$

where $T_0(x) = 1$ and $T_1(x) = x$. Verify that the polynomials defined by the relation (R) above are indeed orthogonal in $C[-1, 1]$ with respect to the inner product in Exercise 28. Verify this as follows:

**a)** Make the change of variables $x = \cos\theta$, and use induction to show that $T_k(\cos\theta) = \cos k\theta$, $k = 0, 1, \ldots$, where $T_k(x)$ is defined by (R).

**b)** Using part a), show that $\langle T_i, T_j \rangle = 0$ when $i \neq j$.

**c)** Use induction to show that $T_k(x)$ is a polynomial of degree $k$, $k = 0, 1, \ldots$.

**d)** Use (R) to calculate $T_2, T_3, T_4$, and $T_5$.

**30.** Let $C[-1, 1]$ have the inner product of Exercise 28, and let $f$ be in $C[-1, 1]$. Use Theorem 13 to prove that $\| f - p^* \| \leq \| f - p \|$ for all $p$ in $\mathcal{P}_n$ if

$$p^*(x) = \frac{a_0}{2} + \sum_{j=1}^{n} a_j T_j(x),$$

where $a_j = \langle f, T_j \rangle$, $j = 0, 1, \ldots, n$.

**31.** The iterated trapezoid rule provides a good estimate of $\int_a^b f(x)\, dx$ when $f(x)$ is periodic in $[a, b]$. In particular, let $N$ be a positive integer, and let $h = (b - a)/N$. Next, define $x_i$ by $x_i = a + ih$, $i = 0, 1, \ldots, N$, and suppose $f(x)$ is in $C[a, b]$. If we define $A(f)$ by

$$A(f) = \frac{h}{2} f(x_0) + h \sum_{j=1}^{N-1} f(x_j) + \frac{h}{2} f(x_N),$$

then $A(f)$ is the iterated trapezoid rule applied to $f(x)$. Using the result in Exercise 30, write a computer program that generates a good approximation to $f(x)$ in $C[-1, 1]$. That is, for an input function $f(x)$ and a specified value of $n$, calculate estimates of $a_0, a_1, \ldots, a_n$, where

$$a_k = \langle f, T_k \rangle \simeq A(fT_k).$$

To do this calculation, make the usual change of variables $x = \cos\theta$ so that

$$a_k = \frac{2}{\pi} \int_0^\pi f(\cos\theta) \cos(k\theta)d\theta, \quad k = 0, 1, \ldots, n.$$

Use the iterated trapezoid rule to estimate each $a_k$. Test your program on $f(x) = e^{2x}$ and note that (R) can be used to evaluate $p^*(x)$ at any point $x$ in $[-1, 1]$.

**32.** Show that if $A$ is a real $(n \times n)$ matrix and if the expression $\langle \mathbf{u}, \mathbf{v} \rangle = \mathbf{u}^T A \mathbf{v}$ defines an inner product on $R^n$, then $A$ must be symmetric and positive definite (see Exercise 3 for the definition of positive definite). [*Hint:* Consider $\langle \mathbf{e}_i, \mathbf{e}_j \rangle$.]

## LINEAR TRANSFORMATIONS

Linear transformations on subspaces of $R^n$ were introduced in Section 3.7. The definition given there extends naturally to the general vector-space setting. In this section and the next, we develop the basic properties of linear transformations, and in Section 5.8 we will use linear transformations and the concept of coordinate vectors to show that an $n$-dimensional vector space is essentially just $R^n$.

If $T: R^n \to R^m$ is a linear transformation, there exists an $(m \times n)$ matrix $A$ such that $T(\mathbf{x}) = A\mathbf{x}$. Although this is not the case in the general vector-space setting, we will show in Section 5.9 that there is still a close relationship between linear transformations and matrices, provided that the domain space is finite dimensional.

We begin with the definition of a linear transformation.

| DEFINITION 8 | Let $U$ and $V$ be vector spaces, and let $T$ be a function from $U$ to $V$, $T: U \to V$. We say that $T$ is a **linear transformation** if for all $\mathbf{u}$ and $\mathbf{w}$ in $U$ and all scalars $a$ $$T(\mathbf{u} + \mathbf{w}) = T(\mathbf{u}) + T(\mathbf{w})$$ and $$T(a\mathbf{u}) = aT(\mathbf{u}).$$ |
| --- | --- |

### Examples of Linear Transformations

To illustrate Definition 8, we now provide several examples of linear transformations.

**EXAMPLE 1**    Let $T: \mathcal{P}_2 \to R^1$ be defined by $T(p) = p(2)$. Verify that $T$ is a linear transformation.

**Solution**    First note that $R^1$ is just the set $R$ of real numbers, but in this context $R$ is regarded as a vector space. To illustrate the definition of $T$, if $p(x) = x^2 - 3x + 1$, then $T(p) = p(2) = -1$.

To verify that $T$ is a linear transformation, let $p(x)$ and $q(x)$ be in $\mathcal{P}_2$ and let $a$ be a scalar. Then $T(p + q) = (p + q)(2) = p(2) + q(2) = T(p) + T(q)$. Likewise, $T(ap) = (ap)(2) = ap(2) = aT(p)$. Thus $T$ is a linear transformation.    ■

In general, if $W$ is any subspace of $C[a, b]$ and if $x_0$ is any number in $[a, b]$, then the function $T: W \to R^1$ defined by $T(f) = f(x_0)$ is a linear transformation.

**EXAMPLE 2**    Let $V$ be a $p$-dimensional vector space with basis $B = \{\mathbf{v}_1, \mathbf{v}_2, \ldots, \mathbf{v}_p\}$. Show that $T: V \to R^p$ defined by $T(\mathbf{v}) = [\mathbf{v}]_B$ is a linear transformation.

**Solution**    That $T$ is a linear transformation is a direct consequence of the lemma in Section 5.4. Specifically, if $\mathbf{u}$ and $\mathbf{v}$ are vectors in $V$, then $T(\mathbf{u} + \mathbf{v}) = [\mathbf{u} + \mathbf{v}]_B = [\mathbf{u}]_B + [\mathbf{v}]_B = T(\mathbf{u}) + T(\mathbf{v})$. Also, if $a$ is a scalar, then $T(a\mathbf{u}) = [a\mathbf{u}]_B = a[\mathbf{u}]_B = aT(\mathbf{u})$.    ■

| | | EXAMPLE 3     Let $T: C[0, 1] \to R^1$ be defined by

$$T(f) = \int_0^1 f(t)\, dt.$$

Prove that $T$ is a linear transformation.

*Solution*     If $f(x)$ and $g(x)$ are functions in $C[0, 1]$, then

$$T(f + g) = \int_0^1 [f(t) + g(t)]\, dt$$

$$= \int_0^1 f(t)\, dt + \int_0^1 g(t)\, dt$$

$$= T(f) + T(g).$$

Likewise, if $a$ is a scalar, the properties of integration give

$$T(af) = \int_0^1 af(t)\, dt$$

$$= a \int_0^1 f(t)\, dt$$

$$= aT(f).$$

Therefore, $T$ is a linear transformation.                                          ◼

| | | EXAMPLE 4     Let $C^1[0, 1]$ denote the set of all functions that have a continuous first derivative in the interval $[0, 1]$. (Note that $C^1[0, 1]$ is a subspace of $C[0, 1]$.) Let $k(x)$ be a fixed function in $C[0, 1]$ and define $T: C^1[0, 1] \to C[0, 1]$ by

$$T(f) = f' + kf.$$

Verify that $T$ is a linear transformation.

*Solution*     To illustrate the definition of $T$, suppose, for example, that $k(x) = x^2$. If $f(x) = \sin x$, then $T(f)$ is the function defined by $T(f)(x) = f'(x) + k(x)f(x) = \cos x + x^2 \sin x$.
To see that $T$ is a linear transformation, let $g$ and $h$ be functions in $C^1[0, 1]$. Then

$$T(g + h) = (g + h)' + k(g + h)$$

$$= g' + h' + kg + kh$$

$$= (g' + kg) + (h' + kh)$$

$$= T(g) + T(h).$$

Also, for a scalar $c$, $T(cg) = (cg)' + k(cg) = c(g' + kg) = cT(g)$. Hence $T$ is a linear transformation.                                          ◼

The linear transformation in Example 4 is an example of a differential operator. We will return to differential operators later and only mention here that the term *operator* is traditional in the study of differential equations. Operator is another term for function or transformation, and we could equally well speak of $T$ as a differential transformation.

For any vector space $V$, the mapping $I: V \to V$ defined by $I(\mathbf{v}) = \mathbf{v}$ is a linear transformation called the *identity transformation*. Between any two vector spaces $U$ and $V$, there is always at least one linear transformation, called the *zero transformation*. If $\boldsymbol{\theta}_V$ is the zero vector in $V$, then the zero transformation $T: U \to V$ is defined by $T(\mathbf{u}) = \boldsymbol{\theta}_V$ for all $\mathbf{u}$ in $U$.

## Properties of Linear Transformations

One of the important features of the two linearity properties in Definition 8 is that if $T: U \to V$ is a linear transformation and if $U$ is a finite-dimensional vector space, then the action of $T$ on $U$ is completely determined by the action of $T$ on a basis for $U$. To see why this statement is true, suppose $U$ has a basis $B = \{\mathbf{u}_1, \mathbf{u}_2, \ldots, \mathbf{u}_p\}$. Then given any $\mathbf{u}$ in $U$, we know that $\mathbf{u}$ can be expressed uniquely as

$$\mathbf{u} = a_1\mathbf{u}_1 + a_2\mathbf{u}_2 + \cdots + a_p\mathbf{u}_p.$$

From this expression it follows that $T(\mathbf{u})$ is given by

$$\begin{aligned}
T(\mathbf{u}) &= T(a_1\mathbf{u}_1 + a_2\mathbf{u}_2 + \cdots + a_p\mathbf{u}_p) \\
&= a_1T(\mathbf{u}_1) + a_2T(\mathbf{u}_2) + \cdots + a_pT(\mathbf{u}_p).
\end{aligned} \tag{1}$$

Clearly Eq. (1) shows that if we know the vectors $T(\mathbf{u}_1), T(\mathbf{u}_2), \ldots, T(\mathbf{u}_p)$, then we know $T(\mathbf{u})$ for any $\mathbf{u}$ in $U$; $T$ is completely determined once $T$ is defined on the basis. The next example illustrates this concept.

EXAMPLE 5   Let $T: \mathcal{P}_3 \to \mathcal{P}_2$ be a linear transformation such that $T(1) = 1 - x$, $T(x) = x + x^2$, $T(x^2) = 1 + 2x$, and $T(x^3) = 2 - x^2$. Find $T(2 - 3x + x^2 - 2x^3)$.

**Solution**   Applying Eq. (1) yields

$$\begin{aligned}
T(2 - 3x + x^2 - 2x^3) &= 2T(1) - 3T(x) + T(x^2) - 2T(x^3) \\
&= 2(1 - x) - 3(x + x^2) + (1 + 2x) - 2(2 - x^2) \\
&= -1 - 3x - x^2.
\end{aligned}$$

Similarly,

$$\begin{aligned}
T(a_0 &+ a_1x + a_2x^2 + a_3x^3) \\
&= a_0T(1) + a_1T(x) + a_2T(x^2) + a_3T(x^3) \\
&= a_0(1 - x) + a_1(x + x^2) + a_2(1 + 2x) + a_3(2 - x^2) \\
&= (a_0 + a_2 + 2a_3) + (-a_0 + a_1 + 2a_2)x + (a_1 - a_3)x^2.
\end{aligned}$$

Before giving further properties of linear transformations, we require several definitions. Let $T: U \to V$ be a linear transformation, and for clarity let us denote the zero vectors in $U$ and $V$ as $\boldsymbol{\theta}_U$ and $\boldsymbol{\theta}_V$, respectively. The *null space* (or *kernel*) of $T$, denoted by $\mathcal{N}(T)$, is the subset of $U$ defined by

$$\mathcal{N}(T) = \{\mathbf{u} \text{ in } U: T(\mathbf{u}) = \boldsymbol{\theta}_V\}.$$

The *range* of $T$, denoted by $\mathcal{R}(T)$, is the subset of $V$ defined by

$$\mathcal{R}(T) = \{\mathbf{v} \text{ in } V: \mathbf{v} = T(\mathbf{u}) \text{ for some } \mathbf{u} \text{ in } U\}.$$

As before, the dimension of $\mathcal{N}(T)$ is called the **nullity** of $T$ and is denoted by nullity($T$). Likewise, the dimension of $\mathcal{R}(T)$ is called the **rank** of $T$ and is denoted by rank($T$). Finally, we say a linear transformation is **one to one** if $T(\mathbf{u}) = T(\mathbf{w})$ implies $\mathbf{u} = \mathbf{w}$ for all $\mathbf{u}$ and $\mathbf{w}$ in $U$. Some of the elementary properties of linear transformations are given in the next theorem.

**THEOREM 14**    Let $T: U \rightarrow V$ be a linear transformation. Then:

    **1.** $T(\boldsymbol{\theta}_U) = \boldsymbol{\theta}_V$.

    **2.** $\mathcal{N}(T)$ is a subspace of $U$.

    **3.** $\mathcal{R}(T)$ is a subspace of $V$.

    **4.** $T$ is one to one if and only if $\mathcal{N}(T) = \{\boldsymbol{\theta}_U\}$; that is, $T$ is one to one if and only if nullity($T$) $= 0$.

**Proof**    To prove property 1, note that $0\boldsymbol{\theta}_U = \boldsymbol{\theta}_U$, so

$$T(\boldsymbol{\theta}_U) = T(0\boldsymbol{\theta}_U) = 0T(\boldsymbol{\theta}_U) = \boldsymbol{\theta}_V.$$

To prove property 2, we must verify that $\mathcal{N}(T)$ satisfies the three properties of Theorem 2 in Section 5.3. It follows from property 1 that $\boldsymbol{\theta}_U$ is in $\mathcal{N}(T)$. Next, let $\mathbf{u}_1$ and $\mathbf{u}_2$ be in $\mathcal{N}(T)$ and let $a$ be a scalar. Then $T(\mathbf{u}_1 + \mathbf{u}_2) = T(\mathbf{u}_1) + T(\mathbf{u}_2) = \boldsymbol{\theta}_V + \boldsymbol{\theta}_V = \boldsymbol{\theta}_V$, so $\mathbf{u}_1 + \mathbf{u}_2$ is in $\mathcal{N}(T)$. Similarly, $T(a\mathbf{u}_1) = aT(\mathbf{u}_1) = a\boldsymbol{\theta}_V = \boldsymbol{\theta}_V$, so $a\mathbf{u}_1$ is in $\mathcal{N}(T)$. Therefore, $\mathcal{N}(T)$ is a subspace of $U$.

The proof of property 3 is left as an exercise. To prove property 4, suppose that $\mathcal{N}(T) = \{\boldsymbol{\theta}_U\}$. In order to show that $T$ is one to one, let $\mathbf{u}$ and $\mathbf{w}$ be vectors in $U$ such that $T(\mathbf{u}) = T(\mathbf{w})$. Then $\boldsymbol{\theta}_V = T(\mathbf{u}) - T(\mathbf{w}) = T(\mathbf{u}) + (-1)T(\mathbf{w}) = T[\mathbf{u} + (-1)\mathbf{w}] = T(\mathbf{u} - \mathbf{w})$. It follows that $\mathbf{u} - \mathbf{w}$ is in $\mathcal{N}(T)$. But $\mathcal{N}(T) = \{\boldsymbol{\theta}_U\}$, so $\mathbf{u} - \mathbf{w} = \boldsymbol{\theta}_U$. Therefore, $\mathbf{u} = \mathbf{w}$ and $T$ is one to one. The converse is Exercise 24.    ∎

When $T: R^n \rightarrow R^m$ is given by $T(\mathbf{x}) = A\mathbf{x}$, with $A$ an $(m \times n)$ matrix, then $\mathcal{N}(T)$ is the null space of $A$ and $\mathcal{R}(T)$ is the range of $A$. In this setting, property 4 of Theorem 14 states that a consistent system of equations $A\mathbf{x} = \mathbf{b}$ has a unique solution if and only if the trivial solution is the unique solution for the homogeneous system $A\mathbf{x} = \boldsymbol{\theta}$.

The following theorem gives additional properties of a linear transformation $T: U \rightarrow V$, where $U$ is a finite-dimensional vector space.

**THEOREM 15**    Let $T: U \rightarrow V$ be a linear transformation and let $U$ be $p$-dimensional, where $B = \{\mathbf{u}_1, \mathbf{u}_2, \ldots, \mathbf{u}_p\}$ is a basis for $U$.

    **1.** $\mathcal{R}(T) = \text{Sp}\{T(\mathbf{u}_1), T(\mathbf{u}_2), \ldots, T(\mathbf{u}_p)\}$.

    **2.** $T$ is one to one if and only if $\{T(\mathbf{u}_1), T(\mathbf{u}_2), \ldots, T(\mathbf{u}_p)\}$ is linearly independent in $V$.

    **3.** rank($T$) $+$ nullity($T$) $= p$.

**Proof**    Property 1 is immediate from Eq. (1). That is, if $\mathbf{v}$ is in $\mathcal{R}(T)$, then $\mathbf{v} = T(\mathbf{u})$ for some $\mathbf{u}$ in $U$. But $B$ is a basis for $U$; so $\mathbf{u}$ is of the form $\mathbf{u} = a_1\mathbf{u}_1 + a_2\mathbf{u}_2 + \cdots + a_p\mathbf{u}_p$; and hence $T(\mathbf{u}) = \mathbf{v} = a_1T(\mathbf{u}_1) + a_2T(\mathbf{u}_2) + \cdots + a_pT(\mathbf{u}_p)$. Therefore, $\mathbf{v}$ is in $\text{Sp}\{T(\mathbf{u}_1), T(\mathbf{u}_2), \ldots, T(\mathbf{u}_p)\}$.

To prove property 2, we can use property 4 of Theorem 14; $T$ is one to one if and only if $\boldsymbol{\theta}_U$ is the only vector in $\mathcal{N}(T)$. In particular, let us suppose that $\mathbf{u}$ is some vector in $\mathcal{N}(T)$, where $\mathbf{u} = b_1\mathbf{u}_1 + b_2\mathbf{u}_2 + \cdots + b_p\mathbf{u}_p$. Then $T(\mathbf{u}) = \boldsymbol{\theta}_V$, or

$$b_1 T(\mathbf{u}_1) + b_2 T(\mathbf{u}_2) + \cdots + b_p T(\mathbf{u}_p) = \boldsymbol{\theta}_V. \tag{2}$$

If $\{T(\mathbf{u}_1), T(\mathbf{u}_2), \ldots, T(\mathbf{u}_p)\}$ is a linearly independent set in $V$, then the only scalars satisfying Eq. (2) are $b_1 = b_2 = \cdots = b_p = 0$. Therefore, $\mathbf{u}$ must be $\boldsymbol{\theta}_U$; so $T$ is one to one. On the other hand, if $T$ is one to one, then there cannot be a nontrivial solution to Eq. (2); for if there were, $\mathcal{N}(T)$ would contain the nonzero vector $\mathbf{u}$.

To prove property 3, we first note that $0 \leq \operatorname{rank}(T) \leq p$ by property 1. We leave the two extreme cases, $\operatorname{rank}(T) = p$ and $\operatorname{rank}(T) = 0$, to the exercises and consider only $0 < \operatorname{rank}(T) < p$. [Note that $\operatorname{rank}(T) < p$ implies that $\operatorname{nullity}(T) \geq 1$, so $T$ is not one to one. We mention this point because we will need to choose a basis for $\mathcal{N}(T)$ below.]

It is conventional to let $r$ denote $\operatorname{rank}(T)$, so let us suppose $\mathcal{R}(T)$ has a basis of $r$ vectors, $\{\mathbf{v}_1, \mathbf{v}_2, \ldots, \mathbf{v}_r\}$. From the definition of $\mathcal{R}(T)$, we know there are vectors $\mathbf{w}_1, \mathbf{w}_2, \ldots, \mathbf{w}_r$, in $U$ such that

$$T(\mathbf{w}_i) = \mathbf{v}_i, \quad 1 \leq i \leq r. \tag{3}$$

Now suppose that $\operatorname{nullity}(T) = k$ and let $\{\mathbf{x}_1, \mathbf{x}_2, \ldots, \mathbf{x}_k\}$ be a basis for $\mathcal{N}(T)$. We now show that the set

$$Q = \{\mathbf{x}_1, \mathbf{x}_2, \ldots, \mathbf{x}_k, \mathbf{w}_1, \mathbf{w}_2, \ldots, \mathbf{w}_r\}$$

is a basis for $U$ (therefore, $k + r = p$, which proves property 3).

We first establish that $Q$ is a linearly independent set in $U$ by considering

$$c_1\mathbf{x}_1 + c_2\mathbf{x}_2 + \cdots + c_k\mathbf{x}_k + a_1\mathbf{w}_1 + a_2\mathbf{w}_2 + \cdots + a_r\mathbf{w}_r = \boldsymbol{\theta}_U. \tag{4}$$

Applying $T$ to both sides of Eq. (4) yields

$$T(c_1\mathbf{x}_1 + \cdots + c_k\mathbf{x}_k + a_1\mathbf{w}_1 + \cdots + a_r\mathbf{w}_r) = T(\boldsymbol{\theta}_U). \tag{5a}$$

Using Eq. (1) and property 1 of Theorem 14, Eq. (5a) becomes

$$c_1 T(\mathbf{x}_1) + \cdots + c_k T(\mathbf{x}_k) + a_1 T(\mathbf{w}_1) + \cdots + a_r T(\mathbf{w}_r) = \boldsymbol{\theta}_V. \tag{5b}$$

Since each $\mathbf{x}_i$ is in $\mathcal{N}(T)$ and $T(\mathbf{w}_i) = \mathbf{v}_i$, Eq. (5b) becomes

$$a_1\mathbf{v}_1 + a_2\mathbf{v}_2 + \cdots + a_r\mathbf{v}_r = \boldsymbol{\theta}_V. \tag{5c}$$

Since the set $\{\mathbf{v}_1, \mathbf{v}_2, \ldots, \mathbf{v}_r\}$ is linearly independent, $a_1 = a_2 = \cdots = a_r = 0$. The vector equation (4) now becomes

$$c_1\mathbf{x}_1 + c_2\mathbf{x}_2 + \cdots + c_k\mathbf{x}_k = \boldsymbol{\theta}_U. \tag{6}$$

But $\{\mathbf{x}_1, \mathbf{x}_2, \ldots, \mathbf{x}_k\}$ is a linearly independent set in $U$, so we must have $c_1 = c_2 = \cdots = c_k = 0$. Therefore, $Q$ is a linearly independent set.

To complete the argument, we need to show that $Q$ is a spanning set for $U$. So let $\mathbf{u}$ be any vector in $U$. Then $\mathbf{v} = T(\mathbf{u})$ is a vector in $\mathcal{R}(T)$; so

$$T(\mathbf{u}) = b_1\mathbf{v}_1 + b_2\mathbf{v}_2 + \cdots + b_r\mathbf{v}_r.$$

Consider an associated vector $\mathbf{x}$ in $U$, where $\mathbf{x}$ is defined by

$$\mathbf{x} = b_1 \mathbf{w}_1 + b_2 \mathbf{w}_2 + \cdots + b_r \mathbf{w}_r. \tag{7}$$

We observe that $T(\mathbf{u} - \mathbf{x}) = \boldsymbol{\theta}_V$; so obviously $\mathbf{u} - \mathbf{x}$ is in $\mathcal{N}(T)$ and can be written as

$$\mathbf{u} - \mathbf{x} = d_1 \mathbf{x}_1 + d_2 \mathbf{x}_2 + \cdots + d_k \mathbf{x}_k. \tag{8}$$

Placing $\mathbf{x}$ on the right-hand side of Eq. (8) and using Eq. (7), we have shown that $\mathbf{u}$ is a linear combination of vectors in $Q$. Thus $Q$ is a basis for $U$, and property 3 is proved since $k + r$ must equal $p$.    ∎

As the following example illustrates, property 1 of Theorem 15 and the techniques of Section 5.4 give a method for obtaining a basis for $\mathcal{R}(T)$.

**EXAMPLE 6**    Let $V$ be the vector space of all $(2 \times 2)$ matrices, and let $T: \mathcal{P}_3 \to V$ be the linear transformation defined by

$$T(a_0 + a_1 x + a_2 x^2 + a_3 x^3) = \begin{bmatrix} a_0 + a_2 & a_0 + a_3 \\ a_1 + a_2 & a_1 + a_3 \end{bmatrix}.$$

Find a basis for $\mathcal{R}(T)$ and determine $\text{rank}(T)$ and $\text{nullity}(T)$. Finally, show that $T$ is not one to one.

*Solution*    By property 1 of Theorem 15, $\mathcal{R}(T) = \text{Sp}\{T(1), T(x), T(x^2), T(x^3)\}$. Thus $\mathcal{R}(T) = \text{Sp}(S)$, where $S = \{A_1, A_2, A_3, A_4\}$ and

$$A_1 = \begin{bmatrix} 1 & 1 \\ 0 & 0 \end{bmatrix}, \quad A_2 = \begin{bmatrix} 0 & 0 \\ 1 & 1 \end{bmatrix}, \quad A_3 = \begin{bmatrix} 1 & 0 \\ 1 & 0 \end{bmatrix}, \quad \text{and} \quad A_4 = \begin{bmatrix} 0 & 1 \\ 0 & 1 \end{bmatrix}.$$

Let $B$ be the natural basis for $V$: $B = \{E_{11}, E_{12}, E_{21}, E_{22}\}$. Form the $(4 \times 4)$ matrix $C$ with column vectors $[A_1]_B, [A_2]_B, [A_3]_B, [A_4]_B$; thus

$$C = \begin{bmatrix} 1 & 0 & 1 & 0 \\ 1 & 0 & 0 & 1 \\ 0 & 1 & 1 & 0 \\ 0 & 1 & 0 & 1 \end{bmatrix}.$$

**EMMY NOETHER**    Emmy Noether (1882–1935) is the most heralded female mathematician of the early twentieth century. Overcoming great obstacles for women in mathematics at the time, she received her doctorate from Göttingen and went on to work with David Hilbert and Felix Klein on the general theory of relativity. Among her most highly regarded results are the representation of noncommutative algebras as linear transformations and Noether's Theorem, which is used to explain the correspondences between certain invariants and physical conservation laws. She fled from Germany in 1933 and spent the last two years of her life on the faculty at Bryn Mawr College in Philadelphia.

The matrix $C^T$ reduces to the matrix

$$D^T = \begin{bmatrix} 1 & 1 & 0 & 0 \\ 0 & 1 & 0 & 1 \\ 0 & 0 & 1 & 1 \\ 0 & 0 & 0 & 0 \end{bmatrix}$$

in echelon form. Therefore,

$$D = \begin{bmatrix} 1 & 0 & 0 & 0 \\ 1 & 1 & 0 & 0 \\ 0 & 0 & 1 & 0 \\ 0 & 1 & 1 & 0 \end{bmatrix},$$

and the nonzero columns of $D$ constitute a basis for the subspace $\text{Sp}\{[A_1]_B, [A_2]_B, [A_3]_B, [A_4]_B\}$ of $R^4$. If the matrices $B_1$, $B_2$, and $B_3$ are defined by

$$B_1 = \begin{bmatrix} 1 & 1 \\ 0 & 0 \end{bmatrix}, \qquad B_2 = \begin{bmatrix} 0 & 1 \\ 0 & 1 \end{bmatrix}, \quad \text{and} \quad B_3 = \begin{bmatrix} 0 & 0 \\ 1 & 1 \end{bmatrix},$$

then $[B_1]_B$, $[B_2]_B$, and $[B_3]_B$ are the nonzero columns of $D$. It now follows from Theorem 5 of Section 5.4 that $\{B_1, B_2, B_3\}$ is a basis for $\mathcal{R}(T)$.

By property 3 of Theorem 15,

$$\dim(\mathcal{P}_3) = \text{rank}(T) + \text{nullity}(T).$$

We have just shown that $\text{rank}(T) = 3$. Since $\dim(\mathcal{P}_3) = 4$, it follows that $\text{nullity}(T) = 1$. In particular, $T$ is not one to one by property 4 of Theorem 14. ∎

EXAMPLE 7    Let $T: \mathcal{P}_2 \to R^1$ be defined by $T(p(x)) = p(2)$. Exhibit a basis for $\mathcal{N}(T)$ and determine the rank and nullity of $T$.

**Solution**    By definition, $T(a_0 + a_1 x + a_2 x^2) = a_0 + 2a_1 + 4a_2$. Thus

$$\mathcal{N}(T) = \{p(x): p(x) \text{ is in } \mathcal{P}_2 \text{ and } a_0 + 2a_1 + 4a_2 = 0\}.$$

In the algebraic specification for $\mathcal{N}(T)$, $a_1$ and $a_2$ can be designated as unconstrained variables, and $a_0 = -2a_1 - 4a_2$. Thus $p(x)$ in $\mathcal{N}(T)$ can be decomposed as

$$p(x) = (-2a_1 - 4a_2) + a_1 x + a_2 x^2 = a_1(-2 + x) + a_2(-4 + x^2).$$

It follows that $\{-2 + x, -4 + x^2\}$ is a basis for $\mathcal{N}(T)$. In particular, $\text{nullity}(T) = 2$. Then $\text{rank}(T) = \dim(\mathcal{P}_2) - \text{nullity}(T) = 3 - 2 = 1$. ∎

We have already noted that if $A$ is an $(m \times n)$ matrix and $T: R^n \to R^m$ is defined by $T(\mathbf{x}) = A\mathbf{x}$, then $\mathcal{R}(T) = \mathcal{R}(A)$ and $\mathcal{N}(T) = \mathcal{N}(A)$. The following corollary, given as a remark in Section 3.5, is now an immediate consequence of these observations and property 3 of Theorem 15.

COROLLARY    If $A$ is an $(m \times n)$ matrix, then

$$n = \text{rank}(A) + \text{nullity}(A).$$

## 5.7     EXERCISES

In Exercises 1–4, $V$ is the vector space of all $(2 \times 2)$ matrices and $A$ has the form

$$A = \begin{bmatrix} a & b \\ c & d \end{bmatrix}.$$

Determine whether the function $T: V \to R^1$ is a linear transformation.

**1.** $T(A) = \det(A)$

**2.** $T(A) = a + 2b - c + d$

**3.** $T(A) = \operatorname{tr}(A)$, where $\operatorname{tr}(A)$ denotes the trace of $A$ and is defined by $\operatorname{tr}(A) = a + d$.

**4.** $T(A) = (a - d)(b - c)$

In Exercises 5–8, determine whether $T$ is a linear transformation.

**5.** $T: C^1[-1, 1] \to R^1$ defined by $T(f) = f'(0)$

**6.** $T: C[0, 1] \to C[0, 1]$ defined by $T(f) = g$, where $g(x) = e^x f(x)$

**7.** $T: P_2 \to P_2$ defined by $T(a_0 + a_1 x + a_2 x^2) = (a_0 + 1) + (a_1 + 1)x + (a_2 + 1)x^2$

**8.** $T: P_2 \to P_2$ defined by $T(p(x)) = p(0) + xp'(x)$

**9.** Suppose that $T: P_2 \to P_3$ is a linear transformation, where $T(1) = 1 + x^2$, $T(x) = x^2 - x^3$, and $T(x^2) = 2 + x^3$.

  **a)** Find $T(p)$, where $p(x) = 3 - 2x + 4x^2$.

  **b)** Give a formula for $T$; that is, find

$$T(a_0 + a_1 x + a_2 x^2).$$

**10.** Suppose that $T: P_2 \to P_4$ is a linear transformation, where $T(1) = x^4$, $T(x + 1) = x^3 - 2x$, and $T(x^2 + 2x + 1) = x$. Find $T(p)$ and $T(q)$, where $p(x) = x^2 + 5x - 1$ and $q(x) = x^2 + 9x + 5$.

**11.** Let $V$ be the set of all $(2 \times 2)$ matrices and suppose that $T: V \to P_2$ is a linear transformation such that $T(E_{11}) = 1 - x$, $T(E_{12}) = 1 + x + x^2$, $T(E_{21}) = 2x - x^2$, and $T(E_{22}) = 2 + x - 2x^2$.

  **a)** Find $T(A)$, where

$$A = \begin{bmatrix} -2 & 2 \\ 3 & 4 \end{bmatrix}.$$

  **b)** Give a formula for $T$; that is, find

$$T\left( \begin{bmatrix} a & b \\ c & d \end{bmatrix} \right).$$

**12.** With $V$ as in Exercise 11, define $T: V \to R^2$ by

$$T\left( \begin{bmatrix} a & b \\ c & d \end{bmatrix} \right) = \begin{bmatrix} a + 2d \\ b - c \end{bmatrix}.$$

  **a)** Prove that $T$ is a linear transformation.

  **b)** Give an algebraic specification for $\mathcal{N}(T)$.

  **c)** Exhibit a basis for $\mathcal{N}(T)$.

  **d)** Determine the nullity and the rank of $T$.

  **e)** Without doing any calculations, argue that $\mathcal{R}(T) = R^2$.

  **f)** Prove $\mathcal{R}(T) = R^2$ as follows: Let $\mathbf{v}$ be in $R^2$,

$$\mathbf{v} = \begin{bmatrix} x \\ y \end{bmatrix}.$$

  Exhibit a $(2 \times 2)$ matrix $A$ in $V$ such that $T(A) = \mathbf{v}$.

**13.** Let $T: P_4 \to P_2$ be the linear transformation defined by $T(p) = p''(x)$.

  **a)** Exhibit a basis for $\mathcal{R}(T)$ and conclude that $\mathcal{R}(T) = P_2$.

  **b)** Determine the nullity of $T$ and conclude that $T$ is not one to one.

  **c)** Give a direct proof that $\mathcal{R}(T) = P_2$; that is, for $p(x) = a_0 + a_1 x + a_2 x^2$ in $P_2$, exhibit a polynomial $q(x)$ in $P_4$ such that $T(q) = p$.

**14.** Define $T: P_4 \to P_3$ by

$$T(a_0 + a_1 x + a_2 x^2 + a_3 x^3 + a_4 x^4)$$
$$= (a_0 - a_1 + 2a_2 - a_3 + a_4)$$
$$+ (-a_0 + 3a_1 - 2a_2 + 3a_3 - a_4)x$$
$$+ (2a_0 - 3a_1 + 5a_2 - a_3 + a_4)x^2$$
$$+ (3a_0 - a_1 + 7a_2 + 2a_3 + 2a_4)x^3.$$

Find a basis for $\mathcal{R}(T)$ (see Example 6) and show that $T$ is not one to one.

**15.** Identify $\mathcal{N}(T)$ and $\mathcal{R}(T)$ for the linear transformation $T$ given in Example 1.

**16.** Identify $\mathcal{N}(T)$ and $\mathcal{R}(T)$ for the linear transformation $T$ given in Example 3.

**17.** Let $I: V \to V$ be defined by $I(\mathbf{v}) = \mathbf{v}$ for each $\mathbf{v}$ in $V$.

  **a)** Prove that $I$ is a linear transformation.

  **b)** Determine $\mathcal{N}(I)$ and $\mathcal{R}(I)$.

**18.** Let $U$ and $V$ be vector spaces and define $T: U \rightarrow V$ by $T(\mathbf{u}) = \boldsymbol{\theta}_V$ for each $\mathbf{u}$ in $U$.

   **a)** Prove that $T$ is a linear transformation.

   **b)** Determine $\mathcal{N}(T)$ and $\mathcal{R}(T)$.

**19.** Suppose that $T: \mathcal{P}_4 \rightarrow \mathcal{P}_2$ is a linear transformation. Enumerate the various possibilities for rank$(T)$ and nullity$(T)$. Can $T$ possibly be one to one?

**20.** Let $T: U \rightarrow V$ be a linear transformation and let $U$ be finite dimensional. Prove that if $\dim(U) > \dim(V)$, then $T$ cannot be one to one.

**21.** Suppose that $T: \mathcal{R}_3 \rightarrow \mathcal{P}_3$ is a linear transformation. Enumerate the various possibilities for rank$(T)$ and nullity$(T)$. Is $\mathcal{R}(T) = \mathcal{P}_3$ a possibility?

**22.** Let $T: U \rightarrow V$ be a linear transformation and let $U$ be finite dimensional. Prove that if $\dim(U) < \dim(V)$, then $\mathcal{R}(T) = V$ is not possible.

**23.** Prove property 3 of Theorem 14.

**24.** Complete the proof of property 4 of Theorem 14 by showing that if $T$ is one to one, then $\mathcal{N}(T) = \{\boldsymbol{\theta}_U\}$.

**25.** Complete the proof of property 3 of Theorem 15 as follows:

   **a)** If rank$(T) = p$, prove that nullity$(T) = 0$.

   **b)** If rank$(T) = 0$, show that nullity$(T) = p$.

**26.** Let $T: R^n \rightarrow R^n$ be defined by $T(\mathbf{x}) = A\mathbf{x}$, where $A$ is an $(n \times n)$ matrix. Use property 4 of Theorem 14 to show that $T$ is one to one if and only if $A$ is nonsingular.

**27.** Let $V$ be the vector space of all $(2 \times 2)$ matrices and define $T: V \rightarrow V$ by $T(A) = A^T$.

   **a)** Show that $T$ is a linear transformation.

   **b)** Determine the nullity and rank of $T$. Conclude that $T$ is one to one and $\mathcal{R}(T) = V$.

   **c)** Show directly that $\mathcal{R}(T) = V$; that is, for $B$ in $V$ exhibit a matrix $C$ in $V$ such that $T(C) = B$.

# OPERATIONS WITH LINEAR TRANSFORMATIONS

We know that a useful arithmetic structure is associated with matrices: Matrices can be added and multiplied, nonsingular matrices have inverses, and so on. Much of this structure is available also for linear transformations. For our explanation we will need some definitions. Let $U$ and $V$ be vector spaces and let $T_1$ and $T_2$ be linear transformations, where $T_1: U \rightarrow V$ and $T_2: U \rightarrow V$. By the **sum** $T_3 = T_1 + T_2$, we mean the function $T_3: U \rightarrow V$, where $T_3(\mathbf{u}) = T_1(\mathbf{u}) + T_2(\mathbf{u})$ for all $\mathbf{u}$ in $U$. The following example illustrates this concept.

 EXAMPLE 1    Let $T_1: \mathcal{P}_4 \rightarrow \mathcal{P}_2$ be given by $T_1(p) = p''(x)$, and suppose that $T_2: \mathcal{P}_4 \rightarrow \mathcal{P}_2$ is defined by $T_2(p) = xp(1)$. If $S = T_1 + T_2$, give the formula for $S$.

*Solution*    By definition, the sum $T_1 + T_2$ is the linear transformation $S: \mathcal{P}_4 \rightarrow \mathcal{P}_2$ defined by $S(p) = T_1(p) + T_2(p) = p''(x) + xp(1)$. ◼

If $T: U \rightarrow V$ is a linear transformation and $a$ is a scalar, then $aT$ denotes the function $aT: U \rightarrow V$ defined by $aT(\mathbf{u}) = a(T(\mathbf{u}))$ for all $\mathbf{u}$ in $U$. Again, we illustrate with an example.

 EXAMPLE 2    Let $V$ be the vector space of all $(2 \times 2)$ matrices and define $T: V \rightarrow R^1$ by $T(A) = 2a - b + 3c + 4d$, where

$$A = \begin{bmatrix} a & b \\ c & d \end{bmatrix}.$$

Give the formula for $3T$.

*Solution* By definition, $3T(A) = 3(T(A)) = 3(2a - b + 3c + 4d) = 6a - 3b + 9c + 12d.$ ▪

It is straightforward to show that the functions $T_1 + T_2$ and $aT$, previously defined, are linear transformations (see Exercises 13 and 14).

Now let $U$, $V$, and $W$ be vector spaces and let $S$ and $T$ be linear transformations, where $S: U \to V$ and $T: V \to W$. The *composition*, $L = T \circ S$, of $S$ and $T$ is defined to be function $L: U \to W$ given by $L(\mathbf{u}) = T(S(\mathbf{u}))$ for all $\mathbf{u}$ in $U$ (see Fig. 5.7).

$$U \xrightarrow{S} V \xrightarrow{T} W$$
$$\mathbf{u} \to S(\mathbf{u}) \to T(S(\mathbf{u}))$$
$$\boxed{\phantom{xx} T \circ S \phantom{xxxx}\uparrow}$$

*Figure 5.7* The composition of linear transformations is a linear transformation (see Example 3).

EXAMPLE 3 Let $S: U \to V$ and $T: V \to W$ be linear transformations. Verify that the composition $L = T \circ S$ is also a linear transformation.

*Solution* Let $\mathbf{u}_1, \mathbf{u}_2$ be vectors in $U$. Then $L(\mathbf{u}_1 + \mathbf{u}_2) = T(S(\mathbf{u}_1 + \mathbf{u}_2))$. Since $S$ is a linear transformation, $S(\mathbf{u}_1 + \mathbf{u}_2) = S(\mathbf{u}_1) + S(\mathbf{u}_2)$. But $T$ is also a linear transformation, so $L(\mathbf{u}_1 + \mathbf{u}_2) = T(S(\mathbf{u}_1) + S(\mathbf{u}_2)) = T(S(\mathbf{u}_1)) + T(S(\mathbf{u}_2)) = L(\mathbf{u}_1) + L(\mathbf{u}_2)$. Similarly, if $\mathbf{u}$ is in $U$ and $a$ is a scalar, $L(a\mathbf{u}) = T(S(a\mathbf{u})) = T(aS(\mathbf{u})) = aT(S(\mathbf{u})) = aL(\mathbf{u})$. This shows that $L = T \circ S$ is a linear transformation. ▪

The next two examples provide specific illustrations of the composition of two linear transformations.

EXAMPLE 4 Let $U$ be the vector space of all $(2 \times 2)$ matrices. Define $S: U \to \mathcal{P}_2$ by $S(A) = (a - c) + (b + 2c)x + (3c - d)x^2$, where

$$A = \begin{bmatrix} a & b \\ c & d \end{bmatrix}.$$

Define $T: \mathcal{P}_2 \to R^2$ by

$$T(a_0 + a_1x + a_2x^2) = \begin{bmatrix} a_0 - a_1 \\ 2a_1 + a_2 \end{bmatrix}.$$

Give the formula for $T \circ S$ and show that $S \circ T$ is not defined.

*Solution* The composition $T \circ S: U \to R^2$ is defined by $(T \circ S)(A) = T(S(A)) = T[(a - c) + (b + 2c)x + (3c - d)x^2]$. Thus

$$(T \circ S)\left(\begin{bmatrix} a & b \\ c & d \end{bmatrix}\right) = \begin{bmatrix} a - b - 3c \\ 2b + 7c - d \end{bmatrix}.$$

If $p(x)$ is in $\mathcal{P}_2$, then $T(p(x)) = \mathbf{v}$, where $\mathbf{v}$ is in $R^2$. Thus $(S \circ T)(p(x)) = S(T(p(x))) = S(\mathbf{v})$. But $\mathbf{v}$ is not in the domain of $S$, so $S(\mathbf{v})$ is not defined. Therefore, $S \circ T$ is undefined. ▪

Example 4 illustrates that, as with matrix multiplication, $T \circ S$ may be defined, whereas $S \circ T$ is not defined. The next example illustrates that even when both are defined, they may be different transformations.

**EXAMPLE 5** Let $S: \mathcal{P}_4 \to \mathcal{P}_4$ be given by $S(p) = p''(x)$ and define $T: \mathcal{P}_4 \to \mathcal{P}_4$ by $T(q) = xq(1)$. Give the formulas for $T \circ S$ and $S \circ T$.

**Solution** The linear transformation $T \circ S: \mathcal{P}_4 \to \mathcal{P}_4$ is defined by

$$(T \circ S)(p) = T(S(p)) = T(p''(x)) = xp''(1),$$

and $S \circ T: \mathcal{P}_4 \to \mathcal{P}_4$ is given by

$$(S \circ T)(p) = S(T(p)) = S(xp(1)) = [xp(1)]'' = \theta(x).$$

In particular, $S \circ T \neq T \circ S$.

## Invertible Transformations

As we have previously noted, linear transformations can be viewed as an extension of the notion of a matrix to general vector spaces. In this subsection we introduce those linear transformations that correspond to nonsingular (or invertible) matrices. First, suppose $X$ and $Y$ are any sets and $f: X \to Y$ is a function; and suppose $\mathcal{R}(f)$ denotes the range of $f$ where $\mathcal{R}(f) \subseteq Y$. Recall that $f$ is **onto** provided that $\mathcal{R}(f) = Y$; that is, $f$ is onto if for each element $y$ in $Y$ there exists an element $x$ in $X$ such that $f(x) = y$.

In order to show that a linear transformation $T: U \to V$ is onto, it is frequently convenient to use the results of Section 5.7 and a dimension argument to determine whether $\mathcal{R}(T) = V$. To be more specific, suppose $V$ has finite dimension. If $\mathcal{R}(T)$ has the same dimension, then, since $\mathcal{R}(T)$ is a subspace of $V$, it must be the case that $\mathcal{R}(T) = V$. Thus in order to show that $T$ is onto when the dimension of $V$ is finite, it suffices to demonstrate that $\text{rank}(T) = \dim(V)$. Alternatively, an elementwise argument can be used to show that $T$ is onto. The next two examples illustrate both procedures.

**EXAMPLE 6** Let $U$ be the subspace of $(2 \times 2)$ matrices defined by

$$U = \{A: A = \begin{bmatrix} a & -b \\ b & a \end{bmatrix}, \quad \text{where } a \text{ and } b \text{ are in } R\},$$

and let $V = \{f(x) \text{ in } C[0, 1]: f(x) = ce^x + de^{-x}, \text{ where } c \text{ and } d \text{ are in } R\}$. Define $T: U \to V$ by

$$T\left( \begin{bmatrix} a & -b \\ b & a \end{bmatrix} \right) = (a + b)e^x + (a - b)e^{-x}.$$

Show that $\mathcal{R}(T) = V$.

**Solution** Note that $U$ has basis $\{A_1, A_2\}$, where

$$A_1 = \begin{bmatrix} 1 & 0 \\ 0 & 1 \end{bmatrix} \quad \text{and} \quad A_2 = \begin{bmatrix} 0 & -1 \\ 1 & 0 \end{bmatrix}.$$

It follows from Theorem 15, property 1, of Section 5.7 that $\mathcal{R}(T) = \text{Sp}\{T(A_1),$ $T(A_2)\} = \text{Sp}\{e^x + e^{-x}, e^x - e^{-x}\}$. It is easily shown that the set $\{e^x + e^{-x}, e^x - e^{-x}\}$ is linearly independent. It follows that $\text{rank}(T) = 2$. Since $\{e^x, e^{-x}\}$ is a linearly independent set and $V = \text{Sp}\{e^x, e^{-x}\}$, the set is a basis for $V$. In particular, $\dim(V) = 2$. Since $\mathcal{R}(T) \subseteq V$ and $\text{rank}(T) = \dim(V)$, it follows that $\mathcal{R}(T) = V$. ◼

**EXAMPLE 7**  Let $T: \mathcal{P} \to \mathcal{P}$ be defined by $T(p) = p''(x)$. Show that $\mathcal{R}(T) = \mathcal{P}$.

**Solution**  Recall that $\mathcal{P}$ is the vector space of all polynomials, with no bound on the degree. We have previously seen that $\mathcal{P}$ does not have a finite basis, so the techniques of Example 6 do not apply. To show that $\mathcal{R}(T) = \mathcal{P}$, let $q(x) = a_0 + a_1 x + \cdots + a_n x^n$ be an arbitrary polynomial in $\mathcal{P}$. We must exhibit a polynomial $p(x)$ in $\mathcal{P}$ such that $T(p) = p''(x) = q(x)$. It is easy to see that $p(x) = (1/2)a_0 x^2 + (1/6)a_1 x^3 + \cdots + [1/(n+1)(n+2)]a_n x^{n+2}$ is one choice for $p(x)$. Thus $T$ is onto. ◼

Let $f: X \to Y$ be a function. If $f$ is both one to one and onto, then the **inverse** of $f$, $f^{-1}: Y \to X$, is the function defined by

$$f^{-1}(y) = x \text{ if and only if } f(x) = y. \tag{1}$$

Therefore, if $T: U \to V$ is a linear transformation that is both one to one and onto, then the inverse function $T^{-1}: V \to U$ is defined. The next two examples illustrate this concept.

**EXAMPLE 8**  Let $T: \mathcal{P}_4 \to \mathcal{P}_3$ be defined by $T(p) = p''(x)$. Show that $T^{-1}$ is not defined.

**Solution**  It is easy to see that $\mathcal{N}(T) = \mathcal{P}_1$. In particular, by property 4 of Theorem 14 (Section 5.7), $T$ is not one to one. Thus $T^{-1}$ is not defined. To illustrate specifically, note that $T(x) = T(x + 1) = \theta(x)$. Thus by formula (1) above, we have both $T^{-1}(\theta(x)) = x$ and $T^{-1}(\theta(x)) = x + 1$. Since $T^{-1}(\theta(x))$ is not uniquely determined, $T^{-1}$ does not exist.

Since $\mathcal{N}(T) = \mathcal{P}_1$, it follows that $\text{nullity}(T) = 2$. By property 3 of Theorem 15 (Section 5.7), $\text{rank}(T) = \dim(\mathcal{P}_4) - \text{nullity}(T) = 5 - 2 = 3$. But $\dim(\mathcal{P}_3) = 4$, so $T$ is not onto. In particular, $x^3$ is in $\mathcal{P}_3$, and it is easy to see that there is no polynomial $p(x)$ in $\mathcal{P}_4$ such that $T(p(x)) = p''(x) = x^3$. Thus $T^{-1}(x^3)$ remains undefined by formula (1). ◼

Example 8 illustrates the following: If $T: U \to V$ is not one to one, then there exists $\mathbf{v}$ in $V$ such that $T^{-1}(\mathbf{v})$ is not uniquely determined by formula (1), since there exists $\mathbf{u}_1$ and $\mathbf{u}_2$ in $U$ such that $\mathbf{u}_1 \neq \mathbf{u}_2$ but $T(\mathbf{u}_1) = \mathbf{v} = T(\mathbf{u}_2)$. On the other hand, if $T$ is not onto, there exists $\mathbf{v}$ in $V$ such that $T^{-1}(\mathbf{v})$ is not defined by formula (1), since there exists no vector $\mathbf{u}$ in $U$ such that $T(\mathbf{u}) = \mathbf{v}$.

**EXAMPLE 9**  Let $T: U \to V$ be the linear transformation defined in Example 6. Show that $T$ is both one to one and onto, and give the formula for $T^{-1}$.

**Solution**  We showed in Example 6 that $T$ is onto. In order to show that $T$ is one to one, it suffices, by Theorem 14, property 4 of Section 5.7, to show that if $A \in \mathcal{N}(T)$, then $A = \mathcal{O}$

[where $\mathcal{O}$ is the $(2 \times 2)$ zero matrix]. Thus suppose that

$$A = \begin{bmatrix} a & -b \\ b & a \end{bmatrix}$$

and $T(A) = \theta(x)$; that is, $(a + b)e^x + (a - b)e^{-x} = \theta(x)$. Since the set $\{e^x, e^{-x}\}$ is linearly independent, it follows that $a + b = 0$ and $a - b = 0$. Therefore, $a = b = 0$ and $A = \mathcal{O}$.

To determine the formula for $T^{-1}$, let $f(x) = ce^x + de^{-x}$ be in $V$. By formula (1), $T^{-1}(f) = A$, where $A$ is a matrix such that $T(A) = f(x)$; that is,

$$T(A) = (a + b)e^x + (a - b)e^{-x} = ce^x + de^{-x}. \tag{2}$$

Since $\{e^x, e^{-x}\}$ is a linearly independent set, Eq. (2) requires that $a + b = c$ and $a - b = d$. This yields $a = (1/2)c + (1/2)d$ and $b = (1/2)c - (1/2)d$. Therefore, the formula for $T^{-1}$ is given by

$$T^{-1}(ce^x + de^{-x}) = (1/2) \begin{bmatrix} c + d & -c + d \\ c - d & c + d \end{bmatrix}. \qquad\blacksquare$$

A linear transformation $T: U \to V$ that is both one to one and onto is called an *invertible* linear transformation. Thus if $T$ is invertible, then the mapping $T^{-1}: V \to U$ exists and is defined by formula (1). The next theorem lists some of the properties of $T^{-1}$.

 THEOREM 16    Let $U$ and $V$ be vector spaces, and let $T: U \to V$ be an invertible linear transformation. Then:

  **1.** $T^{-1}: V \to U$ is a linear transformation.
  **2.** $T^{-1}$ is invertible and $(T^{-1})^{-1} = T$.
  **3.** $T^{-1} \circ T = I_U$ and $T \circ T^{-1} = I_V$, where $I_U$ and $I_V$ are the identity transformations on $U$ and $V$, respectively.

*Proof*    For property 1, we need to show that $T^{-1}: V \to U$ satisfies Definition 8. Suppose that $\mathbf{v}_1$ and $\mathbf{v}_2$ are vectors in $V$. Since $T$ is onto, there are vectors $\mathbf{u}_1$ and $\mathbf{u}_2$ in $U$ such that $T(\mathbf{u}_1) = \mathbf{v}_1$ and $T(\mathbf{u}_1) = \mathbf{v}_2$. By formula (1),

$$T^{-1}(\mathbf{v}_1) = \mathbf{u}_1 \text{ and } T^{-1}(\mathbf{v}_2) = \mathbf{u}_2. \tag{3}$$

Furthermore, $\mathbf{v}_1 + \mathbf{v}_2 = T(\mathbf{u}_1) + T(\mathbf{u}_2) = T(\mathbf{u}_1 + \mathbf{u}_2)$, so by formula (1),

$$T^{-1}(\mathbf{v}_1 + \mathbf{v}_2) = \mathbf{u}_1 + \mathbf{u}_2 = T^{-1}(\mathbf{v}_1) + T^{-1}\mathbf{v}_2.$$

It is equally easy to see that $T^{-1}(c\mathbf{v}) = cT^{-1}(\mathbf{v})$ for all $\mathbf{v}$ in $V$ and for any scalar $c$ (see Exercise 15).

The proof of property 2 requires showing that $T^{-1}$ is both one to one and onto. To see that $T^{-1}$ is one to one, let $\mathbf{v}$ be in $\mathcal{N}(T^{-1})$. Then $T^{-1}(\mathbf{v}) = \theta_U$, so by formula (1), $T(\theta_U) = \mathbf{v}$. By Theorem 14, property 1, of Section 5.7, $\mathbf{v} = \theta_V$ so Theorem 14, property 4, implies that $T$ is one to one. To see that $T^{-1}$ is onto, let $\mathbf{u}$ be an arbitrary vector in $U$. If $\mathbf{v} = T(\mathbf{u})$, then $\mathbf{v}$ is in $V$ and, by formula (1), $T^{-1}(\mathbf{v}) = \mathbf{u}$. Therefore, $T^{-1}$ is onto, and it follows that $T$ is invertible.

That $(T^{-1})^{-1} = T$ is an easy consequence of formula (1), as are the equalities given in property 3, and the proofs are left as exercises. ∎

As might be guessed from the corresponding theorems for nonsingular matrices, other properties of invertible transformations can be established. For example, if $T: U \to V$ is an invertible transformation, then for each vector $\mathbf{b}$ in $V$, $\mathbf{x} = T^{-1}(\mathbf{b})$ is the unique solution of $T(\mathbf{x}) = \mathbf{b}$. Also, if $S$ and $T$ are invertible and $S \circ T$ is defined, then $S \circ T$ is invertible and $(S \circ T)^{-1} = T^{-1} \circ S^{-1}$.

## Isomorphic Vector Spaces

Suppose that a linear transformation $T: U \to V$ is invertible. Since $T$ is both one to one and onto, $T$ establishes an exact pairing between elements of $U$ and $V$. Moreover, because $T$ is a linear transformation, this pairing preserves algebraic properties. Therefore, although $U$ and $V$ may be different sets, they may be regarded as indistinguishable (or equivalent) algebraically. Stated another way, $U$ and $V$ both represent just one underlying vector space but perhaps with different "labels" for the elements. The invertible linear transformation $T$ acts as a translation from one set of labels to another.

If $U$ and $V$ are vector spaces and if $T: U \to V$ is an invertible linear transformation, then $U$ and $V$ are said to be *isomorphic* vector spaces. Also, an invertible transformation $T$ is called an *isomorphism*. For instance, the vector spaces $U$ and $V$ given in Example 6 are isomorphic, as shown in Example 9. The next example provides another illustration.

EXAMPLE 10    Let $U$ be the subspace of $\mathcal{P}_3$ defined by

$$U = \{p(x) = a_0 + a_1 x + a_2 x^2 + a_3 x^3 : a_3 = -2a_0 + 3a_1 + a_2\}.$$

Show that $U$ is isomorphic to $R^3$.

*Solution*    Note that $\dim(U) = 3$ and the set $\{1 - 2x^3, x + 3x^3, x^2 + x^3\}$ is a basis for $U$. Moreover, each polynomial $p(x)$ in $U$ can be decomposed as

$$p(x) = a_0 + a_1 x + a_2 x^2 + a_3 x^3$$
$$= a_0(1 - 2x^3) + a_1(x + 3x^3) + a_2(x^2 + x^3). \tag{4}$$

It is reasonable to expect that an isomorphism $T: U \to R^3$ will map a basis of $U$ to a basis of $R^3$. Since $\{\mathbf{e}_1, \mathbf{e}_2, \mathbf{e}_3\}$ is a basis for $R^3$, we seek a linear transformation $T$ such that

$$T(1 - 2x^3) = \mathbf{e}_1, \qquad T(x + 3x^3) = \mathbf{e}_2, \quad \text{and} \quad T(x^2 + x^3) = \mathbf{e}_3. \tag{5}$$

It follows from Eq. (4) in this example and from Eq. (1) of Section 5.7 that if such a linear transformation exists, then it is defined by

$$T(a_0 + a_1 x + a_2 x^2 + a_3 x^3) = a_0 T(1 - 2x^3) + a_1 T(x + 3x^3) + a_2 T(x^2 + x^3)$$
$$= a_0 \mathbf{e}_1 + a_1 \mathbf{e}_2 + a_2 \mathbf{e}_3.$$

That is,

$$T(a_0 + a_1 x + a_2 x^2 + a_3 x^3) = \begin{bmatrix} a_0 \\ a_1 \\ a_2 \end{bmatrix}. \tag{6}$$

It is straightforward to show that the function $T$ defined by Eq. (6) is a linear transformation. Moreover, the constraints placed on $T$ by (5) imply, by Theorem 15, property 1, of Section 5.7, that $\mathcal{R}(T) = R^3$. Likewise, by Theorem 15, property 2, $T$ is one to one. Therefore, $T$ is an isomorphism and $U$ and $R^3$ are isomorphic vector spaces.
◼

The previous example is actually just a special case of the following theorem, which states that every real $n$-dimensional vector space is isomorphic to $R^n$.

**THEOREM 17**    If $U$ is a real $n$-dimensional vector space, then $U$ and $R^n$ are isomorphic.

*Proof*    To prove this theorem, we need only exhibit the isomorphism, and a coordinate system on $U$ will provide the means. Let $B = \{\mathbf{u}_1, \mathbf{u}_2, \ldots, \mathbf{u}_n\}$ be a basis for $U$, and let $T: U \to R^n$ be the linear transformation defined by

$$T(\mathbf{u}) = [\mathbf{u}]_B.$$

Since $B$ is a basis, $\boldsymbol{\theta}_U$ is the only vector in $\mathcal{N}(T)$; and therefore $T$ is one to one. Furthermore, $T(\mathbf{u}_i)$ is the vector $\mathbf{e}_i$ in $R^n$; so

$$\mathcal{R}(T) = \text{Sp}\{T(\mathbf{u}_1), T(\mathbf{u}_2), \ldots, T(\mathbf{u}_n)\} = \text{Sp}\{\mathbf{e}_1, \mathbf{e}_2, \ldots, \mathbf{e}_n\} = R^n.$$

Hence $T$ is one to one and onto.
◼

As an illustration of Theorem 17, note that $\dim(\mathcal{P}_2) = 3$, so $\mathcal{P}_2$ and $R^3$ are isomorphic. Moreover, if $B = \{1, x, x^2\}$ is the natural basis for $\mathcal{P}_2$, then the linear transformation $T: \mathcal{P}_2 \to R^3$ defined by $T(p) = [p]_B$ is an isomorphism; thus

$$T(a_0 + a_1 x + a_2 x^2) = \begin{bmatrix} a_0 \\ a_1 \\ a_2 \end{bmatrix}.$$

The isomorphism $T$ "pairs" the elements of $\mathcal{P}_2$ with elements of $R^3$, $p(x) \leftrightarrow [p(x)]_B$. Furthermore, under this correspondence the sum of two polynomials, $p(x) + q(x)$, is paired with the sum of the corresponding coordinate vectors:

$$p(x) + q(x) \leftrightarrow [p(x)]_B + [q(x)]_B.$$

Similarly, a scalar multiple, $ap(x)$, of a polynomial $p(x)$ is paired with the corresponding scalar multiple of $[p(x)]_B$:

$$ap(x) \leftrightarrow a[p(x)]_B.$$

In this sense, $\mathcal{P}_2$ and $R^3$ have the same algebraic character.

It is easy to show that if $U$ is isomorphic to $V$ and $V$ is isomorphic to $W$, then $U$ and $W$ are also isomorphic (see Exercise 19). Using this fact, we obtain the following corollary of Theorem 17.

**COROLLARY**    If $U$ and $V$ are real $n$-dimensional vector spaces, then $U$ and $V$ are isomorphic.    ◼

## 5.8     EXERCISES

In Exercises 1–6, the linear transformations $S$, $T$, and $H$ are defined as follows:

$S:\mathcal{P}_3 \to \mathcal{P}_4$ is defined by $S(p) = p'(0)$.

$T:\mathcal{P}_3 \to \mathcal{P}_4$ is defined by $T(p) = (x+2)p(x)$.

$H:\mathcal{P}_4 \to \mathcal{P}_3$ is defined by $H(p) = p'(x) + p(0)$.

1. Give the formula for $S + T$. Calculate $(S + T)(x)$ and $(S + T)(x^2)$.

2. Give the formula for $2T$. Calculate $(2T)(x)$.

3. Give the formula for $H \circ T$. What is the domain for $H \circ T$? Calculate $(H \circ T)(x)$.

4. Give the formula for $T \circ H$. What is the domain for $T \circ H$? Calculate $(T \circ H)(x)$.

5. a) Prove that $T$ is one to one but not onto.
   b) Attempt to define $T^{-1}:\mathcal{P}_4 \to \mathcal{P}_3$ as in formula (1) by setting $T^{-1}(q) = p$ if and only if $T(p) = q$. What is $T^{-1}(x)$?

6. a) Prove that $H$ is onto but not one to one.
   b) Attempt to define $H^{-1}:\mathcal{P}_3 \to \mathcal{P}_4$ as in formula (1) by setting $H^{-1}(q) = p$ if and only if $H(p) = q$. Show that $H^{-1}(x)$ is not uniquely determined.

7. The functions $e^x$, $e^{2x}$, and $e^{3x}$ are linearly independent in $C[0, 1]$. Let $V$ be the subspace of $C[0, 1]$ defined by $V = \text{Sp}\{e^x, e^{2x}, e^{3x}\}$, and let $T:V \to V$ be given by $T(p) = p'(x)$. Show that $T$ is invertible and calculate $T^{-1}(e^x)$, $T^{-1}(e^{2x})$, and $T^{-1}(e^{3x})$. What is $T^{-1}(ae^x + be^{2x} + ce^{3x})$?

8. Let $V$ be the subspace of $C[0, 1]$ defined by $V = \text{Sp}\{\sin x, \cos x, e^{-x}\}$, and let $T:V \to V$ be given by $T(f) = f'(x)$. Given that the set $\{\sin x, \cos x, e^{-x}\}$ is linearly independent, show that $T$ is invertible. Calculate $T^{-1}(\sin x)$, $T^{-1}(\cos x)$, and $T^{-1}(e^{-x})$ and give the formula for $T^{-1}$; that is, determine $T^{-1}(a \sin x + b \cos x + ce^{-x})$.

9. Let $V$ be the vector space of all $(2 \times 2)$ matrices and define $T:V \to V$ by $T(A) = A^T$. Show that $T$ is invertible and give the formula for $T^{-1}$.

10. Let $V$ be the vector space of all $(2 \times 2)$ matrices, and let $Q$ be a given nonsingular $(2 \times 2)$ matrix. If $T:V \to V$ is defined by $T(A) = Q^{-1}AQ$, prove that $T$ is invertible and give the formula for $T^{-1}$.

11. Let $V$ be the vector space of all $(2 \times 2)$ matrices.
    a) Use Theorem 17 to show that $V$ is isomorphic to $R^4$.
    b) Use the corollary to Theorem 17 to show that $V$ is isomorphic to $\mathcal{P}_3$.
    c) Exhibit an isomorphism $T:V \to \mathcal{P}_3$. [Hint: See Example 10.]

12. Let $U$ be the vector space of all $(2 \times 2)$ symmetric matrices.
    a) Use Theorem 17 to show that $U$ is isomorphic to $R^3$.
    b) Use the corollary to Theorem 17 to show that $U$ is isomorphic to $\mathcal{P}_2$.
    c) Exhibit an isomorphism $T:U \to \mathcal{P}_2$.

13. Let $T_1: U \to V$ and $T_2: U \to V$ be linear transformations. Prove that $S: U \to V$, where $S = T_1 + T_2$, is a linear transformation.

14. If $T:U \to V$ is a linear transformation and $a$ is a scalar, show that $aT: U \to V$ is a linear transformation.

15. Complete the proof of property 1 of Theorem 16 by showing that $T^{-1}(c\mathbf{v}) = cT^{-1}(\mathbf{v})$ for all $\mathbf{v}$ in $V$ and for an arbitrary scalar $c$.

16. Complete the proof of property 2 of Theorem 16 by showing that $(T^{-1})^{-1} = T$. [Hint: Use formula 1.]

17. Prove property 3 of Theorem 16.

18. Let $S: U \to V$ and $T: V \to W$ be linear transformations.
    a) Prove that if $S$ and $T$ are both one to one, then $T \circ S$ is one to one.
    b) Prove that if $S$ and $T$ are both onto, then $T \circ S$ is onto.
    c) Prove that if $S$ and $T$ are both invertible, then $T \circ S$ is invertible and $(T \circ S)^{-1} = S^{-1} \circ T^{-1}$.

19. Let $U$, $V$, and $W$ be vector spaces such that $U$ and $V$ are isomorphic and $V$ and $W$ are isomorphic. Use Exercise 18 to show that $U$ and $W$ are isomorphic.

20. Let $U$ and $V$ both be $n$-dimensional vector spaces, and suppose that $T: U \to V$ is a linear transformation.
    a) If $T$ is one to one, prove that $T$ is invertible. [Hint: Use property 3 of Theorem 15 to prove that $\mathcal{R}(T) = V$.]

**b)** If $T$ is onto, prove that $T$ is invertible. [*Hint:* Use property 3 of Theorem 15 and property 4 of Theorem 14 to prove that $T$ is one to one.]

**21.** Define $T: \mathcal{P} \to \mathcal{P}$ by $T(a_0 + a_1 x + \cdots + a_n x^n) = a_0 x + (1/2)a_1 x^2 + \cdots + (1/(n+1))a_n x^{n+1}$. Prove that $T$ is one to one but not onto. Why is this example not a contradiction of part a) of Exercise 20?

**22.** Define $S: \mathcal{P} \to \mathcal{P}$ by $S(p) = p'(x)$. Prove that $S$ is onto but not one to one. Why is this example not a contradiction of part b) of Exercise 20?

In Exercises 23–25, $S: U \to V$ and $T: V \to W$ are linear transformations.

**23.** Show that $\mathcal{N}(S) \subseteq \mathcal{N}(T \circ S)$. Conclude that if $T \circ S$ is one to one, then $S$ is one to one.

**24.** Show that $\mathcal{R}(T \circ S) \subseteq \mathcal{R}(T)$. Conclude that if $T \circ S$ is onto, then $T$ is onto.

**25.** Assume that $U$, $V$, and $W$ all have dimension $n$. Prove that if $T \circ S$ is invertible, then both $T$ and $S$ are invertible. [*Hint:* Use Exercises 20, 23, and 24.]

**26.** Let $A$ be an $(m \times p)$ matrix and $B$ a $(p \times n)$ matrix. Use Exercises 23 and 24 to show that nullity$(B) \leq$ nullity$(AB)$ and rank$(AB) \leq$ rank$(A)$.

**27.** Let $A$ be an $(n \times n)$ matrix, and suppose that $T: R^n \to R^n$ is defined by $T(\mathbf{x}) = A\mathbf{x}$. Show that $T$ is invertible if and only if $A$ is nonsingular. If $T$ is invertible, give a formula for $T^{-1}$.

**28.** Let $A$ and $B$ be $(n \times n)$ matrices such that $AB$ is nonsingular. Use Exercises 25 and 27 to show that each of the matrices $A$ and $B$ is nonsingular.

**29.** Let $U$ and $V$ be vector spaces, and let $L(U, V) = \{T: T$ is a linear transformation from $U$ to $V\}$. With the operations of addition and scalar multiplication defined in this section, show that $L(U, V)$ is a vector space.

---

## 5.9   MATRIX REPRESENTATIONS FOR LINEAR TRANSFORMATIONS

In Section 3.7 we showed that a linear transformation $T: R^n \to R^m$ can be represented as multiplication by an $(m \times n)$ matrix $A$; that is, $T(\mathbf{x}) = A\mathbf{x}$ for all $\mathbf{x}$ in $R^n$. In the general vector-space setting, we have viewed a linear transformation $T: U \to V$ as an extension of this notion. Now suppose that $U$ and $V$ both have finite dimension, say $\dim(U) = n$ and $\dim(V) = m$. By Theorem 17 of Section 5.8, $U$ is isomorphic to $R^n$ and $V$ is isomorphic to $R^m$. To be specific, let $B$ be a basis for $U$ and let $C$ be a basis for $V$. Then each vector $\mathbf{u}$ in $U$ can be represented by the vector $[\mathbf{u}]_B$ in $R^n$, and similarly each vector $\mathbf{v}$ in $V$ can be represented by the vector $[\mathbf{v}]_C$ in $R^m$. In this section we show that $T$ can be represented by an $(m \times n)$ matrix $Q$ in the sense that if $T(\mathbf{u}) = \mathbf{v}$, then $Q[\mathbf{u}]_B = [\mathbf{v}]_C$.

### The Matrix of a Transformation

We begin by defining the matrix of a linear transformation. Thus let $T: U \to V$ be a linear transformation, where $\dim(U) = n$ and $\dim(V) = m$. Let $B = \{\mathbf{u}_1, \mathbf{u}_2, \ldots, \mathbf{u}_n\}$ be a basis for $U$, and let $C = \{\mathbf{v}_1, \mathbf{v}_2, \ldots, \mathbf{v}_m\}$ be a basis for $V$. The *matrix representation* for $T$ with respect to the bases $B$ and $C$ is the $(m \times n)$ matrix $Q$ defined by

$$Q = [\mathbf{Q}_1, \mathbf{Q}_2, \ldots, \mathbf{Q}_n],$$

where

$$\mathbf{Q}_j = [T(\mathbf{u}_j)]_C.$$

Thus to determine $Q$, we first represent each of the vectors $T(\mathbf{u}_1), T(\mathbf{u}_2), \ldots, T(\mathbf{u}_n)$ in terms of the basis $C$ for $V$:

$$
\begin{aligned}
T(\mathbf{u}_1) &= q_{11}\mathbf{v}_1 + q_{21}\mathbf{v}_2 + \cdots + q_{m1}\mathbf{v}_m \\
T(\mathbf{u}_2) &= q_{12}\mathbf{v}_1 + q_{22}\mathbf{v}_2 + \cdots + q_{m2}\mathbf{v}_m \\
&\vdots \qquad \vdots \qquad\qquad \vdots \\
T(\mathbf{u}_n) &= q_{1n}\mathbf{v}_1 + q_{2n}\mathbf{v}_2 + \cdots + q_{mn}\mathbf{v}_m.
\end{aligned}
\tag{1}
$$

It follows from system (1) that

$$
\mathbf{Q}_1 = [T(\mathbf{u}_1)]_C = \begin{bmatrix} q_{11} \\ q_{21} \\ \vdots \\ q_{m1} \end{bmatrix}, \ldots, \mathbf{Q}_n = [T(\mathbf{u}_n)]_C = \begin{bmatrix} q_{1n} \\ q_{2n} \\ \vdots \\ q_{mn} \end{bmatrix}.
\tag{2}
$$

The following example provides a specific illustration.

**EXAMPLE 1**  Let $U$ be the vector space of all $(2 \times 2)$ matrices and define $T: U \to \mathcal{P}_2$ by

$$
T\left( \begin{bmatrix} a & b \\ c & d \end{bmatrix} \right) = (a - d) + (a + 2b)x + (b - 3c)x^2.
$$

Find the matrix of $T$ relative to the natural bases for $U$ and $\mathcal{P}_2$.

*Solution*   Let $B = \{E_{11}, E_{12}, E_{21}, E_{22}\}$ be the natural basis for $U$, and let $C = \{1, x, x^2\}$ be the natural basis for $\mathcal{P}_2$. Then $T(E_{11}) = 1 + x$, $T(E_{12}) = 2x + x^2$, $T(E_{21}) = -3x^2$, and $T(E_{22}) = -1$. In this example system (1) becomes

$$
\begin{aligned}
T(E_{11}) &= \phantom{-}1 + 1x + 0x^2 \\
T(E_{12}) &= \phantom{-}0 + 2x + 1x^2 \\
T(E_{21}) &= \phantom{-}0 + 0x - 3x^2 \\
T(E_{22}) &= -1 + 0x + 0x^2.
\end{aligned}
$$

Therefore, the matrix of $T$ is the $(3 \times 4)$ matrix $Q$ given by

$$
Q = \begin{bmatrix} 1 & 0 & 0 & -1 \\ 1 & 2 & 0 & 0 \\ 0 & 1 & -3 & 0 \end{bmatrix}.
$$

## The Representation Theorem

The next theorem shows that if we translate from general vector spaces to coordinate vectors, the action of a linear transformation $T$ translates to multiplication by its matrix representative.

THEOREM 18    Let $T: U \to V$ be a linear transformation, where $\dim(U) = n$ and $\dim(V) = m$. Let $B$ and $C$ be bases for $U$ and $V$, respectively, and let $Q$ be the matrix of $T$ relative to $B$ and $C$. If $\mathbf{u}$ is a vector in $U$ and if $T(\mathbf{u}) = \mathbf{v}$, then

$$Q[\mathbf{u}]_B = [\mathbf{v}]_C. \qquad (3)$$

Moreover, $Q$ is the unique matrix that satisfies (3).

The representation of $T$ by $Q$ is illustrated in Fig. 5.8. Before giving the proof of Theorem 18, we illustrate the result with an example.

Figure 5.8    The matrix of $T$

EXAMPLE 2    Let $T: U \to \mathcal{P}_2$ be the linear transformation defined in Example 1, and let $Q$ be the matrix representation determined in that example. Show by direct calculation that if $T(A) = p(x)$, then

$$Q[A]_B = [p(x)]_C. \qquad (4)$$

Solution    Recall that $B = \{E_{11}, E_{12}, E_{21}, E_{22}\}$ and $C = \{1, x, x^2\}$. Equation (4) is, of course, an immediate consequence of Eq. (3). To verify Eq. (4) directly, note that if

$$A = \begin{bmatrix} a & b \\ c & d \end{bmatrix},$$

then

$$[A]_B = \begin{bmatrix} a \\ b \\ c \\ d \end{bmatrix}.$$

Further, if $p(x) = T(A)$, then $p(x) = (a - d) + (a + 2b)x + (b - 3c)x^2$, so

$$[p(x)]_C = \begin{bmatrix} a - d \\ a + 2b \\ b - 3c \end{bmatrix}.$$

Therefore,

$$Q[A]_B = \begin{bmatrix} 1 & 0 & 0 & -1 \\ 1 & 2 & 0 & 0 \\ 0 & 1 & -3 & 0 \end{bmatrix} \begin{bmatrix} a \\ b \\ c \\ d \end{bmatrix} = \begin{bmatrix} a - d \\ a + 2b \\ b - 3c \end{bmatrix} = [p(x)]_C.$$

***Proof of Theorem 18*** Let $B = \{\mathbf{u}_1, \mathbf{u}_2, \ldots, \mathbf{u}_n\}$ be the given basis for $U$, let $\mathbf{u}$ be in $U$, and set $T(\mathbf{u}) = \mathbf{v}$. First write $\mathbf{u}$ in terms of the basis vectors:

$$\mathbf{u} = a_1\mathbf{u}_1 + a_2\mathbf{u}_2 + \cdots + a_n\mathbf{u}_n. \tag{5}$$

It follows from Eq. (5) that the coordinate vector for $\mathbf{u}$ is

$$[\mathbf{u}]_B = \begin{bmatrix} a_1 \\ a_2 \\ \vdots \\ a_n \end{bmatrix}.$$

Furthermore, the action of $T$ is completely determined by its action on a basis for $U$ (see Eq. (1) of Section 5.7), so Eq. (5) implies that

$$T(\mathbf{u}) = a_1 T(\mathbf{u}_1) + a_2 T(\mathbf{u}_2) + \cdots + a_n T(\mathbf{u}_n) = \mathbf{v}. \tag{6}$$

The vectors in Eq. (6) are in $V$, and passing to coordinate vectors relative to the basis $C$ yields, by Eq. (10) of Section 5.4,

$$a_1[T(\mathbf{u}_1)]_C + a_2[T(\mathbf{u}_2)]_C + \cdots + a_n[T(\mathbf{u}_n)]_C = [\mathbf{v}]_C. \tag{7}$$

Recall that the matrix $Q$ of $T$ is the $(m \times n)$ matrix $Q = [\mathbf{Q}_1, \mathbf{Q}_2, \ldots, \mathbf{Q}_n]$, where

$$\mathbf{Q}_j = [T(\mathbf{u}_j)]_C.$$

Thus Eq. (7) can be rewritten as

$$a_1\mathbf{Q}_1 + a_2\mathbf{Q}_2 + \cdots + a_n\mathbf{Q}_n = [\mathbf{v}]_C. \tag{8}$$

Since Eq. (8) is equivalent to the matrix equation

$$Q[\mathbf{u}]_B = [\mathbf{v}]_C,$$

this shows that Eq. (3) of Theorem 18 holds. The uniqueness of $Q$ is left as an exercise. ◾

EXAMPLE 3 Let $S: \mathcal{P}_2 \to \mathcal{P}_3$ be the differential operator defined by $S(f) = x^2 f'' - 2f' + xf$. Find the $(4 \times 3)$ matrix $P$ that represents $S$ with respect to the natural bases $C = \{1, x, x^2\}$ and $D = \{1, x, x^2, x^3\}$ for $\mathcal{P}_2$ and $\mathcal{P}_3$, respectively. Also, illustrate that $P$ satisfies Eq. (3) of Theorem 18.

***Solution*** To construct the $(4 \times 3)$ matrix $P$ that represents $S$, we need to find the coordinate vectors of $S(1)$, $S(x)$, and $S(x^2)$ with respect to $D$. We calculate that $S(1) = x$, $S(x) = x^2 - 2$, and $S(x^2) = x^3 + 2x^2 - 4x$; so the coordinate vectors of $S(1)$, $S(x)$, and $S(x^2)$ are

$$[S(1)]_D = \begin{bmatrix} 0 \\ 1 \\ 0 \\ 0 \end{bmatrix}, \quad [S(x)]_D = \begin{bmatrix} -2 \\ 0 \\ 1 \\ 0 \end{bmatrix}, \quad \text{and} \quad [S(x^2)]_D = \begin{bmatrix} 0 \\ -4 \\ 2 \\ 1 \end{bmatrix}.$$

Thus the matrix representation for $S$ is the $(4 \times 3)$ matrix

$$P = \begin{bmatrix} 0 & -2 & 0 \\ 1 & 0 & -4 \\ 0 & 1 & 2 \\ 0 & 0 & 1 \end{bmatrix}.$$

To see that Eq. (3) of Theorem 18 holds, let $p(x) = a_0 + a_1 x + a_2 x^2$ be in $\mathcal{P}_2$. Then $S(p) = -2a_1 + (a_0 - 4a_2)x + (a_1 + 2a_2)x^2 + a_2 x^3$. In this case

$$[p(x)]_C = \begin{bmatrix} a_0 \\ a_1 \\ a_2 \end{bmatrix},$$

and if $S(p) = q(x)$, then

$$[q(x)]_D = \begin{bmatrix} -2a_1 \\ a_0 - 4a_2 \\ a_1 + 2a_2 \\ a_2 \end{bmatrix}.$$

A straightforward calculation shows that $P[p(x)]_C = [q(x)]_D$.    ■

**EXAMPLE 4**    Let $A$ be an $(m \times n)$ matrix and consider the linear transformation $T: R^n \to R^m$ defined by $T(\mathbf{x}) = A\mathbf{x}$. Show that relative to the natural bases for $R^n$ and $R^m$, the matrix for $T$ is $A$.

*Solution*    Let $B = \{\mathbf{e}_1, \mathbf{e}_2, \dots, \mathbf{e}_n\}$ be the natural basis for $R^n$, and let $C$ denote the natural basis for $R^m$. First note that for each vector $\mathbf{y}$ in $R^m$, $\mathbf{y} = [\mathbf{y}]_C$. Now let $Q$ denote the matrix of $T$ relative to $B$ and $C$, $Q = [\mathbf{Q}_1, \mathbf{Q}_2, \dots, \mathbf{Q}_n]$, and write $A = [\mathbf{A}_1, \mathbf{A}_2, \dots, \mathbf{A}_n]$. The definition of $Q$ gives

$$\mathbf{Q}_j = [T(\mathbf{e}_j)]_C = T(\mathbf{e}_j) = A\mathbf{e}_j = \mathbf{A}_j.$$

It now follows that $Q = A$.    ■

If $V$ is a vector space, then linear transformations of the form $T:V \to V$ are of considerable interest and importance. In this case, the same basis $B$ is normally chosen for both the domain and the range of $T$, and we refer to the representation as the matrix of $T$ with respect to $B$. In this case, if $Q$ is the matrix of $T$ and if $\mathbf{v}$ is in $V$, then Eq. (3) of Theorem 18 becomes

$$Q[\mathbf{v}]_B = [T(\mathbf{v})]_B.$$

The next example illustrates this special case.

**EXAMPLE 5**    Let $T: \mathcal{P}_2 \to \mathcal{P}_2$ be the linear transformation defined by $T(p) = xp'(x)$. Find the matrix, $Q$, of $T$ relative to the natural basis for $\mathcal{P}_2$.

*Solution*   Let $B = \{1, x, x^2\}$. Then $T(1) = 0$, $T(x) = x$, and $T(x^2) = 2x^2$. The coordinate vectors for $T(1)$, $T(x)$, $T(x^2)$ relative to $B$ are

$$[T(1)]_B = \begin{bmatrix} 0 \\ 0 \\ 0 \end{bmatrix}, \quad [T(x)]_B = \begin{bmatrix} 0 \\ 1 \\ 0 \end{bmatrix}, \quad \text{and} \quad [T(x^2)]_B = \begin{bmatrix} 0 \\ 0 \\ 2 \end{bmatrix}.$$

It follows that the matrix of $T$ with respect to $B$ is the $(3 \times 3)$ matrix

$$Q = \begin{bmatrix} 0 & 0 & 0 \\ 0 & 1 & 0 \\ 0 & 0 & 2 \end{bmatrix}.$$

If $p(x) = a_0 + a_1 x + a_2 x^2$, then $T[p(x)] = x(a_1 + 2a_2 x) = a_1 x + 2a_2 x^2$. Thus

$$[p(x)]_B = \begin{bmatrix} a_0 \\ a_1 \\ a_2 \end{bmatrix} \quad \text{and} \quad [T(p(x))]_B = \begin{bmatrix} 0 \\ a_1 \\ 2a_2 \end{bmatrix}.$$

A direct calculation verifies that $Q[p(x)]_B = [T(p(x))]_B$. ∎

## Algebraic Properties

In Section 5.8, we defined the algebraic operations of addition, scalar multiplication, and composition for linear transformations. We now examine the matrix representations of the resulting transformations. We begin with the following theorem.

**THEOREM 19**   Let $U$ and $V$ be vector spaces, with $\dim(U) = n$ and $\dim(V) = m$, and suppose that $B$ and $C$ are bases for $U$ and $V$, respectively. Let $T_1$, $T_2$, and $T$ be transformations from $U$ to $V$ and let $Q_1$, $Q_2$, and $Q$ be the matrix representations with respect to $B$ and $C$ for $T_1$, $T_2$, and $T$, respectively. Then:

1. $Q_1 + Q_2$ is the matrix representation for $T_1 + T_2$ with respect to $B$ and $C$.
2. For a scalar $a$, $aQ$ is the matrix representation for $aT$ with respect to $B$ and $C$.

*Proof*   We include here only the proof of property 1. The proof of property 2 is left for Exercises 26 and 27.

To prove property 1, set $T_3 = T_1 + T_2$ and let $Q_3$ be the matrix of $T_3$. By Eq. (3) of Theorem 18, $Q_3$ satisfies the equation

$$Q_3[\mathbf{u}]_B = [T_3(\mathbf{u})]_C \tag{9}$$

for every vector $\mathbf{u}$ in $U$; moreover, any other matrix that satisfies Eq. (9) is equal to $Q_3$. We also know from Theorem 18 that

$$Q_1[\mathbf{u}]_B = [T_1(\mathbf{u})]_C \quad \text{and} \quad Q_2[\mathbf{u}]_B = [T_2(\mathbf{u})]_C \tag{10}$$

for every vector $\mathbf{u}$ in $U$. Using Eq. (10) in Section 5.4 gives

$$[T_1(\mathbf{u}) + T_2(\mathbf{u})]_C = [T_1(\mathbf{u})]_C + [T_2(\mathbf{u})]_C. \tag{11}$$

It follows from Eqs. (10) and (11) that

$$(Q_1 + Q_2)[\mathbf{u}]_B = [T_1(\mathbf{u}) + T_2(\mathbf{u})]_C = [T_3(\mathbf{u})]_C;$$

therefore, $Q_3 = Q_1 + Q_2$. ◀

The following example illustrates the preceding theorem.

EXAMPLE 6    Let $T_1$ and $T_2$ be the linear transformations from $\mathcal{P}_2$ to $R^2$ defined by

$$T_1(p) = \begin{bmatrix} p(0) \\ p(1) \end{bmatrix} \quad \text{and} \quad T_2(p) = \begin{bmatrix} p'(0) \\ p(-1) \end{bmatrix}.$$

Set $T_3 = T_1 + T_2$ and $T_4 = 3T_1$ and let $B = \{1, x, x^2\}$ and $C = \{\mathbf{e}_1, \mathbf{e}_2\}$. Use the definition to calculate the matrices $Q_1$, $Q_2$, $Q_3$, and $Q_4$ for $T_1$, $T_2$, $T_3$, and $T_4$, respectively, relative to the bases $B$ and $C$. Note that $Q_3 = Q_1 + Q_2$ and $Q_4 = 3Q_1$.

**Solution**    Since

$$T_1(1) = \begin{bmatrix} 1 \\ 1 \end{bmatrix}, \quad T_1(x) = \begin{bmatrix} 0 \\ 1 \end{bmatrix}, \quad \text{and} \quad T_1(x^2) = \begin{bmatrix} 0 \\ 1 \end{bmatrix},$$

it follows that $Q_1$ is the $(2 \times 3)$ matrix given by

$$Q_1 = \begin{bmatrix} 1 & 0 & 0 \\ 1 & 1 & 1 \end{bmatrix}.$$

Similarly,

$$T_2(1) = \begin{bmatrix} 0 \\ 1 \end{bmatrix}, \quad T_2(x) = \begin{bmatrix} 1 \\ -1 \end{bmatrix}, \quad \text{and} \quad T_2(x^2) = \begin{bmatrix} 0 \\ 1 \end{bmatrix},$$

so $Q_2$ is given by

$$Q_2 = \begin{bmatrix} 0 & 1 & 0 \\ 1 & -1 & 1 \end{bmatrix}.$$

Now $T_3(p) = T_1(p) + T_2(p)$, so

$$T_3(p) = \begin{bmatrix} p(0) + p'(0) \\ p(1) + p(-1) \end{bmatrix}.$$

Proceeding as before, we obtain

$$T_3(1) = \begin{bmatrix} 1 \\ 2 \end{bmatrix}, \quad T_3(x) = \begin{bmatrix} 1 \\ 0 \end{bmatrix}, \quad \text{and} \quad T_3(x^2) = \begin{bmatrix} 0 \\ 2 \end{bmatrix}.$$

Thus

$$Q_3 = \begin{bmatrix} 1 & 1 & 0 \\ 2 & 0 & 2 \end{bmatrix},$$

and clearly $Q_3 = Q_1 + Q_2$.

The formula for $T_4$ is

$$T_4(p) = 3T_1(p) = 3 \begin{bmatrix} p(0) \\ p(1) \end{bmatrix} = \begin{bmatrix} 3p(0) \\ 3p(1) \end{bmatrix}.$$

The matrix, $Q_4$, for $T_4$ is easily obtained and is given by

$$Q_4 = \begin{bmatrix} 3 & 0 & 0 \\ 3 & 3 & 3 \end{bmatrix}.$$

In particular, $Q_4 = 3Q_1$.    ◼

The following theorem shows that the composition of two linear transformations corresponds to the product of the matrix representations.

**THEOREM 20**    Let $T: U \rightarrow V$ and $S: V \rightarrow W$ be linear transformations, and suppose $\dim(U) = n, \dim(V) = m$, and $\dim(W) = k$. Let $B, C$, and $D$ be bases for $U, V$, and $W$, respectively. If the matrix for $T$ relative to $B$ and $C$ is $Q[Q$ is $(m \times n)]$ and the matrix for $S$ relative to $C$ and $D$ is $P[P$ is $(k \times m)]$, then the matrix representation for $S \circ T$ is $PQ$.

*Proof*    The composition of $T$ and $S$ is illustrated in Fig. 5.9(a), and the matrix representation is illustrated in 5.9(b).

$$U \xrightarrow{T} V \xrightarrow{S} W \qquad\qquad R^n \xrightarrow{Q} R^m \xrightarrow{P} R^k$$

$$\mathbf{u} \longmapsto T(\mathbf{u}) \longmapsto S[T(\mathbf{u})] \qquad\qquad [\mathbf{u}]_B \longmapsto Q[\mathbf{u}]_B \longmapsto PQ[\mathbf{u}]_B$$

$$\text{(a)} \qquad\qquad\qquad\qquad\qquad\qquad \text{(b)}$$

*Figure 5.9*    The matrix for $S \circ T$

To prove Theorem 20, let $N$ be the matrix of $S \circ T$ with respect to the bases $B$ and $D$. Then $N$ is the unique matrix with the property that

$$N[\mathbf{u}]_B = [(S \circ T)(\mathbf{u})]_D \tag{12}$$

for every vector $\mathbf{u}$ in $U$. Similarly, $Q$ and $P$ are characterized by

$$Q[\mathbf{u}]_B = [T(\mathbf{u})]_C \quad \text{and} \quad P[\mathbf{v}]_C = [S(\mathbf{v})]_D \tag{13}$$

for all $\mathbf{u}$ in $U$ and $\mathbf{v}$ in $V$. It follows from Eq. (13) that

$$PQ[\mathbf{u}]_B = P[T(\mathbf{u})]_C = [S(T(\mathbf{u}))]_D = [(S \circ T)(\mathbf{u})]_D.$$

The uniqueness of $N$ in Eq. (12) now implies that $PQ = N$.    ◼

**EXAMPLE 7**    Let $U$ be the vector space of $(2 \times 2)$ matrices. If $T: U \rightarrow \mathcal{P}_2$ is the transformation given in Example 1 and $S: \mathcal{P}_2 \rightarrow \mathcal{P}_3$ is the transformation described in Example 3, give the formula for $S \circ T$. By direct calculation, find the matrix of $S \circ T$ with respect to the bases $B = \{E_{11}, E_{12}, E_{21}, E_{22}\}$ and $D = \{1, x, x^2, x^3\}$ for $U$ and $\mathcal{P}_3$, respectively.

Finally, use Theorem 20 and the matrices found in Examples 1 and 3 to calculate the matrix for $S \circ T$.

**Solution**  Recall that $T: U \rightarrow \mathcal{P}_2$ is given by

$$T\left(\begin{bmatrix} a & b \\ c & d \end{bmatrix}\right) = (a - d) + (a + 2b)x + (b - 3c)x^2,$$

and $S: \mathcal{P}_2 \rightarrow \mathcal{P}_3$ is defined by

$$S(p) = x^2 p'' - 2p' + xp.$$

Therefore, $S \circ T: U \rightarrow \mathcal{P}_3$ is defined by

$$(S \circ T)(A) = S(T(A)) = S((a - d) + (a + 2b)x + (b - 3c)x^2)$$
$$= (-2a - 4b) + (a - 4b + 12c - d)x + (a + 4b - 6c)x^2$$
$$+ (b - 3c)x^3.$$

The matrix, $N$, of $S \circ T$ relative to the given bases $B$ and $D$ is easily determined to be the $(4 \times 4)$ matrix

$$N = \begin{bmatrix} -2 & -4 & 0 & 0 \\ 1 & -4 & 12 & -1 \\ 1 & 4 & -6 & 0 \\ 0 & 1 & -3 & 0 \end{bmatrix}.$$

Moreover, $N = PQ$, where $Q$ is the matrix for $T$ found in Example 1 and $P$ is the matrix for $S$ determined in Example 3. ◼

A particularly useful case of Theorem 20 is the one in which $S$ and $T$ both map $V$ to $V$, $\dim(V) = n$, and the same basis $B$ is used for both the domain and the range. In this case, the composition $S \circ T$ is always defined, and the matrices $P$ and $Q$ for $S$ and $T$, respectively, are both $(n \times n)$ matrices. Using Theorem 20, we can easily show that if $T$ is invertible, then $Q$ is nonsingular, and furthermore the matrix representation for $T^{-1}$ is $Q^{-1}$. The matrix representation for the identity transformation on $V$, $I_V$, is the $(n \times n)$ identity matrix $I$. The matrix representation for the zero transformation on $V$ is the $(n \times n)$ zero matrix. (Observe that the identity and the zero transformations always have the same matrix representations, regardless of what basis we choose for $V$. Thus changing the basis for $V$ may change the matrix representation for $T$ or may leave the representation unchanged.)

## The Vector Space $L(U, V)$ (Optional)

If $U$ and $V$ are vector spaces, then $L(U, V)$ denotes the set of all linear transformations from $U$ to $V$:

$$L(U, V) = \{T: T \text{ is a linear transformation}; T: U \rightarrow V\}.$$

If $T$, $T_1$, and $T_2$ are in $L(U, V)$ and $a$ is a scalar, we have seen in Section 5.8 that $T_1 + T_2$ and $aT$ are again in $L(U, V)$. In fact, with these operations of addition and scalar multiplication, we have the following.

*Remark*     The set $L(U, V)$ is a vector space.

The proof of this remark is Exercise 29 of Section 5.8. We note here only that the zero of $L(U, V)$ is the zero transformation $T_0: U \to V$ defined by $T_0(\mathbf{u}) = \boldsymbol{\theta}_V$ for all $\mathbf{u}$ in $U$. To see this, let $T$ be in $L(U, V)$. Then $(T + T_0)(\mathbf{u}) = T(\mathbf{u}) + T_0(\mathbf{u}) = T(\mathbf{u}) + \boldsymbol{\theta}_V = T(\mathbf{u})$. This shows that $T + T_0 = T$, so $T_0$ is the zero vector in $L(U, V)$.

Now let $R_{mn}$ denote the vector space of $(m \times n)$ real matrices. If $\dim(U) = n$ and $\dim(V) = m$, then we can define a function $\psi: L(U, V) \to R_{mn}$ as follows: Let $B$ and $C$ be bases for $U$ and $V$, respectively. For a transformation $T$ in $L(U, V)$, set $\psi(T) = Q$, where $Q$ is the matrix of $T$ with respect to $B$ and $C$. We will now show that $\psi$ is an isomorphism. In particular, the following theorem holds.

**THEOREM 21**     If $U$ and $V$ are vector spaces such that $\dim(U) = n$ and $\dim(V) = m$, then $L(U, V)$ is isomorphic to $R_{mn}$.

**Proof**     It is an immediate consequence of Theorem 19 that the function $\psi$ defined previously is a linear transformation; that is, if $S$ and $T$ are in $L(U, V)$ and $a$ is a scalar, then $\psi(S + T) = \psi(S) + \psi(T)$ and $\psi(aT) = a\psi(T)$.

To show that $\psi$ maps $L(U, V)$ onto $R_{mn}$, let $Q = [q_{ij}]$ be an $(m \times n)$ matrix. Assume that $B = \{\mathbf{u}_1, \mathbf{u}_2, \ldots, \mathbf{u}_n\}$ and $C = \{\mathbf{v}_1, \mathbf{v}_2, \ldots, \mathbf{v}_m\}$ are the given bases for $U$ and $V$, respectively. Define a subset $\{\mathbf{w}_1, \mathbf{w}_2, \ldots, \mathbf{w}_n\}$ of $V$ as follows:

$$\mathbf{w}_1 = q_{11}\mathbf{v}_1 + q_{21}\mathbf{v}_2 + \cdots + q_{m1}\mathbf{v}_m$$

$$\mathbf{w}_2 = q_{12}\mathbf{v}_1 + q_{22}\mathbf{v}_2 + \cdots + q_{m2}\mathbf{v}_m$$

$$\vdots \qquad \vdots \qquad\qquad \vdots$$

$$\mathbf{w}_n = q_{1n}\mathbf{v}_1 + q_{2n}\mathbf{v}_2 + \cdots + q_{mn}\mathbf{v}_m. \tag{14}$$

Each vector $\mathbf{u}$ in $U$ can be expressed uniquely in the form

$$\mathbf{u} = a_1\mathbf{u}_1 + a_2\mathbf{u}_2 + \cdots + a_n\mathbf{u}_n.$$

If $T: U \to V$ is a function defined by

$$T(\mathbf{u}) = a_1\mathbf{w}_1 + a_2\mathbf{w}_2 + \cdots + a_n\mathbf{w}_n,$$

then $T$ is a linear transformation and $T(\mathbf{u}_j) = \mathbf{w}_j$ for each $j$, $1 \leq j \leq n$. By comparing systems (14) and (1), it becomes clear that the matrix of $T$ with respect to $B$ and $C$ is $Q$; that is, $\psi(T) = Q$.

The proof that $\psi$ is one to one is Exercise 33.  ■

The following example illustrates the method, described in the proof of Theorem 21, for obtaining the transformation when its matrix representation is given.

**EXAMPLE 8**     Let $Q$ be the $(3 \times 4)$ matrix

$$Q = \begin{bmatrix} 1 & 0 & -1 & 0 \\ 0 & 1 & 1 & 0 \\ 2 & 0 & 3 & 1 \end{bmatrix}.$$

Give the formula for a linear transformation $T: \mathcal{P}_3 \to \mathcal{P}_2$ such that the matrix of $T$ relative to the natural bases for $\mathcal{P}_3$ and $\mathcal{P}_2$ is $Q$.

*Solution*  Let $B = \{1, x, x^2, x^3\}$ and let $C = \{1, x, x^2\}$. Following the proof of Theorem 21, we form a subset $\{q_0(x), q_1(x), q_2(x), q_3(x)\}$ of $\mathcal{P}_2$ by using the columns of $Q$. Thus

$$q_0(x) = \quad (1)1 + 0x + 2x^2 = 1 + 2x^2$$
$$q_1(x) = \quad (0)1 + 1x + 0x^2 = x$$
$$q_2(x) = (-1)1 + 1x + 3x^2 = -1 + x + 3x^2$$
$$q_3(x) = \quad (0)1 + 0x + 1x^2 = x^2.$$

If $p(x) = a_0 + a_1 x + a_2 x^2 + a_3 x^3$ is an arbitrary polynomial in $\mathcal{P}_3$, then define $T: \mathcal{P}_3 \to \mathcal{P}_2$ by $T(p(x)) = a_0 q_0(x) + a_1 q_1(x) + a_2 q_2(x) + a_3 q_3(x)$. Thus

$$T(p(x)) = (a_0 - a_2) + (a_1 + a_2)x + (2a_0 + 3a_2 + a_3)x^2.$$

It is straightforward to show that $T$ is a linear transformation. Moreover, $T(1) = q_0(x)$, $T(x) = q_1(x)$, $T(x^2) = q_2(x)$, and $T(x^3) = q_3(x)$. It follows that $Q$ is the matrix of $T$ with respect to $B$ and $C$. ■

Let $U$ and $V$ be vector spaces such that $\dim(U) = n$ and $\dim(V) = m$. Theorem 21 implies that $L(U, V)$ and $R_{mn}$ are essentially the same vector space. Thus, for example, we can now conclude that $L(U, V)$ has dimension $mn$. Furthermore, if $T$ is a linear transformation in $L(U, V)$ and $Q$ is the corresponding matrix in $R_{mn}$, then properties of $T$ can be ascertained by studying $Q$. For example, a vector $\mathbf{u}$ in $U$ is in $\mathcal{N}(T)$ if and only if $[\mathbf{u}]_B$ is in $\mathcal{N}(Q)$ and a vector $\mathbf{v}$ in $V$ is in $\mathcal{R}(T)$ if and only if $[\mathbf{v}]_C$ is in $\mathcal{R}(Q)$. It follows that nullity$(T) =$ nullity$(Q)$ and rank$(T) =$ rank$(Q)$. In summary, the correspondence between $L(U, V)$ and $R_{mn}$ allows both the computational and the theoretical aspects of linear transformations to be studied in the more familiar context of matrices.

## 5.9 EXERCISES

In Exercises 1–10, the linear transformations $S, T, H$ are defined as follows:

$S: \mathcal{P}_3 \to \mathcal{P}_4$ is defined by $S(p) = p'(0)$.

$T: \mathcal{P}_3 \to \mathcal{P}_4$ is defined by $T(p) = (x + 2)p(x)$.

$H: \mathcal{P}_4 \to \mathcal{P}_3$ is defined by $H(p) = p'(x) + p(0)$.

Also, $B = \{1, x, x^2, x^3\}$ is the natural basis for $\mathcal{P}_3$, and $C = \{1, x, x^2, x^3, x^4\}$ is the natural basis for $\mathcal{P}_4$.

**1.** Find the matrix for $S$ with respect to $B$ and $C$.

**2.** Find the matrix for $T$ with respect to $B$ and $C$.

**3. a)** Use the formula for $S + T$ (see Exercise 1 of Section 5.8) to calculate the matrix of $S + T$ relative to $B$ and $C$.

**b)** Use Theorem 19 and the matrices found in Exercises 1 and 2 to obtain the matrix representation of $S + T$.

**4. a)** Use the formula for $2T$ (see Exercise 2 of Section 5.8) to calculate the matrix of $2T$ with respect to $B$ and $C$.

**b)** Use Theorem 19 and the matrix found in Exercise 2 to find the matrix for $2T$.

**5.** Find the matrix for $H$ with respect to $C$ and $B$.

**6. a)** Use the formula for $H \circ T$ (see Exercise 3 of Section 5.8) to determine the matrix of $H \circ T$ with respect to $B$.

*Exercises that are based on optional material.

**b)** Use Theorem 20 and the matrices obtained in Exercises 2 and 5 to obtain the matrix representation for $H \circ T$.

**7. a)** Use the formula for $T \circ H$ (see Exercise 4 of Section 5.8) to determine the matrix of $T \circ H$ with respect to $C$.

**b)** Use Theorem 20 and the matrices obtained in Exercises 2 and 5 to obtain the matrix representation for $T \circ H$.

**8.** Let $p(x) = a_0 + a_1x + a_2x^2 + a_3x^3$ be an arbitrary polynomial in $\mathcal{P}_3$.

**a)** Exhibit the coordinate vectors $[p]_B$ and $[S(p)]_C$.

**b)** If $P$ is the matrix for $S$ obtained in Exercise 1, demonstrate that $P[p]_B = [S(p)]_C$.

**9.** Let $p(x) = a_0 + a_1x + a_2x^2 + a_3x^3$ be an arbitrary polynomial in $\mathcal{P}_3$.

**a)** Exhibit the coordinate vectors $[p]_B$ and $[T(p)]_C$.

**b)** If $Q$ is the matrix for $T$ obtained in Exercise 2, demonstrate that $Q[p]_B = [T(p)]_C$.

**10.** Let $N$ be the matrix representation obtained for $H$ in Exercise 5. Demonstrate that $N[q]_C = [H(q)]_B$ for $q(x) = a_0 + a_1x + a_2x^2 + a_3x^3 + a_4x^4$ in $\mathcal{P}_4$.

**11.** Let $T: V \to V$ be the linear transformation defined in Exercise 7 of Section 5.8, and let $B = \{e^x, e^{2x}, e^{3x}\}$.

**a)** Find the matrix, $Q$, of $T$ with respect to $B$.

**b)** Find the matrix, $P$, of $T^{-1}$ with respect to $B$.

**c)** Show that $P = Q^{-1}$.

**12.** Let $T: V \to V$ be the linear transformation defined in Exercise 8 of Section 5.8, and let $B = \{\sin x, \cos x, e^{-x}\}$. Repeat Exercise 11.

**13.** Let $V$ be the vector space of $(2 \times 2)$ matrices and define $T:V \to V$ by $T(A) = A^T$ (see Exercise 9 of Section 5.8). Let $B = \{E_{11}, E_{12}, E_{21}, E_{22}\}$ be the natural basis for $V$.

**a)** Find the matrix, $Q$, of $T$ with respect to $B$.

**b)** For arbitrary $A$ in $V$, show that $Q[A]_B = [A^T]_B$.

**14.** Let $S: \mathcal{P}_2 \to \mathcal{P}_3$ be given by $S(p) = x^3 p'' - x^2 p' + 3p$. Find the matrix representation of $S$ with respect to the natural bases $B = \{1, x, x^2\}$ for $\mathcal{P}_2$ and $C = \{1, x, x^2, x^3\}$ for $\mathcal{P}_3$.

**15.** Let $S$ be the transformation in Exercise 14, let the basis for $\mathcal{P}_2$ be $B = \{x + 1, x + 2, x^2\}$, and let the basis for $\mathcal{P}_3$ be $C = \{1, x, x^2, x^3\}$. Find the matrix representation for $S$.

**16.** Let $S$ be the transformation in Exercise 14, let the basis for $\mathcal{P}_2$ be $B = \{1, x, x^2\}$, and let the basis for $\mathcal{P}_3$ be $D = \{3, 3x - x^2, 3x^2, x^3\}$. Find the matrix for $S$.

**17.** Let $T: \mathcal{P}_2 \to R^3$ be given by

$$T(p) = \begin{bmatrix} p(0) \\ 3p'(1) \\ p'(1) + p''(0) \end{bmatrix}.$$

Find the representation of $T$ with respect to the natural bases for $\mathcal{P}_2$ and $R^3$.

**18.** Find the representation for the transformation in Exercise 17 with respect to the natural basis for $\mathcal{P}_2$ and the basis $\{\mathbf{u}_1, \mathbf{u}_2, \mathbf{u}_3\}$ for $R^3$, where

$$\mathbf{u}_1 = \begin{bmatrix} 1 \\ 0 \\ 1 \end{bmatrix}, \quad \mathbf{u}_2 = \begin{bmatrix} 0 \\ 1 \\ 1 \end{bmatrix}, \quad \text{and}$$

$$\mathbf{u}_3 = \begin{bmatrix} 1 \\ 1 \\ 1 \end{bmatrix}.$$

**19.** Let $T: V \to V$ be a linear transformation, where $B = \{\mathbf{v}_1, \mathbf{v}_2, \mathbf{v}_3, \mathbf{v}_4\}$ is a basis for $V$. Find the matrix representation of $T$ with respect to $B$ if $T(\mathbf{v}_1) = \mathbf{v}_2$, $T(\mathbf{v}_2) = \mathbf{v}_3$, $T(\mathbf{v}_3) = \mathbf{v}_1 + \mathbf{v}_2$, and $T(\mathbf{v}_4) = \mathbf{v}_1 + 3\mathbf{v}_4$.

**20.** Let $T: R^3 \to R^2$ be given by $T(\mathbf{x}) = A\mathbf{x}$, where

$$A = \begin{bmatrix} 1 & 2 & 1 \\ 3 & 0 & 4 \end{bmatrix}.$$

Find the representation of $T$ with respect to the natural bases for $R^2$ and $R^3$.

**21.** Let $T: \mathcal{P}_2 \to \mathcal{P}_2$ be defined by $T(a_0 + a_1x + a_2x^2) = (-4a_0 - 2a_1) + (3a_0 + 3a_1)x + (-a_0 + 2a_1 + 3a_2)x^2$. Determine the matrix of $T$ relative to the natural basis $B$ for $\mathcal{P}_2$.

**22.** Let $T$ be the linear transformation defined in Exercise 21. If $Q$ is the matrix representation found in Exercise 21, show that $Q[p]_B = [T(p)]_B$ for $p(x) = a_0 + a_1x + a_2x^2$.

**23.** Let $T$ be the linear transformation defined in Exercise 21. Find the matrix of $T$ with respect to the basis $C = \{1 - 3x + 7x^2, 6 - 3x + 2x^2, x^2\}$.

**24.** Complete the proof of Theorem 18 by showing that $Q$ is the unique matrix that satisfies Equation 3. [*Hint:* Suppose $P = [\mathbf{P}_1, \mathbf{P}_2, \dots, \mathbf{P}_n]$ is an $(m \times n)$ matrix such that $P[\mathbf{u}]_B = [T(\mathbf{u})]_C$ for each $\mathbf{u}$ in $U$. By taking $\mathbf{u}$ in $B$, show that $\mathbf{P}_j = \mathbf{Q}_j$ for $1 \leq j \leq n$.]

**25.** Give another proof of property 1 of Theorem 19 by constructing matrix representations for $T_1$, $T_2$, and $T_1 + T_2$.

**26.** Give a proof of property 2 of Theorem 19 by constructing matrix representations for $T$ and $aT$.

**27.** Give a proof of property 2 of Theorem 19 that uses the uniqueness assertion in Theorem 18.

**28.** Let $V$ be an $n$-dimensional vector space, and let $I_V\colon V \to V$ be the identity transformation on $V$. [Recall that $I_V(\mathbf{v}) = \mathbf{v}$ for all $\mathbf{v}$ in $V$.] Show that the matrix representation for $I_V$ with respect to any basis for $V$ is the $(n \times n)$ identity matrix $I$.

**29.** Let $V$ be an $n$-dimensional vector space, and let $T_0\colon V \to V$ be the zero transformation in $V$; that is, $T_0(\mathbf{v}) = \boldsymbol{\theta}_V$ for all $\mathbf{v}$ in $V$. Show that the matrix representation for $T_0$ with respect to any basis for $V$ is the $(n \times n)$ zero matrix.

**30.** Let $V$ be an $n$-dimensional vector space with basis $B$, and let $T\colon V \to V$ be an invertible linear transformation. Let $Q$ be the matrix of $T$ with respect to $B$, and let $P$ be the matrix of $T^{-1}$ with respect to $B$. Prove that $P = Q^{-1}$. [*Hint:* Note that $T^{-1} \circ T = I_V$. Now apply Theorem 20 and Exercise 28.]

In Exercises 31 and 32, $Q$ is the $(3 \times 4)$ matrix given by

$$Q = \begin{bmatrix} 1 & 0 & 2 & 0 \\ 0 & 1 & 0 & 1 \\ -1 & 1 & 0 & -1 \end{bmatrix}.$$

**\*31.** Give the formula for a linear transformation $T\colon \mathcal{P}_3 \to \mathcal{P}_2$ such that $Q$ is the matrix of $T$ with respect to the natural bases for $\mathcal{P}_3$ and $\mathcal{P}_2$.

**\*32.** Let $V$ be the vector space of all $(2 \times 2)$ matrices. Give the formula for a linear transformation $S\colon \mathcal{P}_2 \to V$ such that $Q^T$ is the matrix of $S$ with respect to the natural bases for $\mathcal{P}_2$ and $V$.

**\*33.** Complete the proof of Theorem 21 by showing that the mapping described in the proof of the theorem is one to one.

## 5.10  CHANGE OF BASIS AND DIAGONALIZATION

In Section 5.9, we saw that a linear transformation from $U$ to $V$ could be represented as an $(m \times n)$ matrix when $\dim(U) = n$ and $\dim(V) = m$. A consequence of this representation is that properties of transformations can be studied by examining their corresponding matrix representations. Moreover, we have a great deal of machinery in place for matrix theory; so matrices will provide a suitable analytical and computational framework for studying a linear transformation. To simplify matters somewhat, we consider only transformations from $V$ to $V$, where $\dim(V) = n$. So let $T\colon V \to V$ be a linear transformation and suppose that $Q$ is the matrix representation for $T$ with respect to a basis $B$; that is,

$$\text{if } \mathbf{w} = T(\mathbf{u}), \quad \text{then} \quad [\mathbf{w}]_B = Q[\mathbf{u}]_B. \tag{1}$$

As we know, when we change the basis $B$ for $V$, we may change the matrix representation for $T$. If we are interested in the properties of $T$, then it is reasonable to search for a basis for $V$ that makes the matrix representation for $T$ as simple as possible. Finding such a basis is the subject of this section.

## Diagonalizable Transformations

A particularly nice matrix to deal with computationally is a diagonal matrix. If $T: V \to V$ is a linear transformation whose matrix representation with respect to $B$ is a diagonal matrix,

$$D = \begin{bmatrix} d_1 & 0 & 0 & \cdots & 0 \\ 0 & d_2 & 0 & \cdots & 0 \\ \vdots & & & & \vdots \\ 0 & 0 & 0 & \cdots & d_n \end{bmatrix}, \tag{2}$$

then it is easy to analyze the action of $T$ on $V$, as the following example illustrates.

**EXAMPLE 1**    Let $V$ be a three-dimensional vector space with basis $B = \{\mathbf{v}_1, \mathbf{v}_2, \mathbf{v}_3\}$, and suppose that $T: V \to V$ is a linear transformation with matrix

$$D = \begin{bmatrix} 2 & 0 & 0 \\ 0 & 3 & 0 \\ 0 & 0 & 0 \end{bmatrix}$$

with respect to $B$. Describe the action of $T$ in terms of the basis vectors and determine bases for $\mathcal{N}(T)$ and $\mathcal{R}(T)$.

*Solution*    It follows from the definition of $D$ that $T(\mathbf{v}_1) = 2\mathbf{v}_1$, $T(\mathbf{v}_2) = 3\mathbf{v}_2$, and $T(\mathbf{v}_3) = \boldsymbol{\theta}$. If $\mathbf{u}$ is any vector in $V$ and

$$\mathbf{u} = a\mathbf{v}_1 + b\mathbf{v}_2 + c\mathbf{v}_3,$$

then

$$T(\mathbf{u}) = aT(\mathbf{v}_1) + bT(\mathbf{v}_2) + cT(\mathbf{v}_3).$$

Therefore, the action of $T$ on $\mathbf{u}$ is given by

$$T(\mathbf{u}) = 2a\mathbf{v}_1 + 3b\mathbf{v}_2.$$

It follows that $\mathbf{u}$ is in $\mathcal{N}(T)$ if and only if $a = b = 0$; that is,

$$\mathcal{N}(T) = \mathrm{Sp}\{\mathbf{v}_3\}. \tag{3}$$

Further, $\mathcal{R}(T) = \mathrm{Sp}\{T(\mathbf{v}_1), T(\mathbf{v}_2), T(\mathbf{v}_3)\}$, and since $T(\mathbf{v}_3) = \boldsymbol{\theta}$, it follows that

$$\mathcal{R}(T) = \mathrm{Sp}\{T(\mathbf{v}_1), T(\mathbf{v}_2)\} = \mathrm{Sp}\{2\mathbf{v}_1, 3\mathbf{v}_2\}. \tag{4}$$

One can easily see that the spanning sets given in Eqs. (3) and (4) are linearly independent, so they are bases for $\mathcal{N}(T)$ and $\mathcal{R}(T)$, respectively. ◼

If $T$ is a linear transformation with a matrix representation that is diagonal, then $T$ is called **diagonalizable**. Before characterizing diagonalizable linear transformations, we need to extend the concepts of eigenvalues and eigenvectors to the general vector-space setting. Specifically, a scalar $\lambda$ is called an **eigenvalue** for a linear transformation $T: V \to V$ provided that there is a nonzero vector $\mathbf{v}$ in $V$ such that $T(\mathbf{v}) = \lambda\mathbf{v}$. The vector $\mathbf{v}$ is called an **eigenvector** for $T$ corresponding to $\lambda$. The following example illustrates these concepts.

ᚼᚼᚼ   EXAMPLE 2   Let $T: \mathcal{P}_2 \to \mathcal{P}_2$ be defined by

$$T(a_0 + a_1 x + a_2 x^2) = (2a_1 - 2a_2) + (2a_0 + 3a_2)x + 3a_2 x^2.$$

Show that $C = \{1 + x, 1 - x, x + x^2\}$ is a basis of $V$ consisting of eigenvectors for $T$, and exhibit the matrix of $T$ with respect to $C$.

*Solution*   It is straightforward to show that $C$ is a basis for $\mathcal{P}_2$. Also,

$$
\begin{array}{rcccl}
T(1 + x) &=& 2 + 2x &=& 2(1 + x) \\
T(1 - x) &=& -2 + 2x &=& -2(1 - x) \\
T(x + x^2) &=& 3x + 3x^2 &=& 3(x + x^2).
\end{array}
\tag{5}
$$

Thus $T$ has eigenvalues $2$, $-2$, and $3$ with corresponding eigenvectors $1 + x$, $1 - x$, and $x + x^2$, respectively. Moreover, it follows from (5) that the matrix of $T$ with respect to $C$ is the $(3 \times 3)$ diagonal matrix

$$Q = \begin{bmatrix} 2 & 0 & 0 \\ 0 & -2 & 0 \\ 0 & 0 & 3 \end{bmatrix}.$$

In particular, $T$ is a diagonalizable linear transformation.   ◼

The linear transformation in Example 2 provides an illustration of the following general result.

ᚼᚼᚼ   THEOREM 22   Let $V$ be an $n$-dimensional vector space. A linear transformation $T: V \to V$ is diagonalizable if and only if there exists a basis for $V$ consisting of eigenvectors for $T$.

*Proof*   First, suppose that $B = \{\mathbf{v}_1, \mathbf{v}_2, \ldots, \mathbf{v}_n\}$ is a basis for $V$ consisting entirely of eigenvectors—say, $T(\mathbf{v}_1) = d_1 \mathbf{v}_1$, $T(\mathbf{v}_2) = d_2 \mathbf{v}_2, \ldots, T(\mathbf{v}_n) = d_n \mathbf{v}_n$. It follows that the coordinate vectors for $T(\mathbf{v}_1), T(\mathbf{v}_2), \ldots, T(\mathbf{v}_n)$ are the $n$-dimensional vectors

$$[T(\mathbf{v}_1)]_B = \begin{bmatrix} d_1 \\ 0 \\ \vdots \\ 0 \end{bmatrix}, \quad [T(\mathbf{v}_2)]_B = \begin{bmatrix} 0 \\ d_2 \\ \vdots \\ 0 \end{bmatrix}, \ldots, \quad [T(\mathbf{v}_n)]_B = \begin{bmatrix} 0 \\ 0 \\ \vdots \\ d_n \end{bmatrix}. \tag{6}$$

Therefore, the matrix representation for $T$ with respect to $B$ is the $(n \times n)$ diagonal matrix $D$ given in (2). In particular, $T$ is diagonalizable.

Conversely, assume that $T$ is diagonalizable and that the matrix for $T$ with respect to the basis $B = \{\mathbf{v}_1, \mathbf{v}_2, \ldots, \mathbf{v}_n\}$ is the diagonal matrix $D$ given in (2). Then the coordinate vectors for $T(\mathbf{v}_1), T(\mathbf{v}_2), \ldots, T(\mathbf{v}_n)$ are given by (6), so it follows that

$$
\begin{array}{rcl}
T(\mathbf{v}_1) = d_1 \mathbf{v}_1 + 0\mathbf{v}_2 + \cdots + 0\mathbf{v}_n &=& d_1 \mathbf{v}_1 \\
T(\mathbf{v}_2) = 0\mathbf{v}_1 + d_2 \mathbf{v}_2 + \cdots + 0\mathbf{v}_n &=& d_2 \mathbf{v}_2 \\
\vdots \qquad \vdots \qquad\qquad \vdots \qquad\quad && \vdots \qquad \vdots \\
T(\mathbf{v}_n) = 0\mathbf{v}_1 + 0\mathbf{v}_2 + \cdots + d_n \mathbf{v}_n &=& d_n \mathbf{v}_n.
\end{array}
$$

Thus $B$ consists of eigenvectors for $T$.   ◼

As with matrices, not every linear transformation is diagonalizable. Equivalently, if $T: V \rightarrow V$ is a linear transformation, it may be that no matter what basis we choose for $V$, we never obtain a matrix representation for $T$ that is diagonal. Moreover, even if $T$ is diagonalizable, Theorem 22 provides no procedure for calculating a basis for $V$ consisting of eigenvectors for $T$. Before providing such a procedure, we will examine the relationship between matrix representations of a single transformation with respect to different bases. First we need to facilitate the process of changing bases.

## The Transition Matrix

Let $B$ and $C$ be bases for an $n$-dimensional vector space $V$. Theorem 23, which follows, relates the coordinate vectors $[\mathbf{v}]_B$ and $[\mathbf{v}]_C$ for an arbitrary vector $\mathbf{v}$ in $V$. Using this theorem, we will be able to show later that if $Q$ is the matrix of a linear transformation $T$ with respect to $B$, and if $P$ is the matrix of $T$ relative to $C$, then $Q$ and $P$ are similar. Since we know how to determine whether a matrix is similar to a diagonal matrix, we will be able to determine when $T$ is diagonalizable.

 THEOREM 23    **Change of Basis**    Let $B$ and $C$ be bases for the vector space $V$, with $B = \{\mathbf{u}_1, \mathbf{u}_2, \ldots, \mathbf{u}_n\}$, and let $P$ be the $(n \times n)$ matrix given by $P = [\mathbf{P}_1, \mathbf{P}_2, \ldots, \mathbf{P}_n]$, where the $i$th column of $P$ is

$$\mathbf{P}_i = [\mathbf{u}_i]_C. \tag{7}$$

Then $P$ is a nonsingular matrix and

$$[\mathbf{v}]_C = P[\mathbf{v}]_B \tag{8}$$

for each vector $\mathbf{v}$ in $V$.

**Proof**    Let $I_V$ denote the identity transformation on $V$; that is, $I_V(\mathbf{v}) = \mathbf{v}$ for all $\mathbf{v}$ in $V$. Recall that the $i$th column of the matrix of $I_V$ with respect to $B$ and $C$ is the coordinate vector $[I_V(\mathbf{u}_i)]_C$. But $I_V(\mathbf{u}_i) = \mathbf{u}_i$, so it follows that the matrix $P$ described above is just the matrix representation of $I_V$ with respect to $B$ and $C$. It now follows from Eq. (3) of Theorem 18 that

$$P[\mathbf{v}]_B = [I_V(\mathbf{v})]_C = [\mathbf{v}]_C$$

for each $\mathbf{v}$ in $V$; in particular, Eq. (8) is proved. The proof that $P$ is nonsingular is left as Exercise 17.    ■

The matrix $P$ given in Theorem 23 is called the ***transition matrix***. Since $P$ is nonsingular, we have, in addition to Eq. (8), the relationship

$$[\mathbf{v}]_B = P^{-1}[\mathbf{v}]_C \tag{9}$$

for each vector $\mathbf{v}$ in $V$. The following example illustrates the use of the transition matrix.

 EXAMPLE 3    Let $B$ and $C$ be the bases for $\mathcal{P}_2$ given by $B = \{1, x, x^2\}$ and $C = \{1, x+1, (x+1)^2\}$. Find the transition matrix $P$ such that

$$P[q]_B = [q]_C$$

for each polynomial $q(x)$ in $\mathcal{P}_2$.

***Solution*** Following Theorem 23, we determine the coordinates of $1$, $x$, and $x^2$ in terms of $1$, $x+1$, and $(x+1)^2$. This determination is easy, and we find

$$1 = 1$$
$$x = (x+1) - 1$$
$$x^2 = (x+1)^2 - 2(x+1) + 1.$$

Thus with respect to $C$ the coordinate vectors of $B$ are

$$[1]_C = \begin{bmatrix} 1 \\ 0 \\ 0 \end{bmatrix}, \quad [x]_C = \begin{bmatrix} -1 \\ 1 \\ 0 \end{bmatrix}, \quad \text{and} \quad [x^2]_C = \begin{bmatrix} 1 \\ -2 \\ 1 \end{bmatrix}.$$

The transition matrix $P$ is therefore

$$P = \begin{bmatrix} 1 & -1 & 1 \\ 0 & 1 & -2 \\ 0 & 0 & 1 \end{bmatrix}.$$

In particular, any polynomial $q(x) = a_0 + a_1 x + a_2 x^2$ can be expressed in terms of $1$, $x+1$, and $(x+1)^2$ by forming $[q]_C = P[q]_B$. Forming this, we find

$$[q]_C = \begin{bmatrix} a_0 - a_1 + a_2 \\ a_1 - 2a_2 \\ a_2 \end{bmatrix}.$$

So with respect to $C$, we can write $q(x)$ as $q(x) = (a_0 - a_1 + a_2) + (a_1 - 2a_2)(x+1) + a_2(x+1)^2$ [a result that we can verify directly by multiplying out the new expression for $q(x)$]. ■

## Matrix Representation and Change of Basis

In terms of the transition matrix, we can now state precisely the relationship between the matrix representations of a linear transformation with respect to two different bases $B$ and $C$. Moreover, given a basis $B$, the relationship suggests how to determine a basis $C$ such that the matrix relative to $C$ is a simpler matrix.

**THEOREM 24** Let $B$ and $C$ be bases for the $n$-dimensional vector space $V$, and let $T: V \rightarrow V$ be a linear transformation. If $Q_1$ is the matrix of $T$ with respect to $B$ and if $Q_2$ is the matrix of $T$ with respect to $C$, then

$$Q_2 = P^{-1} Q_1 P, \tag{10}$$

where $P$ is the transition matrix from $C$ to $B$.

***Proof*** First note that the notation is reversed from Theorem 23; $P$ is the transition matrix from $C$ to $B$, so

$$[\mathbf{v}]_B = P[\mathbf{v}]_C \tag{11}$$

for all $\mathbf{v}$ in $V$. Also,

$$P^{-1}[\mathbf{w}]_B = [\mathbf{w}]_C \tag{12}$$

for each $\mathbf{w}$ in $V$. If $\mathbf{v}$ is in $V$ and if $T(\mathbf{v}) = \mathbf{w}$, then (1) implies that

$$Q_1[\mathbf{v}]_B = [\mathbf{w}]_B \text{ and } Q_2[\mathbf{v}]_C = [\mathbf{w}]_C. \tag{13}$$

From the equations given in (11), (12), and (13), we obtain

$$P^{-1}Q_1 P[\mathbf{v}]_C = P^{-1}Q_1[\mathbf{v}]_B = P^{-1}[\mathbf{w}]_B = [\mathbf{w}]_C;$$

that is, the matrix $P^{-1}Q_1 P$ satisfies the same property as $Q_2$ in (13). By the uniqueness of $Q_2$, we conclude that $Q_2 = P^{-1}Q_1 P$. ∎

The following example provides an illustration of Theorem 24.

**EXAMPLE 4**    Let $T: \mathcal{P}_2 \to \mathcal{P}_2$ be the linear transformation given in Example 2, and let $B$ and $C$ be the bases for $\mathcal{P}_2$ given by $B = \{1, x, x^2\}$ and $C = \{1 + x, 1 - x, x + x^2\}$. Calculate the matrix of $T$ with respect to $B$ and use Theorem 24 to find the matrix of $T$ with respect to $C$.

*Solution*    Recall that $T$ is defined by

$$T(a_0 + a_1 x + a_2 x^2) = (2a_1 - 2a_2) + (2a_0 + 3a_2)x + 3a_2 x^2.$$

In particular, $T(1) = 2x$, $T(x) = 2$, and $T(x^2) = -2 + 3x + 3x^2$. Thus

$$[T(1)]_B = \begin{bmatrix} 0 \\ 2 \\ 0 \end{bmatrix}, \quad [T(x)]_B = \begin{bmatrix} 2 \\ 0 \\ 0 \end{bmatrix}, \quad \text{and} \quad [T(x^2)]_B = \begin{bmatrix} -2 \\ 3 \\ 3 \end{bmatrix}.$$

It follows that the matrix of $T$ with respect to $B$ is the matrix $Q_1$ given by

$$Q_1 = \begin{bmatrix} 0 & 2 & -2 \\ 2 & 0 & 3 \\ 0 & 0 & 3 \end{bmatrix}.$$

Now let $P$ be the transition matrix from $C$ to $B$; that is, $P[\mathbf{v}]_C = [\mathbf{v}]_B$ for each vector $\mathbf{v}$ in $V$ (note that the roles of $B$ and $C$ are reversed from Theorem 23). By Theorem 23, $P$ is the $(3 \times 3)$ matrix $P = [\mathbf{P}_1, \mathbf{P}_2, \mathbf{P}_3]$, where

$$\mathbf{P}_1 = [1 + x]_B, \quad \mathbf{P}_2 = [1 - x]_B, \quad \text{and} \quad \mathbf{P}_3 = [x + x^2]_B.$$

Thus $P$ is given by

$$P = \begin{bmatrix} 1 & 1 & 0 \\ 1 & -1 & 1 \\ 0 & 0 & 1 \end{bmatrix}.$$

The inverse of $P$ can be easily be calculated and is given by

$$P^{-1} = (1/2) \begin{bmatrix} 1 & 1 & -1 \\ 1 & -1 & 1 \\ 0 & 0 & 2 \end{bmatrix}.$$

By Theorem 24, the matrix of $T$ with respect to $C$ is the matrix $Q_2$ determined by $Q_2 = P^{-1}Q_1P$. This yields

$$Q_2 = \begin{bmatrix} 2 & 0 & 0 \\ 0 & -2 & 0 \\ 0 & 0 & 3 \end{bmatrix}. \qquad \blacksquare$$

Although the preceding example serves to illustrate the statement of Theorem 2, a comparison of Examples 2 and 4 makes it clear that when the basis $C$ is given, it may be easier to calculate the matrix of $T$ with respect to $C$ directly from the definition. Theorem 24, however, suggests the following idea: If we are given a linear transformation $T: V \rightarrow V$ and the matrix representation, $Q$, for $T$ with respect to a given basis $B$, then we should look for a simple matrix $R$ (diagonal if possible) that is similar to $Q$, $R = S^{-1}QS$. In this case we can use $S^{-1}$ as a transition matrix to obtain a new basis $C$ for $V$, where $[\mathbf{u}]_C = S^{-1}[\mathbf{u}]_B$. With respect to the basis $C$, $T$ will have the matrix representation $R$, where $R = S^{-1}QS$.

Given the transition matrix $S^{-1}$, it is an easy matter to find the actual basis vectors of $C$. In particular, suppose that $B = \{\mathbf{u}_1, \mathbf{u}_2, \ldots, \mathbf{u}_n\}$ is the given basis for $V$, and we wish to find vectors in $C = \{\mathbf{v}_1, \mathbf{v}_2, \ldots, \mathbf{v}_n\}$. Since $[\mathbf{u}]_C = S^{-1}[\mathbf{u}]_B$ for all $\mathbf{u}$ in $V$, we know that $S[\mathbf{u}]_C = [\mathbf{u}]_B$. Moreover, with respect to $C$, $[\mathbf{v}_i]_C = \mathbf{e}_i$. So from $S[\mathbf{v}_i]_C = [\mathbf{v}_i]_B$ we obtain

$$S\mathbf{e}_i = [\mathbf{v}_i]_B, \quad 1 \le i \le n. \tag{14}$$

But if $S = [\mathbf{S}_1, \mathbf{S}_2, \ldots, \mathbf{S}_n]$, then $S\mathbf{e}_i = \mathbf{S}_i$, and Eq. (14) tells us that the coordinate vector of $\mathbf{v}_i$ with respect to the known basis $B$ is the $i$th column of $S$. The procedure just described can be summarized as follows:

## Summary

Let $T: V \rightarrow V$ be a linear transformation and let $B = \{\mathbf{u}_1, \mathbf{u}_2, \ldots, \mathbf{u}_n\}$ be a given basis for $V$.

**Step 1.** Calculate the matrix, $Q$, for $T$ with respect to the basis $B$.

**Step 2.** Use matrix techniques to find a "simple" matrix $R$ and a nonsingular matrix $S$ such that $R = S^{-1}QS$.

**Step 3.** Determine vectors $\mathbf{v}_1, \mathbf{v}_2, \ldots, \mathbf{v}_n$ in $V$ so that $[\mathbf{v}_i]_B = \mathbf{S}_i, 1 \le i \le n$, where $\mathbf{S}_i$ is the $i$th column of $S$.

Then $C = \{\mathbf{v}_1, \mathbf{v}_2, \ldots, \mathbf{v}_n\}$ is a basis for $V$ and $R$ is the matrix of $T$ with respect to $C$.

The case of particular interest is the one in which $Q$ is similar to a diagonal matrix $R$. In this case, if we choose $\{\mathbf{S}_1, \mathbf{S}_2, \ldots, \mathbf{S}_n\}$ to be a basis of $R^n$ consisting of eigenvectors for $Q$, then

$$R = S^{-1}QS = \begin{bmatrix} d_1 & 0 & \cdots & 0 \\ 0 & d_2 & \cdots & 0 \\ \vdots & & & \vdots \\ 0 & 0 & \cdots & d_n \end{bmatrix},$$

where $d_1, d_2, \ldots, d_n$ are the (not necessarily distinct) eigenvalues for $Q$ and where $Q\mathbf{S}_i = d_i\mathbf{S}_i$. Since $R$ is the matrix of $T$ with respect to $C$, $C = \{\mathbf{v}_1, \mathbf{v}_2, \ldots, \mathbf{v}_n\}$ is a basis of $V$ consisting of eigenvectors for $T$; specifically, $T(\mathbf{v}_i) = d_i\mathbf{v}_i$ for $1 \le i \le n$. The following example provides an illustration.

**EXAMPLE 5**    Show that the differential operator $T: \mathcal{P}_2 \to \mathcal{P}_2$ defined by $T(p) = x^2 p'' + (2x - 1)p' + 3p$ is diagonalizable.

*Solution*    With respect to the basis $B = \{1, x, x^2\}$, $T$ has the matrix representation

$$Q = \begin{bmatrix} 3 & -1 & 0 \\ 0 & 5 & -2 \\ 0 & 0 & 9 \end{bmatrix}.$$

Since $Q$ is triangular, we see that the eigenvalues are 3, 5, and 9; and since $Q$ has distinct eigenvalues, $Q$ can be diagonalized where the matrix $S$ of eigenvectors will diagonalize $Q$.

We calculate the eigenvectors $\mathbf{u}_1, \mathbf{u}_2, \mathbf{u}_3$ for $Q$ and form $S = [\mathbf{u}_1, \mathbf{u}_2, \mathbf{u}_3]$, which yields

$$S = \begin{bmatrix} 1 & 1 & 1 \\ 0 & -2 & -6 \\ 0 & 0 & 12 \end{bmatrix}.$$

In this case it follows that

$$S^{-1}QS = \begin{bmatrix} 3 & 0 & 0 \\ 0 & 5 & 0 \\ 0 & 0 & 9 \end{bmatrix} = R.$$

In view of our remarks above, $R$ is the matrix representation for $T$ with respect to the basis $C = \{\mathbf{v}_1, \mathbf{v}_2, \mathbf{v}_3\}$, where $[\mathbf{v}_i]_B = \mathbf{S}_i$, or

$$[\mathbf{v}_1]_B = \begin{bmatrix} 1 \\ 0 \\ 0 \end{bmatrix}, \quad [\mathbf{v}_2]_B = \begin{bmatrix} 1 \\ -2 \\ 0 \end{bmatrix}, \quad \text{and} \quad [\mathbf{v}_3]_B = \begin{bmatrix} 1 \\ -6 \\ 12 \end{bmatrix}.$$

Therefore, the basis $C$ is given precisely as $C = \{1, 1-2x, 1-6x+12x^2\}$. Moreover, it is easy to see that $T(\mathbf{v}_1) = 3\mathbf{v}_1$, $T(\mathbf{v}_2) = 5\mathbf{v}_2$, and $T(\mathbf{v}_3) = 9\mathbf{v}_3$, where $\mathbf{v}_1 = 1$, $\mathbf{v}_2 = 1-2x$, and $\mathbf{v}_3 = 1 - 6x + 12x^2$. ∎

---

## 5.10    EXERCISES

**1.** Let $T: R^2 \to R^2$ be defined by

$$T\left(\begin{bmatrix} x_1 \\ x_2 \end{bmatrix}\right) = \begin{bmatrix} 2x_1 + x_2 \\ x_1 + 2x_2 \end{bmatrix}.$$

Define $\mathbf{u}_1, \mathbf{u}_2$ in $R^2$ by

$$\mathbf{u}_1 = \begin{bmatrix} -1 \\ 1 \end{bmatrix} \quad \text{and} \quad \mathbf{u}_2 = \begin{bmatrix} 1 \\ 1 \end{bmatrix}.$$

Show that $C = \{\mathbf{u}_1, \mathbf{u}_2\}$ is a basis of $R^2$ consisting of eigenvectors for $T$. Calculate the matrix of $T$ with respect to $C$.

2. Let $T: \mathcal{P}_2 \to \mathcal{P}_2$ be defined by

$$T(a_0 + a_1 x + a_2 x^2) = (2a_0 - a_1 - a_2) + (a_0 - a_2)x$$
$$+ (-a_0 + a_1 + 2a_2)x^2.$$

Show that $C = \{1 + x - x^2, 1 + x^2, 1 + x\}$ is a basis of $\mathcal{P}_2$ consisting of eigenvectors for $T$, and find the matrix of $T$ with respect to $C$.

3. Let $V$ be the vector space of $(2 \times 2)$ matrices, and let $T: V \to V$ be defined by

$$T\left(\begin{bmatrix} a & b \\ c & d \end{bmatrix}\right) = \begin{bmatrix} -3a + 5d & 3b - 5c \\ -2c & 2d \end{bmatrix}.$$

If $C = \{A_1, A_2, A_3, A_4\}$, where

$$A_1 = \begin{bmatrix} 1 & 0 \\ 0 & 1 \end{bmatrix}, \qquad A_2 = \begin{bmatrix} 0 & 1 \\ 1 & 0 \end{bmatrix},$$

$$A_3 = \begin{bmatrix} 0 & 1 \\ 0 & 0 \end{bmatrix}, \quad \text{and} \quad A_4 = \begin{bmatrix} 1 & 0 \\ 0 & 0 \end{bmatrix},$$

then show that $C$ is a basis of $V$ consisting of eigenvectors for $T$. Find the matrix of $T$ with respect to $C$.

4. Let $C$ be the basis for $R^2$ given in Exercise 1, and let $B$ be the natural basis for $R^2$. Find the transition matrix and represent the following vectors in terms of $C$:

$$\mathbf{a} = \begin{bmatrix} 4 \\ 2 \end{bmatrix}, \qquad \mathbf{b} = \begin{bmatrix} -2 \\ 0 \end{bmatrix},$$

$$\mathbf{c} = \begin{bmatrix} 9 \\ 5 \end{bmatrix}, \quad \text{and} \quad \mathbf{d} = \begin{bmatrix} a \\ b \end{bmatrix}.$$

5. Let $C$ be the basis for $\mathcal{P}_2$ given in Exercise 2 and let $B = \{1, x, x^2\}$. Find the transition matrix and represent the following polynomials in terms of $C$:

$$p(x) = 2 + x, \quad q(x) = -1 + 2x + 2x^2,$$
$$s(x) = -1 + x^2, \quad \text{and} \quad r(x) = a_0 + a_1 x + a_2 x^2.$$

6. Let $V$ be the vector space of $(2 \times 2)$ matrices, and let $C$ be the basis given in Exercise 3. If $B$ is the natural basis for $V$, $B = \{E_{11}, E_{12}, E_{21}, E_{22}\}$, then find the transition matrix and express the following matrices in terms of the vectors in $C$:

$$A = \begin{bmatrix} 1 & 2 \\ 3 & 4 \end{bmatrix}, \qquad B = \begin{bmatrix} -1 & 1 \\ 0 & 3 \end{bmatrix}, \quad \text{and}$$

$$C = \begin{bmatrix} a & b \\ c & d \end{bmatrix}.$$

7. Find the transition matrix for $R^2$ when $B = \{\mathbf{u}_1, \mathbf{u}_2\}$ and $C = \{\mathbf{w}_1, \mathbf{w}_2\}$:

$$\mathbf{w}_1 = \begin{bmatrix} 2 \\ 1 \end{bmatrix}, \qquad \mathbf{w}_2 = \begin{bmatrix} 1 \\ 2 \end{bmatrix},$$

$$\mathbf{u}_1 = \begin{bmatrix} 1 \\ 1 \end{bmatrix}, \quad \text{and} \quad \mathbf{u}_2 = \begin{bmatrix} 3 \\ 1 \end{bmatrix}.$$

8. Repeat Exercise 7 for the basis vectors

$$\mathbf{w}_1 = \begin{bmatrix} 4 \\ 3 \end{bmatrix}, \qquad \mathbf{w}_2 = \begin{bmatrix} 2 \\ 3 \end{bmatrix},$$

$$\mathbf{u}_1 = \begin{bmatrix} 4 \\ 1 \end{bmatrix}, \quad \text{and} \quad \mathbf{u}_2 = \begin{bmatrix} 2 \\ 1 \end{bmatrix}.$$

9. Let $B = \{1, x, x^2, x^3\}$ and $C = \{x, x + 1, x^2 - 2x, x^3 + 3\}$ be bases for $\mathcal{P}_3$. Find the transition matrix and use it to represent the following in terms of $C$:

$$p(x) = x^2 - 7x + 2, \quad q(x) = x^3 + 9x - 1,$$
$$\text{and} \quad r(x) = x^3 - 2x^2 + 6.$$

10. Represent the following quadratic polynomials in the form $a_0 + a_1 x + a_2 x(x - 1)$ by constructing the appropriate transition matrix:

$$p(x) = x^2 + 5x - 3, \quad q(x) = 2x^2 - 6x + 8,$$
$$\text{and} \quad r(x) = x^2 - 5$$

11. Let $T: R^2 \to R^2$ be the linear transformation defined in Exercise 1. Find the matrix of $T$ with respect to the natural basis $B = \{\mathbf{e}_1, \mathbf{e}_2\}$. If $C$ is the basis for $R^2$ given in Exercise 1, use Theorem 24 to calculate the matrix of $T$ with respect to $C$.

12. Let $T: \mathcal{P}_2 \to \mathcal{P}_2$ be the linear transformation given in Exercise 2. Find the matrix representation of $T$ with respect to the natural basis $B = \{1, x, x^2\}$ and then use Theorem 24 to calculate the matrix of $T$ relative to the basis $C$ given in Exercise 2.

13. Let $V$ and $T$ be as in Exercise 3. Find the matrix representation of $T$ with respect to the natural basis $B = \{E_{11}, E_{12}, E_{21}, E_{22}\}$. If $C$ is the basis for $V$ given in Exercise 3, use Theorem 24 to determine the matrix of $T$ with respect to $C$.

In Exercises 14–16, proceed through the following steps:

a) Find the matrix, $Q$, of $T$ with respect to the natural basis $B$ for $V$.

b) Show that $Q$ is similar to a diagonal matrix; that is, find a nonsingular matrix $S$ and a diagonal matrix $R$ such that $R = S^{-1}QS$.

c) Exhibit a basis $C$ of $V$ such that $R$ is the matrix representation of $T$ with respect to $C$.

d) Calculate the transition matrix, $P$, from $B$ to $C$.

e) Use the transition matrix $P$ and the formula $R[\mathbf{v}]_C = [T(\mathbf{v})]_C$ to calculate $T(\mathbf{w}_1), T(\mathbf{w}_2)$, and $T(\mathbf{w}_3)$.

14. $V = \mathcal{P}_1$ and $T: V \to V$ is defined by $T(a_0 + a_1 x) = (4a_0 + 3a_1) + (-2a_0 - 3a_1)x$. Also,

$$\mathbf{w}_1 = 2 + 3x, \qquad \mathbf{w}_2 = -1 + x, \quad \text{and}$$
$$\mathbf{w}_3 = x.$$

15. $V = \mathcal{P}_2$ and $T: V \to V$ is defined by $T(p) = xp'' + (x + 1)p' + p$. Also,

$$\mathbf{w}_1 = -8 + 7x + x^2, \qquad \mathbf{w}_2 = 5 + x^2, \quad \text{and}$$
$$\mathbf{w}_3 = 4 - 3x + 2x^2.$$

16. $V$ is the vector space of $(2 \times 2)$ matrices and $T: V \to V$ is given by

$$T\left(\begin{bmatrix} a & b \\ c & d \end{bmatrix}\right) = \begin{bmatrix} a - b & 2b - 2c \\ 5c - 3d & 10d \end{bmatrix}.$$

Also,

$$\mathbf{w}_1 = \begin{bmatrix} 0 & 3 \\ 0 & 1 \end{bmatrix}, \qquad \mathbf{w}_2 = \begin{bmatrix} 2 & -3 \\ 1 & 0 \end{bmatrix}, \quad \text{and}$$

$$\mathbf{w}_3 = \begin{bmatrix} 8 & -7 \\ 0 & 2 \end{bmatrix}.$$

17. Complete the proof of Theorem 23 by showing that the transition matrix $P$ is nonsingular. [*Hint:* We have already noted in the proof of Theorem 23 that $P$ is the matrix representation of $I_V$ with respect to the bases $B$ and $C$. Let $Q$ be the matrix representation of $I_V$ with respect to $C$ and $B$. Now apply Theorem 20 with $T = S = I_V$.]

18. Let $V$ be an $n$-dimensional vector space with basis $B$, and assume that $T: V \to V$ is a linear transformation with matrix representation $Q$ relative to $B$.

a) If $\mathbf{v}$ is an eigenvector for $T$ associated with the eigenvalue $\lambda$, then prove that $[\mathbf{v}]_B$ is an eigenvector for $Q$ associated with $\lambda$.

b) If the vector $\mathbf{x}$ in $R^n$ is an eigenvector for $Q$ corresponding to the eigenvalue $\lambda$ and if $\mathbf{v}$ in $V$ is a vector such that $[\mathbf{v}]_B = \mathbf{x}$, prove that $\mathbf{v}$ is an eigenvector for $T$ corresponding to the eigenvalue $\lambda$. [*Hint:* Make use of Eq. (1).]

19. Let $T: V \to V$ be a linear transformation, and let $\lambda$ be an eigenvalue for $T$. Show that $\lambda^2$ is an eigenvalue for $T^2 = T \circ T$.

20. Prove that a linear transformation $T: V \to V$ is one to one if and only if zero is not an eigenvalue for $T$. [*Hint:* Use Theorem 14, property 4, of Section 5.7.]

21. Let $T: V \to V$ be an invertible linear transformation. If $\lambda$ is an eigenvalue for $T$, prove that $\lambda^{-1}$ is an eigenvalue for $T^{-1}$. (Note that $\lambda \neq 0$ by Exercise 20.)

## SUPPLEMENTARY EXERCISES

1. Let $V$ be the set of all $(2 \times 2)$ matrices with real entries and with the usual operation of addition. Suppose, however, that scalar multiplication in $V$ is defined by

$$k\begin{bmatrix} a & b \\ c & d \end{bmatrix} = \begin{bmatrix} ka & 0 \\ 0 & kd \end{bmatrix}.$$

Determine whether $V$ is a real vector space.

**2.** Recall that $\mathcal{F}(R)$ denotes the set of all functions from $R$ to $R$; that is, $\mathcal{F}(R) = \{f : R \to R\}$. A function $g$ in $\mathcal{F}(R)$ is called an even function if $g(-x) = g(x)$ for every $x$ in $R$. Prove that the set of all even functions in $\mathcal{F}(R)$ is a subspace of $\mathcal{F}(R)$.

**3.** In each of parts a)–c), show that the set $S$ is linearly dependent, and write one of the vectors in $S$ as a linear combination of the remaining vectors.

**a)** $S = \{A_1, A_2, A_3, A_4\}$, where

$$A_1 = \begin{bmatrix} 1 & 0 \\ -1 & 1 \end{bmatrix}, \quad A_2 = \begin{bmatrix} -1 & 1 \\ 0 & 1 \end{bmatrix},$$

$$A_3 = \begin{bmatrix} -1 & 3 \\ -2 & 5 \end{bmatrix}, \quad \text{and} \quad A_4 = \begin{bmatrix} -3 & 2 \\ 2 & 0 \end{bmatrix}.$$

**b)** $S = \{p_1(x), p_2(x), p_3(x), p_4(x)\}$, where
$p_1(x) = 1 - x^2 + x^3$, $p_2(x) = -1 + x + x^3$,
$p_3(x) = -1 + 3x - 2x^2 + 5x^3$, and
$p_4(x) = -3 + 2x + 2x^2$.

**c)** $S = \{\mathbf{v}_1, \mathbf{v}_2, \mathbf{v}_3, \mathbf{v}_4\}$, where

$$\mathbf{v}_1 = \begin{bmatrix} 1 \\ 0 \\ -1 \\ 1 \end{bmatrix}, \quad \mathbf{v}_2 = \begin{bmatrix} -1 \\ 1 \\ 0 \\ 1 \end{bmatrix},$$

$$\mathbf{v}_3 = \begin{bmatrix} -1 \\ 3 \\ -2 \\ 5 \end{bmatrix}, \quad \text{and} \quad \mathbf{v}_4 = \begin{bmatrix} -3 \\ 2 \\ 2 \\ 0 \end{bmatrix}.$$

**4.** Let $W$ be the subspace of the set of $(2 \times 2)$ real matrices defined by

$$W = \{A = \begin{bmatrix} a & b \\ c & d \end{bmatrix} : a - 2b + 3c + d = 0\}.$$

**a)** Exhibit a basis $B$ for $W$.

**b)** Find a matrix $A$ in $W$ such that $[A]_B = [2, 1, -2]^T$.

**5.** In $\mathcal{P}_2$, let $S = \{p_1(x), p_2(x), p_3(x)\}$, where $p_1(x) = 1 - x + 2x^2$, $p_2(x) = 2 + 3x + x^2$, and $p_3(x) = 1 - 6x + 5x^2$.

**a)** Obtain an algebraic specification for $\mathrm{Sp}(S)$.

**b)** Determine which of the following polynomials are in $\mathrm{Sp}(S)$:

$q_1(x) = 5 + 5x + 4x^2$, $\quad q_2(x) = 5 - 5x + 8x^2$,

$q_3(x) = -5x + 3x^2$, $\quad$ and $\quad q_4(x) = 5 + 7x^2$.

**c)** Use the algebraic specification obtained in part a) to determine a basis, $B$, of $\mathrm{Sp}(S)$.

**d)** For each polynomial $q_i(x)$, $i = 1, 2, 3, 4$, given in part b), if $q_i(x)$ is in $\mathrm{Sp}(S)$, then find $[q_i(x)]_B$.

**6.** In parts a)–c), find a subset of $S$ that is a basis for $\mathrm{Sp}(S)$. Express each element of $S$ that does not appear in the basis as a linear combination of the basis vectors.

**a)** $S = \{A_1, A_2, A_3, A_4, A_5\}$, where

$$A_1 = \begin{bmatrix} 1 & -2 \\ 1 & -1 \end{bmatrix}, \quad A_2 = \begin{bmatrix} 2 & -3 \\ 4 & -3 \end{bmatrix},$$

$$A_3 = \begin{bmatrix} -1 & 1 \\ -3 & 2 \end{bmatrix}, \quad A_4 = \begin{bmatrix} 1 & -1 \\ 4 & 0 \end{bmatrix}, \quad \text{and}$$

$$A_5 = \begin{bmatrix} 12 & -17 \\ 30 & -11 \end{bmatrix}.$$

**b)** $S = \{p_1(x), p_2(x), p_3(x), p_4(x), p_5(x)\}$, where

$$p_1(x) = 1 - 2x + x^2 - x^3,$$
$$p_2(x) = 2 - 3x + 4x^2 - 3x^3,$$
$$p_3(x) = -1 + x - 3x^2 + 2x^3,$$
$$p_4(x) = 1 - x + 4x^2, \quad \text{and}$$
$$p_5(x) = 12 - 17x + 30x^2 - 11x^3$$

**c)** $S = \{f_1(x), f_2(x), f_3(x), f_4(x), f_5(x)\}$, where

$$f_1(x) = e^x - 2e^{2x} + e^{3x} - e^{4x},$$
$$f_2(x) = 2e^x - 3e^{2x} + 4e^{3x} - 3e^{4x},$$
$$f_3(x) = -e^x + e^{2x} - 3e^{3x} + 2e^{4x},$$
$$f_4(x) = e^x - e^{2x} + 4e^{3x}, \quad \text{and}$$
$$f_5(x) = 12e^x - 17e^{2x} + 30e^{3x} - 11e^{4x}$$

In Exercises 7–11, use the fact that the matrix

$$[A \mid b] = \left[\begin{array}{cccccc|c} 1 & -1 & 3 & 1 & 3 & 2 & a \\ 1 & 0 & 2 & 3 & 2 & 3 & b \\ 0 & -2 & 2 & -4 & 3 & 0 & c \\ 2 & -1 & 5 & 4 & 6 & 7 & d \end{array}\right]$$

is row equivalent to

$$\begin{bmatrix} 1 & 0 & 2 & 3 & 0 & -1 & 4a - 3b - 2c \\ 0 & 1 & -1 & 2 & 0 & 3 & -3a + 3b + c \\ 0 & 0 & 0 & 0 & 1 & 2 & -2a + 2b + c \\ 0 & 0 & 0 & 0 & 0 & 0 & a - 3b - c + d \end{bmatrix}.$$

**7.** Find a basis for $Sp\{A_1, A_2, A_3, A_4\}$, where

$$A_1 = \begin{bmatrix} 1 & -1 & 3 \\ 1 & 3 & 2 \end{bmatrix}, \quad A_2 = \begin{bmatrix} 1 & 0 & 2 \\ 3 & 2 & 3 \end{bmatrix},$$

$$A_3 = \begin{bmatrix} 0 & -2 & 2 \\ -4 & 3 & 0 \end{bmatrix}, \quad \text{and} \quad A_4 = \begin{bmatrix} 2 & -1 & 5 \\ 4 & 6 & 7 \end{bmatrix}.$$

**8.** Let $S = \{p_1(x), p_2(x), p_3(x), p_4(x), p_5(x), p_6(x)\}$, where

$$p_1(x) = 1 + x + 2x^3,$$

$$p_2(x) = -1 - 2x^2 - x^3,$$

$$p_3(x) = 3 + 2x + 2x^2 + 5x^3,$$

$$p_4(x) = 1 + 3x - 4x^2 + 4x^3,$$

$$p_5(x) = 3 + 2x + 3x^2 + 6x^3, \quad \text{and}$$

$$p_6(x) = 2 + 3x + 7x^3.$$

Find a subset of $S$ that is a basis for $Sp(S)$.

**9.** Let $S$ be the set of polynomials given in Exercise 8. Show that $q(x) = 1 + 2x - x^2 + 4x^3$ is in $Sp(S)$, and express $q(x)$ as a linear combination of the basis vector found in Exercise 8.

**10.** If

$$S = \left\{ \begin{bmatrix} 1 & 1 \\ 0 & 2 \end{bmatrix}, \begin{bmatrix} -1 & 0 \\ -2 & -1 \end{bmatrix}, \begin{bmatrix} 3 & 2 \\ 2 & 5 \end{bmatrix}, \right.$$

$$\left. \begin{bmatrix} 1 & 3 \\ -4 & 4 \end{bmatrix}, \begin{bmatrix} 3 & 2 \\ 3 & 6 \end{bmatrix}, \begin{bmatrix} 2 & 3 \\ 0 & 7 \end{bmatrix} \right\},$$

then give an algebraic specification for $Sp(S)$ and use the specification to determine a basis for $Sp(S)$.

**11.** Let $V$ be the vector space for all $(2 \times 3)$ matrices, and suppose that $T: V \to \mathcal{P}_3$ is the linear transformation defined by

$$T\left( \begin{bmatrix} a_{11} & a_{12} & a_{13} \\ a_{21} & a_{22} & a_{23} \end{bmatrix} \right)$$

$$= (a_{11} - a_{12} + 3a_{13} + a_{21} + 3a_{22} + 2a_{23})$$

$$+ (a_{11} + 2a_{13} + 3a_{21} + 2a_{22} + 3a_{23})x$$

$$+ (-2a_{12} + 2a_{13} - 4a_{21} + 3a_{22})x^2$$

$$+ (2a_{11} - a_{12} + 5a_{13} + 4a_{21} + 6a_{22} + 7a_{23})x^3.$$

a) Calculate the matrix of $T$ relative to the natural bases $B$ and $C$ for $V$ and $\mathcal{P}_3$, respectively.

b) Determine the rank and the nullity of $T$.

c) Give an algebraic specification for $\mathcal{R}(T)$ and use the specification to determine a basis for $\mathcal{R}(T)$.

d) Show that $q(x) = 1 + 2x - x^2 + 4x^3$ is in $\mathcal{R}(T)$ and find a matrix $A$ in $V$ such that $T(A) = q(x)$.

e) Find a basis for $\mathcal{N}(T)$.

**12.** Show that there is a linear transformation $T: R^2 \to \mathcal{P}_2$ such that

$$T\left( \begin{bmatrix} 0 \\ 1 \end{bmatrix} \right) = 1 + 2x + x^2 \quad \text{and}$$

$$T\left( \begin{bmatrix} -1 \\ 1 \end{bmatrix} \right) = 2 - x.$$

Give a formula for

$$T\left( \begin{bmatrix} a \\ b \end{bmatrix} \right).$$

**13.** Show that there are infinitely many linear transformations $T: \mathcal{P}_2 \to R^2$ such that

$$T(x) = \begin{bmatrix} 1 \\ 0 \end{bmatrix} \quad \text{and} \quad T(x^2) = \begin{bmatrix} 0 \\ 1 \end{bmatrix}.$$

Give a formula for $T(a + bx + cx^2)$ for one such linear transformation.

**14.** Let $V$ be the vector space of $(2 \times 2)$ matrices, and let $T: V \rightarrow \mathcal{P}_2$ be the linear transformation defined by

$$T\left(\begin{bmatrix} a & b \\ c & d \end{bmatrix}\right) = (a - b + c - 4d) + (b + c + 3d)x + (a + 2c - d)x^2.$$

**a)** Find the matrix of $T$ relative to the natural bases, $B$ and $C$, for $V$ and $\mathcal{P}_2$, respectively.

**b)** Give an algebraic specification for $\mathcal{R}(T)$ and use the specification to obtain a basis $S$ for $\mathcal{R}(T)$.

**c)** For each polynomial $q(x)$ in $S$, find a matrix $A$ in $V$ such that $T(A) = q(x)$. Let $B_1$ denote the set of matrices found.

**d)** Find a basis, $B_2$, for $\mathcal{N}(T)$.

**e)** Show that $B_1 \cup B_2$ is a basis for $V$.

*(Note:* This exercise illustrates the proof that $\text{rank}(T) + \text{nullity}(T) = \dim(V)$.)

## CONCEPTUAL EXERCISES

In Exercises 1–10, answer true or false. Justify your answer by providing a counterexample if the statement is false or an outline of a proof if the statement is true.

**1.** If $a$ is a nonzero scalar and $\mathbf{u}$ and $\mathbf{v}$ are vectors in a vector space $V$ such that $a\mathbf{u} = a\mathbf{v}$, then $\mathbf{u} = \mathbf{v}$.

**2.** If $\mathbf{v}$ is a nonzero vector in a vector space $V$ and $a$ and $b$ are scalars such that $a\mathbf{v} = b\mathbf{v}$, then $a = b$.

**3.** Every vector space $V$ contains a unique vector called the additive inverse of $V$.

**4.** If $V$ consists of all real polynomials of degree exactly $n$ together with the zero polynomial, then $V$ is a vector space.

**5.** If $W$ is a subspace of the vector space $V$ and $\dim(W) = \dim(V) = n$, then $W = V$.

**6.** If $\dim(V) = n$ and $W$ is a subspace of $V$, then $\dim(W) \le n$.

**7.** The subset $\{\boldsymbol{\theta}\}$ of a vector space is linearly dependent.

**8.** Let $S_1$ and $S_2$ be subsets of a vector space $V$ such that $S_1 \subseteq S_2$. If $S_1$ is linearly dependent, then so is $S_2$.

**9.** Let $S_1$ and $S_2$ be subsets of a vector space $V$ such that $S_1 \subseteq S_2$. If $S_1$ is linearly independent, then so is $S_2$.

**10.** Suppose that $S_1 = \{\mathbf{v}_1, \ldots, \mathbf{v}_k\}$ and $S_2 = \{\mathbf{w}_1, \ldots, \mathbf{w}_l\}$ are subsets of a vector space $V$. If $V = \text{Sp}(S_1)$ and $S_2$ is linearly independent, then $l \le k$.

In Exercises 11–19, give a brief answer.

**11.** Let $W$ be a subspace of the vector space $V$. If $\mathbf{u}$ and $\mathbf{v}$ are elements of $V$ such that $\mathbf{u} + \mathbf{v}$ and $\mathbf{u} - \mathbf{v}$ are in $W$, show that $\mathbf{u}$ and $\mathbf{v}$ are in $W$.

**12.** Let $W$ be a subset of a vector space $V$ that satisfies the following properties:

**i)** $\boldsymbol{\theta}$ is in $W$.

**ii)** If $\mathbf{x}$ and $\mathbf{y}$ are in $W$ and $a$ is a scalar, then $a\mathbf{x} + \mathbf{y}$ is in $W$. Prove that $W$ is a subspace of $V$.

**13.** If $W$ is a subspace of a vector space $V$, show that $\text{Sp}(W) = W$.

**14.** Give examples of subsets of $S_1$ and $S_2$ of a vector space $V$ such that $\text{Sp}(S_1) \cap \text{Sp}(S_2) \ne \text{Sp}(S_1 \cap S_2)$.

**15.** If $U$ and $W$ are subspaces of a vector space $V$, then $U + W = \{\mathbf{u} + \mathbf{w}: \mathbf{u} \text{ is in } U \text{ and } \mathbf{w} \text{ is in } W\}$.

**a)** Prove that $U + W$ is a subspace of $V$.

**b)** Let $S_1 = \{\mathbf{x}_1, \ldots, \mathbf{x}_m\}$ and $S_2 = \{\mathbf{y}_1, \ldots, \mathbf{y}_n\}$ be subsets of $V$. Show that $\text{Sp}(S_1 \cup S_2) = \text{Sp}(S_1) + \text{Sp}(S_2)$.

**16.** Let $B = \{\mathbf{v}_1, \ldots, \mathbf{v}_n\}$ be a basis for a vector space $V$, and let $\mathbf{v}$ be a nonzero vector in $V$. Prove that there exists a vector $\mathbf{v}_j$ in $B$, $1 \le j \le n$, such that $\mathbf{v}_j$ can be replaced by $\mathbf{v}$ and the resulting set, $B'$, is still a basis for $V$.

**17.** Let $B = \{\mathbf{v}_1, \ldots, \mathbf{v}_n\}$ be a basis for a vector space $V$, and let $S: V \rightarrow W$ and $T: V \rightarrow W$ be linear transformations such that $S(\mathbf{v}_i) = T(\mathbf{v}_i)$ for $i = 1, 2, \ldots, n$. Show that $S = T$.

18. Let $T: V \to W$ be a linear transformation.

   a) If $T$ is one to one, then show that $T$ carries linearly independent subsets of $V$ to linearly independent subsets of $W$.

   b) If $T$ carries linearly independent subsets of $V$ to linearly independent subsets of $W$, then prove that $T$ is one to one.

19. Give an example of a linear transformation $T: R^2 \to R^2$ such that $\mathcal{N}(T) = \mathcal{R}(T)$.

---

## MATLAB EXERCISES

In these exercises we expand on least-squares approximation of functions, an important topic introduced in Section 5.6. As an inner-product space, we use $C[a, b]$ with an inner product given by

$$\langle f, g \rangle = \int_a^b w(x) f(x) g(x) \, dx.$$

For the inner product just defined, $y = w(x)$ denotes a function that is positive and continuous on $(a, b)$; the function $w$ is called a **weight function**.

Let $y = f(x)$ denote a function we wish to approximate. Let $y = p^*(x)$ denote the best approximation to $f$ in $\mathcal{P}_n$. In particular, if $y = q(x)$ is any polynomial in $\mathcal{P}_n$, then we have

$$\int_a^b w(x)[f(x) - p^*(x)]^2 \, dx \le \int_a^b w(x)[f(x) - q(x)]^2 \, dx. \tag{1}$$

By Theorem 12, the best approximation $p^*$ is characterized by the condition:

$$\langle f - p^*, q \rangle = 0, \quad \text{for all } q \text{ in } \mathcal{P}_n.$$

Let $\{q_j\}_{j=0}^n$ be any basis for $\mathcal{P}_n$. The preceding condition can be replaced by the set of $n + 1$ equations $\langle f - p^*, q_j \rangle = 0, j = 0, 1, \ldots, n$. Equivalently, $p^*$ is characterized by

$$\langle p^*, q_j \rangle = \langle f, q_j \rangle, j = 0, 1, \ldots, n. \tag{2}$$

Now, suppose that $p^*$ has the following representation in terms of the basis:

$$p^*(x) = a_0 q_0(x) + a_1 q_1(x) + \cdots + a_n q_n(x).$$

Inserting this representation into Eq. (2), we obtain a system of $n + 1$ equations in the $n + 1$ unknowns $a_0, a_1, \ldots, a_n$:

$$
\begin{aligned}
a_0 \langle q_0, q_0 \rangle + a_1 \langle q_1, q_0 \rangle + \cdots + a_n \langle q_n, q_0 \rangle &= \langle f, q_0 \rangle \\
a_0 \langle q_0, q_1 \rangle + a_1 \langle q_1, q_1 \rangle + \cdots + a_n \langle q_n, q_1 \rangle &= \langle f, q_1 \rangle \\
&\vdots \\
a_0 \langle q_0, q_n \rangle + a_1 \langle q_1, q_n \rangle + \cdots + a_n \langle q_n, q_n \rangle &= \langle f, q_n \rangle
\end{aligned}
\tag{3}
$$

The equations above are called the **normal equations,** and the coefficient matrix for the system is known as the **Gram matrix**. For notation, let us denote the system (3) by

$$G\mathbf{a} = \mathbf{f} \tag{4}$$

where

$$G = \begin{bmatrix} \langle q_0, q_0 \rangle & \langle q_1, q_0 \rangle & \cdots & \langle q_n, q_0 \rangle \\ \langle q_0, q_1 \rangle & \langle q_1, q_1 \rangle & \cdots & \langle q_n, q_1 \rangle \\ \vdots & & & \vdots \\ \langle q_0, q_n \rangle & \langle q_1, q_n \rangle & \cdots & \langle q_n, q_n \rangle \end{bmatrix}, \quad \mathbf{a} = \begin{bmatrix} a_0 \\ a_1 \\ \vdots \\ a_n \end{bmatrix}, \quad \mathbf{f} = \begin{bmatrix} \langle f, q_0 \rangle \\ \langle f, q_1 \rangle \\ \vdots \\ \langle f, q_n \rangle \end{bmatrix}.$$

Thus, to find the best least-squares polynomial approximation to a function $f$, we can use the following algorithm:

1. choose a basis for $\mathcal{P}_n$
2. set up the Gram matrix $G$ and the vector $\mathbf{f}$ and then solve Eq. (4).

*Note:* The preceding process is not restricted to polynomial approximations of $f$. In particular, without loss of generality, we can replace the subspace $\mathcal{P}_n$ by any finite-dimensional subspace of $C[a, b]$.

1. Let $f(x) = \cos x$, $[a, b] = [0, 1]$, and $w(x) = 1$. Also, let $n = 2$ and $q_j(x) = x^j$ for $j = 0, 1, 2$. Find the best least-squares approximation to $f$ by solving Eq. (4). In setting up the matrix $G$ and the vector $\mathbf{f}$, you can evaluate the inner products using an integral table or by using the MATLAB numerical integration routine `quad8` to estimate the inner products. If you use `quad8`, you might want to test the effects of using different tolerances.

2. In Example 6, Section 5.6, the least-squares approximation problem in Exercise 1 was worked using a different basis for $\mathcal{P}_2$. Verify that you got the same polynomial $p^*$ in Exercise 1 even though the basis was different. On the same MATLAB plot, compare the graph of $y = \cos x$ and $y = p^*(x)$. Next, plot the difference function $y = \cos x - p^*(x)$ and use your graph to estimate the maximum error.

3. Repeat Exercise 1, only this time use the basis from Example 6: $q_0(x) = 1, q_1(x) = x - 1/2$, and $q_2(x) = x^2 - x + 1/6$. What differences are there between the Gram matrix $G$ in this exercise and the matrix $G$ in Exercise 1?

4. If you did not already do so in Exercise 1, calculate by hand the $ij$-th entry of the Gram matrix for the basis of Exercise 1. Is the Gram matrix you find equal to the $(3 \times 3)$ Hilbert matrix? Suppose we were looking for an $n$-th degree polynomial approximation. Would the Gram matrix be the $((n + 1) \times (n + 1))$ Hilbert matrix? If we used an orthogonal basis in Eqs. (3) and (4), would the Gram matrix be a diagonal matrix? (Note that Eq. (4) is ill conditioned when $G$ is the Hilbert matrix, but we would hope that it might be better conditioned when $G$ is a diagonal matrix.)

5. Many applications of mathematics require the use of functions defined by integrals of the form

$$f(x) = \int_0^x g(t) \, dt. \tag{5}$$

Quite often the integral defining $f$ is not an elementary one and can only be evaluated numerically. Some examples are

$$\textbf{a) } g(x) = \int_0^x e^{t^2}\,dt \quad \textbf{b) } f(x) = \int_0^x \frac{\sin t}{t}\,dt \quad \textbf{c) } f(x) = \int_0^x \cos t^2\,dt.$$

These functions are, respectively, the **error function**, the **sine integral**, and the **Fresnel integral**. In each case, the integral defining $f(x)$ must be evaluated numerically.

Rather than calling a numerical integration routine whenever we need the value $f(x)$, we might consider approximating $f$ by a polynomial. That idea is the theme of this exercise.

Now, if we are to approximate $f$ by its best least-squares polynomial approximation $p^*$, we first have to choose a basis for $\mathcal{P}_n$ and then solve the normal equations (represented in Eq. (4) by $\mathbf{Ga} = \mathbf{f}$). As we can see from Eqs. (3) and (4), the vector $\mathbf{f}$ has components $\langle f, q_0 \rangle, \langle f, q_1 \rangle, \ldots, \langle f, q_n \rangle$. Since $f$ itself must be evaluated numerically, we will have to do the same for each of the components $\langle f, q_k \rangle$. However, using a numerical integration routine to estimate $\langle f, q_k \rangle$ requires us to supply a formula of some sort for $f(x)$. In order to avoid this requirement by a numerical integration routine, we use integration by parts to replace evaluations of $f$ by evaluations of $f'$.

In particular, suppose we want to approximate $y = f(x)$ for $x$ in $[0, 1]$. Let us choose $y = \rho(x)$ to be an antiderivative for $q_k(x)$ with the property that $\rho(1)$ is 0. Then, using integration by parts, we have:

$$
\begin{aligned}
\langle f, q_k \rangle &= \int_0^1 f(x)q_k(x)\,dx \\
&= \rho(x)f(x)\big|_0^1 - \int_0^1 \rho(x)f'(x)\,dx \quad (6) \\
&= -\int_0^1 \rho(x)g(x)\,dx.
\end{aligned}
$$

To explain the preceding calculations, we used integration by parts with $u = f(x)$, $dv = q_k(x)dx$, $v = \rho(x)$, and $du = f'(x)\,dx$. To obtain the final result, we used the fact that $\rho(1) = 0$ and $f(0) = 0$, and also the fact that $f'(x) = g(x)$ by the fundamental theorem of calculus.

Let $g(x) = \cos x^2$ and use the preceding ideas to find the best least-squares approximation to the Fresnel integral $f(x)$. Use $n = 2, 4$, and 6. For ease of calculation, use the standard basis for $\mathcal{P}_n$, $q_k(x) = x^k$, $k = 0, 1, \ldots, n$. (Note that this choice of basis will mean that the Gram matrix will be a Hilbert matrix. However, for the small values of $n$ we are using, the Hilbert matrix is not that badly behaved. You can use the MATLAB command `hilb(n)` to create the matrix $G$ in Eq. (4).) In order to find the components of the vector $\mathbf{f}$ on the right-hand side of Eq. (4), use a numerical integration routine such as `quad8`. Because of Eq. (6), the components of $\mathbf{f}$ can be found by evaluating the following integral numerically:

$$\langle f, q_k \rangle = -\int_0^1 \frac{x^{k+1} - 1}{k + 1}\cos(x^2)\,dx.$$

# Appendix:
# An Introduction
# to MATLAB

MATLAB is a powerful tool for scientific computing that can be used for both numerical and graphical purposes. MATLAB was designed to be especially user-friendly for calculations involving matrices and vectors.

In this appendix we introduce enough commands so that you can get started with MATLAB while restricting our discussion to those parts of MATLAB that are of particular value for linear algebra.

## A.1    BASIC OPERATIONS

Open up MATLAB. The window you first see is referred to as the **command window**. The **command line** is the input line next to the MATLAB prompt. You can use MATLAB for simple calculations, such as the following:

```
»8*17+49
ans =
    185
»alpha=sin(1.98)
alpha =
    0.9174
```

A semicolon at the end of a command will suppress screen output:

```
»beta=sqrt(1+0.7*alpha);
»
```

*Note:* If you type a MATLAB command incorrectly and get an error message, you do not need to retype the entire command. Hit the up arrow on the keyboard and you will see your last command repeated. Edit the last command and hit return. Your cursor need not be at the end of the command line when you hit return. Also, continuing to press the up arrow brings past commands back to the command line. This can save some typing when you want to repeat a command.

MATLAB has an extensive online help facility. Type `help` and a topic to get help on a specific topic. For example, `help plot` will give you help with the MATLAB plot command. The command `help help` will list what sort of online help is available.

---

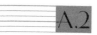 **EXERCISES**

(Hint: `help elfun` describes the elementary mathematical functions.)

1. Evaluate $3.13^2 + |\cos \sqrt{7}|$
2. Evaluate $\tan^{-1} 4.32$

## A.2    ENTERING MATRICES

Suppose we wish to enter the matrix

$$A = \begin{bmatrix} 1 & -1 & 0 \\ 1/2 & 3 & 1/3 \\ 0 & 10 & 1 \end{bmatrix}.$$

To enter $A$, type

```
»A=[1 -1 0; 1/2 3 1/3; 0 10 1]
```

The rows are separated by semicolons, but if it makes viewing a bit easier, the entries can be separated by commas. Notice that we gave the matrix the name $A$. This is not essential but it is good MATLAB form. If you do not name the matrix, MATLAB gives it the default name *ans*. This will be overridden the next time you enter a matrix without naming it.

When the matrix $A$ appears, you might be surprised that the fractions have become decimals. MATLAB's default format gives you a four-place decimal for any fraction it encounters. This format is called *short* format and if you want fractions displayed on the screen instead, you can type

```
»format rat
```

or from the *Options* menu, choose *Numeric format* and then choose *Rat*. You can return to short format in the same way. Now enter the following matrix

$$B = \begin{bmatrix} 2 & 7 & 1/6 & .8 \\ 18/3 & 3/17 & .007 & 6 \\ 2 & -12 & 4 & 1 \end{bmatrix}$$

and notice the difference in output when using *Short*, *Rat*, and *Long* formats.

Suppose after entering the preceding matrix $B$ you realize that $b_{23}$ should have been 0.009 instead of 0.007. To correct the (2, 3) entry of $B$, type

```
»B(2,3)=0.009
```

---

## A.2    EXERCISES

1. Change the (1, 3) entry of $A$ from 0 to 3/7 and name the resulting matrix $Q$.

# THE RREF COMMAND

The MATLAB command `rref(A)` uses elementary row operations to transform $A$ to reduced row echelon form. The rref command is illustrated in Example 5, Section 1.2. As another example, consider the problem of solving the system

$$x_1 + 2x_2 + 2x_3 + x_4 = 3$$
$$2x_2 + 4x_2 + 3x_3 + 4x_4 = 6.$$

First, we create the augmented matrix, $A$:

```
»A=[1 2 2 1 3;2 4 3 4 6]
A =
    1    2    2    1    3
    2    4    3    4    6
```

Next, we row reduce $A$ using the rref command:

```
»B=rref(A)
B =
    1    2    0    5    3
    0    0    1   -2    0
```

Interpreting $B$, we see that the original system is equivalent to

$$x_1 + 2x_2 \quad + 5x_4 = 3$$
$$x_3 - 2x_4 = 0.$$

Therefore, the solution to the system is $x_1 = 3 - 2x_2 - 5x_4$, $x_3 = 2x_4$.

---

## A.3   EXERCISES

**1.** Solve the systems in Exercises 30 and 31, Section 1.2.

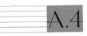

# SURGERY ON MATRICES

MATLAB makes it easy to manipulate matrices and construct new matrices by altering the rows and columns of existing matrices. Enter the $(3 \times 4)$ matrix

$$B = \begin{bmatrix} 1 & 3 & -5 & 0 \\ 9 & 6 & -2 & 1 \\ 0 & 4 & 4 & 1 \end{bmatrix}.$$

Suppose you wish to extract from $B$ the $(2 \times 2)$ block $B_1$ where

$$B_1 = \begin{bmatrix} -5 & 0 \\ -2 & 1 \end{bmatrix}.$$

Type

```
»B1=B([1 2],[3 4])
```

The preceding command says to define a new matrix $B_1$ made from rows 1 and 2 of $B$ and from columns 3 and 4 of $B$. Another way to accomplish the same result is by typing

» B1=B(1:2,3:4)

The colon notation $1:2$ is shorthand and means take all rows, starting with row 1 and ending with row 2. Similarly, the command Q = B(1:2, 2:4) would define $Q$ to be the upper-right ($2 \times 3$) block of $B$. That is, $Q$ would be made from rows 1 and 2 of $B$ and from columns 2, 3, and 4 of $B$. (If you want to define $P$ to consist of rows 1 and 2 along with columns 1, 3, and 4 you could enter P = B[1:2, [1 3 4]]. In particular, the colon notation could not be used to designate the nonconsecutive columns 1, 3, and 4.)

Now, suppose you want to extract the second row of $B$. In this case you would type

» B2=B(2,1:4)

or the shortcut

» B2=B(2,:)

Here, the colon means that *all* the columns are to be included.

Suppose you want the matrix $C$ which is formed from two blocks of $B$:

$$C = \begin{bmatrix} 1 & 3 & -2 & 1 \\ 9 & 6 & 4 & 1 \end{bmatrix}$$

Type

» C1=B(1:2,1:2)
» C2=B(3:4,3:4)
» C= [C1  C2]

The last command treats $C1$ as one big entry and $C2$ as the next big entry. As long as the matrices have the same number of rows it will juxtapose them. On the other hand, if you want the matrix with $C1$ on top of $C2$, type

» C3= [C1;C2]

This treats $C1$ as the *first* row and $C2$ as the *second* row of the matrix. This command works provided $C1$ and $C2$ have the same number of columns. Finally, to extract the $(2, 3)$ entry of the matrix $B$, simply type

» b=B(2,3)

## A.4   EXERCISES

Consider the matrix

$$A = \begin{bmatrix} 1 & 3 & 4 & 2 & -8 \\ 0 & 0 & 8 & 5 & -6 \\ 2 & 3 & 4 & 3 & 7 \\ -1 & -1 & 0 & 6 & 4 \\ 4 & 4 & 3 & 3 & -7 \end{bmatrix}.$$

Create each of the following matrices by performing surgery on $A$.

1. $\begin{bmatrix} 1 & 3 \\ 0 & 0 \end{bmatrix}$

2. $\begin{bmatrix} 0 & 8 & -6 \\ 3 & 4 & 7 \\ 4 & 3 & -7 \end{bmatrix}$

3. $\begin{bmatrix} 1 & 3 & 4 \\ 0 & 0 & 8 \\ 4 & 3 & 7 \\ 0 & 6 & 4 \end{bmatrix}$

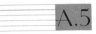

# ELEMENTARY ROW OPERATIONS VIA SURGERY

One way to become proficient with matrix manipulations in MATLAB is by using matrix surgery to execute the elementary row operations required to transform a matrix to reduced echelon form. As an example, consider transforming $A$, where

$$A = \begin{bmatrix} 0 & 2 & 1 & 3 \\ 2 & 3 & 1 & 6 \\ 3 & 2 & 2 & 2 \end{bmatrix}.$$

First we need to interchange rows. Type

```
»A1=A;
»A1(1:2,:)=A(2:1,:)
```

Interpreting the preceding commands, we first let a new matrix $A1$ equal $A$. The next command changes the first and second rows of $A1$ to be the second and first row of $A$ respectively. (Remember that the colon says to change *all* columns of the first and second rows; that is, change the *entire* row.) The result is

$$A1 = \begin{bmatrix} 2 & 3 & 1 & 6 \\ 0 & 2 & 1 & 3 \\ 3 & 2 & 2 & 2 \end{bmatrix}.$$

In general, to obtain a matrix $A1$ from $A$ by interchanging the $i$th and $j$th rows of $A$, the commands are

```
»A1=A;
»A1([i,j],:)=A([j,i],:);
```

Now we need to divide the first row of $A1$ by 2. For clarity, let's choose rational format to display the results

```
»format rat
```

Then type

```
»A2=A1;
»A2(1,:)=(1/2)*A1(1,:)
```

You end up with

$$A2 = \begin{bmatrix} 1 & 3/2 & 1/2 & 3 \\ 0 & 2 & 1 & 3 \\ 3 & 2 & 2 & 2 \end{bmatrix}.$$

Next to eliminate the 3 in the third row, first column, type

```
»A3=A2;
```

To change the third row of $A3$ so that it is the result of adding $-3$ times the first row of $A2$ to the third row of $A2$, type

```
»A3(3,:)= -3*A2(1,:) + A2(3,:)
```

We obtain

$$A3 = \begin{bmatrix} 1 & 3/2 & 1/2 & 3 \\ 0 & 2 & 1 & 3 \\ 0 & -5/2 & 1/2 & -7 \end{bmatrix}.$$

You might wonder why we keep renaming the matrix at each step. This is so we don't override any previous steps. In this way we can backtrack to find an error if it occurs.

---

## A.5    EXERCISES

1. Finish putting the matrix $A$ into reduced row echelon form.

2. Use surgery to put the following matrix into reduced row echelon form

$$B = \begin{bmatrix} 0 & 1 & 2 & -1 \\ 1 & 1 & 1 & 1 \\ 3 & -2 & -6 & 0 \end{bmatrix}.$$

---

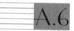 A.6

## GRAPHING CURVES

First, we show you how to graph a curve in the plane. Type

```
»x=0:.1:10;
```

This command defines **x** to be a row vector consisting of all the numbers between 0 and 10 at 0.1 intervals. Thus **x** is made up of 101 points 0.0, 0.1, 0.2, ..., 9.9, 10.0.

Suppose you want to graph the function $y = \cos(3x + 1) + \sin(2x - 3)$ for $0 \le x \le 10$. Type

```
»y=cos(3*x+1)+sin(2*x-3);
```

*Note:* MATLAB preserves data types. If **x** is a vector or even an $(m \times n)$ matrix, then so is $y = \sin(\mathbf{x})$. If $x$ is a scalar then so is $y = \sin(x)$. To see the **x** and **y** values that you will be graphing, type

```
» [x' y']
```

This gives you a (rather large) table of values of **x** and **y**. The ′ notation puts **x** and **y** into columns rather than rows; MATLAB uses $A'$ to denote $A^T$.

Now that the table of values has been generated, we are ready to graph the function $y = \cos(3x + 1) + \sin(2x - 3)$. To see the graph, type

```
»plot(x,y)
```

Suppose you wish to graph the function $y = \sin x$ in the same figure window. Click anywhere on the command window to bring it to the front. Type

```
»y1=sin(x);
```

If you had used $y$ instead of $y1$ above, then the old values of **y** would have been overridden and you would have lost them for good. Also, if you now type

```
»plot(x,y1)
```

the window will be cleared and the first graph lost. So, *before* you use the plot command, type the command

```
»hold on
```

This allows you to plot the new curve and keep the old one. (The `hold off` command releases the window when you are finished superimposing graphs.) If you now type the plot command, you will notice that the figure window does not come to the front. From the menu bar, choose *Window*, and select the figure you want. A better way to keep the figure window in front is to type

```
»figure(gcf),plot(x,y1)
```

The first command brings the current figure to the foreground (gcf stands for get current figure). Note that both curves are colored yellow, which is the default color for a black background. If you want to distinguish between the two curves, type

```
»figure(gcf),plot(x,y1,'g')
```

This will color the second graph green. You may also use 'r', 'm', 'k', 'c', 'b', 'w', 'y' for red, magenta, black, cyan, blue, white, and yellow respectively. (If you want to erase a graph that already exists, just retype the plot command using black for the color. The curve will blend into the background.)

Suppose you want to identify a point of intersection of the two curves you have graphed. Type the command

```
»ginput(1)
```

Then, using your mouse, click on the point of intersection. The $x$ and $y$ coordinates of the point of intersection will appear in the command window. The number 1 in the `ginput` command allows you to click on one point. If you wish to identify and save, say, 5 points, type

```
»v=ginput(5)
```

You can click anywhere in the figure window to collect the five points.

---

## A.6   EXERCISES

1. Consider the two functions
$$y = \cos 2x + \sin x$$
and
$$y = 0.01 \tan x,$$
where
$$0 \le x \le 9.$$
We want to estimate the points where the graphs of these two functions intersect. To that end, prepare an $xy$-table of values, where $x = 0.0, 0.1, 0.2, \ldots, 9.0$ and $y = \cos 2x + \sin x$.

a) Graph the curve you have just defined.

b) Superimpose the curve defined by $y = 0.01 \tan x$, coloring this latter curve red.

c) Note that there appear to be six places where these two curves intersect. Argue that, in reality, there can be only four points where the graphs of the two functions intersect. Can you give a reason for the two "extraneous" intersection points?

d) Estimate the $(x, y)$ coordinates of the actual intersection points.

## A.7    MATRIX OPERATIONS

Let $A$ and $B$ be matrices of the same size and let $s$ be a scalar. The MATLAB command for addition is $A + B$ and the command for scalar multiplication is s*A. The command A + s adds the value $s$ to each entry of $A$.

If $A$ is $(m \times n)$ and $B$ is $(n \times p)$, the command for multiplication is A*B. If $A$ is a nonsingular $(n \times n)$ matrix and $\mathbf{b}$ is an $(n \times 1)$ vector, the command A\b will return the solution to the system $A\mathbf{x} = \mathbf{b}$. If $A$ and $B$ are the same size, the .* command, A.*B, multiplies each entry of $A$ by the corresponding entry of $B$.

*Note:* The standard matrix operations of $+$ and $*$ are defined in MATLAB the same way as they are in linear algebra. The special MATLAB "dotted operations," .+, .−, .*, ./, and .^, are coordinate-wise operations used for matrices (and vectors) of the same size. As an example, suppose we want to prepare a table of values for the expression

$$y = \frac{(x^2 + 3x + 1)\cos(x)}{2 + \sin(x)}.$$

For this table, suppose we want the $x$ values to be $x = 1.0, 1.2, 1.4, \ldots, 29.8, 30.0$. The following MATLAB statements will create the table:

```
»x=1:0.2:30;
»y=( (x.^2+3*x +1).*cos(x) )./(2+sin(x));
»table=[x', y'];
```

## A.7    EXERCISES

1. Use MATLAB to do Exercises 31–41 from Section 1.5.

2. Use the MATLAB \ operation to solve the system in Exercise 27, Section 1.1.

3. Consider the $x$-values given by $x = 2.0, 2.1, \ldots, 4.9, 5.0$. Using these $x$-values, create a table for the expression

$$y = \frac{\tan^{-1}(1 + x^2)}{(1 + x^3)\sqrt{1 + x}}.$$

## A.8    TRANSPOSE, NORM, AND INVERSE

To find the transpose of a matrix $A$, type B = A'. If $\mathbf{x}$ is a vector, the norm command calculates the norm of $\mathbf{x}$. If $\mathbf{x}$ is a column vector, then the MATLAB statements norm(x) and sqrt(x'*x) produce the same value.

To find the inverse of a square matrix $A$, use the command inv(A). The inverse is calculated numerically, using Gaussian elimination. If the MATLAB Gaussian elimination routine suspects that the matrix $A$ is nearly singular, then a warning message is issued.

## A.8    EXERCISES

1. Use MATLAB to find the inverse of the matrix in Exercise 20, Section 1.9.

2. Use the MATLAB inv command to solve the system in Exercise 27, Section 1.1.

**3.** To illustrate the warnings given by MATLAB for singular and nearly singular matrices, consider $A$ and $B$ below

$$A = \begin{bmatrix} 3 & 6 \\ 1 & 2 \end{bmatrix}, \qquad B = \begin{bmatrix} 2 & 4 \\ 1 & 2 \end{bmatrix}.$$

Execute the MATLAB commands `inv(A)` and `inv(B)` and note that MATLAB has actually calculated what it deems to be an inverse for $A$. In particular, MATLAB does not believe that $A$ is singular but it does recognize $A$ as being nearly singular. (Roundoff error causes MATLAB to think $A$ has an inverse. That is, during the first step of reducing $A$, MATLAB multiplies row 1 by the scalar $-0.3333333333333333$ and adds the result to row 2. MATLAB has to use decimal numbers, not fractions. This fact produces a roundoff error since to have an exact result, we must multiply row 1 by $-1/3$, not $-0.3333333333333333$. For matrix $B$ the same roundoff problem does not occur; this time, the first step is to multiply row 1 by $-1/2 = -0.5$ and add the result to row 2.)

## ZEROS, ONES, EYE, AND RAND

MATLAB has commands that generate special matrices. Type the commands

```
»A=zeros(3)
»B=ones(5)
```

As you can see, $A$ is the $(3 \times 3)$ zero matrix, while $B$ is a $(5 \times 5)$ matrix of ones. In general, `zeros(n)` produces the $(n \times n)$ zero matrix and `zeros(m, n)` yields the $(m \times n)$ zero matrix. The `ones` command works the same way. These commands are especially useful when we want to initialize a matrix or vector. The statement `eye(m, n)` creates a matrix with ones on the main diagonal and zeros elsewhere. The command `eye(n)` is shorthand for `eye(n,n)`.

The `rand((m, n)-.5)` command can be used to generate matrices with random entries. This feature is useful, for example, if you want test a conjecture or simulate a series of random events such as traffic flow in a street network.

The `rand(m, n)` command produces a random $(m \times n)$ matrix with entries between 0 and 1. This basic command can then be used to generate other distributions of random matrices. For example, the command `10*rand(m, n)` puts the entries between 0 and 10. The command `rand(m, n)-.5` puts them between $-.5$ and $.5$ and `10*(rand(m, n)-.5)` between $-5$ and 5. The command `round(10*rand(m, n))` gives you a matrix with integer entries between 0 and 10. The command `rand(n)` is shorthand for `rand(n, n)`.

## A.9 EXERCISES

**1.** Create a $(4 \times 5)$ matrix consisting entirely of sevens.

**2.** Experiment with the random commands to generate 10 different homogeneous $(m \times n)$ systems with integer entries, the entries between $-20$ and 20. Make sure at least 6 of your systems have $n$ larger than $m$. Solve the system by first using the `rref` command. Then use pencil and paper to find the form of the solutions. What can you conclude if $n$ is larger than $m$? Compare to Theorem 4. (*Note:* You might notice that both you and a classmate get the same matrix when you type `rand(2,3)`. This is because MATLAB has a default system of selecting the seed for its random number generator. To personalize the `rand` command type

```
»rand('seed', 'yourfirstname
yourlastname')
```

You only need to type this once before you use the first `rand` command. Do not forget the single quotations. (Of course, in practice you can type anything between the second set of single quotations.)

## NUMERICAL ROUTINES IN MATLAB

MATLAB has a variety of different routines that are designed for numerical purposes. Two examples are *polyfit* and *polyval*. The routine polyfit gives the coefficients for a least-squares polynomial fit to data. The routine polyval evaluates a polynomial, given the coefficients and evaluation points. Type

```
»x=1:6
»y=[4, 12, 17, 33, 45, 52]
»a=polyfit(x,y,2)
»b=polyfit(x,y,5)
```

The vector **a** gives the coefficients of the best least-squares fit of degree 2 to the data defined by **x** and **y**. The vector **b** gives the coefficients of the best least-squares fit of degree 5 to the data (since we have 6 data points, this polynomial is the interpolating polynomial).

Type

```
»xe=1:.1:6;
»ye2=polyval(a,xe);
»ye5=polyval(b,xe);
```

The vector **xe** is the set of $x$-evaluation points and the vector **ye2** gives the values of the polynomial defined by **a** at the points in **xe** (the polynomial defined by **a** is the best least-squares fit of degree 2). Similarly, **ye5** gives the values of the interpolating polynomial at the points in **xe**.

You can plot the results in order to see the data and the two fits to the data:

```
»plot(x,y,'o',xe,ye2,'r',xe,ye5,'g')
```

Three other examples of numerical routines available in MATLAB are *quad8*, a program that estimates integrals, *fmins* an optimization program for a real-valued function of several variables, *ode45* a differential-equation solver.

## A.10    EXERCISES

Using the coordinates listed in the following two tables, find the best least-squares linear fit to the data and then find the polynomial interpolator for the data. Plot the data points, the least-squares fit, and the interpolator on the same graph.

**1.**

| $x$ | 1 | 2 | 3 | 4 | 5 |
|---|---|---|---|---|---|
| $y$ | 3.3 | 5.2 | 6.7 | 9.0 | 10.8 |

**2.**

| $x$ | −3 | −2 | −1 | 0 | 1 | 2 | 3 |
|---|---|---|---|---|---|---|---|
| $y$ | 3.3 | 7.8 | 10.5 | 12.2 | 10.9 | 8.2 | 3.1 |

## M-FILES: SCRIPTS AND FUNCTIONS

If you are going to issue a certain sequence of MATLAB commands over and over again, then you should write a MATLAB program that executes this sequence whenever you type a keyword. Such a program is called an *M-file*. These M-files are also a powerful tool when you begin writing long MATLAB programs—M-files are the MATLAB analogs of the subroutines and procedures used in other programming languages.

There are two types of M-files, *scripts* and *functions*. A script is the easiest sort of M-file to visualize. As its name suggests, a script is nothing more than a set of MATLAB instructions that are executed whenever the name of the script is entered.

For example, suppose you are carrying out some data analysis and you want to try various least-squares polynomial fits to a given data set. You are not sure exactly which degree polynomial you want to use, nor are you sure how much of the data you want to fit with a given polynomial. To investigate this typical data analysis problem, you might write the following *script*:

```
»a=polyfit(x,y,n);
»yval=polyval(a,xval);
»plot(x,y,'ro',xval,yval,'g');
```

As you can see, the first instruction takes a given set of $xy$-values (the vectors **x** and **y**) and a given value of $n$ and then generates the coefficients **a** of the best least-squares fit of degree $n$. The second instruction takes a given set of evaluation points, **xval**, and evaluates the least-squares fit at those evaluation points. The last instruction plots the data points (as red circles) and superimposes the graph of the least-squares polynomial (as a green curve). On the basis of this graph, you might want to adjust the degree of the least-squares fit, or the range of data that you want the polynomial to approximate.

Now, place this list of instructions in a file named lsplot.m. Suppose that you enter a set of data points **x** and **y** and choose a polynomial degree, $n$. Also, define a set of evaluation points, **xval**. When you type the name of the script (`lsplot`) on the command line, the script will be executed and you will see the graph of the least-squares fit superimposed on a graph of the data points. If you want to change the degree of the fit, just change the value of $n$ on the command line and type lsplot once again. Similarly, you can alter the data set (**x** and **y**) and the extent of the plot (**xval**) and type lspot to see the effects.

A MATLAB script can be produced with any editor, but MATLAB has a built-in editor that is easy to use. From the File menu select New, After creating the script, give it a name having the form filename.m and save it to a MATLAB folder, so that MATLAB can find the script when you type its name on the command line.

MATLAB *functions* are similar to scripts, except that the variables in the instructions in a function are local rather than global. In this sense, a MATLAB function resembles a function in BASIC or FORTRAN. Following is an example of a function that forms the scalar triple product $\mathbf{u} \cdot \mathbf{v} \times \mathbf{w}$:

```
function c=triple(u,v,w)
x=cross(v,w);
c=dot(u,x);
```

If we are in the MATLAB command window and have three vectors **a**, **b**, and **c**, then we can invoke the triple function to calculate $\mathbf{a} \cdot \mathbf{b} \times \mathbf{c}$:

```
»trip=triple(a,b,c)
```

Note that the function M-file triple used variables named $u$, $v$, $w$, $x$, and $c$, but the call to triple sent in variables named $a$, $b$, and $c$. The variables used in the two MATLAB instructions that define triple are all *local* to the function triple. Thus functions obey standard conventions of mathematical usage; if $f(x, y) = x^2 + y$, then $f(u, v) = u^2 + v$. In other words, the order of the input variables *matter to the function*, but not the names of the input variables. By contrast, a script M-file has no input variables; when a script is invoked it uses the variables that are already in existence in the current MATLAB session. A MATLAB function M-file should be saved under the same file name as the function name, so when we created the function triple, we saved it as triple.m.

## A.11    EXERCISES

1. Write a MATLAB function M-file that calculates the vector triple product $\mathbf{u} \times \mathbf{v} \times \mathbf{w}$. Test your function using the vectors $\mathbf{a} = [1, 1, 2]$, $\mathbf{b} = [2, -2, 1]$, and $\mathbf{c} = [0, 1, 4]$.

2. Use the script lsplot to choose an integer $n$ so that the best least-squares polynomial approximation of degree $n$ or less looks reasonable for the data $(x_i, y_i) = (i, \ln i), i = 1, 2, \ldots, 10$. Restrict $n$ to be between 1 and 5.

# Answers to Selected Odd-Numbered Exercises*

## CHAPTER 1

**Exercises 1.1, p. 12**

**1.** Linear

**3.** Linear

**5.** Nonlinear

**7.** $x_1 + 3x_2 = 7$
$4x_1 - x_2 = 2$

**9.** $x_1 + x_2 = 0$
$3x_1 + 4x_2 = -1$
$-x_1 + 2x_2 = -3$

**11.**

$x - y = 1$
Unique solution
$2x + y = 5$

**13.**

$3x + 2y = 6$
$-6x - 4y = -12$
Infinitely many solutions

**17.** $x_1 = -3t + 4$
$x_2 = 2t - 1$
$x_3 = t$

**19.** $A = \begin{bmatrix} 2 & 1 & 6 \\ 4 & 3 & 8 \end{bmatrix}$

**21.** $Q = \begin{bmatrix} 1 & 4 & -3 \\ 2 & 1 & 1 \\ 3 & 2 & 1 \end{bmatrix}$

**23.** $2x_1 + x_2 = 6$ and $x_1 + 4x_2 = -3$
$4x_1 + 3x_2 = 8$ $\quad\quad 2x_1 + x_2 = 1$
$\quad\quad\quad\quad\quad\quad\quad\quad 3x_1 + 2x_2 = 1$

---

*Many of the problems have answers that contain parameters or answers that can be written in a variety of forms. For problems of this sort, we have presented one possible form of the answer. Your solution may have a different form and still be correct. You can frequently check your solution by inserting it in the original problem or by showing that two different forms for the answer are equivalent.

**25.** $A = \begin{bmatrix} 1 & 1 & -1 \\ 2 & 0 & -1 \end{bmatrix}$, $B = \begin{bmatrix} 1 & 1 & -1 & 2 \\ 2 & 0 & -1 & 1 \end{bmatrix}$

**27.** $A = \begin{bmatrix} 1 & 1 & 2 \\ 3 & 4 & -1 \\ -1 & 1 & 1 \end{bmatrix}$,

$B = \begin{bmatrix} 1 & 1 & 2 & 6 \\ 3 & 4 & -1 & 5 \\ -1 & 1 & 1 & 2 \end{bmatrix}$

**29.** $A = \begin{bmatrix} 1 & 1 & 1 \\ 2 & 3 & 1 \\ 1 & -1 & 3 \end{bmatrix}$, $B = \begin{bmatrix} 1 & 1 & 1 & 1 \\ 2 & 3 & 1 & 2 \\ 1 & -1 & 3 & 2 \end{bmatrix}$

**31.** $\begin{aligned} x_1 + 2x_2 - x_3 &= 1 \\ -x_2 + 3x_3 &= 1 \\ 5x_2 - 2x_3 &= 6 \end{aligned}$

**33.** $\begin{aligned} x_1 + x_2 &= 9 \\ -2x_2 &= -2 \\ -2x_2 &= -21 \end{aligned}$

**35.** $\begin{aligned} x_1 + 2x_2 - x_3 + x_4 &= 1 \\ x_2 + x_3 - x_4 &= 3 \\ 3x_2 + 6x_3 &= 1 \end{aligned}$

**Exercises 1.2, p. 26**

**1. a)** The matrix is in echelon form.
  **b)** The operation $R_1 - 2R_2$ yields reduced
  echelon form $\begin{bmatrix} 1 & 0 \\ 0 & 1 \end{bmatrix}$.

**3. a)** The operations $R_2 - 2R_1$, $(1/2)R_1$, $R_2 - 4R_1$, $(1/5)R_2$ yield echelon form
$$\begin{bmatrix} 1 & 3/2 & 1/2 \\ 0 & 1 & 2/5 \end{bmatrix}.$$

**5. a)** The operations $R_1 \leftrightarrow R_2$, $(1/2)R_1$, $(1/2)R_2$ yield echelon form
$$\begin{bmatrix} 1 & 0 & 1/2 & 2 \\ 0 & 0 & 1 & 3/2 \end{bmatrix}.$$

**7. a)** The matrix is in echelon form.
  **b)** The operations $R_1 - 2R_3$, $R_2 - 4R_3$, $R_1 - 3R_2$ yield reduced echelon form
$$\begin{bmatrix} 1 & 0 & 0 & 5 \\ 0 & 1 & 0 & -2 \\ 0 & 0 & 1 & 1 \end{bmatrix}.$$

**9. a)** The operation $(1/2)R_2$ yields echelon form
$$\begin{bmatrix} 1 & 2 & -1 & -2 \\ 0 & 1 & -1 & -3/2 \\ 0 & 0 & 0 & 1 \end{bmatrix}.$$

**11.** $x_1 = 0$, $x_2 = 0$

**13.** $x_1 = -2 + 5x_3$, $x_2 = 1 - 3x_3$, $x_3$ arbitrary

**15.** The system is inconsistent.

**17.** $x_1 = x_3 = x_4 = 0$; $x_2$ arbitrary

**19.** The system is inconsistent.

**21.** $x_1 = -1 - (1/2)x_2 + (1/2)x_4$, $x_3 = 1 - x_4$, $x_2$ and $x_4$ arbitrary, $x_5 = 0$

**23.** Inconsistent

**25.** $x_1 = 2 - x_2$, $x_2$ arbitrary

**27.** $x_1 = 2 - x_2 + x_3$, $x_2$ and $x_3$ arbitrary

**29.** $x_1 = 3 - 2x_3$, $x_2 = -2 + 3x_3$, $x_3$ arbitrary

**31.** $x_1 = 3 - (7x_4 - 16x_5)/2$, $x_2 = (x_4 + 2x_5)/2$, $x_3 = -2 + (5x_4 - 12x_5)/2$, $x_4$ and $x_5$ arbitrary

**33.** Inconsistent

**35.** Inconsistent

**37.** All values of $a$ except $a = 8$

**39.** $a = 3$ or $a = -3$

**41.** $\alpha = \pi/3$ or $\alpha = 5\pi/3$; $\beta = \pi/6$ or $\beta = 5\pi/6$

**45.** $\begin{bmatrix} 1 & \times & \times \\ 0 & 1 & \times \end{bmatrix}$, $\begin{bmatrix} 1 & \times & \times \\ 0 & 0 & 1 \end{bmatrix}$, $\begin{bmatrix} 1 & \times & \times \\ 0 & 0 & 0 \end{bmatrix}$,

$\begin{bmatrix} 0 & 1 & \times \\ 0 & 0 & 1 \end{bmatrix}$, $\begin{bmatrix} 0 & 1 & \times \\ 0 & 0 & 0 \end{bmatrix}$, $\begin{bmatrix} 0 & 0 & 1 \\ 0 & 0 & 0 \end{bmatrix}$,

$\begin{bmatrix} 0 & 0 & 0 \\ 0 & 0 & 0 \end{bmatrix}$

**47.** The operations $R_2 - 2R_1$, $R_1 + 2R_2$, $-R_2$ transform $B$ to $I$. The operations $R_2 - 3R_1$, $R_1 + R_2$, $(-1/2)R_2$ reduce $C$ to $I$, so the operations $-2R_2$, $R_1 - R_2$, $R_2 + 3R_1$ transform $I$ to $C$. Thus the operations $R_2 - 2R_1$, $R_1 + 2R_2$, $-R_2$, $-2R_2$, $R_1 - R_2$, $R_2 + 3R_1$ transform $B$ to $C$.

**49.** $N = 135$

**51.** The amounts were \$39, \$21, and \$12.

**53.** Let $A$ denote the number of adults, $S$ the number of students, and $C$ the number of children. Possible solutions are: $A = 5k$, $S = 67 - 11k$, $C = 12 + 6k$, where $k = 0, 1, \ldots, 6$.

**55.** $n(n+1)/2$

**57.** $n(n+1)(2n+1)(3n^2 + 3n - 1)/30$

**Exercises 1.3, p. 37**

**1.**
$$\begin{bmatrix} 1 & 1 & 0 & 5/6 \\ 0 & 0 & 1 & 2/3 \\ 0 & 0 & 0 & 0 \\ 0 & 0 & 0 & 0 \end{bmatrix}$$
$n = 3$
$r = 2$
$x_2$

**3.**
$$\begin{bmatrix} 1 & 0 & 4 & 0 & 13/2 \\ 0 & 1 & -1 & 0 & -3/2 \\ 0 & 0 & 0 & 1 & 1/2 \end{bmatrix}$$
$n = 4$
$r = 3$
$x_3$

**5.** $r = 2, r = 1, r = 0$

**7.** Infinitely many solutions

**9.** Infinitely many solutions, a unique solution, or no solution

**11.** A unique solution or infinitely many solutions

**13.** Infinitely many solutions

**15.** A unique solution or infinitely many solutions

**17.** Infinitely many solutions

**19.** There are nontrivial solutions.

**21.** There is only the trivial solution.

**23.** $a = 1$

**25. a)**
$$\begin{bmatrix} 1 & 0 & 0 \\ 0 & 1 & 0 \\ 0 & 0 & 1 \\ 0 & 0 & 0 \end{bmatrix}$$

**27.** $7x + 2y - 30 = 0$

**29.** $-3x^2 + 3xy + y^2 - 54y + 113 = 0$

**Exercises 1.4, p. 44**

**1. a)**
$$\begin{aligned} x_1 \qquad\qquad + x_4 &= 1200 \\ x_1 + x_2 \qquad &= 1000 \\ x_3 + x_4 &= 600 \\ x_2 + x_3 \qquad &= 400 \end{aligned}$$

**b)** $x_1 = 1100, x_2 = -100, x_3 = 500$;

**c)** The minimum value is $x_1 = 600$ and the maximum value is $x_1 = 1000$.

**3.** $x_2 = 800, x_3 = 400, x_4 = 200$

**5.** $I_1 = 0.05, I_2 = 0.6, I_3 = 0.55$

**7.** $I_1 = 35/13, I_2 = 20/13, I_3 = 15/13$

**Exercises 1.5, p. 58**

**1. a)** $\begin{bmatrix} 2 & 0 \\ 2 & 6 \end{bmatrix}$; **b)** $\begin{bmatrix} 0 & 4 \\ 2 & 4 \end{bmatrix}$;

**c)** $\begin{bmatrix} 0 & -6 \\ 6 & 18 \end{bmatrix}$; **d)** $\begin{bmatrix} -6 & 8 \\ 4 & 6 \end{bmatrix}$

**3.** $\begin{bmatrix} -2 & -2 \\ 0 & 0 \end{bmatrix}$ **5.** $\begin{bmatrix} -1 & -1 \\ 0 & 0 \end{bmatrix}$

**7. a)** $\begin{bmatrix} 3 \\ -3 \end{bmatrix}$; **b)** $\begin{bmatrix} 3 \\ 4 \end{bmatrix}$; **c)** $\begin{bmatrix} 0 \\ 0 \end{bmatrix}$

**9. a)** $\begin{bmatrix} 2 \\ 1 \end{bmatrix}$; **b)** $\begin{bmatrix} 0 \\ 1 \end{bmatrix}$; **c)** $\begin{bmatrix} 17 \\ 14 \end{bmatrix}$

**11. a)** $\begin{bmatrix} 2 \\ 3 \end{bmatrix}$; **b)** $\begin{bmatrix} 20 \\ 16 \end{bmatrix}$

**13.** $a_1 = 11/3, a_2 = -4/3$

**15.** $a_1 = -2, a_2 = 0$ **17.** No solution

**19.** $a_1 = 4, a_2 = -3/2$ **21.** $\mathbf{w}_2 = \begin{bmatrix} 1 \\ 3 \end{bmatrix}$

**23.** $\mathbf{w}_3 = \begin{bmatrix} -1 \\ 2 \end{bmatrix}$ **25.** $\begin{bmatrix} -4 & 6 \\ 2 & 12 \end{bmatrix}$

**27.** $\begin{bmatrix} 4 & 12 \\ 4 & 10 \end{bmatrix}$ **29.** $\begin{bmatrix} 0 & 0 \\ 0 & 0 \end{bmatrix}$

**31.** $AB = \begin{bmatrix} 5 & 16 \\ 5 & 18 \end{bmatrix}$, $BA = \begin{bmatrix} 4 & 11 \\ 6 & 19 \end{bmatrix}$

**33.** $A\mathbf{u} = \begin{bmatrix} 11 \\ 13 \end{bmatrix}$, $\mathbf{v}A = [8, 22]$

**35.** 66 **37.** $\begin{bmatrix} 5 & 10 \\ 8 & 12 \\ 15 & 20 \\ 8 & 17 \end{bmatrix}$ **39.** $\begin{bmatrix} 27 \\ 28 \\ 43 \\ 47 \end{bmatrix}$

**41.** $(BA)\mathbf{u} = B(A\mathbf{u}) = \begin{bmatrix} 37 \\ 63 \end{bmatrix}$

**43.** $\mathbf{x} = \begin{bmatrix} x_1 \\ x_2 \\ x_3 \end{bmatrix} = \begin{bmatrix} -2 \\ 3 \\ 0 \end{bmatrix} + x_3 \begin{bmatrix} 1 \\ -2 \\ 1 \end{bmatrix}$

**45.** $\mathbf{x} = \begin{bmatrix} x_1 \\ x_2 \\ x_3 \\ x_4 \\ x_5 \end{bmatrix} = x_3 \begin{bmatrix} 1 \\ -2 \\ 1 \\ 0 \\ 0 \end{bmatrix} + x_5 \begin{bmatrix} 1 \\ -1 \\ 0 \\ -1 \\ 1 \end{bmatrix}$

**47.** $\mathbf{x} = \begin{bmatrix} x_1 \\ x_2 \\ x_3 \\ x_4 \\ x_5 \end{bmatrix} = x_3 \begin{bmatrix} 1 \\ -2 \\ 1 \\ 0 \\ 0 \end{bmatrix} + x_4 \begin{bmatrix} 2 \\ -3 \\ 0 \\ 1 \\ 0 \end{bmatrix} +$

$x_5 \begin{bmatrix} 3 \\ -4 \\ 0 \\ 0 \\ 1 \end{bmatrix}$

**49.** $\mathbf{x} = \begin{bmatrix} x_1 \\ x_2 \\ x_3 \\ x_4 \\ x_5 \end{bmatrix} = x_2 \begin{bmatrix} 1 \\ 1 \\ 0 \\ 0 \\ 0 \end{bmatrix} + x_4 \begin{bmatrix} 2 \\ 0 \\ -2 \\ 1 \\ 0 \end{bmatrix}$

**51.**

| $C(A(B\mathbf{u}))$ | $(CA)(B\mathbf{u})$ | $(C(AB))\mathbf{u}$ | $C((AB)\mathbf{u})$ |
|:---:|:---:|:---:|:---:|
| 12 | 16 | 20 | 16 |

**53. a)** $AB$ is $(2 \times 4)$; $BA$ is undefined.
**b)** Neither is defined.
**c)** $AB$ is undefined; $BA$ is $(6 \times 7)$.
**d)** $AB$ is $(2 \times 2)$; $BA$ is $(3 \times 3)$.
**e)** $AB$ is $(3 \times 1)$; $BA$ is undefined.
**f)** Both are $(2 \times 4)$.
**g)** $AB$ is $(4 \times 4)$, $BA$ is $(1 \times 1)$.

**61. a)** For (i), $A = \begin{bmatrix} 2 & -1 \\ 1 & 1 \end{bmatrix}$, $\mathbf{x} = \begin{bmatrix} x_1 \\ x_2 \end{bmatrix}$,

$\mathbf{b} = \begin{bmatrix} 3 \\ 3 \end{bmatrix}$; for (ii), $A = \begin{bmatrix} 1 & -3 & 1 \\ 1 & -2 & 1 \\ 0 & 1 & -1 \end{bmatrix}$,

$\mathbf{x} = \begin{bmatrix} x_1 \\ x_2 \\ x_3 \end{bmatrix}$, $\mathbf{b} = \begin{bmatrix} 1 \\ 2 \\ -1 \end{bmatrix}$.

**b)** For (i), $x_1 \begin{bmatrix} 2 \\ 1 \end{bmatrix} + x_2 \begin{bmatrix} -1 \\ 1 \end{bmatrix} = \begin{bmatrix} 3 \\ 3 \end{bmatrix}$;

for (ii), $x_1 \begin{bmatrix} 1 \\ 1 \\ 0 \end{bmatrix} + x_2 \begin{bmatrix} -3 \\ -2 \\ 1 \end{bmatrix} +$

$x_3 \begin{bmatrix} 1 \\ 1 \\ -1 \end{bmatrix} = \begin{bmatrix} 1 \\ 2 \\ -1 \end{bmatrix}$.

**c)** For (i), $\mathbf{b} = 2\mathbf{A}_1 + \mathbf{A}_2$;
for (ii), $\mathbf{b} = 2\mathbf{A}_1 + \mathbf{A}_2 + 2\mathbf{A}_3$.

**63.** $B = \begin{bmatrix} 2 & -1 \\ -1 & 1 \end{bmatrix}$

**65. a)** $B = \begin{bmatrix} -1 & 6 \\ 1 & 0 \end{bmatrix}$;    **b)** Not possible;

**c)** $B = \begin{bmatrix} -2a & -2b \\ a & b \end{bmatrix}$,    $a$ and $b$ arbitrary

**Exercises 1.6, p. 69**

**1.** $(DE)F = D(EF) = \begin{bmatrix} 23 & 23 \\ 29 & 29 \end{bmatrix}$

**3.** $DE = \begin{bmatrix} 8 & 15 \\ 11 & 18 \end{bmatrix}$, $ED = \begin{bmatrix} 12 & 27 \\ 7 & 14 \end{bmatrix}$.

**5.** $F\mathbf{u} = F\mathbf{v} = \begin{bmatrix} 0 \\ 0 \end{bmatrix}$    **7.** $\begin{bmatrix} 3 & 4 & 2 \\ 1 & 7 & 6 \end{bmatrix}$

**9.** $\begin{bmatrix} 5 & 5 \\ 9 & 9 \end{bmatrix}$    **11.** $[0 \ \ 0]$    **13.** $-6$

**15.** 36    **17.** 2    **19.** $\sqrt{2}$
**21.** $\sqrt{29}$    **23.** 0    **25.** $2\sqrt{5}$
**29.** $D$ and $F$ are symmetric.
**31.** $AB$ is symmetric if and only if $AB = BA$.
**33.** $\mathbf{x}^T D\mathbf{x} = x_1^2 + 3x_2^2 + (x_1 + x_2)^2 > 0$
**35.** $\begin{bmatrix} -3 & 3 \\ 3 & -3 \end{bmatrix}$    **37.** $\begin{bmatrix} -27 & -9 \\ 27 & 9 \end{bmatrix}$

**39.** $\begin{bmatrix} -12 & 18 & 24 \\ 18 & -27 & -36 \\ 24 & -36 & -48 \end{bmatrix}$

**41. a)** $\mathbf{x} = \begin{bmatrix} -10 \\ 8 \end{bmatrix}$;    **b)** $\mathbf{x} = \begin{bmatrix} 6 \\ -2 \end{bmatrix}$

**57.** $n = 5$,    $m = 7$

**59.** $n = 4$, $m = 6$

**61.** $n = 5$, $m = 5$

**Exercises 1.7, p. 78**

**1.** Linearly independent

**3.** Linearly dependent, $\mathbf{v}_5 = 3\mathbf{v}_1$

**5.** Linearly dependent, $\mathbf{v}_3 = 2\mathbf{v}_1$

**7.** Linearly dependent, $\mathbf{u}_4 = 4\mathbf{u}_5$

**9.** Linearly independent

**11.** Linearly dependent, $\mathbf{u}_4 = 4\mathbf{u}_5$

**13.** Linearly dependent, $\mathbf{u}_4 = \dfrac{16}{5}\mathbf{u}_0 + \dfrac{12}{5}\mathbf{u}_1 - \dfrac{4}{5}\mathbf{u}_2$

**15.** Those in Exercises 5, 6, 13, and 14

**17.** Singular; $x_1 = -2x_2$   **19.** Singular; $x_1 = -2x_2$

**21.** Singular; $x_1 = x_2 = 0$, $x_3$ arbitrary

**23.** Nonsingular

**25.** Singular; $x_2 = x_3 = 0$, $x_1$ arbitrary

**27.** Nonsingular          **29.** $a = 6$

**31.** $b(a - 2) = 4$          **33.** $c - ab = 0$

**35.** $\mathbf{v}_3 = \mathbf{A}_2$          **37.** $\mathbf{v}_2 = (\mathbf{C}_1 + \mathbf{C}_2)/2$

**39.** $\mathbf{u}_3 = (-8\mathbf{F}_1 - 2\mathbf{F}_2 + 9\mathbf{F}_3)/3$

**41.** $\mathbf{b} = -11\mathbf{v}_1 + 7\mathbf{v}_2$          **43.** $\mathbf{b} = 0\mathbf{v}_1 + 0\mathbf{v}_2$

**45.** $\mathbf{b} = -3\mathbf{v}_1 + 2\mathbf{v}_2$

**47. a)** Any value $a$   **b)** Any value $a$

**Exercises 1.8, p. 90**

**1.** $p(t) = (-1/2)t^2 + (9/2)t - 1$

**3.** $p(t) = 2t + 3$

**5.** $p(t) = 2t^3 - 2t^2 + 3t + 1$

**7.** $y = 2e^{2x} + e^{3x}$

**9.** $y = 3e^{-x} + 4e^x + e^{2x}$

**11.** $\displaystyle\int_0^{3h} f(t)\,dt \approx \dfrac{3h}{2}[f(h) + f(2h)]$

**13.** $\displaystyle\int_0^{3h} f(t)\,dt$

$\approx \dfrac{3h}{8}[f(0) + 3f(h) + 3f(2h) + f(3h)]$

**15.** $\displaystyle\int_0^h f(t)\,dt \approx \dfrac{h}{2}[-f(-h) + 3f(0)]$

**17.** $f'(0) \approx [-f(0) + f(h)]/h$

**19.** $f'(0) \approx [-3f(0) + 4f(h) - f(2h)]/(2h)$

**21.** $f''(0) \approx [f(-h) - 2f(0) + f(h)]/h^2$

**27.** $p(t) = t^3 + 2t^2 + 3t + 2$

**29.** $p(t) = t^3 + t^2 + 4t + 3$

**35.** $f'(a) \approx \dfrac{1}{12h}$
$\times [f(a - 2h) - 8f(a - h) + 8f(a + h) - f(a + 2h)]$

**Exercises 1.9, p. 102**

**5.** $x_1 = -3$, $x_2 = 1.5$

**7.** $x_1 = 14$, $x_2 = -20$, $x_3 = 8$

**9.** If $B = (b_{ij})$ is a $(3 \times 3)$ matrix such that $AB = I$, then $0b_{11} + 0b_{21} + 0b_{31} = 1$. Since this is impossible, no such matrix exists.

**13.** $\begin{bmatrix} 3 & -1 \\ -2 & 1 \end{bmatrix}$

**15.** $\begin{bmatrix} -1/3 & 2/3 \\ 2/3 & -1/3 \end{bmatrix}$   **17.** $\begin{bmatrix} 1 & 0 & 0 \\ -2 & 1 & 0 \\ 5 & -4 & 1 \end{bmatrix}$

**19.** $\begin{bmatrix} 1 & -2 & 0 \\ 3 & -3 & -1 \\ -6 & 7 & 2 \end{bmatrix}$

**21.** $\begin{bmatrix} -1/2 & -2/3 & -1/6 & 7/6 \\ 1 & 1/3 & 1/3 & -4/3 \\ 0 & -1/3 & -1/3 & 1/3 \\ -1/2 & 1 & 1/2 & 1/2 \end{bmatrix}$

**23.** $A^{-1} = (1/10) \begin{bmatrix} 3 & 2 \\ -2 & 2 \end{bmatrix}$

**25.** $A$ has no inverse          **27.** $\lambda = 2$ and $\lambda = -2$

**29.** $x_1 = 6$, $x_2 = -8$          **31.** $x_1 = 18$, $x_2 = 13$

**33.** $x_1 = 5/2$, $x_2 = 5/2$

**35.** $Q^{-1} = C^{-1}A^{-1} = \begin{bmatrix} -3 & 1 \\ 3 & 5 \end{bmatrix}$

**37.** $Q^{-1} = (A^{-1})^T = \begin{bmatrix} 3 & 0 \\ 1 & 2 \end{bmatrix}$

**39.** $Q^{-1} = (A^{-1})^T (C^{-1})^T = \begin{bmatrix} -3 & 3 \\ 1 & 5 \end{bmatrix}$

**41.** $Q^{-1} = BC^{-1} = \begin{bmatrix} 1 & 5 \\ -1 & 4 \end{bmatrix}$

**43.** $Q^{-1} = (1/2)A^{-1} = \begin{bmatrix} 3/2 & 1/2 \\ 0 & 1 \end{bmatrix}$

**45.** $Q^{-1} = B(C^{-1}A^{-1}) = \begin{bmatrix} 3 & 11 \\ -3 & 7 \end{bmatrix}$

**47.** $B = \begin{bmatrix} 1 & 10 \\ 15 & 12 \\ 3 & 3 \end{bmatrix}$; $\quad C = \begin{bmatrix} 13 & 12 & 8 \\ 2 & 3 & 5 \end{bmatrix}$

**49.** $(AB)^{-1} = B^{-1}A^{-1} = \begin{bmatrix} 2 & 35 & 1 \\ 14 & 35 & 34 \\ 23 & 12 & 70 \end{bmatrix}$,

$(3A)^{-1} = \dfrac{1}{3}A^{-1} = \begin{bmatrix} 1/3 & 2/3 & 5/3 \\ 1 & 1/3 & 2 \\ 2/3 & 8/3 & 1/3 \end{bmatrix}$,

$(A^T)^{-1} = (A^{-1})^T = \begin{bmatrix} 1 & 3 & 2 \\ 2 & 1 & 8 \\ 5 & 6 & 1 \end{bmatrix}$

**63.** $b_0 = -5$, $\quad b_1 = 2$

**64.** $b_0 = -7$, $\quad b_1 = 0$

# CHAPTER 2

## Exercises 2.1, p. 126

**1.**

For vector $AB$ the $x$-component is $-4 - 0 = 4$ and the $y$-component is $3 - (-2) = 5$. For vector $CD$ the $x$-component is $1 - 5 = -4$ and the $y$-component is $4 - (-1) = 5$. The vectors are equal.

**3.**

For vector $AB$ the $x$-component is $0 - (-4) = 4$ and the $y$-component is $1 - (-2) = 3$. For vector $CD$ the $x$-component is $3 - 0 = 3$ and the $y$-component is $2 - (-2) = 4$. The vectors are not equal.

**5. a)** For **u**: $\|\mathbf{u}\| = \sqrt{(2 - (-3))^2 + (2 - 5)^2} = \sqrt{34}$.

For **v**: $\|\mathbf{v}\| = \sqrt{(-2 - 3)^2 + (7 - 4)^2} = \sqrt{34}$.

Therefore, $\|\mathbf{u}\| = \|\mathbf{v}\|$.

**b)** Segment $AB$ has slope $(2 - 5)/(2 - (-3)) = -3/5$.
Segment $CD$ has slope $(7 - 4)/(-2 - 3) = 3/(-5)$.

**c)** For vector $AB$ the $x$-component is $2 - (-3) = 5$ and the $y$-component $2 - 5 = -3$. For vector $CD$ the $x$-component is $-2 - 3 = -5$ and the $y$-component is $7 - 4 = 3$. The vectors are not equal.

**d)**

**7.** $D = (-2, 5)$

**9.** $D = (-1, 1)$

**11.** $v_1 = 5, v_2 = 3$

**13.** $v_1 = -6, v_2 = 5$

**15.** $B = (3, 3)$

**17.** $A = (2, 4)$

**19. a)** $B = (3, 2), \quad C = (5, 0)$

**b)**

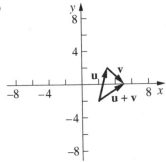

**21. a)** $Q = (7, 1)$

**b)**

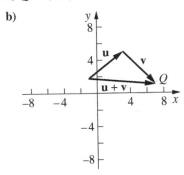

**23. a)** $B = (-1, 4), \quad C = (0, -1)$

**b)**

**25. a)** $B = (3, 3), \quad C = (6, 1)$

**b)**

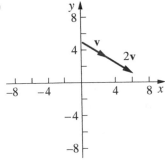

**27. a)** $D = (6, -3)$

**b)**

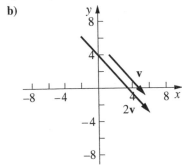

**29.** $\dfrac{1}{5} \begin{bmatrix} 3 \\ 4 \end{bmatrix}$

**31.** $\dfrac{3}{\sqrt{13}}\mathbf{i} - \dfrac{2}{\sqrt{13}}\mathbf{j}$

**33.** $B = (1, -2)$

**35.** $B = (1/3, -7)$

**37.** $\mathbf{u} + \mathbf{v} = \begin{bmatrix} 2 \\ 4 \end{bmatrix}, \qquad \mathbf{u} - 3\mathbf{v} = \begin{bmatrix} -6 \\ 8 \end{bmatrix}$

**39.** $\mathbf{u} + \mathbf{v} = 4\mathbf{i} + \mathbf{j}, \qquad \mathbf{u} - 3\mathbf{v} = -4\mathbf{i} - 7\mathbf{j}$

**Exercises 2.2, p. 134**

**1.**

$$d(P, Q) = \sqrt{(0 - 1)^2 + (2 - 2)^2 + (2 - 1)^2} = \sqrt{2}$$

**3.**

$z$

$\bullet\, Q = (0, 0, 1)$

$y$

$\bullet\, P = (1, 0, 0)$

$x$

$d(P, Q) = \sqrt{(0 - 1)^2 + (0 - 0)^2 + (1 - 0)^2} = \sqrt{2}$

**5.** $M = (1, 4, 4)$;

$d(M, O) = \sqrt{(0 - 1)^2 + (0 - 4)^2 + (0 - 4)^2} = \sqrt{33}$

**7.** $B = (0, 3/2, -3/2)$,
$C = (1, 3, 0)$,
$D = (2, 9/2, 3/2)$

**9.** line

**11.** plane

**19. a)** $v = \begin{bmatrix} 3 \\ 2 \\ -3 \end{bmatrix}$

**b)** $D = (2, 4, -2);\quad v\begin{bmatrix} 3 \\ 2 \\ -3 \end{bmatrix}$

**21. a)** $v = \begin{bmatrix} 0 \\ 5 \\ -7 \end{bmatrix}$

**b)** $D = (-1, 7, -6)$

**23.** $\lambda = 2$

**25.** $A = (-2, 3, -1)$

**27. a)** $u + 2v = \begin{bmatrix} 7 \\ 7 \\ 10 \end{bmatrix}$

**b)** $\|u - v\| = 3$

**c)** $w\begin{bmatrix} -1 \\ 1/2 \\ -1 \end{bmatrix}$

**29. a)** $u + 2v = \begin{bmatrix} -1 \\ 1 \\ 2 \end{bmatrix}$

**b)** $\|u - v\| = \sqrt{150}$

**c)** $w\begin{bmatrix} 7/2 \\ -5 \\ 1/2 \end{bmatrix}$

**31.** $u = 2k$

**33.** $u = -\dfrac{5}{3}v = \begin{bmatrix} 5/3 \\ -10/3 \\ -10/3 \end{bmatrix}$

**35.** $u = \begin{bmatrix} -2 \\ -4 \\ -1 \end{bmatrix}$

**Exercises 2.3, p. 146**

**1.** $-2$

**3.** $-1$

**5.** $\cos\theta = \dfrac{11}{\sqrt{290}}$

**7.** $\cos\theta = \dfrac{1}{6}$

**9.** $\theta = \dfrac{\pi}{6}$

**11.** $\theta = \dfrac{\pi}{2}$

**13.** $u = i + 3j + 4k$

**15.** $u = 3i + 4k$

**17.** $u = -i + 3j + k$

**19.** $R = (33/10, 11/10)$

**21.** $R = (-3, -1)$

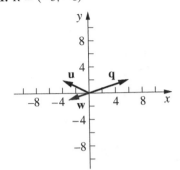

**23.** $\mathbf{u}_1 = \begin{bmatrix} 5 \\ 5 \end{bmatrix}, \quad \mathbf{u}_2 = \begin{bmatrix} 2 \\ -2 \end{bmatrix}$

**25.** $\mathbf{u}_1 = \begin{bmatrix} 2 \\ 4 \\ 2 \end{bmatrix}, \quad \mathbf{u}_2 = \begin{bmatrix} 4 \\ 0 \\ -4 \end{bmatrix}$

**33.** $\begin{bmatrix} -2 \\ 2 \\ 8 \end{bmatrix}$

**35.** $3\mathbf{i} - \mathbf{j} - 5\mathbf{k}$

**37.** $\begin{bmatrix} -2 \\ -5 \\ 4 \end{bmatrix}$

**39.** $\begin{bmatrix} 2 \\ -3 \\ 1 \end{bmatrix}$

**41.** $\begin{bmatrix} 1 \\ 1 \\ -4 \end{bmatrix}$

**43.** $4\sqrt{6}$ square units
**45.** $3\sqrt{11}$ square units
**47.** 24 cubic units
**49.** not coplanar

**Exercises 2.4, p. 157**
**1.** $x = 2 + 3t, y = 4 + 2t,$
   $z = -3 + 4t$

**3.** $x = t, y = 4 - 2t, z = 1 + 3t$
**5.** The lines are parallel.
**7.** The lines are not parallel.
**9.** $x = 1 + 3t, y = 2 + 4t, z = 1 - t$
**11.** The line intersects the plane at
    $P = (-1, 4, 1)$.
**13.** The line intersects the plane at
    $P = (-8, -13, 36)$.
**15.** $6x + y - z = 16$
**17.** $-7x - y + 4z = 5$
**19.** $2x - 7y - 3z = 1$
**21.** $\mathbf{n} = \begin{bmatrix} 2/3 \\ 1/3 \\ -2/3 \end{bmatrix}$
**23.** $x + 2y - 2z = 17$
**25.** $x = 4 - t, y = 5 + t, z = t$

## CHAPTER 3

**Exercises 3.1, p. 166**
**1.**

**3.**

**5.**

**7.**

**9.**

**11.**

**13.**

$x + 3y = 0$

**15.**

$x + y = 0$

**17.**

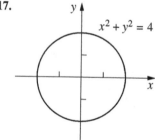

$x^2 + y^2 = 4$

**19.** $W$ is the plane with equation $x + y + 2z = 0$.

**21.** $W$ is the set of points on the upper half of the sphere $x^2 + y^2 + z^2 = 1$.

**23.** $W = \left\{ \begin{bmatrix} a \\ 0 \end{bmatrix} : a \text{ any real number} \right\}$

**25.** $W = \left\{ \begin{bmatrix} a \\ 2 \end{bmatrix} : a \text{ any real number} \right\}$

**27.** $W = \left\{ \begin{bmatrix} x_1 \\ x_2 \\ x_3 \end{bmatrix} : x_1 + x_2 - 2x_3 = 0 \right\}$

**29.** $W = \left\{ \begin{bmatrix} 0 \\ x_2 \\ x_3 \end{bmatrix} : x_2, x_3 \text{ any real number} \right\}$

**Exercises 3.2, p. 174**

**1.** $W$ is a subspace. $W$ is the set of points on the line with equation $x = 2y$.

**3.** $W$ is not a subspace.

**5.** $W$ is the subspace consisting of the points on the $y$-axis.

**7.** $W$ is not a subspace.

**9.** $W$ is the subspace consisting of the points on the plane $2x - y - z = 0$.

**11.** $W$ is not a subspace.

**13.** $W$ is not a subspace.

**15.** $W$ is the subspace consisting of the points on the line with parametric equations $x = 2t$, $y = -t$, $z = t$.

**17.** $W$ is the subspace consisting of the points on the $x$-axis.

**19.** $W$ is the set of points on the plane $x + 2y + 3z = 0$.

**23.** $W$ is the line formed by the two intersecting planes $x + 2y + 2z = 0$ and $x + 3y = 0$. The line has parametric equations $x = -6t$, $y = 2t$, $z = t$.

**25.** $W$ is the set of points on the plane $x - z = 0$.

**Exercises 3.3, p. 186**

**1.** $\text{Sp}(S) = \{\mathbf{x}: x_1 + x_2 = 0\}$; $\text{Sp}(S)$ is the line with equation $x + y = 0$.

**3.** $\text{Sp}(S) = \{\mathbf{e}\}$; $\text{Sp}(S)$ is the point $(0, 0)$.

**5.** $\text{Sp}(S) = R^2$

**7.** $\text{Sp}(S) = \{\mathbf{x}: 3x_1 + 2x_2 = 0\}$; $\text{Sp}(S)$ is the line with equation $3x + 2y = 0$.

**9.** $\text{Sp}(S) = R^2$

**11.** $\text{Sp}(S) = \{\mathbf{x}: x_1 + x_2 = 0\}$; $\text{Sp}(S)$ is the line with equation $x + y = 0$.

**13.** $\text{Sp}(S) = \{\mathbf{x}: x_2 + x_3 = 0 \text{ and } x_1 = 0\}$; $\text{Sp}(S)$ is the line through $(0, 0, 0)$ and $(0, -1, 1)$. The parametric equations for the line are $x = 0$, $y = -t$, $z = t$.

**15.** $\text{Sp}(S) = \{\mathbf{x}: 2x_1 - x_2 + x_3 = 0\}$; $\text{Sp}(S)$ is the plane with equation $2x - y + z = 0$.

**17.** $\text{Sp}(S) = R^3$

**19.** $\text{Sp}(S) = \{\mathbf{x}: x_2 + x_3 = 0\}$; $\text{Sp}(S)$ is the plane with equation $y + z = 0$.

**21.** The vectors $\mathbf{u}$ in b), c), and e) are in $\text{Sp}(S)$; for b), $\mathbf{u} = \mathbf{x}$; for c), $\mathbf{u} = \mathbf{v}$; for e), $\mathbf{u} = 3\mathbf{v} - 4\mathbf{x}$.

**23.** d and e

**25.** x and y

**27.** $\mathcal{N}(A) = \{\mathbf{x} \text{ in } R^2: -x_1 + 3x_2 = 0\}$; $\mathcal{R}(A) = \{\mathbf{x} \text{ in } R^2: 2x_1 + x_2 = 0\}$

**29.** $\mathcal{N}(A) = \{\boldsymbol{\theta}\}$; $\mathcal{R}(A) = R^2$

**31.** $\mathcal{N}(A) = \{\mathbf{x} \text{ in } R^3: x_1 + 2x_2 = 0 \text{ and } x_3 = 0\}$; $\mathcal{R}(A) = R^2$

**33.** $\mathcal{N}(A) = \{\mathbf{x} \text{ in } R^2: x_2 = 0\}$; $\mathcal{R}(A) = \{\mathbf{x} \text{ in } R^3: x_2 = 2x_1 \text{ and } x_3 = 3x_1\}$

**35.** $\mathcal{N}(A) = \{\mathbf{x} \text{ in } R^3: x_1 = -7x_3 \text{ and } x_2 = 2x_3\}$; $\mathcal{R}(A) = \{\mathbf{x} \text{ in } R^3: -4x_1 + 2x_2 + x_3 = 0\}$

**37.** $\mathcal{N}(A) = \{\boldsymbol{\theta}\}$; $\mathcal{R}(A) = R^3$

**39. a)** The vectors $\mathbf{b}$ in ii), v), and vi) are in $\mathcal{R}(A)$.

   **b)** For ii), $\mathbf{x} = [1, 0]^T$ is one choice; for v), $\mathbf{x} = [0, 1]^T$ is one choice; for vi), $\mathbf{x} = [0, 0]^T$ is one choice.

   **c)** For ii), $\mathbf{b} = \mathbf{A}_1$; for v), $\mathbf{b} = \mathbf{A}_2$, for vi), $\mathbf{b} = 0\mathbf{A}_1 + 0\mathbf{A}_2$.

**41. a)** The vectors $\mathbf{b}$ in i), iii), v), and vi) are in $\mathcal{R}(A)$.

   **b)** For i), $\mathbf{x} = [-1, 1, 0]^T$ is one choice; for iii), $\mathbf{x} = [-2, 3, 0]^T$ is one choice; for v), $\mathbf{x} = [-2, 1, 0]^T$ is one choice; for vi), $\mathbf{x} = [0, 0, 0]^T$ is one choice.

   **c)** For i), $\mathbf{b} = -\mathbf{A}_1 + \mathbf{A}_2$; for iii), $\mathbf{b} = -2\mathbf{A}_1 + 3\mathbf{A}_2$; for v), $\mathbf{b} = -2\mathbf{A}_1 + \mathbf{A}_2$; for vi), $\mathbf{b} = 0\mathbf{A}_1 + 0\mathbf{A}_2 + 0\mathbf{A}_3$.

**47.** $\mathbf{w}_1 = [-2, 1, 3]^T$, $\mathbf{w}_2 = [0, 3, 2]^T$

**49.** $\mathbf{w}_1 = [1, 2, 2]^T$, $\mathbf{w}_2 = [0, 3, 1]^T$

**Exercises 3.4, p. 200**

**1.** $\{[1, 0, 1, 0]^T, [-1, 1, 0, 1]^T\}$

**3.** $\{[1, 1, 0, 0]^T, [-1, 0, 1, 0]^T, [3, 0, 0, 1]^T\}$

**5.** $\{[-1, 1, 0, 0]^T, [0, 0, 1, 0]^T, [0, 0, 0, 1]^T\}$

**7.** $\{[2, 1, -1, 0]^T, [-1, 0, 0, 1]^T\}$

**9. a)** $\mathbf{x} = 2\begin{bmatrix} 1 \\ 0 \\ 1 \\ 0 \end{bmatrix} + \begin{bmatrix} -1 \\ 1 \\ 0 \\ 1 \end{bmatrix}$;　**b)** $\mathbf{x}$ is not in $W$.

   **c)** $\mathbf{x} = -3\begin{bmatrix} -1 \\ 1 \\ 0 \\ 1 \end{bmatrix}$;　**d)** $\mathbf{x} = 2\begin{bmatrix} 1 \\ 0 \\ 1 \\ 0 \end{bmatrix}$

**11. a)** $B = \begin{bmatrix} 1 & 0 & 1 & 1 \\ 0 & 1 & 1 & -1 \\ 0 & 0 & 0 & 0 \end{bmatrix}$

   **b)** A basis for $\mathcal{N}(A)$ is $\{[-1, -1, 1, 0]^T, [-1, 1, 0, 1]^T\}$.

   **c)** $\{\mathbf{A}_1, \mathbf{A}_2\}$ is a basis for the column space of $A$; $\mathbf{A}_3 = \mathbf{A}_1 + \mathbf{A}_2$ and $\mathbf{A}_4 = \mathbf{A}_1 - \mathbf{A}_2$.

**d)** $\{[1, 0, 1, 1], [0, 1, 1, -1]\}$ is a basis for the row space of $A$.

**13. a)** $B = \begin{bmatrix} 1 & 0 & -1 & 2 \\ 0 & 1 & 1 & -1 \\ 0 & 0 & 0 & 0 \\ 0 & 0 & 0 & 0 \end{bmatrix}$

**b)** A basis for $\mathcal{N}(A)$ is $\{[1, -1, 1, 0]^T, [-2, 1, 0, 1]^T\}$.

**c)** $\{\mathbf{A}_1, \mathbf{A}_2\}$ is a basis for the column space of $A$; $\mathbf{A}_3 = -\mathbf{A}_1 + \mathbf{A}_2$ and $\mathbf{A}_4 = 2\mathbf{A}_1 - \mathbf{A}_2$.

**d)** $\{[1, 0, -1, 2], [0, 1, 1, -1]\}$ is a basis for the row space of $A$.

**15. a)** $B = \begin{bmatrix} 1 & 2 & 0 \\ 0 & 0 & 1 \\ 0 & 0 & 0 \end{bmatrix}$

**b)** A basis for $\mathcal{N}(A)$ is $\{[-2, 1, 0]^T\}$.

**c)** $\{\mathbf{A}_1, \mathbf{A}_3\}$ is a basis for the column space of $A$; $\mathbf{A}_2 = 2\mathbf{A}_1$.

**d)** $\{[1, 2, 0], [0, 0, 1]\}$ is a basis for the row space of $A$.

**17.** $\{[1, 3, 1]^T, [0, -1, -1]^T\}$ is a basis for $\mathcal{R}(A)$.

**19.** $\{[1, 2, 2, 0]^T, [0, 1, -2, 1]^T\}$ is a basis for $\mathcal{R}(A)$.

**21. a)** $\{[1, 2]^T\}$;   **b)** $\{[1, 2]^T\}$

**23. a)** $\{[1, 2, 1]^T, [2, 5, 0]^T\}$;
**b)** $\{[1, 2, 1]^T, [0, 1, -2]^T\}$

**25. a)** $\{[0, 1, 0]^T\}$;   **b)** $\{[-1, 1, 0]^T, [0, 0, 1]^T\}$
**c)** $\{[-1, 1, 0]^T\}$

**27.** $-2\mathbf{v}_1 - 3\mathbf{v}_2 + \mathbf{v}_3 = \boldsymbol{\theta}$, so $S$ is linearly dependent. Since $\mathbf{v}_3 = 2\mathbf{v}_1 + 3\mathbf{v}_2$, if $\mathbf{v} = a_1\mathbf{v}_1 + a_2\mathbf{v}_2 + a_3\mathbf{v}_3$ is in $Sp\{\mathbf{v}_1, \mathbf{v}_2, \mathbf{v}_3\}$, then $\mathbf{v} = (a_1 + 2a_3)\mathbf{v}_1 + (a_2 + 3a_3)\mathbf{v}_2$. Therefore $\mathbf{v}$ is in $Sp\{\mathbf{v}_1, \mathbf{v}_2\}$.

**29.** The subsets are $\{\mathbf{v}_1, \mathbf{v}_2, \mathbf{v}_3\}, \{\mathbf{v}_1, \mathbf{v}_2, \mathbf{v}_4\}$, $\{\mathbf{v}_1, \mathbf{v}_3, \mathbf{v}_4\}$.

**33.** $S$ is not a basis.

**35.** $S$ is not a basis.

**Exercises 3.5, p. 212**

**1.** $S$ does not span $R^2$.

**3.** $S$ is linearly dependent.

**5.** $S$ is linearly dependent and does not span $R^2$.

**7.** $S$ does not span $R^3$.

**9.** $S$ is linearly dependent.

**11.** $S$ is a basis.

**13.** $S$ is not a basis.

**15.** $\dim(W) = 3$

**17.** $\dim(W) = 2$

**19.** $\dim(W) = 1$

**21.** $\{[-2, 1]^T\}$ is a basis for $\mathcal{N}(A)$; nullity$(A) = 1$; rank$(A) = 1$.

**23.** $\{[-5, -2, 1]^T\}$ is a basis for $\mathcal{N}(A)$; nullity$(A) = 1$; rank$(A) = 2$.

**25.** $\{[1, -1, 1]^T, [0, 2, 3]^T\}$ is a basis for $\mathcal{R}(A)$; rank$(A) = 2$; nullity$(A) = 1$.

**27. a)** $\{[1, 1, -2], [0, -1, 1]^T, [0, 0, 1]^T\}$ is a basis for $W$; $\dim(W) = 3$.

**b)** $\{[1, 2, -1, 1]^T, [0, 1, -1, 1]^T, [0, 0, -1, 4]^T\}$ is a basis for $W$; $\dim(W) = 3$.

**29.** $\dim(W) = 2$

**33. a)** rank$(A) \le 3$ and nullity$(A) \ge 0$.

**b)** rank$(A) \le 3$ and nullity$(A) \ge 1$.

**c)** rank$(A) \le 4$ and nullity$(A) \ge 0$.

**Exercises 3.6, p. 224**

**5.** $\mathbf{u}_1^T\mathbf{u}_3 = 0$ requires $a + b + c = 0$; $\mathbf{u}_2^T\mathbf{u}_3 = 0$ requires $2a + 2b - 4c = 0$; therefore $c = 0$ and $a + b = 0$.

**7.** $\mathbf{u}_1^T\mathbf{u}_2 = 0$ forces $a = 3$; then $\mathbf{u}_2^T\mathbf{u}_3 = 0$ requires $-8 - b + 3c = 0$, while $\mathbf{u}_1^T\mathbf{u}_3 = 0$ requires $4 + b + c = 0$; therefore $b = -5, c = 1$.

**9.** $\mathbf{v} = (2/3)\mathbf{u}_1 - (1/2)\mathbf{u}_2 + (1/6)\mathbf{u}_3$

**11.** $\mathbf{v} = 3\mathbf{u}_1$

**13.** $\mathbf{u}_1 = \begin{bmatrix} 0 \\ 0 \\ 1 \\ 0 \end{bmatrix}$, $\mathbf{u}_2 = \begin{bmatrix} 1 \\ 1 \\ 0 \\ 1 \end{bmatrix}$, $\mathbf{u}_3 = \begin{bmatrix} 1/3 \\ -2/3 \\ 0 \\ 1/3 \end{bmatrix}$

**15.** $\mathbf{u}_1 = \begin{bmatrix} 1 \\ 1 \\ 0 \end{bmatrix}$, $\mathbf{u}_2 = \begin{bmatrix} 1 \\ -1 \\ -1 \end{bmatrix}$, $\mathbf{u}_3 = \begin{bmatrix} 2 \\ -2 \\ 4 \end{bmatrix}$

**17.** $\mathbf{u}_1 = \begin{bmatrix} 0 \\ 1 \\ 0 \\ 1 \end{bmatrix}$, $\mathbf{u}_2 = \begin{bmatrix} -1 \\ -1 \\ 0 \\ 1 \end{bmatrix}$, $\mathbf{u}_3 = \begin{bmatrix} -2/3 \\ 1/3 \\ 1 \\ -1/3 \end{bmatrix}$

**19.** For the null space: $\begin{bmatrix} -3 \\ -1 \\ 1 \\ 0 \end{bmatrix}$, $\begin{bmatrix} 7/11 \\ -27/11 \\ -6/11 \\ 1 \end{bmatrix}$;

for the range space: $\begin{bmatrix} 1 \\ 2 \\ 1 \end{bmatrix}$, $\begin{bmatrix} -11/6 \\ 8/6 \\ -5/6 \end{bmatrix}$

## Exercises 3.7, p. 239

**1. a)** $\begin{bmatrix} 0 \\ 0 \end{bmatrix}$; **b)** $\begin{bmatrix} -1 \\ 0 \end{bmatrix}$; **c)** $\begin{bmatrix} 1 \\ -1 \end{bmatrix}$;

**d)** $\begin{bmatrix} -2 \\ 1 \end{bmatrix}$

**3.** c) is not but a), b), and d) are.

**9.** $F$ is a linear transformation.

**11.** $F$ is not a linear transformation.

**13.** $F$ is a linear transformation.

**15.** $F$ is a linear transformation.

**17.** $F$ is not a linear transformation.

**19. a)** $\begin{bmatrix} 3 \\ 1 \\ -1 \end{bmatrix}$; **b)** $\begin{bmatrix} 0 \\ -1 \\ -2 \end{bmatrix}$; **c)** $\begin{bmatrix} 7 \\ 2 \\ -3 \end{bmatrix}$,

**21.** $T\left( \begin{bmatrix} x_1 \\ x_2 \end{bmatrix} \right) = \begin{bmatrix} x_1 + x_2 \\ x_1 - 2x_2 \end{bmatrix}$

**23.** $T\left( \begin{bmatrix} x_1 \\ x_2 \\ x_3 \end{bmatrix} \right) = \begin{bmatrix} -\frac{1}{2}x_1 - \frac{1}{2}x_2 + \frac{1}{2}x_3 \\ \frac{1}{2}x_1 + \frac{1}{2}x_2 + \frac{1}{2}x_3 \end{bmatrix}$

**25.** $A = \begin{bmatrix} 1 & 3 \\ 2 & 1 \end{bmatrix}$; $\mathcal{N}(T) = \{\boldsymbol{\theta}\}$; $\mathcal{R}(T) = R^2$;

rank$(T) = 2$; nullity$(T) = 0$

**27.** $A = [3 \ 2]$; $\mathcal{N}(T) = \{\mathbf{x} \text{ in } R^2: \ 3x_1 + 2x_2 = 0\}$; $\mathcal{R}(T) = R^1$; rank$(T) = 1$; nullity$(T) = 1$

**29.** $A = \begin{bmatrix} 1 & -1 & 0 \\ 0 & 1 & -1 \end{bmatrix}$; $\mathcal{N}(T) = \{\mathbf{x} \text{ in } R^3: x_1 = x_3$

and $x_2 = x_3\}$; $\mathcal{R}(T) = R^2$; rank$(T) = 2$; nullity$(T) = 1$

## Exercises 3.8, p. 254

**1.** $\mathbf{x}^* = \begin{bmatrix} -5/13 \\ 7/13 \end{bmatrix}$

**3.** $\mathbf{x}^* = \begin{bmatrix} (28/74) - 3x_3 \\ (27/74) + x_3 \\ x_3 \end{bmatrix}$, $x_3$ arbitrary

**5.** $\mathbf{x}^* = \begin{bmatrix} 2x_2 + 26/7 \\ -x_2 \end{bmatrix}$, $x_2$ arbitrary

**7.** $y = 1.3t + 1.1$      **9.** $y = 1.5t$

**11.** $y = 0.5t^2 + 0.1t$      **13.** $y = 0.25t^2 + 2.15t + 0.45$

## Exercises 3.9, p. 266

**1.** $\mathbf{w}^* = \begin{bmatrix} 1/2 \\ 3 \\ 11/2 \end{bmatrix}$      **3.** $\mathbf{w}^* = \begin{bmatrix} 1 \\ 1 \\ 1 \end{bmatrix}$

**5.** $\mathbf{w}^* = \begin{bmatrix} 4 \\ 2 \\ 2 \end{bmatrix}$      **7.** $\mathbf{w}^* = \begin{bmatrix} 3 \\ -1 \\ 2 \end{bmatrix}$

**9.** $\mathbf{w}^* = \begin{bmatrix} 0 \\ 1 \\ -1 \end{bmatrix}$

**11.** $\mathbf{w}^* = \frac{4}{5}\begin{bmatrix} 2 \\ 1 \\ 0 \end{bmatrix} + \frac{11}{2}\begin{bmatrix} -1/5 \\ 2/5 \\ 1 \end{bmatrix}$

**13.** $\mathbf{w}^* = \begin{bmatrix} 1 \\ 1 \\ 0 \end{bmatrix} + 4\begin{bmatrix} 1/2 \\ -1/2 \\ 1 \end{bmatrix}$

**15.** $\mathbf{w}^* = 2\begin{bmatrix} 1 \\ -1 \\ 1 \end{bmatrix} + \begin{bmatrix} 1 \\ 1 \\ 0 \end{bmatrix}$

## CHAPTER 4

## Exercises 4.1, p. 279

**1.** $\lambda = 1$, $\mathbf{x} = a\begin{bmatrix} -1 \\ 1 \end{bmatrix}$, $a \neq 0$;

$\lambda = 3$, $\mathbf{x} = a\begin{bmatrix} 0 \\ 1 \end{bmatrix}$, $a \neq 0$

**3.** $\lambda = 1$, $\mathbf{x} = a\begin{bmatrix} 1 \\ 1 \end{bmatrix}$, $a \neq 0$;

$\lambda = 3$, $\mathbf{x} = a\begin{bmatrix} -1 \\ 1 \end{bmatrix}$, $a \neq 0$

**5.** $\lambda = 1$, $\mathbf{x} = a \begin{bmatrix} -1 \\ 1 \end{bmatrix}$, $a \neq 0$;

$\lambda = 3$, $\mathbf{x} = a \begin{bmatrix} 1 \\ 1 \end{bmatrix}$, $a \neq 0$

**7.** $\lambda = 1$, $\mathbf{x} = a \begin{bmatrix} 0 \\ 1 \end{bmatrix}$, $a \neq 0$

**9.** $\lambda = 0$, $\mathbf{x} = a \begin{bmatrix} -1 \\ 1 \end{bmatrix}$, $a \neq 0$;

$\lambda = 5$, $\mathbf{x} = a \begin{bmatrix} 2 \\ 3 \end{bmatrix}$, $a \neq 0$

**11.** $\lambda = 2$, $\mathbf{x} = a \begin{bmatrix} -1 \\ 1 \end{bmatrix}$, $a \neq 0$

**Exercises 4.2, p. 288**

**1.** $M_{11} = \begin{bmatrix} 1 & 3 & -1 \\ 2 & 4 & 1 \\ 2 & 0 & -2 \end{bmatrix}$; $A_{11} = 18$

**3.** $M_{31} = \begin{bmatrix} -1 & 3 & 1 \\ 1 & 3 & -1 \\ 2 & 0 & -2 \end{bmatrix}$; $A_{31} = 0$

**5.** $M_{34} = \begin{bmatrix} 2 & -1 & 3 \\ 4 & 1 & 3 \\ 2 & 2 & 0 \end{bmatrix}$; $A_{34} = 0$

**7.** $\det(A) = 0$    **9.** $\det(A) = 0$; $A$ is singular.
**11.** $\det(A) = -1$; $A$ is nonsingular.
**13.** $\det(A) = 6$; $A$ is nonsingular.
**15.** $\det(A) = 20$; $A$ is nonsingular.
**17.** $\det(A) = 6$; $A$ is nonsingular.
**19.** $\det(A) = 36$; $A$ is nonsingular.
**21.** $y = 2x - 1$    **27.** $5$    **29.** $3/5$

**Exercises 4.3, p. 296**

**1.** $\det(A) = \begin{vmatrix} 1 & 2 & 1 \\ 3 & 0 & 2 \\ -1 & 1 & 3 \end{vmatrix} \overset{\substack{R_2 - 3R_1 \\ R_3 + R_1}}{=} \begin{vmatrix} 1 & 2 & 1 \\ 0 & -6 & -1 \\ 0 & 3 & 4 \end{vmatrix}$

$= \begin{vmatrix} -6 & -1 \\ 3 & 4 \end{vmatrix} = -21$

**3.** $\det(A) = \begin{vmatrix} 3 & 6 & 9 \\ 2 & 0 & 2 \\ 1 & 2 & 0 \end{vmatrix} = (3)(2) \begin{vmatrix} 1 & 2 & 3 \\ 1 & 0 & 1 \\ 1 & 2 & 0 \end{vmatrix}$

$\overset{\substack{R_2 - R_1 \\ R_3 - R_1}}{=} 6 \begin{vmatrix} 1 & 2 & 3 \\ 0 & -2 & -2 \\ 0 & 0 & -3 \end{vmatrix} = 6 \begin{vmatrix} -2 & -2 \\ 0 & -3 \end{vmatrix} = 36$

**5.** $\det(A) = \begin{vmatrix} 2 & 4 & -3 \\ 3 & 2 & 5 \\ 2 & 3 & 4 \end{vmatrix} = (\tfrac{1}{2}) \begin{vmatrix} 2 & 4 & -3 \\ 6 & 4 & 10 \\ 2 & 3 & 4 \end{vmatrix}$

$\overset{\substack{R_2 - 3R_1 \\ R_3 - R_1}}{=} (\tfrac{1}{2}) \begin{vmatrix} 2 & 4 & -3 \\ 0 & -8 & 19 \\ 0 & -1 & 7 \end{vmatrix}$

$= \begin{vmatrix} -8 & 19 \\ -1 & 7 \end{vmatrix} = -37$

**7.** $\begin{vmatrix} 1 & 0 & 0 & 0 \\ 2 & 0 & 0 & 3 \\ 1 & 1 & 0 & 1 \\ 1 & 4 & 2 & 2 \end{vmatrix} = (-1) \begin{vmatrix} 1 & 0 & 0 & 0 \\ 2 & 3 & 0 & 0 \\ 1 & 1 & 0 & 1 \\ 1 & 2 & 2 & 4 \end{vmatrix}$

$= \begin{vmatrix} 1 & 0 & 0 & 0 \\ 2 & 3 & 0 & 0 \\ 1 & 1 & 1 & 0 \\ 1 & 2 & 4 & 2 \end{vmatrix} = 6$

**9.** $\begin{vmatrix} 0 & 0 & 2 & 0 \\ 0 & 0 & 1 & 3 \\ 0 & 4 & 1 & 3 \\ 2 & 1 & 5 & 6 \end{vmatrix} = (-1) \begin{vmatrix} 2 & 0 & 0 & 0 \\ 1 & 0 & 0 & 3 \\ 1 & 4 & 0 & 3 \\ 5 & 1 & 2 & 6 \end{vmatrix}$

$= \begin{vmatrix} 2 & 0 & 0 & 0 \\ 1 & 3 & 0 & 0 \\ 1 & 3 & 0 & 4 \\ 5 & 6 & 2 & 1 \end{vmatrix}$

$= (-1) \begin{vmatrix} 2 & 0 & 0 & 0 \\ 1 & 3 & 0 & 0 \\ 1 & 3 & 4 & 0 \\ 5 & 6 & 1 & 2 \end{vmatrix} = -48$

**11.** $\begin{vmatrix} 0 & 0 & 1 & 0 \\ 0 & 2 & 6 & 3 \\ 2 & 4 & 1 & 5 \\ 0 & 0 & 0 & 4 \end{vmatrix} = (-1) \begin{vmatrix} 2 & 4 & 1 & 5 \\ 0 & 2 & 6 & 3 \\ 0 & 0 & 1 & 0 \\ 0 & 0 & 0 & 4 \end{vmatrix} = -16$

**13.** $\det(B) = 3\det(A) = 6$

**15.** $\det(B) = -\det(A) = -2$

**17.** $\det(B) = -2\det(A) = -4$

**19.** $R_4 - \frac{1}{2}R_1$ gives $\begin{vmatrix} 2 & 4 & 2 & 6 \\ 1 & 3 & 2 & 1 \\ 2 & 1 & 2 & 3 \\ 0 & 0 & 0 & -2 \end{vmatrix}$

$= (-2) \begin{vmatrix} 2 & 4 & 2 \\ 1 & 3 & 2 \\ 2 & 1 & 2 \end{vmatrix} = (-2) \begin{vmatrix} 2 & 4 & 2 \\ 0 & 1 & 1 \\ 0 & -3 & 0 \end{vmatrix}$

$= (-2)(2) \begin{vmatrix} 1 & 1 \\ -3 & 0 \end{vmatrix} = -12.$

**21.** $R_4 - 2R_3$ gives $\begin{vmatrix} 0 & 4 & 1 & 3 \\ 0 & 2 & 2 & 1 \\ 1 & 3 & 1 & 2 \\ 0 & -4 & -1 & 0 \end{vmatrix}$

$= \begin{vmatrix} 4 & 1 & 3 \\ 2 & 2 & 1 \\ -4 & -1 & 0 \end{vmatrix} = \begin{vmatrix} 4 & 1 & 3 \\ 2 & 2 & 1 \\ 0 & 0 & 3 \end{vmatrix}$

$= 3 \begin{vmatrix} 4 & 1 \\ 2 & 2 \end{vmatrix} = 18.$

**Exercises 4.4, p. 305**

**1.** $p(t) = (1 - t)(3 - t); \quad \lambda = 1, \lambda = 3$

**3.** $p(t) = t^2 - 4t + 3 = (t - 3)(t - 1); \quad \lambda = 1, \lambda = 3$

**5.** $p(t) = t^2 - 4t + 4 = (t - 2)^2; \quad \lambda = 2$, algebraic multiplicity 2

**7.** $p(t) = -t^3 + t^2 + t - 1 = -(t - 1)^2(t + 1);$ $\lambda = 1$, algebraic multiplicity 2; $\lambda = -1$, algebraic multiplicity 1

**9.** $p(t) = -t^3 + 2t^2 + t - 2 = -(t - 2)(t - 1)(t + 1);$ $\lambda = 2, \lambda = 1, \lambda = -1$

**11.** $p(t) = -t^3 + 6t^2 - 12t + 8 = -(t - 2)^3; \quad \lambda = 2,$ algebraic multiplicity 3

**13.** $p(t) = t^4 - 18t^3 + 97t^2 - 180t + 100 =$ $(t - 1)(t - 2)(t - 5)(t - 10); \lambda = 1, \lambda = 2, \lambda = 5,$ $\lambda = 10$

**Exercises 4.5, p. 314**

**1.** **x** is an eigenvector if and only if $\mathbf{x} = \begin{bmatrix} -x_2 \\ x_2 \end{bmatrix}$, $x_2 \neq 0$; basis consists of $\begin{bmatrix} -1 \\ 1 \end{bmatrix}$; algebraic and geometric multiplicities are 1.

**3.** **x** is an eigenvector if and only if $\mathbf{x} = \begin{bmatrix} -x_2 \\ x_2 \end{bmatrix}, x_2 \neq 0$; basis consists of $\begin{bmatrix} -1 \\ 1 \end{bmatrix}$; algebraic multiplicity is 2 and geometric multiplicity is 1.

**5.** **x** is an eigenvector if and only if $\mathbf{x} = \begin{bmatrix} a \\ -a \\ 2a \end{bmatrix}, a \neq 0$; basis consists of $\begin{bmatrix} 1 \\ -1 \\ 2 \end{bmatrix}$; algebraic and geometric multiplicities are 1.

**7.** **x** is an eigenvector if and only if $\mathbf{x} = \begin{bmatrix} x_4 \\ -x_4 \\ -x_4 \\ x_4 \end{bmatrix}$, $x_4 \neq 0$; basis consists of $\begin{bmatrix} 1 \\ -1 \\ -1 \\ 1 \end{bmatrix}$; algebraic and geometric multiplicities are 1.

**9.** **x** is an eigenvector if and only if $\mathbf{x} = \begin{bmatrix} x_4 \\ x_4 \\ x_4 \\ x_4 \end{bmatrix}$, $x_4 \neq 0$; basis consists of $\begin{bmatrix} 1 \\ 1 \\ 1 \\ 1 \end{bmatrix}$; algebraic and geometric multiplicities are 1.

**11.** $\mathbf{x}$ is an eigenvector if and only if

$$\mathbf{x} = \begin{bmatrix} -x_2 - x_3 - x_4 \\ x_2 \\ x_3 \\ x_4 \end{bmatrix};$$

basis consists of $\begin{bmatrix} -1 \\ 1 \\ 0 \\ 0 \end{bmatrix}, \begin{bmatrix} -1 \\ 0 \\ 1 \\ 0 \end{bmatrix},$

$\begin{bmatrix} -1 \\ 0 \\ 0 \\ 1 \end{bmatrix}$; algebraic and geometric multiplicities are 3.

**13.** For $\lambda = 2$, $\mathbf{x} = \begin{bmatrix} x_1 \\ -2x_3 \\ x_3 \end{bmatrix} = x_1 \begin{bmatrix} 1 \\ 0 \\ 0 \end{bmatrix} +$

$x_3 \begin{bmatrix} 0 \\ -2 \\ 1 \end{bmatrix}$; for $\lambda = 3$, $\mathbf{x} = \begin{bmatrix} x_2 \\ x_2 \\ 0 \end{bmatrix}$; the matrix is

not defective.

**15.** For $\lambda = 2$, $\mathbf{x} = \begin{bmatrix} x_1 \\ x_2 \\ 0 \end{bmatrix} = x_1 \begin{bmatrix} 1 \\ 0 \\ 0 \end{bmatrix} + x_2 \begin{bmatrix} 0 \\ 1 \\ 0 \end{bmatrix};$

for $\lambda = 1$, $\mathbf{x} = \begin{bmatrix} -3x_3 \\ -x_3 \\ x_3 \end{bmatrix}$; the matrix is not

defective.

**17.** For $\lambda = 2$, $\mathbf{x} = \begin{bmatrix} x_1 \\ -x_1 \\ 2x_1 \end{bmatrix}$; for $\lambda = 1$, $\mathbf{x} =$

$\begin{bmatrix} -3x_2 \\ x_2 \\ -7x_2 \end{bmatrix}$; for $\lambda = -1$; $\mathbf{x} = \begin{bmatrix} x_1 \\ 2x_1 \\ 2x_1 \end{bmatrix}$; the

matrix is not defective.

**19.** For $\lambda = 1$, eigenvectors are $\mathbf{u}_1 = \begin{bmatrix} 1 \\ 0 \\ 0 \end{bmatrix}$, $\mathbf{u}_2 =$

$\begin{bmatrix} 0 \\ 1 \\ 2 \end{bmatrix}$; for $\lambda = 2$, $\mathbf{u}_3 = \begin{bmatrix} 1 \\ 2 \\ 3 \end{bmatrix}$. Therefore $\mathbf{x} =$

$\mathbf{u}_1 + 2\mathbf{u}_2 + \mathbf{u}_3$, and thus $A^{10}\mathbf{x} = \mathbf{u}_1 + 2\mathbf{u}_2 + 2^{10}\mathbf{u}_3 =$

$\begin{bmatrix} 1025 \\ 2050 \\ 3076 \end{bmatrix}$.

**Exercises 4.6, p. 324**

**1.** $3 + 2i$  **3.** $7 - 3i$

**5.** 6  **7.** 17

**9.** $-5 + 5i$  **11.** $17 - 6i$

**13.** $(10 - 11i)/17$  **15.** $(3 + i)/2$

**17.** 1

**19.** $\lambda = 4 + 2i$, $\mathbf{x} = a \begin{bmatrix} 4 \\ -1 + i \end{bmatrix};$

$\lambda = 4 - 2i$, $\mathbf{x} = a \begin{bmatrix} 4 \\ -1 - i \end{bmatrix}$

**21.** $\lambda = i$, $\mathbf{x} = a \begin{bmatrix} -2 + i \\ 5 \end{bmatrix};$

$\lambda = -i$, $\mathbf{x} = a \begin{bmatrix} -2 - i \\ 5 \end{bmatrix}$

**23.** $\lambda = 2$, $\mathbf{x} = a \begin{bmatrix} -1 \\ 0 \\ 1 \end{bmatrix}$; $\lambda = 2 + 3i$,

$\mathbf{x} = a \begin{bmatrix} -5 + 3i \\ 3 + 3i \\ 2 \end{bmatrix}$; $\lambda = 2 - 3i$,

$\mathbf{x} = a \begin{bmatrix} -5 - 3i \\ 3 - 3i \\ 2 \end{bmatrix}$

**25.** $x = 2 - i$, $y = 3 - 2i$

**27.** $\sqrt{6}$  **29.** 4

**Exercises 4.7, p. 336**

**1.** $A$ is symmetric, so $A$ is diagonalizable. For $S =$

$$\begin{bmatrix} 1 & -1 \\ 1 & 1 \end{bmatrix}, S^{-1}AS = \begin{bmatrix} 1 & 0 \\ 0 & 3 \end{bmatrix} \text{ and } S^{-1}A^5S =$$

$$\begin{bmatrix} 1 & 0 \\ 0 & 243 \end{bmatrix}; \text{ therefore } A^5 = \begin{bmatrix} 122 & -121 \\ -121 & 122 \end{bmatrix}.$$

**3.** $A$ is not diagonalizable; $\lambda = -1$ is the only eigenvalue

and $\mathbf{x} = a \begin{bmatrix} 1 \\ 1 \end{bmatrix}$, $a \neq 0$, are the only eigenvectors.

**5.** $A$ is diagonalizable since $A$ has distinct eigenvalues. For

$$S = \begin{bmatrix} -1 & 0 \\ 10 & 1 \end{bmatrix}, S^{-1}AS = \begin{bmatrix} 1 & 0 \\ 0 & 2 \end{bmatrix}$$

and $S^{-1}A^5S = \begin{bmatrix} 1 & 0 \\ 0 & 32 \end{bmatrix}$; therefore

$$A^5 = \begin{bmatrix} 1 & 0 \\ 310 & 32 \end{bmatrix}.$$

**7.** $A$ is not diagonalizable; $\lambda = 1$ is the only eigenvalue and it has geometric multiplicity 2. A basis for the eigenspace consists of $[1, 1, 0]^T$ and $[2, 0, 1]^T$.

**9.** $A$ is diagonalizable since $A$ has distinct eigen-

values. For $S = \begin{bmatrix} -3 & -1 & 1 \\ 1 & 1 & 2 \\ -7 & -2 & 2 \end{bmatrix}$,

$$S^{-1}AS = \begin{bmatrix} 1 & 0 & 0 \\ 0 & 2 & 0 \\ 0 & 0 & -1 \end{bmatrix}. \text{ Therefore}$$

$$A^5 = \begin{bmatrix} 163 & -11 & -71 \\ -172 & 10 & 75 \\ 324 & -22 & -141 \end{bmatrix}.$$

**11.** $A$ is not diagonalizable; $\lambda = 1$ has algebraic multiplicity 2 and geometric multiplicity 1.

**13.** $Q$ is orthogonal.

**15.** $Q$ is not orthogonal since the columns are not orthonormal.

**17.** $Q$ is orthogonal.

**19.** $\alpha = 1/\sqrt{2}$, $\beta = 1/\sqrt{6}$, $a = -1/\sqrt{3}$, $b = 1/\sqrt{3}$, $c = 1/\sqrt{3}$

**33.** $\lambda = 2$, $\mathbf{u} = \dfrac{1}{\sqrt{2}} \begin{bmatrix} 1 \\ -1 \end{bmatrix}$, $\mathbf{v} = \dfrac{1}{\sqrt{2}} \begin{bmatrix} 1 \\ 1 \end{bmatrix}$,

$$Q = [\mathbf{u}, \mathbf{v}], Q^TAQ = \begin{bmatrix} 2 & -2 \\ 0 & 2 \end{bmatrix}$$

**35.** $\lambda = 1$, $\mathbf{u} = \dfrac{1}{\sqrt{2}} \begin{bmatrix} 1 \\ 1 \end{bmatrix}$, $\mathbf{v} = \dfrac{1}{\sqrt{2}} \begin{bmatrix} 1 \\ -1 \end{bmatrix}$,

$$Q = [\mathbf{u}, \mathbf{v}], Q^TAQ = \begin{bmatrix} 1 & 0 \\ 0 & 3 \end{bmatrix}$$

**Exercises 4.8, p. 349**

**1.** $\mathbf{x}_1 = \begin{bmatrix} 4 \\ 2 \end{bmatrix}$, $\mathbf{x}_2 = \begin{bmatrix} 2 \\ 4 \end{bmatrix}$,

$$\mathbf{x}_3 = \begin{bmatrix} 4 \\ 2 \end{bmatrix}, \mathbf{x}_4 = \begin{bmatrix} 2 \\ 4 \end{bmatrix}$$

**3.** $\mathbf{x}_1 = \begin{bmatrix} 80 \\ 112 \end{bmatrix}$, $\mathbf{x}_2 = \begin{bmatrix} 68 \\ 124 \end{bmatrix}$,

$$\mathbf{x}_3 = \begin{bmatrix} 65 \\ 127 \end{bmatrix}, \mathbf{x}_4 = \begin{bmatrix} 64.25 \\ 127.75 \end{bmatrix}$$

**5.** $\mathbf{x}_1 = \begin{bmatrix} 7 \\ 1 \end{bmatrix}$, $\mathbf{x}_2 = \begin{bmatrix} 11 \\ 8 \end{bmatrix}$,

$$\mathbf{x}_3 = \begin{bmatrix} 43 \\ 19 \end{bmatrix}, \mathbf{x}_4 = \begin{bmatrix} 119 \\ 62 \end{bmatrix}$$

**7.** $\mathbf{x}_k = 3(1)^k \begin{bmatrix} 1 \\ 1 \end{bmatrix} + (-1)^k \begin{bmatrix} -1 \\ 1 \end{bmatrix} =$

$$\begin{bmatrix} 3 + (-1)^{k+1} \\ 3 + (-1)^k \end{bmatrix}; \mathbf{x}_4 = \begin{bmatrix} 2 \\ 4 \end{bmatrix},$$

$$\mathbf{x}_{10} = \begin{bmatrix} 2 \\ 4 \end{bmatrix}; \text{ the sequence } \{\mathbf{x}_k\} \text{ has no limit,}$$

but $\|\mathbf{x}_k\| \leq \sqrt{20}$.

**9.** $\mathbf{x}_k = 64(1)^k \begin{bmatrix} 1 \\ 2 \end{bmatrix} - 64(1/4)^k \begin{bmatrix} -1 \\ 1 \end{bmatrix} =$

$$64 \begin{bmatrix} 1 + (1/4)^k \\ 2 - (1/4)^k \end{bmatrix}; \mathbf{x}_4 = \begin{bmatrix} 64.25 \\ 127.75 \end{bmatrix},$$

$$\mathbf{x}_{10} = \begin{bmatrix} 64.00006 \\ 127.99994 \end{bmatrix}; \text{ the sequence } \{\mathbf{x}_k\} \text{ con-}$$

verges to $[64, 128]^T$.

**11.** $\mathbf{x}_k = (3/4)(3)^k \begin{bmatrix} 2 \\ 1 \end{bmatrix} + (5/4)(-1)^k \begin{bmatrix} -2 \\ 1 \end{bmatrix} =$

$\dfrac{1}{4} \begin{bmatrix} 6(3)^k - 10(-1)^k \\ 3(3)^k + 5(-1)^k \end{bmatrix}$; $\mathbf{x}_4 = \begin{bmatrix} 119 \\ 62 \end{bmatrix}$;

$\mathbf{x}_{10} = \begin{bmatrix} 88571 \\ 44288 \end{bmatrix}$; the sequence $\{\mathbf{x}_k\}$ has no limit

and $\|\mathbf{x}_k\| \to \infty$.

**13.** $\mathbf{x}_k = -2(1)^k \begin{bmatrix} -3 \\ 1 \\ -7 \end{bmatrix} - 2(2)^k \begin{bmatrix} -1 \\ 1 \\ -2 \end{bmatrix} -$

$5(-1)^k \begin{bmatrix} 1 \\ 2 \\ 2 \end{bmatrix} = \begin{bmatrix} 6 + 2(2)^k - 5(-1)^k \\ -2 - 2(2)^k - 10(-1)^k \\ 14 + 4(2)^k - 10(-1)^k \end{bmatrix}$;

$\mathbf{x}_4 = \begin{bmatrix} 33 \\ -44 \\ 68 \end{bmatrix}$; $\mathbf{x}_{10} = \begin{bmatrix} 2049 \\ -2060 \\ 4100 \end{bmatrix}$;

the sequence $\{\mathbf{x}_k\}$ has no limit and $\|\mathbf{x}_k\| \to \infty$.

**15.** $\mathbf{x}(t) = 3e^{2t} \begin{bmatrix} 2 \\ 1 \end{bmatrix} - 2e^{-t} \begin{bmatrix} 1 \\ 1 \end{bmatrix}$

**17.** $\mathbf{x}(t) = \begin{bmatrix} 0 \\ -2 \\ 2 \end{bmatrix} - e^{2t} \begin{bmatrix} -2 \\ -3 \\ 1 \end{bmatrix} + e^{3t} \begin{bmatrix} 1 \\ 2 \\ 0 \end{bmatrix}$

**21.** $\alpha = -.18$; $\mathbf{x}_k = \dfrac{16}{118}(1)^k \begin{bmatrix} 3 \\ 10 \end{bmatrix} +$

$\dfrac{7}{118}(-.18)^k \begin{bmatrix} 10 \\ -6 \end{bmatrix}$; the limit is $\dfrac{16}{118} \begin{bmatrix} 3 \\ 10 \end{bmatrix}$.

## CHAPTER 5

**Exercises 5.2, p. 366**

**1.** $\begin{bmatrix} 0 & -7 & 5 \\ -11 & -3 & -12 \end{bmatrix}$, $\begin{bmatrix} 12 & -22 & 38 \\ -50 & -6 & -15 \end{bmatrix}$,

$\begin{bmatrix} 7 & -21 & 28 \\ -42 & -7 & -14 \end{bmatrix}$

**3.** $e^x - 2\sin x$, $e^x - 2\sin x + 3\sqrt{x^2 + 1}$, $-2e^x - \sin x + 3\sqrt{x^2 + 1}$

**5.** $c_1 = -2 + c_3$, $c_2 = 3 - c_3$, $c_3$ arbitrary

**7.** Not a vector space         **9.** Not a vector space

**11.** Not a vector space         **13.** A vector space

**15.** Not a vector space         **25.** A vector space

**27.** Not a vector space         **29.** A vector space

**Exercises 5.3, p. 373**

**1.** Not a subspace         **3.** A subspace

**5.** A subspace         **7.** Not a subspace

**9.** A subspace         **11.** Not a subspace

**13.** A subspace         **15.** Not a subspace

**17.** $p(x) = -p_1(x) + 3p_2(x) - 2p_3(x)$

**19.** $A = (-1 - 2x)B_1 + (2 + 3x)B_2 + xB_3 - 3B_4$, $x$ arbitrary

**21.** $\cos 2x = -\sin^2 x + \cos^2 x$

**23.** $W = \mathrm{Sp}\{1, x^2\}$

**25.** In Exercise 2, $W = \mathrm{Sp}\left\{\begin{bmatrix} 1 & 1 & 0 \\ 0 & 0 & 0 \end{bmatrix},\right.$

$\begin{bmatrix} -2 & 0 & 1 \\ 0 & 0 & 0 \end{bmatrix}, \begin{bmatrix} 0 & 0 & 0 \\ 1 & 0 & 0 \end{bmatrix}, \begin{bmatrix} 0 & 0 & 0 \\ 0 & 1 & 0 \end{bmatrix},$

$\left.\begin{bmatrix} 0 & 0 & 0 \\ 0 & 0 & 1 \end{bmatrix}\right\}$; in Exercise 3, $W =$

$\mathrm{Sp}\left\{\begin{bmatrix} -1 & -1 & 1 \\ 0 & 0 & 0 \end{bmatrix}, \begin{bmatrix} 0 & 0 & 0 \\ 1 & 0 & 0 \end{bmatrix},\right.$

$\left.\begin{bmatrix} 0 & 0 & 0 \\ 0 & 1 & 0 \end{bmatrix}\right\}$; in Exercise 5, $W =$

$\mathrm{Sp}\{-1 + x, -2 + x^2\}$; in Exercise 6, $W = \mathrm{Sp}\{1, -4x + x^2\}$; in Exercise 8, $W = \mathrm{Sp}\{1 - x^2, x\}$

**27.** $W = \mathrm{Sp}\{B_1, B_2, E_{12}, E_{13}, E_{21}, E_{23}, E_{31}, E_{32}\}$,

where $B_1 = \begin{bmatrix} -1 & 0 & 0 \\ 0 & 1 & 0 \\ 0 & 0 & 0 \end{bmatrix}$ and

$B_2 = \begin{bmatrix} -1 & 0 & 0 \\ 0 & 0 & 0 \\ 0 & 0 & 1 \end{bmatrix}$

**29.** $A = B + C$ where $B = (A + A^T)/2$ and $C = (A - A^T)/2$

**31. a)** $W = \text{Sp}\{E_{12}, E_{13}, E_{23}\}$;

**b)** $W = \text{Sp}\left\{\begin{bmatrix} -1 & 0 & 0 \\ 0 & 1 & 0 \\ 0 & 0 & 0 \end{bmatrix}, \begin{bmatrix} -1 & 0 & 0 \\ 0 & 0 & 0 \\ 0 & 0 & 1 \end{bmatrix}, \right.$

$\left. \begin{bmatrix} 0 & -1 & 0 \\ 0 & 0 & 1 \\ 0 & 0 & 0 \end{bmatrix}, \begin{bmatrix} 0 & 0 & 1 \\ 0 & 0 & 0 \\ 0 & 0 & 0 \end{bmatrix} \right\}$;

**c)** $W = \text{Sp}\left\{\begin{bmatrix} 1 & 1 & 0 \\ 0 & 0 & 0 \\ 0 & 0 & 0 \end{bmatrix}, \begin{bmatrix} 0 & 0 & 1 \\ 0 & 0 & 1 \\ 0 & 0 & 0 \end{bmatrix}, \right.$

$\left. \begin{bmatrix} 0 & 0 & 0 \\ 0 & 1 & 0 \\ 0 & 0 & 1 \end{bmatrix} \right\}$;

**d)** $W = \text{Sp}\left\{\begin{bmatrix} 1 & 0 & 0 \\ 0 & 1 & 0 \\ 0 & 0 & 1 \end{bmatrix}, \begin{bmatrix} 0 & -1 & 1 \\ 0 & 0 & 1 \\ 0 & 0 & 0 \end{bmatrix}, \right.$

$\left. \begin{bmatrix} 0 & 0 & 1 \\ 0 & 0 & 0 \\ 0 & 0 & 0 \end{bmatrix} \right\}$

**33.** $x_1 = -6a + 5b + 37c + 15d$;
$x_2 = 3a - 2b - 17c - 7d$;
$x_3 = -a + b + 5c + 2d$;   $x_4 = 2c + d$;
$C = -12B_1 + 6B_2 - B_3 - B_4$;
$D = 8B_1 - 3B_2 + B_3 + B_4$

**Exercises 5.4, p. 386**

**1.** $\left\{\begin{bmatrix} -1 & 1 \\ 0 & 0 \end{bmatrix}, \begin{bmatrix} -1 & 0 \\ 1 & 0 \end{bmatrix}, \begin{bmatrix} -1 & 0 \\ 0 & 1 \end{bmatrix}\right\}$

**3.** $\{E_{12}, E_{21}, E_{22}\}$          **5.** $\{1 + x^2, x - 2x^2\}$

**7.** $\{x, x^2\}$

**9.** $\{-9x + 3x^2 + x^3, 8x - 6x^2 + x^4\}$

**13. a)** $[2 \quad -1 \quad 3 \quad 2]^T$;   **b)** $[1 \quad 0 \quad -1 \quad 1]^T$;
**c)** $[2 \quad 3 \quad 0 \quad 0]^T$

**15.** Linearly independent

**17.** Linearly dependent

**19.** Linearly dependent

**21.** Linearly independent

**23.** $\{p_1(x), p_2(x)\}$          **25.** $\{A_1, A_2, A_3\}$

**27.** $[-4 \quad 11 \quad -3]^T$

**31.** $[a + b - 2c + 7d, -b + 2c - 4d, c - 2d, d]^T$

**38.** The set $\{\mathbf{u}, \mathbf{v}\}$ is linearly dependent if and only if one of the vectors is a scalar multiple of the other.
**a)** Linearly independent;
**b)** Linearly independent;   **c)** Linearly dependent;
**d)** Linearly dependent;     **e)** Linearly dependent

**Exercises 5.5, p. 390**

**1. b)** $\{E_{11}, E_{21}, E_{22}, E_{31}, E_{32}, E_{33}\}$ is a basis for $V_1$.
$\{E_{11}, E_{12}, E_{13}, E_{22}, E_{23}, E_{33}\}$ is a basis for $V_2$.
**c)** $\dim(V) = 9$, $\dim(V_1) = 6$, $\dim(V_2) = 6$

**3.** $V_1 \cap V_2 = \left\{\begin{bmatrix} a_{11} & 0 & 0 \\ 0 & a_{22} & 0 \\ 0 & 0 & a_{33} \end{bmatrix} : a_{11}, a_{22}, a_{33}\right.$

arbitrary real numbers}; $\dim(V_1 \cap V_2) = 3$

**5.** $\dim(W) = 3$          **7.** $\dim(W) = 3$

**9. iii)** The set $S$ is linearly dependent.

**11. ii)** The set $S$ does not span $V$.

**13. iii)** The set $S$ is linearly dependent.

**21. a)** $A = \begin{bmatrix} 1 & -1 & 1 \\ 0 & 1 & -2 \\ 0 & 0 & 1 \end{bmatrix}$; **b)** $[5 \quad 2 \quad 1]^T$

**23.** $A^{-1} = \begin{bmatrix} 1 & 1 & 1 \\ 0 & 1 & 2 \\ 0 & 0 & 1 \end{bmatrix}$; **a)** $p(x) =$

$6 + 11x + 7x^2$;
**b)** $p(x) = 4 + 2x - x^2$; **c)** $p(x) = 5 + x$;
**d)** $p(x) = 8 - 2x - x^2$

**Exercises 5.6, p. 401**

**9.** $\langle \mathbf{x}, \mathbf{y} \rangle = -3$, $\|\mathbf{x}\| = \sqrt{5}$, $\|\mathbf{y}\| = \sqrt{2}$,
$\|\mathbf{x} - \mathbf{y}\| = \sqrt{13}$

**11.** $\langle p, q \rangle = 52$, $\|p\| = 3\sqrt{6}$, $\|q\| = 3\sqrt{6}$,
$\|p - q\| = 2$

**13.** For $\langle \mathbf{x}, \mathbf{y} \rangle = \mathbf{x}^T\mathbf{y}$, the graph of $S$ is the circle with equation $x^2 + y^2 = 1$. For $\langle \mathbf{x}, \mathbf{y} \rangle = 4x_1 y_1 + x_2 y_2$, the graph of $S$ is the ellipse with equation $4x^2 + y^2 = 1$.

**15.** $a_1 = 7$, $a_2 = 4$

**17.** $q = (-5/3)p_0 - 5p_1 - 4p_2$

**19.** $p_0 = 1$, $p_1 = x$, $p_2 = x^2 - 2$, $p_3 = x^3 - (17/5)x$,
$p_4 = x^4 - (31/7)x^2 + 72/35$

**25.** $p^*(x) = (3/2)x^2 - (3/5)x + 1/20$

**27.** $p^*(x) \cong 0.841471 p_0(x) - 0.467544 p_1(x) - 0.430920 p_2(x) + 0.07882 p_3(x)$

**29. d)** $T_2(x) = 2x^2 - 1$, $T_3(x) = 4x^3 - 3x$, $T_4(x) = 8x^4 - 8x^2 + 1$, $T_5(x) = 16x^5 - 20x^3 + 5x$

**Exercises 5.7, p. 410**

**1.** Not a linear transformation

**3.** A linear transformation

**5.** A linear transformation

**7.** Not a linear transformation

**9. a)** $11 + x^2 + 6x^3$;

**b)** $T(a_0 + a_1x + a_2x^2) = (a_0 + 2a_2) + (a_0 + a_1)x^2 + (-a_1 + a_2)x^3$

**11. a)** $8 + 14x - 9x^2$;

**b)** $T\left(\begin{bmatrix} a & b \\ c & d \end{bmatrix}\right) = (a + b + 2d) + (-a + b + 2c + d)x + (b - c - 2d)x^2$

**13. a)** $\{2, 6x, 12x^2\}$ is a basis for $\mathcal{R}(T)$.

**b)** Nullity$(T) = 2$

**c)** $T[(a_0/2)x^2 + (a_1/6)x^3 + (a_2/12)x^4] = a_0 + a_1x + a_2x^2$

**15.** $\mathcal{N}(T) = \{a_0 + a_1x + a_2x^2 : a_0 + 2a_1 + 4a_2 = 0\}$; $\mathcal{R}(T) = R^1$

**17. b)** $\mathcal{N}(I) = \{\boldsymbol{\theta}\}$; $\mathcal{R}(I) = V$

**19.**

| rank$(T)$ | 3 | 2 | 1 | 0 |
|---|---|---|---|---|
| nullity$(T)$ | 2 | 3 | 4 | 5 |

$T$ cannot be one-to-one.

**21.**

| rank$(T)$ | 3 | 2 | 1 | 0 |
|---|---|---|---|---|
| nullity$(T)$ | 0 | 1 | 2 | 3 |

$\mathcal{R}(T) = P_3$ is not possible.

**27. b)** Nullity$(T) = 0$; rank$(T) = 4$

**Exercises 5.8, p. 418**

**1.** $(S + T)(p) = p'(0) + (x + 2)p(x)$; $(S + T)(x) = 1 + 2x + x^2$; $(S + T)(x^2) = 2x^2 + x^3$

**3.** $(H \circ T)(p) = p(x) + (x + 2)p'(x) + 2p(0)$; $(H \circ T)(x) = 2x + 2$

**5. b)** There is no polynomial $p$ in $P_3$ such that $T(p) = x$, so $T^{-1}(x)$ is not defined.

**7.** $T^{-1}(e^x) = e^x$; $T^{-1}(e^{2x}) = (1/2)e^{2x}$; $T^{-1}(e^{3x}) = (1/3)e^{3x}$; $T^{-1}(ae^x + be^{2x} + ce^{3x}) = ae^x + (b/2)e^{2x} + (c/3)e^{3x}$

**9.** $T^{-1}(A) = A^T$

**11. c)** $T\left(\begin{bmatrix} a & b \\ c & d \end{bmatrix}\right) = a + bx + cx^2 + dx^3$

**Exercises 5.9, p. 429**

**1.** $\begin{bmatrix} 0 & 1 & 0 & 0 \\ 0 & 0 & 0 & 0 \\ 0 & 0 & 0 & 0 \\ 0 & 0 & 0 & 0 \\ 0 & 0 & 0 & 0 \end{bmatrix}$

**3.** $\begin{bmatrix} 2 & 1 & 0 & 0 \\ 1 & 2 & 0 & 0 \\ 0 & 1 & 2 & 0 \\ 0 & 0 & 1 & 2 \\ 0 & 0 & 0 & 1 \end{bmatrix}$

**5.** $\begin{bmatrix} 1 & 1 & 0 & 0 & 0 \\ 0 & 0 & 2 & 0 & 0 \\ 0 & 0 & 0 & 3 & 0 \\ 0 & 0 & 0 & 0 & 4 \end{bmatrix}$

**7.** $\begin{bmatrix} 2 & 2 & 0 & 0 & 0 \\ 1 & 1 & 4 & 0 & 0 \\ 0 & 0 & 2 & 6 & 0 \\ 0 & 0 & 0 & 3 & 8 \\ 0 & 0 & 0 & 0 & 4 \end{bmatrix}$

**9. a)** $[p]_B = \begin{bmatrix} a_0 \\ a_1 \\ a_2 \\ a_3 \end{bmatrix}$,

$[T(p)]_C = \begin{bmatrix} 2a_0 \\ a_0 + 2a_1 \\ a_1 + 2a_2 \\ a_2 + 2a_3 \\ a_3 \end{bmatrix}$

**11. a)** $Q = \begin{bmatrix} 1 & 0 & 0 \\ 0 & 2 & 0 \\ 0 & 0 & 3 \end{bmatrix}$;

**b)** $P = \begin{bmatrix} 1 & 0 & 0 \\ 0 & 1/2 & 0 \\ 0 & 0 & 1/3 \end{bmatrix}$

**13. a)** $Q = \begin{bmatrix} 1 & 0 & 0 & 0 \\ 0 & 0 & 1 & 0 \\ 0 & 1 & 0 & 0 \\ 0 & 0 & 0 & 1 \end{bmatrix}$

**15.** $\begin{bmatrix} 3 & 6 & 0 \\ 3 & 3 & 0 \\ -1 & -1 & 3 \\ 0 & 0 & 0 \end{bmatrix}$

**17.** $\begin{bmatrix} 1 & 0 & 0 \\ 0 & 3 & 6 \\ 0 & 1 & 4 \end{bmatrix}$

**19.** $\begin{bmatrix} 0 & 0 & 1 & 1 \\ 1 & 0 & 1 & 0 \\ 0 & 1 & 0 & 0 \\ 0 & 0 & 0 & 3 \end{bmatrix}$

**21.** $\begin{bmatrix} -4 & -2 & 0 \\ 3 & 3 & 0 \\ -1 & 2 & 3 \end{bmatrix}$

**23.** $\begin{bmatrix} 2 & 0 & 0 \\ 0 & -3 & 0 \\ 0 & 0 & 3 \end{bmatrix}$

**31.** $T(a_0 + a_1 x + a_2 x^2 + a_3 x^3) = (a_0 + 2a_2) + (a_1 + a_3)x + (-a_0 + a_1 - a_3)x^2$

**Exercises 5.10, p. 438**

**1.** $T(\mathbf{u}_1) = \mathbf{u}_1, \quad T(\mathbf{u}_2) = 3\mathbf{u}_2, \quad \begin{bmatrix} 1 & 0 \\ 0 & 3 \end{bmatrix}$

**3.** $T(A_1) = 2A_1, T(A_2) = -2A_2, T(A_3) = 3A_3,$

$T(A_4) = -3A_4, \quad \begin{bmatrix} 2 & 0 & 0 & 0 \\ 0 & -2 & 0 & 0 \\ 0 & 0 & 3 & 0 \\ 0 & 0 & 0 & -3 \end{bmatrix}$

**5.** $\begin{bmatrix} 1 & -1 & -1 \\ 1 & -1 & 0 \\ -1 & 2 & 1 \end{bmatrix}$;

$p(x) = (1 + x - x^2) + (1 + x^2);$
$q(x) = -5(1 + x - x^2) - 3(1 + x^2) + 7(1 + x);$
$s(x) = -2(1 + x - x^2) - (1 + x^2) + 2(1 + x);$
$r(x) = (a_0 - a_1 - a_2)(1 + x - x^2)$
$\qquad + (a_0 - a_1)(1 + x^2)$
$\qquad + (-a_0 + 2a_1 + a_2)(1 + x)$

**7.** $\begin{bmatrix} 1/3 & 5/3 \\ 1/3 & -1/3 \end{bmatrix}$

**9.** $\begin{bmatrix} -1 & 1 & 2 & 3 \\ 1 & 0 & 0 & -3 \\ 0 & 0 & 1 & 0 \\ 0 & 0 & 0 & 1 \end{bmatrix}$

$p(x) = -7x + 2(x + 1) + (x^2 - 2x);$
$q(x) = 13x - 4(x + 1) + (x^3 + 3);$
$r(x) = -7x + 3(x + 1) - 2(x^2 - 2x) + (x^3 + 3)$

**11.** The matrix of $T$ with respect to $B$ is

$Q_1 = \begin{bmatrix} 2 & 1 \\ 1 & 2 \end{bmatrix}$. The transition matrix from $C$ to

$B$ is $P = \begin{bmatrix} -1 & 1 \\ 1 & 1 \end{bmatrix}$. The matrix of $T$ with respect

to $C$ is $Q_2$, where $Q_2 = P^{-1}Q_1P = \begin{bmatrix} 1 & 0 \\ 0 & 3 \end{bmatrix}$.

**13.** The matrix of $T$ with respect to $B$ is

$Q_1 = \begin{bmatrix} -3 & 0 & 0 & 5 \\ 0 & 3 & -5 & 0 \\ 0 & 0 & -2 & 0 \\ 0 & 0 & 0 & 2 \end{bmatrix}$. This transition

matrix from $C$ to $B$ is $P = \begin{bmatrix} 1 & 0 & 0 & 1 \\ 0 & 1 & 1 & 0 \\ 0 & 1 & 0 & 0 \\ 1 & 0 & 0 & 0 \end{bmatrix}$. The

matrix of $T$ with respect to $C$ is $Q_2$, where $Q_2 =$

$P^{-1}Q_1P = \begin{bmatrix} 2 & 0 & 0 & 0 \\ 0 & -2 & 0 & 0 \\ 0 & 0 & 3 & 0 \\ 0 & 0 & 0 & -3 \end{bmatrix}$.

**15. a)** $Q = \begin{bmatrix} 1 & 1 & 0 \\ 0 & 2 & 4 \\ 0 & 0 & 3 \end{bmatrix}$;

**b)** $S = \begin{bmatrix} 1 & 1 & 2 \\ 0 & 1 & 4 \\ 0 & 0 & 1 \end{bmatrix}$; $R = \begin{bmatrix} 1 & 0 & 0 \\ 0 & 2 & 0 \\ 0 & 0 & 3 \end{bmatrix}$;

**c)** $C = \{1, 1 + x, 2 + 4x + x^2\}$;

**d)** $P = \begin{bmatrix} 1 & -1 & 2 \\ 0 & 1 & -4 \\ 0 & 0 & 1 \end{bmatrix}$;

**e)** $T(\mathbf{w}_1) = -1 + 18x + 3x^2$;
$T(\mathbf{w}_2) = 5 + 4x + 3x^2$;
$T(\mathbf{w}_3) = 1 + 2x + 6x^2$

# INDEX